Professional Cloud Architect – Google Cloud Certification Guide

Second Edition

Build a solid foundation in Google Cloud Platform
to achieve the most lucrative IT certification

Konrad Cłapa

Brian Gerrard

BIRMINGHAM—MUMBAI

Professional Cloud Architect – Google Cloud Certification Guide
Second Edition

Group Product Manager: Rahul Nair

Publishing Product Manager: Rahul Nair

Senior Editor: Sangeeta Purkayastha

Content Development Editor: Nihar Kapadia

Technical Editor: Nithik Cheruvakodan

Copy Editor: Safis Editing

Project Coordinator: Shagun Saini

Proofreader: Safis Editing

Indexer: Hemangini Bari

Production Designer: Aparna Bhagat

Marketing Coordinator: Nimisha Dua and Sanjana Gupta

First published: October 2019
Second edition: January 2022
Production reference: 1101221

Published by Packt Publishing Ltd.
Livery Place
35 Livery Street
Birmingham
B3 2PB, UK.

ISBN 978-1-80181-229-0

www.packt.com

To my wife and parents, for their constant support.

– Konrad Cłapa

To Linda, for her constant support and understanding.

– Brian Gerrard

Foreword

I came to know Konrad Cłapa on LinkedIn. We both have an interest in Google Cloud and have both become fully certified on Google Cloud. Then we met at Google Cloud Next '19, where Konrad invited me to co-author a book to teach people how to use Google Cloud – this book.

I had had a failed writing experience before and I knew it takes a lot of effort to write a book, so I didn't agree to co-author it, but I did write the foreword for the first edition of the book, published in 2019.

Those 2 years passed quickly and so many new services have been released on Google Cloud since then. Google Cloud Training and Certification released an upgraded version of the exam for Google Cloud Certified Professional Cloud Architect in March 2021. Even though my certification won't expire until September 2021, I took the beta exam and passed.

As expected, a lot of new content has been added to the exam, and new services such as Google Kubernetes Engine and Anthos are tested in the new exam. These changes made the first edition of the book irrelevant.

I am glad Konrad and Brian have spent time refreshing their book to reflect the changes in the exam syllabus. This will be the first book ever published on the topic since the new exam was released and it will provide much-needed guidance for people to learn about the most up-to-date services from Google in order to pass the exam and advance their careers.

A better job, a better life. I achieved so much more after I became certified on a number of cloud vendors. I encourage people to learn the cloud and plan for a better career. This book gives you what you need to pass one of the most sought-after certifications, and also the highest-paid certification, according to some sources online.

We didn't get a chance to meet again after Google Cloud Next '19. Google Cloud Next '20 and '21 were online only due to COVID-19. But we kept in touch on LinkedIn and I am aware that Konrad has become a Google Cloud Certified Fellow, the most prestigious certification from Google, and one of my own career goals. I am happy about his achievement.

Even though I don't know Brian Gerrard in person, since Konrad and Brian are colleagues and they co-authored the first edition of the book, we connected on LinkedIn. Brian has decade-long experience on VMware and he claimed to have many VMware-related certifications. Brian just moved to the public cloud in recent years. His transition from data center-centric technology to the public cloud is an inspiration for people facing the same dilemma – stop doubting the public cloud; rather, embrace it to further your career advancement. There are many similar success stories on LinkedIn for people to use as a reference and as inspiration for their own career moves. LinkedIn is a professional social media platform where you can connect with people with a common interest, learn from each other, and grow together to reach your own professional goals.

I feel honored to be given this opportunity again to write the foreword to this second edition. And I understand why Konrad wanted me to write it. For the past 5 years, I have inspired thousands of people to learn the cloud and find their purpose. I am the right person to introduce this book to you, which will help you learn Google Cloud and become certified. And great things will happen after becoming certified in Google Cloud.

Yujun Liang

Fully Certified on GCP

Cloud Certification King on LinkedIn

Contributors

About the authors

Konrad Cłapa is a Certified Google Trainer and Lead Cloud Architect working for Atos R&D. He has over 12 years' experience in the IT industry. He holds over 40 IT certification. This includes all 12/12 active Google Cloud Platform certifications making him the first in the world to achieve it. He is also listed among 40 individuals who hold Google Cloud Certified Fellow certificate. Sharing knowledge has always been important to him, so he contributes to the community by acting as a leader for a local Google Cloud Developer group. Funny fact about Konrad is that till now he never failed a GCP exam attempt including multiple beta exams that he has taken.

First of all, I would like to thank my lovely wife Kinga for the patience and understanding of my passion. It is difficult to be a wife of a geek. I would also like to thank my parents that always supported me in any decisions I have taken in my life. Last but not the least I thank Brian for being a fellow for multiple journeys and above all being a great friend!

Brian Gerrard is currently a DevOps Engineer from Scotland with over 15 years' experience in the IT industry. As well as holding the Google Certified Professional Architect and Google Certified Associate Engineer certifications , he is certified in Azure, AWS, Terraform and VMware. Brian is a firm believer in lifelong learning, and you will regularly find him contributing to his local user groups.

I would like to thank my wife and children for their support. Also, thanks to Konrad for constantly pushing the Google community to achieve more!

About the reviewers

Dr. Artem Nikulchenko is a chief software architect at Teamwork Commerce, a Google Cloud Platform Partner that specializes in the development of retail management systems. Artem spearheaded the usage of Google Cloud Platform in teamwork products from the very first publicly available version of the platform.

Artem has a Ph.D. in computer science and holds an associate professor position at National Technical University Kharkiv Polytechnic Institute. He teaches courses on databases, software architecture, and public clouds.

As a big fan of Google Cloud, Artem leads his local Google Developer Group and delivers talks about Google Cloud Platform at specialized conferences around the world.

> *Having worked with GCP for over 10 years, I still found this book very useful while preparing for my Google Cloud Architect certification exam. Then, I was invited to become a reviewer of that same book's newest edition. It's a great honor for me and I'd like to thank the authors, as well as Packt Publishing, for this exceptional opportunity.*

Artur Zejfer has been working in the IT industry for more than 20 years, ranging across application support, database administration, automation, and architect roles. This has given him a broad base of skills and the ability to work with a diverse range of clients. He holds a master's degree in computer science and several industry-recognized certifications from Oracle, Google, The Open Group, and so on. He currently works for Atos R&D as a database architect focusing on automating daily operations. Artur has a passion for learning and information that he continues to pursue daily.

Above all the previously stated, he is a father, husband, son, brother, and friend.

> *I'd like to thank my wife, Kamila, and our son, Franek, for their daily support and patience. To my parents, siblings, relatives, friends, and mentors (you know who you are), thank you for guiding and supporting me.*

Shouvik Basak is a solution architect at a leading Fortune 500 global IT services organization. He specializes in architecting cloud-based solutions and data center infrastructure technologies. In a career spanning more than 20 years in technology, he has worked extensively on public, private, and hybrid cloud delivery, traditional infrastructure, and operations, primarily for global enterprise customers. He has led multiple programs in the technology, service management, and integration areas and has worked hands-on in multiple technical roles.

To my mentors and friends, who have kept me motivated and curious and helped me navigate my journey and find joy in learning and doing what I do. I would also like to thank Packt Publishing for the opportunity to review this wonderful book.

Vijaykumar Jangamashetti (VJ) is a cloud solutions architect at Rackspace Technology, with a specialization in Google Cloud Platform, and is 7X Google Cloud Platform-certified. VJ is passionate about data and analytics and a strong customer advocate of educating on and promoting the power of data. As a Google Cloud Platform expert, VJ has led multiple efforts in strengthening alliance partnerships with Google Cloud through the achievement of MSP credentials, specialization awards, and expertise badges for the respective organizations he has worked in. With 15+ years of IT experience working with customers across the globe with multiple positions as an ETL architect, enterprise data architect, and cloud architect, he has built a strong reputation as a customer champion and a trusted advisor. He goes by the name @vijaykumarpj on LinkedIn and Twitter.

I'd like to thank my wife, Jyoti, and our daughter, Shriya, for their continued support and encouragement with everything that I do with great patience. I genuinely appreciate what you both have done for me and I love you both. I'd also like to thank my grandparents, parents, siblings, relatives, friends, colleagues, and mentors for helping me to be who I am today, and I greatly appreciate you all. Thanks to Packt for providing me with the opportunity to review this wonderful book.

Jarosław Gajewski holds the lead architect and distinguished expert positions in Atos. He is responsible for designing multi- and hybrid cloud solutions for cloud-agnostic and cloud-native services.

His technical knowledge and experience are backed by multiple industry-standard certificates. He is already part of an elite group of Google Cloud Certified Fellows. He holds the Google Cloud Certified Professional and other Google, VMware, Dell, Microsoft, and AWS certifications.

As someone who is passionate about the cloud, outside of his work, he is also an active community speaker and one of the Google Developer group leads for GDG Cloud Bydgoszcz.

In his free time, he loves to enjoy time with his wife, two daughters, and son, play board games, and constantly increase his knowledge.

I'd like to thank my wife Weronika for her patience and constant support.

Maciej Stopa is a multi-certified cloud solution architect experienced in Azure, Google Cloud Platform, AWS, Red Hat, IBM, Oracle, and VMware. With more than 17 years of experience in IT, he has gained deep on-premises, HPC, and distributed systems experience while working for a leading systems integrator in Poland. He transformed through virtualization and hybrid cloud, then architected a custom-tailored public cloud offering for the Polish market. After moving to Microsoft, he enjoyed working in a corporate environment, spending a couple of years as a cloud solution architect for enterprise customers. He now supports a multi-national organization called Digital and Cloud Services in Deutsche Telekom as a lead cloud solution architect, also leading an internal community of practice called Cloud Architect Ninjas.

I'd like to thank my beloved wife, Beata, and our children, Oliwia and Oskar, for their daily support, patience, and encouragement with everything that I do. I'd like to thank my parents, for giving me everything I needed to become who I am, my Mom, for her endless patience, and my Dad, for starting his IT journey living in a small Polish city by finishing offline snail-mailed courses almost 35 years ago! A spark that ignited my interests.

Dr. Nabil Hadj-Ahmed is a Google Cloud authorized trainer, a cloud architect, and a Google Cloud developer expert with over 20 years of experience working in real-world, challenging, enterprise, and demanding environments. Nabil facilitates Google Cloud training and brings a wealth of experience to enhance the learning experience of Google Cloud.

Nabil holds a Ph.D. and an MSc from Leeds Beckett University, where he also taught during his doctoral research. He also manages and speaks at Google Developer groups, organizing monthly meetup events and workshops focusing on Google technologies.

Pawel Piwowarek is a highly technical IT professional with a master's degree in computer science and over 18 years of industry experience designing, implementing, and supporting a wide range of IT solutions. He is an experienced technical leader and communicator who works with executives, managers, suppliers, and technical peers on large-scale projects with critical business impact. He maintains a keen interest in emerging and disruptive technologies and continuously adopts skillsets backed by relevant vendors' accreditations to match evolving business needs.

Table of Contents

Section 2: Manage, Design, and Plan a Cloud Solution Architecture

4

Working with Google Compute Engine

5

Exploring Google App Engine as a Compute Option

6

Managing Kubernetes Clusters with Google Kubernetes Engine

7

Deploying Cloud-Native Workloads with Cloud Run

10

Networking Options in GCP

11

Exploring Storage and Database Options in GCP – Part 1

12

Exploring Storage and Database Options in GCP – Part 2

13

Analyzing Big Data Options

14

Putting Machine Learning to Work

Section 3: Secure, Manage and Monitor a Google Cloud Solution

15

Security and Compliance

16

Google Cloud Management Options

17
Monitoring Your Infrastructure

Section 4: Exam Focus

18
Case Studies

19

Test Your Knowledge

Index

Other Books You May Enjoy

Preface

Google Cloud Platform (GCP) is a leading cloud offering that has grown exponentially year on year. GCP offers an array of services that can be leveraged by various organizations to bring the best out of their infrastructure. This book is a complete guide to GCP and will teach you various methods to effectively utilize GCP services for your business needs. You will also become acquainted with the topics required to pass Google's Professional Cloud Architect certification exam.

Following the Professional Cloud Architect certification's official exam syllabus, you will be introduced to GCP. You will then be taught about the core services that GCP offers, such as computing, storage, and network. Additionally, you will learn methods of how to scale and automate your cloud infrastructure and make it compliant and secure. Finally, you will also learn how to process big data and embrace machine learning services.

By the end of this book, you will have all the information required to ace Google's Professional Cloud Architect exam and become an expert in GCP services.

Who this book is for

If you are a cloud architect, cloud engineer, administrator, or anyone who would like to learn different ways to implement Google Cloud services in your organization, as well as get yourself certified with the Professional Cloud Architect's certificate, then this is the book for you.

What this book covers

Chapter 1, GCP Cloud Architect Professional, discusses the benefits of becoming a certified architect, how to register for the exam, and what to expect when you are in the test center.

Chapter 2, Getting Started with Google Cloud Platform, covers the basics of GCP and how it positions itself on the market. You will learn about all the major GCP services that are available.

Chapter 3, Google Cloud Platform Core Services, examines the most important GCP services, including computing, storage, networking, big data, and machine learning.

Chapter 4, Working with Google Compute Engine, examines how to create and run virtual machine instances on top of the **Google Compute Engine (GCE)** service.

Chapter 5, Exploring Google App Engine as a Compute Option, discusses how to define and run applications on Google App Engine.

Chapter 6, Managing Kubernetes Clusters with Google Kubernetes Engine, explains the basis of containers and microservices. It looks at running and managing Kubernetes clusters on the **Google Kubernetes Engine (GKE)** service.

Chapter 7, Deploying Cloud-Native Workloads with Cloud Run, discusses running cloud-native workloads in GCP with a serverless experience. Cloud Run does this without the need to understand complex Kubernetes resource definitions.

Chapter 8, Managing Cloud-Native Workloads with Anthos, introduces one of the newest and most exciting GCP products available. We will learn how we can run cloud-native workloads on Kubernetes anywhere. This includes not only all three major public cloud providers, but also on-premises. We will see how to keep the Anthos clusters in sync with predefined configuration and polices as well as how to control and observe traffic in a microservice architecture using Anthos Service Mesh.

Chapter 9, Running Serverless Functions with Google Cloud Functions, looks into running serverless functions on Google Cloud Functions.

Chapter 10, Networking Options in GCP, discusses Google's networking services. Understanding networking is key to completing the architect exam. We will introduce you to concepts such as **Virtual Private Cloud (VPC)** before diving further into other concepts such as **Virtual Private Network (VPN)**, networks, subnetworks, and routes.

Chapter 11, Exploring Storage and Database Options in GCP – Part 1, considers different storage options. This will allow us to choose the right storage for a given use case. We will discuss object storage alongside relational and non-relational databases.

Chapter 12, Exploring Storage and Database Options in GCP – Part 2, looks at storage options such as Cloud Spanner and BigTable.

Chapter 13, Analyzing Big Data Options, discusses how big data is another key topic in the architect exam. Understanding what big data is, and what services GCP offers to handle the complexities of data analytics, will really help you in the test center when taking the exam. In this chapter, we will look at the various services that are available, and when we might choose one over the other.

Chapter 14, Putting Machine Learning to Work, examines **Machine Learning** (**ML**) in general as well as GCP-related services. This will allow us to understand the use cases and possible implementations of machine learning using Google Cloud.

Chapter 15, Security and Compliance, covers security, which is a feature of all GCP services. In this chapter, we will cover IAM in more detail than we have in previous chapters, to allow you to understand custom roles and service accounts. Additionally, we will look at Google's commitments to compliance through the **Payment Card Industry** (**PCI**) regulations.

Chapter 16, Google Cloud Management Options, shows you that there are several ways to manage your GCP infrastructure and its services. In this chapter, we will look at how to manage your GCP infrastructure and the key management options that are available, including Cloud Shell, SDK, and G-Cloud, and the steps that are needed to access or install these tools.

Chapter 17, Monitoring Your Infrastructure, looks at monitoring your infrastructure using Stackdriver.

Chapter 18, Case Studies, discusses how, in the exam, some questions may refer you to several case studies. You should be familiar with these case studies before you take the exam. These involve hypothetical business and solution concepts. In this chapter, we will cover how to find these case studies; additionally, we will also take a look at an example case study and analyze it in order to design an appropriate solution.

Chapter 19, Test Your Knowledge, goes through exam tips and sample tests.

To get the most out of this book

As the practical examples throughout the book involve the use of GCP, a GCP free-tier account is required.

OS requirements
Windows, macOS X, and Linux (any)

Download the color images

We also provide a PDF file that has color images of the screenshots/diagrams used in this book. You can download it here: `https://static.packt-cdn.com/downloads/9781801812290_ColorImages.pdf`.

Conventions used

There are a number of text conventions used throughout this book.

`Code in text`: Indicates code words in the text, database table names, folder names, filenames, file extensions, pathnames, dummy URLs, user input, and Twitter handles. Here is an example: "Now, we need to update our configuration file. Let's save this and call it `multi.yaml`."

A block of code is set as follows:

```
apiVersion: apps/v1
kind: Deployment
metadata:
  name: nginx-deployment
  labels:
    app: nginx
spec:
  replicas: 3
```

Any command-line input or output is written as follows:

```
kubectl apply -f definition.yaml
```

Bold: Indicates a new term, an important word, or words that you see on screen. For example, words in menus or dialog boxes appear in the text like this. Here is an example: "Let's check out the **Deployment Manager** menu, where we can see that our deployments have been successful."

> **Tips or important notes**
> Appear like this.

Get in touch

Feedback from our readers is always welcome.

General feedback: If you have questions about any aspect of this book, mention the book title in the subject of your message and email us at `customercare@packtpub.com`.

Errata: Although we have taken every care to ensure the accuracy of our content, mistakes do happen. If you have found a mistake in this book, we would be grateful if you would report this to us. Please visit www.packtpub.com/support/errata, selecting your book, clicking on the Errata Submission Form link, and entering the details.

Piracy: If you come across any illegal copies of our works in any form on the internet, we would be grateful if you would provide us with the location address or website name. Please contact us at copyright@packt.com with a link to the material.

If you are interested in becoming an author: If there is a topic that you have expertise in and you are interested in either writing or contributing to a book, please visit authors.packtpub.com.

Share Your Thoughts

Once you've read *Professional Cloud Architect Google Cloud Certification Guide*, we'd love to hear your thoughts! Scan the QR code below to go straight to the Amazon review page for this book and share your feedback.

https://packt.link/r/1801812292

Your review is important to us and the tech community and will help us make sure we're delivering excellent quality content.

Section 1:
Introduction to GCP

This section will introduce us to Google Cloud Platform and outline the Professional Cloud Architect exam.

This part of the book comprises the following chapters:

- *Chapter 1, GCP Cloud Architect Professional*
- *Chapter 2, Getting Started with Google Cloud Platform*
- *Chapter 3, Google Cloud Platform Core Services*

1
GCP Cloud Architect Professional

The shift to the cloud is not a new thing, and for many years, companies have been utilizing cost-effective solutions from public cloud vendors to move away from the traditional on-premises architecture. The speed at which technology is moving now makes it increasingly difficult for companies managing their own infrastructure to get the most out of their IT systems.

While **Amazon Web Services (AWS)** and Microsoft Azure currently lead the race with enterprise-scale companies, **Google Cloud Platform (GCP)** is one of the most popular solutions among IT professionals, and interest in it is steadily increasing. It seems that Google is playing the long game very well. In Q3 2018, ex-CEO of Google Cloud, Diane Greene, estimated that only 10% of workloads are in the public cloud, showing the massive scope for market share still available.

Given that companies are continuously moving to multi-cloud solutions to distribute their workloads or have more control over where and how their data is stored, this means that IT cloud architects and engineers need to understand more than just the current top two providers.

Furthermore, the *2020 global pandemic* accelerated cloud adoption as companies shifted to home working, and collaboration tools such as *Google Meet* became vital in companies for maintaining stability. It also highlighted that legacy IT models proved a significant risk to businesses due to the delay in being able to scale when needed, for example.

This book, of course, will focus on Google technologies. Many of you may have experience with other public cloud vendors, such as AWS or Microsoft Azure, but we will also cater to those who are new to the public cloud. The goal of this book is to help you pass the **Google Professional Cloud Architect** exam. This book is suitable for both levels of experience. In this chapter, we will look at why you would take this exam, inform you about how to register for the exam, and brief you on what to expect from the exam.

We will cover the following topics in this chapter:

- Understanding the benefits of being a certified architect
- Registering for the exam
- What to expect from the exam
- Suggested hints and tips

Understanding the benefits of being a certified architect

Studying for an exam can be a daunting prospect. Many hours need to be spent to achieve a certification, and it's not always an easy decision to dedicate a lot of personal time to achieve this goal. That said, if you currently work in the IT industry, you will know that the landscape has changed over several years. The public cloud is no longer something that worries companies, and more enterprises are shifting away from traditional on-premises solutions, meaning that the time you invest in learning new technologies will be beneficial to your career.

But *why take the exam?* There are several reasons why you would take this exam, such as the following:

- You have used GCP for some time and want to have an industry-recognized certification that reflects your current skill set.
- You want to achieve a new role or promotion and show that you can dedicate your own time to learning new skills that you don't get to use every day.
- There is no better way to showcase your skills than having industry-led certifications.
- You want to get acquainted with modern stack development technologies.
- You have a desire to become a multi-cloud specialist and want to be certified across the *Big 3* public cloud vendors.

> **Important Note**
>
> A Forbes article recently showed that the **Google Cloud Certified Professional Cloud Architect** is the highest-paid certification of 2019 and 2020. You can read it at `https://www.forbes.com/sites/louiscolumbus/2020/02/10/15-top-paying-it-certifications-in-2020/?sh=390a9e48358e`.

Whatever your reason for taking the exam, it is important to be realistic about your expectations.

Registering for the exam

The cost of the **GCP Professional Architect** exam is around 200 USD (this may change by the time you are reading this), and it can be booked in several languages, such as English, Japanese, Spanish, and Portuguese. In mid-2020, Google introduced the ability to take the exam remotely from your own home. The registration process is the same. You can register for the exam by going through the following steps:

1. The first step is to visit the Google certification web page. There are two links to this:

   - `https://cloud.google.com/certification`
   - `https://cloud.google.com/certification/register`

2. Click on the preferred language to schedule your exam, as shown in the following screenshot:

Register for your certification

Refer to the chart below to find which Google Cloud Certifications are offered in multiple languages.

To schedule your exam, select your preferred language. Each language requires a separate Google Cloud Webassessor account.

Select your preferred language to schedule an exam

| English | Japanese | Spanish |

Figure 1.1 – Select your preferred language

3. Next, you will be redirected to the **Webassessor** login page. You will need a Webassessor account to book the exam. You can follow the guide on the **Webassessor** page to create a new account if needed.

4. Next, click on the **REGISTER FOR AN EXAM** button, as shown in the following screenshot:

Receipts   Register For An Exam   My Assessments   **Home**

You last logged in 18 May 2021 at 1:57AM MST.

Make sure you review the retake policy and recertification eligibility criteria before you take an exam. There is a limit on the number of times you can take an exam and a waiting period between attempts (even if you are taking the same exam in a different language). It is your responsibility to adhere to these terms and conditions to avoid possible suspension or rejection of exam results.

Launching your online exam? Due to high volume, you may experience additional wait time (15-20 mins) before connecting with a proctor. Do not disconnect. We appreciate your patience!

REGISTER FOR AN EXAM

Figure 1.2 – The REGISTER FOR AN EXAM button

5. Browse to the **Google Cloud Certified – Professional Cloud Architect** exam and expand the plus (+) sign. You will have options to sit the exam at a test center (**Onsite Proctored**) or remotely (**Remote Proctored**), as follows:

Figure 1.3 – Selecting Remote Proctored or Onsite Proctored

6. If you choose to sit the exam at a test center, you will be prompted to select a location, as shown in the following screenshot:

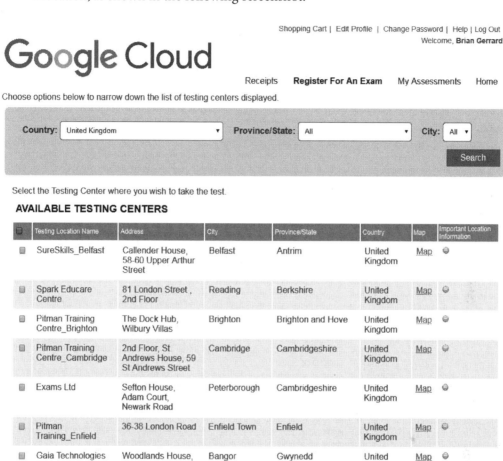

Figure 1.4 – Selecting a test center (if applicable)

7. Next, select a date and time, as shown in the following screenshot. Note that the time is local to the test center:

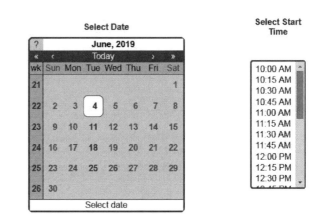

Figure 1.5 – Selecting a date and time

8. Finally, review and click **Check Out**. At this point, you can pay for the exam and you are ready to go. Submit your coupon or voucher code if you have one, as shown here:

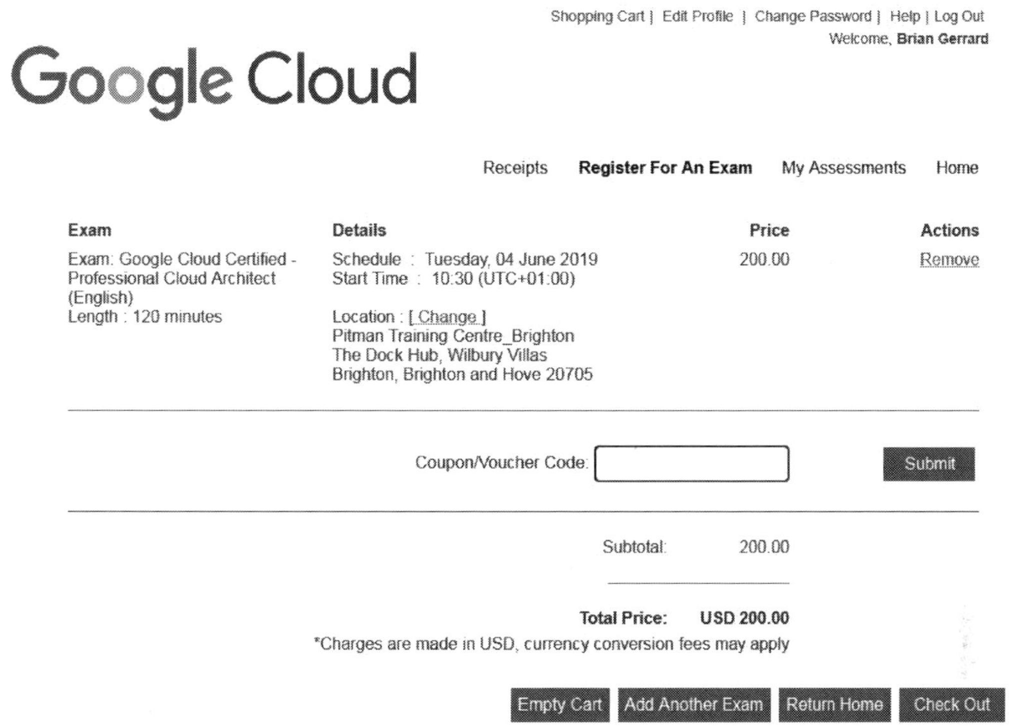
Shopping Cart | Edit Profile | Change Password | Help | Log Out
Welcome, Brian Gerrard
Google Cloud
Receipts
Register For An Exam
My Assessments
Home
Exam
Details
Price
Actions
Exam: Google Cloud Certified - Professional Cloud Architect (English)
Length : 120 minutes
Schedule : Tuesday, 04 June 2019
Start Time : 10:30 (UTC+01:00)
Location : [Change]
Pitman Training Centre_Brighton
The Dock Hub, Wilbury Villas
Brighton, Brighton and Hove 20705
200.00
Remove
Coupon/Voucher Code:
Submit
Subtotal:
200.00
Total Price:
USD 200.00
*Charges are made in USD, currency conversion fees may apply
Empty Cart
Add Another Exam
Return Home
Check Out

Figure 1.6 – Confirming the purchase

Please bear in mind that you can change the selected date once the exam has been booked. Rescheduling exams up to 72 hours for onsite or 24 hours for remote can be done at no extra cost. Note that a rescheduling fee will be charged for any changes that are made inside these timeframes.

This section has shown us how to register for the exam. The main to recognize is that we now have the option to sit the exam at home. In the next section, we will look at what to expect from the exam.

What to expect from the exam

There are several resources that Google advises you to take advantage of to prepare for the exam. These consist of online training courses, instructor-led training, and practical labs. All of this information can be found on the cloud architect web page at `https://cloud.google.com/certification/cloud-architect`.

In addition, by visiting the exam guide web page at `https://cloud.google.com/certification/guides/professional-cloud-architect/`, you can see the expected subject knowledge of the exam applicants. The exam blueprint is critical for any exam, and GCP Architect is no different. You should review this guide and make sure you understand each section.

Like most exams, some real-life experience will also help you. The exam was created with cloud architects in mind who have experience with software development and multi-cloud/hybrid-cloud environments. That said, there is no reason why you cannot pass this exam with the correct amount of study and exposure to a GCP environment, even if you don't have practical, hands-on experience.

Google offers **Qwiklabs**, a self-study platform that can be used to gain experience in the services offered. It is recommended that you sign up to familiarize yourself with GCP's layout and services. Qwiklabs can be paid for either through a monthly subscription, which will give you unlimited access to the labs, or by purchasing credits. Each lab will cost a certain number of credits, depending on the complexity of the lab. The typical cost of 10 credits is 10 USD and there are discounts for bulk buys. GCP Essentials gives a great introduction to GCP that can be found at `https://google.qwiklabs.com/quests/23?utm_source=gcp&utm_medium=site&utm_campaign=certification`. It takes around 5 hours to complete this lab.

The exam itself will consist of multiple-choice questions that will require one or more answers to be selected. In addition to this, you will be quizzed on the case studies of fictional companies. However, you will have access to these case studies before the exam, and you can refer to them during the exam. In *Chapter 18, Case Studies*, we will go over these in more detail. There will be around 60 questions in the exam, and you will have 2 hours to complete them. You will receive an on-screen message stating only a pass or fail, with no indication of your score. Google believes that scored results are not meaningful for the examinee and can be misinterpreted. A confirmation email will also be delivered to your registered email address confirming the result.

Passing the exam will validate your skills for 2 years. Then, you are required to recertify by sitting the full and latest exam again. Should you be unsuccessful in your attempt, you must wait 14 days before you can retake. If you fail a second attempt, you must wait 60 days, while for a third failed attempt, you must wait 1 full year before you can retake the exam. A full fee is required for each attempt.

Online proctored exams

Due to the COVID-19 pandemic, as of early 2020, Google accelerated its program to deliver online proctored exams. In H2 of 2020, the *Professional Data Engineer* exam became the first Google exam to be offered online and the Professional Cloud Architect exam soon followed. There is no difference in terms of price, length, or the content of the exam compared to the traditional test center method. However, there are differences in the minutes leading up to your exam. You must download the **Sentinel** software and have full administrative control over your machine. If you are using a corporate machine, this may cause issues. There are also system requirements that must be met; for example, the OS must be Windows 8.1 or 10, or Mac OS X 10.13-11.1. Your web browser requires the latest version of Chrome, Firefox, or Safari. Additionally, a webcam is required. You are also required to have your face scanned for a biometrics profile and this must be populated before the exam.

When the time comes to sit your exam, you should be in a secure, quiet, and well-lit room. You will be required to show the surrounding room with your webcam. You will also require a mirror or your phone to show its screen if the webcam is integrated. There can be no other people in the room, nor is any food, drink, or other paper or writing instruments allowed. A full list of testing requirements can be found on the Google Cloud certification web page `https://support.google.com/cloud-certification/answer/9907748?hl=en`.

When you have completed the exam, you will be informed of your result, the same as you would in the test center, with a message stating only pass or fail.

After a few days, you will get confirmation that the results have been sent to Google for verification. In a week, you should get an official confirmation, along with a link to your certificate.

Suggested hints and tips

In the exam, we recommend that you make use of the fact that you can mark questions for review and come back to them later. It is a personal preference, of course, but we suggest that you don't puzzle over a question for too long. You will have around 2 minutes per question to provide an answer. Some of the answers to the questions will jump straight out of the screen at you, while others will take you more time to determine the correct answer. If you are spending too long on a question, then mark it for review and move on, as it's important to get to the end of the test to ensure that you have scored the maximum number of marks.

We also recommend booking the exam to give you an incentive. It is easy to procrastinate or worry too much that you are not fully prepared. This is a natural feeling but having an end date in sight gives you focus and determination. We recommend that you print out the exam guide and work through each point to ensure that you understand each objective.

Additionally, 2 hours is a long time. Ensure that you book the exam at a time of day when you are the most alert, to give yourself the best chance of success. With the option of the remote exam, it should become easier to find a slot that suits you, but you must be sure to find a space that is both private and quiet. Additionally, ensure you have a stable internet connection and enough laptop power if this is the type of device you are using. For some, attending a test center may still be the preferred option.

Summary

In this chapter, we covered what to expect from the exam and how to register for it, as well as the benefits of being a GCP Certified Architect. Throughout this book, we will introduce you to the services that are needed for a successful outcome. This book's ultimate goal is to assist you in passing the exam; however, we encourage you to do more reading, use Qwiklabs, or play around in the GCP console if you wish to deep dive into a particular topic or service that you encounter while reading this book.

In the next chapter, we will get started with GCP.

Further reading

Read the following article for more information regarding what was covered in this chapter:

- **Google Cloud Certificate**: `https://cloud.google.com/certification`.

2

Getting Started with Google Cloud Platform

In this chapter, we will introduce the concept of cloud computing to better understand what **Google Cloud Platform** (**GCP**) is. We will take a look at GCP resources and their hierarchy. After that, we will create our first account and set up a project. Additionally, we will discuss the billing options that are available. We will examine how to create a billing account and associate it with the project. Finally, we will take a look at how to export the billing information. It is important to have this introduction before we start talking about GCP services. This will both help you to pass the exam and to implement the basic setup of GCP for real-life scenarios before you even begin using the services. We actively encourage you to set up your own free-tier Google Cloud account in order to acquire hands-on exposure and gain confidence.

In this chapter, we will cover the following topics :

- Introducing the cloud
- Understanding GCP
- Exam tips

> **Exam Tip**
>
> Having a good understanding of GCP resources is vital in order to pass the
> **GCP Cloud Architect** exam. Make sure that you go through this chapter
> carefully and attentively. Read it multiple times if required, and play around
> with the creation of projects and billing accounts using your free-tier account.
> Try exporting billing data to both files and BigQuery. You need to remember
> individual **Identity and Access Management (IAM)** roles for billing. Make
> sure that you have a good understanding of the scope of the services.

Introducing the cloud

Before we jump into GCP, first, let's learn what the cloud is, as per the following diagram:

Figure 2.1 – What the cloud is

It is true—*there is no cloud: it's just someone else's computer*. With the cloud, what we are
actually doing is accessing resources and consuming services that are hosted on someone
else's computer. If we want to be more precise, the cloud is a pool of computers.

Now, let's take a look at a more accurate and professional definition used by Google
that comes from the United States National Institute of Standards and Technology
(`https://csrc.nist.gov/publications/detail/sp/800-145/final`):

> *"Cloud computing is a model for enabling ubiquitous, convenient,
> on-demand network access to a shared pool of configurable computing
> resources (for example, networks, servers, storage, applications, and
> services) that can be rapidly provisioned and released with minimal
> management effort or service provider interaction. This cloud model
> is composed of five essential characteristics, three service models,
> and four deployment models."*

The five essential characteristics of the cloud are as follows:

- **On-demand self-service**: Services are provisioned automatically without manual provider intervention, and you only pay for what is used.
- **Broad network access**: Resources are available throughout the network.
- **Resource pooling**: Resources are pooled from a shared pool, giving the user a sense of location independence. For some of the resources, the location might be restricted.
- **Rapid elasticity**: Services can be elastically provisioned and de-provisioned with the capacity being managed by the provider.
- **Measured service**: Resource usage is monitored and can be reported on.

The four deployment models are as follows:

- **Private cloud**: This is used by specific organizations but can be managed by third parties.
- **Public cloud**: This is used by the general public.
- **Community cloud**: This is used by specific communities.
- **Hybrid cloud**: This is composed of two or more different clouds.

When we look at GCP, it fulfills all of the five characteristics and fits into the public cloud deployment model. In the next section, we will take a look at GCP itself.

Understanding GCP

Google has been developing its own tools to deliver services such as Gmail, YouTube, and Google Workspace for years. These tools have been converted into services that can be consumed by others. Consumers are given the amazing scalability that Google must use for their own purposes. GCP allows you to choose from computing, storage, networking, big data, and **Machine Learning** (**ML**) services to build your application on top of them. The number of services is constantly growing, and new announcements are made on an almost weekly basis. New services and features are released, first, as alpha versions, then as beta versions, and finally, they are made globally available. The early releases are available even earlier for selected customers and partners. This allows the services to be tested by external parties even before their official release!

Google supports several service models, including the following:

- **Infrastructure-as-a-Service (IaaS)**
- **Platform-as-a-Service (PaaS)**
- **Container-as-a-Service (CaaS)**
- **Function-as-a-Service (FaaS)**
- **Managed services**

As you can see, the range of services in GCP is very broad. Let's quickly analyze this range of services offered by GCP. We will start from very simple IaaS, such as a traditional data center, and end with using FaaS, where we can run code without the need to manage any server infrastructure. The choice of service depends on our requirements. Put simply, if we require flexibility and control over our **Virtual Machines (VMs)**, we would use **Compute Engine**. This service allows us to provision VM instances or simply lift and shift machines from our existing environment. However, the trade-off is that you are responsible for managing all of the layers above the VM instance. That includes the operating system, any middleware, and any applications on top of it.

When we move away from IaaS toward PaaS, CaaS, or FaaS, the responsibility of maintaining the infrastructure is taken away from us. With **Cloud Functions**, all we really care about is the coding of a function in a language supported by GCP. Once it's done and published, we access it through the HTTP(S) protocol.

Finally, as we move to managed services, we simply start to consume services that bring us a particular business value without having to worry about any underlying parts. They can be used in **Software-as-a-Service (SaaS)** models and consumed through APIs. An example of this is **Dataprep**, which is a data service that allows you to clean up and prepare your data for further analysis. Another example is the pretrained ML model, **Vision API**. Developers can consume this service by using the RESTful API to analyze images without having to write any code, except for the call itself.

Hopefully, now you understand that GCP is much more than just a hosting service. It provides you with sets of tools, services, and resources that will help you to develop and deliver your applications. The choice of the services you will use depends entirely on the set of requirements you have. If that feels overwhelming, then don't worry. This book is written to help you to go through GCP step by step.

In *Chapter 3, Google Cloud Platform Core Services*, you will get an overview of the most important GCP services. In the following chapters, we will dive into each of them in more detail to get you prepared for the exam.

GCP differentiators

Every cloud provider has something that differentiates it from others. Each provider has its own strategy in terms of how to deliver value to customers, and the same is true for GCP. Let's take a look at what the key GCP features are that make it stand out from the crowd:

- **Google Cloud's operations suite** (formerly known as **The Google Network**): The Google Network is something that differentiates GCP from other cloud providers. Google claims that around 40% of the world's internet traffic is carried by the Google Network, making it the largest network on the globe. This allows the Google Network to respond with very low latency, as close to the end user as possible.

- **Global scope**: GCP was developed with global availability in mind. You will note that services such as load balancing are available globally rather than regionally, unlike other providers. This allows the client to concentrate on development and embrace out-of-the-box high availability and elasticity.

- **ML services**: GCP offers a great number of ML services for both data scientists and regular developers who might have limited knowledge of ML. The ML services allow pretrained models to be used, as well as offering *AutoML* services. The latter allows you to train ML models without knowing how they are actually created. The portfolio of these services is growing very quickly. The key goal of Google is to enable enterprises with ML to make faster and smarter decisions.

- **Developer-focused**: GCP was built with a focus on developers. If you look at the history of GCP, it started in 2008 with a preview release of App Engine, which is a fully serverless platform, allowing developers to initially run their applications written in Python, before support for other languages such as Java and Go were added. It provides out-of-the-box load balancing and autoscaling. Developers simply need to choose the platform they want to develop on and they can start coding. Also, if you look at **Google Cloud's operations suite** (formerly known as **Stackdriver**, a GCP monitoring tool) itself, it provides several tools that can be directly integrated with an application. This allows the developer to use them to monitor and debug their application. Google makes it very clear that GCP was created for developers to help them with their challenges. Having achieved this goal, they are now aiming toward large enterprises.

- **Pricing**: The VM instances are priced per second with a minimum runtime of one minute. This allows you to run the machines for short tests and not have to pay for a full hour of use.

- **Service-Level Agreement (SLA)**: GCP provides the customer agreement with the level of service that will be delivered for the service. This is usually defined as a **Service-Level Objective (SLO)**, which covers a Monthly Uptime Percentage for the service. If the SLO is not met, the customer is eligible for financial credits. Note that this percentage depends on the service and that alpha and beta features are not included with any SLA.

- **Security**: Google uses its many years of experience in running services such as Gmail in GCP. Your data is always encrypted with a choice of Google or customer-managed keys.

- **Carbon neutral**: This might not be the most important feature when it comes to functionality, but it is worth knowing. Google data centers are carbon-neutral, meaning that 100% of the energy used to power them comes from renewable energy. This includes the GCP data centers.

GCP locations

As we have already mentioned, GCP has a global footprint that includes North America, South America, Europe, Asia, and Australia. The locations are further split into regions and zones.

It is your decision where your application should be located to provide low latency and high availability:

- **A region** is defined by Google as an independent geographic area that is divided into multiple zones. Locations within regions should have round-trip network latencies of under 1 ms in 95% of cases.

- **A zone** is a deployment area for GCP resources. Note that a zone does not correspond to a single data center; it can consist of multiple buildings. Even though a zone provides a certain amount of fault protection, a zone is considered a **single point of failure (SPOF)**. Therefore, you should consider placing your application across multiple zones to provide fault tolerance.

- **Network edge locations** are connections to GCP services located in a particular metropolitan area.

At the time of writing, GCP has the following:

- 28 regions

- 85 zones

- 146 network edge locations

These numbers are growing rapidly, and, at the time of writing, Google has announced an additional two regions at the Google Cloud Next conference. For the most up-to-date information, please refer to `https://cloud.google.com/about/locations`. The following map shows the current and future regions and zones across the globe:

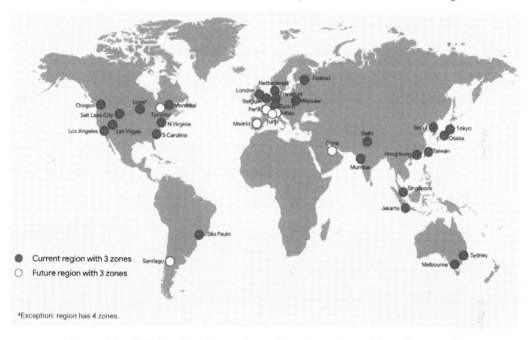

Figure 2.2 – GCP locations (Source: https://cloud.google.com/about/locations/)

The preceding map shows current regions in blue and planned regions in white. It should also be noted that not all services are available in each region. For example, **Cloud Functions**, after being made globally available, was only introduced in a limited number of locations.

Resource manager

GCP consists of containers such as organizations, folders, and projects to hierarchically group your resources. This allows you to manage their configuration and access control. The resources can be managed programmatically using APIs. Also, Google provides tools such as *Google Cloud Console* and *command-line utilities*, which are wrappers around the API calls. Now, let's take a look at the hierarchy presented in the following diagram and familiarize ourselves with each of the resources:

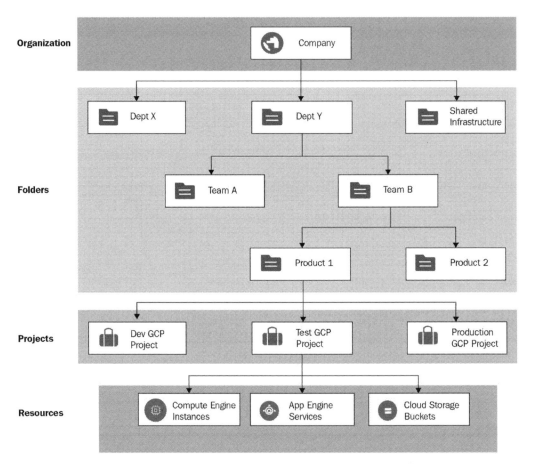

Figure 2.3 – The resource manager hierarchy (Source: https://cloud.google.com/resource-manager/docs/cloud-platform-resource-hierarchy, License: https://creativecommons.org/licenses/by/4.0/legalcode)

The preceding diagram shows the resource manager hierarchy. Starting from the top, we have an **Organization** that can be mapped to a company. Next, we have **Folders** that can represent a company's departments. Next, we have **Projects**, which further divide the actual company projects or environments, such as development and production. Finally, underneath **Projects**, we have GCP **Resources**. We will take a look at each of these in the following sections.

Organizations

At the top of the hierarchy, we have the organization. However, note that this is an optional resource, and you can use GCP very well without it. The organization is only available to users of **Google Workspace** (formerly *G-Suite*) and **Cloud Identity**, which are products outside of GCP.

To provide some context, Google Workspace is a bundle of collaboration tools, including Gmail, Google Drive, Hangouts, and Google Docs. Users use these tools, which are stored in the Google Workspace domain.

Cloud Identity is an **Identity-as-a-Service (IDaaS)** offering. Similarly, it allows you to create a domain and to manage your users, applications, and device accounts from a single point. You can learn more about Cloud Identity in *Chapter 15, Security and Compliance.*

A single Google Workspace or Cloud Identity account can only be associated with a single organization. This implies that the organization is bound to one domain only. In both Google Workspace and Cloud Identity, there is a defined role of super administrators. When you create the organization, those users will have the highest privileges in the organization and underlying resources. Please ensure that this account is not used for day-to-day operations.

Instead, the super administrator should assign the role of organization administrator to designated users. This role is further used to define IAM policies, resource hierarchy, and delegate permissions using IAM roles.

Important Note

With the creation of a new organization, all users from the domain get project creator and Billing Account Creator IAM roles. This allows them to create new projects in that organization. Again, we will take a closer look at this in *Chapter 15, Security and Compliance.*

Folders

Folders are logical containers that can group projects or other folders. They can be used to assign IAM policies. Again, the use of folders is optional and is only available when an organization resource exists. The use case for using folders is to group projects that will use the same IAM policies.

Projects

Projects are the smallest logical containers that group resources. Every resource within GCP needs to belong to exactly one project. Each project is managed separately, and IAM roles can be assigned per project to control the access in a fine-grained way.

Projects have three identification attributes:

- **Project ID**: This is a globally unique immutable ID generated by Google.

- **Project name**: This is a unique name provided by a user.

- **Project number**: This is a globally unique number generated by Google.

In most cases, you will use the project ID to identify your project. To manage resources within GCP, you will always need to identify which project they belong to by either the project ID or the project number. You can create multiple projects, but there is a quota that limits the number of projects per account. If you reach the quota, you will need to submit a request to extend it.

Resources' scope

Now that we know the physical and logical separation of GCP resources, let's take a look at their scope. The resources can be either *global*, *regional*, or *zonal*. This indicates how accessible the resource is to other resources. For example, a global image can be used in any region to provision VMs. On the other hand, a VM that needs to belong to a particular subnet must reside in the same region for which the subnet was configured.

Even though the resources have a narrow scope, bear in mind that they still need to have unique names within the project, meaning you can't have two VMs with the same name within one project.

OK, let's take a look at the resources and their scope. You might not be completely familiar with the following resources, but don't worry; they will be explained in more detail in the coming chapters.

Global resources

Global resources are globally available within the same project and can be accessed from any zone. These include the following objects:

- **Addresses**: These are reserved external IP addresses and can be used by global load balancers.

- **Images**: These are either predefined or user-customized. They can be used to provision VMs.

- **Snapshots**: Snapshots of a persistent disk allow the creation of new disks and VMs. Note that you can also expose a snapshot to a different project. Snapshots can also act as a backup for VMs.

- **Instance templates**: These can be used for the creation of managed instance groups.

- **Virtual Private Cloud (VPC) networks**: These are virtual networks that you can connect your workloads to.

- **Firewall**: These are defined per VPC but are globally accessible.

- **Routes**: Routes allow you to direct your network traffic and are assigned to VPCs, but they are also considered global.

Regional resources

Regional resources are only accessible by other resources within the same region. These include the following objects:

- **Addresses**: Static, external IP addresses can only be used by instances that are in the same region.

- **Subnets**: These are associated with VPC networks and allow the assignment of IP addresses to VMs.

- **Regional managed instance groups**: These allow you to scale groups of instances. The scope can be set to either regions or zones.

- **Regional persistent disks**: These provide replicated, persistent storage to VM instances. They can also be shared between projects for the creation of snapshots and images, but not disk attachments.

Zonal resources

Zonal resources are only accessible by other resources within the same zone. These include the following objects:

- **VM instances**: These reside in a particular zone.

- **Zonal persistent disks**: These provide persistent storage to VM instances. They can also be shared as disks between projects for the creation of snapshots and images, but not disk attachments.

- **Machine types**: These define the hardware configuration for your VM instances and are defined for any particular zone.

- **Zonal managed instance groups**: These allow you to autoscale groups of instances. The scope can be set to either regions or zones.

Now that we understand the theory, let's take a look at how to create a project. Note that if you have not done so yet, navigate to `https://cloud.google.com/free` to create your free-tier GCP account.

Managing projects

To create a new project, perform the following steps:

1. Log in to the GCP console at `https://console.cloud.google.com`. Then, click on the drop-down arrow next to the name of the project you are currently logged into. A **Select a project** window will pop up. Click on **NEW PROJECT** in the upper-right corner:

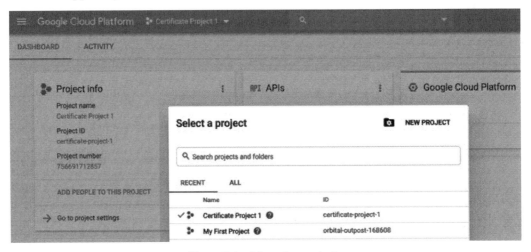

Figure 2.4 – Managing projects

2. Fill in the name and choose the billing account. You can attach the project to an organization or a folder. Choose the default billing account. In the following steps, we will show you how to create a new billing account and associate it with the project we are now creating. Click on the **CREATE** button, as shown in the following screenshot:

New Project

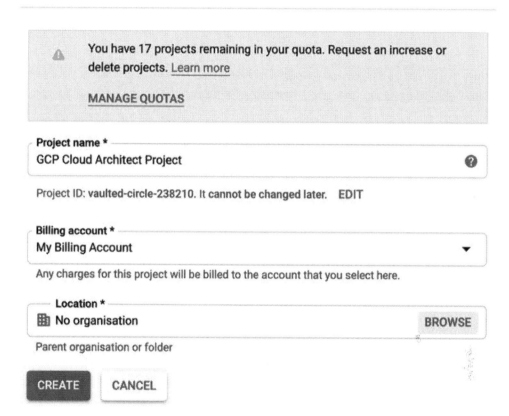

You have 17 projects remaining in your quota. Request an increase or delete projects. Learn more

MANAGE QUOTAS

Project name *
GCP Cloud Architect Project

Project ID: vaulted-circle-238210. It cannot be changed later.   EDIT

Billing account *
My Billing Account

Any charges for this project will be billed to the account that you select here.

Location *
No organisation   BROWSE

Parent organisation or folder

CREATE   CANCEL

Figure 2.5 – The New Project pane

Note that the **Billing account** option will not be shown if you don't own an organization and use a private account.

3. A new project has been created. You can now manage it from the GCP console:

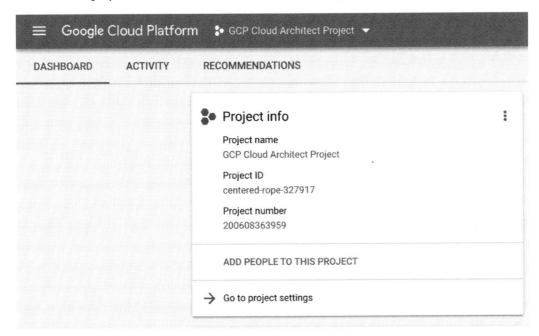

Figure 2.6 – The Project info pane

4. To start using the GCP services, click on the hamburger icon. A menu will pop up. You can access all of the GCP services from here, as shown in the following screenshot:

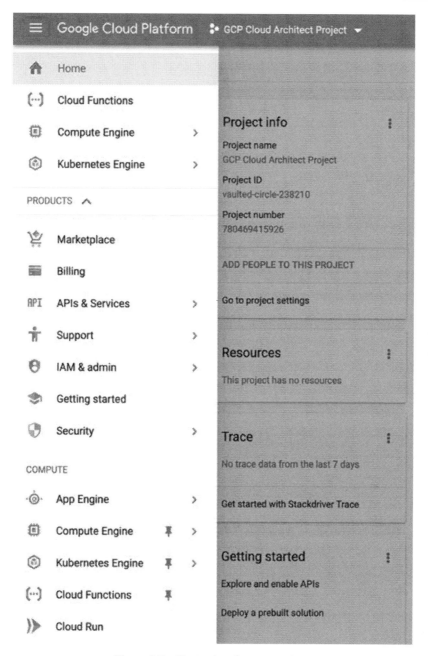

Figure 2.7 – Start using the new project

In the following chapter of this book, we will take a look at each of the services that are relevant to the exam. Don't get scared by the number of options available.

Granting permissions

In the IAM section of *Chapter 15, Security and Compliance,* you will find more details about how to assign permissions to your GCP resources.

For the sake of this introduction, we will now learn how to add a member and assign previously defined roles to them. Essentially, roles are the settings of permissions.

Here are the step-by-step instructions to grant permissions:

1. To add a new member to your project, go to the **IAM** section of the **IAM & admin** pane.

2. Select the **MEMBERS** tab and click on **ADD**. Now, select a member and choose a role. Click on **Save** to confirm:

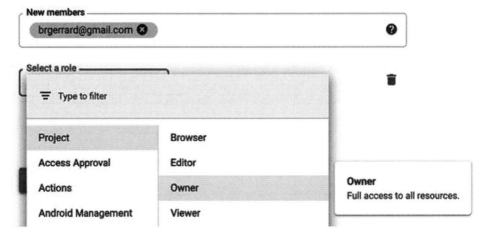

Figure 2.8 – Adding members to roles

3. The user has been added and has been granted the permissions of the defined role:

Figure 2.9 – Users added to the role

`Brian Gerrard` has been sent an invitation to join the project as an owner. The triangle with an exclamation mark will be displayed until the invitation has been accepted.

Billing

Depending on your company structure, you might have different requirements regarding billing. With GCP, you have the option to create a single or multiple billing accounts. As shown in the following diagram, the billing accounts can be associated with one or more projects. The actual payment details are created in the payment profiles that are attached to the billing account, as follows:

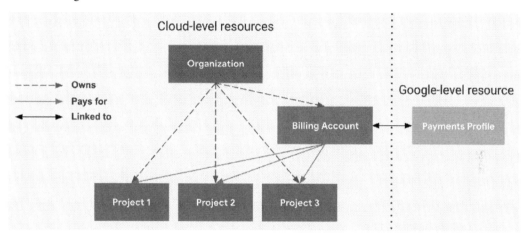

Figure 2.10 – Google Cloud billing (Source: https://cloud.google.com/billing/docs/how-to/billing-access?hl=pl, License: https://creativecommons.org/licenses/by/4.0/legalcode)

Here, you can see that the smallest entity you are billed for is a single project. Therefore, you cannot split your bill inside the project. This affects how you can split the billing within your organization. Do you have multiple departments that need separate billing—for example, finance, engineering, and human resources—or do you manage it centrally?

In the first scenario, you might want multiple projects with multiple billing accounts; however, in the latter scenario, you might require multiple projects with a single billing account.

Managing billing accounts

The first billing account will be created upon the creation of your GCP account. However, as we have just learned, you might require multiple billing accounts.

To create a new billing account, perform the following steps:

1. Navigate to the GCP console and choose **Billing** from the left-hand side navigation pane. Click on the drop-down menu that shows your billing account and click on **MANAGE BILLING ACCOUNTS**.

2. You will be presented with the existing billing accounts. Click on **Create account**:

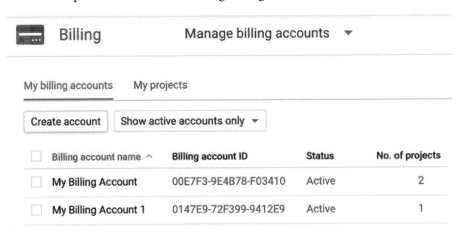

Figure 2.11 – My billing accounts

3. In the next window, name your billing account, as shown in the following screenshot:

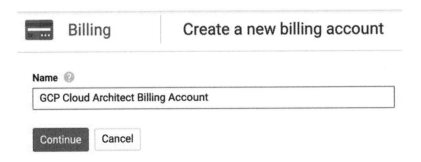

Figure 2.12 – Creating a new billing account

4. Choose the country, and the currency will be updated for you. Click on the **Confirm** button:

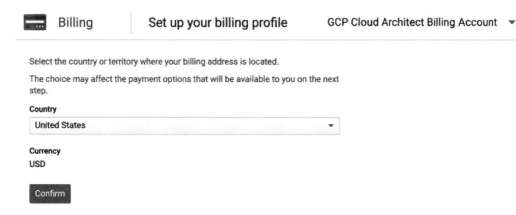

Figure 2.13 – Setting up the billing profile

5. Now, you can choose an existing payment profile or create a new one. Note that we do not see any existing profiles. This is because my existing payment profiles are set to Polish PLN, while the new billing profile is set to USD. Fill in the customer information and scroll down to **Payment method**:

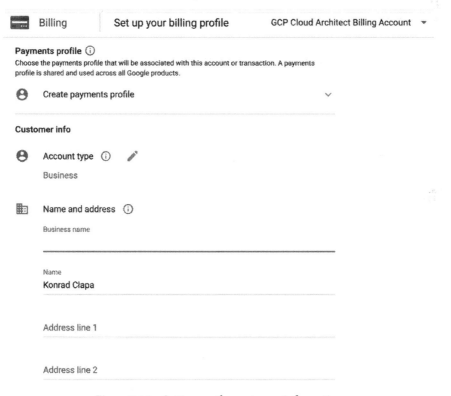

Figure 2.14 – Setting up the customer information

6. Fill in your payment details, and click on the **Submit and enable billing** button:

Figure 2.15 – Payment details

7. Now, your billing account has been created, and you can manage it from the **Billing** window:

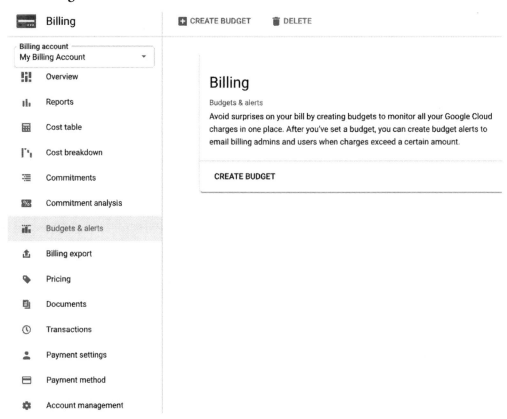

Figure 2.16 – The billing account has been created

We can now assign a project to the newly created billing account.

Assigning a project to a billing account

As mentioned already, you can assign multiple projects to one billing account. In the following screenshot, you can see that we now have three billing accounts and multiple projects assigned to them. Our newly created billing account has no project assigned to it; therefore, let's move our GCP Cloud Architect project to that billing account, as follows:

1. Click on **Billing** and then click on **Account Management**. Now, click on the three-dots next to the project name and choose **Change billing**:

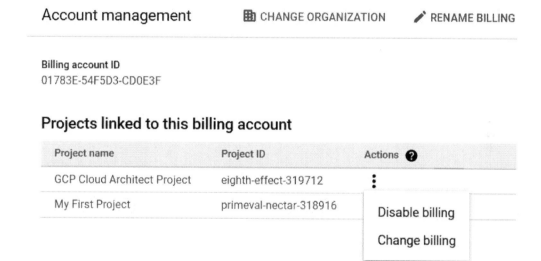

Figure 2.17 – Changing the billing account

2.   In the next window, we select the billing account we want the project to be attached to and click on **SET ACCOUNT**:

Figure 2.18 – Selecting the billing account for the project

The project is now attached to its proper billing account.

Exporting billing

GCP allows you to export the billing information to a **BigQuery** dataset. This can be useful if you need to prepare reports or carry out an analysis of the cost of your cloud consumption.

> **Important Note**
> We will learn about BigQuery and Google Storage in the big data and storage chapters of this book. To understand billing exports, you just need to know that BigQuery is a GCP data warehouse service.

To perform the export, follow these steps:

1.   Go to **Billing** and choose **Billing export**. Select the **BIGQUERY EXPORT** option. There are different levels of details available for exports:

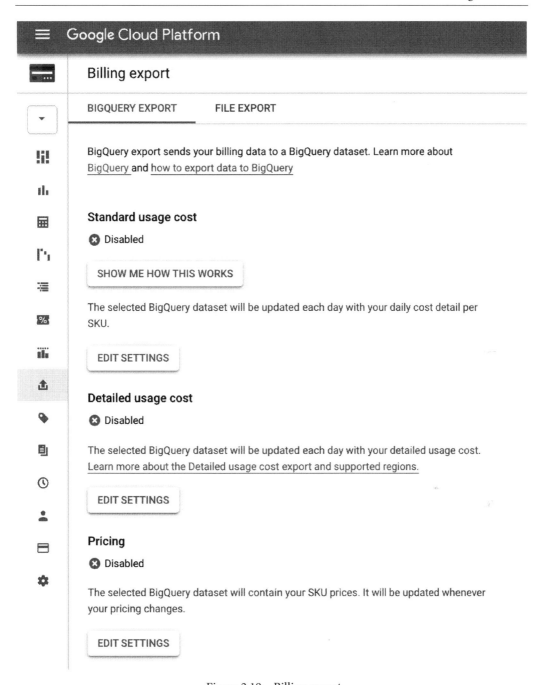

Figure 2.19 – Billing export

2. To export a standard report, click on the **EDIT SETTINGS** in the **Standard usage cost** section. Then, fill in the information regarding the dataset and click on **SAVE**. If you currently have no datasets set up in BigQuery, then you will be prompted to create one from the drop-down menu:

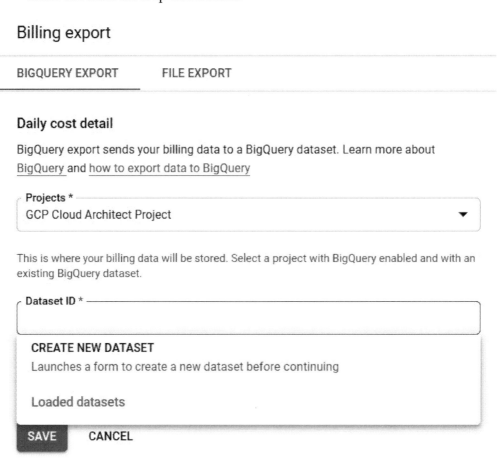

Figure 2.20 – Daily cost detail

3. Next, you can create a new dataset with the values you require:

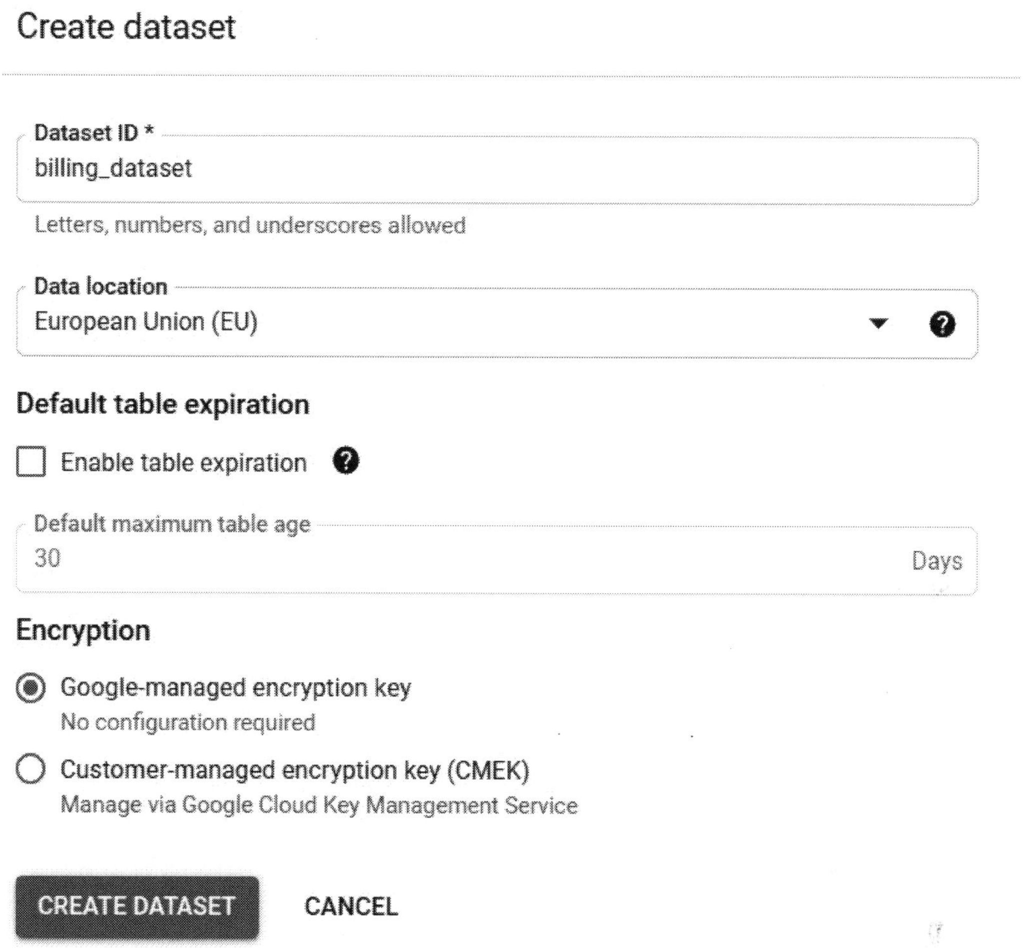

Create dataset

Dataset ID *

billing_dataset

Letters, numbers, and underscores allowed

Data location

European Union (EU)   ▼   ❓

Default table expiration

☐ Enable table expiration ❓

Default maximum table age

30   Days

Encryption

◉ Google-managed encryption key
   No configuration required

○ Customer-managed encryption key (CMEK)
   Manage via Google Cloud Key Management Service

[CREATE DATASET]   CANCEL

Figure 2.21 – Dataset values

4. After the data has been exported to BigQuery, you can perform queries on it. For example, you can check which service has generated the most costs:

Figure 2.22 – BigQuery billing query (Source: https://cloud.google.com/billing/docs/how-to/visualize-data, License: https://creativecommons.org/licenses/by/4.0/legalcode)

This information is very useful when you wish to create all sorts of billing reports. In addition to the reporting, we would also like to be informed, upfront, whether we are exceeding our budget. In the next section, let's examine how this can be done.

Budgets and alerts

Budgets and alerts can be set for each billing account or project. You can set up a specific threshold. Once the amount spent is higher than the defined threshold, billing administrators and billing account users will be notified. This will not stop the usage of any services, and charges will continue to apply for the running resources. By default, there are three alert thresholds: **50%**, **90%**, and **100%**. Both the number of thresholds and their values can be modified:

Figure 2.23 – Creating a budget

There are two types of notification targets: email and a Pub/Sub topic. If the mail channel is chosen, the billing administrators and users can be notified or a specific notification channel with an associated email address can be selected. If a Pub/Sub topic is selected, an already existing topic can be selected or a new topic can be created.

> **Exam Tip**
> If the alerts and budgets are attached to a billing account, and you have multiple projects attached to the alerts, this will count toward the total cost generated in all of those projects together. Remember the default thresholds for the alerts.

Billing account roles

Surely, you would want to have control over who has access to your billing and who can manage the payments. The following list shows the roles that can be used to control the billing:

- **Billing Account Creator**: This is used for the initial billing setup, including signing up for GCP with a credit card.

- **Billing Account Administrator**: This is the owner of the billing account. This role is allowed to link and unlink projects and manage other users' roles for the billing account. This role can manage payment instruments, billing exports, and view cost information.

- **Billing Account User**: In combination with the project creator role, the Billing Account User role is allowed to create new projects linked to the billing account on which the role has been granted.

- **Billing Account Viewer**: This role allows access to view the billing information. It can be used by the finance team.

- **Billing Account Costs Manager**: This role allows you to view and export the cost information of the billing account.

- **Project Billing Manager**: This role enables the attachment of the project to a billing account without rights to resources.

> **Exam Tip**
> Make sure you understand the billing roles; in particular, ensure you have a good understanding of who can manage new billing accounts and who can only view the data.

Summary

In this chapter, we learned about the basics of GCP. We discussed resources and their scopes and hierarchies. We set up our first account, created permissions for other users to access it, and configured billing. We also learned how to export billing information. Finally, we learned how to set up alerts and budgets to control the cost of GCP usage.

In the next chapter, we will take a look at GCP's core services, and, in the chapters that follow, we will continue to deep dive into each of them.

Further reading

For more information on GCP billing and security, please refer to the following resources:

- **IAM**: `https://cloud.google.com/billing/docs/how-to/billing-access`

- **Visualizing billing**: `https://cloud.google.com/billing/docs/how-to/visualize-data?hl=pl`

- **SLA**: `https://cloud.google.com/terms/sla/`

- **Security in GCP**: `https://cloud.google.com/security/`

- **Comparing GCP services to AWS and Azure**: `https://cloud.google.com/free/docs/aws-azure-gcp-service-comparison`

3
Google Cloud Platform Core Services

Before we do a deep dive into **Google Cloud Platform (GCP)** services, let's have a tour to introduce all of the most important core services. This will help us to understand the overall picture in a much better way. It is important to be familiar with all of the core services, not only for the sake of the exam—it will also allow you to choose the best fit for your use case.

Google divides the services into the following logical groups, and they will be the topics we will cover in this chapter:

- Understanding computing and hosting services
- Exploring storage services
- Getting to know about networking services
- Going through big data services
- Understanding **Machine Learning (ML)** services
- Learning about identity services

> **Exam Tip**
>
> As a cloud architect, you need to understand how most of the services work from a high level. This chapter should answer some of the fundamental questions in the exam. Note that Google releases new services very often; however, there is always a delay between a new service release and the exam being updated with new content.

Understanding computing and hosting services

We are given a variety of options when it comes to **computing** in GCP. Depending on our requirements and flexibility, we can choose from one of the following four options, which we will be looking into in the upcoming sections:

- **Infrastructure-as-a-Service (IaaS): Google Compute Engine (GCE)**

- **Container-as-a-Service (CaaS): Google Kubernetes Engine (GKE)**

- **Platform-as-a-Service (PaaS): Google App Engine (GAE)**

- **Function-as-a-Service (FaaS): Cloud Functions**

> **Exam Tip**
>
> Note that there are additional compute options that might not yet appear on the exam but were announced in 2019. **GKE On-Prem** is a GKE service that can be installed on your local environment and managed from your Google Console. **Cloud Run** is an FaaS offering that allows you to define containers that will listen for HTTP requests. This allows you to use languages that are not supported by Cloud Functions. To read more about these services, check the *Further reading* links.

- **Fully managed container platform: Cloud Run**

The choice we make may depend on several factors. For example, do we need full control over our infrastructure, or do we want a fully managed service? Starting with **Compute Engine**, we have control over the **Virtual Machine (VM)** instance. This gives us the most flexibility but also implies that we need to take care of the stack above it. With **Cloud Functions**, we are very much constrained by the supported programming languages (JavaScript, Python, Node.js, Java, .NET, Ruby, PHP, and Go). The advantage of Cloud Functions is that you don't need to worry about infrastructure and scaling. You only concentrate on developing your functions. If you need to use a language that is not supported by Cloud Functions, you will not be able to use it.

The computing options in GCP are as shown in the following diagram:

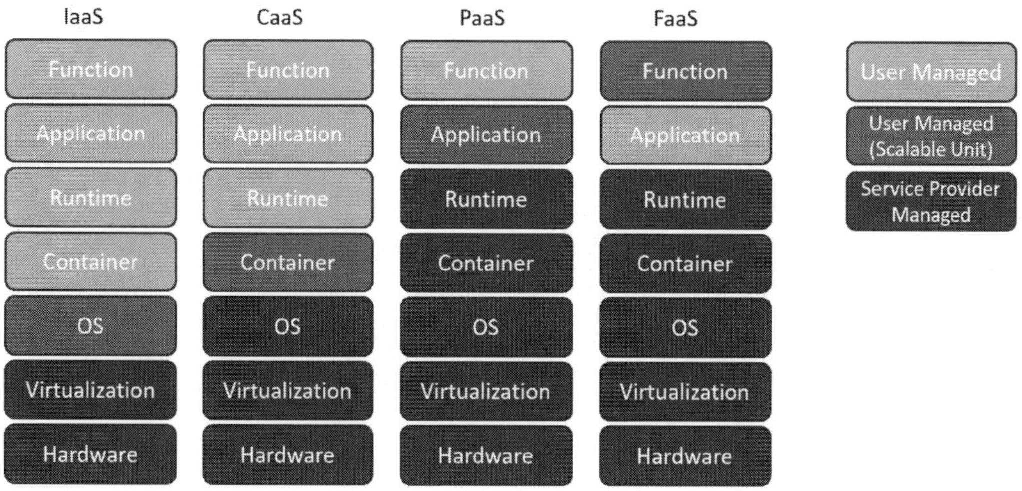

Figure 3.1 – Computing options

Let's have a look at each of the compute options and see what is managed by Google for us against the flexibility that we are given:

- **GCE**: GCE is an IaaS offering. It allows the most flexibility as it provides compute infrastructure to provision VM instances. This means that you have control of the virtualized hardware and operating system. Note, this can be limited to available machine types. You can use standard GCP images or your own custom image. You can control where your VMs and storage are located in terms of regions and zones. You have granular control over the network, including firewalls and load balancing. With the use of an instance group, you can autoscale your control and your capacity as needed. Compute Engine is suitable in most cases but might not be an optimal solution.

- **GKE**: GKE is a CaaS offering. It allows you to create Kubernetes clusters on demand, which takes away all of the heavy lifting of installing the clusters yourself. It leverages Compute Engine for hosting the cluster nodes, but the customer does not need to bother with the infrastructure and can concentrate on writing the code. The provisioned cluster can be automatically updated and scaled. The GCP software-defined networks are integrated with GKE and allow users to create network objects, such as load balancers, on demand when the application is deployed. Several services integrate with GKE, such as Artifact Registry, which allows you to store and scan your container images.

- **App Engine**: App Engine is a PaaS offering. It allows you to concentrate on writing your code, while Google takes care of hosting, scaling, monitoring, and updates. It is targeted at developers who do not need to understand the complexity of the infrastructure. GAE offers two types of environments, as follows:

  - **Standard**: With sets of common languages supported, including Python, Go, Java, Node.js, PHP, Ruby, and Go.

  - **Flexible**: Even more languages, with the possibility of creating a custom runtime. With a flexible environment, you lose some out-of-the-box integration, but you gain more flexibility.

GAE is tightly integrated with GCP services, including databases and storage. It allows versioning of your application for easy rollouts and rollbacks:

- **Cloud Functions**: Cloud Functions is a FaaS offering. It allows you to concentrate on writing your functions in one of the supported languages. It is ideal for executing simple tasks for data processing, mobile backends, and IoT. This service is completely serverless and all of the layers below it are managed by Google. The functions can be executed using an event trigger or HTTP endpoint.

- **Cloud Run**: Brings together the simplicity of FaaS and portability of CaaS. It allows you to develop and deploy self-scaling containerized applications on a fully managed serverless platform. It is compatible with Knative so you can move your workloads to any environment that can run Kubernetes in the cloud or on-premises.

- **Anthos**: Anthos is a modern application management platform that provides a consistent development and operations experience for cloud and on-premises environments. Anthos is not a compute option itself but allows you to run Google Kubernetes Engine and Cloud Run on Anthos in multi-cloud and hybrid environments.

- **Google Cloud VMware Engine (GCVE)** is a fully managed native VMware Cloud Foundation software stack hosted in GCP. It allows you to accelerate the move to GCP by lifting and shifting your VMs hosted on vSphere into Google Cloud *as is*.

Now that we have studied compute services, let's have a look at storage services in the next section.

Exploring storage services

Storage is an essential part of cloud computing as it saves the data and state of your applications. GCP offers a wide variety of storage, from object storage to managed databases. The different storage services that we will be looking at are as follows:

- **Cloud Storage**: Cloud Storage is a fully managed, object-oriented storage service with a virtually infinite capacity. It allows the creation of buckets that store your data and allow access through APIs and tools such as gsutil. It comes with different storage classes and locations to best suit your needs in terms of how often your data will be accessed and where it should be located. Keep in mind that the price differs for each tier. Making a conscious decision will allow you to cut costs. You can choose from the following options:

  - **Standard**: The highest availability in multiple geolocations

  - **Nearline**: For data accessed less than once a month

  - **Coldline**: Very low cost for data accessed less than once a quarter

  - **Archive**: The lowest cost for data accessed less than once a year

> **Important Note**
>
> Previously, Google Cloud Storage offered slightly different storage classes than the previously mentioned ones. The exam may not have updated this as yet, so it is important to also know the older options, as follows:
>
> **Multi-regional**: The highest availability in multiple geolocations
>
> **Regional**: High availability with fixed locations
>
> **Nearline**: Low-cost, for data accessed less than once a month
>
> **Coldline**: The lowest cost for backup and disaster recovery

With Cloud Storage, you do not need to worry about running out of capacity. The following list informs us of other Google Cloud Storage options:

- **Cloud Filestore**: Filestore is a managed file storage service. It allows users to provision a **Network Attached Storage (NAS)** service that can be integrated with GCE and GKE. It comes with two performance tiers—**standard** and **premium**, which offer different **Input/Output operations Per Second (IOPS)** and throughputs.

- **Cloud SQL**: Cloud SQL is a fully-managed relational database service for either a MySQL, PostgreSQL, or SQL Server database. It offers data replication, backups, data exports, and monitoring. It is ideal when you need to move your current instances from on-premises and want to delegate the maintenance of the database to Google.

- **Cloud Datastore**: Cloud Datastore is a fully managed non-SQL database. It is ideal for applications that rely on highly available structured data at scale. The scaling and high availability are achieved with a distributed architecture and are abstracted from the user. There is only one database available per project. Cloud Datastore offers SQL-like language to query your data. It has been superseded by Cloud Firestore.

- **Cloud Firestore**: Cloud Firestore is the next generation of Cloud Datastore with several enhanced features. It can run in Native or Datastore mode. The former is compatible with Cloud Datastore. Google has already started moving all Datastore clients to Cloud Firestore without any downtime or any user intervention. All new projects should be created in Cloud Firestore instead of Datastore.

- **Cloud Spanner**: Cloud Spanner is a fully managed, globally distributed database service. It offers the strong consistency of a relational database with non-relational database scaling capabilities. Users can define a schema and leverage industry-standard **American National Standards Institute (ANSI)** 2011 SQL. It delivers high-performance transactions, with a 99.999% availability **Service-Level Agreement (SLA)**, meaning there is almost no downtime. Cloud Spanner is aimed at use cases such as financial trading, insurance, global call centers, telecoms, gaming, and e-commerce. Global consistency makes it ideal for globally accessible applications.

- **Bigtable**: Bigtable is a fully managed, massive scale, NoSQL database service with a consistent sub-10ms latency for large analytical and operational workloads. It is used by Google to deliver services such as Gmail and Google Maps. It is ideal for fintech, IoT, and ML storage use cases. It integrates easily with big data product families such as **Dataproc** and **Dataflow**. It is based on open source Apache HBase, enabling the use of its API. The cost of Bigtable is much higher than Datastore, so the database should be chosen with great care.

- **Custom databases**: You can also choose to use Compute Engine to install a database of your choice, such as MongoDB; however, that would be an unmanaged service.

- **Persistent Disks**: These are durable network storage devices that can be accessed by our instances as if they were physical disks. They are located independently from our VM instances and can be detached and moved to keep data safe even after a VM is deleted.

With this, we conclude our look at storage services; let's have a look at networking services in the next section.

Getting to know about networking services

GCP networking is based on **Software-Defined Networks** (**SDNs**), which allow users to deliver all networking services programmatically. All of the services are fully managed, leaving users with the task of configuring them according to their requirements. The networking services that we will be looking at are as follows:

- **Virtual Private Cloud** (**VPC**): The VPC is the foundation of GCP networking. Projects can contain multiple VPC networks. Unless you create an organizational policy that prohibits it, new projects start with a default network (an auto mode VPC network) that has one subnetwork (subnet) in each region. You can think of it as a cloud version of a physical network. Each VPC network can contain one or more regional subnets. A VPC creates a global logical boundary that allows communication between resources within the same VPC network, subject to applicable network firewall rules. To allow communication between VPCs, traffic needs to traverse the internet or use VPC peering.

- **Load balancer**: A load balancer allows the distribution of traffic between your workloads. They are available for GCE, GAE, and GKE. For GCE, you can choose from load balancers with global or regional scopes. The choice will also depend on the network type. The following load balancers are available:

  - HTTP(S) load balancer

  - SSL proxy

  - TCP proxy

  - External network load balancer

  - Internal TCP/UDP load balancer

  - Internal HTTP(S) load balancer

- **Cloud Router**: Cloud Router is a service that allows you to dynamically exchange routes between VPC and on-premises networks by using **Border Gateway Protocol** (**BGP**): `https://www.wikipedia.org/wiki/Border_Gateway_Protocol`. It eliminates the need for the creation of static routes.

- **Virtual Private Network** (**VPN**): VPNs allow a connection between your on-premises network and GCP VPC through an IPsec tunnel over the internet. Only site-to-site VPNs are supported. Traffic in transit is encrypted. Both static and dynamic routing are supported, with the latter requiring a cloud router. Using a VPN should be considered an initial method of connecting your environment to GCP as it entails the lowest cost. If there are low-latency, high-reliability, and high-bandwidth requirements, then Cloud Interconnect should be considered.

- **Cloud Interconnect**: If there is a need for low latency and a highly available connection between your on-premises and Google Cloud VPC networks, then interconnect should be considered. In this case, the traffic does not traverse the internet. There are two interconnect options, which are as follows:

  - **Dedicated Interconnect**: 10 or 100 Gbps piped directly to a Google datacenter
  - **Partner Interconnect**: 50 Mbps-50 Gbps piped through a Google partner

- **Cloud DNS**: Cloud DNS is a managed DNS service with a 100% SLA. It resolves domain names into corresponding IP addresses. It can be used to publish and manage millions of DNS zones and records with ease. Cloud DNS can also host private zones accessible only from one or more VPC networks that you specify.

- **Cloud Content Delivery Network (CDN)**: Cloud CDN is a service that allows the caching of HTTP(S) load balanced content, from various types of backends, including Cloud Storage buckets. Caching reduces content delivery time and cost. It can also protect you from a **Distributed Denial-of-Service (DDoS)** attack. Data is cached on Google's globally distributed edge points. On the first request, when content is not cached, data is retrieved from a backend origin. The subsequent requests for the same data will be served directly from the cache until the expiration time is reached.

- **Cloud NAT**: Cloud NAT is a regional service that allows VMs without external IPs to communicate with the internet. It's a distributed, software-defined managed service that can be configured to automatically scale the number of NAT IP addresses that it uses. It works with both GCE and GKE. It is a better alternative for NAT instances that need to be managed by users.

- **Firewall**: GCP Firewall is a service that allows for micro-segmentation. Firewall rules are created per VPC and can be based on IPs, IP ranges, tags, and service accounts. Several firewall rules are created by default but can be modified.

- **Identity-Aware Proxy (IAP)**: IAP is a service that replaces the VPN when a user is working from an untrusted network. It controls access to your application based on user identity, device status, and IP address. It is part of Google's BeyondCorp (https://cloud.google.com/beyondcorp) zero trust security model.

- **Cloud Armor**: Cloud Armor is a service that allows protection against infrastructure DDoS attacks using Google's global infrastructure and security systems. It integrates with global HTTP(S) load balancers and blocks traffic based on IP addresses or ranges. The preview mode allows users to analyze the attack pattern without cutting off regular users.

Phew! We have covered a lot about networking services. Now, let's look at big data services in the following section.

Going through big data services

Big data services enable the user to process large amounts of data to provide answers to complex problems. GCP offers many services that tightly integrate to create an **End-to-End (E2E)** data analysis pipeline. These services are as follows:

- **BigQuery**: BigQuery is a highly scalable and fully managed cloud data warehouse. It allows users to perform analytics operations with built-in ML. BigQuery is completely serverless and can host petabytes of data. The underlying infrastructure scales seamlessly and allows parallel data processing. The data can be stored in BigQuery Storage, Cloud Storage, Bigtable, Sheets, or Google Drive. The user defines datasets containing tables. BigQuery uses familiar ANSI-compliant SQL for queries and provides ODBC and JDBC drivers. Users can choose from two types of payment models—one is flexible and involves paying for storage and queries, and the other involves a flat rate with stable monthly costs. It is ideal for use cases such as predictive analysis, IoT, and log analysis, and integrates with GCP's big data product family.

- **Pub/Sub**: This is a fully managed asynchronous messaging service that allows you to loosely couple your application components. It is serverless with global availability. Your application can publish messages to a topic or subscribe to it to pull messages. Pub/Sub also offers push-based delivery of messages as HTTP POST requests to **Webhooks**.

- **Dataproc**: Dataproc is a fully managed **Apache Spark** and **Hadoop** cluster service. It allows users to create clusters on demand and use them only when data processing is needed. It is billed per second. It allows users to move already existing, on-premises clusters to the cloud without refactoring the code. The use of pre-emptible instances can further lower the cost.

- **Cloud Dataflow**: Cloud Dataflow is a fully managed service for processing data in streams and batches. It is based on open source Apache Beam, is completely serverless, and offers almost limitless capacity. It will manage resources and job balancing for the user. It can be used for use cases such as online fraud analytics, IoT, healthcare, and logistics.

- **Dataprep**: This is a tool that can be used to perform data preparation and visualization. We can explore and transform data without any coding skills being required. Data can be interactively prepared for further analysis.

- **Datalab**: Datalab is a tool built into **Jupyter** (formerly **IPython**) that allows users to explore, analyze, and transform data. It also allows users to build ML data models and leverages Compute Engine.

- **Data Studio**: This is a tool that allows you to consume data from sources and visualize it in the form of reports and dashboards.

- **Cloud Composer**: This is a fully managed service based on open source **Apache Airflow**. It allows you to create and orchestrate big data pipelines.

- **Data Fusion**: This is a fully managed enterprise data integration service. It provides a UI that allows you to build and manage pipelines to clean, prepare, blend, transfer, and transform data.

Finally, let's study ML services in the next section.

Understanding machine learning services

One of the strongest points of Google is its long-term experience with **Machine Learning (ML)**. GCP offers several services around ML. You can choose between a pre-trained model or train a model yourself. The various services included under ML are as follows:

- **Pretrained APIs**: ML APIs are services that allow you to leverage several pre-trained models, enabling you to analyze a video. Currently, the following APIs are available:

  - Google Cloud Video Intelligence
  - Google Cloud Speech
  - Google Cloud Vision
  - Google Cloud Natural Language
  - Google Cloud Translation
  - Google Recommendations AI

The following list of models can be used without any background knowledge of how they work. As an example, we can analyze text for sentiment analysis:

- **AutoML**: AutoML is a service that can be used by developers to train models without having extensive knowledge of data science. As an example, by providing labeled samples to AutoML, it can be trained to recognize objects that are not recognizable by the Vision API. The following are the labeled samples of AutoML:

  - AutoML Translation
  - AutoML Natural Language
  - Video Intelligence
  - AutoML Tables

- **Dialogflow**: This is a service that allows you to build conversation applications that can interact with human beings. The interface can interact with many compatible platforms, such as Slack or Google Assistant. It can also integrate with **Firebase** functions to integrate with third-party platforms using common APIs.

- **AI Platform**: This was a fully managed service to allow the E2E development of a machine learning model. Before it went to general availability, Google released Vertex AI and deprecated AI Platform.

- **Vertex AI**: This is a unified machine learning platform to build, deploy, and scale AI models. It integrates AutoML and AI Platform together into a unified API, client library, and user interface. With Vertex AI, you can perform both AutoML training and custom training. For both of those options, you can save models, deploy models, and request predictions using Vertex AI.

ML services will be discussed further in *Chapter 14, Putting Machine Learning to Work*. In the next section, we will introduce *Google's identity and access management* services.

Learning about identity services

Identity and Access Management (**IAM**) is one of the most important aspects of any cloud. It allows you to control who has access to the cloud but can also provide identity services to your applications. In short, this is achieved by a combination of roles and permissions. The roles are assigned to either users or groups. Let's have a look at the options we have in GCP:

- **IAM**: IAM allows the GCP admin to control authorization to GCP services. Administrators can create roles with granular permissions. Roles can then be assigned to users, or preferably, a group of users.

- **Cloud Identity**: Cloud Identity is an **Identity-as-a-Service** (**IDaaS**) offering. It sits outside of GCP but can be easily integrated with GCP. It allows you to create organizations, groups, and users, and manage them centrally. If you already have an existing user catalog, you can synchronize it with Cloud Identity.

IAM is very important to understand because it underpins how your GCP architecture will be created. We will discuss this more in *Chapter 15, Security and Compliance*.

Summary

In this chapter, we learned about GCP services and gathered them in specific groups: compute and hosting, storage, networking, big data, ML, and identity services. This allowed us to get a broad overview of what GCP offers us. That should give you a little bit more confidence in what GCP actually is, but you probably also understand that there is quite some work ahead of us. But don't worry, we'll get there together!

Once you've finished going through this chapter, let's switch to *Chapter 4, Working with Google Compute Engine*, where we will finally get some hands-on experience with deploying our first services to GCP. This is getting exciting!

Further reading

You can refer to the following links to gain more information:

- **GCP core services and products**: `https://cloud.google.com/products/`.
- **Cloud Run**: `https://cloud.google.com/run/`
- **GKE On-Prem**: `https://cloud.google.com/gke-on-prem/`

Section 2: Manage, Design, and Plan a Cloud Solution Architecture

In this section, we will focus on the various GCP services in more detail. By examining these services, we will demonstrate how to manage, design, and plan solutions based on GCP.

This part of the book comprises the following chapters:

4
Working with Google Compute Engine

Google Compute Engine (GCE) is one of the fundamental services inside **Google Cloud Platform (GCP)**. While the public cloud continues to move on from traditional **Virtual Machines (VMs)**, there are still use cases for these machines and, just like other vendors, GCE allows us to create and run VMs on GCP. Google refers to a VM in GCP as a Compute Engine instance. Compute Engine makes it easy to find the VM to match our requirements, whether it is a small-sized VM or a large data-processing VM.

GCE is a purely **Infrastructure-as-a-Service (IaaS)** solution; therefore, you will need to manage and scale your VM as necessary, but this makes it an ideal solution for **lift and shift** migration from on-premises into the public cloud. You can use your own customized OS as you do within your own data center or you can use some predefined Google, Windows, or Linux images. You can also bring your own license for Windows, but this comes with some considerations. Throughout the GCE section of this chapter, we will look at how we can deploy a simple GCE instance, the options available to us when we deploy, and more complex solutions that enable us to scale out with ease.

In this chapter, we will take a deeper look into Compute Engine. Specifically, we will cover the following topics:

- Deploying our first GCE instance
- Deployment options
- Instance templates and instance groups
- Autoscaling
- Autohealing
- Quotas and limits
- IAM roles
- Pricing

Deploying our first GCE instance

Let's begin this chapter with the basics of provisioning a new VM. We can do this from the GCP console. In this section, we will look at the very basics needed to deploy a VM. We will look at the deployment options in more detail in the next section of this chapter:

1. First, we should sign into the GCP console, then browse to the navigation menu, and go to **Compute Engine | VM instances**, as shown in the following screenshot:

> **Important Note**
> You may be prompted to enable the Compute Engine API when using Compute Engine for the first time.

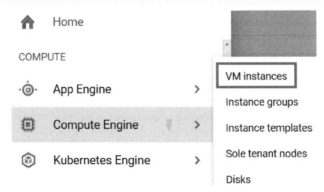

Figure 4.1 – Browsing to VM instances

2. Click **ENABLE** to enable the Compute Engine API (this is a one-time enablement when we are creating our first Compute Engine instance):

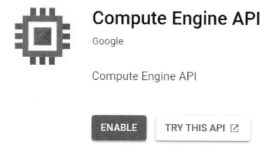

Figure 4.2 – Enabling API

3. Click **CREATE INSTANCE**, as shown in the following screenshot:

Figure 4.3 – Creating an instance

4. Give your VM a name; in this example, we called it `cloudarchitect`. We can select a region and a zone along with the size of the machine. Some zones are more expensive than others and you will notice that, depending on the zone and machine type, we can see the estimation of the cost of our instance change:

Figure 4.4 – Selecting a region and zone

5. If we look at the options under the **Machine configuration** menu, we can select the machine family we want. This gives us the option to select machines for common workloads, high-performance workloads, memory-intensive, or optimized for machine learning. The following screenshot shows us selecting the **E2** series of machine from the **General-purpose** machine family:

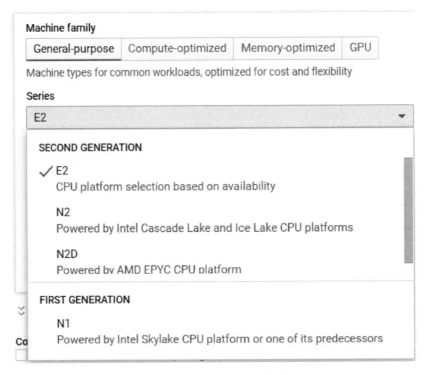

Figure 4.5 – Selecting a machine configuration

6. However, if this does not meet our requirements, we can also select a custom machine type and select the exact resources we need. We should think of 1 vCPU as 1 hyper-threaded core:

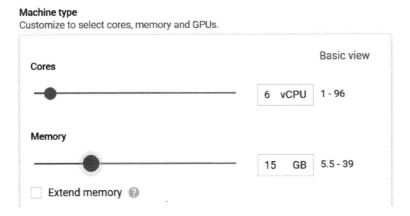

Figure 4.6 – Custom type

7. The boot disk selection allows us to select the image we require. For now, let's select **Windows Server 2019 Datacenter**, as shown in the following screenshot (please note that Windows Server instances are no longer eligible as part of the Free Tier trial):

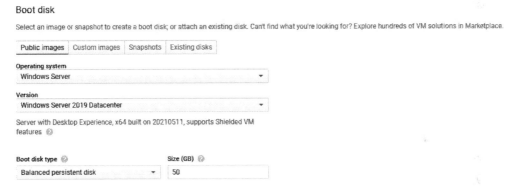

Figure 4.7 – Selecting a boot disk

8. Leave everything else as default; we will look at other settings in more detail shortly in this section. Click **Create** to begin the deployment.

9. Now that we have a VM, we need to connect to it. Within the **Compute Instance** section, we will now see our new VM. Simply click on the arrow beside **RDP** and select **Set Windows password**. Once we've set our password, click on the **RDP** button:

INSTANCES
INSTANCE SCHEDULE
Filter Enter property name or value
Status
Name
Zone
Recommendations
In use by
Internal IP
External IP
Connect
cluodarchitect
europe-west2-b
10.154.0.2 (nic0)
34.89.37.52
RDP
Set Windows password
View gcloud command to reset password
Download the RDP file
Learn about Windows auth

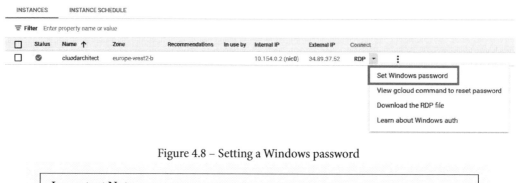

Figure 4.8 – Setting a Windows password

> **Important Note**
>
> **Remote Desktop Protocol (RDP)** allows us to connect to another Windows server over a network connection.

10. Click **SET**, as shown in the following screenshot:

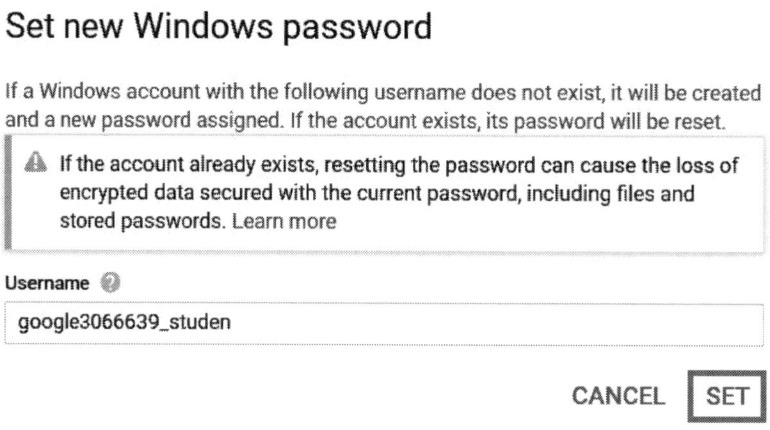

Set new Windows password
If a Windows account with the following username does not exist, it will be created and a new password assigned. If the account exists, its password will be reset.
If the account already exists, resetting the password can cause the loss of encrypted data secured with the current password, including files and stored passwords. Learn more
Username
google3066639_studen
CANCEL
SET

Figure 4.9 – Setting a password

11. We can now copy this password and use this to RDP to our GCE instance:

Figure 4.10 – Copying a password

12. If we created a Compute Engine instance with a Linux-based OS, then we simply need to click **SSH**, as shown in the following screenshot:

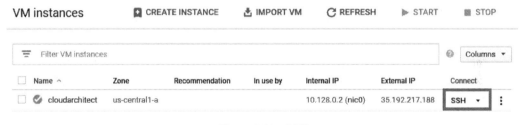

Figure 4.11 – SSH

> **Exam Tip**
> If you do not have an external IP, then a bastion host should be used, also referred to as **terminal servers**. If you need access to resources that have internal IP addresses only, then bastion hosts are configured with external IP addresses and act as a gateway to your internal resources.

As expected, we can also deploy a GCE instance from the command line. The CLI of choice to create a VM is gcloud via Cloud Shell. We will look at Cloud Shell in more detail in *Chapter 16, Google Cloud Management Options*, but for now, just understand that it is a command line available directly from the GCP console, and it gives us the ability to quickly create our VM instances:

1. To activate it, click on the Cloud Shell icon in the top right-hand corner:

Figure 4.12 – Activating Cloud Shell

One feature to note is that following the aforementioned process to create a VM from the GUI, underneath the **Create** button, you will find the **Equivalent REST or command line** options, as shown in the following screenshot:

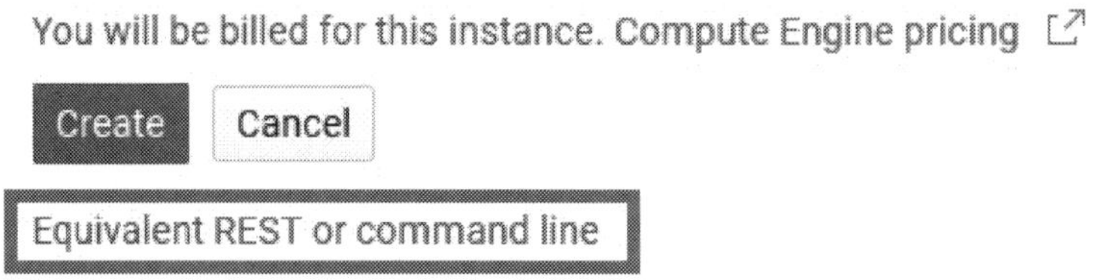

You will be billed for this instance. Compute Engine pricing ⌐⌐

Create   Cancel

Equivalent REST or command line

Figure 4.13 – REST or command line

2. Click on the **command line** option to open up the exact CLI you would need to create using `gcloud` commands:

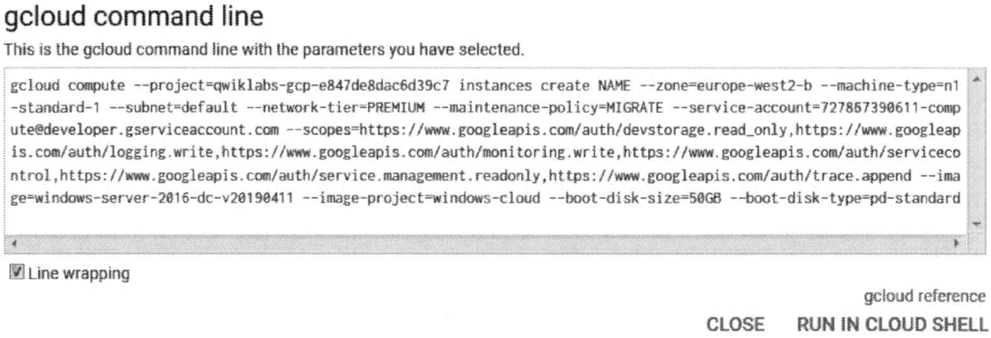

gcloud command line

This is the gcloud command line with the parameters you have selected.

```
gcloud compute --project=qwiklabs-gcp-e847de8dac6d39c7 instances create NAME --zone=europe-west2-b --machine-type=n1
-standard-1 --subnet=default --network-tier=PREMIUM --maintenance-policy=MIGRATE --service-account=727867390611-comp
ute@developer.gserviceaccount.com --scopes=https://www.googleapis.com/auth/devstorage.read_only,https://www.googleap
is.com/auth/logging.write,https://www.googleapis.com/auth/monitoring.write,https://www.googleapis.com/auth/serviceco
ntrol,https://www.googleapis.com/auth/service.management.readonly,https://www.googleapis.com/auth/trace.append --ima
ge=windows-server-2016-dc-v20190411 --image-project=windows-cloud --boot-disk-size=50GB --boot-disk-type=pd-standard
```

☑ Line wrapping

gcloud reference

CLOSE   RUN IN CLOUD SHELL

Figure 4.14 – A command line example

You can copy the text or click **RUN IN CLOUD SHELL,** which will activate your Cloud Shell instance and execute the request.

Deployment options

You will notice that there are some options we left as default. Let's look at these in a bit more detail to make sure we understand all of the settings required to create a Compute Engine instance.

Region

Regions are geographical locations that are made up of three or more zones. We need to select a region where we can run our VM. The requirements may be related to where most traffic is expected. As we have mentioned, some regions are more expensive than others:

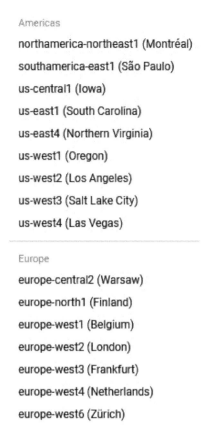

Figure 4.15 – Regions

Make sure the selected region makes sense based on your requirements.

Zone

Make sure you select a zone that suits your requirements. Consider network latency and select a region or zone close to your point of service:

Figure 4.16 – Zones

All zones in a region are connected through a high-bandwidth and low-latency network – usually below 5 minutes for a round trip between each zone.

Boot disk

We have already seen that many predefined images can be selected. The default storage for these images is a balanced persistent disk. This type of disk is backed by **Solid State Drives (SSDs)** and balances performance and cost. This can be changed to a standard persistent disk, which is backed by standard HDD, or SSD persistent disks, which are backed by SSDs. The default size will change depending on the OS image selected, but this can be adjusted:

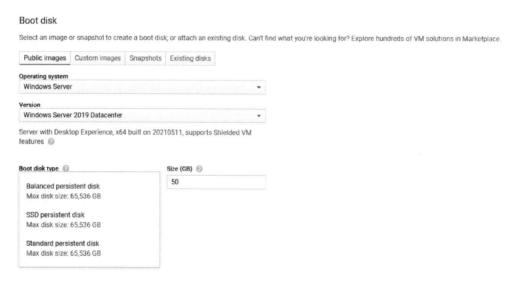

Figure 4.17 – A boot disk type

Changes from the default will again impact the cost of your instance.

Custom images are available per project and can be created from source disks, images, snapshots, or images stored in cloud storage.

Snapshots

It is possible to snapshot a persistent disk and use this as part of a new instance creation, even if is still attached to a running instance. Snapshots can be used to create a new custom image or instance. Snapshots can be created for a number of reasons, one of which is data protection. It is recommended to have a snapshot schedule to reduce data loss. Snapshots are also global resources, which means they are accessible by any resource in the same project.

To create a snapshot from the console, we should browse to the navigation menu and then to **Compute Engine | Snapshots**. Then, we must give our snapshot a name and select the source disk we wish to work with. Lastly, we can select the location we wish to store the snapshot, as shown in the following screenshot:

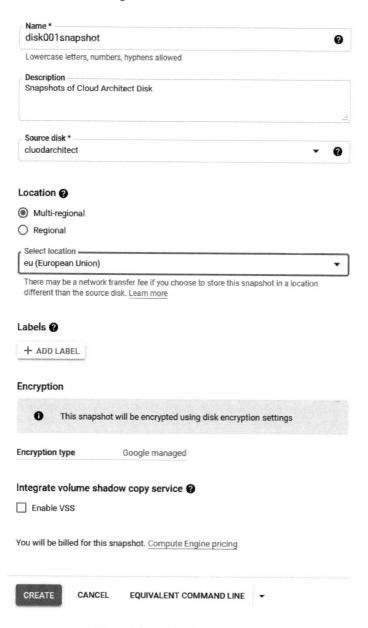

Figure 4.18 – Creating a snapshot

The following diagram shows how the process of multiple snapshots works. The first snapshot will be a full snapshot of all the data on the disk, and subsequent snapshots will be incremental:

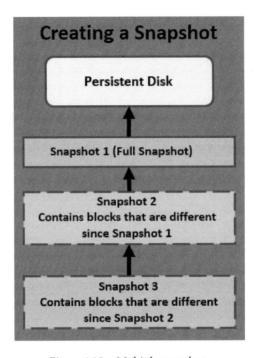

Figure 4.19 – Multiple snapshots

> **Important Note**
>
> Snapshots are incremental and, therefore, will contain blocks that are different from the previous snapshot. Therefore, if you perform regular snapshots, the cost is less than performing a regular full image of the disk. Each snapshot is stored across multiple locations within GCP for redundancy. Snapshots can be stored across projects with the correct permissions.

The exam will not go into great detail on snapshots, but more information can be found here: https://cloud.google.com/compute/docs/disks/create-snapshots.

Existing disks

Existing disks can also be attached to a new instance. To create a new disk, we can browse to the navigation menu and go to **Compute Engine | Disk**. The following screenshot shows us creating a new blank disk:

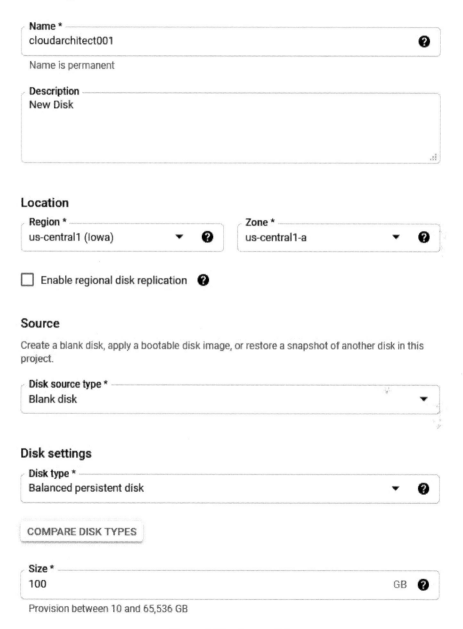

Figure 4.20 – A new disk

Once successfully created, we can use this new disk when we deploy a new Compute Engine instance. The following screenshot shows how this would look when we click on the **Existing disks** tab. We can see all of the disks available to us:

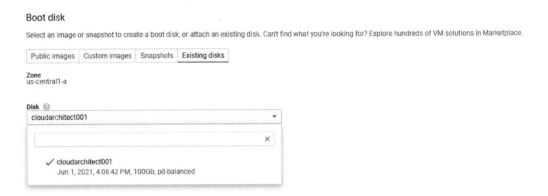

Figure 4.21 – Existing disks

We can also see, from the preceding screenshot, that we can use a snapshot of a disk as our boot disk. We discussed how to take snapshots earlier in this chapter.

Labels

There are a number of additional options that can be modified. To group-related resources, it can be beneficial to label your VM instances. This can help with organizing and filtering for billing and reporting. Labels work with key-value pairs and can be used, for example, to differentiate between projects, environments, and so on. Simply click **Add label** and you will be presented with a popup to add your key-value pair, which will be saved and added into the main **Create Instance** screen, as follows:

Figure 4.22 – Labels

The preceding screenshot is an example of this, where we can label an instance as the production environment.

Confidential VM service

Enable this option to encrypt data while in use. This will keep data encrypted in memory during processing without Google having access to the encryption keys:

Confidential VM service ⊘
☐ Enable the Confidential Computing service on this VM instance.

Figure 4.23 – Confidential VM service

Container

Enable this option to deploy and launch a Docker container using a **Container-Optimized OS (COS)**. Note you can only deploy one container for each VM instance. This is separate to **Google Kubernetes Engine (GKE)**, which we will discuss in *Chapter 6, Managing Kubernetes Clusters with Google Kubernetes Engine*:

Container ⊘
☐ Deploy a container image to this VM instance. Learn more

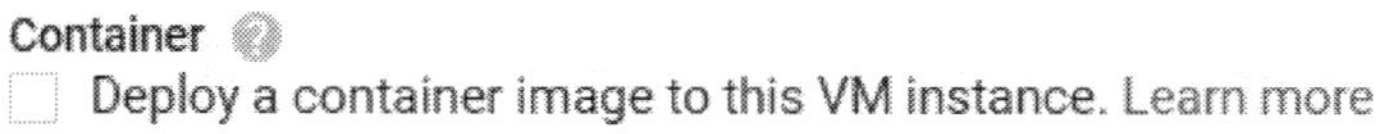

Figure 4.24 – Container

The preceding figure shows the simple checkbox to deploy a container image.

Deletion protection

Enable this to prevent your GCE instance from accidental deletion. Checking this box will set the `deletionProtection` property on the instance resource. Usually, only critical VM instances that need to stay running indefinitely would have this option checked. Even after this is checked, instances can still be reset, stopped, or even removed after a project is terminated. Only users who have `compute.instance.create` permissions can modify this flag to allow a protected VM to be deleted.

Reservations

Reservations can be created for VM instances in specific zones using custom or predefined machine types. Use reservations to ensure resources are available for your workloads when you need them; however, as soon as you create a reservation, you will immediately begin paying for it until the reservation is deleted. Increases in demand should be considered before using reservations. This option allows you to select an existing reservation, create a new one, or use none.

Metadata

Adding metadata to your GCE instance allows future queries to pull information about the instance. Metadata is stored on a metadata server and can be queried from the Compute Engine API or from the instance itself. We can pull information such as hostname, instance ID, or any custom metadata we apply. We can also provide configuration information to applications using metadata, which will negate the need to store this data in the application itself.

We also use metadata to reference the startup script to be executed during our instance deployment. Let's assume we host our startup script called `startup.sh` on a Cloud Storage bucket called `deployments`. To ensure it is executed, we need to add the path to our bucket and the startup script:

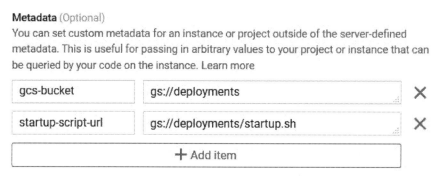

Figure 4.25 – Metadata

The preceding screenshot shows how this would look in the console.

Startup scripts

When populating the variables for a GCE deployment, we can also set a startup script if we wish. This is a script that will run when your instance boots up or restarts. Common examples would be to install specific software or ensure services are started. These scripts are specified through the same metadata server we previously mentioned and use the startup script metadata keys. Again, these scripts can be added via `gcloud` commands as well as at the console. Let's look at the example commands from the CLI. This is installing `apache2` and populating the main page. Please note that after running this code, GCP will ask us to confirm the zone:

```
gcloud compute instances create cloudarchitect --tags http-
server \
--metadata startup-script='#! /bin/bash
# Installs apache and a custom homepage
```

```
sudo su -
apt-get update
apt-get install -y apache2
cat <<EOF > /var/www/html/index.html
<html><body><h1>Hello World</h1>
<p>This page was created from a simple start up script!</p>
</body></html>
EOF'
```

It is also possible to specify a script that resides on Google Cloud Storage. Again, from the gcloud CLI, we can specify our bucket location. In this example, our bucket is called cloudarchitectbucket:

```
gcloud compute instances create example-instance --scopes
storage-ro \
      --metadata startup-script-url=gs://cloudarchitectbucket/
startupscript.sh
```

> **Exam Tip**
>
> If we want to specify a shutdown script, then we will browse to the metadata section and add shutdown-script as the key and add the contents of the script as the value.

We should note that startup scripts will only be executed when a network is available.

Preemptibility

Preemptibility brings the cost of an instance down but will generally only last a maximum of 24 hours before it is terminated. Certain actions, such as stopping and starting an instance, will reset this counter. It might sound strange to deploy VMs that have such a limited lifecycle, but if we have fault tolerance at an application level, then utilizing preemptible instances can result in significant cost savings. Let's take the example of batch-processing jobs.

These could run on preemptible instances, and if some of the instances are terminated, then the process will slow down but not stop entirely. This allows batch processing to occur without any additional workload on existing instances. We should note, however, that due to the nature of preemptible instances, there is no GCP **Service-Level Agreement** (**SLA**) applied, and they can be removed by the provider with only 30 seconds' notification.

To set up a preemptible instance, simply select **On** under **Availability policy** while creating a new instance:

Figure 4.26 – Preemptibility

Availability policy

Compute Engine will perform maintenance on its infrastructure, which may require your VM instances to be moved to another host. GCE will live-migrate your instance if the instance's availability policy was set to use this feature. As a result, your applications will not suffer from any downtime but may witness some performance degradation. Live migration is the default setting for an instance.

Alternatively, if you have built-in high availability at the application level, then you may wish to change this setting to terminate and restart on another host. This setting means that your instance would be shut down cleanly and restarted on a fresh host. Google will report any maintenance issues and how it affects your instance, depending on the setting selected.

Automatic restart

If underlying hardware causes your instance to crash, then GCE offers a setting to automatically restart the instance. This is set to **On (recommended)** by default. You can set this to **Off** by selecting from the drop-down menu:

Figure 4.27 – Automatic restart

Google will report any automatic restart under **Operations** from the **Compute Engine** menu, as shown in the preceding screenshot. Once we have selected this, we can view any alerts:

Operations

Operations are REST requests that affect resources at the global, region, or zone level Learn more

Operation summary	Target	User	Time (GMT)	Status
⊘ compute.projects.setCommonInstanceMetadata	qwiklabs-gcp-37865da19b691f65	qwiklabs-gcp-37865da19b691f65@qwiklabs-gcp-37865da19b691f65.iam.gserviceaccount.com	Start: Jun 7, 2019, 8:19:22 PM End: Jun 7, 2019, 8:19:28 PM	Done
⊘ compute.projects.setCommonInstanceMetadata	qwiklabs-gcp-37865da19b691f65	qwiklabs-gcp-37865da19b691f65@qwiklabs-gcp-37865da19b691f65.iam.gserviceaccount.com	Start: Jun 7, 2019, 8:19:18 PM End: Jun 7, 2019, 8:19:22 PM	Done

Figure 4.28 – Operations

The preceding screenshot shows what these alerts look like on the **Operations** screen.

Shielded VM

Let's now look under the security section. The first option is Shielded VM. GCP offers the ability to harden your VM instance with security controls, which will defend against rootkits, bootkits, and kernel-level malware. GCP uses a **virtual Trusted Platform Module (vTPM)** to provide a virtual root of trust to verify the identity of the VM and ensure they are part of a specified project or region. The vTPM generates and stores encryption keys at the guest OS level. It should be noted that this does not add any extra cost to your VM deployment.

Deletion rule

Under the **Disks** section, we will find the **Deletion rule**. This option allows us to either delete or keep the boot disk when the instance is deleted:

Figure 4.29 – Disk options

If there are specific use cases for keeping your boot disk, then make sure the checkbox is removed. You can also select how your data will be encrypted. By default, a Google-managed key will be used, but you can change this to use other options.

Node affinity labels

Sole tenancy was introduced to GCE in 2018 and is a physical Compute Engine server designed for your dedicated use. In other words, the underlying host hardware and hypervisor handles only your GCE instances. A use case for this setup could be security requirements. Many companies have compliance or regulations that require a physical separation of their compute resources.

The following diagram shows this split. We can see that, on the left-hand side, different customers share the same hardware but, on the right-hand side, we have dedicated hardware for this specific customer and only their VMs reside on it:

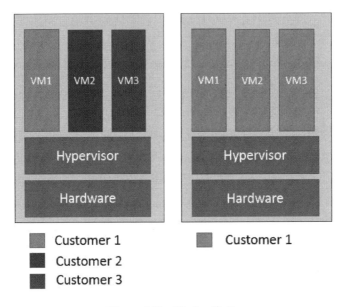

Figure 4.30 – Node affinity

VMs will still have the same live-migration functionality and shared instances, but there are cost implications. Not all regions and zones support sole tenancy.

When we create a VM, we have the option to add a label that would define where the new instance would be deployed. To use sole tenancy, we first have to create a sole-tenant node from the console under **Compute Engine | Sole tenant nodes**. Note that we could also use gcloud commands for this. Click on **Create a node template**, and set **Region** and **Node type**. The following screenshot shows the different options available. We can also utilize labels to give a key/pair value, such as Environment:HighSecureArea:

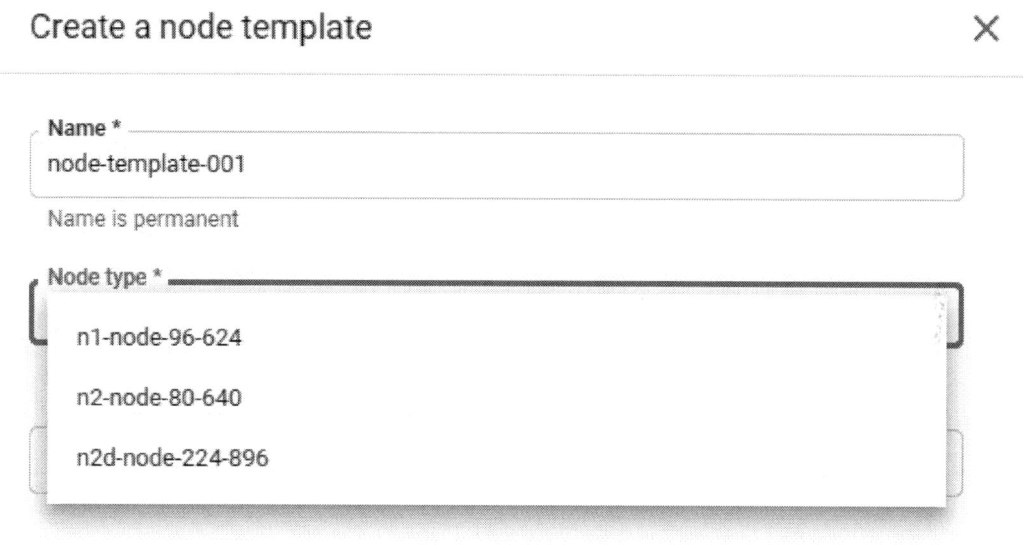

Create a node template   ✕

Name *

node-template-001

Name is permanent

Node type *

  n1-node-96-624

  n2-node-80-640

  n2d-node-224-896

Figure 4.31 – Creating a node template

Once the template has been created, on the same menu page, we can now create a sole-tenant node. Again, we can give a name, select a region and a template, and define the number of nodes we need. Note that the region needs to match the region you created the template in:

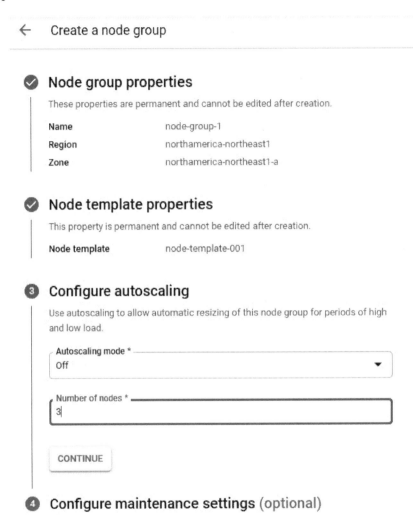

Figure 4.32 – Sole-tenant node

We can now create a VM from within the sole tenancy. Some more advanced settings can be made, but we will look at these in more depth in the coming chapters:

- For firewalls, refer to *Chapter 10, Networking Options in GCP.*

- For security and encryption settings, refer to *Chapter 15, Security and Compliance.*

GPUs and TPUs

Along with standard vCPUs, Compute Engine also offers **Graphics Processing Units (GPUs)**. These can be used on graphics-intensive workloads such as 3D rendering or virtual applications. We should note here that GPUs can only be attached to predefined or custom-machine types and are only available in certain zones. They are also still eligible for discounts that we receive from standard vCPUs (please note that we will discuss sustained use discounts in more detail later in this chapter). When we are creating a new instance, we can add a GPU by expanding the **CPU platform and GPU** section, as shown in the following screenshot:

Figure 4.33 – GPU configuration

Tensor Processing Units (**TPUs**) are custom-developed application-specific integrated circuits designed using Google's experience in **Machine Learning** (**ML**) and can be used to maximize performance and flexibility in building TensorFlow compute clusters and other ML workloads. We can access TPUs from the navigation menu and go to **Compute Engine | TPUs**. Once we enable the API, we can create our first TPU node. From the following screenshot, you can see that we can assign **Zone**, **TPU type**, **TPU software version**, **Network**, and **IP address range**. The TPU should be in the same zone as the Compute Engine instance you wish to connect from:

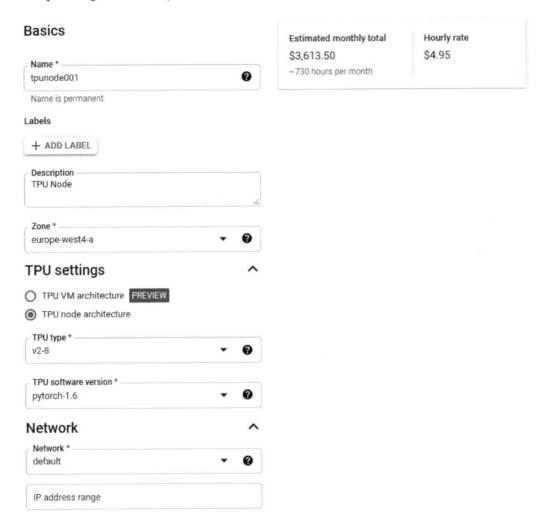

Figure 4.34 – TPU configuration

Under the Management section of TPU configuration, we can also enable preemptibility on TPU nodes.

Instance templates and instance groups

Even when we think of on-premises architecture, many of the key requirements are around high availability and scalability. Of course, this does not change when we architect in the public cloud, but they do become a lot easier and cheaper to do!

We have previously seen how we can deploy individual GCE instances, but not many organizations will move to the public cloud to host a single VM. Business needs depend on the ability to react to demand and react to any instance failures.

Each of the VM instances deployed into the instance group comes from the same instance template, which defines the machine type, boot disk images, labels, and other instance properties that we spoke about previously in this chapter. Instance templates are global resources, which means they are not tied to a specific zone or region. Zonal resources in the template itself will restrict the template to the zone where that resource resides. For example, the template may include a disk that is tied to a specific zone.

It's important to understand that there are two types of instance groups:

- **Managed instance groups**: This type of instance group allows your workloads to be scalable and highly available via automated services in the groups, such as autoscaling or autohealing. Google recommends using this type of group unless it is unavoidable due to pre-existing configurations or a requirement to group dissimilar instances.

- **Unmanaged instance groups**: This type of instance group allows for load balancing across a fleet of VMs that are not identical. They are user-managed, therefore autoscaling and autohealing are not supported.

Let's look at an example of creating a new instance template and group:

1. From the navigation menu, we should browse to **Compute Engine | Instance templates**:

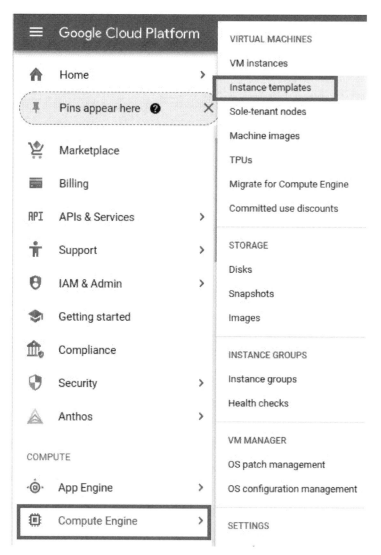

Figure 4.35 – Instance templates

2. We can name and update settings as if we were creating a new VM instance. In previous examples, we set a startup script from `gcloud` commands but, in this example, let's set it up from the console. We add this in the **Metadata** options and use the `startup-script-url` key and `gs://cloudarchitect/startup.sh` as our value:

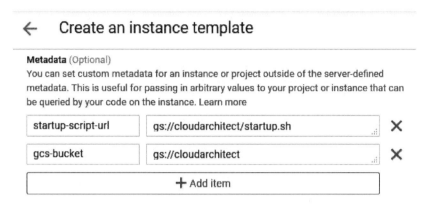

Figure 4.36 – Metadata

3. Click on **Instance Groups**, and then create a new instance group:

Instance Groups

Instance groups let you organize VM instances or use them in a load-balancing backend service. You can group existing instances or create a group based on an instance template. Learn more

Figure 4.37 – Creating an instance group

Let's look at the different options that we can specify when creating an instance group.

Setting the location

Here, we can set whether we want multiple or single zones. This selection will be based on your availability requirements. If you require high availability, then it's best to go with multiple zones; however, you should note that this restricts your group type to *managed only*. It also gives an additional field called **Target distribution shape**, where the default value of **Even** is set. By default, regional-managed instance groups will distribute managed instances evenly across selected zones. However, there may be a need to change this if, for example, you need some hardware that is not available in selected zones. Other shapes are available, but it should be noted that the **Balanced** and **Any** options do not support autoscaling, canary updates, or proactive instance redistribution. You will need to delete the default autoscaling configuration in order to select **Balanced** or **Any**:

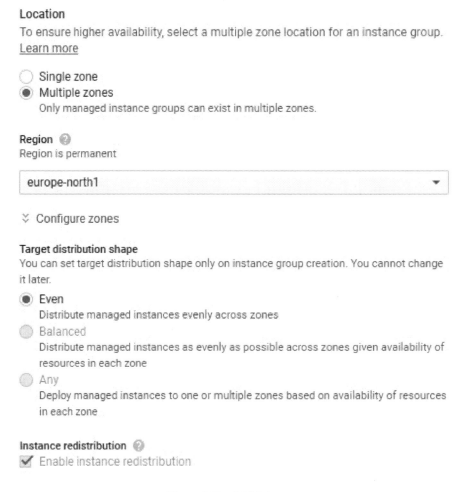

Figure 4.38 – Multiple zones

We can see in the preceding screenshot that, with **Multiple zones** selected, we are told that **Only managed instance groups can exist**. Additionally, if we select the **Configure zones** drop-down menu, we can select zones within the region that we wish to distribute the instances.

Port name mapping

If we select the **Single zone** option, then we are presented with an optional setting called **Port Name Mapping**. We can use this in conjunction with a load balancer. We can specify a port name and associated port number and map incoming traffic to this specific number.

Of course, we also need to specify the instance template we want to use for this managed group. This option is only available if we select a managed instance group in the group type options. We also need to select the number of instances to be deployed by the instance group.

We have the ability to turn autoscaling on, off, or up. Autoscaling allows the dynamic growth or, indeed, deletion of your VM instances as demand increases or decreases. We will speak more on autoscaling in this chapter.

When we have populated everything we need, we can click **Create Instance Group**. The group will now create the number of VMs we have specified in the instance group. Under **Compute Engine | Instance groups**, we can see the running instances connected to the instance group.

Autoscaling

We mentioned autoscaling earlier, which deserves a full section to itself. Autoscaling is a fundamental principle of cloud computing. It allows resources to be elastic and can increase and decrease the number of instances based on demand. As a reminder, we can only use autoscaling with managed instance groups. This is because only managed instance groups will use a dedicated template, which, in turn, can be used as a basis for a pool of homogeneous VM instances.

Once autoscaling is enabled in our instance group, it also enables many settings under an **autoscaling policy**. These policies can be based on CPU usage, HTTP load balancing usage, or Google Cloud operations suite-monitoring metrics. We should also note here that it is possible to autoscale based on custom metrics, so we are not reliant only on out-of-the-box metrics.

The following example is based on CPU usage, which is the simplest form of autoscaling. The autoscaler will collect a CPU utilization of instances in a group and decide whether it is necessary to scale the group or whether it should maintain the current number of VM instances.

Looking at the following screenshot, let's take a look at the settings we should populate:

- **Target CPU usage**: This is set at 60%. This means the autoscaler should keep an average CPU usage of 60% among all vCPUs in the instance group.

- **Minimum number of instances**: This is the minimum number of instances that the autoscaler should scale in.

- **Maximum number of instances**: This is the maximum number of instances that the autoscaler should scale out.

- **Predictive autoscaling:** Managed instance groups can be configured to automatically add or remove virtual machine instances based on load. This may not suit all applications if, for example, they can take a few minutes to initialize. Predictive autoscaling forecasts scaling metrics based on historical trends and are recomputed every few minutes. It requires at least 3 days of history to gather a service usage pattern, therefore it cannot be enabled when creating a new autoscaling configuration. It can also only be enabled when a CPU utilization metric is applied.

- **Cool down period**: This number indicates the number of seconds the autoscaler will wait after a VM instance has started before the autoscaler starts collecting information from it. For scale-in decisions, it must consider usage data from all instances, regardless of whether an instance is still within its cool down period. For scale-out decisions, it must ignore data from instances that are still within their cool down period. If predictive mode is enabled, the cool down period informs the predictive autoscaler that it should scale out further to ensure applications are initialized when the load arrives.

  Generally, this is the time you expect your application to initialize. The default time is 60 seconds and anything below this could be deemed to give false information to the autoscaler. However, it is recommended that you test how long your application takes to initialize:

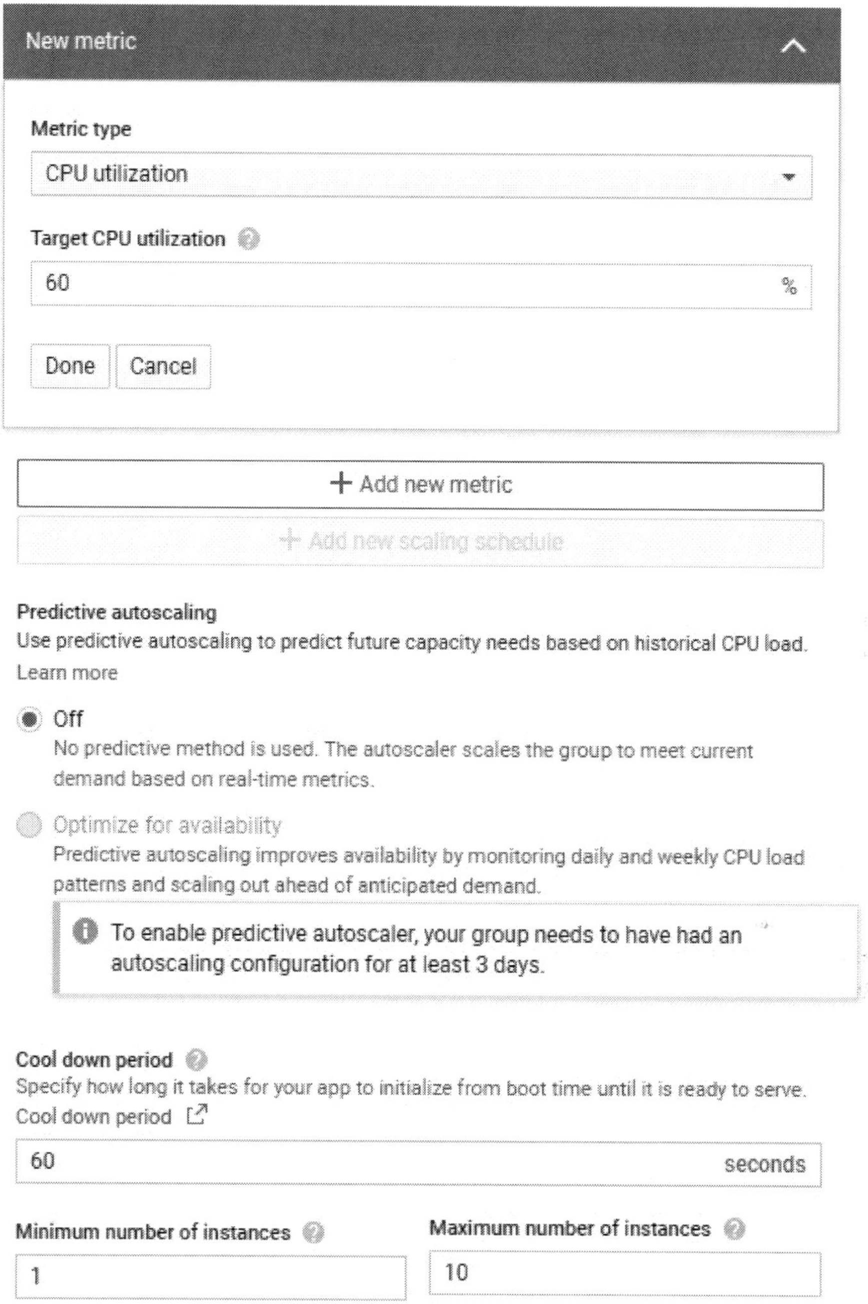

New metric   ∧

Metric type

CPU utilization   ▾

Target CPU utilization ⊘

60   %

Done   Cancel

+ Add new metric

+ Add new scaling schedule

Predictive autoscaling
Use predictive autoscaling to predict future capacity needs based on historical CPU load.
Learn more

◉ Off
No predictive method is used. The autoscaler scales the group to meet current demand based on real-time metrics.

◯ Optimize for availability
Predictive autoscaling improves availability by monitoring daily and weekly CPU load patterns and scaling out ahead of anticipated demand.

> ⓘ To enable predictive autoscaler, your group needs to have had an autoscaling configuration for at least 3 days.

Cool down period ⊘
Specify how long it takes for your app to initialize from boot time until it is ready to serve.
Cool down period ↗

60   seconds

Minimum number of instances ⊘

1

Maximum number of instances ⊘

10

Figure 4.39 – Autoscaling – CPU utilization

We should also understand that, as our managed instance group grows, the impact of adding the same-sized VM decreases. Let's clarify what we mean here. Say we have set a CPU utilization of 75% and a minimum of three instances in our group. The autoscaler is checking to see whether the aggregate of the VM instances averages above 75%. If the autoscaler adds a fourth VM, it adds a 25% increased capacity to the group.

If we have a maximum of 10 VMs in our group, then the tenth VM is only contributing 10% more capacity – so the impact of the tenth node is not the same as the fourth node. We should keep this in mind when setting utilization and maximum capacity. It's also important to note that autoscaling will always act conservatively and round up the statistics. It would start an extra VM instance that isn't really needed, rather than possibly running out of resources.

Scaling based on HTTP load balancing will scale based on the load of your VM instances. A load balancer will spread the load over backend services that are configured when you create an HTTP load balancer. When instance groups are used for the backend, external load balancers offer two balancing modes – **utilization**, which allows us to specify a maximum target for average backend utilization of all instances in our instance group, and **rate**, where we must specify a target number of requests per second. This is on a per-instance basis or a per-group basis.

The **Target HTTP load balancing utilization** value in the autoscaling policy should be a fraction of what is configured in your load balancer setting. For example, if you set the policy to 100 requests per second, then it would be sensible to scale slightly below this and set the usage in the policy to maybe 80 requests per second (80%):

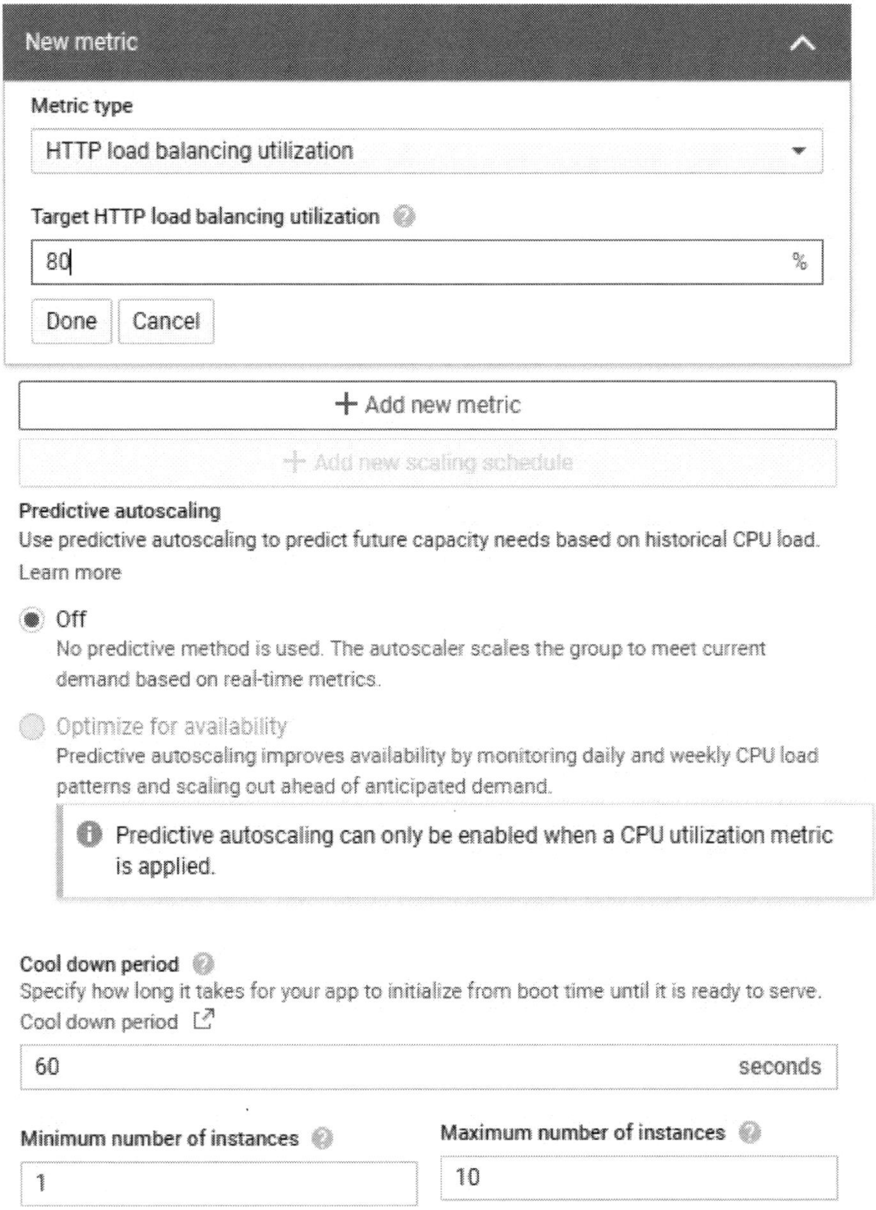

New metric ^

Metric type

HTTP load balancing utilization ▼

Target HTTP load balancing utilization ?

80 %

Done   Cancel

＋ Add new metric

＋ Add new scaling schedule

Predictive autoscaling
Use predictive autoscaling to predict future capacity needs based on historical CPU load.
Learn more

◉ Off
No predictive method is used. The autoscaler scales the group to meet current
demand based on real-time metrics.

◯ Optimize for availability
Predictive autoscaling improves availability by monitoring daily and weekly CPU load
patterns and scaling out ahead of anticipated demand.

ⓘ Predictive autoscaling can only be enabled when a CPU utilization metric
is applied.

Cool down period ?
Specify how long it takes for your app to initialize from boot time until it is ready to serve.
Cool down period ↗

60 seconds

Minimum number of instances ? **Maximum number of instances** ?

1 10

Figure 4.40 – Autoscaling – HTTP utilization

> **Tip**
> We will discuss load balancers in more detail in *Chapter 10, Networking Options in GCP*.

We also can scale on Google Cloud operations suite metrics, where the selected metric will provide data for each instance in the managed instance group or the entire group. These metrics can either be out-of-the-box or custom metrics you have created. Note that at the time of writing, in some documentation, the option is still referred to as **Stackdriver** in the settings; however, you should be aware that this was rebranded as Google Cloud's operations suite.

> **Important Note**
> If you have a requirement to scale down to zero instances from time to time, then you should use per-group metrics.

Let's look at another example, using a custom metric that Google offers as a demonstration metric, `custom.googleapis.com/appdemo_queue_depth_01`.

Utilization target type is set to **Gauge** in this example, because this will tell the autoscaler to compute the average value of the data collected over the last few minutes and compare it to the target value:

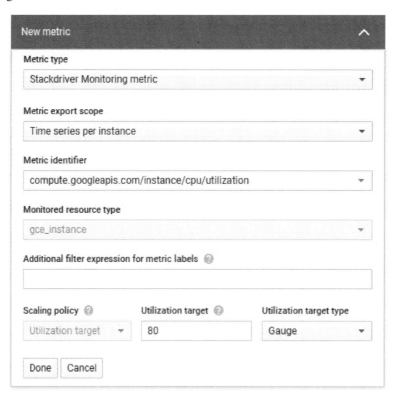

Figure 4.41 – Autoscaling – Stackdriver (Google Cloud's operations suite) metrics

Let's assume we now have a startup script on our instance template, which will invoke another script responsible for generating these custom metrics. We can see, from the charts monitoring tab within our instance group, that the load started to increase on our instance groups around 5:55 P.M. but dropped again around 6 P.M.:

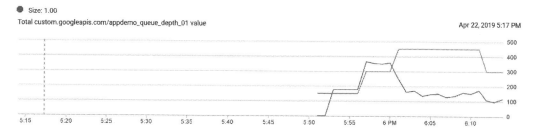

Figure 4.42 – Monitoring load

Given the spike in our queue depth, we can expect that the **autoscaling policy** would have generated a new instance. If we check the autoscaler logs, we can confirm this. It then added a third instance, before reducing back to two instances when the demand dropped again:

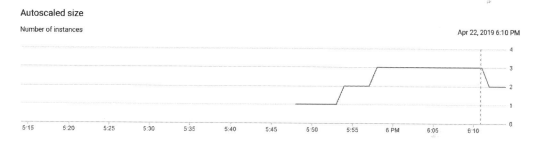

Figure 4.43 – Adding and removing instances

This is true elastic computing! These are small examples of how autoscaling works, and we advise that you ensure you can create your own policies and replicate any load that's responsible for increasing and decreasing your machine instances.

> **Important Note**
> You can only create one autoscaler per managed instance group.

Autohealing

Autohealing is also part of the managed instance group settings but merits its own section in order to discuss it further. GCP's managed instance groups are responsible for validating whether each VM instance in our group is running and ready to accept client requests. To perform this validation, it needs a **health check**, which is basically a probe that contacts each member of the instance group to check their current health. The policy can be based on certain protocols, namely HTTP(S), TCP, or SSL.

We also need to configure the criteria to inform the health check how often to check the instance, the acceptable amount of time that it can get a no response, and the number of consecutive failures to its probe. These settings define when a VM would be classified as unhealthy. If that specific instance is no longer healthy, the autoscaler will add a new instance:

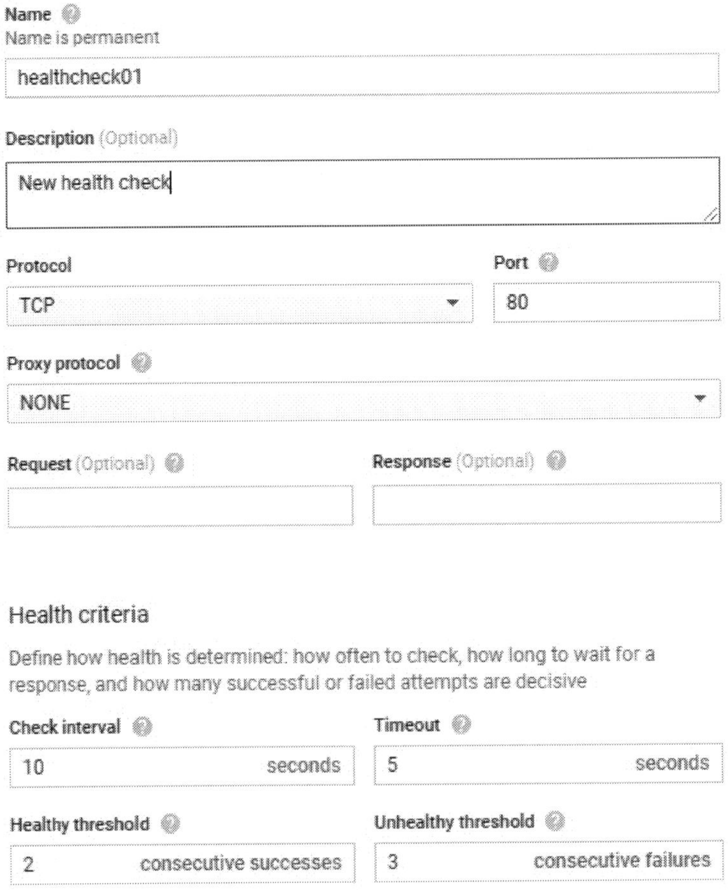

Name
Name is permanent

> healthcheck01

Description (Optional)

> New health check

Protocol   Port

> TCP ▼   80

Proxy protocol

> NONE ▼

Request (Optional)   Response (Optional)

Health criteria

Define how health is determined: how often to check, how long to wait for a response, and how many successful or failed attempts are decisive

Check interval   Timeout

> 10   seconds   5   seconds

Healthy threshold   Unhealthy threshold

> 2   consecutive successes   3   consecutive failures

Figure 4.44 – Autohealing configuration

Within the health checks, we also have to specify the healthy threshold. This figure is used to determine how many continuous successful checks must be returned before an unhealthy instance can be marked as healthy and traffic is directed to it.

We can then apply this health check as an autohealing policy in our instance group. The following screenshot shows the health check selected in this example:

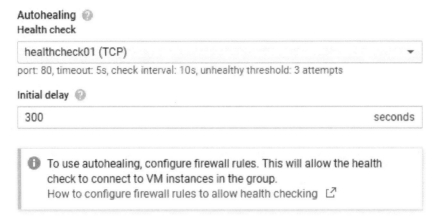

Figure 4.45 – Autohealing information

Autohealing policies can also improve the availability of your application. In the next section, we will look at containers on Compute Engine.

Containers on Compute Engine

As an alternative to running GKE, GCP offers the ability to run containers on Compute Engine. Containers will be covered more in *Chapter 6, Managing Kubernetes Clusters with Google Kubernetes Engine*; however, it's important to note that containers can be run on both Linux and Windows server VM instances or container-optimized operating systems offered inside of Compute Engine. Docker and Podman are two common container technologies that let us run containerized applications.

We should note that a Container-Optimized OS does have some limitations:

- It does not include a package manager, so we cannot install software packages directly on an instance.

- It does not support execution of non-containerized applications.

- The kernel is locked down.

- It is not supported outside of the GCP environment.

Running a simple Windows container on Compute Engine

Let's assume we have a Windows VM up and running with the *Windows Server 2019 DC core for containers* image. We can start RDPing to it, as we did in the *Deploying our first GCE instance* section. As the container is running a core version of Windows, it is running an OS with minimal UI. All we can see is the Command Prompt window.

If we run the docker images command, we can see what images are installed by default:

Figure 4.46 – Docker images

Let's create a new image and run it:

1. Run the mkdir my-new-container command.

2. Run the cd my-new-container command.

3. Run the mkdir content command.

4. Run the notepad content\index.html command.

5. Enter the following text to create a simple **Internet Information Services (IIS)** server:

    ```
    <html>
      <head>
        <title>Windows containers</title>
      </head>
      <body>
        <p>This is my test windows container!</p>
      </body>
    </html>
    ```

6. Use Notepad to create a file called Dockerfile.

7. Enter the following text to create the content of `Dockerfile`:

```
FROM mcr.microsoft.com/windows/servercore/
iis:windowsservercore-ltsc2019
RUN powershell -NoProfile -Command Remove-Item -Recurse
C:\inetpub\wwwroot\*
WORKDIR /inetpub/wwwroot
COPY content/ .
```

8. Let's build the Docker image and store it in the Google Container Registry by running the following command (please note the . at the end of the command): `docker build -t gcr.io/my-project-id/iis-site-windows ..`

9. You will see this completed successfully when the output returns something such as `Successfully tagged gcr.io/my-project-id/iis-site-windows:latest`.

10. If you rerun Docker images, you will now see the newly created image available.

11. Let's now run a Windows container with the `docker run -d -p 80:80 gcr.io/my-project-id/iis-site-windows` command.

12. Finally, let's browse the external IP of the VM instance.

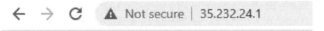

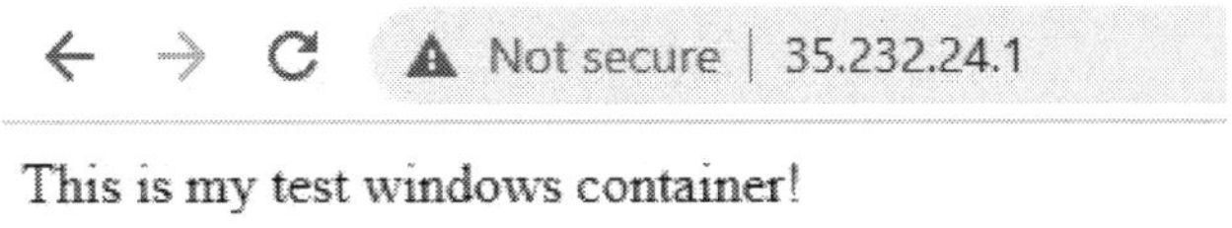

This is my test windows container!

Figure 4.47 – Web server on Docker

13. We can see from the preceding image that we have successfully run a very simple web server running on a Windows container.

> **Tip**
> It is important to note that containers built on earlier versions of Windows do not work in Compute Engine instances that have more recent versions of Windows.

A quick look at Google Cloud VMware Engine

Announced in May 2020, Google Cloud VMware Engine is a fully managed service that allows us to run a VMware platform in Google Cloud. Google will manage the infrastructure, networking, and management services so that you can use the VMware platform efficiently and securely. In short, this is VMware-as-a-service that can be deployed in around 30 minutes. It runs using VMware Cloud Foundation on dedicated Google bare-metal servers and can integrate with Google's big data and ML services.

The service is sold based on hyperconverged nodes with VMware services deployed. ESXi, vSAN, and NSX-T sit on top of bare-metal servers, while vCenter, NSX Manager, and HCX are also installed to automate deployment, monitoring, patching, and upgrades. Google is responsible for all of this, while the customer will retain responsibility for any VMs and VMware management tools and services, such as the vRealize suite. Licensing is also fully integrated into the service; therefore, the consumers are not required to worry about any VMware licensing issues relating to cores per socket.

> **Tip**
> The Professional Cloud Architect exam does not go deep into the Google Cloud VMware Engine service; however, you should be aware that the service exists, as it can be a milestone for companies who want to migrate quickly into Google Cloud using the *lift and shift* approach.

Use cases

There are many use cases for Google Cloud VMware Engine, such as data center extensions or migrations to allow companies to scale into the public cloud with guaranteed compatibility of their existing workloads. Disaster recovery is also another huge benefit of this service, as companies can leverage Google's global infrastructure to improve availability. HCX is used in both migrations and disaster recovery. A dedicated interconnect link between the on-premises data center and Google Cloud allows an easy migration of VMs and services between the two endpoints. Google is really trying to sell this as the quickest and easiest way into the cloud. This may be an important thing for some companies, who do not want to feel pressured into retooling their workforce or refactoring their applications to meet objectives to migrate into the cloud while maintaining operational continuity.

One important thing to also note is that **role-based access control** (**RBAC**) and billing is all under your Google account. It is all under one banner. This allows the VMware platform to integrate easily into Google's native services.

There are some prerequisites and requirements before we can use the service. At a high level, here are a few considerations. First, we need to enable the **VMware Engine API**. We can do this directly from the GCP main menu:

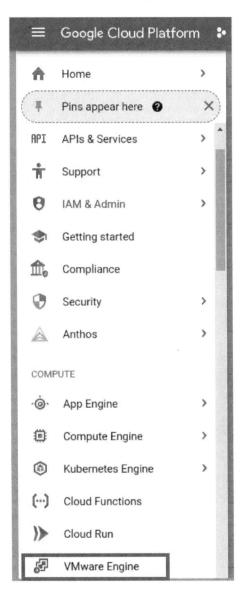

Figure 4.48 – VMware Engine

We then must set up private service access, which is a private connection between your **Virtual Private Cloud** (**VPC**) and networks in VMware Engine. You are also required to reserve address ranges that will not overlap with any of your on-premises subnets, VPC subnets, or planned workload subnets. Finally, VMware Engine has a specific set of IAM roles, so consideration should be taken to ensure the principle of least privilege is applied.

Quotas and limits

Compute Engine comes with a predefined quota. VM instances are part of regional quotas and therefore limits are applied to the number of VM instances that can exist in a given region. These default quotas can be changed in the console via the hamburger menu and go to **IAM & Admin | Quotas**. From this menu, we can review the current quotas and request an increase to these limits. We recommend you are aware of the limits for each service, as this can have an impact on your scalability.

IAM roles

Access to GCE is secured with IAMs. Let's have a look at the list of predefined roles, together with a short description for each:

- **Compute admin role**: This has the right to access all Compute Engine resources.

- **Compute image user role**: This has the right to list and read images.

- **Compute instance admin (v1) role**: This has the right to access full management of Compute Engine instances, instance groups, disks, snapshots, and images. It also has read access to all Compute Engine networking resources.

- **Compute instance admin role**: This has the right to create, modify, and delete VM instances. Additionally, it has the right to create, modify, and delete disks, and to configure shielded VM settings.

- **Compute load balancer admin role**: This has the right to create, modify, and delete load balancers and associated resources.

- **Compute network admin role**: This has the right to create, modify, and delete networking resources, except for firewall rules and SSL certificates. Additionally, this role has read-only rights to firewall rules, SSL certificates, and instances (to view their ephemeral IP addresses). With this role, you cannot create, start, stop, or delete instances.

- **Compute network user role**: This has the right to access a shared VPC network.

- **Compute network viewer role**: This has read-only rights over all networking resources.

- **Compute OS admin login role**: This has the right to log on to a Compute Engine instance as an administrator.

- **Compute organization firewall policy admin role**: This has full control of Compute Engine organization firewall policies.

- **Compute organization firewall policy user role**: This can view or use Compute Engine firewall policies to associate with the organization or folders.

- **Compute organization security policy admin role**: This has full control of Compute Engine organization security policies.

- **Compute organization firewall policy user role**: This can view or use Compute Engine security policies to associate with the organization or folders.

- **Compute organization resource admin role**: This has full control of Compute Engine firewall policy associations to the organization or folders.

- **Compute OS login role**: This has the right to log on to a Compute Engine instance as an administrator.

- **Compute OS login external user role**: This is available only at the organizational level. It provides access for an external user to set OS login information associated with this organization.

- **Compute packet mirroring admin role**: This provides access to specify resources that are to be mirrored.

- **Compute packet mirroring user Role**: This provides access to use resources that are mirrored.

- **Compute public IP admin role**: This provides full control of public IP address management for Compute Engine.

- **Compute security admin role**: This has the right to create, modify, and delete firewall rules and SSL certificates. This role also has the right to configure shielded VM settings.

- **Compute storage admin role**: This has the right to create, modify, and delete disks, images, and snapshots.

- **Compute viewer role**: This has read-only access to Compute Engine resources. It does not have the right to read the data stored on them.

- **Compute shared VPC admin role**: This has the right to administer a shared VPC host project. This role is on an organization by an organization admin.

- **Patch deployment admin role**: This provides full access to patch deployments.

- **Patch deployment viewer role**: This provides access to view patch deployments.

- **Path job executor role**: This provides access to execute patch jobs.

- **Patch job viewer role**: This provides access to get a list of patch jobs.

- **DNS administrator role**: This has read-write rights to all cloud DNS resources.

- **DNS peer role**: This has the right to target networks with DNS peering zones. Note that at the time of writing, this is in beta.

- **DNS reader role**: This has read-only access to all cloud DNS resources.

- **Service account admin role**: This has the right to create and manage service accounts.

- **Create service account role**: This has the right to create service accounts.

- **Delete service account role**: This has the right to delete service accounts.

- **Service account key admin role**: This has the right to create and manage service account keys. The role has the right to rotate keys.

- **Service account token creator role**: This has the right to impersonate service accounts.

- **Service account user role**: This has the right to run operations as the service account.

- **Workload identity user role**: This has the right to impersonate service accounts from GKE workloads. For less granular access, you can also use primitive roles of owner, editor, and viewer, but we should always use the principle of least privilege.

> **Exam Tip**
>
> If you want to debug an issue in a VM instance, grant the compute instance admin role and not the compute admin role. The latter has full control of all Compute Engine resources, whereas the former has less privilege.

In the next section, we will look at pricing.

Pricing

Google's billing model means that you are charged for vCPUs, GPUs, and GB of memory per 1 second, with a 1-minute minimum. However, Google also offers the opportunity to significantly reduce monthly billing. Sustained use discounts reduce the cost of running specific GCE resources.

Sustained use discounts are applied to specific Compute Engine resources automatically and can result in monthly savings on vCPU and memory for the following resources:

- General-purpose custom and predefined machine types
- Compute-optimized machine types
- Memory-optimized machine types

Sole-tenant nodes will also receive discounts. We discussesd them in more detail in the preceding sections. Additionally, savings are also applied to GPU devices.

If we run one of the preceding resources for more than 25% of a month, then GCE will discount every incremental minute you use for the instance automatically. Discounts will increase with usage, and anything up to a 30% discount per month can be expected. For example, general-purpose N2 and N2D predefined and custom images and compute-optimized machine types can provide us with up to 20% discounts. For general-purpose N1 predefined and custom machine types, sole-tenant nodes and GPUs can provide us with up to 30% discounts. Full discounts can only be taken advantage of if VM instances are created on the first day of the month, as discounts are reset at the beginning of each month. If we deployed instances around the middle of the month, then we would expect a discount of around 10%.

One key thing to note is how the billing is calculated. At a high level, let's look at an example of two different machine types created in the same region but running at different times of the month:

- An *n1–standard–4* instance with 4 vCPUs and 15 GB memory from the beginning of the month until halfway through the month
- An *n1–standard–16* instance with 16 vCPUs and 60 GB memory halfway through the month until the end of the month

In this example, Compute Engine will organize the machine types into individual vCPU and memory resources and combine their usage. It will break them down to the following:

- 4 vCPUs for the full month
- 12 vCPUs for half the month
- 15 GB of memory for the full month
- 45 GB of memory for half the month

So, we can see that the discount from the 4 vCPUs and 15 GB memory created in the *n1–standard–4* instance transfers over to the *n1–standard–16* instance, meaning we have a full 30% discount on 4 vCPUs and 15 GB memory. The remaining 12 vCPUs and 45 GB memory attached to the *n1–standard–16* instance would only receive a discount from week 2 onwards, meaning a 10% discount.

Another method offered for discounts is **committed use** discounts, whereby we can purchase a specific amount of vCPU and memory for an agreed term of 1 or 3 years. Discounts can reach 57% for most custom machine types or even 70% for more memory-optimized machine types. There are no upfront costs, but discounts are applied to your monthly billing. You will be billed for the selected vCPU and memory each month for the agreed term.

Discounts are applied via purchase commitments. Let's say, for example, we make a commitment for 8 cores but run 16 cores for 10 hours. We would receive the discount on the 8 cores for the 10 hours, but we would be billed as standard for the remaining 8 cores. The remaining cores would, however, qualify for sustained use discounts. Likewise, if we did not use the 8 committed cores in a monthly cycle, we would still be billed for them, so we should ensure that we only commit to what we will use. There are some other important caveats to committed use discounts.

Discounts are applied to resources in the following order:

1.   Custom machine types

2.   Sole-tenant node groups

3.   Predefined machine types

Let's take another example to make this clearer. Let's say we have a custom machine with 5 vCPUs and 50 GB of memory along with a single predefined machine. If we purchase 10 vCPUs and 15 GB of memory for committed use, the discount would apply first to our 5 vCPUs of the custom machine type and the remaining 5 discounted vCPUs would be applied to the predefined machine type. Likewise, the discount for the full 15 GB of committed use memory would be applied to our custom type memory.

Summary

In this chapter, we introduced GCP's IaaS offering – Compute Engine. This is a basic offering by Google and aligns with a traditional VM. We discussed how to deploy an instance and how to add to instance groups to scale our services automatically, so we can be confident now of how easy it is to get a VM instance running in GCP. Additionally, we looked at the various optional settings we can select when deploying a Compute Engine instance. We have also introduced containers and how VMware Engine can speed up the move to public cloud adoption. In the next chapter, we will move away from IaaS and introduce GKE.

Further reading

We recommend that you review the following URLs for further information:

- **Compute Engine**: `https://cloud.google.com/compute/docs/`
- **Compute Engine IAM roles and permissions**: `https://cloud.google.com/compute/docs/access/iam`

5
Exploring Google App Engine as a Compute Option

App Engine is a **Platform-as-a-Service (PaaS)** offering. It is the fastest way to get your application running with Google Cloud. It is suitable for web, mobile, and IoT applications, takes away the overhead of managing the execution environment, and scales quickly on demand. Multiple languages, such as **Node.js**, **Java**, **Ruby**, **C#**, **Go**, **Python**, and **PHP**, are supported. This way, the developer can concentrate on solely delivering the code. The applications are versioned, and traffic can be directed to multiple versions, allowing us to perform A/B or canary tests. Applications in App Engine can be secured with firewalls, IAM roles, and SSL certificates, and can be scanned for common vulnerabilities using the Web Security Scanner service.

We will cover the following topics in this chapter:

- App Engine components
- Choosing the right location
- Working with App Engine
- Environment types

- Deploying an App Engine application

- Versions

- Splitting traffic

- Migrating traffic

- Firewall rules

- Settings

- Scaling

- Cron jobs

- Memcache

- IAM

- Quotas and limits

- Pricing

> **Exam Tip**
>
> Expect a couple of questions on App Engine in the Cloud Architect exam. However, there is another (Cloud Developer) exam that tests your knowledge of App Engine in detail. For this exam, make sure you know how App Engine works, the two types of App Engine environments – namely standard and flexible – the two types of Memcache and use cases for them, versioning, how to split migrate traffic, what cron jobs are for, custom domains, and what SSL certificates can be used.

App Engine components

First, we need to understand that each project can only host one App Engine application.

The application can have multiple services with multiple versions, as shown in the following diagram:

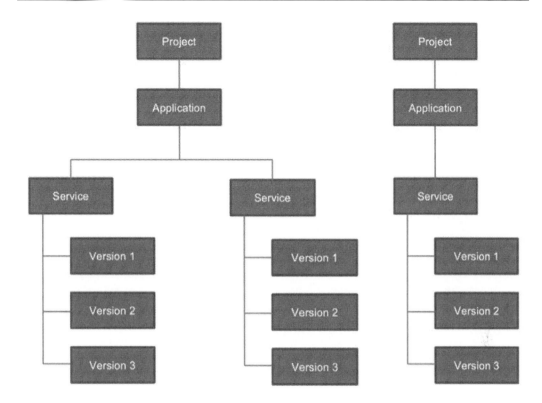

Figure 5.1 – App Engine components

Which version is served to the end user is based on the network traffic's configuration. We decide on the percentage of traffic that should be directed to a particular version. This means that it is very easy to make new rollouts and possibly even rollbacks.

Choosing the right location

Applications in App Engine are deployed regionally. This means that the infrastructure that's used to host it is spread across the zones within this region for high availability. The main consideration when it comes to choosing the region is where your end users will be connecting from. However, you should also remember that your app might use other GCP resources. This has an impact on delays as well as costs. Consult the documentation to see which regions the App Engine service is available in as this might change.

> **Important Note**
> Once the application has been deployed, you cannot change its region.

Working with App Engine

The deployment itself is fairly easy. We define an `app.yaml` file that defines the application and develop the code. By using `gcloud app deploy`, the application will be deployed to App Engine:

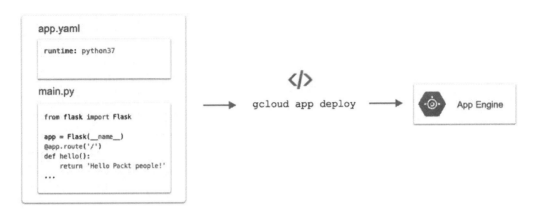

Figure 5.2 – Working with App Engine

The preceding example is very simple, and you can create far more sophisticated applications. The Cloud Architect exam does not require you to have deep knowledge of how to define the `app.yaml` file or how to write applications. However, we suggest that you have a look at the *Further reading* section as it might help you understand App Engine concepts better.

Environment types

App Engine comes with two types of environments, namely **standard** and **flexible**. If you don't have any special requirements, such as unsupported languages or need to customize the execution environment, always go for standard. Keep in mind that flexible App Engine will allow you to migrate your workloads more easily as your workload will already be containerized. Let's have a look at these environment types.

App Engine standard environment

The standard environment uses **containers** running in GCP. These are standardized for each available execution environment. The traffic to your application is distributed using load balancing. The application can scale down to zero if it is not used and can be scaled up within seconds when the demand rises. The following execution environments are supported:

- Python 2.7 and 3.7
- Java 8 and 11
- Node.js 8 and 10
- PHP 5.5, 7.2, and 7.3
- Go 1.9, 1.11, and 1.12

> **Exam Tip**
> App Engine standard is often also defined as a sandbox for developers.

We will now look at the flexible environment.

Flexible environment

The flexible environment uses GCE **virtual machine instances**. It also scales up and down automatically and distributes traffic using load balancing. However, it always requires at least a single instance to run. Starting the instances takes minutes, while in standard environments, it takes seconds. The following execution environments are supported:

- Java 8
- Python 2.7 and 3.6
- Node.js
- Ruby
- PHP 5.6, 7.0, 7.1, and 7.2
- .NET Core
- Go 1.9, 1.10, and 1.11
- Custom

Note that the runtimes can be customized. You can even create your own runtime. This can be done by supplying a custom Docker image or **Dockerfile**.

Exam Tip

As you may have noticed, the App Engine standard environment can scale down to zero, while the flexible environment will always run at least one instance. This has an impact on the cost of running your application.

An App Engine flexible environment service allows you to access root accounts on your instances via a secure shell, known as SSH. However, by default, this is disabled. Remember that the instances will be restarted weekly so that the necessary patches are applied.

Deploying an App Engine application

We have already seen how applications are deployed to App Engine at a high level. Now, let's have a look at the actual steps we need to take. Here, we will provision a `Hello World` application. This application leverages the **Python Flask web server**. As you can probably imagine, the application will display static `Hello World` text on the website. Let's get started:

1. To start, go to the Google Cloud Console and switch to the project that your application will be deployed to. From the hamburger menu, choose **App Engine**. On the welcome screen, click the **Create Application** button:

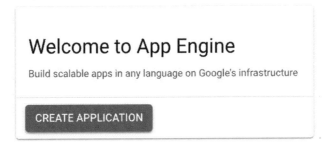

Figure 5.3 – Welcome to App Engine

2. In the **Create app** window, choose a region and click **Create app**, as shown in the following screenshot:

Create app

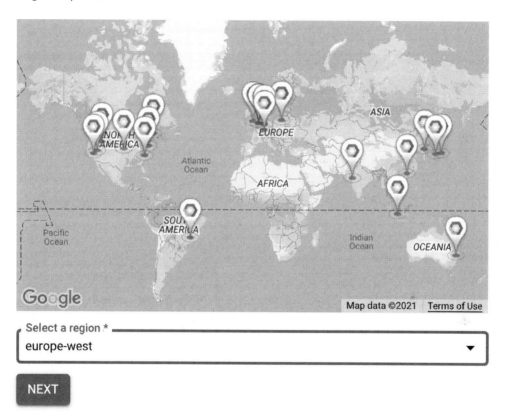

Region

Region is permanent.

Figure 5.4 – Choosing a region

We have chosen `europe-west` as our region.

3. In the **Get started** window, choose the runtime language. We have selected **Python**:

Get started
Resourc
Language
Python
Node.js
Java
Go
PHP
.NET
Ruby
Other
I'LL DO THIS L
Deploy with Google Cloud SDK
DOWNLOAD THE CLOUD SDK
Initialize your SDK
$ gcloud init
Deploy to App Engine
$ gcloud app deploy

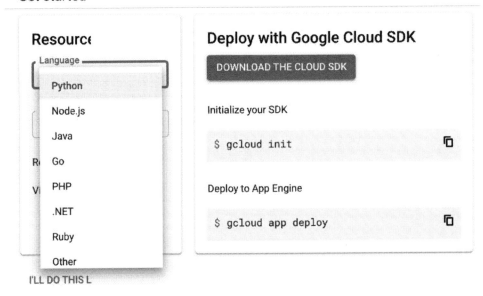

Figure 5.5 – Choosing a language

4. From the **Environment** dropdown, choose either **Standard** or **Flexible**. As we do not need runtime customization, we have chosen the **Standard** environment:

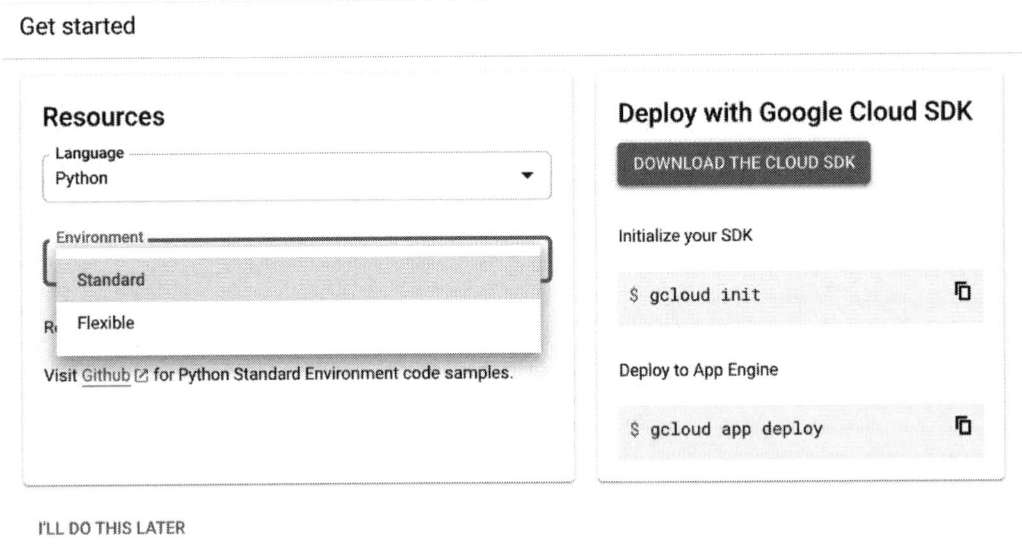

Get started
Resources
Language
Python
Environment
Standard
Flexible
Visit Github for Python Standard Environment code samples.
I'LL DO THIS LATER
Deploy with Google Cloud SDK
DOWNLOAD THE CLOUD SDK
Initialize your SDK
$ gcloud init
Deploy to App Engine
$ gcloud app deploy

Figure 5.6 – Choosing an environment

5. Now, we can either use the installation SDK on our machine or use the Cloud Shell machine. To learn how to use both those tools, check out *Chapter 16, Google Cloud Management Options.*

    We will open the Cloud Shell as it comes with the SDK already installed and configured. Open the console and run the following command:

    ```
    gcloud config set project $PROJECT
    ```

    Here, <project_id> is the ID of the project you used in the Google Cloud Console.

6. Now, let's download a sample Python application that Google provides on GitHub:

    ```
    git clone  https://github.com/GoogleCloudPlatform/python-
    docs-samples
    ```

7. Change directory to browse to the application:

    ```
    cd  python-docs-samples/appengine/standard_python3/hello_
    world
    ```

8. Now, you can use any text editor to view the content of the main.py file, which contains our application code. Open the file in an editor by running the following command:

    ```
    cloudshell edit main.py
    ```

9. You will see that the application is using the **Flask web server** and displays `Hello World!` on the `main` page:

```
main.py  ×
 1    # Copyright 2018 Google LLC
 2    #
 3    # Licensed under the Apache License, Version 2.0 (the "License");
 4    # you may not use this file except in compliance with the License.
 5    # You may obtain a copy of the License at
 6    #
 7    #      http://www.apache.org/licenses/LICENSE-2.0
 8    #
 9    # Unless required by applicable law or agreed to in writing, software
10    # distributed under the License is distributed on an "AS IS" BASIS,
11    # WITHOUT WARRANTIES OR CONDITIONS OF ANY KIND, either express or implied.
12    # See the License for the specific language governing permissions and
13    # limitations under the License.
14
15    # [START gae_python38_app]
16    # [START gae_python3_app]
17    from flask import Flask
18
19
20    # If `entrypoint` is not defined in app.yaml, App Engine will look for an app
21    # called `app` in `main.py`.
22    app = Flask(__name__)
23
24
25    @app.route('/')
26    def hello():
27        """Return a friendly HTTP greeting."""
28        return 'Hello World!'
29
30
31    if __name__ == '__main__':
32        # This is used when running locally only. When deploying to Google App
33        # Engine, a webserver process such as Gunicorn will serve the app. This
34        # can be configured by adding an `entrypoint` to app.yaml.
35        app.run(host='127.0.0.1', port=8080, debug=True)
36    # [END gae_python3_app]
37    # [END gae_python38_app]
38
```

Figure 5.7 – The main.py file

10. If we have a look at that `app.yaml` file, we will see that we only need to define the runtime type, without any additional parameters:

```
app.yaml ×
1    # Copyright 2021 Google LLC
2    #
3    # Licensed under the Apache License, Version 2.0 (the "License");
4    # you may not use this file except in compliance with the License.
5    # You may obtain a copy of the License at
6    #
7    #        http://www.apache.org/licenses/LICENSE-2.0
8    #
9    # Unless required by applicable law or agreed to in writing, software
10   # distributed under the License is distributed on an "AS IS" BASIS,
11   # WITHOUT WARRANTIES OR CONDITIONS OF ANY KIND, either express or implied.
12   # See the License for the specific language governing permissions and
13   # limitations under the License.
14
15   runtime: python39
16
```

Figure 5.8 – The app.yaml file

11. Finally, we will have a look at the `requirements.txt` file, which defines the modules that are used in our Python code:

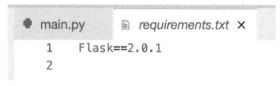

Figure 5.9 – The requirements.txt file

12. Now that we know what the configuration and code are, we can deploy the application to App Engine. Being in the folder where all the files are, run the following command:

```
gcloud app deploy app.yaml --project $PROJECT
```

Confirm this action when you are asked in the console. It may take a minute or two to deploy.

13. Once the application has been deployed, we can check the URL that's been assigned to the application by running the following command:

```
gcloud app browse
```

14. Copy the URL and paste it into your browser. You will see that the application is already running in App Engine. Simple, isn't it?

Figure 5.10 – Viewing the application

Next, let's look at versions.

Versions

Now, let's imagine that we want to update the application with new content:

1. Let's modify the welcome message to `Hello Packt people!`:

```
24    @app.route('/')
25    def hello():
26        """Return a friendly HTTP greeting."""
27        return 'Hello Packt people!'
```

Figure 5.11 – Modifying the application

2. We will save the changes and deploy the application again:

```
gcloud app deploy app.yaml --project <project_id>
```

3. Now, if we switch to the Google Cloud Console and go to **App Engine | Versions**, we will see that a new version of the application has been deployed:

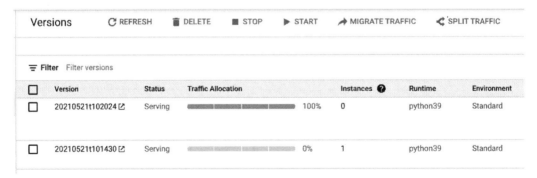

Figure 5.12 – Traffic allocation

Note that all the traffic is directed toward the new version.

Go back to your browser and refresh to see that the new version of the application has been deployed:

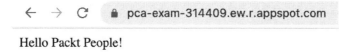

pca-exam-314409.ew.r.appspot.com
Hello Packt People!

Figure 5.13 – Viewing the new application version

In the next section, we will look at splitting traffic.

Splitting traffic

Now, imagine that we want to test the changes that we've made on a small number of users. We can do that by clicking on **Split traffic**, which can be found in the top-right corner. This will bring us to a window where we can choose how much traffic is directed to each version of the application. Choose an appropriate percentage and click the **Save** button:

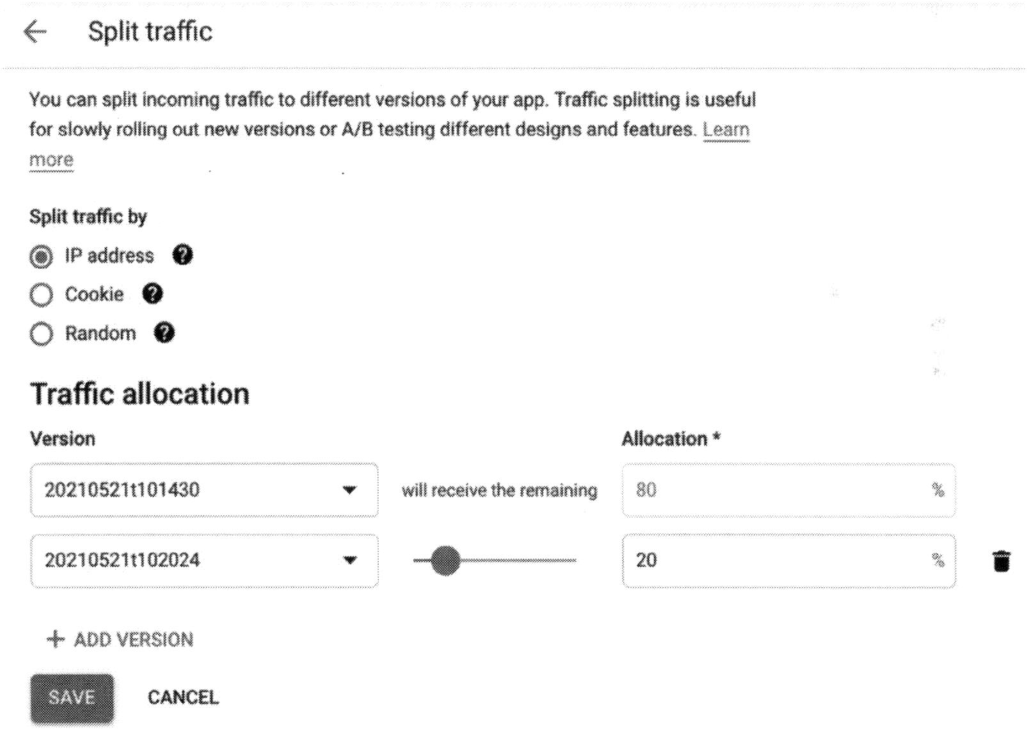

Split traffic
You can split incoming traffic to different versions of your app. Traffic splitting is useful for slowly rolling out new versions or A/B testing different designs and features. Learn more
Split traffic by
IP address
Cookie
Random
Traffic allocation
Version
Allocation *
20210521t101430
will receive the remaining
80
%
20210521t102024
20
%
+ ADD VERSION
SAVE
CANCEL

Figure 5.14 – Split traffic

> **Important Note**
> If you don't see the old version, click the **Add version** button.

Migrating traffic

Instead of splitting the traffic, we can also migrate the traffic at once. There are also gradual traffic migrating options so that we can gracefully change the version. Follow these steps to do so:

1. Select the checkbox next to the new version and click **MIGRATE TRAFFIC**, which can be found at top of the screen. From the popup window, click **MIGRATE**, as shown in the following screenshot:

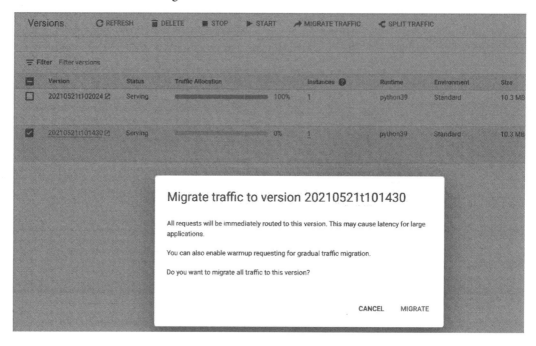

Figure 5.15 – Migrating traffic

The traffic will now be migrated to the new version.

> **Exam Tip**
> Pay special attention to how you switch traffic between different versions. This can be used for both rolling out the new version as well as rolling back to the last stable version.

2. Now, if we check the console, we will see that all the traffic has been allocated to the new version:

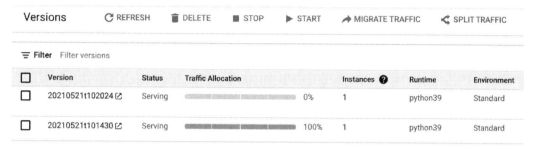

Figure 5.16 – Traffic migrated to the old version

3. If we browse to the URL, we will see that the new version of the application is now being served:

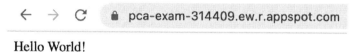

Hello World!

Figure 5.17 – Viewing the application

Here, we can see the old version of the application.

Firewall rules

The firewall for App Engine is pretty simple. It contains a list of rules for allowing or denying traffic to your application from a specific IP range. Note that these rules apply to all the resources of the application. The rules are ordered by priority, with a value of 1 being the most important and 2147483647 being the least important:

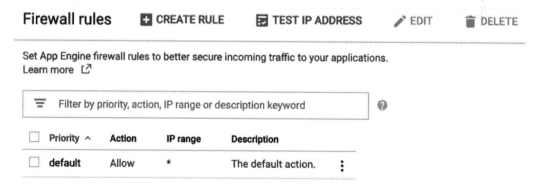

Figure 5.18 – Firewall rules

The default rule, which allows all traffic from all IP ranges, has the lowest priority and is always evaluated at the end.

Settings

From the hamburger menu, go to **App Engine | Settings**. Here, you will find two important settings: **Custom domain** and **SSL certificates**. Let's go over these now.

Custom domain

As you already know, when you deploy an application, you are assigned a URL in the form of `<project_id>.appspot.com`.

However, you can add a custom domain or register a new domain. You do this from the **App Engine | Setting | Custom domains** menu:

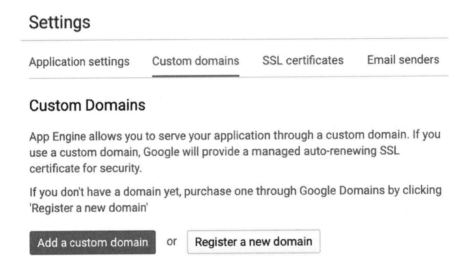

Figure 5.19 – Custom Domains

If you choose to register a new domain, you will be able to purchase it from the Google Domains service.

SSL certificates

Since the traffic in the App Engine is load-balanced and uses SSL, GCP offers globally distributed SSL endpoints so that you can serve your application users. An application with a custom domain has a managed SSL certificate assigned to it by default. The certificate will be provisioned and renewed before expiration automatically. When you remove the custom domain, the certificate will be revoked:

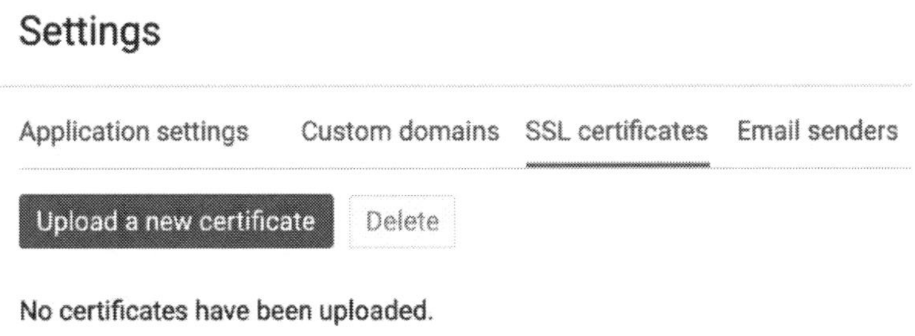

Settings

Application settings   Custom domains   SSL certificates   Email senders

Upload a new certificate   Delete

No certificates have been uploaded.

Figure 5.20 – SSL certificates

If you wish to use your own certificate, you are responsible for managing its life cycle.

Scaling

One of the most important features of App Engine is its ability to scale several instances. We have a choice regarding the level of automation we wish to use. App Engine offers three options, as follows:

- **Manual scaling**: In this setup, you specify the number of instances that will run, no matter what the load will be. Since the instances keep the memory state, they can be used for applications that depend on them.

- **Automatic scaling**: In this setup, several instances depend on the request rate, response latencies, and other application metrics. It also allows you to specify the number of instances that should always run independently of the load.

- **Basic scaling**: In this setup, an instance is created when a request is received by the application. The instance will be shut down when the application becomes idle. It can be used for apps that are driven by user activity.

> **Important Note**
>
> Scaling is a very important topic for App Engine. We want to make sure that the application can handle the load, but we also want to control the cost. Remember that you pay for the time it takes to run the instances. You can control the scaling behavior using parameters in the YAML that defines your application. Check the *Further reading* section regarding App Engine scaling to find out more.

Cron jobs

With cron jobs, you can schedule tasks that run at a defined time or regular intervals. The use case for cron jobs includes administration tasks that need to reoccur. For example, perhaps you need to send out an email every day that includes a report about the environment.

For each language, cron jobs are configured a little bit differently. See the *Further reading* section to find detailed configuration information for various languages. The cron jobs are defined in YAML format and placed in the `cron.yaml` file.

The following is a YAML file that will run the task every 24 hours:

1. The actual task is to run it using the handler defined under the `url` parameter:

    ```yaml
    cron:
    - description: "daily summary job"
      url: /tasks/summary
      target: beta
      schedule: every 24 hours
    ```

2. To deploy the `cron` job, use the following command:

    ```
    gcloud app deploy cron.yaml --project <project_id>
    ```

3. Once deployed, the jobs will be visible via Cloud Scheduler. In the Google Cloud Console, under **App Engine | Cron jobs**, click the **GO TO CLOUD SCHEDULER** button:

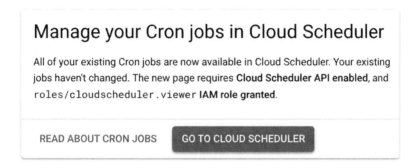

Figure 5.21 – Cron jobs

Click on the **APP ENGINE CRON JOBS** tab:

Figure 5.22 – Cron job summary

With that, your newly created job has been created and will run every 24 hours. Note that you might need to enable the Cloud Scheduler API if you have not used it before.

> **Exam Tip**
>
> Remember that cron jobs are a way of triggering jobs periodically and are an alternative to using Compute Engine with native third-party tools.

Memcache

Caching is a common way of speeding up how we can access frequently accessed data. This includes session data, user preferences, or any other queries that don't change often. If multiple queries are accessing the same data, it is a perfect candidate to be cached. Memcache is a service that's built into App Engine. It allows you to keep key-value pairs in memory that can be accessed much faster than querying a database. There are two service levels for Memcache, as follows:

- **Shared**: This is the default and free version of Memcache. Note that this service provides cache capacity on best effort basis. The resources are shared with multiple applications within the App Engine platform.

- **Dedicated**: This is an optional and paid version of Memcache. It provides a fixed cache capacity that's dedicated to your application. It is paid per GB/hour. This should be used for applications that require predictable performance.

You can add values to be cached by accessing the **App Engine | Memcache** menu:

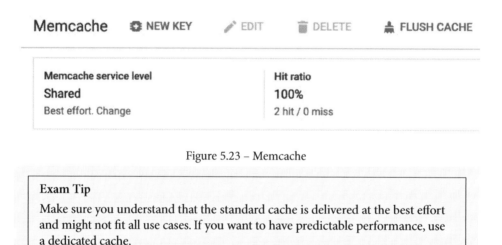

Figure 5.23 – Memcache

> **Exam Tip**
>
> Make sure you understand that the standard cache is delivered at the best effort and might not fit all use cases. If you want to have predictable performance, use a dedicated cache.

Next, we will look at the IAM roles required for App Engine.

IAM

Access to Google App Engine is secured with IAM. Let's have a look at a list of predefined roles, along with a short description of each:

- **App Engine Admin**: Has the right to read, write, and modify access to all application configurations and settings.

- **App Engine Creator:** Has the right to create App Engine resources for the project.

- **App Engine Service Admin**: Has read-only permissions to application configuration and settings. It also allows write access to service and version settings, though it does not allow us to deploy versions of apps.

- **App Engine Deployer**: Provides read-only access to application configuration and settings. It allows us to deploy and create new versions and delete old ones. However, we cannot modify an existing version traffic configuration.

- **App Engine Viewer**: Provides read-only access to application configuration and settings.

- **App Engine Code Viewer**: Provides read-only access application configuration, settings, and deployed code.

For less granular access, you can also use primitive roles such as **Owner**, **Editor**, and **Viewer**.

Quotas and limits

Google App Engine comes with predefined quotas. These default quotas can be changed via the hamburger menu, under **IAM & Admin | Quotas**. From this menu, we can review the current quotas and request an increase to these limits. You should be aware of the limits for each service as this can have an impact on your scalability.

For App Engine, we should be aware of the following quotas:

- **Free quotas**: For each application, you are allowed a certain number of resources for free. This quota can only be exceeded for paid applications.

- **Spending limits**: This quota is used to control the limits of your spending. It can be set by the **project owner** or **billing administrator**.

- **Safety limits**: This quota is set by Google to protect App Engine.

Pricing

The price of App Engine consists of multiple factors and differs for standard and flexible environments. For standard environment instances, the manual and basic scaling services are billed at hourly rates based on uptime. For flexible environments, the applications are deployed in virtual machine instances that are billed on a per-second basis with a minimum of 1-minute usage.

On top of that, you need to include the cost of additional resources that are used by your application. To get the most recent prices, take a look at the following link: `https://cloud.google.com/appengine/pricing`.

Summary

In this chapter, we had a look at App Engine, which is a PaaS offering. We distinguished between two types of environments, namely standard and flexible. Then, we looked at how to deploy an App Engine application and how to update it to newer versions. We also learned how to split and migrate traffic between the versions. Finally, we learned about cron jobs, which allow us to run scheduled jobs.

In the next chapter, we will have a look at Cloud Functions, which is a **Function-as-a-Service (FaaS)** offering.

Further reading

To find out more about App Engine, check out the following links:

- **app.yaml reference**: `https://cloud.google.com/appengine/docs/standard/python/config/appref`
- **Environments**: `https://cloud.google.com/appengine/docs/the-appengine-environments`
- **Memcache**: `https://cloud.google.com/appengine/docs/standard/python/memcache/`
- **Firewall**: `https://cloud.google.com/appengine/docs/standard/python/creating-firewalls`
- **Cron Jobs for Python**: `https://cloud.google.com/appengine/docs/standard/python/config/cron`

- **Cron Jobs for Java**: `https://cloud.google.com/appengine/docs/standard/java/config/cron`

- **Cron Jobs for Go**: `https://cloud.google.com/appengine/docs/standard/go/config/cron`

- **Custom domains**: `https://cloud.google.com/appengine/docs/standard/python/mapping-custom-domains`

- **SSL certificates**: `https://cloud.google.com/appengine/docs/standard/python/securing-custom-domains-with-ssl`

- **App Engine scaling**: `https://cloud.google.com/appengine/docs/standard/python/how-instances-are-managed`

6
Managing Kubernetes Clusters with Google Kubernetes Engine

In the previous chapter, we took a deep dive into Google Compute Engine, which provides **Infrastructure-as-a-Service (IaaS)**. In this chapter, we will look at a **Container-as-a-Service (CaaS)** offering. **Google Kubernetes Engine (GKE)** allows us to create managed Kubernetes clusters on demand. Before we start talking about GKE, we need to understand a few concepts, such as microservices, containers, and **Kubernetes** itself.

Exam Tips

GKE is heavily tested in the cloud architect exam. Make sure you understand the basic concepts of containers, microservices, Kubernetes, and GKE-specific topics. Pay special attention to the *Kubernetes* section. A lot of questions are related to Kubernetes rather than being GKE-specific. Make sure that you understand the Kubernetes architecture and resources, pay special attention to networking and services so that you know how the applications are accessed, understand how you can secure clusters with IAM and RBAC, and, finally, understand how you can manage, scale, and upgrade GKE clusters.

If you have never heard of these before, don't worry – we will take you through all the basic concepts. We will cover the following topics in this chapter:

- An introduction to microservices

- Containers

- Kubernetes

- Google Kubernetes Engine

An introduction to microservices

Let's start by going over the concept of microservices. In the legacy world, applications were delivered in a monolithic architecture. This meant that multiple services were hosted together on a single node. In the microservice architecture, the application is divided into several microservices, each hosted on a separate node, like so:

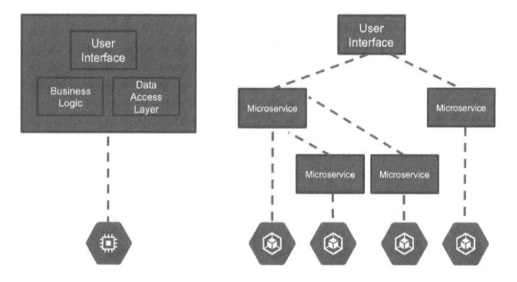

Figure 6.1 – Monolithic versus microservice

Each microservice is responsible for a single piece of functionality. The microservices are loosely coupled and can be developed and managed separately. They communicate with each other using APIs. Thanks to that, each microservice can even be developed in a different programming language. When you need to upgrade your application, you can upgrade a single service without affecting other components. By splitting the application into microservices, you also have control over how and when you scale your application. You can granularly scale the services that require scaling without touching the others. Finally, microservices allow you to embrace CI/CD and deliver functionalities faster as deployments can be rolled out in a very controlled way.

> **Important Note**
>
> **Continuous integration and continuous delivery and/or continuous deployment (CI/CD)** is a methodology of streamlining software delivery. **Continuous integration** is a practice where developers frequently submit code to a common repository. The code is reviewed and tested. After validation, automatic builds are triggered. **Continuous delivery** allows you to automate the release process so that the software can be deployed to the target environment at any point in time. In **continuous deployment**, any changes that are made by a developer that pass all the tests are automatically deployed to the production environment.

Containers

To understand containers, let's compare them to traditional virtual machines. While virtual machines virtualize hardware, containers virtualize the operating system. They abstract the application, along with all its dependencies, into one unit. Multiple containers can be hosted on one operating system running as an isolated process:

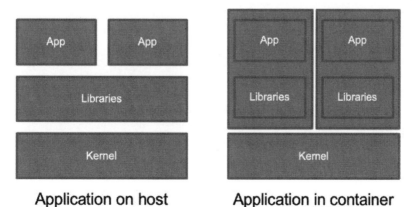

Figure 6.2 – Applications in containers

Containers bring the following advantages:

- **Isolation**: Applications can use their libraries without conflicting with libraries from other applications.

- **Resource limitation**: Applications can be limited to the resource's usage.

- **Portability**: Applications are self-contained with all their dependencies and are not tied to an OS or a cloud provider.

- **Lightweight**: The footprint of the application is much smaller as the containers share a common kernel.

The software that allows the containers to run is called the **container runtime**.

While there are many container runtimes available, Google recommends using **containerd** (`https://containerd.io`). For many years, the standard was the **Docker** runtime, but this has changed recently. **Containerd** was identified as the most secure and efficient and has become a new standard for Kubernetes and therefore also for GKE. If you are running your GKE nodes with Docker, Google recommends that you plan for a migration. Note that you can still build your containers using Docker as this is a separate process that happens outside of the Kubernetes cluster.

Kubernetes

Kubernetes, also known as K8s, is an open source container orchestrator that was initially developed by Google and donated to the Cloud Native Computing Foundation. It allows you to deploy, scale, and manage containerized applications. As an open source platform, it can run on multiple environments both on-premises as well as in the public cloud. It is suitable for both stateless as well as stateful applications.

> **Exam Tip**
>
> Kubernetes is an important exam topic. Fortunately, the exam does not require you to have in-depth knowledge of it. In this section, we will talk about both the management layer and Kubernetes objects. We want you to understand the management layer because it is necessary to understand GKE itself. When it comes to Kubernetes objects, make sure that you understand at least the ones mentioned in this book, including Pods, Deployments, Services, and Namespaces. Kubernetes itself deserves its own book, and there are many available on the market. If you feel like you want to learn more, refer to the *Further reading* section.

Kubernetes architecture

In the following diagram, we can see the basic architecture of a Kubernetes cluster. The cluster consists of multiple nodes. At a high level, the master nodes are responsible for managing the cluster, while the worker nodes host the workloads. The worker nodes host so-called Pods, which are the most atomic units of Kubernetes. These Pods can contain one or more containers. Access to the containers in the Pods is provided using services. In the following diagram, we can see a Kubernetes cluster and the services that are hosted on each type of node:

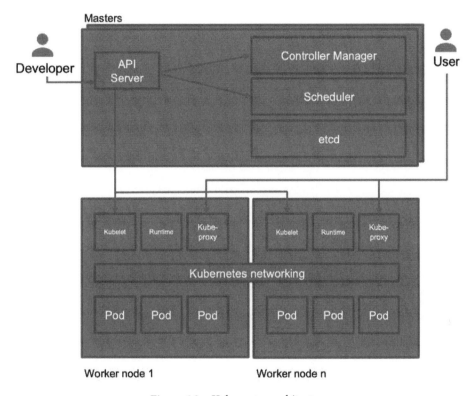

Figure 6.3 – Kubernetes architecture

Now, let's have a closer look at master and worker nodes.

The master nodes

The master node is a control plane that takes care of maintaining the desired state of the cluster. It monitors the Kubernetes object definitions (YAML files) and makes sure that they are scheduled on the worker nodes.

> **Important Note**
>
> **YAML Ain't Markup Language (YAML)** is a human-friendly data serialization standard, mainly used for configuration files. It is an alternative for formats such as XML or JSON.

It is essentially a control plane for the cluster. It works as follows:

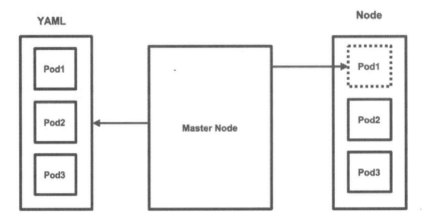

Figure 6.4 – Control plane

The master node runs multiple processes:

- **API server**: Exposes the Kubernetes API. It is the frontend of the control plane.

- **Controller manager**: Multiple controllers are responsible for the overall health of the cluster.

- **etcd**: A database that hosts the cluster state information.

- **Scheduler**: Responsible for placing the Pods across the nodes to balance resource consumption.

A cluster can run perfectly with just one master, but multiple nodes should be run for high availability and redundancy purposes. Without the master, the control plane is essentially down. All the cluster management operations you perform go through the master API. So, for production workloads, it is recommended that you have *multiple master* node configurations.

Worker nodes

A worker node can be a virtual machine or even a physical server. In the case of GKE, it is a GCE virtual machine instance. Worker nodes are responsible for running containerized applications. Worker nodes are managed by the master node. They run the following services:

- **kubelet**: This reads the Pod specification and makes sure that the right containers run in the Pods. It interacts directly with the master node.

- **kube-proxy**: This is a network proxy running on each node. It enables the usage of services (we will learn about services shortly).

- **Container runtime**: This is responsible for running containers.

Kubernetes objects

Kubernetes objects are **records of intent** that are defined in YAML format. They are declarative. Once created, Kubernetes will take care of keeping them in the state that's been declared in the definition file. Some examples of the most important objects are as follows:

- Pods
- ReplicaSets
- Replication controllers
- Deployments
- Namespaces

It would take hundreds of pages to describe all the available Kubernetes objects, so for the exam, we will concentrate on the preceding ones. Let's create an example `definition.yaml` file that contains the following content. This deployment will deploy two Pods with containers using the `nginx` image:

```
apiVersion: apps/v1
kind: Deployment
metadata:
  name: nginx-deployment
  labels:
    app: nginx
spec:
  replicas: 3
```

```
  selector:
    matchLabels:
      app: nginx
  template:
    metadata:
      labels:
        app: nginx
    spec:
      containers:
      - name: nginx
        image: nginx:1.7.9
        ports:
        - containerPort: 80
```

No matter what kind of object we define, we need to have the following data in it:

- `apiVersion`: The version of the Kubernetes API we want to use

- `kind`: The kind of object to be created

- `metadata`: Data that helps uniquely identify the object, such as its name

- `spec`: The specification of the object, which depends on its type

To create or update an existing object, we can use the following command:

```
kubectl apply -f definition.yaml
```

Here, `definition.yaml` is the file that contains an object definition. To run our first deployment, we would have to save the preceding definition in the `definition.yaml` file and run the `kubectl` command.

There are multiple commands you can use to manage Kubernetes. `kubectl` is the most used as it allows us to create, delete, and update Kubernetes objects. Take a look at the following link to see what operations can be performed using `kubectl`: `https://kubernetes.io/docs/reference/kubectl/overview/`. Note that `kubectl` is installed in the GCP Cloud Shell console by default, but if you want to use it from any other machine, it needs to be installed.

Now, let's have a look at each object, starting with Pods.

Selectors and Labels

You will notice that Kubernetes objects have parameters called **labels** and **selectors**.

Those parameters are used to associate different objects with each other. Say you want to associate a Deployment with a Service. In the Deployment definition, you would use a property label such as app: myapp, while in the Service definition, you would use a selector such as app: myapp.

Pods

A Pod is an atomic unit of deployment in Kubernetes. A Pod contains one or more containers and storage resources. Usually, there would be a single container within a Pod. Additional containers can be added to the Pod when we need small helper services. Each Pod has a unique IP address that is shared with the containers inside it. Pods are ephemeral by nature and are recreated when they need to be rescheduled. If they use no persistent volumes, the volume's content vanishes when a Pod is recreated. To create a Pod, we can use a kind value of Pod and define what image we want to use, like so:

```
apiVersion: v1
kind: Pod
metadata:
  name: my-pod
  labels:
    app: myapp
spec:
  containers:
  - name: my-container
    image: nginx:1.7.9
```

Here, we can see a definition of a Pod with a container that's been deployed from an nginx image.

ReplicaSets

A ReplicaSet object is used to manage the number of Pods that are running at a given time. A ReplicaSet monitors how many Pods are running and deploys new ones to reach the desired number of replicas. To define a ReplicaSet, you can use a kind value of `ReplicaSet`. The number of Pods to run is defined under the `replicas` parameter:

```
apiVersion: apps/v1
kind: ReplicaSet
metadata:
  name: frontend
  labels:
    app: guestbook
    tier: frontend
spec:
  # modify replicas according to your case
  replicas: 3
  selector:
    matchLabels:
      tier: frontend
  template:
    metadata:
      labels:
        tier: frontend
    spec:
      containers:
      - name: php-redis
        image: gcr.io/google_samples/gb-frontend:v3
```

ReplicaSets are successors of replication controller objects. It is not very common to create ReplicaSets. Instead, you should create Deployments, which we will have a look at in the next section.

Deployments

Deployments are used to deploy, update, and control Pods. These deployments create ReplicaSets without the need to define them separately. By stating how many replicas are needed, the appropriate ReplicaSet object will be created for you. By changing the image in the container, we can update the application to a new version. Deployment objects support both canary and Blue/Green deployment methods.

> **Important Note**
>
> In a **canary** deployment, we deploy a new version of the application to a
> subset of users. Once we are sure that the new version works properly, the
> application is updated for all the users. In a **blue/green** deployment, we use two
> environments, with only one active at a time. After updating the inactive one to
> a new version and testing it, we switch the traffic and make it the active one.

To create a deployment object, use a kind value of `Deployment`, like so:

```yaml
apiVersion: apps/v1
kind: Deployment
metadata:
  name: deployment-demo
  labels:
    app: nginx
spec:
  replicas: 3
  selector:
    matchLabels:
      app: nginx
  template:
    metadata:
      labels:
        app: nginx
    spec:
      containers:
      - name: nginx
        image: nginx:1.7.9
        ports:
        - containerPort: 80
```

In the preceding example, we created a deployment with three replicas from the
`nginx:1.7.9` image. The deployment object will make sure that three replicas
will be running at all times.

Namespaces

Namespaces are essentially virtual clusters within a Kubernetes cluster. In big environments, there can be multiple teams developing an application. By creating namespaces, users are allowed to reuse the names of resources. These names need to be unique within the namespaces but not across the cluster. By default, a Kubernetes cluster comes with three predefined namespaces:

- `default`: A default namespace for objects with no other namespace

- `kube-system`: Used for resources that are created by Kubernetes

- `kube-public`: Reserved for future use:

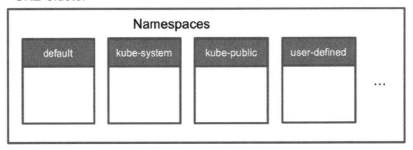

Figure 6.5 – Namespaces

Additional namespaces can be created as needed by running the following command:

```
kubectl create namespace <namespace-name>
```

Here, `<namespace-name>` is the name of the new namespace.

To deploy to the new namespace, you should use the `--namespace` flag, like so:

```
kubectl --namespace=<namespace-name> run nginx --image=nginx
```

Alternatively, you can define the namespace attribute in the object definition.

Namespaces can be isolated from each other using network policies. To learn more about network policies, check the *Further reading* section of this chapter. You can also limit the resources that are available to a namespace by using resource quotas. The following quota requests/reserves a total of 1 CPU and 1 GB of memory. It also limits the CPU to 2 and the memory to 2 GB:

```
apiVersion: v1
kind: ResourceQuota
```

```
metadata:
  name: quota-demo
spec:
  hard:
    requests.cpu: "1"
    requests.memory: 1Gi
    limits.cpu: "2"
    limits.memory: 2Gi
```

As you can see, namespaces are a good way of separating your environment. Before you decide to deploy a new Kubernetes cluster, you might want to have a look at creating a new namespace instead.

Services

Services are used to group Pods into a single endpoint. As we know, Pods come and go. A service has a stable IP address, so requests can be sent to it and forwarded to a Pod. What algorithm is used to perform the forwarding depends on the type of service. We will have a look at each type of service in the next section. Let's take a look at a simple definition of a service. Here, we are using a kind value of Service.

As we mentioned previously, you can use a selector in the service definition and a label in the Pod definition to assign the Pod to a service.

The following is a simple service definition:

```
apiVersion: v1
kind: Service
metadata:
  name: service-demo
spec:
  selector:
    app: myapp
  ports:
  - protocol: TCP
    port: 80
    targetPort: 9376
```

Let's take a look at the types of services.

Types of services

In this section, we will have a look at the most important service types. Services differ by how they handle traffic and whether they expose Pods externally or internally. The services we will discuss are as follows:

- `ClusterIP`
- `NodePort`
- `LoadBalancer`
- `ExternalName`

Let's discuss each service in detail:

- `ClusterIP`: This is a default service that uses an internal `ClusterIP` to expose Pods. This means that services are not available from outside the cluster. The use case for `ClusterIP` is internal communication between the microservices within the cluster:

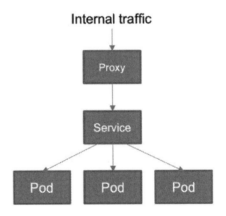

Figure 6.6 – The ClusterIPservice type

The following is a sample definition of a `Service` of the `ClusterIP` type:

```
apiVersion: v1
kind: Service
metadata:
  name: clusterip-demo
spec:
  selector:
    app: myapp
```

```
type: ClusterIP
ports:
- name: http
  port: 80
  targetPort: 80
  protocol: TCP
```

- NodePort: This simply exposes each node outside of the cluster. The Pods can be accessed using `<NodeIP>:<NodePort>`. If there are multiple nodes, then multiple IP addresses with the same port will be exposed:

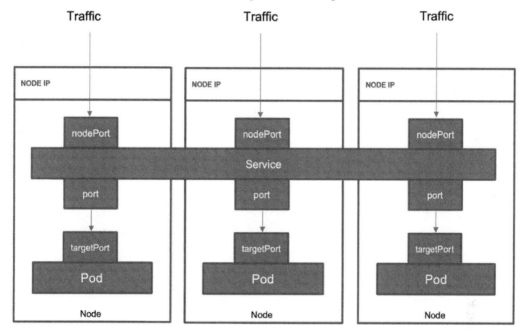

Figure 6.7 – The NodePort service type

The following is a sample definition of a `Service` of the `NodePort` type:

```
apiVersion: v1
kind: Service
metadata:
  name: nodeport-demo
spec:
  selector:
    app: myapp
```

```
type: NodePort
ports:
- name: http
  port: 80
  targetPort: 80
  nodePort: 30080
  protocol: TCP
```

- LoadBalancer: This will dynamically create a provider load balancer. In the case of GCP, a network load balancer is created for you. Remember that it uses objects from outside of Kubernetes and generates additional costs:

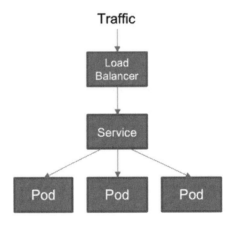

Figure 6.8 – The LoadBalancer service type

The following is a sample definition of a Service of the LoadBalancer type:

```
kind: Service
apiVersion: v1
metadata:
  name: loadbalancer-demo
spec:
  selector:
    app: myapp
  ports:
  - protocol: TCP
    port: 80
    targetPort: 9376
    clusterIP: 10.115.240.5
```

```
  loadBalancerIP: 70.10.10.19
  type: LoadBalancer
status:
  loadBalancer:
    ingress:
    - ip: 160.160.160.155
```

- ExternalName: This service is exposed using a DNS name specified in the ExternalName spec. The following is a sample definition of a Service of the ExternalName type:

```
kind: Service
apiVersion: v1
metadata:
  name: externalname-demo
spec:
  type: ExternalName
  externalName: my.app.example.com
```

- Ingress: This is an object that allows HTTP(S) traffic to be routed according to the defined rules (paths). It can be associated with one or more Service objects. These services are further associated with Pods. In the case of GCP, the ingress controller creates HTTP(S) load balancers. These load balancers are configured automatically using the definition in the Ingress object:

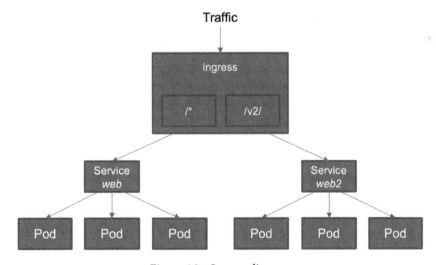

Figure 6.9 – Ingress diagram

Let's have a look at the YAML definition. The ingress is defined with a `kind` value of `Ingress`. From here, you define rules. Depending on the path, you direct the traffic to the associated service. In the following example, `/*` traffic is directed to the web if `/v2/*` traffic is directed to the `web2` service:

```yaml
apiVersion: networking.k8s.io/v1
kind: Ingress
metadata:
    name: example-ingress
spec:
    rules:
    - http:
        paths:
        - path: /*
          pathType: Prefix
          backend:
            service:
              name: web
              port:
                number: 8080
        - path: /v2/*
          pathType: Prefix
          backend:
            service:
              name: web2
              port:
                number: 8080
```

This sums up the list of the most important Kubernetes objects. In the next section, we will have a closer look at GKE.

Exam Tip

In specialization exams such as Google Cloud Certified Developer, you can expect more deep-dive questions on Kubernetes. You might see questions about resources such as `StatefulSets` `https://kubernetes.io/docs/concepts/workloads/controllers/statefulset)` or DeamonSets `https://kubernetes.io/docs/concepts/workloads/controllers/daemonset)`. Although we do not expect such questions in the PCA exam, we encourage you to have a look at the official Kubernetes documentation.

Google Kubernetes Engine

GKE is a fully managed service that allows us to provision Kubernetes clusters on demand. It offloads the burden of deploying clusters manually and provides managed master nodes. It also comes with several benefits that manual deployment does not offer, such as the following:

- Automated cluster provisioning
- Automated cluster scaling
- Automated upgrades
- Auto-repair
- Integrated load balancing
- Node pools
- Integration with the Google Cloud operations suite for monitoring and logging

A GKE cluster can be deployed in two modes: **zonal** or **regional**. In a zonal deployment, only one master node is deployed. In a regional deployment, three masters are deployed in different zones. This is shown in the following diagram:

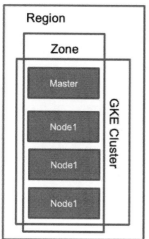 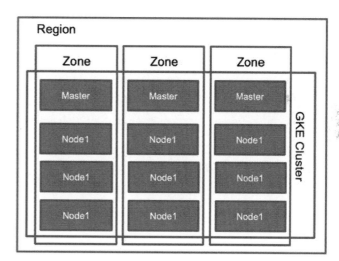

Figure 6.10 – GKE clusters

To be provided with a higher availability SLA and have zero downtime when upgrading the management plane, you should deploy regional clusters. In this setup, the masters can be upgraded one by one so that the management plane is functional during the upgrade period.

GKE Autopilot

GKE Autopilot is a new mode of operation for GKE clusters next to the standard one. This is Google's attempt to provide the customer with an even wider scope of services than GKE standard mode does. In the case of GKE Autopilot, it is GKE itself that provisions and manages the cluster, nodes, and node pools, providing you with an optimized cluster and a fully managed experience. You no longer need to worry about the health of your nodes or Pods. Those are monitored and managed by Google. The SLA covers both the control plane as well as the Pods. Another important aspect is you don't need to worry about the capacity required to host your Pods as this is taken care of for you by the service.

With GKE Autopilot, you pay for the CPU, memory, and storage that your Pods request while they are running not for the GKE cluster itself. You can learn more about GKE Autopilot here: `https://cloud.google.com/kubernetes-engine/docs/concepts/autopilot-overview`.

Node pools

Node pools are used to put worker nodes into groups with the same configuration. When you create your first cluster, all the nodes are put into the default node pool. You might want to have multiple node pools if you want to have groups with specific characteristics, such as local SSDs, minimum CPU, a specific node image, or using a preemptible instance:

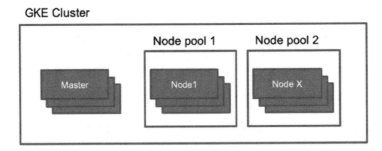

Figure 6.11 – Node pools

Node pools might be useful if your workloads have special resource requirements. You can use the concept of **node taints** and **Pod tolerances** to allow your workload to be scheduled on a particular node. In the *Further reading* section, you will find a link to documentation on how to use node taints.

> **Exam Tip**
>
> Pay special attention to taints and tolerances as this is a topic that might pop up in the exam. Understand how you allow Pods to run on a particular node.

Node pools are managed with the `gcloud container node-pools` command.

We will have a look at how we can use this command to scale our node pools later, in the *Resizing the cluster* section.

Container-Optimized OS (COS)

By default, nodes in your Kubernetes Engine use Google's Container-Optimized OS. It is a locked-down version of Chromium OS that runs containerized applications. Images are maintained and updated by Google. Updates are downloaded automatically in the background. As it is stripped of unnecessary features, the attack surface is smaller than in the case of other Linux distributions.

Note that this OS is not good for running non-containerized applications or when you need enterprise support from a Linux provider. Use Container-Optimized OS for nodes unless you have a very good reason to use another Linux distribution. While there are still images with Docker runtimes, Google suggests using the ones that run the containerd runtime instead.

Storage

The easiest way to use persistent storage in GKE is to use GCP services such as Cloud SQL, Datastore, or Cloud Storage. However, you can also expose storage directly to your Pods using Kubernetes abstraction layers. Storage is delivered to Pod containers using volumes. These volumes can be backed either by ephemeral or durable storage. While ephemeral storage is good for scratch space, to persist the state, durable storage is needed:

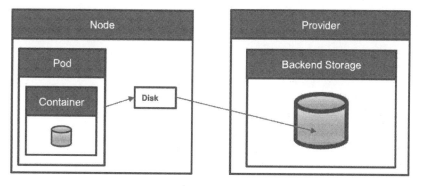

Figure 6.12 – Kubernetes storage

When a Pod crashes and is redeployed, the files that are stored on a Pod's local disk will be lost. To keep the state, you need to use external storage outside of the Pod. To do this, you can use **PersistentVolumes (PVs)**, whose lifespans are not bound to the Pod's lifespan. In GKE, those volumes are usually backed by Google Cloud Computer Engine Persistent Disks and can be provisioned dynamically by using a **PersistentVolumeClaim (PVC)**. An example of a claim is shown here. Here, we are requesting a volume of 20 GB, with the access mode allowing us to attach it to one node:

```
apiVersion: v1
kind: PersistentVolumeClaim
metadata:
  name: claim-demo
spec:
  accessModes:
    - ReadWriteOnce
  resources:
    requests:
      storage: 20Gi
```

To use this claim as a volume for the Pod, you need to refer to the claim in the Pod definition:

```
apiVersion: v1
kind: Pod
metadata:
  name: mypod
spec:
  containers:
    - name: myfrontend
      image: nginx
      volumeMounts:
      - mountPath: "/var/www/html"
        name: mypd
  volumes:
    - name: mypd
      persistentVolumeClaim:
        claimName: claim-demo
```

To learn more about PersistentVolumes, refer to the *Further reading* section.

GKE cluster management

We have finally gone through the theory that's needed to understand GKE. Now, let's have a look at some practical examples of managing a GKE cluster. We will start by deploying a cluster and then look at the operations for scaling and upgrading.

There are a couple of tools you can use to manage a cluster, including the following:

- Google Cloud Console
- The gcloud command-line interface
- The REST API

For exam purposes, we will concentrate on the first two tools. Let's get to work!

Creating a GKE cluster

The simplest way to deploy a cluster is to use the Google Cloud Console. This is also a good way to see all the available options without having to read the command-line reference. Let's get started:

1. From the hamburger menu, choose **Kubernetes Engine | Clusters**. From the pop-up window, click on the **CREATE** button, as shown in the following screenshot:

> **Important Note**
> If you are using the GKE for the first time, you need to enable the Kubernetes API.

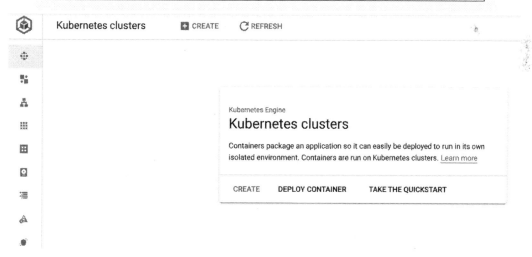

Figure 6.13 – Creating a Kubernetes cluster

2.   Click on **Create cluster**. You will be able to choose the mode. We will go with Standard mode as this gives you more options to choose from and will help you understand GKE better. Click on **CONFIGURE** next to the **GKE Standard** section:

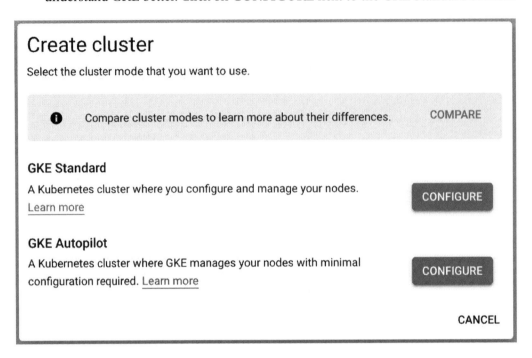

Figure 6.14 – Creating a cluster

3.   In the following pane, you can choose a template for your cluster, depending on the workload type. We will go with **Standard cluster** as we want to deploy a simple web application. On the right-hand side, we can choose more detailed settings for the cluster. Let's have a closer look at the available options:

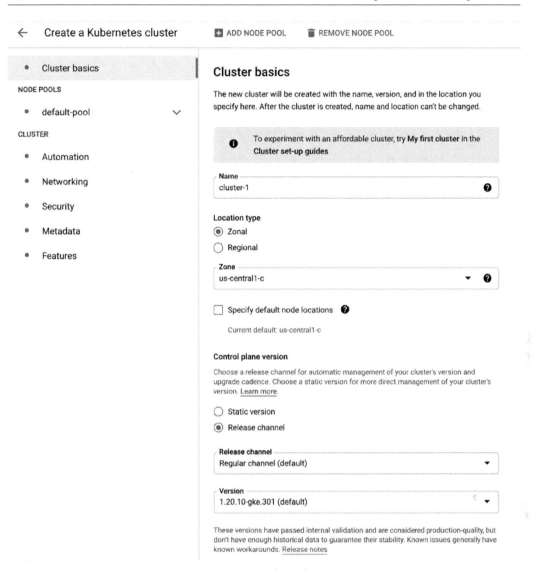

Figure 6.15 – Cluster basics

4.   First, choose the name of your cluster. Next, decide whether you want the cluster to be **Zonal** or **Regional**. If we choose **Zonal**, we will see that we are asked for a **Zone** to deploy to, as shown in the following screenshot:

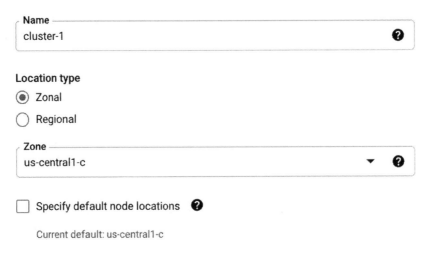

Figure 6.16 – Zonal cluster

5.   If we choose **Regional**, we will have to choose a region, as shown in the following screenshot:

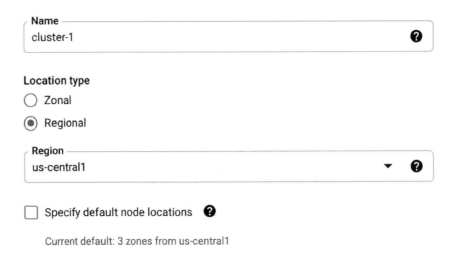

Figure 6.17 – Regional cluster

6. No matter which **Location type** we select, we need to choose a **Master version**. By default, the most stable version is selected. We will keep the default value as-is:

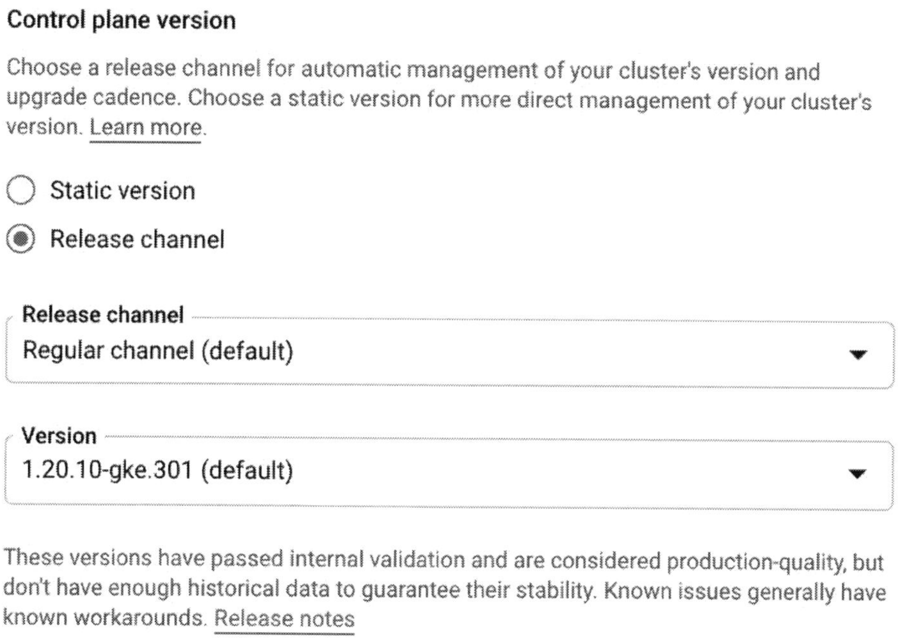

Control plane version

Choose a release channel for automatic management of your cluster's version and upgrade cadence. Choose a static version for more direct management of your cluster's version. Learn more.

○ Static version

◉ Release channel

Release channel
Regular channel (default)   ▼

Version
1.20.10-gke.301 (default)   ▼

These versions have passed internal validation and are considered production-quality, but don't have enough historical data to guarantee their stability. Known issues generally have known workarounds. Release notes

Figure 6.18 – Control plane version

In this window, you can also choose the release channel. Here, you have three options:

- **Rapid channel**: Used by early adopters. Allows you to use the newest features in a couple of weeks from the **General Availability (GA)** release of the Kubernetes minor version. Note that Google does not provide any SLA for this option.

- **Regular channel**: Provides a compromise between the reliability and available features. Available after 2-3 months after the rapid channel's release.

- **Stable channel**: This is the most stable and well tested. Available after 2-3 months after the regular channel's release. Use this version when reliability is a priority for you.

7. Click on **default-pool** in the left-hand menu to configure the node pool's settings. Remember that there can be one or more pools in a cluster. As we mentioned previously, pools group nodes with the same characteristics. In this section, we can choose the **Name** parameter for the pool, its **Size**, and define some characteristics such as **auto-scaling** and **node locations**. By default, the auto-repair and auto-upgrade options are enabled. Finally, you can define the **maximum surge** (number of nodes) and **maximum unavailable** nodes during the upgrade. We will learn more about these options later in this chapter:

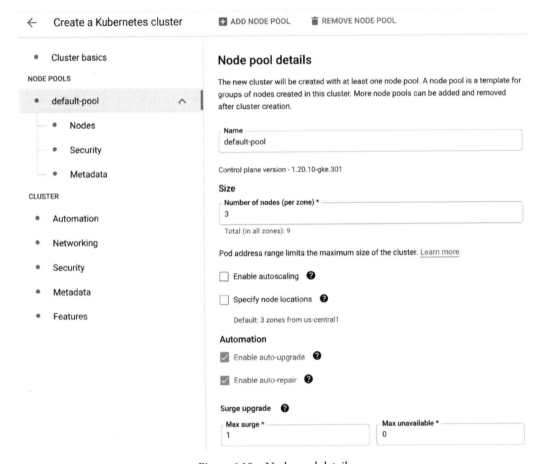

Figure 6.19 – Node pool details

8. When we click on the **Nodes** menu, we are presented with more settings. Here, we can choose the image for the nodes and the type of machines that will be used.

If we choose several vCPUs, then the memory amount will be automatically filled in for us. Furthermore, we can choose the node's disk type and size. We can encrypt the boot disk with the Customer-Managed Encryption Key and we are given an option to use the preemptible nodes. Finally, we can set a maximum number of Pods per node and assign network tags to control access to nodes using firewalls:

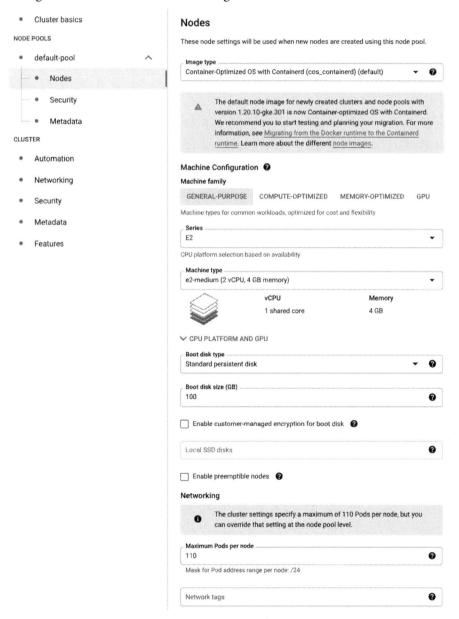

Figure 6.20 – Nodes

Click on the **Security** section. Here, we can see that the service account that's being used is the **Compute Engine** default service account. This is very similar to how the GCE security settings work. However, note that this account will be used by the workloads that have been deployed to the node pool. Remember to use the least privileges principle:

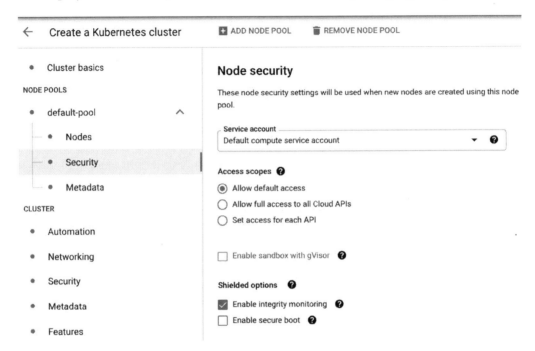

Figure 6.21 – Node security

We are also given the option to enable sandboxing with gVisor (`https://github.com/google/gvisor`) and options for Shielded nodes.

In the **Metadata** section, we can set **Kubernetes labels** and **Node taints,** as well as the metadata for the node's GCE instances:

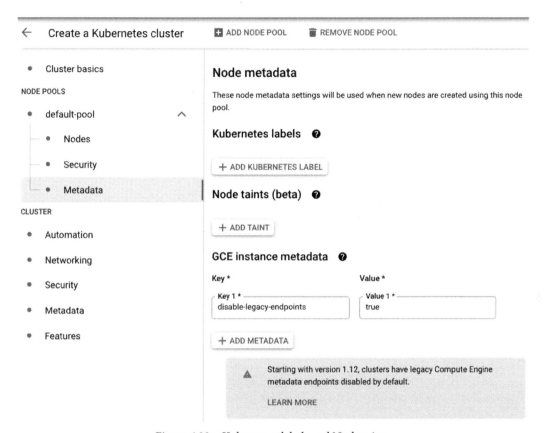

Figure 6.22 – Kubernetes labels and Node taints

With that, we have finished configuring the first node pool. If additional node pools are required, they can be created by clicking the **ADD NODE POOL** link on top of the screen. The new node pool will be listed under the **NODE POOLS** section. In this tutorial, we will continue using a single node pool. The following screenshot only shows what happens when you decide to add a new node pool:

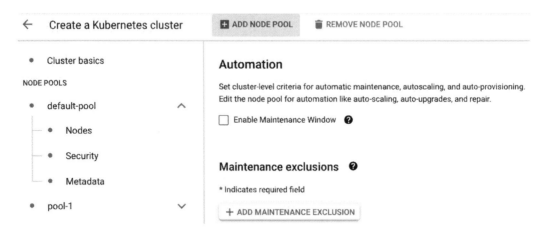

Figure 6.23 – Adding node pools

Let's move on to the **Automation** section. Here, you can set a maintenance window for the cluster, which will define when your clusters can be upgraded by Google. You can also enable notifications for upgrades, **Vertical Pod Autoscaling**, and **Node auto-provisioning**. For the auto-scaling profile, you can change from the standard **Balanced** mode to **Optimized**, which aggressively removes your nodes (this is optimized for batch workloads that are not sensitive to startup latency):

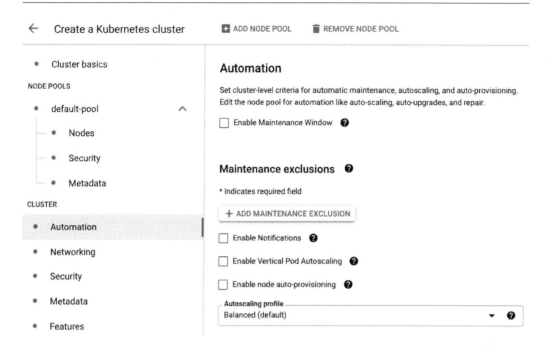

Figure 6.24 – Automation

Next, let's look at the **Networking** section.

Networking

Here, we can choose whether we want to use a VPC from the project or use a shared VPC. Let's get started:

> **Important Note**
> In this case, we have a service project that uses a shared VPC.

1. First, we must choose the subnet from the VPC that will be used by the nodes:

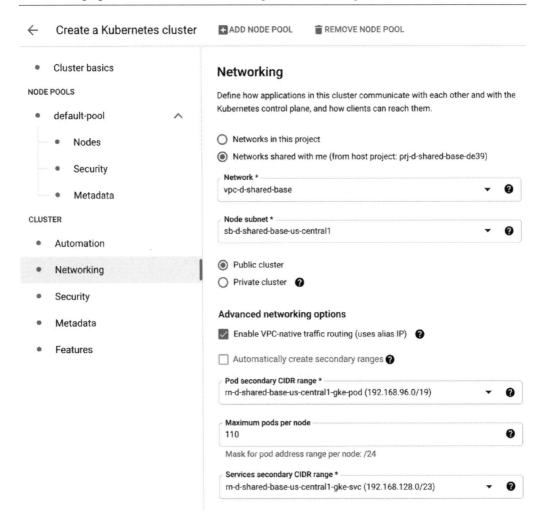

Figure 6.25 – Networking

2. Next, we will be presented with the option of using a public or private cluster. Private means that the nodes will have private IP addresses only. You can also uncheck **Access the control plane using external IP address** to disallow connecting to the control plane from the internet. If you check the **Enable control plane global access** box, this will allow you to access the control plan from any GCP region or on-premises. For **Control Plane IP range**, fill in the IP range you want to use for the control plane:

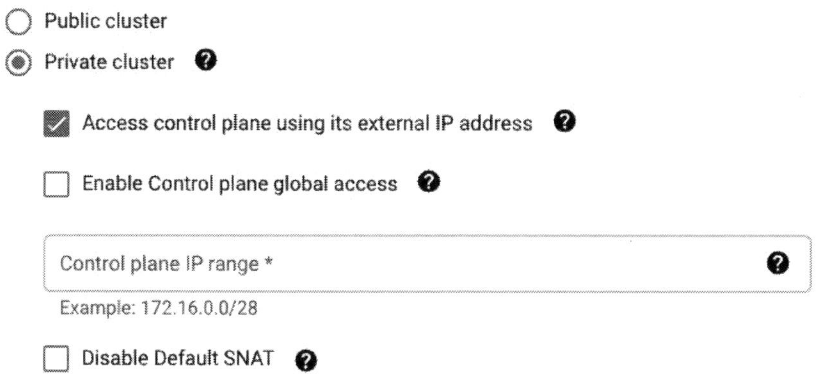

○ Public cluster

◉ Private cluster ❷

☑ Access control plane using its external IP address ❷

☐ Enable Control plane global access ❷

Control plane IP range * ❷

Example: 172.16.0.0/28

☐ Disable Default SNAT ❷

Figure 6.26 – Private cluster

> **Important Note**
>
> If you plan to use privately used public IPs (`https://cloud.google.com/architecture/configuring-privately-used-public-ips-for-GKE`), you need to check the **Disable Default SNAT** option.

3. Keep **Public cluster** selected and move to the **Advanced networking options** section. If we stay with the default **VPC-native** traffic routing, we will be able to use alias IP ranges from the shared VPC. This is Google's recommended best practice setup. We choose the provided Pod and service IP ranges and leave the default maximum Pods as-is per node number:

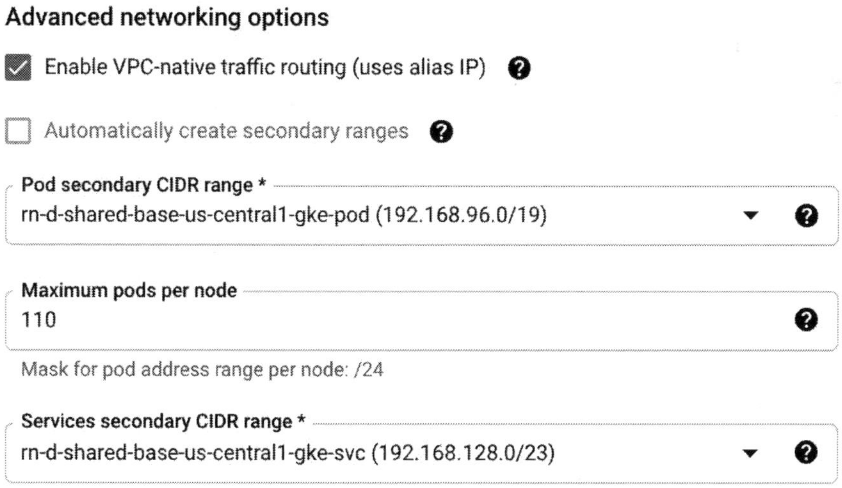

Advanced networking options

☑ Enable VPC-native traffic routing (uses alias IP) ❷

☐ Automatically create secondary ranges ❷

Pod secondary CIDR range *
rn-d-shared-base-us-central1-gke-pod (192.168.96.0/19)   ▼ ❷

Maximum pods per node
110   ❷

Mask for pod address range per node: /24

Services secondary CIDR range *
rn-d-shared-base-us-central1-gke-svc (192.168.128.0/23)   ▼ ❷

Figure 6.27 – Advanced networking options

4. To be able to use a Kubernetes ingress resource, we must keep HTTP load balancing enabled:

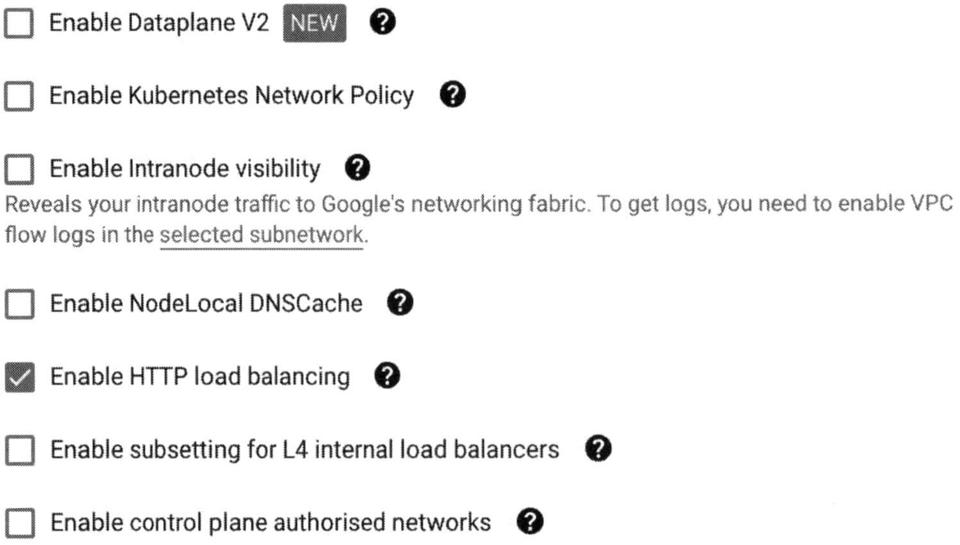

☐ Enable Dataplane V2 NEW ❷

☐ Enable Kubernetes Network Policy ❷

☐ Enable Intranode visibility ❷
Reveals your intranode traffic to Google's networking fabric. To get logs, you need to enable VPC flow logs in the selected subnetwork.

☐ Enable NodeLocal DNSCache ❷

☑ Enable HTTP load balancing ❷

☐ Enable subsetting for L4 internal load balancers ❷

☐ Enable control plane authorised networks ❷

Figure 6.28 – HTTP load balancing

As you can see, there are a couple of interesting features you can enable in this section, as follows:

- **Enable Kubernetes Network Policy**: This allows you to allow or disallow network traffic within the cluster.

- **Enable Intranode visibility**: This allows you to gain insight into the network flows between the nodes.

- **Enable control plane authorized networks**: This allows you to define which networks you can connect to your control plane from.

Now, we will have a look at the **Security** options.

5. In the **Security** section, we have a couple of authentication and authorization settings that are disabled by default:

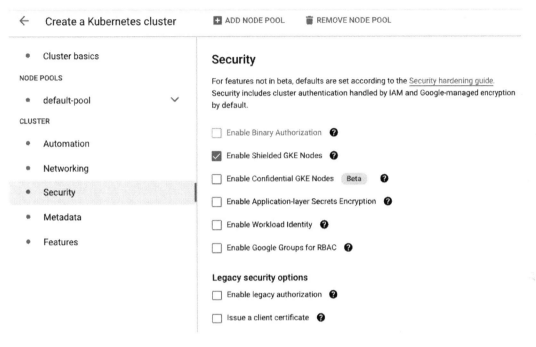

Figure 6.29 – Security

You can enable a couple of very useful services here, as follows:

-   **Binary Authorization**: Disallows running unsigned images on your cluster

-   **Shielded GKE Nodes**: Provides a strong cryptographic identity for nodes in the cluster

-   **Confidential GKE nodes**: Encrypts the memory of your nodes with keys that Google does not have access to

-   **Application-layer Secrets Encryption**: Uses Cloud KMS to encrypt secrets stored in etcd databases

-   **Workload Identity**: Allows you to use your workloads to access the Google API securely by mapping Kubernetes service accounts to Google service accounts

- **Google Groups for RBAC**: Maps the Google Groups to the roles and cluster roles in your cluster

There are also some legacy security options that you should not use unless you have a special use case and you are confident with the security tradeoffs.

In the **Metadata** section, you can put some optional descriptions and labels in your cluster:

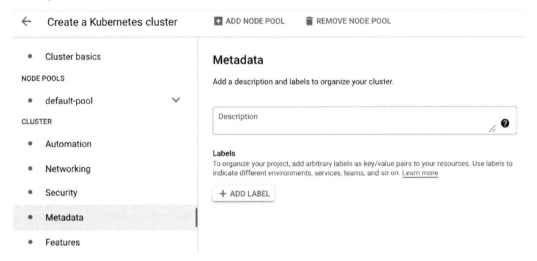

Figure 6.30 – Metadata

Finally, we can move on to the **Features** section.

6. In the **Features** section, we can enable new GKE monitoring functionality that is available for your Kubernetes version. You will learn more about GKE monitoring in *Chapter 17, Monitoring Your Infrastructure*:

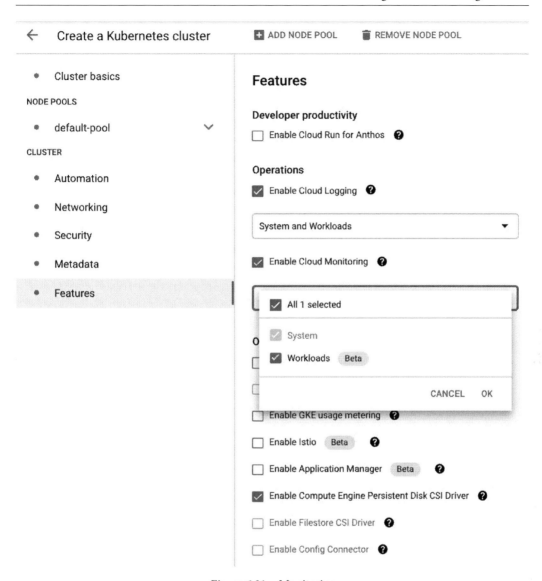

Figure 6.31 – Monitoring

7. We will leave the system and workload logging and monitoring options as-is. Besides monitoring, there are some interesting features such as Cloud Run for Anthos and Config Connector (we will learn more about these in *Chapter 8, Managing Cloud-Native Workloads with Anthos*). For exam purposes, have a look at the *Exam Tip* box to understand the most important ones:

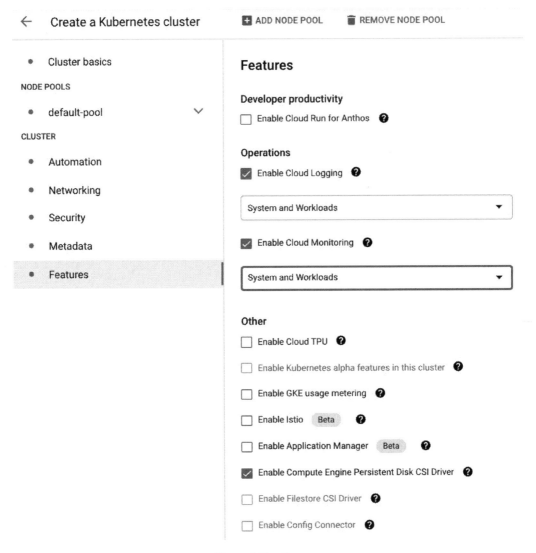

Figure 6.32 – Features

> **Exam Tip**
>
> It might be worth remembering that we can do the following:
>
> **Enable Cloud TPU**: We will discuss this in *Chapter 14, Putting Machine Learning to Work.*
>
> **Enable Istio (beta)**: This is a service mesh product that allows us to control and observe network traffic.

8. Now that we have populated all the settings, we can create the cluster by clicking on the **Create** button. Alternatively, we can generate a REST API call or command line by clicking on the respective hyperlinks:

Figure 6.33 – REST or command line

9. Before clicking on **Create**, let's have a look at the command line by clicking on the **command line** link. As usual, you can just copy this into Cloud Shell and execute it. In the following code, you can see that we used some features that are available in beta mode, such as the `gcloud beta container` command:

```
gcloud beta container --project "prj-bu1-d-sample-
base-6159" clusters create "standard-cluster-1" --zone
"us-central1-c" --no-enable-basic-auth --cluster-version
"1.19.9-gke.1900" --release-channel "regular" --machine-
type "e2-medium" --image-type "COS_CONTAINERD" --disk-
type "pd-standard" --disk-size "100" --metadata disable-
legacy-endpoints=true --scopes "https://www.googleapis.
com/auth/devstorage.read_only","https://www.googleapis.
com/auth/logging.write","https://www.googleapis.com/
auth/monitoring","https://www.googleapis.com/auth/
servicecontrol","https://www.googleapis.com/auth/service.
management.readonly","https://www.googleapis.com/auth/
trace.append" --num-nodes "3" --enable-stackdriver-
kubernetes --no-enable-ip-alias --network "projects/
prj-d-shared-base-de39/global/networks/vpc-d-shared-base"
--subnetwork "projects/prj-d-shared-base-de39/regions/
us-central1/subnetworks/sb-d-shared-base-us-central1"
--no-enable-intra-node-visibility --no-enable-master-
authorized-networks --addons HorizontalPodAutoscaling,
HttpLoadBalancing,GcePersistentDiskCsiDriver --enable-
autoupgrade --enable-autorepair --max-surge-upgrade 1
--max-unavailable-upgrade 0 --enable-shielded-nodes
--node-locations "us-central1-c"
```

> **Important Note**
> This code is an example and may differ slightly if you play with the deployment yourself.

10. Now, we can click on **Create** and wait until the cluster is created. Once this has happened, we will see a green tick next to the cluster's name:

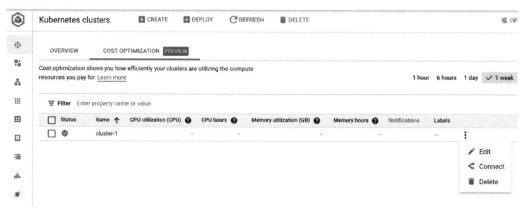

Figure 6.34 – Provisioned cluster

11. After clicking on the three dots symbol and the **Connect** option, we will be presented with information regarding how to connect to the cluster:

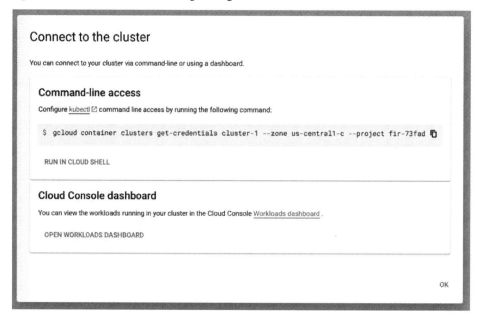

Figure 6.35 – Connect to the cluster

This information can be copied to Google Cloud Shell so that we can authenticate it against the newly created cluster. In the next section, we will use it and deploy our first application.

Deploying our first application

Now that we have created a cluster, we can deploy our first application. We will provision a simple NGINX web server using three Pods. For this purpose, we will use the `Deployment` object. Then, we will expose the application using the `Service` object.

To demonstrate different ways of creating Kubernetes objects, we will use both `kubectl` and the Google Cloud Console. Once they have been successfully deployed, we will check their connectivity. Let's get started:

> **Exam Tip**
>
> Expect to see questions on GKE and Kubernetes command-line tools. Remember that `gcloud` is used to manage the GKE cluster, while `kubectl` is a native Kubernetes tool. So, as an example, if you want to scale a GKE cluster, you would use `gcloud`, while to scale a deployment, you would use `kubectl`.

1. Let's open Cloud Shell and run the following command, which we copied from the Google Cloud Console:

```
gcloud container clusters get-credentials standard-
cluster-1 --zone us-central1-a --project qwiklabs-gcp-
21ec218e55edd052
```

> **Important Note**
>
> You need to adjust the cluster name and the project ID so that they match your environment.

When you are asked for authorization, confirm it. This will configure the credentials for `kubectl`. Now, we can deploy Kubernetes resources to the cluster.

2. Now, let's open Cloud Shell in editor mode and create a `deploy.yaml` file with the sample `Deployment` definition. You can find a similar example in the official Kubernetes documentation: `https://kubernetes.io/docs/concepts/workloads/controllers/deployment/#creating-a-deployment`. Save it and run the `kubectl apply -f deploy.yaml` file:

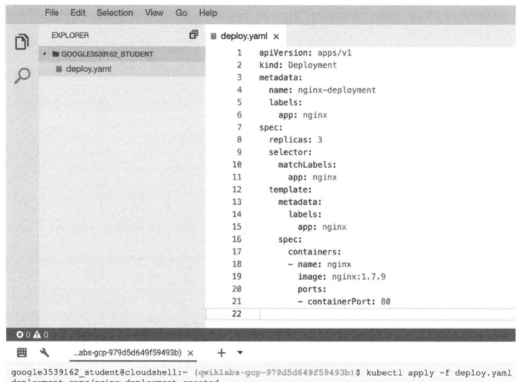

Figure 6.36 – The deploy.yaml file

3. To verify that the Pods have been created, we can use the `kubectl get pods` command:

```
google3539162_student@cloudshell:~ (qwiklabs-gcp-979d5d649f59493b)$ kubectl get pods
NAME                                READY   STATUS    RESTARTS   AGE
nginx-deployment-5c689d88bb-2d7pq   1/1     Running   0          2m33s
nginx-deployment-5c689d88bb-srtn8   1/1     Running   0          2m33s
nginx-deployment-5c689d88bb-z4mkp   1/1     Running   0          2m33s
```

Figure 6.37 – Pods

4. Now, we need to go back to the console and check the **Workloads** menu. We will see that `nginx-deployment` is present. Click on **Name** to see details about it, as shown in the following screenshot:

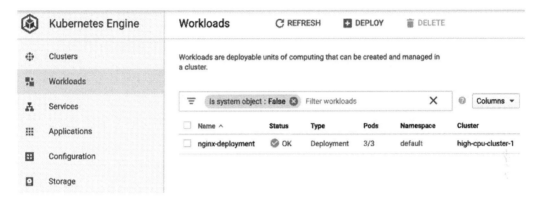

Figure 6.38 – Workloads

5. Click on the `nginx-deployment` link in the **Name** column to move to a detailed view. At the top of the detailed view, we will be asked if we want to expose the service. Click on the **Expose** button, as shown in the following screenshot:

Figure 6.39 – Exposing a Deployment

6. Now, we can choose a **Port** and a **Target port**, a **Protocol**, and the most important type of Service. We will choose a **Load balancer**. If you click on **View YAML**, you will see a definition of the service. You could copy it and use kubectl to deploy it from the shell. Instead, we will click on the **Expose** button to see how this is done from the GUI:

Figure 6.40 – Service settings

7. It will take a couple of seconds to deploy the service. Once deployed, it will be visible in **Services,** under the **Kubernetes Engine** menu. Find the nginx-deployment-services service and click on its name to see the following details. Find the **Load balancer IP** value and copy it:

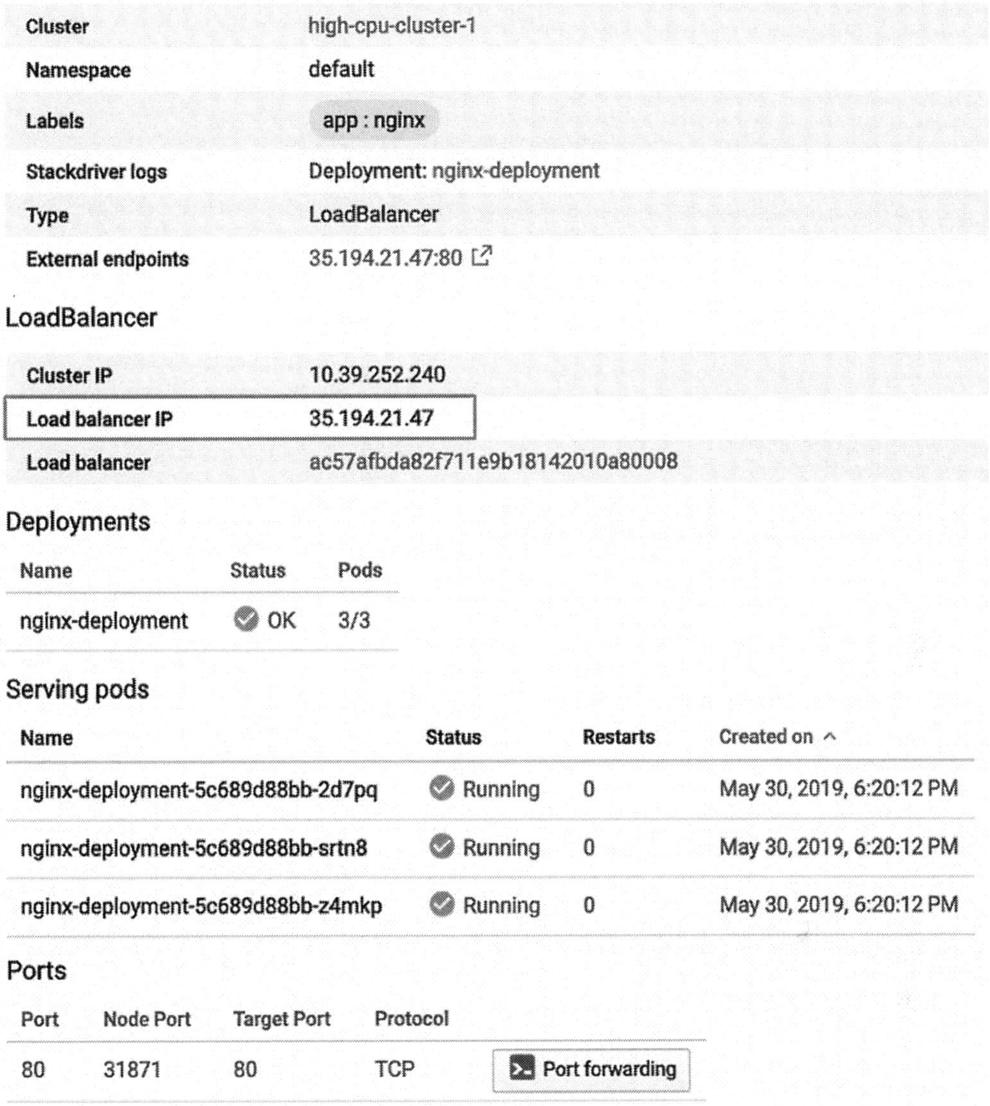

Cluster	high-cpu-cluster-1
Namespace	default
Labels	app : nginx
Stackdriver logs	Deployment: nginx-deployment
Type	LoadBalancer
External endpoints	35.194.21.47:80 ⎘

LoadBalancer

Cluster IP	10.39.252.240
Load balancer IP	35.194.21.47
Load balancer	ac57afbda82f711e9b18142010a80008

Deployments

Name	Status	Pods
nginx-deployment	✅ OK	3/3

Serving pods

Name	Status	Restarts	Created on ⌃
nginx-deployment-5c689d88bb-2d7pq	✅ Running	0	May 30, 2019, 6:20:12 PM
nginx-deployment-5c689d88bb-srtn8	✅ Running	0	May 30, 2019, 6:20:12 PM
nginx-deployment-5c689d88bb-z4mkp	✅ Running	0	May 30, 2019, 6:20:12 PM

Ports

Port	Node Port	Target Port	Protocol	
80	31871	80	TCP	▶ Port forwarding

Figure 6.41 – Service details

8. Paste the IP into your web browser or click on the link next to the **External endpoints** key. You will see the following NGINX welcome message:

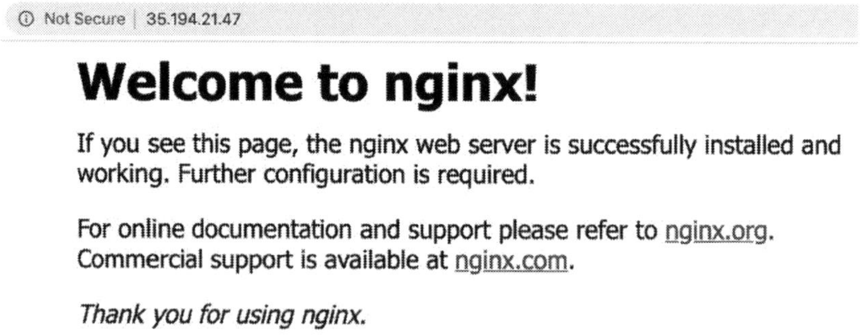

ⓘ Not Secure | 35.194.21.47

Welcome to nginx!

If you see this page, the nginx web server is successfully installed and working. Further configuration is required.

For online documentation and support please refer to nginx.org. Commercial support is available at nginx.com.

Thank you for using nginx.

Figure 6.42 – Accessing the application

With that, we have successfully deployed our first application to a GKE cluster. As you have seen, you can do this by using either the GUI or the command line. The Google Cloud Console allows you to deploy Kubernetes objects without having to define the YAML files manually. It also visualizes the most useful ones and their relationships. With the GUI, you can also perform some second-day operations. At this point, we encourage you to get some hands-on experience and play around with deploying your applications using either of these methods.

Cluster second-day operations

So far, we have created a cluster and our first application has been deployed. Everything is up and running. Now, let's have a look at second-day operations such as upgrades and scaling. As you already know, these operations can be quite time-consuming if you deploy a cluster manually. When you use GKE, it takes care of automating those tasks for you. All you need to do is initiate this or even allow GKE to decide when the actions should be triggered. Let's start with upgrades.

Upgrading the cluster

Google Kubernetes allows us to simply upgrade cluster components without having to install anything manually. The master and the nodes are upgraded separately. Remember that masters can only work with nodes up to two minor versions older than their version. Let's get started:

1. Before you start running any commands, set the default zone by running the following command:

```
gcloud config set compute/zone us-central1-a
```

2. To check the current version of the master and the nodes, use the following command:

```
gcloud container clusters describe $CLUSTER_NAME
```

3. Google upgrades masters automatically but you can also trigger upgrades for the master manually by running the following command:

```
gcloud container clusters upgrade $CLUSTER_NAME --master
```

4. Once your master has been upgraded, you can upgrade the nodes by running the following command:

```
gcloud container clusters upgrade $CLUSTER_NAME
```

GKE will attempt to reschedule the Pods from the node being upgraded. The node will be replaced with the new one with the desired version. When the nodes register with the master, they are marked as schedulable.

> **Important Note**
> Although you can downgrade your node, Google does not recommend this.
> You can downgrade your nodes to one patch version lower than the master.

Auto-upgrades

Auto-upgrade is enabled by default for newly created clusters. The nodes are upgraded so that they can keep up with the master's version. The upgrade takes place during a chosen maintenance window. Only one node is upgraded at a time, and only within one node pool of the cluster. During the upgrade, the Pods residing in the node being upgraded are rescheduled. If it isn't possible to reschedule, the Pod goes into pending mode. To enable auto-upgrade, use the --enable-autoupgrade flag when creating or updating your cluster.

Auto-repair

The auto-repair option allows you to keep the nodes of a cluster healthy. It monitors the state of the nodes' health and recreates them when needed. Recreation is triggered when the node reports NotReady or does not report at all for approximately 10 minutes. This will also trigger if the node is out of boot disk space for approximately 30 minutes. Before recreating, the node is drained. This might be unsuccessful if it is unresponsive. To enable auto-repair, use the --enable-autorepair flag when creating or updating your cluster.

Resizing the cluster

The GKE cluster can be resized by increasing or decreasing the number of nodes in a node pool. To perform a resize, use the following command:

```
gcloud container clusters resize $CLUSTER_NAME --node-pool
$POOL_NAME –num-nodes $NUM_NODES
```

Here, we have the following options:

- $CLUSTER_NAME: The cluster's name
- $POOL_NAME: The name of the node pool to resize
- $NUM_NODES: The number of nodes to run in the pool

When you increase the size of the cluster, new Pods might be scheduled on new nodes, but the old Pods will not be migrated. When you decrease the size of the cluster, the Pods hosted on the removed nodes will be deleted. They will only be recreated on other nodes if they are managed by the replication controller. To drain the nodes before removal, you can use the beta command:

```
gcloud beta container clusters resize $CLUSTER_NAME --node-pool
$POOL_NAME –num-nodes $NUM_NODES
```

Autoscaling a cluster

You can also set your cluster to autoscale. This scaling event can be triggered by changes in workloads and resource usage. Autoscaling monitors your nodes and checks whether they should be increased or decreased. The maximum and the minimum number of nodes to run in the cluster are defined in the following command:

```
gcloud container clusters create $CLUSTER_NAME --num-nodes $NUM
--enable-autoscaling --min-nodes $MIN_NODES --max-nodes $MAX_
NODES --zone $COMPUTE_ZONE
```

Here, we have the following options:

- $CLUSTER_NAME: The cluster's name
- $NUM: The initial number of nodes
- $MIN_NODES: The minimum number of nodes
- $MAX_NODES: The maximum number of nodes

You can also change the autoscaling settings using the following command:

```
gcloud container clusters update $CLUSTER_NAME --enable-
autoscaling --min-nodes $MIN_NODES --max-nodes $MAX_NODES
--zone $COMPUTE_ZONE --node-pool default-pool
```

Here, we have the following options:

- $CLUSTER_NAME: The cluster's name
- $MIN_NODES: The minimum number of nodes
- $MAX_NODES: The maximum number of nodes

To disable autoscaling for a particular node, use the following `--no-enable-autoscaling` flag:

```
gcloud container clusters update $CLUSTER_NAME --no-enable-
autoscaling
```

IAM

Access to GKE is secured with IAM. Let's have a look at a list of predefined roles, along with a short description of each:

- **Kubernetes Engine Admin**: Has the right to access the management of clusters and their Kubernetes API objects
- **Kubernetes Engine Cluster Admin**: Has the right to access the management of clusters
- **Kubernetes Engine Cluster Viewer**: Has read-only access to clusters
- **Kubernetes Engine Developer**: Has full access to Kubernetes API objects inside clusters
- **Kubernetes Engine Host Service Agent User**: Has access to the GKE Host Service Agent
- **Kubernetes Engine Viewer**: Has read-only access to GKE resources

Kubernetes role-based access control

Native Kubernetes **role-based access control** (**RBAC**) can be used in combination with Cloud IAM. While Cloud IAM works at a project level, RBAC grants permissions to Kubernetes resources. Privileges are granted at the cluster or namespace level. The following is an example of a `Role` object that grants read access to all the Pods in a `mynamespace` namespace:

```
kind: Role
apiVersion: rbac.authorization.k8s.io/v1
metadata:
namespace: mynamespace
name: pod-reader
rules:
- apiGroups: [""] # "" indicates the core API group
  resources: ["pods"]
  verbs: ["get", "watch", "list"]
```

Now, let's discuss Artifact Registry.

Artifact Registry

The container images that we use for application deployments to Kubernetes are stored in container repositories. Docker Hub (`hub.docker.com`) is a public image repository. We can use it to pull public images. But what if we want a local repository where we want to store our images? Google Cloud Platform comes with a service called Artifact Registry (the evolution of Google Container Registry). This is essentially a single place where you can store, perform vulnerability scans on, and control access to your images. As it is hosted on GCP, it is also faster to use than Docker Hub. GKE clusters can access the registry that resides in the same project by default.

To run images that are stored in Artifact Registry, use the following command:

```
kubectl run $NAME --image=$LOCATION-docker.pkg.dev/$PROJECT-
ID/$REPOSITORY/$IMAGE:$TAG
```

Here, we have the following options:

- $NAME: Pod name
- $LOCATION: The regional or multi-regional location (`https://cloud.google.com/artifact-registry/docs/repo-organize#locations`) of the repository

- $REPOSITORY: The image repository's name

- $PROJECT-ID: The ID of the GCP project

- $IMAGE: The image we will use as part of the deployment

- $TAG: The image's tag

You can also use $LOCATION-docker.pkg.dev/$PROJECT-ID/$REPOSITORY /$IMAGE:$TAG in the Kubernetes YAML definition as the image parameter.

Cloud Build

Cloud Build is a service that originates from Container Builder. It was initially used to build container images. Google created this service to evolve it into a CI/CD service. When the service was rebranded, additional functionalities were introduced. Cloud Build runs one or more build steps to produce artifacts. These build steps use so-called Cloud Builders, which are containers with a particular command-line tool installed on them. These include git, docker, kubectl, maven, gcloud, gsutil, and many others. These build steps are defined in YAML configuration files. The following YAML configuration file uses the Docker Cloud Builder to build a container image and then push it to Artifact Registry:

```
steps:
- name: 'gcr.io/cloud-builders/docker'
  args: ['build', '-t', 'us-central1-docker.pkg.dev/ my-
project/my-image', '.']
- name: 'gcr.io/cloud-builders/docker'
  args: ['push', 'us-central1-docker.pkg.dev/ my-project/my-
image']
```

If standard builders are not enough, you can either search for a community cloud builder or create one of your own. This means that you can use whatever tools you need. To learn more about custom Cloud Builders, have a look at the *Further reading* section.

The build can either be run manually or triggered by a code repository. Cloud Build integrates with common code repositories such as Cloud Source Repository, GitHub, and Bitbucket.

Best practices for building containers

Google has defined a set of best practices for building the containers, which results in a shorter time build, as well as smaller and more secure images. The full list of those recommendations can be found here: `https://cloud.google.com/architecture/best-practices-for-building-containers`. For the exam, you should know about those with the highest importance. These recommendations have been categorized according to their importance in the following lists:

- **High importance**:

  - Package a single app per container.
  - Properly handle PID 1, signal handling, and zombie processes.
  - Optimize for the Docker build cache.

- **Medium importance**:

  - Remove unnecessary tools.
  - Build the smallest image possible.
  - Scan images for vulnerabilities.
  - Properly tag your images.

The details for each of these recommendations can be found in the documentation at the aforementioned link.

Quotas and limits

GKE comes with the following limits:

- A maximum of 50 clusters per zone, plus 50 regional clusters per region
- A maximum of 15,000 nodes per cluster
- A maximum of 1,000 nodes per cluster if you use the GKE ingress controller
- A maximum of 1,000 nodes per node pool zone
- 110 Pods per node

Note that GKE uses Compute Engine to host nodes, so Compute Engine quotas also apply.

Additionally, there are resource quotas for the cluster itself. To view the quotas, use the `kubectl get resourcequota gke-resource-quotas -o yaml` command. Note that the quotas cannot be removed as they are there to protect the stability of the cluster.

Pricing

Under the hood, Kubernetes Engine uses Compute Engine services. You are billed for every virtual machine instance that is running as a node of the cluster. Because Kubernetes Engine abstracts master machines, you are not charged for them. You pay a monthly fee for the control plane. You will also be charged for the load balancers that are backing your `Service` and `Ingress` resources.

> **Exam Tip**
>
> Make sure you know the pricing model for the exam. Remember that you pay for the nodes and the control plan fee.

Summary

In this chapter, we learned about GKE, as well as microservices and containers. We went through basic Kubernetes concepts and described the most important Kubernetes objects. We also looked at the advantages of using GKE, including automated deployment, autoscaling, and auto-upgrades. We deployed a cluster and looked at second-day operations. We also looked at how to connect to a cluster with the `kubectl` command. If you feel like doing some additional reading, have a look at the links that are provided in the *Further reading* section.

In the next chapter, we will talk about the Cloud Run service, which allows you to run cloud-native workloads without having to provision GKE clusters.

Further reading

To learn more about the topics that were covered in this chapter, take a look at the following resources:

- **Kubernetes**: `https://kubernetes.io`
- **Microservices**: `https://microservices.io/`
- **Kubernetes tale**: `https://www.youtube.com/watch?v=4ht22ReBjno&t=31s`
- **kubectl**: `https://kubernetes.io/docs/reference/kubectl/overview/`
- **Network Overview**: `https://cloud.google.com/kubernetes-engine/docs/concepts/network-overview`

- **Services**: https://cloud.google.com/kubernetes-engine/docs/concepts/service

- **Ingress**: https://cloud.google.com/kubernetes-engine/docs/concepts/ingress

- **Node pools**: https://cloud.google.com/kubernetes-engine/docs/concepts/node-pools

- **Node taints**: https://cloud.google.com/kubernetes-engine/docs/how-to/node-taints

- **Autoscaler**: https://cloud.google.com/kubernetes-engine/docs/concepts/cluster-autoscaler

- **Upgrading a cluster**: https://cloud.google.com/kubernetes-engine/docs/how-to/upgrading-a-cluster

- **PersistentVolumes**: https://kubernetes.io/docs/concepts/storage/persistent-volumes/

- **Network Policies**: https://kubernetes.io/docs/concepts/services-networking/network-policies/

- **Quotas**: https://cloud.google.com/kubernetes-engine/quotas

- **Container Registry**: https://cloud.google.com/container-registry/docs/overview

- **Cloud Build**: https://cloud.google.com/cloud-build/docs/configuring-builds/create-basic-configuration

- **Cloud builders**: https://cloud.google.com/cloud-build/docs/cloud-builders

- **Kubernetes RBAC**: https://kubernetes.io/docs/reference/access-authn-authz/rbac/

7
Deploying Cloud-Native Workloads with Cloud Run

In the previous chapter, we took a deep dive into **Google Kubernetes Engine (GKE)**, which provides Kubernetes as a Service. In this chapter, we will look at the **Cloud Run** offering. **Google Cloud Run** allows us to run containerized workloads on a fully managed serverless platform. It brings the experience you get from GKE one level up by simplifying the process of developing and deploying applications. The service is based on the open source **Knative** (https://knative.dev/docs/serving) project, so Cloud Run workloads can be ported to any platform that runs Kubernetes. With Cloud Run, you get full integration with Google Cloud services such as Cloud IAM, Cloud Build, and Google Cloud's operations suite. All you have to do is build your application in one of your favorite languages. Once you've done this, you can deploy it to Cloud Run in seconds. The service will take care of scaling and keeping the application live. You will only be charged for the resources that are used, not for the underlying cluster.

In this chapter, we will cover the following topics:

- Introduction to using Cloud Run
- Deploying services to Cloud Run
- Cloud Run IAM roles
- Cloud Run pricing and limitations

> **Exam Tip**
>
> Cloud Run is an important exam topic. The Professional Cloud Architect exam has been updated to contain more and more cloud-native technologies as this is the direction Google is focusing on. Cloud Run is similar to App Engine in that it gives excellent developer experience as it is fully managed and lots of underlying implementation details are abstracted from the user. The difference is that it is based on Kubernetes and Knative, which makes it very portable. Compared to the previous version of the exam, the number of questions for App Engine has been reduced and there has been a shift to test your Cloud Run knowledge instead.
>
> If you want to understand how Cloud Run works under the hood, you might want to do a deep dive into Knative itself. However, you do not need to do so to pass the PCA exam, nor to use Cloud Run.

Using Cloud Run

As we have already mentioned, deploying applications to Cloud Run is a seamless experience. The following diagram shows a simplified flow for building a container and deploying it to Cloud Run:

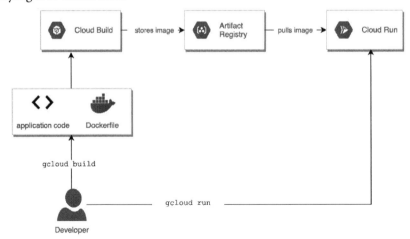

Figure 7.1 – Building a Cloud Run service

You start by developing your containerized application, which can listen for HTTPS or gRPC (`https://grpc.io/`) requests. To build the application from code, you can use the Google Cloud Build service and store the image of your container in Artifact Registry. Next, you must tell Cloud Run where your container is stored and define some parameters, such as the maximum number of replicas you want to run at once or how the application should be triggered. You request to deploy and in a couple of seconds, your app is ready to serve your users.

Cloud Run will take care of running all the Kubernetes resources that are responsible for scaling the application and load balancing the traffic to your Cloud Run service. It will also send logs to Cloud Logging and deliver metrics to Cloud Monitoring.

If you wish to deploy the new version of the application, you can do so directly from the Google Console. The new version might include changes in the application code, which results in a new container being built. Alternatively, it might include making changes to parameters, such as the maximum number of container instances for the service. The new version of the application is called a Cloud Run service **revision** (`https://github.com/knative/specs/blob/main/specs/serving/knative-api-specification-1.0.md#revision`) and is in line with Knative naming convention:

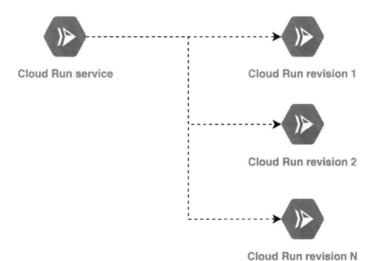

Figure 7.2 – Cloud Run revisions

Can the same be achieved with GKE? Of course. The difference is that with Cloud Run, all the Kubernetes resources that you would need to create in GKE, such as Service, HorizontalPodAutoscalers, and Deployments, are abstracted from you. This helps you develop and deploy cloud-native workloads without having to master the Kubernetes internals.

Cloud Run containers

In the previous section, we looked at a flow for developing and deploying a Cloud Run application. The fundamental task in that flow was building the container. This is because the deployment itself is automated by GCP and the implementation details are not of concern to the developer. Cloud Run containers need to fulfill several requirements to be able to execute. This is well described in the Container runtime contract, which you can find here: `https://cloud.google.com/run/docs/reference/container-contract`. Let's have a quick look at a short list of requirements:

- You can use any *programming language* for your application.

- Executables must be *compatible with Linux 64-bit* (Linux x86_64 ABI format).

- Your application must listen on *address* `0.0.0.0` and a port you define in the Cloud Run config. By default, the port is set to `8080`. The configured port will be set as the `PORT` environmental variable in the container.

- The container should listen for HTTPS or gRPC requests and *TLS should not be implemented* directly in the container. TLS is implemented in Cloud Run and proxies the requests.

- The container instance needs to return the *response within the timeout* specified during the deployment of the service. The container will be terminated if there are more than 20 timeouts in a row.

- The response must contain *only printable non-whitespace ASCII characters* (no colons).

Also, note that any data that's written to the filesystem resides in the container instance's memory and will not persist when the container is stopped.

Cloud Run triggers

As we have already learned, the Cloud Run service can be triggered over HTTPS or gRPC. However, these are not the only available options. Thanks to the integration with other Google Cloud services, there is a set of triggers that can be used with Cloud Run:

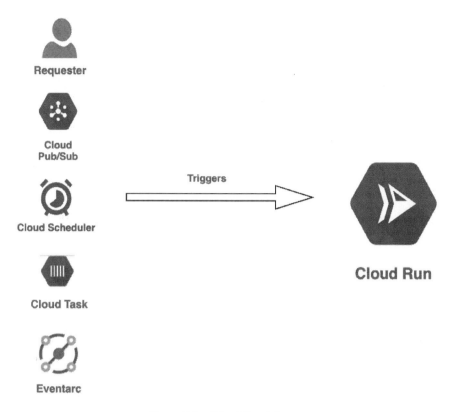

Figure 7.3 – Cloud Run triggers

These triggers are as follows:

- **HTTPS or gRPC request**: This is the most general way of calling Cloud Run and can be used to create a web API, middleware, reverse proxy, or web applications.

- **Pub/Sub**: This can use Cloud Run as a webhook where Pub/Sub messages will be pushed.

- **Cloud Scheduler**: This allows you to run Cloud Run at a scheduled time.

- **Cloud Task**: Asynchronously executes the Cloud Run service.

- **Eventarc**: Connects Cloud Run to Eventarc-supported events.

Consult the Google Cloud Run documentation page to understand how you can use these for your use case. If none of these triggers fulfill your use case, you might want to have a look at **Eventarc**, which gives you even more flexibility. Eventarc is based on the Knative Eventing (`https://knative.dev/docs/eventing/`) project and provides even more triggers.

> **Exam Tip**
>
> We do not expect questions on Eventarc in the PCA exam. But please keep an eye on the exam guide as this can change without notice. At a minimum, you should remember that Eventarc allows you to trigger events based on Pub/Sub and Audit Logs. The latter is extremely powerful as all the Google Cloud services can generate Audit Logs. To learn more about Eventarc, check out `https://cloud.google.com/eventarc/docs/creating-triggers`.

Deploying to Cloud Run

To be able to use Cloud Run, you need to enable the Cloud Run API in the API library. If you want to simply test an application that is already containerized, you can deploy it to Cloud Run by running the following command in Cloud Shell:

```
gcloud run deploy [SERVICE] --image gcr.io/[PROJECT-ID]/[IMAGE]
```

This will deploy the Cloud Run service called `[SERVICE]` using the image stored in the `gcr.io/[PROJECT-ID]/[IMAGE]` path.

> **Important Note**
>
> If you have not configured the default region yet, you will be prompted to do so.

For the exam, you should know about the advanced settings you can set for your Cloud Run service. So, let's have a look at how we can deploy the service from the Cloud console:

1. From the hamburger menu, choose **Cloud Run**. You will see the **Cloud Run** welcome page:

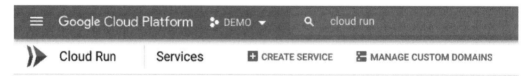

Figure 7.4 – Cloud Run welcome page

2. Click on the **CREATE SERVICE** link. Fill in the name of the service and choose the region where your service will be hosted. Click **NEXT** to move to section 2:

Cloud Run
Create service
1 Service settings
A service exposes a unique endpoint and automatically scales the underlying infrastructure to handle incoming requests. Service name and region cannot be changed.
Service name *
pca-cloud-run
Region *
us-central1 (Iowa)
How to pick a region?
NEXT

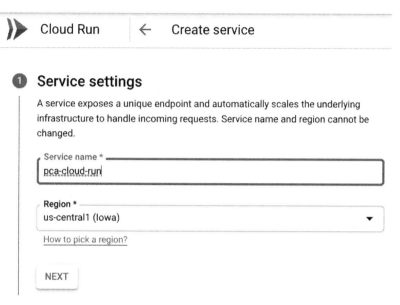

Figure 7.5 – Service settings

3. In section 2, specify the path to the container image you want to use for the deployment and click **NEXT**:

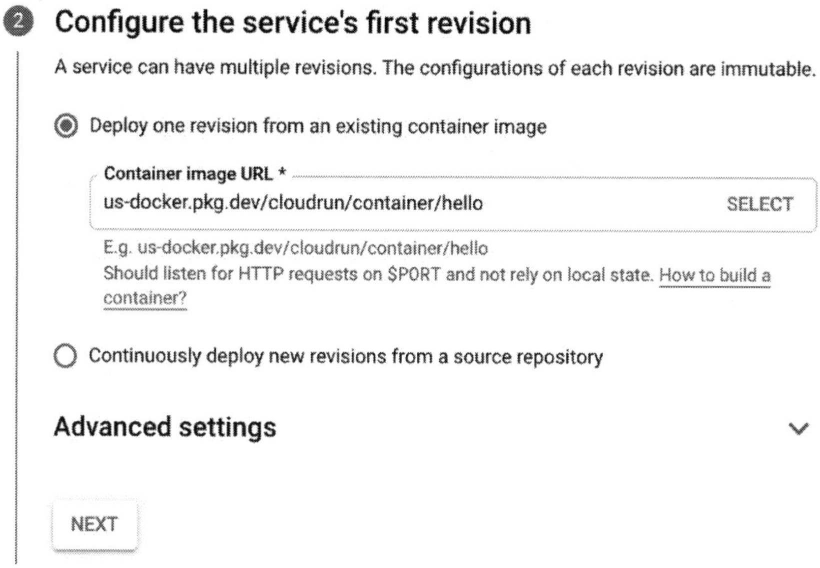

2 Configure the service's first revision
A service can have multiple revisions. The configurations of each revision are immutable.
Deploy one revision from an existing container image
Container image URL *
us-docker.pkg.dev/cloudrun/container/hello
SELECT
E.g. us-docker.pkg.dev/cloudrun/container/hello
Should listen for HTTP requests on $PORT and not rely on local state. How to build a container?
Continuously deploy new revisions from a source repository
Advanced settings
NEXT

Figure 7.6 – Configure the service's first revision

4. Alternatively, you can use the second option; that is, **Continuously deploy new revisions from a source repository**. Below, you will see that if we choose this option, we will have to provide the repository where our code resides. Cloud Build will use this code to build an image for you, store it in the Container Registry, and deploy it to Cloud Run. On every pull request, the flow will execute again. This way, you can get a seamless GitOps flow for your Cloud Run service. Click the **ADVANCED OPTIONS** dropdown:

 Set up with Cloud Build   ×

With continuous deployment powered by Cloud Build, changes to your source repository are automatically built into container images in Container Registry and deployed to Cloud Run.
Your code should listen for HTTP requests on $PORT. Your repository must include a Dockerfile or source code in Go, Node.js, Python, Java or .NET Core in order to be built into a container image.

1 Source repository

Repository Provider
GitHub   ▼

Repository *
konradclapa/hello-world-py   ▼

Can't find your repository? Manage connected repositories

☐ I understand that GitHub content for the selected repositories will be transferred to this GCP project to provide the connected service. Members of this GCP project with sufficient permissions will be able to create and run triggers on these repositories, based on transferred GitHub content. I also understand that content from all GitHub app triggers in this GCP project may be transferred to GitHub in order to provide functionality like showing trigger names in GitHub build results. This will apply to all existing and future GitHub App triggers in this project. Learn more

∨ ADVANCED OPTIONS

NEXT

2 Build Configuration

Figure 7.7 – Source repository

5. In the **Build Configuration** step, you can configure the branch that will trigger the flow, as well as the build type. You can either provide a Dockerfile with your image manifest or use Google Cloud Buildpacks (`https://cloud.google.com/blog/products/containers-kubernetes/google-cloud-now-supports-buildpacks`) for the supported programming languages:

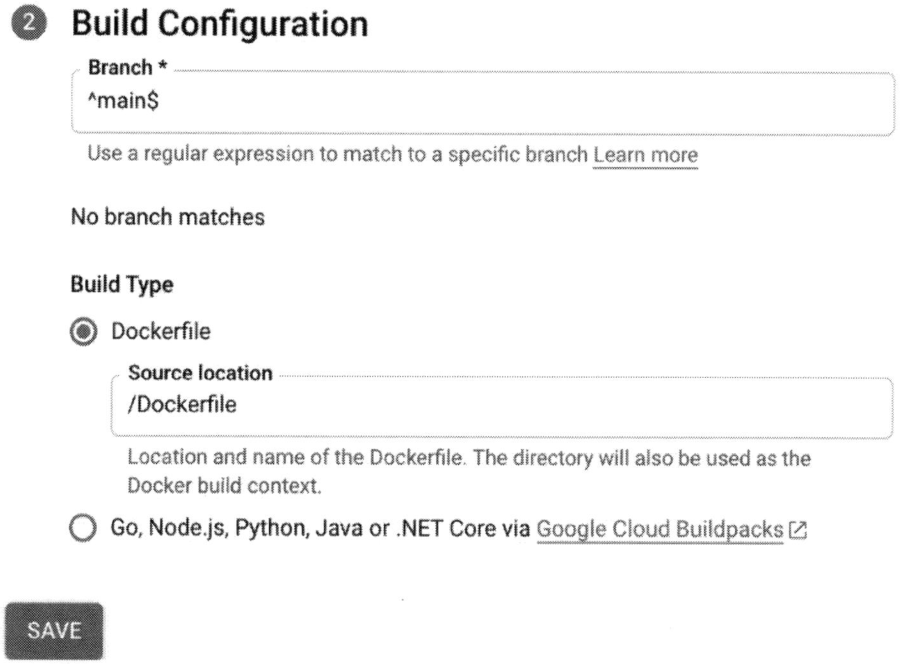

2 Build Configuration

Branch *

^main$

Use a regular expression to match to a specific branch Learn more

No branch matches

Build Type

◉ Dockerfile

Source location

/Dockerfile

Location and name of the Dockerfile. The directory will also be used as the Docker build context.

○ Go, Node.js, Python, Java or .NET Core via Google Cloud Buildpacks ☒

SAVE

Figure 7.8 – Build Configuration

6. In our scenario, we will continue our deployment using an existing container image. So, we must move back to the menu from *Step 3* and move to the **Advanced settings** section. This section contains multiple tabs. As you will see, most of those setting are parameters that you can also find in `Pod` or `Deployments` Kubernetes resources manifests. Some other settings that you might not be familiar with come from the Knative Service (`https://knative.dev/docs/serving`) manifest.

In the **CONTAINER** tab, we can do the following:

*   Set a custom container port.
*   Define a command with an argument that should be executed by the container.
*   Allocate memory and CPU.
*   Set a request timeout.

* Configure **Maximum requests per container.**
* Set autoscaling regarding the minimum and the maximum number of instances:

Advanced settings   ∧

CONTAINER   VARIABLES & SECRETS   CONNECTIONS   SECURITY

General

Container port
8080

Requests will be sent to the container on this port. We recommend listening on $PORT instead of this specific number.

Container command

Leave blank to use the entry point command defined in the container image.

Container arguments

Arguments passed to the entry point command.

Capacity

Memory allocated
512 MiB   ▼

Memory to allocate to each container instance.

CPU allocated
1   ▼

Number of vCPUs allocated to each container instance.

Request timeout
300   seconds

Time within which a response must be returned (maximum 3600 seconds).

Maximum requests per container
80

The maximum number of concurrent requests that can reach each container instance. What is concurrency?

Autoscaling ❓

Minimum number of instances *
0

Maximum number of instances
100

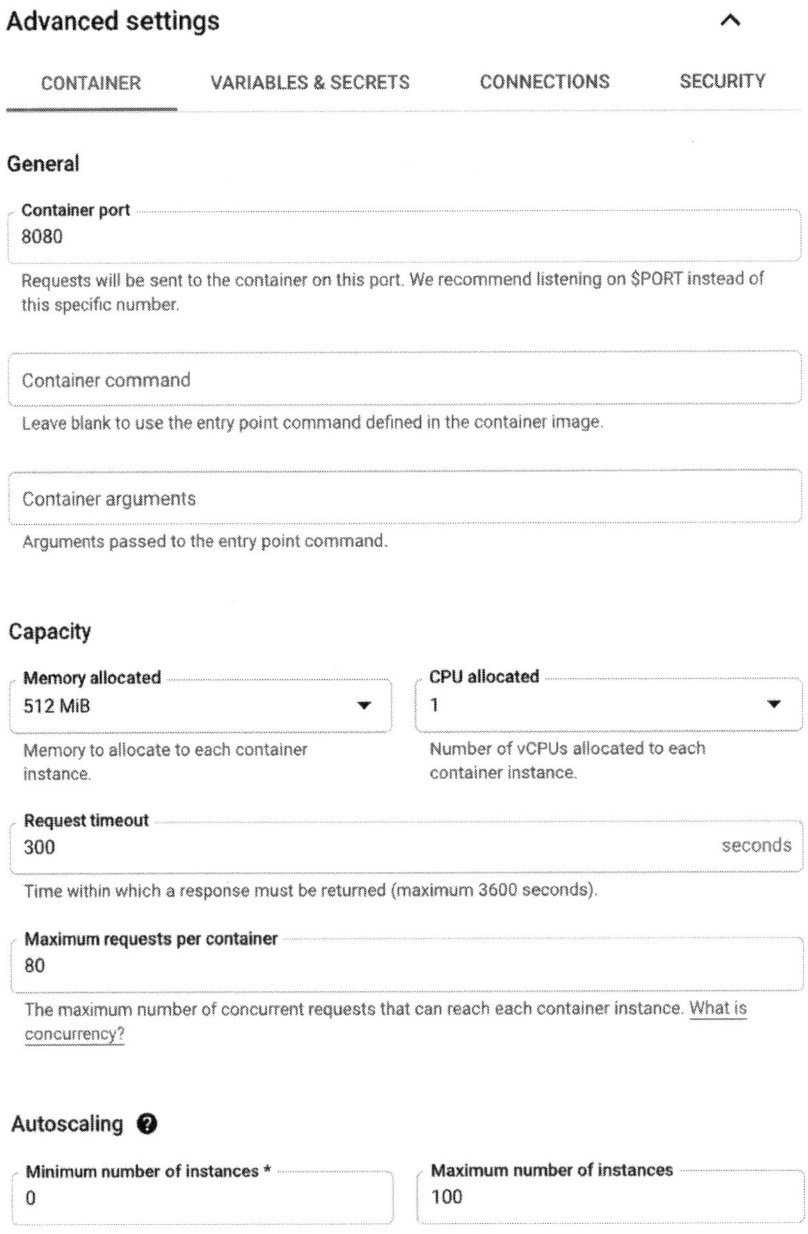

Figure 7.9 – Advanced settings

7. In the **VARIABLES & SECRETS** tab, you can add environmental variables and secrets. These environmental variables can be used by your application to store configurations. Secrets can be useful for passing credentials to your application. To learn more about using secrets, go to `https://cloud.google.com/run/docs/configuring/secrets`:

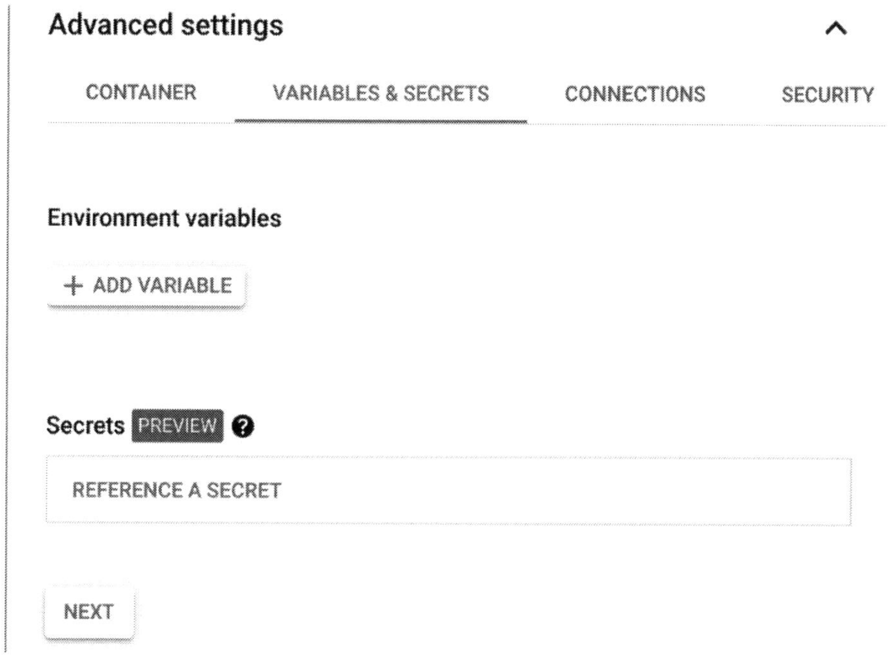

Figure 7.10 – VARIABLES & SECRETS

8. In the **CONNECTIONS** tab, you can enable **HTTP/2 connections** (`https://`
    `cloud.google.com/run/docs/configuring/http2`) for your service.
    Note that by default, Cloud Run uses HTTP/1. You can also create a connection
    to Cloud SQL for persisting data. As you may recall, all the data that's saved in the
    container will disappear when the container is stopped. Storing the
    data in Cloud SQL will allow you to create stateful applications. Finally, you can
    create a VPC connector to communicate with any of your workloads that are
    connected to VPC:

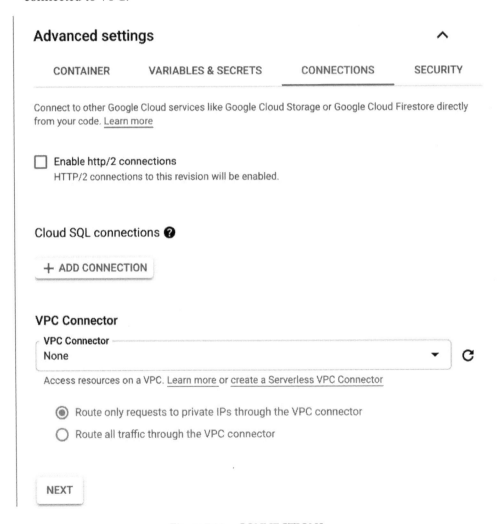

Figure 7.11 – CONNECTIONS

9. In the last tab, called **SECURITY**, you can configure the service account that will be used by your service. You can also configure Binary Authorization (you will learn more about Binary Authorization in *Chapter 8*, *Managing Cloud-Native Workloads with Anthos*) and a customer-managed encryption key. We will leave the default settings as is and click **NEXT**:

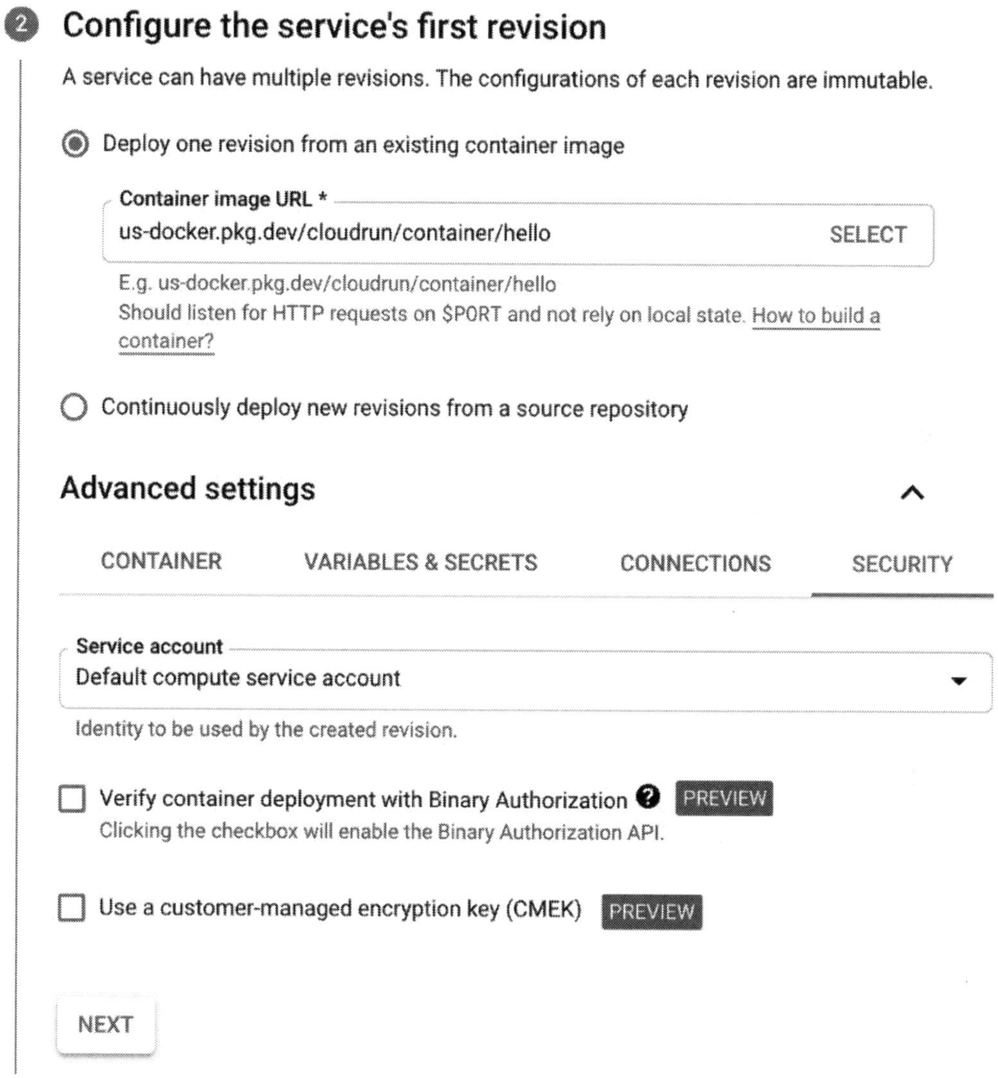

② Configure the service's first revision

A service can have multiple revisions. The configurations of each revision are immutable.

◉ Deploy one revision from an existing container image

Container image URL *

```
us-docker.pkg.dev/cloudrun/container/hello                    SELECT
```

E.g. us-docker.pkg.dev/cloudrun/container/hello
Should listen for HTTP requests on $PORT and not rely on local state. How to build a container?

○ Continuously deploy new revisions from a source repository

Advanced settings   ⌃

| CONTAINER | VARIABLES & SECRETS | CONNECTIONS | SECURITY |

Service account

```
Default compute service account                                ▾
```

Identity to be used by the created revision.

☐ Verify container deployment with Binary Authorization ❓ PREVIEW
Clicking the checkbox will enable the Binary Authorization API.

☐ Use a customer-managed encryption key (CMEK) PREVIEW

NEXT

Figure 7.12 – SECURITY

10. In stage 3, we define how the service will be triggered. In the **Ingress** section, we define which traffic is allowed. We can either allow all traffic, allow internal traffic and traffic from Cloud Load Balancing, or allow internal traffic only. We must also choose the authentication method. We can either allow unauthenticated invocations for public access or use Cloud IAM for authentication. By clicking **+ ADD EVENTARC TRIGGER**, we can define the trigger for the service:

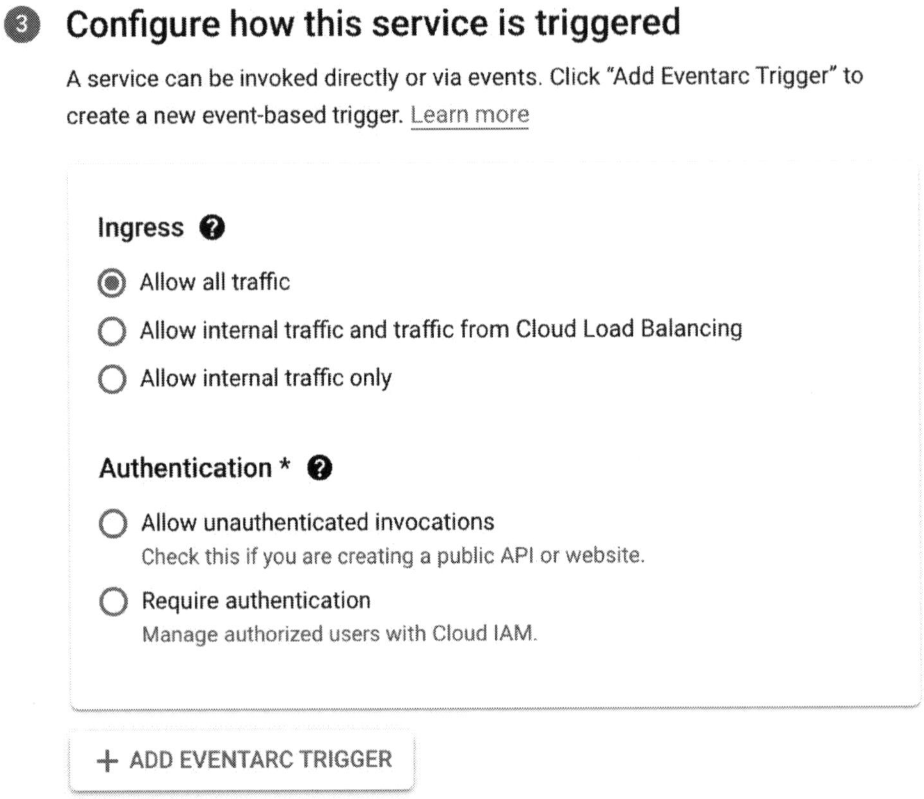

③ Configure how this service is triggered

A service can be invoked directly or via events. Click "Add Eventarc Trigger" to create a new event-based trigger. Learn more

Ingress ❓

◉ Allow all traffic

○ Allow internal traffic and traffic from Cloud Load Balancing

○ Allow internal traffic only

Authentication * ❓

○ Allow unauthenticated invocations
    Check this if you are creating a public API or website.

○ Require authentication
    Manage authorized users with Cloud IAM.

+ ADD EVENTARC TRIGGER

Figure 7.13 – Configure how this service is triggered

11. We will use the default trigger in this case, so we can click on the **DEPLOY** button. After a couple of seconds, we will see that a single revision of the service was deployed. All the requests will be directed to that revision. Let's click on the **URL** link and see whether the application is available on the internet:

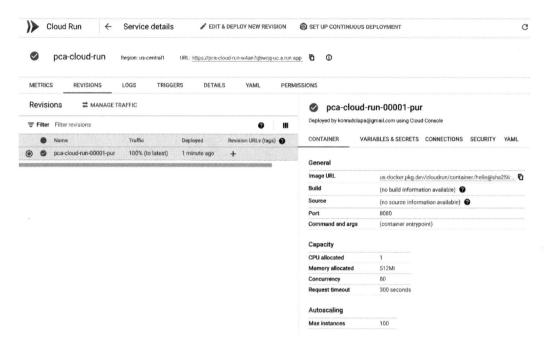

Figure 7.14 – Deployed Cloud Run service

As we can see, the application has been successfully deployed and can be accessed from the internet:

Figure 7.15 - Deployed Application

Congratulations – you have deployed your first Cloud Run service! Now, let's learn how to deploy a new revision of the application.

Deploying a new revision

To deploy a new revision of the application, return to the Cloud Run service details and follow these steps:

1. Click on the **EDIT & DEPLOY NEW REVISION** button:

Figure 7.16 – EDIT & DEPLOY NEW REVISION

2. Let's choose one of the **Capacity** parameters to change:

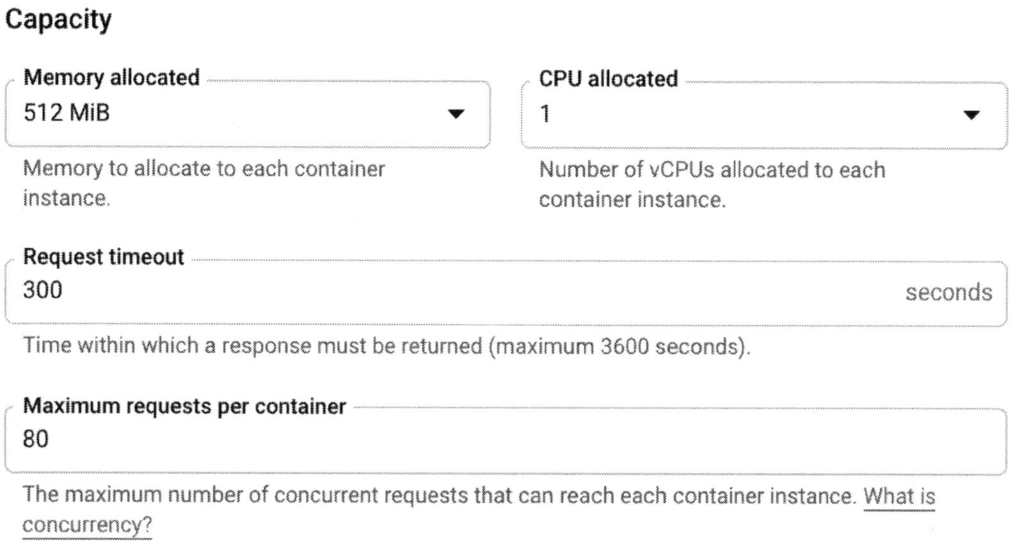

Capacity

Memory allocated

512 MiB ▼

Memory to allocate to each container instance.

CPU allocated

1 ▼

Number of vCPUs allocated to each container instance.

Request timeout

300   seconds

Time within which a response must be returned (maximum 3600 seconds).

Maximum requests per container

80

The maximum number of concurrent requests that can reach each container instance. What is concurrency?

Figure 7.17 – Changing the capacity

3. We will edit the **Maximum requests per container** attribute and change it from 80 to 1. This means that each container instance will only be able to serve a single request. By default, each container can serve 80 requests. We will leave the **Serve this revision immediately** option as is so that all the traffic will be directed to the new revision instead of using existing splits. Click on the **DEPLOY** button:

> **Exam Tip**
>
> Concurrency is one of the differentiators regarding Cloud Run and Cloud Functions. In Cloud Function, each function execution can only serve a single request.

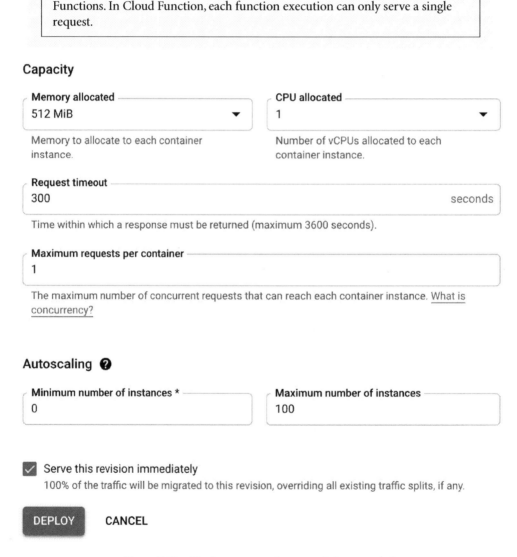

Figure 7.18 – Maximum requests per container equals 1

4. After waiting a couple of seconds, you will see that a new revision has been deployed. Note that 100% of the traffic is automatically routed to the new revision:

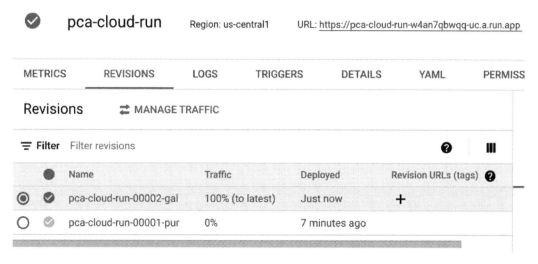

Figure 7.19 – New revision deployed

5. If we click on the **MANAGE TRAFFIC** link, a menu will appear. In this menu, you can set a custom amount of percentage for traffic to a specific revision. This might be useful for performing tests and rollbacks. Set this as a **50:50** split and click the **SAVE** button:

Figure 7.20 – Manage traffic

6. In the **Service details** section, we will see that the traffic has been split between two revisions:

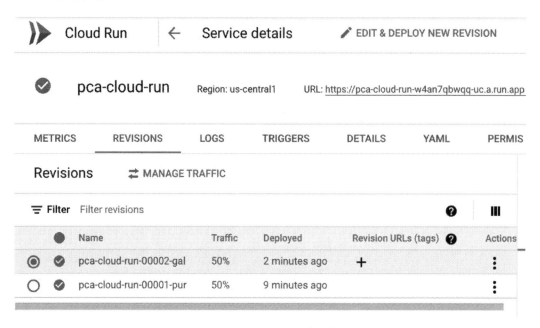

Figure 7.21 – Service details

With that, we have learned how to deploy new revisions of a Cloud Run service and how to manage the traffic to route a certain amount of traffic to a particular revision. This can, for example, help you run canary deployments on a small set of users. If you want to learn how to deploy a new revision using continuous deployment, visit Konrad's YouTube channel: `https://www.youtube.com/watch?v=QjBbOKb9yns`.

Mapping custom domains

As we saw in the previous sections, for each of the Cloud Run services that are deployed, an automatic URL is generated. You might want to map your domain instead of using the generated one. This is possible with the mapping custom domains feature. It requires that you do the following:

- Map a custom domain to a service.
- Add the DNS records to your domain registrar.

If you do not own a domain, you can register a domain with the Cloud Domains service directly from the Cloud Run console.

Note that this feature is only available in a few regions. To find the list of all the supported regions and see the step-by-step procedure for mapping the custom domains, check out `https://cloud.google.com/run/docs/mapping-custom-domains`.

IAM roles

Access to Cloud Run is secured with IAM. Let's have a look at a list of predefined roles, along with a short description of each:

- **Cloud Run admin** (`roles/run.admin`): Has the right to create, update, and delete services. You can also get and set IAM policies. Needs additional permission to deploy services.
- **Cloud Run developer** (`roles/run.developer`): Has the right to create, update, and delete services. Can also get but *not* set IAM policies.
- **Cloud Run viewer** (`roles/run.viewer`): Has the right to view services and get IAM policies.
- **Cloud Run invoker** (`roles/run.invoker`): Has the right to invoke services.

Quotas and limits

The list of quotas and limits for Cloud Run is quite long, so please consult `https://cloud.google.com/run/quotas` for a detailed list. For the exam, you might want to remember some of the most important ones.

Cloud Run comes with the following limits:

- 1,000 services per region
- 1,000 revisions per service
- 1,000 container instances per service (extendable)
- 8 GB memory per container instance
- 4 vCPUs per container instance
- 8 GB writable in-memory storage
- 60-minute maximum timeout
- 250 concurrent requests per container instance

> **Exam Tips**
>
> Remember that Cloud Run has a 60-minute timeout, while Cloud Function has a 9-minute (540s) timeout. This means that Cloud Run can be a solution for cases where Cloud Function would time out. However, keep the cost aspects of long-running container instances in mind. Also, Cloud Run can serve up to 250 concurrent requests while Cloud Function can only serve a single thread.

Pricing

As Cloud Run is a fully managed service, you are charged per use and do not have to worry about the underlying infrastructure. It is quite important to understand what this means as we have learned that containers are provisioned and de-provisioned as requests to access the applications are triggered. In the case of Cloud Run, the charge applies when the application is running, and you are billed to the nearest 100 milliseconds. A charge applies to the time when the following occurs:

- The container instance is starting.

- The container instance is shut down and it is handling the SIGTERM (`https://cloud.google.com/blog/products/containers-kubernetes/kubernetes-best-practices-terminating-with-grace`) signal.

- At least one instance is serving the request.

The active billable time begins with the start of the first request and ends at the end of the last request:

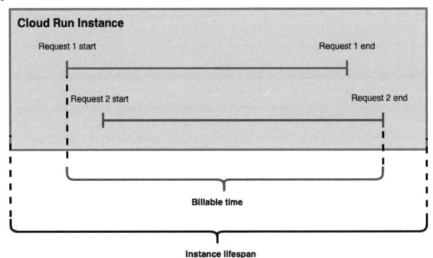

Figure 7.22 – Cloud Run billing time

Cloud Run comes with a free tier of 2 million requests and the first million have 180,000 vCPU per second and 360,000 GiB per second of memory. There is also a free egress of 1 GiB within North America.

Note that if you set a minimum number of container instances, you will be always billed for those running containers. By default, your Cloud Run service scales to zero and there is no charge for idle time.

Summary

In this chapter, we learned about Cloud Run, which is a service that allows you to run cloud-native workloads on Google Cloud serverlessly. Cloud Run abstracts all the implementation details of Kubernetes and Knative away from the developer and allows a seamless deployment experience. The developer does not need to understand the complex Kubernetes resource definitions to define how the application should behave under load. Scaling and load balancing are done under the hood based on the parameters that are defined during the deployment. Cloud Run integrates with many GCP services such as Cloud IAM and the Cloud operations suite for logging and monitoring.

We also deployed the Cloud Run service and learned how new revisions can be deployed. Finally, we learned how to control traffic between various revisions.

In the next chapter, we will talk about Anthos, a GCP hybrid multi-cloud platform that allows you to manage cloud-native workloads both in the public cloud as well as in on-premises data centers.

Further reading

For more information on the topics that were covered in this chapter, take a look at the following resources:

- **Overview**: `https://cloud.google.com/run/docs`
- **Developing the Cloud Run service**: `https://cloud.google.com/run/docs/developing`
- **Deploying to Cloud Run**: `https://cloud.google.com/run/docs/deploying`
- **Monitoring Cloud Run**: `https://cloud.google.com/run/docs/monitoring`
- **Cloud Run authentication**: `https://cloud.google.com/run/docs/authenticating/overview`
- **Limits and quotas**: `https://cloud.google.com/run/quotas`
- **Pricing**: `https://cloud.google.com/run/pricing`

8
Managing Cloud-Native Workloads with Anthos

In the previous chapters, we took a deep dive into **Google Kubernetes Engine (GKE)** and Cloud Run, which provide orchestration for cloud-native workloads. In this chapter, we will look at **Anthos**; a hybrid multi-cloud platform that allows you to run your cloud-native workloads in a consistent and controlled way in any environment, whether in the public cloud, on-premises, or even at the edge.

It is important to understand that Anthos is developed in a very agile way. A new version is released every 3 months. Therefore, we will not make reference in this chapter to any particular version of Anthos. Instead, we will explain to you the main concepts and make reference to the most up-to-date documentation so you can stay up to date and be ready for the exam.

> **Exam Tip**
>
> As Anthos is a very hot topic, it is very likely to appear in the PCA exam. Note that Anthos is a very wide topic and deservers a book of its own, however, this chapter will give you a good introduction to help you pass the exam.
>
> For the PCA exam, be prepared with a high-level understanding of all the Anthos services described in this chapter. Even though you should not expect deep-dive questions on how Anthos works and how to configure the services involved, we encourage you to try out Anthos Qwiklabs to better understand it.

We will cover the following topics in the chapter:

- What is Anthos?
- Anthos cluster deployment options
- Anthos Config Management
- Anthos Service Mesh
- Anthos Binary Authorization
- Migrate for Anthos and GKE
- Cloud Run for Anthos

Anthos components

Anthos is not a single service but rather a set of services that are combined into a platform. It allows you to manage and observe your cloud-native workloads wherever they are deployed. As we can see in *Figure 8.1*, Anthos consists of a set of services that provide the following:

- Infrastructure management
- Cluster management
- Service management
- Policy management
- Configuration management:

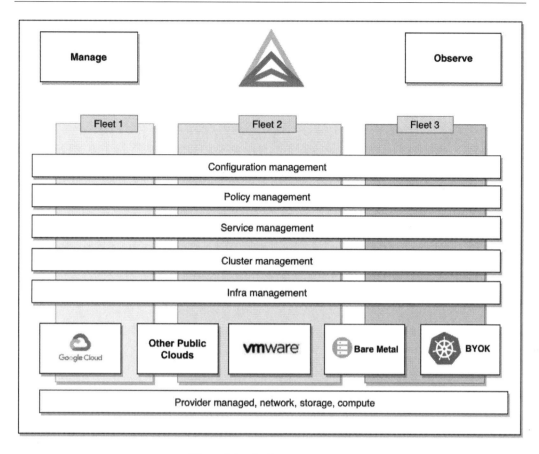

Figure 8.1 – Anthos components

Anthos allows you to group your Kubernetes resources into fleets/environs to manage them as a single entity. We will have a closer look at fleets later in this chapter.

Anthos clusters

Anthos clusters allow you to work with multiple Kubernetes clusters and provide consistent and secure environments for your cloud-native workloads. Anthos can deploy Anthos clusters in **Google Cloud Platform** (**GCP**) using GKE, on-premises, and other public clouds. You can also attach already-existing Kubernetes clusters and take advantage of some Anthos features without having to provision a new Anthos cluster and migrate your workloads.

Anthos Connect Agent

Anthos Connect Agent can connect any Kubernetes cluster to GCP. By connecting a cluster to GKE Hub, you are able to access the cluster directly from Cloud Console and interact with the hosted workloads. The agent runs as a Kubernetes Deployment called Connect Agent and establishes an encrypted connection with the GKE hub:

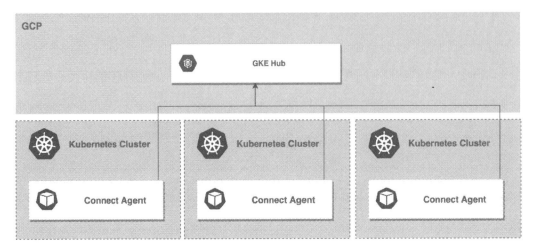

Figure 8.2 – Anthos Connect agents

For scenarios where the cluster cannot access the internet directly, the agent can be configured to use NAT or proxies for the egress to the GKE hub. Once you have the cluster registered in the GKE hub, you get a GKE-like experience of interacting with your Kubernetes cluster.

Fleets (formerly environs)

Fleets (formerly called environs) allow you to logically organize **fleet-aware resources** such as Kubernetes clusters to allow easier administration. As an example, you can apply unified configuration or policies on your resources to achieve consistency within your fleet.

Fleets have the following constraint: A single fleet can be associated with a single GCP project called the **fleet host project** and the fleet project can have only one fleet. This constraint results in isolation of resources on the project level.

Fleets can be used to work with **fleet-enabled components** such as the following:

- **Workload identity pools** – Allows you to uniformly authorize workloads in the pool to external services

- **Anthos Config Management** – Allows you to uniformly apply configuration and enforce policies on clusters and resources in the fleet

- **Anthos Service Mesh** – Allows you to create a service mesh across the resources in the fleet

- **Multi Cluster Ingress (MCI)** – Allows you to create a common ingress for the clusters and service endpoints in the fleet to provide load balancing

Another important element of fleets is the concept of sameness. An object in different contexts but with the same name can be treated as the same entity. This includes the following contexts:

- Namespace sameness

- Service sameness

- Identity sameness when accessing external resources

- Identity sameness within a fleet

As an example, for namespace sameness, namespaces with the same name across different clusters in the same fleet are treated as a single entity.

Anthos cluster deployment options

Anthos comes with multiple deployment options allowing you to host cloud-native workloads almost anywhere. As was already said, Anthos is a very fast-developing platform. Therefore, you should always consult the documentation to find the most recent list of supported endpoints and features, at `https://cloud.google.com/anthos/deployment-options`. The following diagram shows the deployment options available and planned at the time of writing this book:

Figure 8.3 – Anthos deployment options

Also note that you can attach Kubernetes clusters that are provisioned using a managed Kubernetes service in **Azure Kubernetes Service** (**AKS**) and **Amazon Elastic Kubernetes Service** (**EKS**). If you inspect the preceding link you may notice that new Anthos features are always introduced to GKE (that is, on GCP) first. This is because GKE fits very well into the Anthos ecosystem and leverages GCP infrastructure. You can also expect that clusters that have been provisioned outside of Anthos and were later attached might have some limitations in terms of features due to technical constraints.

Now let's have a high-level look at each of the deployment options.

Note that in *Chapter 6, Managing Kubernetes Clusters with Google Kubernetes Engine*, we went through an extensive review of the GKE service. We encourage you to revisit the chapter if you would like to get more information on this deployment option. To enable Anthos for GKE follow the step-by-step guide you can find here: `https://cloud.google.com/anthos/docs/setup/cloud`.

Anthos clusters on VMware (GKE on-prem)

Anthos clusters on VMware (GKE on-prem) was the first deployment option that brought GKE to data centers on premises. It can run on your existing virtualization platform based on **VMware vSphere**. Anthos communicates with vSphere as an infrastructure management layer via the **vCenter** API to provision **Virtual Machines** (**VMs**) that host the Kubernetes nodes. This way we are able to provision both the control plane and the workload clusters for the GKE on-prem deployment.

As vSphere is one of the most mature and widely adopted virtualization platforms on the market, it has a very sophisticated set of features including software-defined networking, storage, and advanced APIs. It is also considered a state-of-the-art foundation for private clouds. As vSphere removes the management overhead by providing automation for software-defined infrastructure, it was a natural choice for Google to start with vSphere as the first endpoint for GKE on-prem. You must be aware though that this comes with some costs, as you need to purchase vSphere licenses on top of the regular licenses.

GKE on-prem components

In *Chapter 6, Managing Kubernetes Clusters with Google Kubernetes Engine*, we learned that the management plane for the GKE clusters resides in GCP and we as consumers do not need to worry about it. GCP takes care of the provisioning and management of both the control and data planes of GKE Kubernetes clusters.

When we move to on-premises or another cloud provider, the management plane resides outside of GCP. In most of the non-GCP Anthos clusters, the management plane is hosted on a so-called **admin cluster** as per *Figure 8.4*:

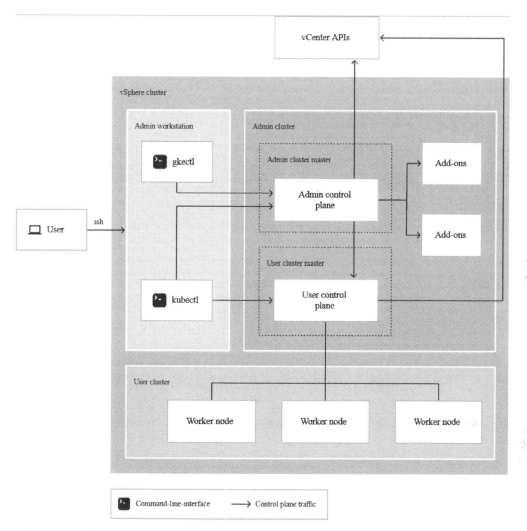

Figure 8.4 – GKE on-prem components (Source: `https://cloud.google.com/anthos/clusters/docs/on-prem/overview?hl=pl`)

> **Important Note**
>
> This architecture is constantly being refined by Google with some attempts to minimize or remove the admin cluster role. Therefore, be aware that this might change in the future.

An admin cluster is a Kubernetes cluster that is provisioned as the base layer of the Anthos cluster and runs the following components:

- **Admin cluster control plane**: This hosts the Kubernetes API, scheduler, and controllers for the admin cluster

- **User cluster control plane**: These are nodes of the user cluster control plane. They host the Kubernetes API, scheduler, and controllers for the user clusters

- **Add-ons**: Runs Kubernetes add-ons such as Google Cloud's operations suite

It is important to note that the master nodes of the **user clusters** (workload clusters) run in the admin cluster, not in the user cluster itself.

In *Figure 8.4* you can also see the **Admin workstation,** which is a Linux-based VM. This machine contains all the tools required to download, provision, and manage the GKE on-prem cluster.

Load balancing

Load balancing is needed for both the management plane of Anthos on-premises and also for exposing the Kubernetes services. There is a choice of three load balancing modes:

- **Integrated** – Uses F5 BIG-IP load balancers that need to be provisioned outside of the Anthos clusters. There is deep integration with F5 via the API so when services are deployed in the Anthos cluster, operators take care of creating objects in the F5 appliance without any manual interaction needed. Note that F5 licenses are not included in the cost of Anthos

- **Bundled** – The load balancer is provisioned during the Anthos deployment. It is based on the open source Google Seesaw load balancer project. To learn more about this project, visit `https://github.com/google/seesaw`

- **Manual** – Allows you to integrate with other third-party load balancers

The choice of the right load balancing mode depends on multiple factors including your network architecture, support for particular features, and cost limitations. You might need to consult your data center network architect before taking the decision on which load balancing mode to use.

Deployment of GKE on-prem clusters

As you can imagine, the deployment of an on-prem cluster is not as straightforward as a deployment of a GKE on Google Cloud. As of today, there is no way to deploy the GKE on-prem clusters from the Google Cloud Console directly. For GKE on-prem you will use command-line tools called `gkeadm` and `gkectl` that can be run directly from your admin workstation residing on premises.

The high-level steps of deploying GKE on-prem are as follows:

1. Deploy and/or prepare the vSphere infrastructure.
2. Prepare your Anthos GCP project and a service account.
3. Deploy the admin workstation and download the Anthos images.
4. Deploy the integrated, manual, or bounded load balancers for the admin cluster.
5. Deploy the admin cluster.
6. Deploy the integrated, manual, or bounded load balancers for the admin cluster.
7. Deploy the user cluster.
8. Configure additional services (such as Anthos Service Mesh, Config Management, and so on).

Note that this procedure can change, so for a step-by-step installation guide for GKE on-prem clusters, visit `https://cloud.google.com/anthos/clusters/docs/on-prem/overview?hl=pl`.

Anthos on AWS

Anthos clusters on AWS (GKE on AWS) allow you to extend your cloud-native platform to the AWS cloud. It leverages AWS-native services including the following:

- EC2 VMs
- **Elastic Block Storage (EBS)**
- **Elastic Load Balancer (ELB)**

This allows you to leverage the benefits of Anthos but also consume AWS services natively.

Anthos on AWS components

Anthos on AWS already follows the architectural decision to reduce the footprint or completely remove the admin cluster (see the *GKE on-prem components* section). Therefore, there are two components to Anthos clusters on AWS:

- **Management service**: This allows us to install, update, and manage the user clusters via the AWS API

- **User cluster**: Runs the user workloads

The following figure shows the architecture of Anthos on AWS:

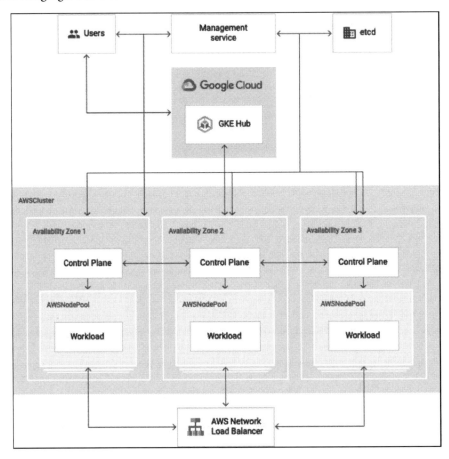

Figure 8.5 – Anthos on AWS (Source: https://cloud.google.com/anthos/clusters/ docs/aws/concepts/architecture?hl=pl)

As we can see in the diagram, both the management service and the users cluster are located in AWS and are connected to the GKE hub located in GCP.

Load balancing

Anthos on AWS uses the AWS-native ELB so there is no need install or configure an additional load balancer. This eliminates the need for additional tools to manage third-party products and gives you the best-in-class load balancing option deeply integrated with the AWS ecosystem.

Deployment of Anthos on AWS

The deployment of Anthos on AWS consists of the following steps:

1. Prepare the AWS account.

2. Install the management service.

3. Create user clusters to run your workloads.

You can find the step-by-step installation procedure by following the link: `https://cloud.google.com/anthos/clusters/docs/aws/how-to/installation-overview?hl=pl`.

Anthos on Azure

At the time of writing this chapter, the preview of Anthos on Azure has been announced. The capabilities at this time are limited. You can deploy the Anthos cluster and workload, but some management options are not there yet. As an example, you can connect to the cluster using the Connect gateway but you cannot use Terraform to manage your clusters. However, Google has announced this will be solved soon.

Anthos on Azure components

The architecture of Anthos on Azure is very similar to what we have already seen with AWS. Therefore, there are two components to Anthos clusters on Azure:

- **Management service**: This allows us to install, update, and manage the user clusters via the Azure API

- **User cluster**: This runs the user workloads

The following figure shows the architecture of Anthos on Azure:

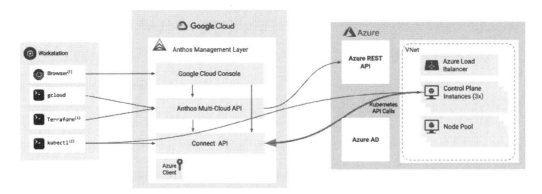

Figure 8.6 – Anthos on Azure (Source: `https://cloud.google.com/anthos/clusters/docs/azure/concepts/architecture`)

Let's have a closer look at each of the components of Anthos on Azure.

Management service

The management service of Anthos on Azure consists of the following:

- The **Anthos multi-cloud API** that accepts the `gcloud` command to provision and manage the Anthos clusters

- **AzureClient**, a secure connection to Azure using a X.509 key pair, with the private key stored in GCP and the public key in Azure

- **App Registration**, which allows the Anthos cluster to create resources in Azure using AzureClient

- The **Connect API**, which allows management of the cluster directly from Google Cloud Console

User cluster

The user cluster has two components: a control plane and at least one node pool. The control plane is responsible for storing the configuration in a highly available `etcd` database. The control plane can manage multiple node pools. The node pool consists of VMs that act as worker nodes.

Load balancing

Anthos on Azure uses the Azure-native Azure Load Balancer for both the cluster control planes and workloads. The load balancer is automatically provisioned by Anthos automation when the user deploys a Kubernetes `Service` of type `Loadbalancer`.

Deployment of Anthos on Azure

The deployment of Anthos on Azure consists of the following steps:

1. Prepare the Azure account.

2. Install the management service.

3. Create the user clusters.

4. Create node pools.

You can find the step-by-step installation procedure by following the link: `https://cloud.google.com/anthos/clusters/docs/azure/how-to/installation-overview`.

Anthos clusters on bare metal

With Anthos on bare metal, you can take advantage of your existing infrastructure and don't need vSphere as the virtualization layer. As you are running Anthos directly on the hardware, you get the best performance possible, including low network latency. The cost of using Anthos clusters on bare metal is reduced by not having to pay for vSphere licenses. Another benefit is that you can reduce latency by moving the Anthos clusters to the edge of the network.

Figure 8.7 shows the three layers of an Anthos cluster on bare metal: the hardware, operating system, and Anthos itself. You can install the cluster on the nodes running CentOS, RHEL, or Ubuntu:

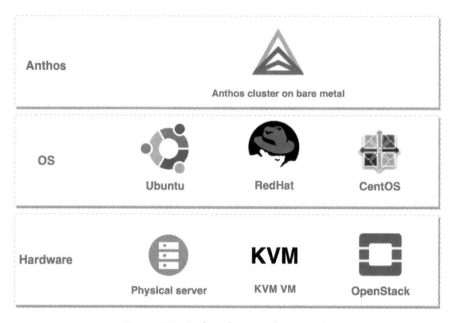

Figure 8.7 – Anthos cluster on bare metal

Consult the documentation for the exact supported versions of your chosen OS.

The Anthos cluster nodes can be also installed on VMs so you can take advantage of your existing hypervisors.

In this deployment option you are responsible for providing the hardware and managing the operating system of the cluster nodes. Google is responsible for providing you the Anthos binaries. You manage the Anthos cluster yourself.

Anthos on bare metal cluster types

Anthos clusters on bare metal consist of two types of clusters:

- **Admin clusters** to control the resources of your clusters
- **User clusters** to run workloads

You can also choose to deploy the cluster in the following modes:

- **Hybrid cluster**: Clusters that combine administration tasks and workloads, as well as controlling other user clusters. The first cluster acts as both the admin and user clusters while other clusters act as user clusters

- **Standalone cluster**: A single standalone Anthos cluster on bare metal

- **Multi-cluster**: A single management cluster with one or more user clusters

This gives you a lot of flexibility in terms of architecting your cluster. You can either choose to have a standalone cluster or manage multiple clusters with an admin cluster.

Load balancing modes

As in other deployment options, you need to make a choice on a load balancer for both the control plane and workloads. With bare metal you can choose from the following:

- **Bundled load balancer**: Where the load balancer is deployed on a dedicated pool of worker nodes on your control plane cluster nodes

- **Manual load balancer mode**: Where you deploy the load balancer outside of the cluster. You can use either **MetalLB** or **F5 BIG-IP**

Note that for the bundled load balancer there is a requirement that all nodes are in the same L2 subnet as it uses ARP broadcasts.

Summary of Anthos clusters on bare metal

Anthos clusters on bare metal cover all use cases where there is a need for high performance and direct access to underlying hardware. One such use case is in telco scenarios. Another interesting feature is the capability of hosting VMs using an open source project called Kubevirt (`https://kubevirt.io`). To learn more about Anthos clusters on bare metal have a look at the following link: `https://cloud.google.com/anthos/clusters/docs/bare-metal`.

Anthos Config Management

Anthos Config Management comes with a suite of components that provide you with constant configuration and policies across multiple Anthos clusters. The components are interoperable but can also be used independently of each other. *Figure 8.8* shows three components included in the service:

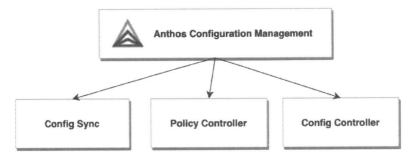

Figure 8.8 – Anthos Configuration Management

Let's look at the components in more detail:

- **Config Sync** continuously reconciles the state of your clusters with a central set of configurations stored in one or more Git repositories. This feature lets you manage common configurations with an auditable, transactional, and version-controlled deployment process that can span hybrid or multi-cloud environments:

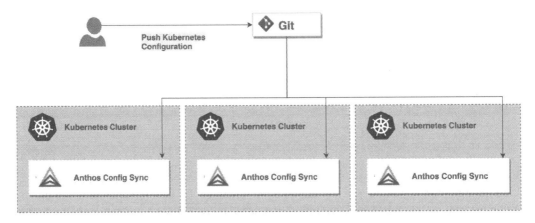

Figure 8.9 – Anthos Configuration Manager

- **Policy Controller** enables the enforcement of fully programmable policies. You can use these policies to actively block non-compliant API requests, or simply to audit the configuration of your clusters and report violations. Policy Controller is based on the open source Open Policy Agent Gatekeeper project and comes with a library of pre-built policies for common security and compliance checks:

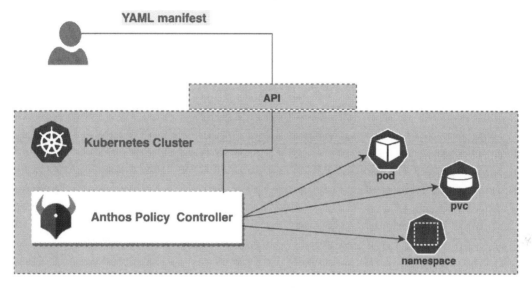

Figure 8.10 – Anthos Policy Controller

The policies are enforced by using objects called constraints. For example, you can use a constraint to require each namespace to have at least one label, or restrict the repositories a given container image can be pulled from. You can also create your own polices with the use of constraint templates. You can find the Google-developed constraint library at https://cloud.google.com/anthos-config-management/docs/reference/constraint-template-library.

As policies are defined as Kubernetes objects, they can be pushed directly to the cluster with the use of a Git repository and the Config Sync service.

As we can see, Config Management is a very powerful service that can help you keep control of your Anthos clusters.

Config Connector allows you to provision and manage GCP resources using Kubernetes manifests. This way, you gain a single API to provide both GCP and Kubernetes resources:

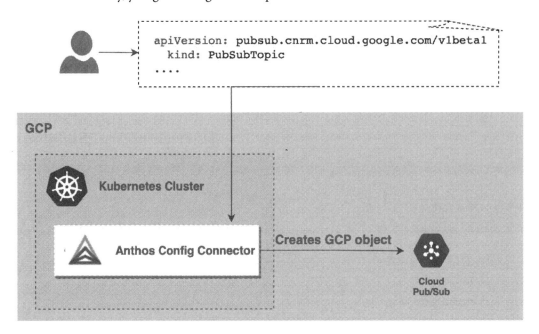

Figure 8.11 – Anthos Config Connector

Config Connector comes with **Custom Resource Definitions (CRDs)** and associated controllers for almost all GPC services. If you want to learn more about the resources supported, visit `https://cloud.google.com/config-connector/docs/reference/overview`.

The Config Controller service, at the time of writing this book, is in a preview state. It is a Google-hosted service that combines the Config Connector and Config Sync services to allow GitOps operations for Google Cloud and Anthos resources. To achieve this, an administrator defines the desired state of the resources using Config Connector CRDs and stores them in a Git repository. Config Sync makes sure the desired state is enforced.

> **Important Note**
> It is possible that rebranding of this service might happen without any notice, so please refer to the link: `https://cloud.google.com/anthos-config-management/docs/concepts/config-controller-overview` to learn about current status of the service.

Service management with Anthos Service Mesh

Anthos Service Mesh is a fully managed service mesh for microservices architectures. It is based on an open source project, started by Google, called Istio. Google is gradually integrating Istio's functionalities with other Google Cloud services such as the Cloud operations suite to provide an enterprise-grade service mesh offering. Let's have a look at Istio first to understand how it works so we can better understand Anthos Service Mesh.

Istio

Istio is an open source service mesh project. It runs in Kubernetes but may also integrate with traditional workloads hosted on VMs. It provides a programable and application-aware network. With the use of open source Envoy proxies, the traffic between microservices is intercepted and can be controlled, secured, and observed. This allows us to gain full control and visibility of the traffic between complex microservice-based applications. As we see in *Figure 8.12*, Istio injects Envoy sidecar proxies to the Kubernetes Pods:

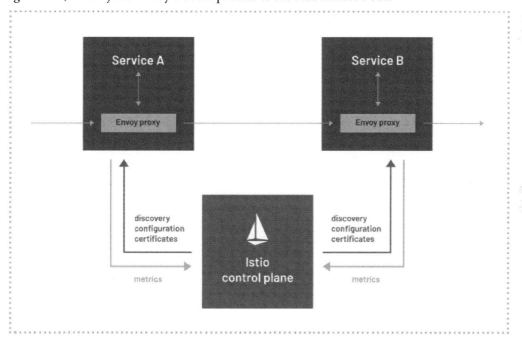

Figure 8.12 – Istio (Source: `https://istio.io/latest/`)

This way, all the ingress and egress traffic needs to pass through the proxies. The Istio control plane is a Kubernetes application that runs on your cluster. It gathers the metrics and controls network traffic based on the characteristics defined in the Kubernetes manifest.

With Istio you can perform the following tasks:

- **Request routing**: Route requests to multiple versions of a microservice

- **Fault injection**: Inject faults to test the resiliency of the application

- **Traffic shifting**: Gradually migrate traffic between different versions of a microservice to another

- **Query metrics**: Query for Istio metrics using **Prometheus**

- **Visualize metrics**: Use the Istio Dashboard to monitor mesh traffic using **Grafana**

- **Access external services**: Configure the Envoy proxy to pass through requests for unknown services

- **Visualize the service mesh**: Use the Kiali web-based graphical user interface to view service graphs of the mesh and your Istio configuration objects

- **Encrypt the traffic**: Enforce encryption of the traffic between microservices using mTLS

> **Exam Tip**
>
> Make sure you understand well all the capabilities of Istio and Anthos Service Mesh: request routing; fault injection; traffic shifting; querying metrics; visualizing metrics; accessing external services; visualizing your mesh.

Configuring Istio

You can install Istio on you any Kubernetes cluster by following the official guide at `https://istio.io/latest/docs/setup/getting-started`. Once you have Istio installed you can define for which namespace you want the sidecar proxies to be injected by labeling the namespace:

```
kubectl label namespace default istio-injection=enabled
```

In the guide mentioned above, you download the `Istio` repository that contains a sample application called `Bookinfo`. Deploy the application to the default namespace by running the following command:

```
kubectl apply -f samples/bookinfo/platform/kube/bookinfo.yaml
```

You can list the Pods by running the following command:

```
kubectl get pods
```

When you run the preceding commands, you will see the sidecar proxies have been automatically added to the Pods. As we see here, 2/2 containers (the workload and the proxy) are reported as **READY**:

NAME	READY	STATUS	RESTARTS	AGE
details-v1-558b8b4b76-2llld	2/2	Running	0	2m41s
productpage-v1-6987489c74-lpkgl	2/2	Running	0	2m40s
ratings-v1-7dc98c7588-vzftc	2/2	Running	0	2m41s
reviews-v1-7f99cc4496-gdxfn	2/2	Running	0	2m41s
reviews-v2-7d79d5bd5d-8zzqd	2/2	Running	0	2m41s
reviews-v3-7dbcdcbc56-m8dph	2/2	Running	0	2m41s

Figure 8.13 – Bookinfo application pods

Using Istio

As we have already seen, Istio has a lot of capabilities. As an example, you can perform traffic shifting. Let's say we want to split the traffic equally between the `reviews:v1` and `reviews:v3` services.

You can define this in a Kubernetes manifest with a `VirtualService` object and apply it using the `kubetctl apply` command:

```
apiVersion: networking.istio.io/v1beta1
kind: VirtualService
metadata:
  name: reviews
spec:
  hosts:
    - reviews
  http:
  - route:
    - destination:
        host: reviews
        subset: v1
      weight: 50
    - destination:
        host: reviews
        subset: v3
      weight: 50
```

Istio will make sure that the incoming traffic is split evenly between those two services.

> **Exam Tip**
>
> It is not required for the PCA exam to have in-depth knowledge of Istio, but if
> you would like to learn more on how to use it, you can find a step-by-step guide at
> `https://istio.io/latest/docs/setup/getting-started/`.

Using Anthos Service Mesh

Now that we know what Istio is, let's have a look at **Anthos Service Mesh,** which is a
managed version of Istio. Note that as usual, the features for Anthos Service Mesh will be
first introduced to GKE on GCP and next to the remaining flavors of Anthos clusters. As
the list is pretty long, have a look at the up-the-date list at `https://cloud.google.`
`com/service-mesh/docs/supported-features`.

As Anthos Service Mesh is simply an Anthos-verified and optimized distribution of Istio,
you can use the Istio CRDs as you would with the open source version.

The additional advantages that come from Anthos Service Mesh are due to the integration
with the GCP ecosystem. This means you get a single-pane-of-glass view in the Google
Cloud Console for your mesh. You can visualize all your services and traffic between them
and create alerts in Cloud Monitoring. You can access it from the **Service Mesh** menu in
the Anthos console:

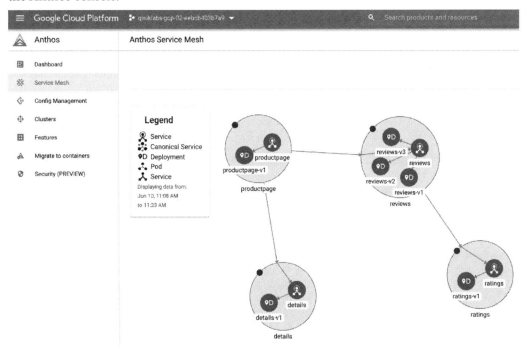

Figure 8.14 – Service Mesh visualization

You can also get details of the traffic per service using the **Traffic** option from the left-hand menu in Anthos Service Mesh:

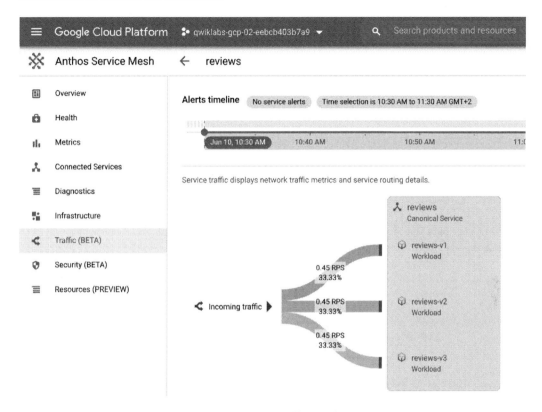

Figure 8.15 – Service traffic visualization

This will show you how much traffic is routed to each version.

Service - Level Objectives

Another very useful feature is that you can create so-called **Service-Level Objectives (SLOs)** based on **Service-Level Indicators (SLIs)**. SLIs measure how well you service is performing. The metrics can be based either on availability or latency:

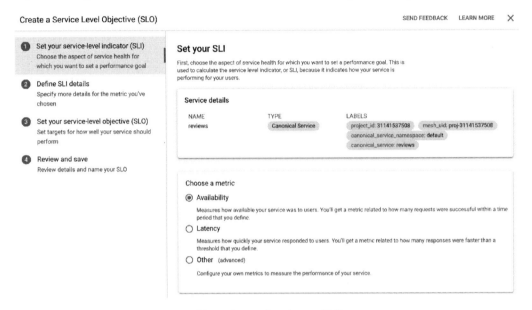

Figure 8.16 – Creating an SLO

You can also choose to use an advanced option and define your own metric.

Summary of Anthos Service Mesh

As we have learned here, Anthos Service Mesh is a very powerful tool that allows you to get control of the traffic within your Anthos clusters. It also gives brilliant insights into the health of your application by being able to see metrics relevant to this.

If you want to get hands-on experience with Anthos Service Mesh, please check the *GSP656 -Traffic Management with Anthos Service Mesh* lab at `https://www.qwiklabs.com/`.

Anthos Multi Cluster Ingress (MCI)

Anthos MCI is a service available under your Anthos subscription. It is built on the architecture of Google's external HTTP(S) Load Balancing service with proxies deployed at over 100 Google **points of presence (PoPs)** around the world. As we see in *Figure 8.17*, MCI provides a single IP for the app independent of where the app is deployed.

> **Exam Tip**
>
> MCI should be used when there is a need for load balancing for multi-cluster and multi-regional applications. It's a controller for the external HTTP(S) Load Balancer that provides ingress for traffic coming from the internet to one or more Anthos clusters.

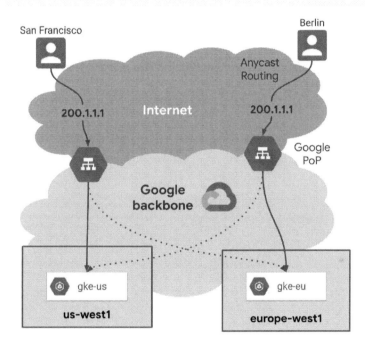

Figure 8.17 – Anthos MCI (Source: https://cloud.google.com/kubernetes-engine/docs/concepts/multi-cluster-ingress)

Anthos MCI comes with two very powerful features supporting the multi cluster setup.

MCI's proximity-based routing directs the users to the cluster nearest to their location. MCI's health checks allow us to perform seamless cluster upgrades and traffic failovers.

You can learn more about working with MCI at `https://cloud.google.com/ kubernetes-engine/docs/concepts/multi-cluster-ingress`.

Anthos Binary Authorization

Binary Authorization is a Google Cloud service aimed at providing security for your containerized software supply chain. It reduces the risk of deploying defective, vulnerable, or unauthorized software.

It allows you to create policies that kick in when there is an attempt to deploy a container on one of the supported platforms. It is done by means of so-called **attestations** that certify the images for the deployments.

At the time of writing this book, Binary Authorization supports the following platforms:

- GKE
- Cloud Run
- Anthos clusters on VMware

Binary Authorization compliments the suite of Google software supply chain services that includes Cloud Source Repositories, Cloud Build, Artifact Registry, and Container Analysis:

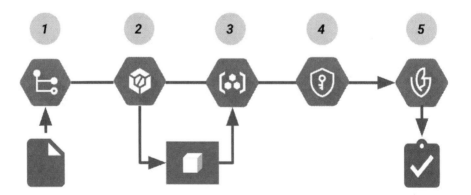

Figure 8.18 – The Cloud Build pipeline that creates a Binary Authorization attestation

(Source: `https://cloud.google.com/binary-authorization/docs/cloud-build?hl=zh-tw`)

As we see in the preceding diagram, the pipeline works as follows:

1. The developer pushes the code to build the container image into **Cloud Source Repositories**.

2. **Cloud Build** builds the container image.

3. **Cloud Build** pushes the container image to **Artifact Registry.**

4. **Cloud Key Management Service** creates a cryptographic key pair to sign the container image. The signature is then stored in an attestation.

5. During deployment, the attestor in **Binary Authorization** verifies the attestation using the public key from the key pair.

Use of Binary Authorization should be considered a best practice for the deployment of production workloads.

Migrate for Anthos and GKE

Migrate for Anthos and GKE allows us to modernize traditional VM-hosted applications by extracting and migrating them into containers that can run on top of GKE or Anthos clusters. This comes with the following benefits:

- **Better density** by using containers to optimize usage of cluster resources

- A **security-optimized node kernel** with no need to update the operating system

- **Integrate traditional apps with modern services** including Anthos Service Mesh, Cloud Logging, Cloud Monitoring, and other GCP-native services to offload infrastructure-related functionalities to GCP

- **Unified policy and configuration management** with use of declarative definitions

- **Modern image-based management and orchestration** through integration with CI/CD tools

As of the time of writing this book, the following target platforms are supported:

- GKE

- Anthos clusters on GCP

- Anthos clusters on VMware

- Anthos clusters on AWS

The service is available for both Windows and Linux VMs as sources for the migration.

For Linux VMs, the migration process includes the following steps:

1. Swapping the VM's OS kernel to the kernel used by the GKE node
2. Setting up the network interface, DNS, logging, and health status
3. Running the application and services found in the user space of the VM
4. Removal of the VM or hardware-related services

For Windows VMs, a Dockerfile with the container image definition and a ZIP file with the application content are generated. An official Microsoft Windows Server image is used.

The migration process is divided into multiple phases:

1. Discovery phase
2. Migration planning phase
3. Landing zone phase
4. Migration and deployment phase
5. Operate and optimize phase

If you want to learn more about the architecture of Migrate for Anthos and GKE, and the detailed procedure for migration, visit `https://cloud.google.com/migrate/anthos/docs/concepts`.

Cloud Run for Anthos

In *Chapter 7, Deploying Cloud-Native Workloads with Cloud Run*, we learned about Google Cloud Run, which allows us to run serverless-like cloud-native workloads on GCP. With Cloud Run for Anthos this capability is available to be executed on Anthos clusters either in GCP, public clouds, or on-premises. As Cloud Run for Anthos is powered by the open source Knative (`https://knative.dev`) project, the workloads are portable to any Kubernetes cluster.

For Anthos-enabled projects, when you create a Cloud Run service, you should choose **Cloud Run for Anthos** rather than **Cloud Run (fully managed)** for the deployment platform:

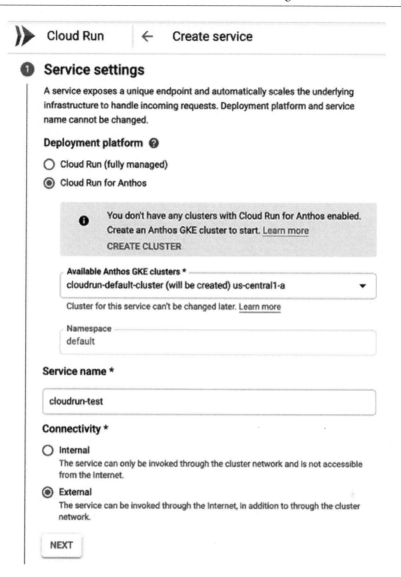

Figure 8.19 – Cloud Run for Anthos

If you don't have any Anthos clusters with Cloud Run enabled, the cluster will be created for you. If you want to create a cluster with Cloud Run enabled, add the following flags to the `gcloud` command:

```
gcloud container clusters create CLUSTER_NAME \
   --addons=HttpLoadBalancing,CloudRun \
   --machine-type=n1-standard-2 \
   --enable-stackdriver-kubernetes
```

Note that you need to have the default zone and region specified for this command to run correctly. Once executed successfully, you can deploy the Cloud Run service on your cluster.

Cloud Run (fully managed) versus Cloud Run for Anthos

In the following table we have a simple summary of the differences between Cloud Run (fully managed) and Cloud Run for Anthos:

Feature	Cloud Run	Cloud Run for Anthos
Price	Pay-per-use	Anthos cluster cost
Compute	CPU and memory limits	Anthos cluster nodes' capabilities (includes GPUs)
Isolation	Uses gVisor sandbox	Anthos cluster isolation
Scaling	1,000 containers with extensible quotas	Anthos cluster-based
Domains	Available	
VPC access	Serverless VPC access	Direct access to VPC
Service mesh	Not connected to Istio Service Mesh	Services connected to Istio Service Mesh
Execution environment	Google-native infrastructure	Anthos cluster

As we can see, the differences are not only in the pricing model and execution environment but also in the functionalities provided. The choice of which option to run your workloads on needs to be based on your requirements. Each of the services has its pros and cons.

Quotas and limits

Anthos comes with a set of quotas and limitations. These are in place to make sure you get the best performance, and you are protected from provisioning too many resources. As the quotas and limits might change, it is best to refer to the documentation to find the most up-to-date quotas, at `https://cloud.google.com/anthos/clusters/docs/on-prem/concepts/scalability`.

As an example, you can see what quotas are applicable to Anthos clusters on VMware (GKE on-prem) at the time of writing this book:

- You can deploy a maximum of 20 user clusters per admin cluster.

- For each user cluster:

  - You must create a minimum of 3 nodes.

  - You can create a maximum of 250 nodes.

  - You can create a maximum of 7,500 pods:

- For each node, you can create a maximum of 110 pods.

- For each Google Cloud project, you can register a maximum of 15 user clusters in the GKE hub, but you can submit a request to increase your quota.

Now let's review the Anthos pricing.

Pricing

Anthos clusters are charged per vCPU of the worker nodes in the user clusters. This excludes both the admin cluster and the master node. There are two charging models you can choose from:

- **Pay-as-you-go** pricing, where you are billed at the current applicable rates for Anthos-managed clusters as you use them. You can start using pay-as-you-go Anthos without any long-term commitment

- **Subscription** pricing, where you pay a monthly charge for your Anthos deployments. You can benefit from a discounted price for long-term subscription commitments

As the actual pricing might change, please refer to the documentation for the price list, at `https://cloud.google.com/anthos/pricing`.

Summary

In this chapter, we learned about Anthos and its most important features. We went over the Anthos deployment options, including **GKE (Google Cloud)**, **on-premises (VMware)**, **on-premises (bare metal)**, **AWS**, **attached clusters**, and **Azure**. We looked at how to control Anthos clusters' configuration in sync with the defined configuration and enforce policies using **Anthos Config Management**. We learned how to control and observe traffic in microservice architectures using **Anthos Service Mesh**. We also understood how we can distribute inbound traffic using **Anthos MCI**. Finally, we learned how to run serverless-like cloud-native workloads on Anthos clusters using **Cloud Run on Anthos**. We compared this to running the workload on **Cloud Run (fully managed)**. In the next chapter, we will have a look at running serverless functions with Google Cloud Functions.

Further reading

You can refer to the following links for more information:

- **Anthos main page**: `https://cloud.google.com/anthos/docs/concepts/overview`

- **Anthos on VMware**: `https://cloud.google.com/anthos/clusters/docs/on-prem/`

- **Anthos clusters on bare metal**: `https://cloud.google.com/anthos/clusters/docs/bare-metal/1.6/concepts/about-bare-metal`

- **Anthos on AWS**: `https://cloud.google.com/anthos/clusters/docs/aws/concepts/architecture`

- **Anthos on Azure**: `https://cloud.google.com/anthos/clusters/docs/azure/`

- **Athos Configuration Management**: `https://cloud.google.com/anthos/config-management`

- **Anthos Service Mesh**: `https://cloud.google.com/anthos/service-mesh`

- **Istio**: `https://istio.io/latest/docs`

- **Anthos for Anthos and GKE**: `https://cloud.google.com/migrate/anthos/docs/concepts`

- **Cloud Run on Anthos**: `https://cloud.google.com/anthos/run/`

- **Multi Cluster Ingress**: `https://cloud.google.com/kubernetes-engine/docs/concepts/multi-cluster-ingress`

- **Config Connector**: `https://cloud.google.com/config-connector`

9

Running Serverless Functions with Google Cloud Functions

In this chapter, we will finally talk about fully serverless compute options, that is, Cloud Functions. This means no more servers and no more containers. This service is leveraging them in the backend, but they aren't visible to the end user. All we need to care about now is the code. Cloud Functions is a **Function-as-a-Service (FaaS)** offering. This means that you write a function in one of the languages supported by GCP and it can be triggered by an event or via HTTP. GCP takes care of provisioning and scaling the resources that are needed to run your functions.

> **Important Note**
>
> How does Cloud Functions work in the backend? Again, you don't need to bother with GCP's backend infrastructure, which runs the functions for you. However, being an engineer, I bet you will still search for answers on your own. Cloud Functions uses containers to set an isolated environment for your function. These are called Cloud Functions instances. If multiple functions are executed in parallel, multiple instances are created.

> **Exam Tip**
>
> Expect Cloud Functions questions to appear in the Cloud Architect exam. You will need to understand what Cloud Functions is and what the most common use cases are. Being able to tell the difference between two types of functions, namely HTTP and backend functions, is also important. Knowing when you would use Cloud Functions rather than other compute options, as well as remembering what programming languages are supported, is crucial. Finally, be sure that you can deploy a function both from the Google Cloud Console and the command line.

In this chapter, we will cover the following topics:

- Main Cloud Functions characteristics
- Use cases
- Runtime environments
- Types of Cloud Functions
- Events and triggers
- Other considerations
- Deploying Cloud Functions
- IAM
- Quotas and limits
- Pricing

Main Cloud Functions characteristics

The following are the key Cloud Functions characteristics:

- **Serverless**: Cloud Functions are completely serverless. The underlying infrastructure is abstracted from the end user.
- **Event-driven**: Cloud Functions are event-driven. There are triggered in response to an event or HTTP request. This means that they are only invoked when needed and do not produce any cost when inactive.

- **Stateless**: Cloud Functions do not store state nor data. This allows them to work independently and scale as needed. It is very important to understand that each invocation has an execution environment and does not share global variable memory or filesystems. To share state across function invocations, your function should use a service such as Cloud Datastore or Cloud Storage.

- **Autoscaling**: Cloud Functions scale from zero to the desired scale. Scaling is managed by GCP without any end user intervention. Autoscaling limits can be set to control the cost of execution. This is important as failures in the design might cause large spikes, resulting in your bill reaching the clouds.

Now that we are aware of the main characteristics, let's look at some use cases.

Use cases

Now that we have a basic understanding of Cloud Functions, let's have a look at numerous use cases. Remember that, in each of these use cases, you can still use other compute options. However, it is a matter of delivering the solution quickly, taking advantage of in-built autoscaling, and paying only for what we have used.

Application backends

Instead of using virtual machines for backend computing, you can simply use functions. Let's have a look at some example backends:

- **IoT backends**: In the IoT world, there's a large number of devices that send data to the backend. Cloud Functions allow you to process this data and auto-scale it when needed. This happens without any human intervention.

- **Mobile backends**: Cloud Functions can process data that's delivered by your mobile applications. It can interact with all the GCP services to make use of big data, machine learning capabilities, and so on. There is no need to use any virtual machines and you can go completely serverless.

- **Third-party API integrations**: You can use functions to integrate with any third-party system that provides an API. This will allow you to extend your application with additional features that are delivered by other providers.

Next, let's have a look at some data processing examples.

Real-time data processing systems

When it comes to **event-driven data processing**, Cloud Functions can be triggered whenever a predefined event occurs. When this happens, it can preprocess the data that's passed for analysis with GCP big data services:

- **Real-time stream processing**: When messages arrive in the Pub/Sub, Cloud Functions can be triggered to analyze or enrich the messages to prepare them for further data processing steps in the pipeline.

- **Real-time files processing**: When files are uploaded to your Cloud Storage bucket, they can be immediately processed. For example, thumbnails can be created or analyzed using GCP AI APIs.

Next, let's look at examples of smart applications.

Smart applications

Smart applications allow users to perform various tasks in a smarter way by using a data-driven experience. Some of these are as follows:

- **Chatbots and virtual assistants**: You can connect your text or voice platforms to Cloud Functions to integrate them with other GCP services, such as **DialogFlow** (see *Chapter 14, Putting Machine Learning to Work*), to give the user a natural conversation experience. The conversation logic can be defined in DialogFlow without any programming skills. Integration with third-party applications can be created to provide services such as weather information or the purchase of goods.

- **Video and image analysis**: You can use Cloud Functions to interact with the various GCP AI building blocks, such as video and image AIs. When a user uploads an image or video to your application, Cloud Functions can immediately trigger the related API and return the analysis. It may even perform actions, depending on the results of that analysis.

- **Lightweight APIs and webhooks**: Since Cloud Functions can be triggered using HTTP, you can expose your application to the external world for programmatic consumption. You don't need to build your API from scratch.

Now, let's cover some runtime environment examples.

Runtime environments

Cloud Functions are executed in a fully managed environment. The infrastructure and software that's needed to run the function are handled for you. Each function is single-threaded and is run in an isolated environment with the intended context. You don't need to take care of any updates for that environment. They are auto-updated for you and scaled as needed.

Currently, several runtimes are supported by Cloud Functions, namely the following:

- Node.js 10, 12, and 14
- Python 3.7, 3.8, and 3.9
- Go 1.11 and 1.13
- Java 11
- .NET Core 3.1
- Ruby 2.6 and 2.7
- PHP 7.4

When you define a function, you can also define the requirements or dependencies file in which you state which modules or libraries your function is dependent on. However, remember that those libraries will be loaded when your function is executed. This causes delays in terms of execution. We will talk about this in more detail in the *Cold start* section of this chapter.

In the next section, we will look at types of Cloud Functions.

Types of Cloud Functions

There are two types of Cloud Functions: HTTP functions and background functions. They differ in the way they are triggered. Let's have a look at each.

HTTP functions

HTTP functions are invoked by HTTP(S) requests. The POST, PUT, GET, DELETE, and OPTIONS HTTP methods are accepted. Arguments can be provided to the function using the request body:

Figure 9.1 – HTTP request

The invocation can be defined as synchronous as it can return a response that's been constructed within the function.

> **Interesting Fact**
>
> Don't expect a question on this on the exam. However, it might be interesting to know that Cloud Functions handles HTTP requests using common frameworks. For Node.js, this is Express 4.16.3, for Python, this is Flask 1.0.2, and for Go, this is the standard http.HadlerFunc interface.

Background functions

Background functions are invoked by events such as changes in the Cloud Storage bucket, messages in the **Cloud Pub/Sup** topic, or one of the supported **Firebase** events:

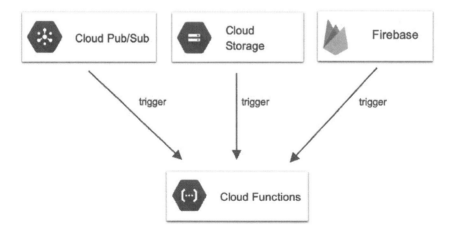

Figure 9.2 – Background functions

In the preceding diagram, we can see various triggers for **Cloud Functions**; that is, **Cloud Pub/Sub**, **Cloud Storage**, and **Firebase**.

Next, let's take a look at events.

Events

Events can be defined as things happening in or outside the GCP environment. When they occur, you might want certain actions to be triggered. An example of an event might be a file that's been added to Cloud Storage, a change that was made to your database table, or a new resource that has been provisioned to GCP, to name a few. These events can come from one of the following providers:

- HTTP
- Cloud Storage
- Cloud Pub/Sub
- Cloud Logging via Pub/Sub sink
- Cloud Firestore
- Firebase Realtime Database, Storage, and Authentication

If you create a sink to forward the logs to Pub/Sub, then you can trigger Cloud Functions (for more details, check out *Chapter 17, Monitoring Your Infrastructure*).

Next, let's look at triggers.

Triggers

For your function to react to an event, a trigger needs to be configured. The actual binding of the trigger happens at deployment time. We will have a look at how to deploy functions with different kinds of triggers in the *Deploying Cloud Functions* section.

Other considerations

When using Cloud Functions, you should be aware of a couple of features and considerations. Let's have a look at these now.

Cloud SQL connectivity

As we mentioned previously, Cloud Functions is stateless and the state needs to be saved on external storage or in a database. This can be done with external storage such as Cloud Storage or a database such as Cloud SQL. In general, any external storage can be used. We introduced Cloud SQL in *Chapter 3, Google Cloud Platform Core Services*. To remind you, it is a managed MySQL, Postgres, or MS SQL database. With Cloud Functions, you can connect to Cloud SQL using a local socket interface that's provided in the Cloud Functions execution environment. It eliminates the need to expose your database to a public network.

Connecting to internal resources in a VPC network

If your function needs to access services within a VPC, you can connect to it directly by passing a public network. To do this, you need to create a serverless VPC access connector from the network menu and refer to the connector when you deploy the function. Note that this does not work with Shared VPC and legacy networks.

Environmental variables

Cloud Functions allows you to set environment variables that are available during the runtime of the function. These variables are stored in the function's backend and follow the same life cycle as the function itself. These variables are set using the `--set-env-vars` flag; for example:

```
gcloud functions deploy env_vars --runtime python37 --set-env-
vars FOO=bar --trigger-http
```

> **Important Note**
> The first time you use Cloud Functions, you will be asked to enable the API.

Next, let's take a look at cold starts.

Cold start

As we mentioned previously, Cloud Functions executes using function instances. These new instances are created in the following cases:

- When the function is deployed
- Scaling up is required to handle the load
- When replacing an existing instance is triggered

Cold starts can impact the performance of your application. Google comes with a set of tips and tricks to help us reduce the impact of cold starts. Check out the *Further reading* section for a link to a detailed guide.

Local emulator

Deploying functions to GCP takes time. If you want to speed up tests, you can use a local emulator. This only works with Node.js and allows you to deploy, run, and debug your functions.

In the next section, we will learn how to deploy a Cloud Function.

Deploying Cloud Functions

Cloud Functions can be deployed using a CLI, the Google Cloud Console, or with APIs. In this section, we will have a look at the first two methods since it's likely that you will be tested on them in the exam.

Deploying Cloud Functions with the Google Cloud Console

To deploy Cloud Functions from the Google Cloud Console, follow these steps:

1. Select **Cloud Functions** from the hamburger menu. You will see the **Cloud Functions** window. Click on **CREATE FUNCTION**:

Figure 9.3 – The Cloud Functions menu

2. Fill in the name of your function and the region where it will be hosted:

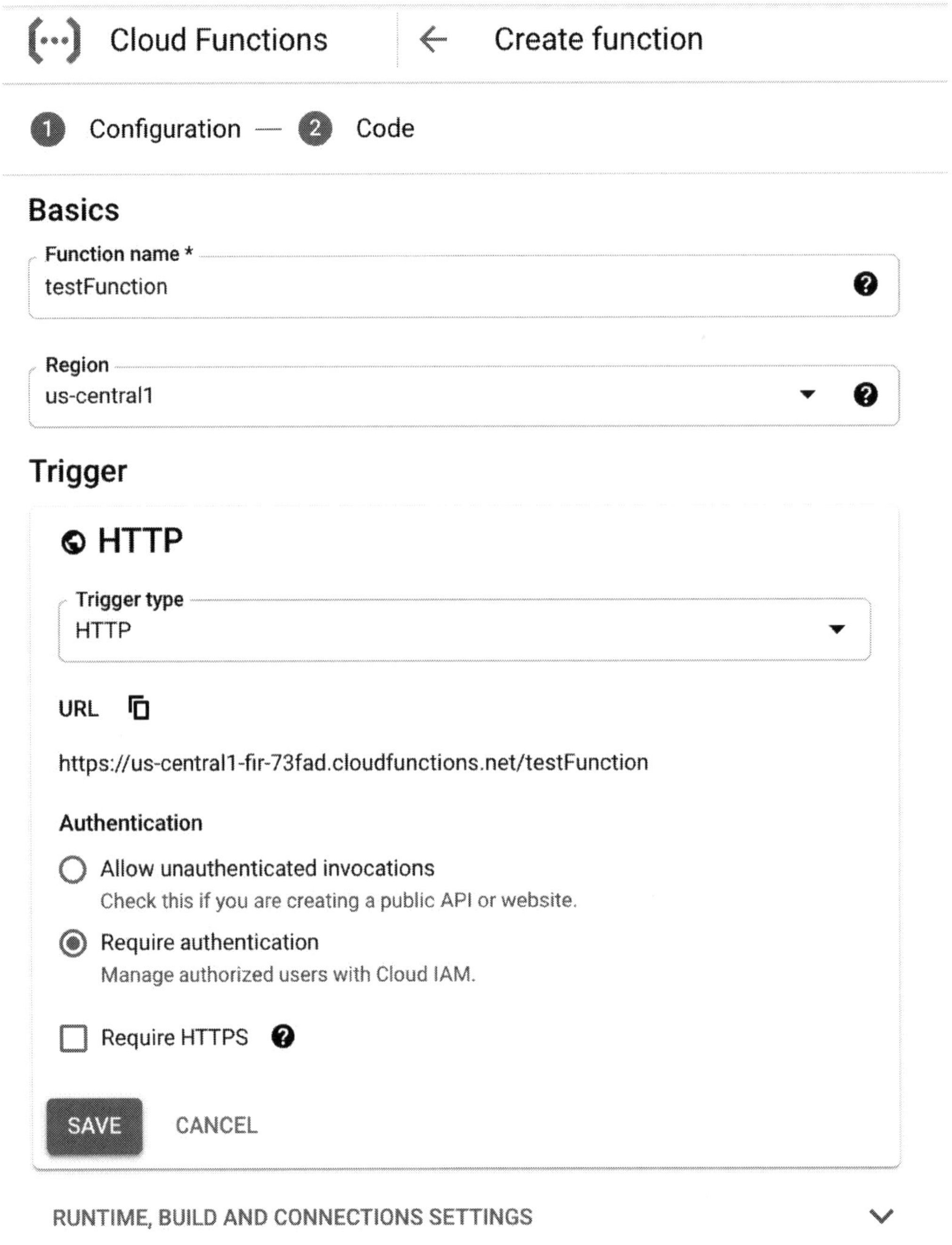

Figure 9.4 – Create function

3. Choose the trigger type from the drop-down menu:

Trigger

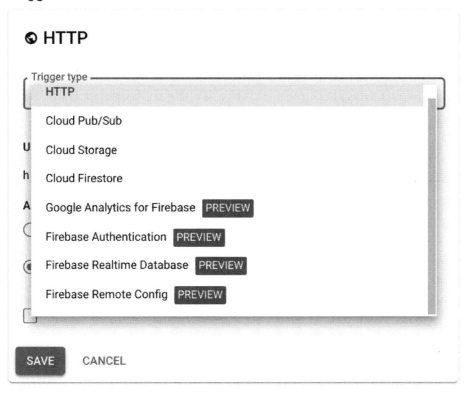

Figure 9.5 – Trigger

4. Click the **SAVE** button. If you have chosen to use an **HTTP** trigger, the URL to call your function with will be generated for you in the **URL** section, like so:

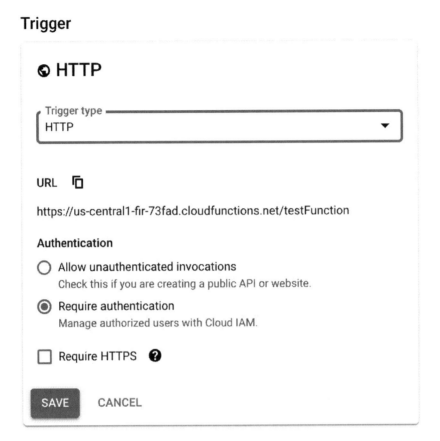

Figure 9.6 – Cloud Function URL

5. If you want to set more advanced settings, click on **RUNTIME, BUILD AND CONNECTION SETTINGS**. In the **RUNTIME** tab, you can set **Memory allocated** and **Timeout**. You can also define the service account that will run the function. Finally, you can define the minimum and the maximum number of instances:

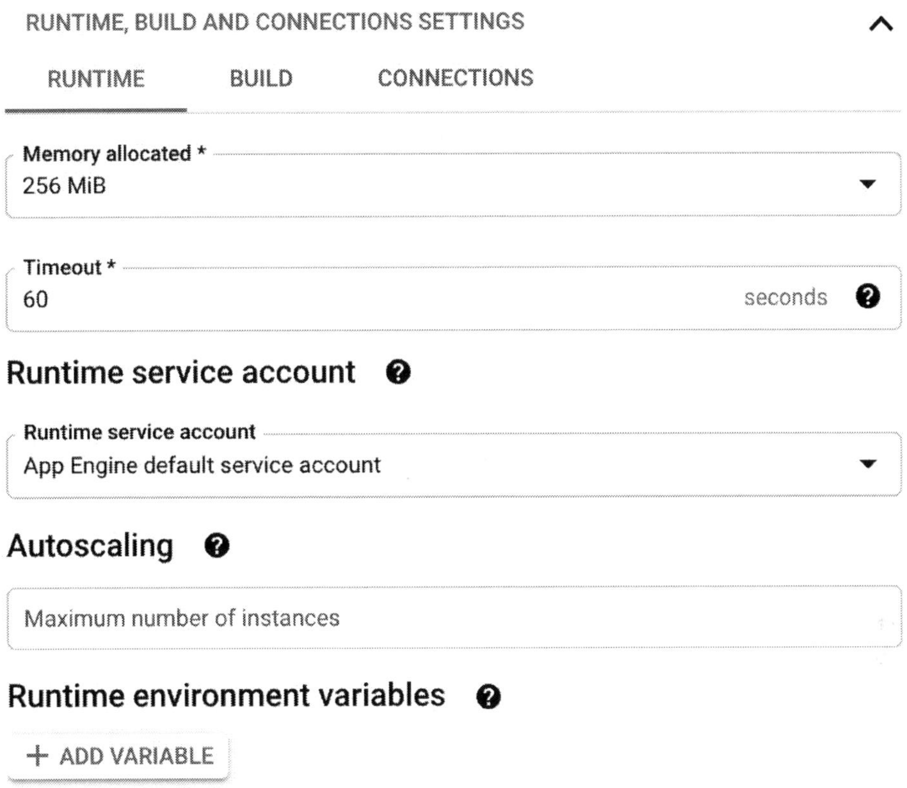

RUNTIME, BUILD AND CONNECTIONS SETTINGS

RUNTIME   BUILD   CONNECTIONS

Memory allocated *
256 MiB   ▼

Timeout *
60   seconds ❓

Runtime service account ❓

Runtime service account
App Engine default service account   ▼

Autoscaling ❓

Maximum number of instances

Runtime environment variables ❓

＋ ADD VARIABLE

Figure 9.7 – Runtime options

6. In the **BUILD** tab, you can define the variables and worker pools that will be used
    to build the function:

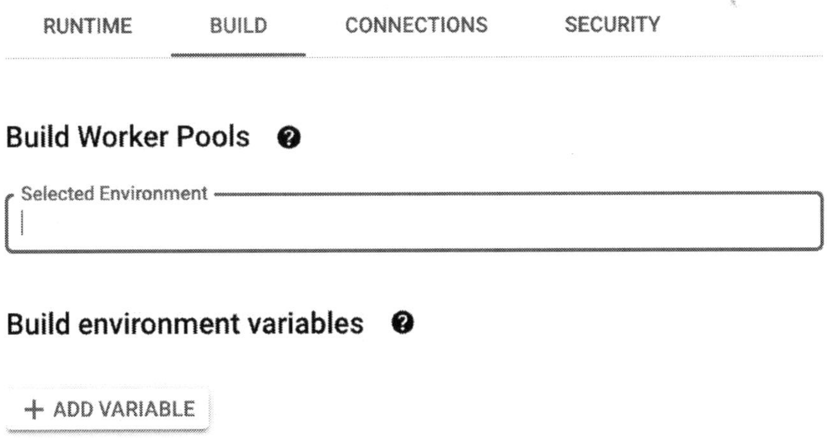

RUNTIME   BUILD   CONNECTIONS   SECURITY

Build Worker Pools ❓

Selected Environment

Build environment variables ❓

＋ ADD VARIABLE

Figure 9.8 – Build options

7. In the **CONNECTIONS** tab, you can define various ingress settings. This can limit where the traffic to trigger the function can come from. You may wish to create a connector so that the function can connect to your VPC:

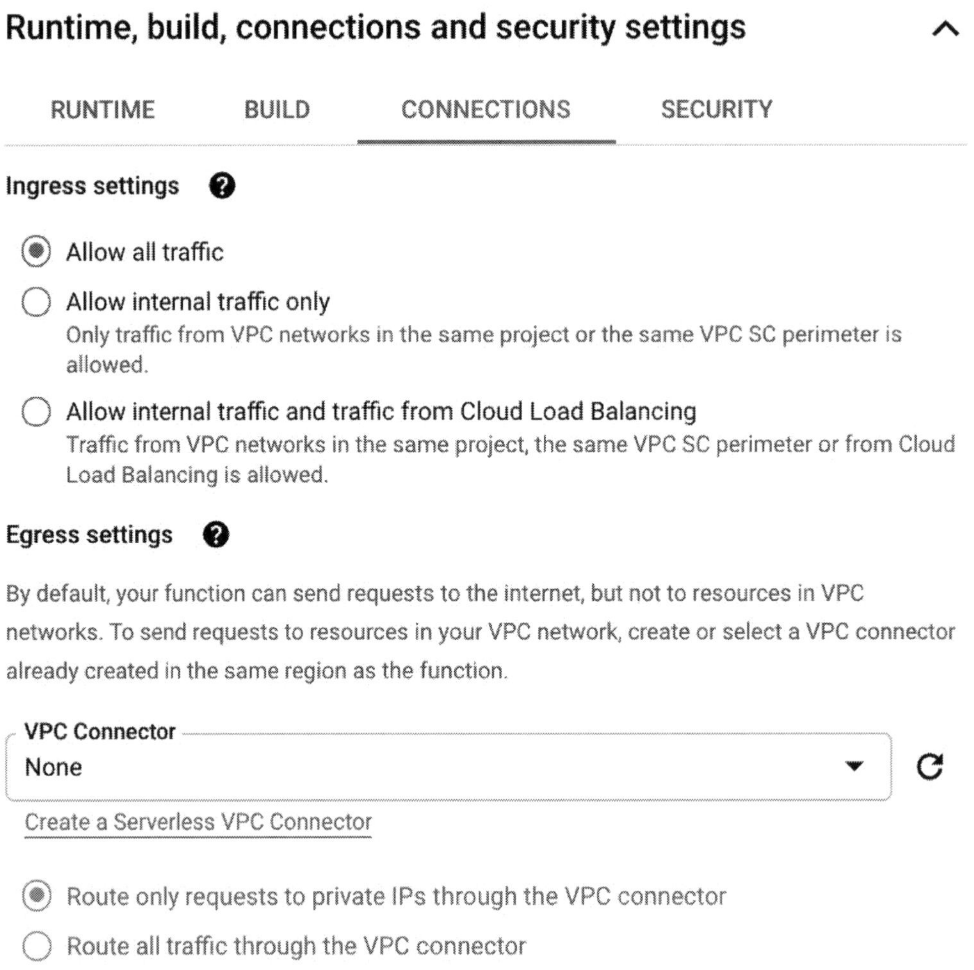

Runtime, build, connections and security settings   ∧

RUNTIME	BUILD	CONNECTIONS	SECURITY

Ingress settings ❷

◉ Allow all traffic

○ Allow internal traffic only
Only traffic from VPC networks in the same project or the same VPC SC perimeter is allowed.

○ Allow internal traffic and traffic from Cloud Load Balancing
Traffic from VPC networks in the same project, the same VPC SC perimeter or from Cloud Load Balancing is allowed.

Egress settings ❷

By default, your function can send requests to the internet, but not to resources in VPC networks. To send requests to resources in your VPC network, create or select a VPC connector already created in the same region as the function.

┌ VPC Connector ──────────────────────────────────────┐
│ None   ▼ │ C
└───┘

Create a Serverless VPC Connector

◉ Route only requests to private IPs through the VPC connector

○ Route all traffic through the VPC connector

Figure 9.9 – CONNECTIONS

8. In the **SECURITY** tab, you can set up a secret that can be consumed by the function:

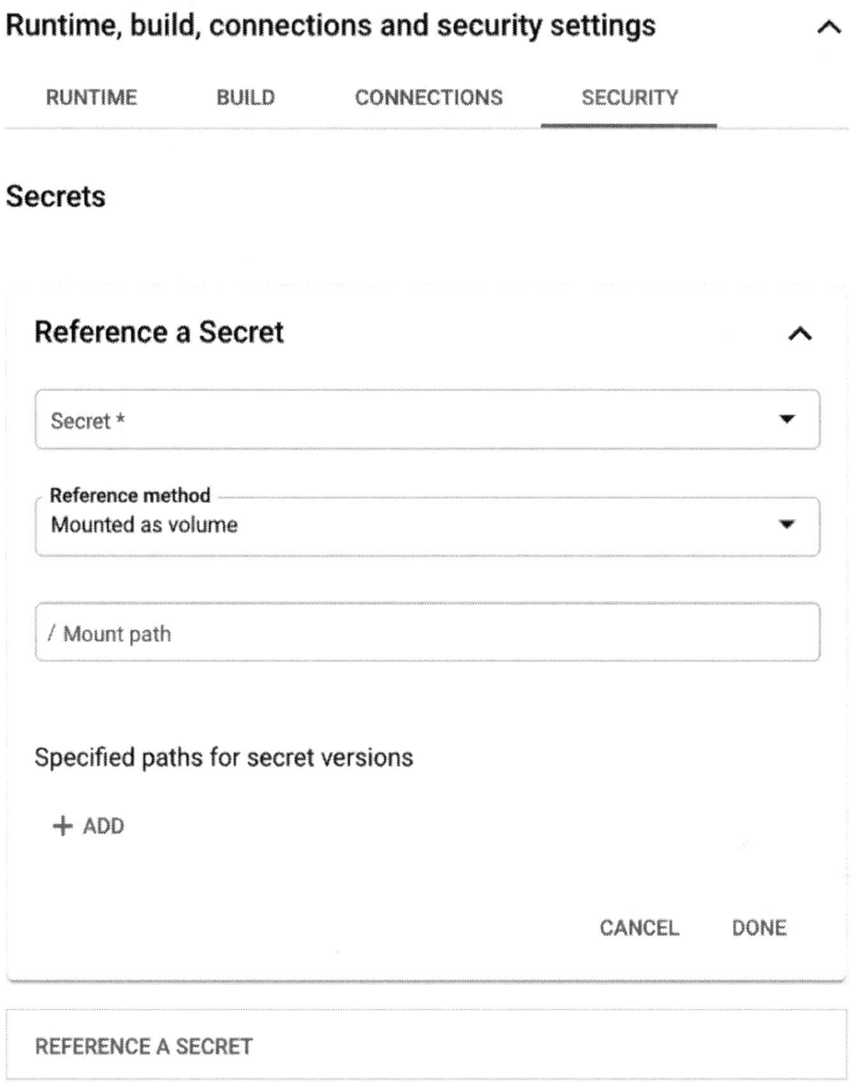

Runtime, build, connections and security settings   ∧

RUNTIME   BUILD   CONNECTIONS   SECURITY

Secrets

Reference a Secret   ∧

Secret *   ▼

Reference method
Mounted as volume   ▼

/ Mount path

Specified paths for secret versions

\+ ADD

CANCEL   DONE

REFERENCE A SECRET

Figure 9.10 – SECURITY

9. Click the **Next** button. Select how you will provide your code. You can either use **Inline Editor**, upload it from your local machine (**ZIP Upload**) or **ZIP from Cloud Storage**, or even use **Cloud Source repository**:

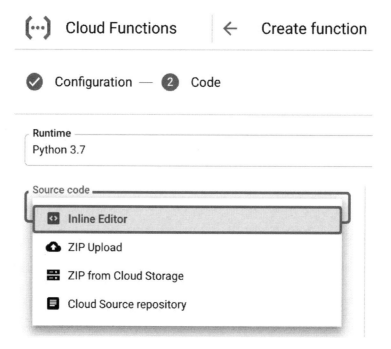

Figure 9.11 – Source code

10. From the **Runtime** dropdown, choose the programming language you will use to write your functions. For this example, we decided to use the inline editor for Python 3.7. Therefore, we need to provide two files: `main.py`, where we will define the function, and `requirements.txt`, with dependencies:

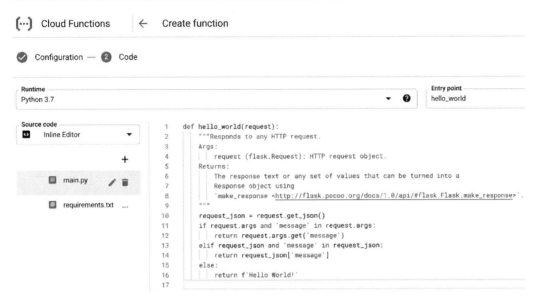

Figure 9.12 – The main.py file

11. In the **Entry point** field, we must define the name of the entry point; for example, `hello_world`:

Figure 9.13 – Entry point

12. Now, we can simply deploy the function by clicking on the **DEPLOY** button:

Figure 9.14 – DEPLOY

13. Once your function has been deployed, you will be able to see it in the **Cloud Functions** list:

Figure 9.15 – Function deployed

Now, your function is ready to execute.

Deploying functions with the gcloud command

Now that we have seen how to deploy the function using the Google Cloud Console, it will be easier to explain the parameters and flags for the gcloud command.

To deploy Cloud Functions, we can use the following command:

```
gcloud deploy cloud functions $FUNCTION_NAME \
--region=$REGION \
--entry-point=$ENTRY_POINT \
--memory=$MEMORY \
--runtime=$RUNTIME \
--service-account=$SERVICE_ACCOUNT\
--source=$SOURCE \
--stage-bucket=$STAGE_BUCKET \
--timeout=$TIMEOUT \
--retry
```

Here, we have the following options:

- $REGION: The region of the function.

- $ENTRY_POINT: The name of the function (as defined in the source code).

- $MEMORY: The limit on the amount of memory that can be used. The allowed values are 128 MB, 256 MB, 512 MB, 1,024 MB, and 2,048 MB.

- $SERVICE_ACCOUNT: The IAM service account associated with the function.

- $SOURCE: The source code's location. Can be either Cloud Storage, a source repository, or the local filesystem.

- $STAGE_BUCKET: If a function is deployed from a local directory, it defines the name of the Cloud Storage bucket that the source code will be stored in.

- $TIMEOUT: The function's execution timeout.

- --retry: Applies only to background functions. If present, it defines that the function should retry running if it's not executed successfully.

Next, let's define our triggers.

Triggers

After defining the necessary parameters, you can define the following triggers, depending on how you want your function to be initiated.

To define an HTTP trigger, use the following command:

```
--trigger-http
```

An endpoint will be assigned to the function.

To trigger a function on changes to a Cloud Storage bucket, use the following command:

```
--trigger-bucket=$TRIGGER_BUCKET
```

Here, we have the following option:

- $TRIGGER_BUCKET: The Google Cloud Storage bucket name. Every change that's made to the files in this bucket will trigger function execution.

To trigger a function on messages that are arriving in a Pub/Sub queue, use the following command:

```
--trigger-topic=$TRIGGER_TOPIC
```

Here, we have the following option:

- $TRIGGER_TOPIC: The name of the Pub/Sub topic. Messages arriving in the queue will trigger this function. The message's content will be passed to the function.

For other sources, such as Firebase, use the following command:

```
--trigger-event=$EVENT_TYPE
--trigger-resource=$RESOURCE
```

Here, we have the following options:

- $EVENT_TYPE: The action that should trigger the function
- $RESOURCE: A resource from which the event occurs

Let's have a look at an example of configuring a trigger from Pub/Sub:

```
gcloud functions deploy hello_pubsub --runtime python37
--trigger-topic mytopic
```

This will deploy a function called `help_pubsub`, where there will be a message arriving in the `mytopic` Pub/Sub topic.

> **Important Note**
>
> You may be interested in looking at some more advanced triggers, such as using Firebase authentication. Check out `https://cloud.google.com/functions/docs/calling/` for examples for every possible trigger.

In the next section, we will review the IAM roles that are available for Cloud Functions.

IAM

Access to Google Cloud Functions is secured with IAM. Let's have a look at a list of predefined roles, along with a short description of each:

- **Cloud Function Admin**: Has the right to create, update, and delete functions. Can set IAM policies and view source code.
- **Cloud Functions Developer**: Has the right to create, update, and delete functions, as well as view source code. Cannot set IAM policies.
- **Cloud Functions Viewer**: Has the right to view functions. Cannot get IAM policies, nor view the source code.
- **Cloud Function Invoker**: Has the right to invoke an HTTP function using its public URL.

Note that for the Cloud Functions Developer role to work, you must also assign the user the IAM Service Account User role on the Cloud Functions runtime service account.

Quotas and limits

Google Cloud Functions come with predefined quotas. These default quotas can be changed via the hamburger menu via **IAM & Admin | Quotas**. From this menu, we can review the current quotas and request an increase to these limits. We recommend that you become familiar with the limits for each service as this can have an impact on your scalability. For Cloud Functions, we should be aware of the following three types of quotas:

- **Resource limits**: Defines the total amount of resources your functions can consume
- **Time limits**: Defines how long things can run for
- **Rate limits**: Defines the rate at which you can call the Cloud Functions API

The list of values is quite extensive. Check out the *Further reading* section if you wish to see a detailed list.

Pricing

The price of Cloud Functions consists of multiple factors. These include the number of **Invocations**, **Compute time**, and network rate (**Networking**). These are shown in the following diagram:

Figure 9.16 – Cloud Functions pricing

Remember that there is a monthly free usage tier that you can play around with without generating any cost. At the time of writing this book, it consists of 2 million invocations, 1 million seconds of compute time, and 5 GB of egress network traffic. Enjoy it!

Summary

In this chapter, we talked about Cloud Functions and several use cases where it works perfectly. We talked about two types of functions, namely HTTP and background functions, and also understood that functions can be executed via a particular event or an HTTP request. Finally, we looked at how a function can be deployed both with the Google Cloud Console and with the gcloud command. For the exam, it is important to understand the use cases of Cloud Functions and when using them could be to our advantage.

With this chapter, we have concluded with the Google Compute options. In the next chapter, we will have a look at networking.

Further reading

For more information regarding the topics that were covered in this chapter, take a look at the following resources:

- **Cloud Functions behind the scenes**: https://cloud.google.com/functions/docs/concepts/exec

- **Cloud Functions and VPC**: https://cloud.google.com/functions/docs/connecting-vpc

- **Local Emulator**: https://cloud.google.com/functions/docs/emulator

- **Cold Starts**: `https://cloud.google.com/functions/docs/bestpractices/tips`

- **Quotas**: `https://cloud.google.com/functions/quotas`

- **Pricing**: `https://cloud.google.com/functions/pricing-summary/`

- **The gcloud command**: `https://cloud.google.com/sdk/gcloud/reference/functions/deploy`

- **Cloud Run**: `https://cloud.google.com/run/`

10
Networking Options in GCP

We already know that compute is the most fundamental cloud feature. But even if we are able to do the computation without connecting to our resources, we get no value. Networking covers many types of connections. We need to be able to connect to the Google Cloud Console and the **Google Cloud Platform** (**GCP**) API. We may want to connect our on-premises data center to GCP either through a **Virtual Private Network** (**VPN**) or through a high bandwidth interconnect. Finally, we might need to have load-balanced connectivity to **Virtual Machine** (**VM**) instances. GCP networking will help us with all of that.

In this chapter, we will go through all the theory that we need to know so that we understand how workloads communicate internally and externally with GCP. We will also have a look at all the basic networking services.

We will cover the following topics:

- Exploring GCP networking
- Understanding Virtual Private Clouds
- Load balancing

- **Network Address Translation** (NAT)
- Hybrid connectivity
- DNS
- Firewall rules
- Private access

Exploring GCP networking

The Google network is something that differs from other clouds. To understand the huge amount of investment Google has made in networking, we should have a look at the following map (https://cloud.google.com/about/locations/#network-tab). This map shows hundreds of thousands of fiber optic cables running between 85 zones and 146 **points of presence** (**PoP**). Keep in mind that this view is from October 2021 and that it is still growing:

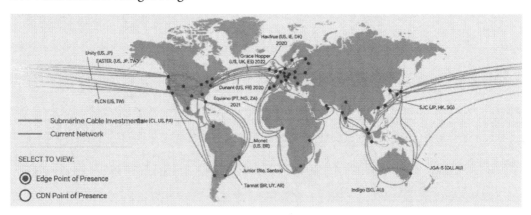

Figure 10.1 – Network .ocations (Source: https://cloud.google.com/about/locations/#network-tab. License: https://creativecommons.org/licenses/by/4.0/legalcode)

Having such a massive network infrastructure allows you to connect GCP at a location very close to your **Internet Service Provider** (**ISP**). In fact, GCP offers two network service tiers, as follows:

- **Premium**: The Premium Tier provides high-performance routing. On top of that, it offers global load balancing and a **Content Delivery Network** (**CDN**) service. It is aimed at use cases where global presence is required and has the best user experience in mind. This tier comes with **Service-Level Agreements** (**SLAs**).

- **Standard**: The Standard Tier is a lower performance network with no SLAs attached. The CDN service is not available and load balancers are regional. It is aimed at use cases where cost is the main deciding factor. The GCP networking that's exposed to the user is based on a **Software-Defined Network (SDN)** called **Andromeda**. This platform is an orchestration point for all network services in GCP. Fortunately, this is abstracted from the user and there is no need to understand how Andromeda works itself.

> **Exam Tip**
> Interestingly enough, networking is not the key topic of the exam; however, there is a GCP Certified Network Engineer exam that will test your GCP networking knowledge thoroughly. It is impossible to understand other GCP services without understanding the basics of networking. Therefore, in this chapter, you will learn about Google's global network and GCP's networking services.

Understanding Virtual Private Clouds

The fundamental concept of the GCP network is a **Virtual Private Cloud (VPC)**, which is also simply called a **network**. As you learned in *Chapter 2, Getting Started with Google Cloud Platform*, GCP can be divided into projects that logically isolate Google Cloud resources. Within a project, you can create multiple VPCs.

By default, up to five networks can be created per project (the quota can be extended by contacting support). Multiple VPCs make it possible to separate GCP resources such as VMs, containers, and so on at a network level. A VPC has a **global** scope, and it can span all GCP regions. To allow connectivity between VMs residing in different VPCs, you have two options: you can create a shared VPC or peer the VPCs. We will have a look at each option in detail later in this chapter.

Furthermore, the VPCs are divided into regional subnetworks, also known as **subnets**, that have associated IP ranges that are used to assign addresses to resources.

When you create a new project, a default network is created for you. Subnets are created for each region and have allocated non-overlapping CIDR blocks.

> **Important Note**
> **Classless Inter-Domain Routing (CIDR)** is an IP addressing schema that replaces the classful A, B, C system. It is based on variable-length subnet masks. In CIDR, the prefixes of the subnet can be defined as an arbitrary number, making the network mask length more flexible. This means that organizations can utilize IP address schemas more efficiently.

Also, default firewall rules are created to allow us to ingress ICMP, RDP, and SSH from anywhere. Any traffic within the default network is also allowed. The following VPC networks screenshot is from the **VPC networks** section of the GCP portal:

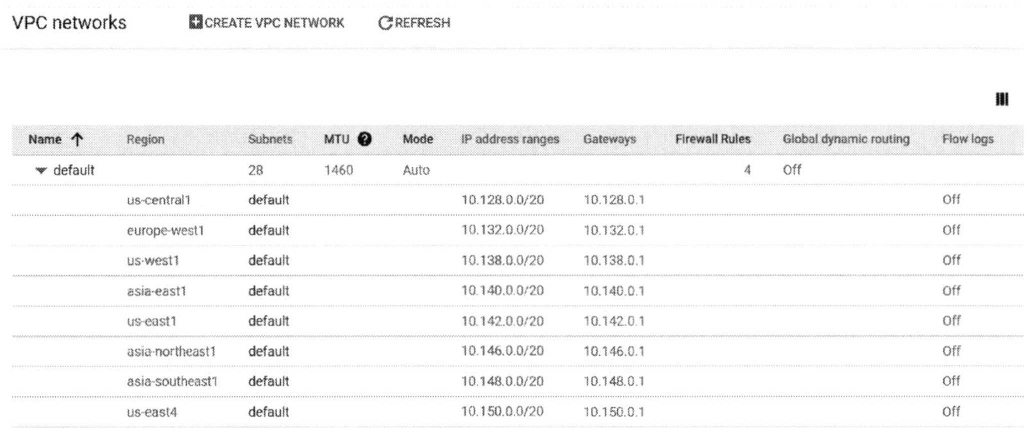

VPC networks   + CREATE VPC NETWORK   ⟳ REFRESH

Name ↑	Region	Subnets	MTU ❓	Mode	IP address ranges	Gateways	Firewall Rules	Global dynamic routing	Flow logs
▼ default		28	1460	Auto			4	Off	
	us-central1	default			10.128.0.0/20	10.128.0.1			Off
	europe-west1	default			10.132.0.0/20	10.132.0.1			Off
	us-west1	default			10.138.0.0/20	10.138.0.1			Off
	asia-east1	default			10.140.0.0/20	10.140.0.1			Off
	us-east1	default			10.142.0.0/20	10.142.0.1			Off
	asia-northeast1	default			10.146.0.0/20	10.146.0.1			Off
	asia-southeast1	default			10.148.0.0/20	10.148.0.1			Off
	us-east4	default			10.150.0.0/20	10.150.0.1			Off

Figure 10.2 – VPC networks

If you create a new VPC, you have two modes to choose from:

- **Auto mode**: Automatically creates one subnet per region with predefined IP ranges with the /20 mask from the 10.128.0.0/9 CIDR block. Each subnet is expandable to the /16 mask.

- **Custom mode**: It does not create subnets automatically and delegates complete control to the user. You decide how many subnets should be created and in which regions, dynamic routing mode (either regional or global) and MTU size. You can also specify if you wish for Flow Logs and private Google access to be enabled.

When creating a subnet, you must define one primary range and can also define up to five secondary ranges (though this is optional):

- **Primary IP address range**: For this range, addresses can be assigned from RFC 1918 CIDR address spaces and should not overlap in the same network. These can be assigned to a VM primary internal IP addresses, VM alias IP addresses, and the IP addresses of internal load balancers. Note that there are always four addresses reserved in this range.

- **Secondary IP address range**: For this range, addresses can be assigned from the RFC 1918 CIDR address space and can only be used for alias IP addresses. There are no addresses reserved in those ranges.

> **Important Note**
> Alias IP addresses can be assigned to a VM if there are multiple services running on it. You can map them to the alias IP that's assigned to that VM. It is also used in the Google Kubernetes Engine Pods. For more information, refer to the *Further reading* section of this chapter.

It is possible to convert an auto mode network in a custom mode network, but not the other way round. Remember to not use IP ranges that overlap between VPCs or on-premises if you will be connecting those networks either through VPC peering or VPNs.

Connectivity

It is time to understand how the connectivity between the VM instances works in VPC. We have already stated that networks are global and that subnets are regional. Now, let's have a look at VM networking. We should note that VMs can have two types of IP addresses:

- **Internal IP address**: Assigned within the VM operating system
- **External IP address (optional)**: Assigned to a VM but not visible in the operating system

The internal IP will be always assigned to the VMs. The external IP can be either created automatically for you or you can create an IP address yourself. If you don't want to use this type of address, you need to set the address to **None** when you request the VM. Note that the external IP address is not visible to the VM itself. Which IP address will be used to initiate a connection depends on the following scenarios:

- VMs with the same network can communicate using the internal IP, even if they are in a different region.
- VMs in a different network can communicate using external IPs, even if they are in the same regions.

Let's have a look at the following diagram:

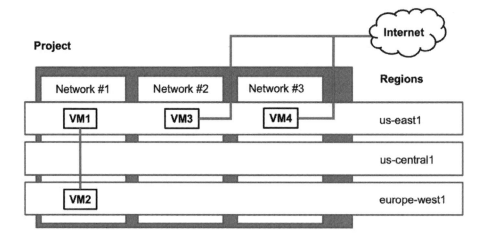

Figure 10.3 – Communication flow

In this scenario, **VM1** and **VM2** can communicate using internal IPs. **VM3** and **VM4** need to communicate using external IPs. Note that the traffic between **VM3** and **VM4** does not need to traverse the internet but is routed through the Google Edge router.

Cost

It is very important to understand how network traffic flows work as it can impact your billing. The general rule of thumb is that the following traffic is free:

- Ingress traffic
- Egress within the same zones using internal IPs
- Egress to a different GCP service within the same region using an external IP address or an internal IP address

> **Important Note**
> This free traffic does not include a number of services that haven't been mentioned in this book yet: Cloud Memorystore for Redis, Cloud Filestore, GKE, and Cloud SQL.

You will be charged for the following traffic:

- Egress between zones within the regions

- Egress between regions

- Internet egress (note: VPN traffic is treated as egress)

> **Important Note**
>
> For current pricing, please refer to `https://cloud.google.com/vpc/network-pricing`.

VPC Flow Logs

VPC Flow Logs allow you to record network flows to and from VM instances. The flows are recorded in 5-second intervals. Note that only the flows are recorded rather than the full network packet capture. The logs contain information regarding the source and destination VPC, and the instance start and end times. VPC Flow Logs are enabled at the subnet level and can be used for real-time security analysis, expense optimization, forensics, or network monitoring.

Cross-VPC connectivity

In some cases, you might need to provide connectivity between two VPCs. As an example, departments in your organization are merging and now they need connectivity to services residing in their respective VPCs.

To do this, there are currently two options:

- Shared VPC

- VPC peering

Let's have a look at both these options.

Shared VPC

In this model, we have a single VPC that is shared between different projects. The project where the shared VPC is created is called the **host project**. The projects that can use the VPC are called **service projects**. In the following diagram, we can see we have two service projects (**Service Project A** and **Service Project B**):

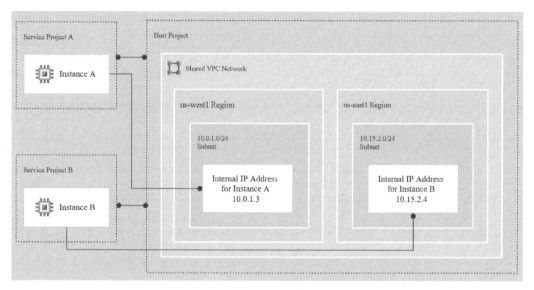

Figure 10.4 – Shared VPC (Source: https://cloud.google.com/vpc/docs/shared-vpc.
License: https://creativecommons.org/licenses/by/4.0/legalcode)

To create a shared project, a shared VPC admin role is required (`roles/compute.xpnAdmin`). The shared VPC admin can further delegate the permissions to the following:

- **Network admin**: Full control over networks, excluding firewall rules and SSL certificates
- **Security admin**: Control over firewall and SSL certificates

Users in the service project can provision VMs that are in a shared VPC. To be able to do so, they need to have a network user role assigned. Note that it can be assigned either at a project or subnet level.

VPC network peering

With VPC peering, you can connect two existing VPCs, regardless of whether they belong to the same project or organization. In this scenario, the administration of each VPC stays separated.

Each site of the peering is set up independently and peering is only established once both sides are configured. The project owner/editor and network admin roles are allowed to perform the configuration. It is important to remember that the CIDR prefixes cannot overlap between peering VPCs' subnets. Once peering has been established, every internal IP becomes accessible across peered networks. Multiple peers can be created per VPC, but transitive peering is not supported. This means that only connectivity between directly peered VPCs is allowed. You cannot bridge the traffic between two VPCs via another VPC. To understand this better, take a look at the following diagram:

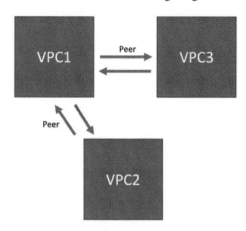

Figure 10.5 – VPC peering

In this scenario, **VPC1** is peered with **VPC2** and **VPC3**. There is no communication between **VPC2** and **VPC3** until peering between those two is configured. Note that peering can also be established with a shared VPC.

Choosing between shared VPC and VPC peering

There are two main factors that will allow you to choose between a shared VPC and VPC peering, as follows:

- If VPCs exist in different organizations, choose VPC peering.
- If you need a shared governance model, choose a shared VPC.

> **Important Note**
> In real-life scenarios, you might have more detailed requirements for your cross-VPC communication, so we encourage you to do further reading on the subject.

Load balancing

Load balancing is one of the most important features of GCP networking. It allows you to distribute a workload between your scaling resources. It works with GCE, GAE, and GKE.

Load balancing in GCP is one of those topics that can be difficult to comprehend at the beginning. There are many types of load balancers, and the Google documentation makes it slightly difficult to map them to what you can see in the console. When we go to the Google Cloud Console (`https://console.cloud.google.com`) and navigate to **NETWORKING | Network Services | Load Balancing**, and finally click on **Create load balancer**, we will be presented with the following configuration options:

Figure 10.6 – Load balancer options

When you look at the documentation, it distinguishes between the following load balancing options. We will look at these in more detail in the *Load balancer types* section:

- HTTP(S) load balancing (external and internal)
- SSL proxy load balancing
- TCP proxy load balancing
- Network load balancing
- Internal TCP/UDP load balancing

You can clearly see that this does not match the GUI options. Note that to configure an internal TCP/UDP load balancer, you need to choose either **TCP Load Balancing** or **UDP Load Balancing** and then choose the **Only between my VMs** option:

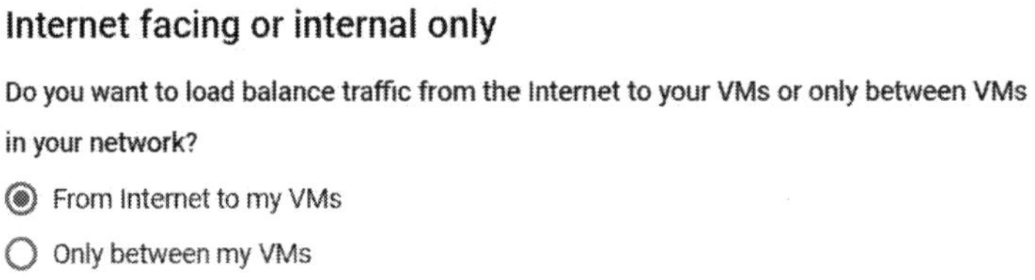

Internet facing or internal only

Do you want to load balance traffic from the Internet to your VMs or only between VMs in your network?

◉ From Internet to my VMs
◯ Only between my VMs

Figure 10.7 – Internal load balancer

Thankfully, the exam does not require you to know how to exactly configure each load balancing method and instead concentrates on the differences between them. However, you will need it when you put your knowledge into practice.

> **Important Note**
>
> Refer to the following how-to guide. All the options are described step by step: `https://cloud.google.com/load-balancing/docs/how-to`.

You might need to perform a couple of labs (use a service such as `Qwiklabs.com`) to feel comfortable with load balancer configuration. For our discussion, we will stick to the documentation definitions as they are also in line with the exam guidelines.

Global versus regional load balancing

Load balancing can be delivered on a regional or global level. This means that for regional load balancing, the balanced resources will reside within one region, whereas in global load balancing, the resources can reside in many regions. The feature that distinguishes GCP from other cloud providers is that some of the load balancing options are available globally. You don't really need to worry about placing the load balancer in the right region:

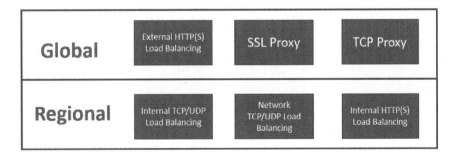

Figure 10.8 – Global versus regional load balancing

As shown in the preceding diagram, the internal and network load balancers are regional only.

External versus internal

We can also distinguish between load balancers in terms of whether they are external or internal. In most scenarios, you would like to expose an application to the internet. This would be the perfect use case for an external load balancer. However, you may also want to load balance traffic in the backend of your application for high availability scenarios. In this case, you would use an internal load balancer, which does not allow connectivity from outside of the VPC.

Proxy versus load balancer

There is an important difference between a proxy and a load balancer in terms of the source IP reaching your backend VM. In the case of a proxy, the source IP is swapped to the proxy's IP as the connection is terminated at the proxy. In the case of a load balancer, the source IP is preserved. Keep this in mind when you configure your firewall rules using the source IP.

Load balancer types

Keeping in mind the key differences we mentioned previously, let's have a look at each load balancing type:

- **HTTP(S) load balancing**: One of the load balancers that requires special attention is the HTTP(S) load balancer. **External HTTP(S)** load balancers are global and allow external connectivity. It supports both IPv4 and IPv6. It can be only used for HTTP and HTTPS traffic but offers a couple of additional features, such as the following:

  - CDN caching

  - Integrates with Cloud Armor

  - Supports URL maps

  - Hosts SSL certificates

  - Supports Cloud Storage

  - Supports session affinity

  - Supports the **Quick UDP Internet Connections** (**QUIC**) protocol

- **Internal HTTP(S)** load balancers are regional and accessible only in the selected region of the VPC. They *do not* support the following:

  - Cloud CDN

  - Cloud Armor

  - Storage buckets

  - Google-managed SSL certificates

  - SSL policies

> **Important Note**
> Session affinity sticks the client session to one VM instance as long as the instance is healthy.

- **SSL proxy load balancing**: The SSL proxy terminates the user's SSL (TLS connections) and is intended for non-HTTP(S) traffic. It is global and allows external connectivity that supports both IPv4 and IPv6. The traffic from the proxy to the machines can use either the TCP or SSL protocols.

- **TCP proxy load balancing**: The TCP proxy terminates non-HTTP traffic that does not require SSL. It is global and allows external connectivity that supports both IPv4 and IPv6.

- **Network TCP/UDP load balancing**: Network load balancing uses a non-proxied load balancer that distributes traffic-based inbound IP protocol data such as addresses, ports, and protocol types. It is regional and external with support for IPv4 only. The network load balancer collects VMs to be load balanced into a logical group called a **target pool**.

- **Internal TCP/UDP load balancing**: Internal load balancing is a non-proxied form of load balancing. It is regional and internal with support for IPv4 only. As an example, it can be used for three-tier applications where web services need to load balance an internal connection to the application tier.

Next, let's compare these different types of load balancers.

Comparison

Now that we have learned about each load balancer, let's have a look at a table that will help us put the most important features into one area:

Load balancer type	Traffic type	Preserve Client IP	Global or regional	Load balancing scheme	Load balancer destination ports	Proxy or pass-through
External HTTP(S)	HTTP or HTTPS	No	Global*	EXTERNAL	HTTP on 80 or 8080; HTTPS on 443	Proxy
Internal HTTP(S)	HTTP or HTTPS	No	Regional	INTERNAL_MANAGED	HTTP on 80 or 8080; HTTPS on 443	Proxy
SSL Proxy	TCP with SSL offload	No	Global*	EXTERNAL	25, 43, 110, 143, 195, 443, 465, 587, 700, 993, 995, 1883, 3389, 5222, 5432, 5671, 5672, 5900, 5901, 6379, 8085, 8099, 9092, 9200, and 9300	Proxy
TCP Proxy	TCP without SSL offload	No	Global*	EXTERNAL	25, 43, 110, 143, 195, 443, 465, 587, 700, 993, 995, 1883, 3389, 5222, 5432, 5671, 5672, 5900, 5901, 6379, 8085, 8099, 9092, 9200, and 9300	Proxy
External Network TCP/UDP	TCP, UDP, ESP, or ICMP (Preview)	Yes	Regional	EXTERNAL	Any	Pass-through
Internal TCP/UDP	TCP or UDP	Yes	Regional backends, regional frontends (global access supported)	INTERNAL	Any	Pass-through

Figure 10.9 – Load balancer comparison (Source: https://cloud.google.com/load-balancing/docs/choosing-load-balancer. License: https://creativecommons.org/licenses/by/4.0/legalcode)

Looking at *Figure 8.9*, think about the use cases for each of the balancers. A good example could be a three-tier application. Which load balancer would you use to balance each tier?

Choosing the right load balancer

To choose the right load balancer, let's have look at the following diagram provided by Google:

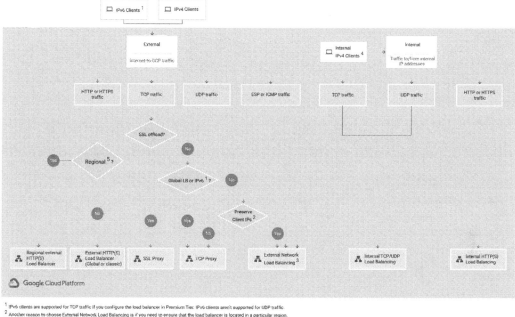

Figure 10.10 – Load Balancer considerations (Source: https://cloud.google.com/load-balancing/docs/choosing-load-balancer. License: https://creativecommons.org/licenses/by/4.0/legalcode)

Let's go through the preceding diagram step by step:

1. First, we need to choose whether we want the load balancer to be accessible externally or internally. For external exposure, we choose what traffic we want to balance.

2. For HTTP and HTTPS traffic, we use an HTTP(S) load balancer.

3. For TCP traffic with an SSL offload, we would go for the SSL proxy. If we don't need the offload SSL but need IPv6 or global scope support, we would choose the TCP proxy.

4. Then, we need to check whether we need to preserve client IPs. If yes, we go for the network load balancer; if not, we stay with the TCP proxy. The network load balancer can be also used for UDP traffic that does not need IPv6 or global scope.

5. For internal load balancing, use an internal TCP/UDP load balancer.

As you can see, choosing the appropriate load balancer can be quite an intimidating task. However, if you follow the preceding flow chart, you should be able to choose the best option.

Now that we have understood how load balancing works, we will look at NAT.

NAT

NAT is a service that translates source and/or destination addresses when traffic passes through a routing device. In the case of GCP, NAT allows us to hide the original IP address of our VM when communicating with external networks. In the case of GCP, it allows VMs with internal addresses to access the internet.

There are currently two options for NAT, as follows:

- NAT gateway
- Cloud NAT

Google recommends using Cloud NAT over NAT gateway. If you are still using NAT gateway, Google recommends that you migrate it to Cloud NAT as it is a managed and self-scaling service.

NAT gateway

Google allows us to provision a VM that will act as a NAT gateway. This way, you are exposing only one VM to the internet. The gateway machine needs to be configured with the `--can-ip-forward` parameter, which allows traffic forwarding. You will also need to create default routes for the subnets that should be using the gateway. As you can see, this solution does not look scalable and introduces the concept of single points of failure.

To eliminate this problem, you can create multiple gateways and put them in managed instance groups. Next, you configure the routing rule to the NAT gateways with the same priority. In this case, GCP uses **equal-cost multi-path** (**ECMP**) to distribute the traffic between the NAT gateways.

> **Important Note**
> To find out how to create highly available NAT gateways, complete the *Building High Availability and High Bandwidth NAT Gateways* lab at `https://www.qwiklabs.com/focuses/612?parent=catalog`.

If this sounds complicated, fortunately, there is an easier solution. Yes, you guessed right! Cloud NAT.

Cloud NAT

Cloud NAT is a regional self-scaling service that's fully managed by Google. It allows VMs to access the internet without the need for an external IP address. It does not, however, allow inbound internet traffic to the VMs. This service is provided by Google SDN, so there are no gateway instances to manage. In fact, under the hood, there are no actual proxy VMs.

In terms of bandwidth, each VM gets exactly the same bandwidth it would get if it had an external IP.

Hybrid connectivity

By hybrid connectivity, we mean connectivity between GCP and your on-premises data center. It is important if you want to connect through a secure channel to GCP and not simply traverse the internet. There are a number of ways this connectivity can be achieved. The method you choose will depend on your reliability, bandwidth, and latency requirements.

Now, let's have a look at some possible hybrid connectivity options, that is, VPN Interconnect and peering.

VPN

Cloud VPN is a regional service that will securely connect your on-premises network to GCP VPC using an IPSec tunnel. All traffic traversing the internet through the tunnel is encrypted. Both the **IKEv1** and **IKEv2** ciphers are supported. The VPN connection requires a Cloud VPN gateway, an on-premises VPN gateway, and two VPN tunnels that are set up from the perspective of each gateway. A connection is established when both tunnels are created. The on-premise gateway can be either a hardware or software device. There is a special requirement that the MTU of your on-premises gateway should not be higher than 1,460 bytes. VPN supports both static and dynamic routes. Dynamic routes are managed by the routers in the VPC network and use **Border Gateway Protocol (BGP)**, while static routes are created manually and support route next hops.

At the time of writing, Google offers two types of VPN gateways: HA VPN and Classic VPN.

HA VPN

An HA VPN, as you may suspect, is a highly available VPN solution that allows us to connect our on-premises network to a GCP VPC in a single region. Due to its highly available nature, an HA VPN offers a 99.99% SLA on service availability. When we create this type of VPN, GCP automatically creates two external IP addresses – one for each of its fixed interfaces and each HA VPN gateway interface supports multiple tunnels. We should note that it *is* possible to configure an HA VPN with only a single active interface and one external IP, however this will not offer the SLA mentioned. There are some requirements that need to be in place to achieve the 99.99% availability SLA. Let's discuss this in more detail:

- Availability is guaranteed only on the Google Cloud side of the connection, which means end-to-end availability will be dependent on the correct configuration of the peer VPN gateway. If the correct configuration is in place, then both sides are Google Cloud gateways and end-to-end 99.99% availability will be guaranteed. In order to achieve high availability when both VPN gateways are in VPC networks, we are required to use two HA VPN gateways, and both must be in the same region.

- Although both gateways must be in the same region, if our VPC network is configured for **global dynamic routing** mode, the routes to the subnets that the gateways share can be in any region. If we configure our VPC network for **regional dynamic routing** mode, then only routes to subnets in the same region will be shared with the peer network. Learned routes are applied only to subnets in the same region as the VPN tunnel.

- HA VPN must also reject Google Cloud IP addresses if they are configured in an external VPN gateway resource; for example, using the external IP address of a VM instance as the external IP address for the external VPN gateway resource. HA VPN must be used on both sides of a Google Cloud network in order to get a fully supported HA VPN topology.

We must also ensure that we configure two VPN tunnels from the perspective of the Cloud VPN gateway. This comes with specific requirements depending on our design:

- **Two peer VPN gateway devices**: This configuration requires that each of the tunnels from each interface on the Cloud VPN gateway must be connected to its own peer gateway.

- **Single peer VPN gateway device with two interfaces**: This configuration requires that each of the tunnels from each interface on the Cloud VPN gateway must be connected to its own interface on the peer gateway.

- **Single peer VPN gateway device with a single interface**: This configuration requires both tunnels from each interface on the Cloud VPN gateway must be connected to the same interface on the peer gateway.

- A peer VPN device must be configured with the appropriate redundancy. The device vendor will specify details of a redundant configuration, and this may differ depending on the vendor.

- If our design requires two peer devices, then each peer device should be connected to a different HA VPN gateway interface. If the peer side is from another provider, for example Azure, then VPN connections should be configured with appropriate redundancy on the Azure side as well.

- Finally, our peer VPN gateway device must support dynamic (BGP) routing.

Classic VPN

Classic VPN gateways have a single interface and a single external IP address. They support tunnels that use BGP or static routing and will provide an SLA of 99.9% service availability. We will not dwell too much on classic VPNs. From Q4 2021, we will no longer be able to use static routing to create classic VPN tunnels that connect to another classic VPN gateway nor connect a classic VPC network to another cloud provider network. You will also be unable to create a new classic VPN tunnel. Google encourages us to migrate our production traffic to an HA VPC.

Interconnects

Interconnect is a layer-2 connectivity method that incurs a monthly cost. You would use it when you need low latency and highly available connectivity between GCP and your on-premise network and you are planning for large data transfers.

It comes in two flavors, as follows:

- **Dedicated Interconnect**: The connection is established with Google Edge. Google charges us on an hourly basis and the cost is dependent on the size of the circuit (that is, 10 Gbps or 100 Gpbs). There is also a charge for egress traffic from a VPC network through a Dedicated Interconnect connection.

- **Partner Interconnect**: The connection is established with the Google partner network. Google also charges us on an hourly basis for VLAN attachments, depending on their capacity and egress traffic from a VPC network through a Partner Interconnect connection is also chargeable.

The connections can be scaled by introducing multiple links. For Dedicated Interconnect, each connection delivers 10-Gbps or 100-Gbps circuits. Up to eight 10-Gbps connections can be created, giving us a maximum of 80 Gbps total per interconnect or 2 x 100-Gbps (200 Gbps) circuits. With Partner Interconnect connections, bandwidth ranges from 50 Mbps to 50 Gbps. Interconnect comes with an uptime SLA of either 99.9% or 99.99%. This depends on your configuration and number of connections.

For more information on pricing scenarios, we recommend that you review `https://cloud.google.com/network-connectivity/docs/interconnect/pricing`.

Peering

Peering is a layer-3 connectivity method. It provides connectivity to services such as Google Workspace, YouTube, and Google APIs with public IP addresses. It allows us to establish connectivity with higher availability and latency. Note that those connections exist outside of GCP. Peering has no maintenance costs and also comes in two flavors, as follows:

- **Direct Peering**
- **Carrier Peering**

Direct Peering offers 10-Gbps connections per link established with a GCP PoP, which are points where the Google network connects with the rest of the internet. Carrier Peering bandwidth depends on the provider. Note that peering provides no SLA.

Choosing the right connectivity method

In general, Google's recommendation is to start the connectivity with Cloud VPN and move to Interconnect if needed. Again, Google comes with a nice flow diagram that will help you make the right choice when it comes to the best connectivity method for your situation:

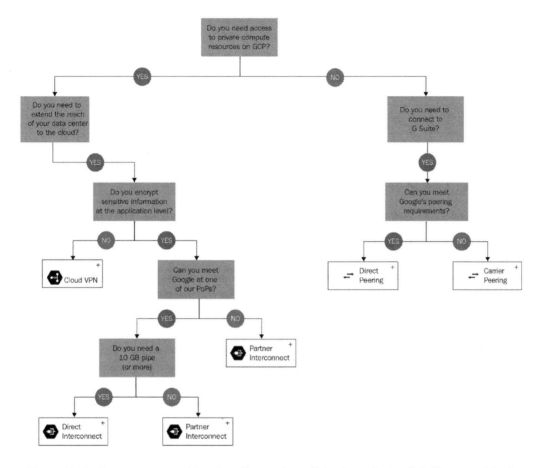

Figure 10.11 – Interconnect considerations (Source: https://cloud.google.com/hybrid-connectivity/)

This concludes the hybrid connectivity section. Again, think twice before you go for Interconnect connectivity. Unless you have high bandwidth and low latency requirements, start with VPN and only move to Interconnect if you aren't getting the desired results. In a later section, we will look at the **Domain Name System (DNS)**, which is critical for proper hostnames and URL resolution.

Network Connectivity Center

Network Connectivity Center is a hub-and-spoke model for managing our network connectivity in Google Cloud. It allows us to connect our on-premises or other public cloud networks together using Google's network as a **Wide Area Network (WAN)** for data transfer. Using this service enables access to the global range and reliability of Google's network.

Using the hub-and-spoke model, sites are connected using various kinds of on-premises connections to connect to each other. For example, Data Center A could be connected to a VPC via a Cloud VPN, and Data Center B could be connected to the same VPC via Dedicated Interconnect. These sites are then connected via a Network Connectivity Center hub associated with the VPC.

DNS

DNS allows the resolution of domain names into IP addresses. There are a couple of concepts you need to understand when it comes to DNS in GCP, such as the following:

- DNS resolution
- Cloud DNS
- **DNS Security (DNSSEC)**

DNS resolution

VPCs come with internal DNS services. Machines get their internal names registered automatically within an internal zone. This allows VMs within the same network to access each other using the internal DNS names. The DNS record follows the life cycle of the VM. It's created when the VM is created and is deleted when the VM is deleted. This means that names are created when the instance is deployed and are removed when the instance is deleted. Note that the records are only created for internal IPs (not external and alias IPs). The resolution only works for VMs within the same VPC.

As you probably know, there are many types of DNS records (A, MX, SRV, CNAME, and so on). The actual records that are created in this case are so-called **A** records. These are records that translate the hostname into an IP address. They are created using the following pattern:

```
<INSTANCE_NAME>.c.<PROJECT_ID>.internal
```

Here, INSTANCE_NAME is the hostname that is auto-generated by GCP and PROJECT_ID is the ID of the project in which the VM is deployed.

When a VM is provisioned, the IP settings are configured automatically. The VMs DNS server setting is also configured and is pointing to its metadata server. For public name resolutions, queries are forwarded to Google's public DNS servers. For external IPs, the records are not registered automatically. They can be registered in external DNS servers or in a DNS zone hosted in the Cloud DNS service.

Cloud DNS

Cloud DNS is a managed service that allows you to host millions of DNS records without the need to manage any servers or software. As this is hosted on the same infrastructure on which Google is hosted, it provides an uptime SLA of 100%.

Cloud DNS allows us to create managed zones that will contain multiple records. To migrate from your current provider, you can export the zones and then import them into Cloud DNS. The records can be managed using APIs and the `gcloud` command.

DNSSEC

DNSSEC is a DNS extension that allows the authentication of domain lookup responses. It protects the requester from the manipulation and poisoning of DNS request responses. In GCP, DNSSEC can be enabled per DNS zone. Note that it also needs to be configured at your domain registrar. On top of that, the requester needs to make sure that the resolver on their workstation validates signatures for DNSSEC-signed domains.

> **Important Note**
>
> For more details, refer to `https://cloud.google.com/dns/docs/dnssec`.

VPC firewall rules

A firewall is either a hardware or software device that filters network traffic that's passing through it. This filtering can be done based on many conditions, such as the source, target IPs, protocol, or ports. It allows you to secure your network from unwanted access.

The firewall rules allow you to control traffic flow to and from VM-based instances. Firewall rules work independently of the VM operating system and are always enforced if put in an enabled state. VPC acts as a distributed firewall that leverages micro-segmentation. This means that the firewall rules are enforced per VM, even if the machines reside in the same network. It should be noted that it does not have the ability to analyze the contents of data packets. The firewall rules are constructed of the following components:

- **Ingress (inbound) firewall rules**:

  - **Priority 0**: `65545` with a default value of `1000`

  - **Action**: `allow` or `deny`

  - **Enforcement**: `enabled` or `disabled`

- **Target (destination)**: All instances in the network, tag, and service account
- **Source**: Address range, subnet, service account, and network tag

- **Protocol and ports**: Allow all or specify a protocol(s) and port(s) **egress (outbound) firewall**:

  - **Priority 0**: `65545` with a default value of `1000`
  - **Action**: `allow` or `deny`
  - **Enforcement**: `enabled` or `disabled`
  - **Target (source)**: All instances in the network, tag, and service account
  - **Destination**: Address range and subnet
  - **Protocol and ports**: Allow all or specify a protocol(s) and port(s)

We can further divide these firewall rules as follows:

- Default firewall rules
- Implied rules
- Always allowed traffic rules
- Always denied rules
- User-defined rules
- GKE firewall rules

The preceding rules are the actual rules that you would define once you have an understanding of what traffic you need for your infrastructure and application to communicate. The **default rules** are defined by Google to provide the basic protection and functionality that are needed so that you can manage your environment. Now, let's have a closer look at each of them.

Default rules

There are a number of `allow` ingress firewall rules with a priority of `65534` that are created for the default network, as follows:

- `default-allow-internal`: Ingress connections for all protocols and ports between instances in the VPC
- `default-allow-ssh`: Ingress connections on TCP port `22` from any source to any instance in the VPC

- `default-allow-rdp`: Ingress connections on TCP port `3389` from any source to any instance in the VPC

- `default-allow-icmp`: Ingress ICMP traffic from any source to any instance in the VPC:

	Name	Type	Targets	Filters	Protocols/ports	Action	Priority	Network ⌃
☐	default-allow-http	Ingress	http-server	IP ranges: 0.0.0.0/0	tcp:80	Allow	1000	default
☐	default-allow-https	Ingress	https-server	IP ranges: 0.0.0.0/0	tcp:443	Allow	1000	default
☐	default-allow-icmp	Ingress	Apply to all	IP ranges: 0.0.0.0/0	icmp	Allow	65534	default
☐	default-allow-internal	Ingress	Apply to all	IP ranges: 10.128.0.0/9	tcp:0-65535 udp:0-65535 icmp	Allow	65534	default
☐	default-allow-rdp	Ingress	Apply to all	IP ranges: 0.0.0.0/0	tcp:3389	Allow	65534	default
☐	default-allow-ssh	Ingress	Apply to all	IP ranges: 0.0.0.0/0	tcp:22	Allow	65534	default

Figure 10.12 – Firewall rules

There are also predefined rules for HTTP and HTTPS traffic. The targets for those rules are tags. You can assign those tags to your VMs to allow this type of traffic from any source.

Implied rules

There are two implied firewall rules with the lowest possible priority (`65535`), as follows:

- **Deny ingress rule** with source `0.0.0.0/0`
- **Allow egress rule** with destination `0.0.0.0/0`

At this point, it may be beneficial just to clarify that `65535` is the lowest possible priority, and `0` is the highest. Also, the IP range `0.0.0.0/0` is equivalent to all IPv4 addresses. The rules cannot be removed but can be overridden by any rules that have higher priority.

Always allowed traffic rules

There are certain types of traffic that are always allowed from a VM, as follows:

- Traffic to a metadata server
- DHCP traffic
- DNS traffic
- NTP traffic

Always denied rules

There are also types of traffic that are always blocked, as follows:

- GRE traffic
- Protocols other than TCP, UDP, ICMP, AH, ESP, SCTP and IPIP
- Egress SMTP traffic on TCP port 25

User-defined rules

Finally, user-defined rules are the rules that you would define to allow communication that's needed for your application that does not match the default, always allowed, or implied rules:

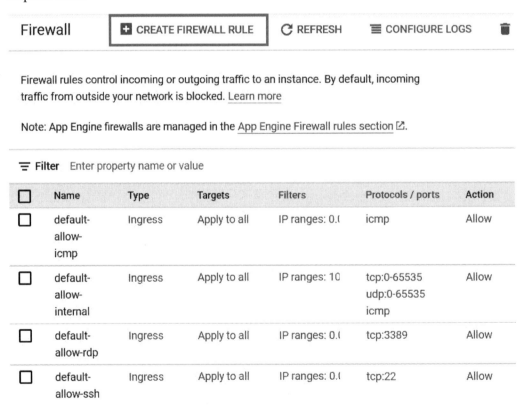

	Name	Type	Targets	Filters	Protocols / ports	Action
☐	default-allow-icmp	Ingress	Apply to all	IP ranges: 0.(	icmp	Allow
☐	default-allow-internal	Ingress	Apply to all	IP ranges: 10	tcp:0-65535 udp:0-65535 icmp	Allow
☐	default-allow-rdp	Ingress	Apply to all	IP ranges: 0.(	tcp:3389	Allow
☐	default-allow-ssh	Ingress	Apply to all	IP ranges: 0.(	tcp:22	Allow

Figure 10.13 – Create firewall rule

These rules can be created by going to the **Navigation** menu, **VPC network | Firewall**, and clicking **CREATE FIREWALL RULE**.

Firewall logging

Firewall logging allows you to verify whether your firewall rules are functioning correctly. It can be enabled for new and existing firewall rules. The logs are injected into the Google Cloud operations suite (formerly Stackdriver).

Hierarchical firewall policies

Hierarchical firewall policies allow us to create and enforce consistent policies across our organization. They can be assigned to our organization as a whole or to individual folders. Like VPC firewall rules, hierarchical firewall policies contain rules that can deny or allow connections but can additionally delegate evaluation to lower-level policies or VPC network firewall rules with the `goto_next` action. This allows organization-wide admins to manage firewall rules in one place.

We should note that creating a policy at organization or folder node level does not automatically apply a rule to the node – the policy needs to be associated with nodes in the organization and a single policy can be associated with multiple nodes. Policies are containers for firewall rules and when we associate a policy with an organization or folder, the rules are applied immediately. We can swap policies for a node, which atomically swaps all the firewall rules applied to a VM instance under that node. Rules associated with the organization node are evaluated first and any folders and VPC networks in the organization will inherit this policy. If policies are applied to a folder, then all folders and VPC networks in this folder will inherit its associated policy. Hierarchical policies cannot be associated with projects. The levels of hierarchy at which firewall rules can be applied are shown in the following diagram:

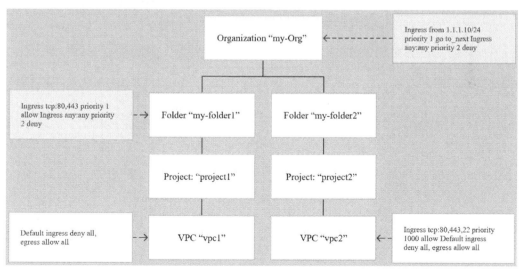

Figure 10.14 – Hierarchical policy inheritance (Source: https://cloud.google.com/vpc/docs/firewall-policies)

Hierarchical firewall policy rules must have a specified priority that will be unique to each policy. This is unlike VPC firewall rules, which can have multiple rules that have the same priority. Additionally, firewall policy rules do not have names, but rather the policy itself has an ID and a name, and each rule has a unique priority number. Rules are then evaluated in priority order starting with the highest priority rule, which is represented by the lowest number. For example, a rule with priority number 100 would override a rule with 200.

To create a firewall policy from Google Cloud Shell, use the following code and replace your organization ID and folder ID:

```
gcloud compute firewall-policies create \        [--organization
ORG_ID] | --folder FOLDER_ID] \        --short-name SHORT_NAME
```

We would then add the rule the policy by using the following. We have used an example org ID:

```
gcloud compute firewall-policies rules create 1000
\       --action=allow \        --description="allow-scan-probe"
\       --layer4-configs=tcp:123 \       --firewall-policy=example-
firewall-policy \       --organization=123456789\       --src-ip-
ranges=10.100.0.1/32
```

Finally, associate the firewall policy with the organization node. We have used an example org ID:

```
gcloud compute firewall-policies associations create
\       --firewall-policy=example-firewall-policy \
--organization=123456789
```

In the next section, we will look at private access options.

Private access options

Google provides various options to let VM instances reach supported APIs and services without the need for an external IP address. Depending on your use case you can configure one or all of the options available and they operate independently of each other. As a high-level overview, here are the reasons for using each option:

- **Private Service Connect for Google APIs**: Used to connect to Google APIs and services using an endpoint in our VPC network if on-premises and GCP resources don't require an external IP address.

- **Private Google Access**: Used to connect to Google APIs and services without giving our GCP resources external IP addresses.

- **Private Google Access for on-premises hosts**: Used to connect to Google APIs and services through a VPC network if your on-premises host does not require an external IP address.

- **Private Service Connect for services**: Used to connect to supported services in another VPC network without assigning an external IP address to our GCP resources.

- **Private Services Access**: Used to connect to specific Google or third-party services without assigning our GPC or third-party resources an external IP address.

- **Serverless VPC Access**: This is used to connect directly from a serverless Google service to resources in a VPC network using internal IP addresses.

There are also DNS considerations when using private access, so it is important to look further into each option and understand its impact. As an example, if we wanted to use the **Private Google Access for on-premises** host option, our on-premises network must have DNS zones and records configured so that Google domain names resolve to the set of IP address for either `private.googleapis.com` or `restricted.googleapis.com`.

> **Important Note**
>
> For more details, check out the Google documentation at `https://cloud.google.com/vpc/docs/private-access-options`.

Summary

In this chapter, we have gone through basic networking concepts in GCP. We have learned about VPC, load balancing, firewall, DNS, and hybrid connectivity. Make sure that you understand how you connect VMs to the GCP network, as well as how to protect and load balance them. Now that you have an understanding of different ways to connect to your on-premises data center, we suggest that you get some hands-on experience. Set up your first VPC, create firewall rules, and deploy and manage a VM instance group with a load balancer of your choice. If you have any problems doing this, return to this book and check this chapter or *Chapter 4, Working with Google Compute Engine*.

In *Chapter 11, Exploring Storage and Database Options in GCP – Part 1*, and *Chapter 12, Exploring Storage and Database Options in GCP – Part 2*, we will see how we can store data. This is essential for stateful workloads.

Further reading

The overview of networking services that we provided in this chapter should be good enough for the exam. If you still feel like you need a deeper knowledge of GCP networking, check out the following links:

- **VPC**: https://cloud.google.com/vpc/docs/
- **Firewalls**: https://cloud.google.com/vpc/docs/firewalls
- **Load balancing**: https://cloud.google.com/load-balancing/docs/
- **Interconnects**: https://cloud.google.com/interconnect/docs/
- **VPN**: https://cloud.google.com/vpn/docs/
- **DNS**: https://cloud.google.com/dns/docs/
- **NAT**: https://cloud.google.com/nat/docs/
- **Alias IP addresses**: https://cloud.google.com/vpc/docs/alias-ip

11
Exploring Storage and Database Options in GCP – Part 1

In the previous two chapters, we learned about important topics regarding networking and compute services. Now, we will continue by looking at another fundamental offering from GCP – **storage**. Every application needs to store data, but not all data is the same. Data can be structured, unstructured, relational, or transactional, and GCP offers services to meet these requirements. Your application may even need to use multiple storage services to achieve your needs.

In this chapter, we will look at the different types of storage offered by Google and explain what should be considered before selecting a particular service. Google provides numerous storage options and covering all of these in a single chapter may make the facts difficult for you to digest. Therefore, we have divided this chapter into two parts.

In this part, we will consider which storage option we should choose and look into the following topics:

- Choosing the right storage option
- Understanding Cloud Storage
- Understanding Cloud Firestore
- Understanding Cloud SQL

Although BigQuery can be considered a storage option, we will look at that product in *Chapter 13, Analyzing Big Data Options.*

Let's start this chapter by looking at when we should select a specific storage service. After that, we will look at each service individually while concentrating on exam topics.

Choosing the right storage option

As we mentioned at the beginning of this chapter, various storage services are offered by Google. You must understand what the correct storage to use is for your requirements. Google provides a nice flow chart that we can walk through. It is easy to follow and shows how requirements will dictate which storage option to select. Take some time to look at the following decision tree. This diagram works through some key questions to make sure that the storage service we select will fulfill our requirements:

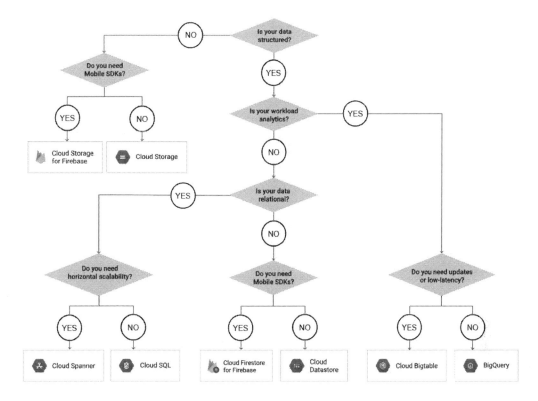

Figure 11.1 – Storage options

With the preceding diagram in mind, let's walk through an example:

1. First, we need to understand whether our data will be structured. Different services will be recommended, depending on this answer.

2. If our data is structured, then we should check whether our workload is for analytics.

3. If our data is not for analytics, then we should check whether our data is relational.

4. If our data is relational, then we need to know whether we require horizontal scaling.

5. If we do, then we should select Cloud Spanner. If not, we should select Cloud SQL.

As shown in the preceding diagram, there are various outcomes, depending on our requirements. There are a lot of storage services offered by GCP, but if we follow this flow chart, we should be able to choose the best option.

Additionally, Google offers the following information, which may help you understand the product you require:

CATEGORY	PRODUCT	GOOD FOR
Object Storage	Cloud Storage	Streaming videos. Image and web asset libraries. Data lakes.
Block Storage	Persistent disk	Disks for virtual machines. Shared read-only data across multiple VMs. Creating durable backups of running VMs. Storage for databases.
Block Storage	Local SSD	Flash-optimized databases. Hot caching layer for analytics. Application scratch disk.
Archival Storage	Cloud Storage	Data analytics. Rendering and media processing. Application migrations. Web content management.
Data Transfer	Data Transfer Service	Collecting research data. Moving ML/AI training datasets. Migrating from S3 to Google Cloud.
Data Transfer	Transfer Appliance	Transfer data for archival, migrations, or analytics. Capturing sensor data for ML or analytics. Moving data from bandwidth-constrained locations.

> **Exam Tip**
>
> Understanding these options is critical. You may be presented with a scenario where relational databases are needed over non-relational databases, or where you need to select an option that is suitable for structured data. You also need to understand the limits of storage; as an example, let's say you are told that you need to assess a service that offers a NoSQL database and can scale to terabytes of data. After reading this chapter, you should be able to map this scenario to a service.

In the next section, we will discuss data consistency.

Data consistency

Data consistency refers to how the storage service handles transactions and how data is written to a database. As you go through this chapter, make sure that you review the consistency of each service, as this is one of the main design factors when choosing a product or service.

We will also take this chance to explain ACID. This is a key term in data consistency, and we will refer to this several times throughout this chapter.

ACID is an acronym for the following attributes:

- **Atomicity**: This is where a transaction involves two or more pieces of information, and then all the pieces are committed or none at all are. For example, when performing a bank transfer, the debit and credit of the funds would be treated as a single transaction. If either the debit or credit fails, then both will fail.

- **Consistency**: If the aforementioned failure occurs, then all the data would be returned to the state before the transaction began.

- **Isolation**: The bank transfer would be isolated from any other transaction. In our example, this means that we would not debit from the bank until the transfer was complete.

- **Durability**: Even in the event of failure, the data would be available in its correct state.

> **Exam Tip**
>
> It's also important for you to be able to identify storage services that support structured data, low latency, or horizontal scaling. Likewise, you should be able to identify storage services that offer strong consistency or support ACID properties.

Now, let's look more closely at each of these services. We will begin with Cloud Storage.

Understanding Cloud Storage

Google Cloud Storage is a service for storing objects in Google Cloud. It is fully managed and can scale dynamically. Objects are referred to as immutable pieces of data consisting of a file of any format. Some use cases are video transcoding, video streaming, static web pages, and backups. It is designed to provide secure and durable storage while also offering optimal pricing and performance for your requirements through different storage classes.

Cloud Storage uses the concept of buckets; you may be familiar with this term if you have used AWS S3 storage. A bucket is a basic container where your data will reside and is attached to a GCP project, such as other GCP services. Each bucket name is globally unique and once created, you cannot change it. There is no minimum or maximum storage size, and we only pay for what we use. Access to our buckets can be controlled in several ways. We will learn more about security in *Chapter 15, Security and Compliance*, but as an overview, we have the following main methods:

- **Cloud Identity and Access Management (IAM)**: We will speak about IAM in more detail in *Chapter 15, Security and Compliance*. IAM will grant access to buckets and the objects inside them. This gives us a centralized way to manage permissions rather than providing fine-grained control over individual objects. IAM policies are used throughout GCP, and permissions are applied to all the objects in a bucket.

- **Access Control Lists (ACLs)**: ACLs are only used by Cloud Storage. This allows us to grant read or write access for individual objects. It is not recommended that you use this method, but there may be occasions when it is required. For example, you may wish to customize access to individual objects inside a bucket.

- **Signed URLs**: This gives time-limited read or write access to an object inside your bucket through a dedicated URL. Anyone who receives this URL can access the object for the time that was specified when the URL was generated.

We will also mention encryption in *Chapter 15, Security and Compliance*. By default, Cloud Storage will always encrypt your data on the server side before it is written to disk. There are three options available for server-side encryption:

- **Google-Managed Encryption Keys**: This is where Cloud Storage will manage encryption keys on behalf of the customer, with no need for further setup.

- **Customer-Supplied Encryption Keys (CSEKs)**: This is where the customer creates and manages their encryption keys.

- **Customer-Managed Encryption Keys (CMEKs)**: This is where the customer generates and manages their encryption keys using GCP's **Key Management Service (KMS)**.

There is also the **client-side encryption** option, where encryption occurs before data is sent to Cloud Storage and additional encryption takes place at the server side.

Bucket locations

Bucket locations allow us to specificity a location for storing our data. There are the following different location types:

- **Region**: This is a specific location, such as London.
- **Dual-region**: Dual-region is a pair of regions such as Iowa and South Carolina. Dual regions are geo-redundant, meaning that data is stored in at least two separate geographic places and will be separated by 100 miles, ensuring maximum availability for our data. Geo-redundancy occurs asynchronously.
- **Multi-regions**: A multi-region is a large area such as the EU and will contain two or more geographic places. Multi-regions are also geo-redundant. Of course, storing data in multiple locations will come at an increased cost.

Bucket locations are permanent, so some consideration should be taken before you select your preferred option. Data should be stored in a location that is convenient for your business users. For example, if you wish to optimize latency and network bandwidth for users in the same region, then region-based locations are ideal. However, if you also have additional requirements for higher availability, then consider dual-region to take advantage of this geo-redundancy.

Storage classes

We previously mentioned storage classes, and we should make it clear that it's vital to understand the different offerings to be successful in this exam. Let's take a look at these in more detail:

- **Standard**: This is the default setting for a new storage bucket. There is no minimum storage, and this is the best option for frequently accessed data and/or data that's only stored for small periods. When used alongside a multi- or dual region, the availability SLA for standard storage is 99.95%. When used in a single region, the availability SLA is 99.9%. Google also publishes what is known as typical monthly availability and for multi-region and dual-region this is > 99.99% while for regional, it is 99.99%.
- **Nearline**: Use the Nearline storage class for data that will be read or modified no more than once per month – for example, backup data. Nearline offers a slightly lower SLA than standard but this is a trade-off for lower at rest storage costs. When used alongside a multi- or dual region, the availability SLA for Nearline storage is 99.9% (the typical monthly availability is 99.95%). When used in a single region, then the availability SLA is 99.0% (the typical monthly availability is 99.9%). Nearline has very low cost-per-GB storage, but it does come with a retrieval cost. There is a 30-day minimum storage duration.

- **Coldline**: Use the Coldline storage class for data that is accessed no more than once per quarter; for example, for disaster recovery. It is a very low cost and highly durable service. When used alongside a multi- or dual region, the availability SLA for Coldline storage is 99.9% (the typical monthly availability is 99.95%). When used in a single region, then the availability SLA is 99.0% (the typical monthly availability is 99.9%). This class offers lower cost-per-GB storage than Nearline but comes with a higher retrieval cost. There is a 90-day minimum storage duration.

- **Archive**: Use Archive storage for long-term preservation of data that won't be accessed more than once a year. This is the lowest cost storage available and unlike many other cloud storage vendors, the data will be available in milliseconds rather than hours or days. There is a 365-day minimum storage duration. When used alongside a multi- or dual region, the typical monthly availability for archive storage is 99.95% with an SLA of 99.9%. When used in a single region, then the typical monthly availability is 99.9% with an SLA of 99.0%.

These different classes are summarized in the following diagram. Please note that the SLA and typical monthly availability may show different percentage values:

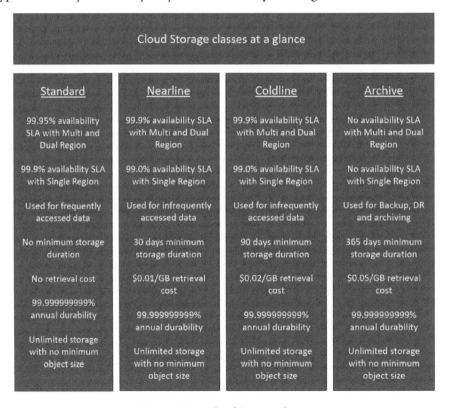

Figure 11.2 – Cloud Storage classes

You can edit Cloud Storage buckets to move between these storage classes. Note that there are additional storage classes that cannot be set using Cloud Console:

- **Multi-region storage**: This is equivalent to standard storage but can only be used for objects stored in multi-regions or dual regions.

- **Regional storage**: This is equivalent to standard storage but can only be used for objects stored in regions.

- **Durable Reduced Availability (DRA) storage**: This can be compared to standard storage but the DRA storage has a higher pricing for operations and a lower performance, especially in terms of availability, where it has an SLA of 99%.

Buckets get a default storage class upon their creation, and any objects inside it will inherit this class unless otherwise specified. We can change the default storage class of our bucket, but it will only apply to new objects after the change; the existing objects will remain in the original class. We can also effectively move data between buckets by using the Cloud Storage Transfer Service. However, note that moving data between locations incurs network usage costs. Additionally, we should be aware of extra costs that may be applicable. As Nearline, Coldline, and Archive storage are used to store infrequently accessed data, Google may apply retrieval or early deletion fees. A retrieval cost will be applied when we copy, read, or rewrite data or metadata that is stored in one of these storage classes.

Data consistency

Cloud Storage will provide both strong consistency and eventual consistency in certain circumstances.

Strong consistency can be expected in the following circumstances:

- When uploading data to Cloud Storage, meaning the data will always be available to read after a write or update operation.

- Once we delete the data successfully, the files will be instantly unavailable.

Eventual consistency can be expected in the following circumstance:

- When access to resources is revoked. It will typically take around 1 minute for access to be revoked, though in some cases, this may take even longer.

Cloud Storage FUSE

Cloud Storage cannot be mounted to a Google Compute Engine instance. However, if this is something that you would like to explore, GCP currently offers third-party integration using an open source FUSE adapter that will allow you to mount a storage bucket as a filesystem on Linux. This is available free of charge and is not officially supported; however, normal Cloud Storage charges are applicable.

Creating and using a bucket

Now that we have a good understanding of storage classes, let's take a look at how to create a bucket. We will also learn how to copy files into our bucket and change the storage policy of an object.

We have two options to create a bucket – either through a console or using gsutil. We will learn more about gsutil in *Chapter 16, Google Cloud Management Options*, but for the context of this chapter, it's enough for you to know that it is a dedicated command-line tool that will make RESTful API calls to your Cloud Storage service. Let's look at how to create a bucket from the console by going through the following steps:

1. Browse to **STORAGE** from the navigation menu. Then, select **Cloud Storage | Browser**:

Figure 11.3 – Navigating to Cloud Storage

2. Click on **CREATE BUCKET**, as shown in the following screenshot:

Store and retrieve your data

Get started by creating a bucket — a container where you can organize and control access to your data and files in Cloud Storage.

CREATE BUCKET   TAKE QUICKSTART

Figure 11.4 – CREATE BUCKET

3. Give the bucket a name. Remember that this must be globally unique:

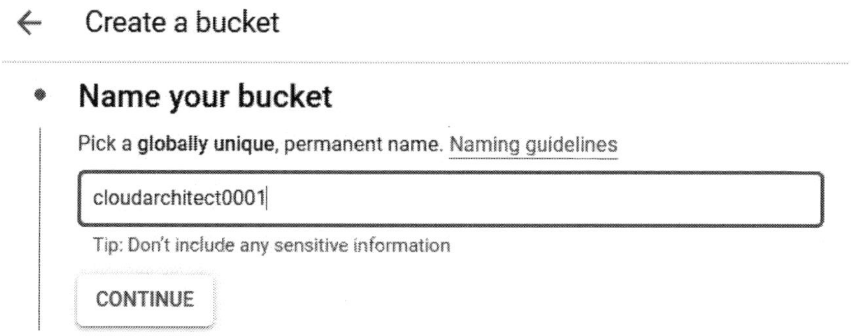

← Create a bucket

● Name your bucket

Pick a **globally unique**, permanent name. Naming guidelines

    cloudarchitect0001

Tip: Don't include any sensitive information

CONTINUE

Figure 11.5 – Name your bucket

4. Select the location for your bucket:

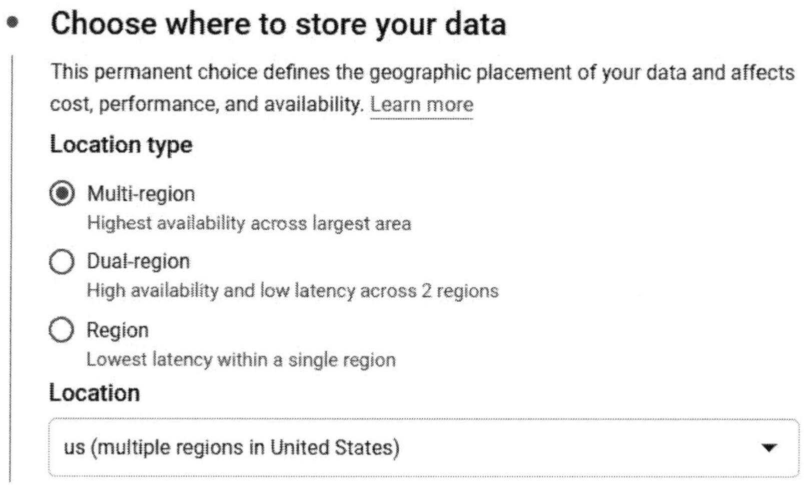

● Choose where to store your data

This permanent choice defines the geographic placement of your data and affects cost, performance, and availability. Learn more

Location type

◉ Multi-region
    Highest availability across largest area

○ Dual-region
    High availability and low latency across 2 regions

○ Region
    Lowest latency within a single region

Location

    us (multiple regions in United States)   ▼

Figure 11.6 – Location type

5. Select a storage class that fits your needs. Select a location. You will notice that the location will either be a zone or a region, depending on whether your selection is **Multi-region** or **Region**. Bear in mind that your selection will have an impact on the cost:

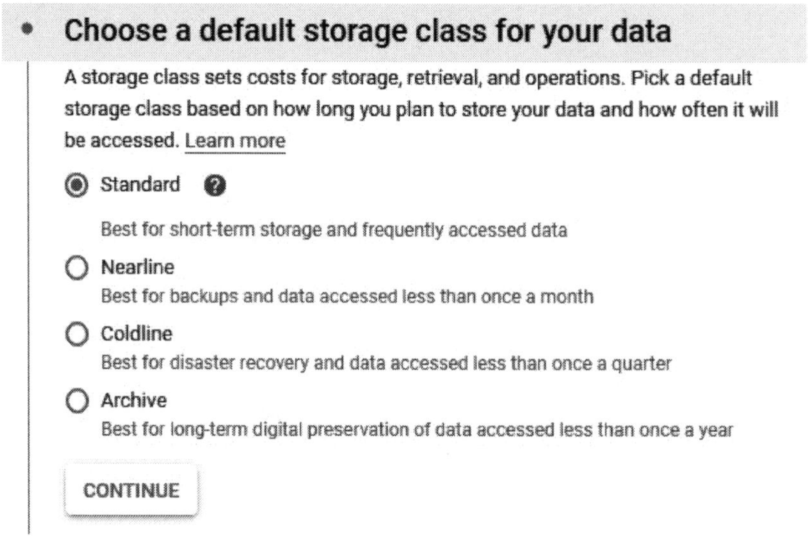

Figure 11.7 – Storage class options

6. Select either an ACL or IAM access control model:

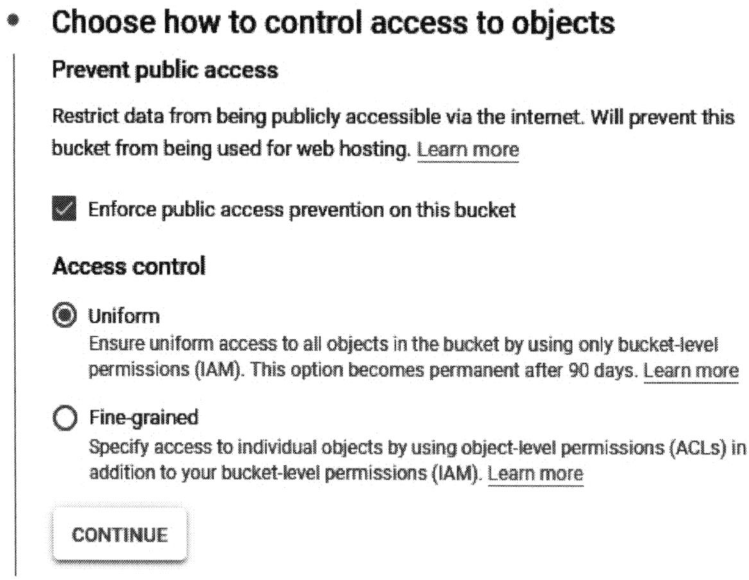

Figure 11.8 – Access control options

7. We can also set more advanced settings that will show the encryption and retention policies. By default, Google will manage our keys. A retention policy can also be set. This will offer a minimum duration in which objects in the bucket will be protected from deletion:

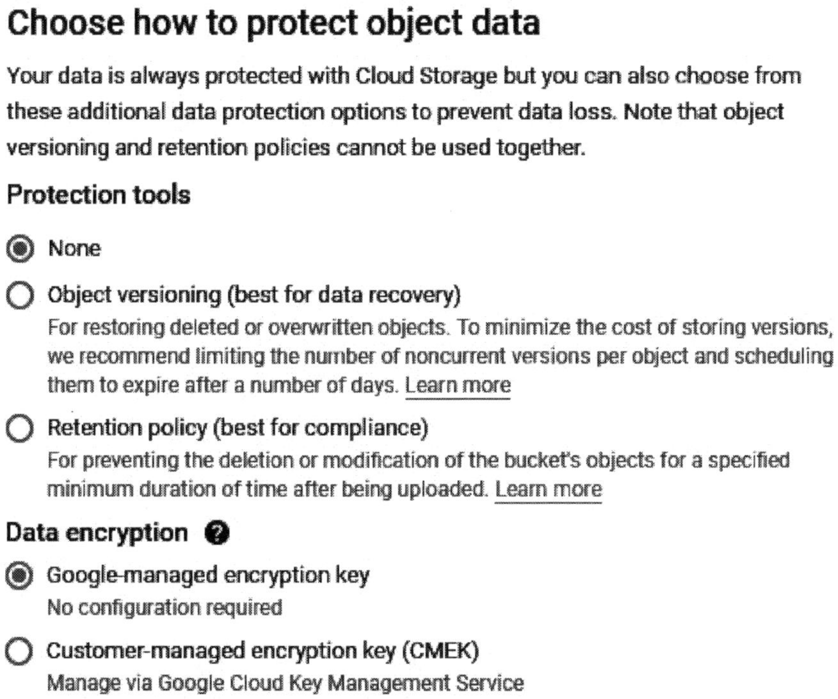

Choose how to protect object data

Your data is always protected with Cloud Storage but you can also choose from these additional data protection options to prevent data loss. Note that object versioning and retention policies cannot be used together.

Protection tools

◉ None

◯ Object versioning (best for data recovery)
For restoring deleted or overwritten objects. To minimize the cost of storing versions, we recommend limiting the number of noncurrent versions per object and scheduling them to expire after a number of days. Learn more

◯ Retention policy (best for compliance)
For preventing the deletion or modification of the bucket's objects for a specified minimum duration of time after being uploaded. Learn more

Data encryption ❷

◉ Google-managed encryption key
No configuration required

◯ Customer-managed encryption key (CMEK)
Manage via Google Cloud Key Management Service

Figure 11.9 – Optional advanced settings

8. Click **Create** and we are done.

As you can see, this is a pretty simple process. Let's make it even simpler by creating it from our dedicated command-line tool, gsutil, which we can access from Cloud Shell:

1. In Cloud Shell, we can run the following command:

```
gsutil mb -c <storage class> -l <location> gs://<bucket
name>
```

Let's look at the code in a little more detail:

- <storage class> is the class we would like to apply to our bucket.
- <location> is the region we want to create our bucket in.
- <bucket name> is the unique name we want to assign to our bucket.

2. Let's create a new bucket called `cloudarchitect001` in the `us-east1` region and apply the `regional` storage class:

```
gsutil mb -c regional -l us-east1 gs://cloudarchitect001
```

3. Now, we have a bucket with no data inside. Let's use `gsutil` and move some objects into our bucket with the following syntax:

```
gsutil cp <filename> gs://<bucketname>
```

Here, `<filename>` is the name of the file you wish to copy, while `<bucketname>` is the destination bucket.

4. In this example, let's copy over a file called `conf.yaml` to our new bucket, called `cloudarchitect001`:

```
gsutil cp conf.yaml gs://cloudarchitect001
```

5. Let's look at how to change the storage class of a file. The storage class of an individual object can only be put inside a bucket using `gsutil`. We should use the following syntax:

```
gsutil rewrite -s <storage class> gs://<bucket
name>/<file name>
```

6. Let's change our file, `conf.yaml`, so that it uses Coldline storage:

```
gsutil rewrite -s coldline gs://cloudarchitect001/conf.
yaml
```

Great! So, we now know how to manage our buckets. In the next section, we will take a look at some key features of Cloud Storage.

Versioning and life cycle management

Now, let's take a look at versioning and life cycle management. These are important features offered by Cloud Storage and are of particular significance for the exam.

> **Exam Tip**
> Cloud Storage offers an array of features. To succeed in the exam, you must understand the versioning and life cycle management features of Cloud Storage. Like the storage classes, you should review these and make sure you are comfortable before moving on to future sections of this chapter.

Versioning

Versioning can be enabled to retrieve objects that we have deleted or overwritten. Note that, at this point, this will increase storage costs, but this may be worth it for you to be able to roll back to previous versions of important files. The additional costs come from the archived versions of each object that is created each time we overwrite or delete the live version of an object. The archived version of the file will retain the original name but will also be appended by a generation number to identify it. Let's go through the process of versioning:

1. To enable versioning, we should use the `gsutil` command:

```
gsutil versioning set on gs://<bucket name>
```

Here, `<bucket name>` is the bucket that we want to enable versioning on.

Let's look at the following screenshot, which shows how this looks. In this example, we are enabling versioning on our `cloudarchitect` bucket and then confirming that versioning is indeed enabled:

```
google3339831_student@cloudshell:~ (qwiklabs-gcp-e7f0f69cdda1b280)$ gsutil versioning set on gs://cloudarchitect
Enabling versioning for gs://cloudarchitect/...
google3339831_student@cloudshell:~ (qwiklabs-gcp-e7f0f69cdda1b280)$ gsutil versioning get gs://cloudarchitect
gs://cloudarchitect: Enabled
```

Figure 11.10 – Set versioning

2. Now, let's copy a file called `vm.yaml` to our bucket. We can use the `-v` switch to version it:

```
google3339831_student@cloudshell:~ (qwiklabs-gcp-e7f0f69cdda1b280)$ gsutil cp -v vm.yaml gs://cloudarchitect
Copying file://vm.yaml [Content-Type=application/octet-stream]...
Created: gs://cloudarchitect/vm.yaml#1557763393469362

Operation completed over 1 objects/492.0 B.
```

Figure 11.11 – Copying the file

3. If we modify this file, we can list the available versions by running a command with the following syntax:

```
gsutil ls -a gs://<bucket name>/<filename>
```

Let's run this command on our file, named `vm.yaml`, which resides in our `cloudarchitect` bucket. We can see that we have several archived versions available:

```
google3339831_student@cloudshell:~ (qwiklabs-gcp-e7f0f69cdda1b280)$ gsutil ls -a gs://cloudarchitect/vm.yaml
gs://cloudarchitect/vm.yaml#1557760768160333
gs://cloudarchitect/vm.yaml#1557763393469362
gs://cloudarchitect/vm.yaml#1557763527069403
```

Figure 11.12 – Viewing the different versions

We can turn versioning on and off whenever we want. Any available archived versions will remain when we turn it off, but we should remember that we will not have any archived versions until we enable this option.

Life cycle management

Archived files could quickly get out of hand and impact our billing unnecessarily. To avoid this, we can utilize life cycle management policies. Life cycle management configurations can be assigned to a bucket. These files are a set of rules that can be applied to current or future objects in the bucket. When any of the objects meet the guidelines of the configuration, Cloud Storage can perform actions automatically.

One of the most common use cases for using life cycle management policies is when we want to downgrade the storage class of objects after a set period. For example, there may be a scenario where data needs to be accessed frequently up to 30 days after it is moved to Cloud Storage, and after that, it will only be accessed once a year. It makes no sense to keep this data in regional or multi-regional storage, so we can use life cycle management to move this to Coldline storage after 30 days. Perhaps objects are not needed at all after 1 year, in which case we can use a policy to delete these objects. This helps keep costs down. Let's learn how we can apply a policy to a bucket.

The first thing we need to do is create a life cycle configuration file. As we mentioned previously, these files contain a set of rules that we want to apply to our bucket. If the policy contains more than one rule, then an object has to match all of the conditions before the action will be taken. It might be possible that a single object could be subject to multiple actions; in this case, Cloud Storage will perform only one of the actions before re-evaluating any additional actions.

We should also note that a `Delete` action will take precedence over a `SetStorageClass` action. Additionally, if an object has two rules applied to it to move the object to Nearline or Coldline, then the object will always move to the Coldline storage class if both rules use the same condition. A configuration file can be created in JSON or XML.

In the following example, we will create a simple configuration file in JSON format that will delete files after 60 days. We will also delete archived files after 30 days. Let's save this as `lifecycle.json`:

```
{
    "lifecycle": {
        "rule": [{
            "action": {
                "type": "Delete"
```

```
            },
            "condition": {
                "age": 60,
                "isLive": true
            }
        }, {
            "action": {
                "type": "Delete"
            },
            "condition": {
                "age": 30,
                "isLive": false
            }
        }]
    }
}
```

Exam Tip

If the value of isLive is true, then this lifecycle condition will only match objects in a live state; however, if the value is set to false, the lifecycle condition will only match archived objects. We should also note that objects in non-versioned buckets are considered live.

We can also use gsutil to enable this policy on our buckets using the following syntax:

```
gsutil lifecycle set <lifecycle policy name> gs://<bucket name>
```

Here, <lifecycle policy name> is the file we have created with our policy, while <bucket name> is the unique bucket name we want to apply the policy to. The following code shows how to apply our lifecycle.json file to our cloudarchitect bucket:

```
gsutil lifecycle set lifecycle.json gs://cloudarchitect
```

We mentioned earlier that a common use case for `lifecycle` would be to move objects to a cheaper storage class after a set period. Let's look at an example that would map to a common scenario. Suppose we have objects in our `cloudarchitect` bucket that we want to access frequently for 90 days. After this time, we only need to access the data monthly. Finally, after 180 days, we will only access the data yearly. We can translate these requirements into storage classes and create the following policy, which will help keep our costs to a minimum.

Let's break this down a little since we now have a policy with two rules that each have two conditions. Any storage object with an age greater than `90` days and that has the `REGIONAL` storage class applied to it will be moved to `NEARLINE` storage. Any object with an age greater than `180` days and that has the `NEARLINE` storage class applied to it will be moved to `ARCHIVE` storage:

```
{
    "lifecycle": {
        "rule": [{
            "action": {
                "type": "SetStorageClass",
                "storageClass": "NEARLINE"
            },
            "condition": {
                "age": 90,
                "matchesStorageClass": ["REGIONAL"]
            }
        },
        {
            "action": {
                "type": "SetStorageClass",
                "storageClass": "ARCHIVE"
            },
            "condition": {
                "age": 180,
                "matchesStorageClass": ["NEARLINE"]

            {
```

> **Exam Tip**
>
> At least one condition is required. If you enter an incorrect action or condition, then you will receive a 400 bad request error response.

Next, let's check out retention policies and locks.

Retention policies and locks

Bucket locks allow us to configure data retention policies for a Cloud Storage bucket. This means we can govern how long objects in the bucket must be retained and prevent the policy from being reduced or removed.

We can create a retention policy by running the following command:

```
gsutil retention set 60s "gs://<bucketname>"
```

This sets the policy for 60 seconds. We can also set it to 60d for 60 days, 1m for 1 month, or 10y for 10 years. The output of setting this policy will be similar to the following:

```
Retention Policy (UNLOCKED):
    Duration: 60 Second(s)
    Effective Time: Thu, 01 Jul 2021 05:49:05 GMT
```

Note that if a bucket does not have a retention policy, then we can delete or replace objects at any time. However, if a policy is applied, then the objects in the bucket can only be replaced or deleted once their age is older than the retention policy period.

> **Exam Tip**
>
> Retention policies and object versioning are exclusive features, which means that for a given bucket, only one of these can be enabled at a time.

Object holds

Object holds are metadata flags that can be placed on individual objects, which means they cannot be replaced or deleted. We can, however, still edit the metadata of an object that has been placed on hold.

There are two types of holds and an object can have one, both, or neither hold applied. When an object is stored in a bucket without a retention policy, both hold types behave in the same way. However, if a retention policy has been applied to the bucket, the holds have different effects on an object when the hold is released:

- **Event-based hold**: This resets the object's time in the bucket for the retention period.

- **Temporary hold**: This does not affect the object's time in the bucket for the retention period.

Let's look at an example to make things a little clearer. Let's say we have two objects – Object A and Object B – that we add to a storage bucket that has a 1-month retention period. We apply an **event-based hold** on Object A and a **temporary hold** on Object B. Due to the retention period alone, we would usually be able to delete both objects after 1 month. However, because we applied an **object hold** to each object, we are unable to do so. If we release the hold on Object A, then due to the **event-based hold**, the object must remain in the bucket for another 1 month before we can delete it. If we release the hold on Object B, we can immediately delete this due to the **temporary hold** not affecting the object's time in the bucket.

Transferring data

There will be cases where we want to transfer files to a bucket from on-premises or another cloud-based storage, and Google offers many ways to do so. There are some considerations that we should bear in mind to make sure that we select the right option. The size of the data and the available bandwidth will be the deciding factors. Let's take a quick look at a chart to show how long it would take to transfer some set data sizes over a specific bandwidth:

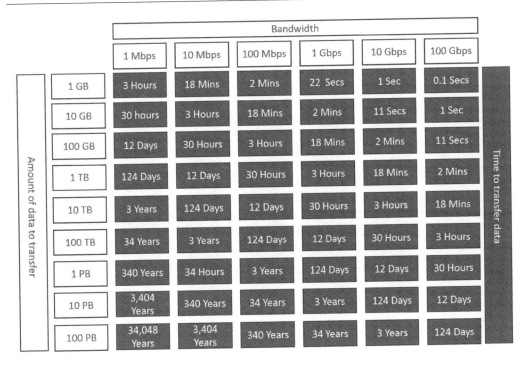

Figure 11.13 – Data transfer guidance

Next, Let's look at some methods of transferring data.

Cloud Storage Transfer Service

Cloud Storage Transfer Service provides us with the option to transfer or back up our data from online sources to a data sink. Let's say, for example, that we want to move data from our AWS S3 bucket into our Cloud Storage bucket. S3 would be our source and the destination Cloud Storage bucket would be our data sink. We can also use Cloud Storage Transfer Service to move data from an HTTP/HTTP(s) source or even another Cloud Storage bucket. To make these data migrations or synchronizations easier, Cloud Storage Transfer Service offers several options:

- We can schedule a one-time transfer operation or a recurring operation.
- We can delete existing objects in the destination data sink if they don't have any corresponding objects in the source.

- We can delete source objects once we have transferred them.

- We can schedule periodic synchronizations between the source and destination using folders based on file creation dates, filenames, or even the time of day you wish to import data.

> **Exam Tip**
>
> You can also use `gsutil` to transfer data between Cloud Storage and other locations. You can speed up the process of transferring files on-premises by using the `-m` option to enable a multi-threaded copy. If you plan to upload larger files, `gsutil` will split these files into several smaller chunks and upload these in parallel.
>
> It is recommended that you use Cloud Storage Transfer Service when transferring data from Amazon S3 to Cloud Storage.

Google Transfer Appliance

If we look at *Figure 9.13*, we can see that there are some pretty large transfer times. If we have petabytes of storage to transfer, then we should use Transfer Appliance. This is a hardware storage device that allows secure offline data migration. It can be set up in our data center and is rack-mountable. We simply fill it with data and then ship it to an ingest location where Google will upload it to Cloud Storage.

Google offers the option of a 40 TB or 300 TB transfer appliance. The following is a quote from `https://cloud.google.com/transfer-appliance/docs/4.0/security-and-encryption`:

> *"After uploading your data, we sanitize the drive media*
> *in the appliance you returned by applying NIST 800-88 standards*
> *for purging information..."*

A common use case for Transfer Appliance is to move large amounts of existing backups from on-premises to cheaper Cloud Storage using the Coldline storage class. It would take more than 1 week to perform this upload over the network.

Now, we will have a look at IAM.

Understanding IAM

Access to Google Cloud Storage is secured with IAM. Let's have a look at the following list of predefined roles and their details:

- **Storage Object Creator**: Has rights to create objects but does not give permissions to view, delete, or overwrite objects

- **Storage Object Viewer**: Has rights to view objects and their metadata, but not the ACL, and has rights to list the objects in a bucket

- **Storage Object Admin**: Has full control over objects and can create, view, and delete objects

- **Storage Admin**: Has full control over buckets and objects

- **Storage HMAC Key Admin**: Has full control over HMAC keys in a project and can only be applied to a project

Quotas and limits

Google Cloud Storage comes with predefined quotas. These default quotas can be changed via the **Navigation** menu, under the **IAM & Admin | Quotas** section. From this menu, we can review the current quotas and request an increase to these limits. We recommend that you familiarize yourself with the limits of each service as this can have an impact on your scalability. For Cloud Storage, we should be aware of the following limits:

- Individual objects are limited to a maximum size of 5 TiB.

- Updates to an individual object are limited to one per second.

- There is an initial limit of 1,000 writes per second per bucket.

- There is an initial limit of 5,000 reads per second per bucket.

- There is a limit of 100 ACL entries per object.

- There is a limit of one bucket creation operation every 2 seconds.

- There is a limit of one bucket deletion operation every 2 seconds.

Pricing

Pricing for Google Cloud Storage is based on four components:

- **Data storage**: This applies to at-rest data that is stored in Cloud Storage, is charged per GB per month, and the cost depends on the location and class of the storage.
- **Network usage**: This applies when object data or metadata is read from or moved between our buckets.
- **Operations usage**: This applies when you perform actions within Cloud Storage that make changes or retrieve information about buckets and their objects. The cost depends on the class of the storage.
- **Retrieval and early deletion fees**: This applies when accessing data from the Nearline, Coldline, and Archive storage classes. Retrieval costs will apply when we read, copy, or rewrite data or metadata. The minimum storage duration applies to data stored in Nearline, Coldline, and Archive storage. You will still be charged for the duration of an object, even if the file is deleted before the minimal period.

Understanding Cloud Firestore

It's wise to note early on in this section that Google rebranded their previous Cloud Datastore product with a newer major version called **Cloud Firestore**. However, it is also important to understand the relationship between both as Firestore gives the option of Native mode and Datastore mode, with the latter using the traditional Datastore system's behaviors with the Firestore storage layer, which eliminates some of Datastore's limitations.

Cloud Datastore is a NoSQL database that is built to ease application development. It uses a distributed architecture that is highly scalable, and because it is serverless, we do not have to worry about the underlying infrastructure. Cloud Datastore distributes our data over several machines and uses masterless, synchronous replication over a wide geographical area.

Firestore builds on this but also accelerates the development of mobile, IoT, and web applications. It offers built-in live synchronization, as well as an offline mode that increases the efficiency of developing real-time applications. This includes workloads consisting of live asset tracking, real-time analytics, social media profiles, and gaming leaderboards.

Firestore also offers very **high availability** (**HA**) on our data. With automatic multi-region replication and strong consistency, it offers a 99.999% guarantee.

Before we go any further into the details, we don't want to make any assumptions that you know what a NoSQL database is. SQL databases are far more well-known by non-database administrators in the industry. A SQL database is primarily a relational database that is based on tables consisting of several rows of data that have predefined schemas.

Compare that to the concept of a NoSQL database, which is a non-relational database based around key-value pairs that do not have to adhere to any schema definitions. Ultimately, this allows us to scale efficiently; therefore, we can see how it becomes a lot easier to add or remove resources as we need to. This elasticity makes Cloud Datastore perfect for transactional information, such as real-time inventories, ACID transactions that will always provide data that is valid, or for providing user profiles to keep a record of user experience based on past activities or preferences. However, it is also important to note that NoSQL databases may not be the perfect fit for every scenario and consideration should be taken when deciding on what database to select, particularly regarding the efficiency of querying your data. OK; so, now that we know what a NoSQL database is, let's look at what makes up a Datastore database, as relationships between data objects are addressed differently than other databases that you may be familiar with. A traditional SQL database would be made up of tables, rows, and columns. In Cloud Datastore, an entity is the equivalent of a row, and a kind is the equivalent of a table. Entities are data objects that can have one or more named properties.

Each entity has a key that identifies it. Let's look at the following table to compare the terminology that is used with SQL databases and Cloud Datastore:

Concept	SQL Database	Cloud Datastore
Category of object	Table	Kind
One object	Row	Entity
Individual data for an object	Column	Property
Unique ID for an object	Primary Key	Key

Figure 11.14 – Terminology comparison

Now, let's look at the different types of modes that are offered in more detail.

Cloud Firestore in Datastore mode or Native mode

When we create a new database, we must select one of the modes. However, we cannot use a mixture of modes within the same project. So, it is recommended to think about your design and what your application is built for.

Native mode offers all the new features of the revamped product. It takes the best of Cloud Datastore and the Firebase real-time database. Firebase was originally designed for mobile applications that required synced states across clients in real time. As such, Firestore takes advantage of this and offers a new, strongly consistent storage layer, as well as real-time updates. Additionally, it offers a collection and document data model and mobile and web client libraries. Native mode can scale automatically to millions of concurrent clients.

> **Exam Tip**
>
> While Firestore is backward compatible with Datastore, the new data model, real-time updates, and mobile and web client libraries are not. You must use Native mode to gain access to these features.

Datastore mode supports the Datastore API, so there is no requirement to change any existing Datastore applications. If your architecture requires the use of an established Datastore server architecture, then Datastore mode allows for this and removes some of the limitations from Datastore, mainly that Datastore mode offers strong consistency unless eventual consistency is specified. Datastore mode can scale automatically to millions of writes per second.

> **Exam Tip**
>
> Data objects in Firestore in Datastore mode are known as entities.

Upgrading to Firestore

New projects that require a Datastore database should use Firestore in Datastore mode. However, starting in 2021, existing Datastore databases will be automatically upgraded without the need to update your application code. Google will notify users of the schedule for the upgrade, which does not require downtime.

Creating and using Cloud Datastore

The first thing we need to do is select a mode before we can utilize Cloud Firestore. Let's look at creating a database in Datastore mode and run some queries on the entities that we create. Before we do so, let's remind ourselves that Datastore is a managed service. As we go through this process, you will note that we are directly creating our entities without provisioning any underlying infrastructure first. You should also note that, like all storage services from GCP, Cloud Datastore automatically encrypts all data before it's written to disk. Follow these steps to create a Firestore in Datastore mode:

1. From our GCP Console, browse to **DATABASES Firestore**:

Figure 11.15 – Selecting Firestore

2. We are now required to choose an operational mode. **Native mode** is the official Firestore mode, which is the next major version of Cloud Datastore and offers new features, such as real-time updates and mobile and web client libraries. Datastore mode uses traditional Cloud Datastore system behavior. In our example, we will use **Datastore mode**:

	Native mode	Datastore mode
	Enable all of Cloud Firestore's features, with offline support and real-time synchronization. SELECT NATIVE MODE	Leverage Cloud Datastore's system behavior on top of Cloud Firestore's powerful storage layer. SELECT DATASTORE MODE
API	Firestore	Datastore
Scalability	Automatically scales to millions of concurrent clients	Automatically scales to millions of writes per second
App engine support	Not supported in the App Engine standard Python 2.7 and PHP 5.5 runtimes	All runtimes
Max writes per second	10,000	No limit
Real-time updates	✓	✗
Mobile/web client libraries with offline data persistence	✓	✗
Query consistency	Strong	Strong
Data model	Documents / collections	Entities / kinds
Web console	Firestore page in Google Cloud Platform and Firebase	Datastore page in Google Cloud Platform

Figure 11.16 – Choosing Datastore mode

3.   Select a location for your Datastore database and click **CREATE DATABASE:**

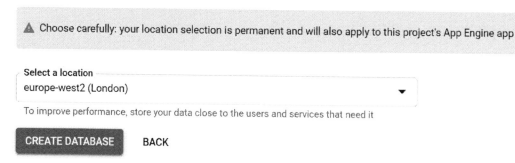

Figure 11.17 – Selecting a location

4.   Once the database is ready, we will be directed to the **Entities** menu. Click **CREATE ENTITY** to create our first Datastore entity:

Figure 11.18 – Creating an entity

We can now give our entity a namespace, a **Kind** (a table, in SQL terminology), and a key identifier, which will be auto-generated. Let's leave our namespace as the default and create a new kind called exam:

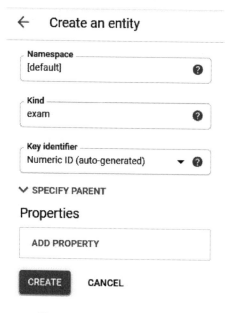

Figure 11.19 – Create an entity

5. Click **ADD PROPERTY** to specify a name – in this case, `title`. We can also select from several types, but in this example, we want to use **String**. Finally, we will give it the value of `Professional Cloud Architect`. Click **DONE** to add the property:

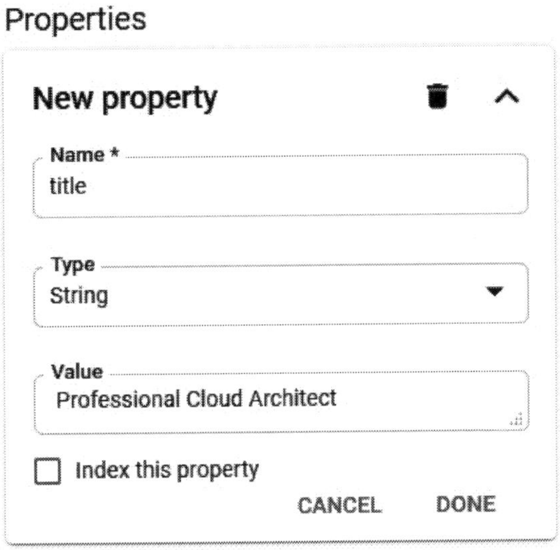

Figure 11.20 – Adding entity properties

6. We can repeat *Step 5* to add another property. This time, we will use `cost` as the name, **Integer** as the type, and `200` as the value. When we have added all of the properties we want in our entity, click **CREATE**. Let's also create two new entities with the `exam` kinds for the `Associate Cloud Engineer` exam and the `Professional Cloud Developer` exam:

	Name/ID ↑	cost	title
☐	id=5071211717459968	200	Professional Cloud Developer
☐	id=5634161670881280	200	Professional Cloud Architect
☐	id=5644004762845184	100	Associate Cloud Engineer

Kind: exam   ☰ FILTER ENTITIES

Figure 11.21 – Creating an entity

7. Now, we can filter our entities to a query based on cost or title. Let's look for information on the Professional Cloud Developer exam:

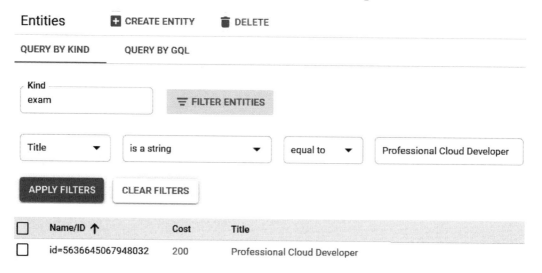

Figure 11.22 – Filter entities

8. We can also use **QUERY BY GQL** and enter a SQL-like query to get the same results:

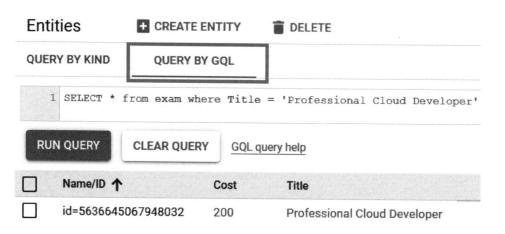

Figure 11.23 – Executing the query

With that, we have seen how easy it is to create a Datastore database and query the entities we create. Now, let's move on and look at some of the differences between Datastore and Firestore.

Summary of Datastore mode versus Native mode

Cloud Firestore in Native mode is the complete re-branded product. It takes the best of Cloud Datastore and the Firebase real-time database to offer the same conceptual NoSQL database as Datastore, but as Firebase is built for low-latency mobile applications, it also includes the following new features:

- A new strongly consistent storage layer
- A collect and document data model
- Real-time updates
- Mobile and web client libraries

Cloud Firestore in Datastore mode uses the same Datastore system behavior but will access the Firestore storage layer, which will remove some limitations, such as the following:

- No longer limited to eventual consistency, as all queries become strongly consistent
- No longer limited to a 25 entity group limit
- No longer limited to 1 write per second to an entity group

IAM

Access to Google Cloud Datastore is secured with IAM. Let's have a look at the list of predefined roles and their details:

- **Datastore owner with an AppEngine app admin**: Has full access to Datastore mode
- **Datastore owner without an AppEngine app admin**: Has access to Datastore mode but cannot enable admin access, check whether Datastore mode admin is enabled, disable Datastore mode writes, or check whether Datastore mode writes are disabled
- **Datastore user**: Has read/write access to data in a Datastore mode database. Mainly used by developers or service accounts

- **Datastore viewer**: Has rights to read all Datastore mode resources

- **Datastore import-export admin**: Has full access to manage imports and exports

- **Datastore index admin**: Has full access to manage index definitions

Quotas and limits

Google Cloud Datastore comes with predefined quotas. These default quotas can be changed by going to the **Navigation** menu, under the **IAM & Admin | Quotas** section. From this menu, we can review the current quotas and request an increase to these limits. We recommend that you familiarize yourself with the limits for each service as this can have an impact on your scalability. Cloud Firestore offers a free quota that allows us to get started at no cost:

- There is a 1 GiB limit on stored data.

- There is a limit of 50,000 reads per day.

- There is a limit of 20,000 writes per day.

- There is a limit of 20,000 deletes per day.

- There is a network egress limit of 10 GiB per month.

With the free tier, there are the following standard limits:

- There is a maximum depth of subcollections of 100.

- There is a maximum document size of 6 KiB.

- There is a maximum document size of 1 MiB.

- There is a maximum writes per second per database of 10,000.

- There is a maximum API request size of 10 MiB.

- There is a maximum of 500 writes that can be passed to a commit operation or performed in a transaction.

- There is a maximum of 500 field transformations that can be performed on a single-document Commit operation or in a transaction.

Pricing

Pricing for Google Cloud Firestore offers a free quota to get us started, as mentioned previously.

If these limits are exceeded, there will be a charge that will fluctuate, depending on the location of your data. General pricing is per 100,00 documents for reads, writes, and deletes. Stored data is charged per GB per month.

Understanding Cloud SQL

Given the name, it won't be a major surprise to hear that Cloud SQL is a database service that makes it easy to set up, maintain, and manage your relational PostgreSQL, MySQL, or SQL Server database on Google Cloud.

Although we are provisioning the underlying instances, it is a fully managed service that is capable of handling up to 64 TB of storage. Cloud SQL databases are relational, which means that they are organized into tables, rows, and columns. As an alternative, we can install the SQL Server application image onto a Compute Engine instance, but Cloud SQL offers many benefits that come from being fully managed by Google – for example, scalability, patching, and updates are applied automatically, automated backups are provided, and it offers HA out-of-the-box. Again, it is important to highlight that although these benefits may look great, we should also be mindful that there are some unsupported functions and that consideration should be taken before committing to Cloud SQL.

> **Exam Tip**
> Cloud SQL can accommodate up to 64 TB of storage. If you need to handle larger amounts of data, then you should look at alternative services, such as Cloud Spanner.

Now, let's look at some of the features offered by Cloud SQL.

Cloud SQL for MySQL offers us the following:

- MySQL currently offers support for MySQL 5.6, 5.7, and 8.0 and can provide up to a maximum of 624 GB of RAM and 64 TB of storage when selecting a high memory instance type.

- There's data replication between multiple zones with automatic failover.

- Fully managed MySQL Community Edition databases are available in the cloud.

- There's point-in-time recovery and on-demand backups.

- There's instance cloning.

- It offers integration with GCPs monitoring and logging solutions – Cloud Operations.

Cloud SQL for PostgreSQL offers us the following:

- A fully managed PostgreSQL database in the cloud with up to 64 TB of storage, depending on whether the instance has dedicated or shared vCPUs

- Custom machine types with up to 624 GB RAM and 96 CPUs

- Data replication between multiple zones with automatic failover

- Instance cloning

- On-demand backups

- Integration with GCPs monitoring and logging solutions – Cloud Operations logging and monitoring

Cloud SQL for SQL Server offers us the following:

- A fully-managed SQL Server database in the cloud.

- Custom machine types with up to 624 GB RAM and 96 CPUs.

- Up to 64 TB of storage.

- Custom data encrypted in Google's internal networks and database tables, temporary files, and backups.

- Databases can be imported using BAK and SQL files.

- Instance cloning.

- Integration with Cloud Operations logging and monitoring.

- Data replication between multiple regions.

- HA through regional persistent disks.

Now that we know the main features, let's look at some of the things to bear in mind when we create a new instance:

- **Selecting an instance**: Similar to other GCP services, we have the option to select a location for our instances. It makes sense to place our database instance close to the services that depend on it. We should understand our database requirements and have a baseline of active connections, memory, and CPU usage to allow us to select the correct machine type. If we over-spec, this will have an impact on our cost, and likewise, if we under-spec, we may impact our performance or availability if resources are exhausted.

- **Selecting region**: We have the option to select the region that our instance will be deployed to. Be mindful that the region cannot be changed after deployment, but the zone can be changed at any time. For HA, we can select multiple zones, which offers automatic failover to another zone in our selected region. From a performance standpoint, we should be looking to deploy our instances close to the services that are using them. We will look at HA in more detail later in this chapter.

- **Selecting storage**: When creating an instance, we can select different storage tiers. Depending on our requirements, we may wish to select an SSD for lower latency and higher throughput; however, we can also select an HDD if we don't require such a high-performing disk.

- **Selecting encryption**: When creating an instance, we can choose to have Google manage our encryption keys, which is the default, or select a customer-managed key, which is managed via the Google KMS service.

Selecting the correct capacity to fit your database size is also extremely important because once you have created your instance, you cannot decrease the capacity. If we over-spec our storage, then we will be paying for unused space. If we under-spec our storage, then we can cause issues with availability. One method to avoid this is through the automatic storage increase setting. If this is enabled, your storage is checked every 30 seconds to ensure that the storage has not fallen below a set threshold size. If it has, then additional storage will be automatically added to your instance. The threshold's size depends on the amount of storage your instance currently has provisioned, and it cannot be larger than 25 GB. This sounds great, but we should also be mindful that if we have spikes in demand, then we will suffer a permanent increase in storage cost. We should also be mindful that creating or increasing storage capacity to 30 TB or greater could lead to increased latency for operations such as backups:

- **Selecting an IP address**: We can select from a public or a private IP address. The default is to use a public IP address, which will block all IP addresses. So, we must add specific IP addresses or ranges to open our instances up. To use a private IP address, we must enable Google's Service Networking API. This is required for each project. If we wish to use a private IP address, we need to ensure that we have VPC peering set up between the Google service VPC network where our instance resides and our VPC network. This is shown in the following diagram:

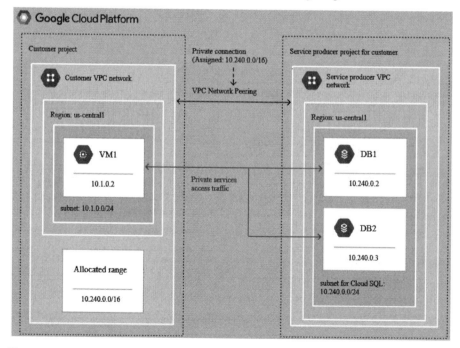

Figure 11.24 – VPC peering (Source: https://cloud.google.com/sql/docs/postgres/private-ip. License: https://creativecommons.org/licenses/by/4.0/legalcode)

We discussed VPC peering in more detail in *Chapter 10, Networking Options in GCP*. Using a private IP will help lower network latency and improve security as traffic will never be exposed to the internet; however, we should also note that to access a Cloud SQL instance on its private IP address from other GCP resources, the resource must be in the same region.

> **Important Note**
>
> It is recommended that you use a private IP address if you wish to access a Cloud SQL instance from an application that is running in Google's container service; that is, Google Kubernetes Engine.

- **Automatic backups**: Enabling automatic backups will have a small impact on performance; however, we should be willing to accept this to take advantage of features such as read replicas, cloning, or point-in-time recovery. We can select where our backups are located. However, by default, backups are stored in the closest multi-region location, so they should only be customized based on unique design decisions. Additionally, we can select how many automatic backups are stored. This defaults to 7 and again, unless there is a specific reason to change this, then it is not recommended to modify it. Also, please note that if multiple zones are selected, then automatic backups are enabled by default and cannot be disabled.

- **Maintenance windows**: When working with this offering, we should also specify a maintenance window. We can choose a specific day and 1-hour time slot when updates can be applied. GCP will not initiate any update to that instance within this specified window. Please note that if no window is specified, then potentially disruptive updates can occur at any time.

Data consistency

Cloud SQL is a relational database that offers strong consistency and support for ACID transactions.

Creating and managing Cloud SQL

Now that we have an understanding of the concepts, let's look at how to create a new MySQL instance:

1. Go to the navigation menu and go to **DATABASES | SQL**:

Figure 11.25 – Selecting SQL

2. Click on **Create an instance**.

3. Select the database engine you require. In our example, we will select **MySQL**:

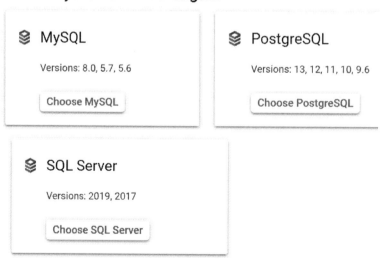

Figure 11.26 – Choose your database engine

4. Give the instance a name and a password. You can either enter your own password or click **Generate** to receive a random password. Additionally, you can select a location and database version. We will leave the defaults in this example as-is:

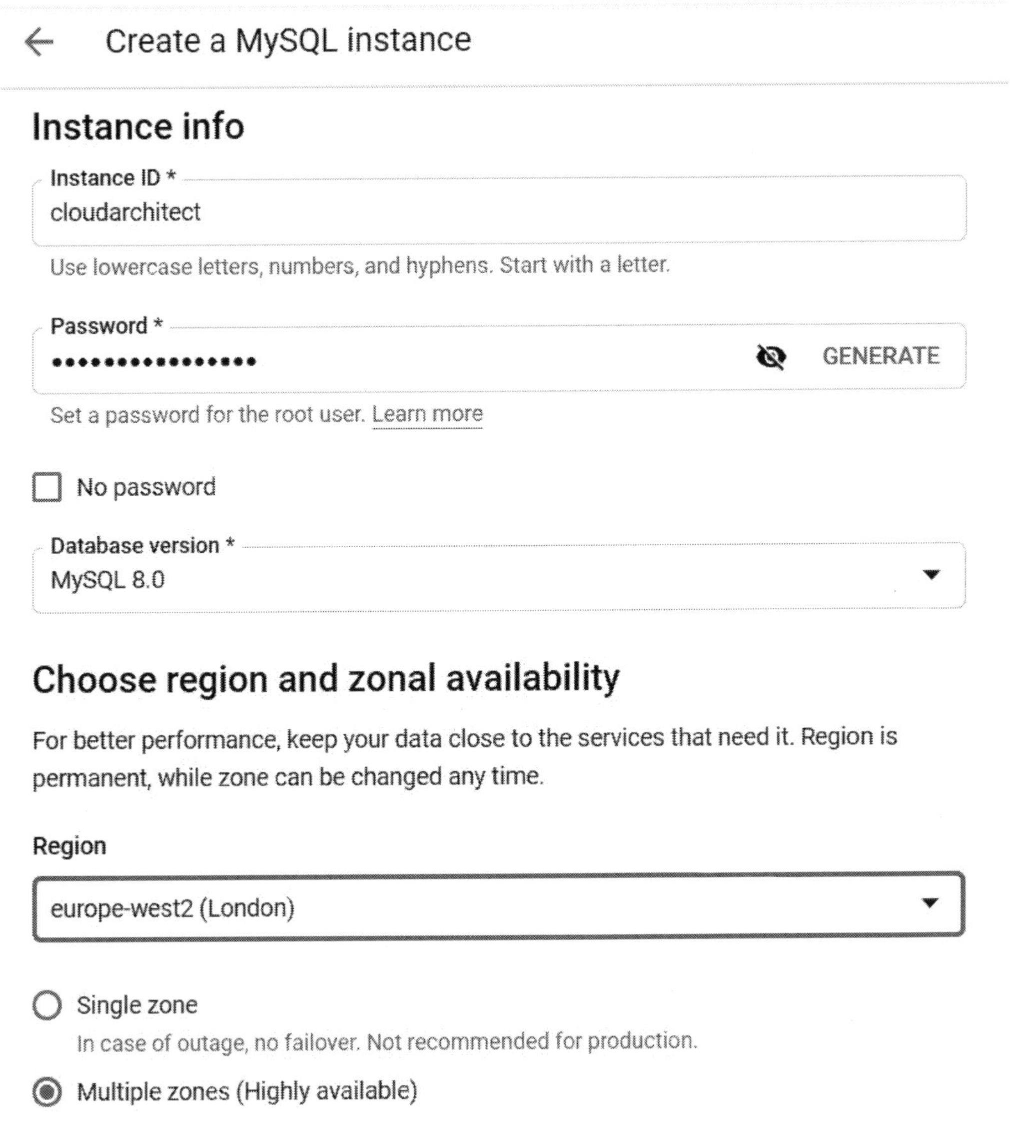

←   Create a MySQL instance

Instance info

Instance ID *

cloudarchitect

Use lowercase letters, numbers, and hyphens. Start with a letter.

Password *

••••••••••••••••   ⊘   GENERATE

Set a password for the root user. Learn more

☐ No password

Database version *

MySQL 8.0   ▼

Choose region and zonal availability

For better performance, keep your data close to the services that need it. Region is permanent, while zone can be changed any time.

Region

europe-west2 (London)   ▼

◯ Single zone
    In case of outage, no failover. Not recommended for production.

◉ Multiple zones (Highly available)

Figure 11.27 – Create a MySQL instance

5. Now, let's look at some of the custom configurations. First, we must select our machine type and storage options:

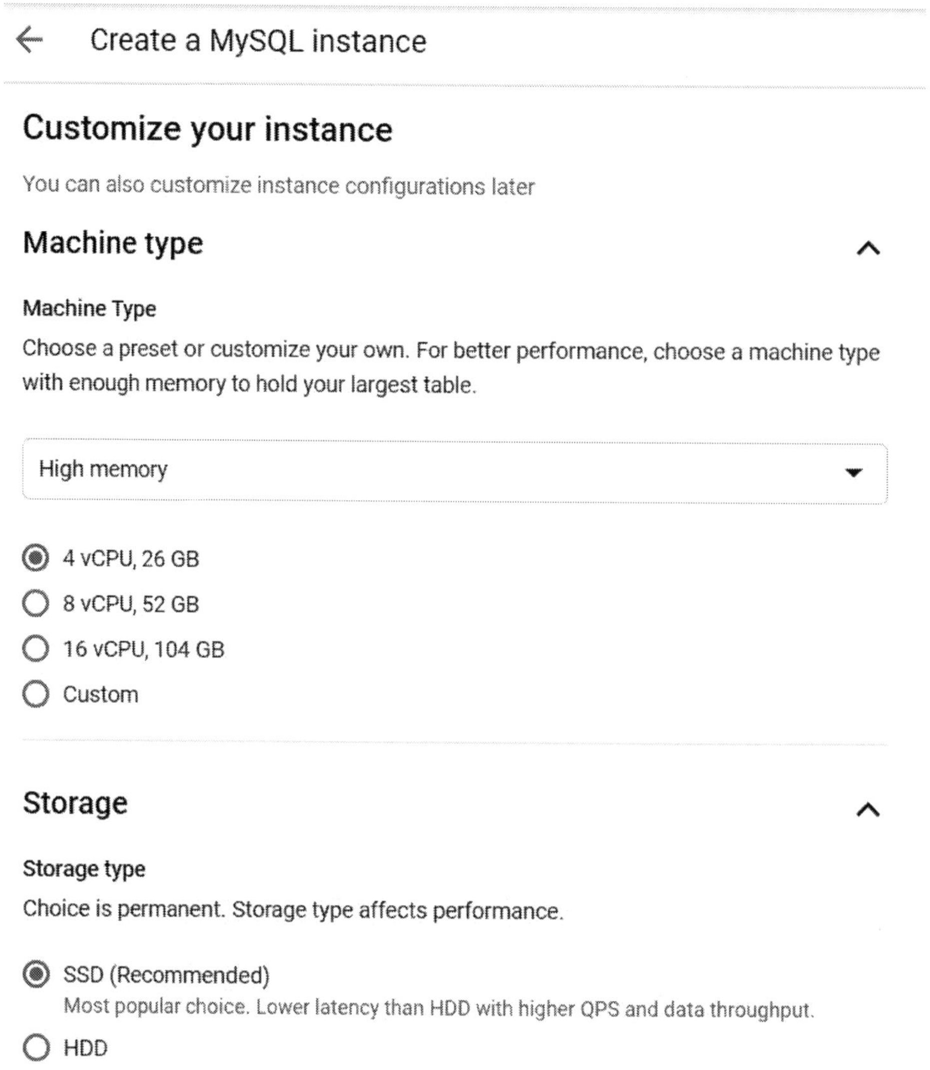

←   Create a MySQL instance

Customize your instance

You can also customize instance configurations later

Machine type   ⌃

Machine Type

Choose a preset or customize your own. For better performance, choose a machine type with enough memory to hold your largest table.

High memory   ▼

- ◉ 4 vCPU, 26 GB
- ○ 8 vCPU, 52 GB
- ○ 16 vCPU, 104 GB
- ○ Custom

Storage   ⌃

Storage type

Choice is permanent. Storage type affects performance.

- ◉ SSD (Recommended)
  Most popular choice. Lower latency than HDD with higher QPS and data throughput.
- ○ HDD

Figure 11.28 – Selecting the machine type and storage

We can also set the storage capacity and encryption options to enable the use of customer-managed encryption keys. In the preceding screenshot, we are using the default settings.

6. Next, we can choose whether we want a private or public IP address for our instance:

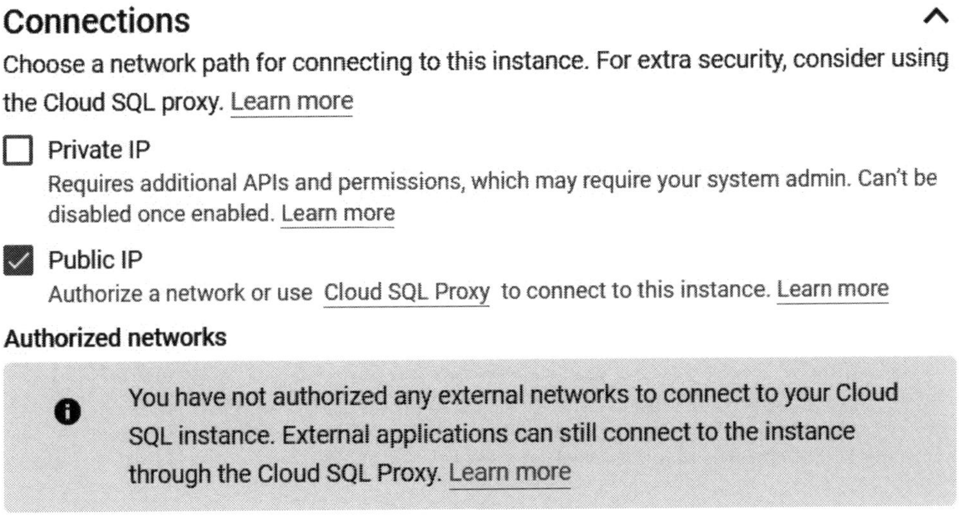

Connections   ⌃

Choose a network path for connecting to this instance. For extra security, consider using the Cloud SQL proxy. Learn more

☐ **Private IP**
Requires additional APIs and permissions, which may require your system admin. Can't be disabled once enabled. Learn more

☑ **Public IP**
Authorize a network or use Cloud SQL Proxy to connect to this instance. Learn more

Authorized networks

> ⓘ You have not authorized any external networks to connect to your Cloud SQL instance. External applications can still connect to the instance through the Cloud SQL Proxy. Learn more

Figure 11.29 – Selecting a connection type

7. Provide 4 hours for a backup. Also, ensure that you check the **Create failover replica** option if required:

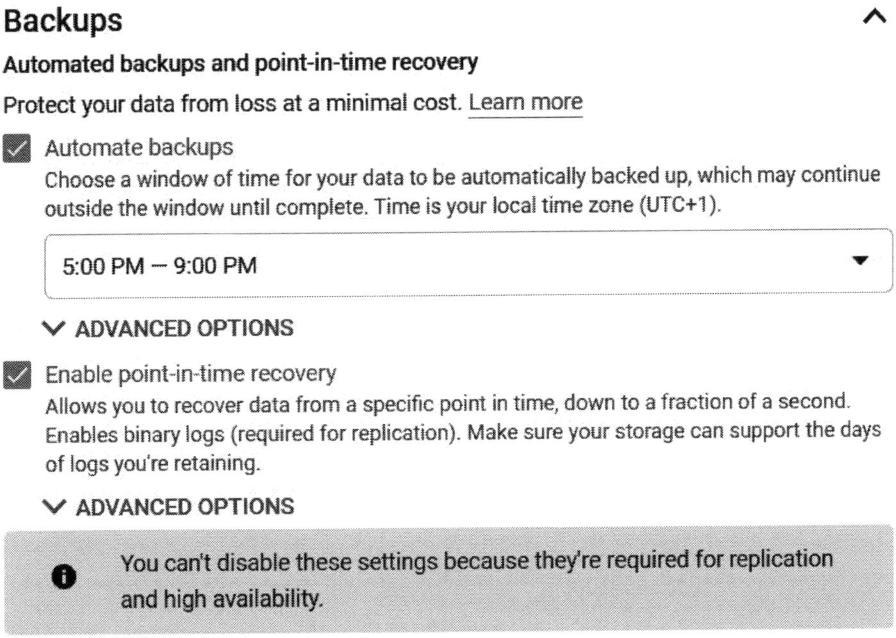

Backups   ⌃

Automated backups and point-in-time recovery

Protect your data from loss at a minimal cost. Learn more

☑ Automate backups
Choose a window of time for your data to be automatically backed up, which may continue outside the window until complete. Time is your local time zone (UTC+1).

5:00 PM — 9:00 PM   ▼

⌄ ADVANCED OPTIONS

☑ Enable point-in-time recovery
Allows you to recover data from a specific point in time, down to a fraction of a second. Enables binary logs (required for replication). Make sure your storage can support the days of logs you're retaining.

⌄ ADVANCED OPTIONS

> ⓘ You can't disable these settings because they're required for replication and high availability.

Figure 11.30 – Creating a backup schedule

8.   Set a maintenance schedule by selecting a day and 1-hour time slot:

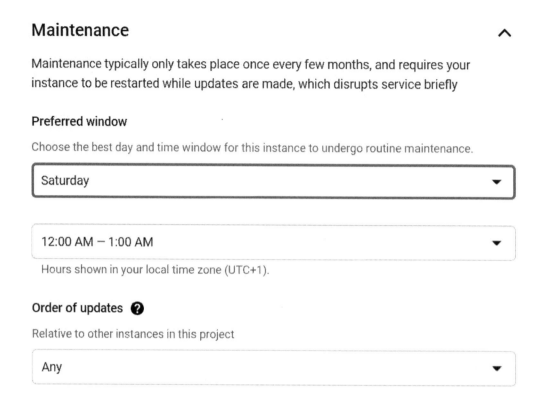

Maintenance   ∧

Maintenance typically only takes place once every few months, and requires your
instance to be restarted while updates are made, which disrupts service briefly

Preferred window

Choose the best day and time window for this instance to undergo routine maintenance.

Saturday ▼

12:00 AM – 1:00 AM ▼

Hours shown in your local time zone (UTC+1).

Order of updates ❷

Relative to other instances in this project

Any ▼

Figure 11.31 – Creating maintenance windows

9.   At this point, we can also add any labels we require. Finally, click **CREATE**.

Like other services, we can create an instance by using the command-line tools available
to us. Earlier in this chapter, we touched on some command-line tools, and likewise,
we can use `gcloud` to create a new instance. We can run the following syntax to create
a new database:

```
gcloud sql instances create <instance name> --database-
version=<DATABASE version> --cpu=<cpu size> --memory=<RAM size>
--region=<region name>
```

Let's look at this code in a little more detail:

- `<instance name>` is the name of our database instance.
- `<DATABASE version>` is the name of the specific version of MySQL or
  PostgreSQL you wish to create.

- `<cpu size>` and `<RAM size>` are the sizes of the resources we wish to create.

- `<region name>` is the region we wish to deploy our instance to.

Let's create a new PostgreSQL DB with version 9.6 called `cloudarchitect001` and allocate 4 CPUs and 3,840 MiB of RAM. We will deploy this instance in the `us-central` region. Please note that this command may ask you to enable the API. Click **Yes**:

```
gcloud sql instances create cloudarchitect001 --database-
version=POSTGRES_9_6  --cpu=1 --memory=3840MiB --region=us-
central
```

> **Exam Tip**
>
> You can directly map your on-premises MySQL, SQL, or PostgreSQL database to Cloud SQL without having to convert it into a different format. This makes it one of the common options for companies looking to experiment with public cloud services.

Now that we have created a new instance by console and command line, let's look at some important features in more detail – read replicas and failover replicas.

Read replicas

Cloud SQL offers the ability to replicate our master instance to one or more read replicas. This is essentially a copy of the master that will register changes that are made to the master in the replica in almost real time.

> **Tip**
>
> We should highlight here that read replicas do not provide HA, and we cannot failover to a read replica from a master. They also do not fall in line with any maintenance window that we may have specified when creating the master instance.

There are several scenarios that Cloud SQL offers for read replication:

- **Read replica**: This offers additional read capacity and an analytics target to optimize performance on the master.

- **Cross-region read replica**: This offers the same as a standard read replica but also offers disaster recovery capabilities, improved read performance, and the ability to migrate between regions.

- **External read replica**: This replicates to a MySQL instance that is external to Cloud SQL. It can help reduce latency if you are connecting from an on-premises network and also offers a migration path to other platforms.

- **Replication from an external server**: This is where an external MySQL instance is the master and is being replicated into Cloud SQL. This also offers data replication to GCP.

Enabling read replicas is a simple process. Let's learn how to do this from our GCP Console:

1. Browse once more to **Database | SQL**. Let's add a replica to our existing `cloudarchitect001` instance. We simply need to open our options menu and select **Create read replica**:

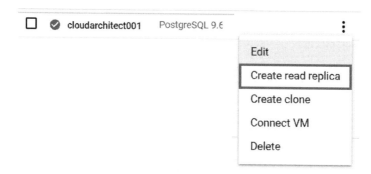

Figure 11.32 – Create read replica

> **Exam Tip**
>
> Before we can create a read replica, the following requirements must be met: binary logging must be enabled and at least one backup must have been created since binary logging was enabled.

Simply give the instance a name, select a region, and click **Create**. We will see configuration options similar to those we used when we created a master instance:

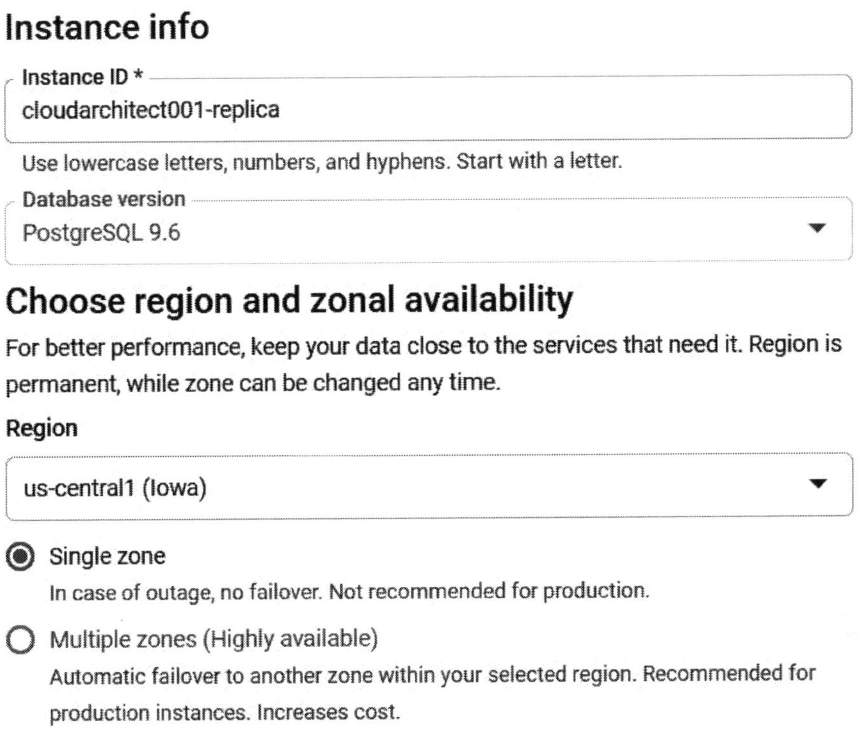

Instance info
Instance ID *
cloudarchitect001-replica
Use lowercase letters, numbers, and hyphens. Start with a letter.
Database version
PostgreSQL 9.6
Choose region and zonal availability
For better performance, keep your data close to the services that need it. Region is permanent, while zone can be changed any time.
Region
us-central1 (Iowa)
Single zone
In case of outage, no failover. Not recommended for production.
Multiple zones (Highly available)
Automatic failover to another zone within your selected region. Recommended for production instances. Increases cost.

Figure 11.33 – Creating a replica

2. Once the read replica has been created, we will see the following in our normal instance view:

SQL
Instances
+ CREATE INSTANCE
Filter
Enter property name or value
Instance ID
cloudarchitect001
cloudarchitect001-replica

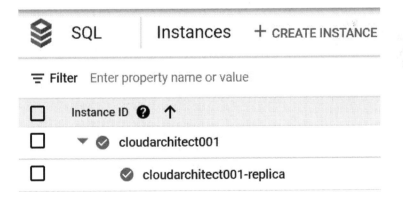

Figure 11.34 – Viewing the read replica

In this section, we looked at read replicas and the various options available. In the next section, we will look at failover replicas.

High availability

I am sure we are all familiar with the term HA. The purpose of this is, of course, to reduce the downtime of a service and in terms of Cloud SQL, to reduce the downtime when a zone or instance becomes unavailable. Public clouds are not immune to downtime and zonal outages can occur, as well as instances becoming corrupted. By enabling HA, our data continues to be available to client applications. As we discussed in the previous section, when deploying a new Cloud SQL instance, we can select a multiple zone configuration to enable HA, which means two separate instances are created within the same region but in different zones. The first instance is configured as the primary, while the second is used as a standby. Through synchronous replication to each zones persistent disk, all writes that are made to the primary instance will be replicated to the disks in both zones before the transaction is confirmed as completed. In the event of a zone or instance failure, the persistent disk is attached to the standby instance, which will then become the new primary instance. Users are then routed to this new primary instance. This process is described as a *failover*. It is important to note that this configuration will remain even when the original primary instance comes back online. This is because once the original primary instance becomes available once more, it is destroyed, recreated, and becomes the new standby instance. If there is a need to have the primary instance in the original zone, then a *failback* can be performed. This process is the same as a *failover* but is where we are making the decision.

Please note that until Q1 2021, legacy MySQL had an HA option for using failover replicas. This is no longer available from Cloud Console.

Backup and recovery

We mentioned backup and recovery previously when we created a new instance. We can create a backup schedule and trigger an on-demand backup from our console or command line whenever required. If we want to edit our instance, we have to check the backup schedule that we have configured or change the backup time if necessary:

Figure 11.35 – Editing the backup schedule

Backups are a way to restore our data from a certain time in the event of corruption or data loss. Cloud SQL gives us the option to restore data for the original instance or a different instance. Both methods will overwrite all of the current data on the target instance.

Let's look at how we can restore from the console:

1. From our MySQL deployment, we can click on the **BACKUPS** tab and then scroll to the bottom of the page for the specific backup we would like to restore:

Figure 11.36 – Selecting a backup

2. If we don't have any replicas or we have deleted them, then we can proceed. You will notice that we can restore directly back to the source instance or select another instance:

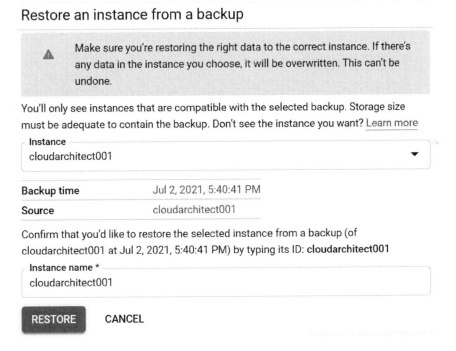

Figure 11.37 – Restoring a backup

In the next section, we will look at how to migrate data.

Database migration service

GCP now offers a service that allows us to easily migrate databases to Cloud SQL from on-premises, Compute Engine, or even other clouds. In essence, this is a *lift and shift* for MySQL and PostgreSQL workloads in Cloud SQL. This is an ideal first step for organizations looking to move existing services into a public cloud as it means less infrastructure to manage and also enjoying the HA, DR, and performance benefits of Google Cloud.

Instance cloning

We previously mentioned that we can clone our instances. This will create a copy of our source instance, but it will be completely independent. This does not mean that we have a cluster or read-only replica in place. Once the cloning is complete, any changes to the source instance will not be reflected in the new cloned instance and vice versa. Instance IP addresses and replicas are not copied to the new cloned instance and must be configured again on the cloned instance. Similarly, any backups that are taken from the source instance are not replicated to the cloned instance.

This can be done from our GCP Console or by using our `gcloud` command-line tool:

1. Let's look at the syntax that we would use to perform this:

    ```
    gcloud sql instances clone <instance source name> <target
    instance name>
    ```

    Here, `<instance source name>` is the name of the instance you wish to clone, while `<target instance name>` is the name you wish to assign to the cloned instance.

2. Let's look at how to clone our `cloudarchitect001` instance:

    ```
    gcloud sql instances clone cloudarchitect001
    cloudarchitect001cloned
    ```

We will call the cloned instance `cloudarchitect001cloned`.

IAM

Access to Google Cloud SQL is secured with IAM. Let's have a look at the list of predefined roles and their details:

- **Owner**: Has full access and control over all GCP resources
- **Editor**: Has read-write access to all SQL resources

- **Viewer**: Has read-only access to all Google Cloud resources, including Cloud SQL resources

- **Cloud SQL Admin**: Has full control of all Cloud SQL resources

- **Cloud SQL Editor**: Has rights to manage specific instances; can't see or modify permissions or modify users for SSL certificates; cannot import data or restore from a backup nor clone, delete, or promote instances; and cannot stop or start replicas or delete databases, replicas, or backups

- **Cloud SQL Viewer**: Has read-only rights to all Cloud SQL resources

- **Cloud SQL Client**: Has access to cloud SQL instances from App Engine and Cloud SQL Proxy

- **Cloud SQL Instance User**: Allows access to a Cloud SQL resource

Quotas and limits

Google Cloud SQL comes with predefined quotas. These default quotas can be changed via the **Navigation** menu, under the **IAM & Admin | Quotas** section. From this menu, we can review the current quotas and request an increase to these limits. We recommend that you familiarize yourself with the limits for each service as this can have an impact on your scalability. For Cloud SQL, we should be aware of some important limits.

> **Exam Tip**
> MySQL (second generation) and PostgreSQL have a storage limit of 10 TB.

Other limits to be aware of include the following:

- There is a limit of 100 instances per project.

- There is a maximum storage limit of 64 TB.

Pricing

Pricing for Cloud SQL is based on CPU and memory pricing, storage and networking pricing, and instance pricing.

For CPU and memory, it is dependent on location, the number of CPUs, and the amount of memory you plan to use. Read replicas are charged at the same rate as standalone instances.

For storage and networking, it is dependent on location, per GB of storage used per month, and the amount of egress networking from Cloud SQL.

Instance pricing is also dependent on where the instance is located and the shared-core machine type.

Summary

In this chapter, we covered the storage options available to us by looking at which ones were most appropriate for common requirements. We also learned about Google Cloud Storage, Cloud Firestore, and Cloud SQL.

With Google Cloud Storage, we looked at use cases, storage classes, and some main features of the service. We also covered some considerations to bear in mind when transferring data. It's clear that Cloud Storage offers a lot of flexibility, but when we need to store more structured data, we need to look at alternatives.

With Cloud Datastore, we learned that this service is a NoSQL database and is ideal for your situation, should your application rely on highly available and structured data. Also, Cloud Datastore can scale from zero up to terabytes of data with ease and is ideal for ACID transactions. We also learned that it offers eventual or strong consistency; however, if we have different requirements and a need for a relational database that has full SQL support for **Online Transaction Processing (OLTP)**, then we should consider Cloud SQL.

For Cloud SQL, we learned that we have different offerings – MySQL, SQL Server, and PostgreSQL. We reviewed how to create and manage our instances, how to create replicas, and how to restore our instances.

In the next chapter, we will continue looking at GCP storage options by covering Cloud Spanner and Bigtable.

Further reading

Read the following articles for more information on the topics that were covered in this chapter:

- **Cloud Storage**: https://cloud.google.com/storage/docs/
- **Cloud Datastore**: https://cloud.google.com/datastore/docs/
- **Cloud SQL**: https://cloud.google.com/sql/docs/

- **Cloud SQL pricing**: `https://cloud.google.com/sql/pricing`

- **Importing data into Cloud SQL**: `https://cloud.google.com/sql/docs/mysql/import-export/importing`

- **Exporting data from Cloud SQL**: `https://cloud.google.com/sql/docs/mysql/import-export/exporting`

12

Exploring Storage and Database Options in GCP – Part 2

In the first part of our storage and database exploration, we looked at several services. In this chapter, we will focus on the remaining core database options.

The concepts of these services may sound similar to those we discussed in the previous chapter. For example, Cloud Spanner has similarities to Cloud SQL, while Bigtable may have you thinking about Cloud Datastore. In this chapter, we will not only look at the Cloud Spanner and Bigtable services but also show you how they differ and why you may need to select these over the other offerings.

We cover the following topics in this chapter:

- Cloud Spanner
- Bigtable

Cloud Spanner

There may be situations where you require horizontal scaling and Cloud SQL will not fit these requirements. Enter Cloud Spanner. Cloud Spanner is a cloud-native, fully managed offering that is designed specifically to combine relational database features, such as support for ACID transactions and SQL queries, with the horizontal scaling of a non-relational database. We should look to use Cloud Spanner when we have requirements for high queries per second or to deliver over multiple regions. Unlike most databases, Cloud Spanner is globally distributed and provides a strongly consistent database service with high performance.

> **Important Note**
> To reiterate, Cloud Spanner is strongly consistent.

It also offers an availability SLA of >=99.999% when you're using a multi-regional instance and is capable of providing up to 10,000 queries per second of reads or 2,000 queries per second of writes. It is important to understand that Cloud Spanner is SQL-like and has a schema; however, because of its high availability, it is ideal for mission-critical workloads. Its key use cases are from the financial and retail industries.

> **Exam Tip**
> With horizontal scalability, it will also support applications hosting across multiple regions. Remember that Cloud Spanner is ideal for workloads that require strong consistency.

Let's look at the configuration Cloud Spanner. We must create a Cloud Spanner instance inside our GCP project to do this.

Instance configurations

When we create a new instance, we should select an instance configuration. This will determine where our instance will reside and the replication of the databases in the instance. We can select between the following:

- **Multi-regional**: By using this instance, we will gain a higher SLA of 99.999% – or a downtime of approximately 5 minutes per year – but it will be more costly. Multi-regional allows the database's data to be replicated in multiple zones across multiple regions, allowing us to read data with low latency from locations. However, because replicas will be spread across more than one region, our applications will see a small increase in write latency.

- **Regional**: This will result in a 99.99% SLA, which is still very high and equivalent to approximately only 52 minutes of downtime per year. Regional instances should be selected if users and services are within the same region. This will offer the lowest latency. As you can see, the requirements will dictate the best option. We cannot change the instance's configuration after creation. Regional configurations will contain three read/write replicas that allow us to meet any governance requirements regarding where our data is located.

Node count

We are also required to select the number of nodes to allocate to our instance. This will determine the amount of CPU/RAM and storage resources that are available to our instance. Each node will provide up to 2 TB of storage, and it is recommended that a minimum of three nodes be used for production environments. We can change the number of nodes after creation to scale up or down.

Processing units

Cloud Spanner now supports processing units. 1,000 processing units is equivalent to 1 node and each increment of 100 units will behave like 1/10th of a node.

Replication

We mentioned replicas previously, and it's important to take a closer look at replication within Cloud Spanner. The underlying distributed filesystem that Cloud Spanner is built on will automatically replicate at the byte level. However, to provide additional data availability and geographic locality, Cloud Spanner will also replicate data by creating copies (replicas) of the rows that Cloud Spanner organized data into. These copies are then stored in a different geographic area. One of these replicas is elected to act as the leader and will be responsible for handling writes. Cloud Spanner has three types of replicas:

- **Read/Write**: This type of replication will maintain a full copy of our data and is eligible to become a leader. This is the only type of replication that's available to single-region instances.

- **Read-Only**: This type of replication will only support reads and cannot become a leader. It will maintain a full copy of our data, which has been replicated from our read/write replica. Read-Only is only available in multi-regional configurations.

- **Witness**: This type of replication doesn't support reads, nor does it maintain a full copy of our data. Witness replication makes it easier for us to achieve quorums for writes without the compute resources that are required by a read/write replica. Witness is only available in multi-regional configurations.

TrueTime

TrueTime is a globally distributed clock built on GPS and atomic clocks. It returns a time interval that is guaranteed to contain the clock's actual time. TrueTime is provided to applications on Google Servers, which allows applications to generate monotonically increasing timestamps. Cloud Spanner uses TrueTime to assign timestamps to transactions whenever Cloud Spanner deems the transaction to have taken place.

Data consistency

If you are looking for guaranteed strong consistency, then Cloud Spanner is the database offering for you! This is all down to the fact it is designed for the cloud and, therefore, will negate a lot of the constraints of other database offerings. Note that Cloud Spanner provides external consistency, which is a stronger property than strong consistency. This is the strictest consistency property for **transaction-processing systems**.

When we speak about data consistency concerning Cloud Spanner, it is wise to raise awareness of the concept of the **CAP theorem**. This theorem says that a database can only have two out of three of the following properties:

- **C: Consistency**. This implies a single value for shared data.
- **A: Availability**. 100% for both reads and updates.
- **P: Partitions**. Tolerance for network partitions.

This means that systems can be made up of *CA*, *CP*, or *AP*. The theorem is about 100% availability, but we know that systems will not offer 100% availability; therefore, system developers are forced to think seriously about the trade-off. If we believe that some network partitions are inevitable at some point in a system's life cycle, then a distributed system should be designed to forfeit consistency or availability – but only during a partition. Cloud Spanner, in times of a partition, will forfeit availability to ensure consistency. Given that Spanner offers 99.999% availability, which equates to less than 5.26 minutes of downtime per year, this is deemed to be high enough that we don't need to worry about availability trade-offs.

Encryption

By default, all data in Cloud Spanner will use Google-managed default encryption. When **Customer-Managed Encryption Keys (CMEK)** are enabled, Cloud Spanner will use our Cloud **Key Management Service (KMS)** keys to protect data at rest. To use CMEK, we must specify the Cloud KMS key when the database is created. As of June 2021, Cloud Spanner supports **Cloud External Key Manager (Cloud EKM)** when using CMEK.

Point-in-time recovery

Cloud Spanner offers protection against accidental write or deletions. This is known as **Point-in-Time Recovery (PITR)**. If, for example, an application rollout corrupts a database, then PITR can recover your data from a point in time from the past 7 days. PITR works by allowing us to configure the database's `version_retention_period` to retain all the versions of the data and its schema. Retention periods can range from 1 hour to 7 days. We can restore either the entire database or a portion of it, but we should also consider performance when we set longer retention periods as this will use more system resources, particularly on those databases that frequently overwrite data.

Next, let's look at how we can create our first Spanner instance.

Creating a Cloud Spanner instance

Let's look at actually creating a Cloud Spanner instance. We will also create a database – that is, a table – and run a query on it:

1.   Browse to **DATABASES | Spanner**, as shown in the following screenshot:

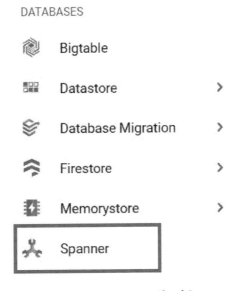

Figure 12.1 – Browsing to Cloud Spanner

2. Choose to create an instance, and then enter an instance name. Please note that you may have to enable the API. **ID** will be auto-populated based on our name, but this can be modified if needed. We can also select our regional configuration and our compute capacity. Click on **Create** to provision the instance:

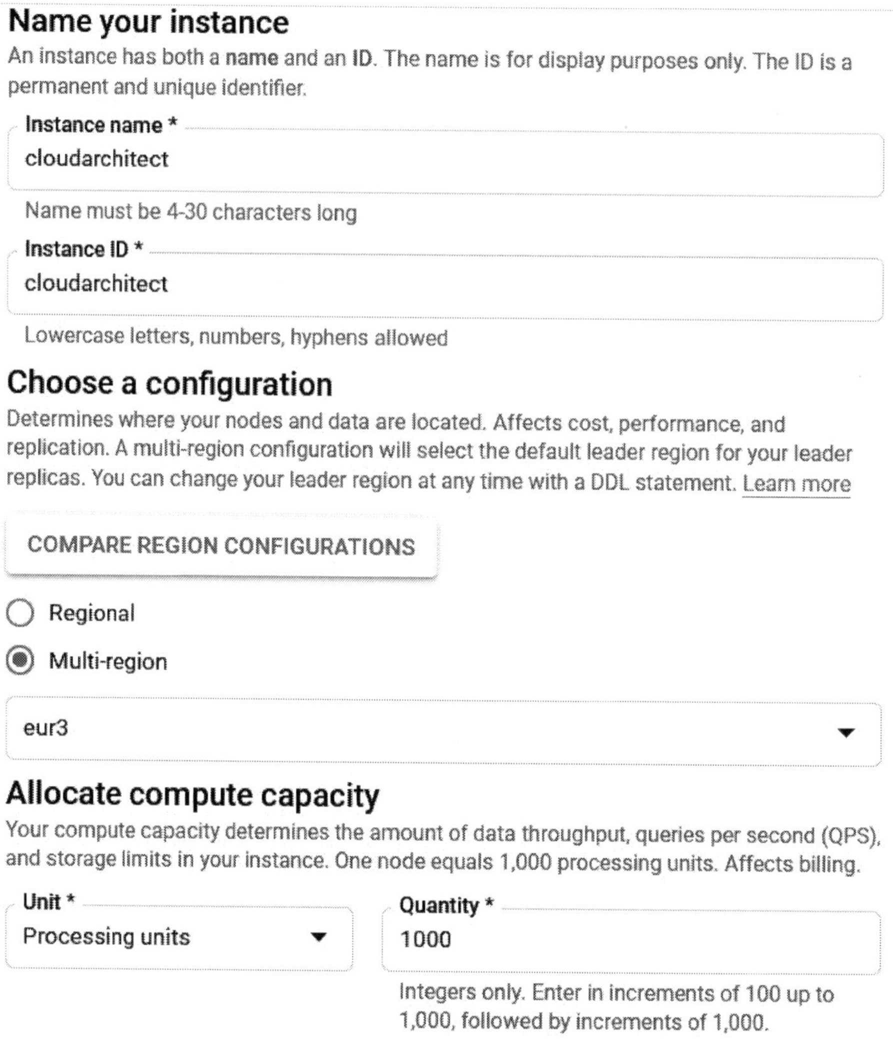

Name your instance

An instance has both a **name** and an **ID**. The name is for display purposes only. The ID is a permanent and unique identifier.

Instance name *

cloudarchitect

Name must be 4-30 characters long

Instance ID *

cloudarchitect

Lowercase letters, numbers, hyphens allowed

Choose a configuration

Determines where your nodes and data are located. Affects cost, performance, and replication. A multi-region configuration will select the default leader region for your leader replicas. You can change your leader region at any time with a DDL statement. Learn more

COMPARE REGION CONFIGURATIONS

○ Regional

◉ Multi-region

eur3   ▼

Allocate compute capacity

Your compute capacity determines the amount of data throughput, queries per second (QPS), and storage limits in your instance. One node equals 1,000 processing units. Affects billing.

Unit *   Quantity *

Processing units   ▼   1000

Integers only. Enter in increments of 100 up to 1,000, followed by increments of 1,000.

Figure 12.2 – Creating a new instance

3. Once our instance has been created, click on **Create database**:

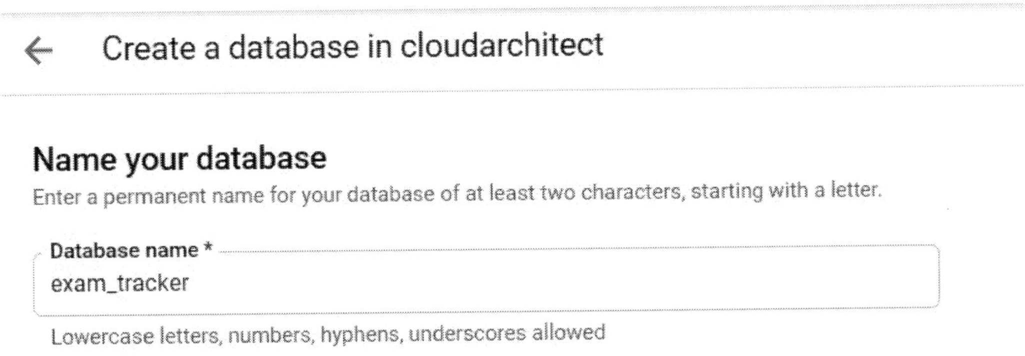

← Create a database in cloudarchitect

Name your database

Enter a permanent name for your database of at least two characters, starting with a letter.

Database name *
exam_tracker

Lowercase letters, numbers, hyphens, underscores allowed

Figure 12.3 – Creating a database

4. Now, we can create a table. Let's create a table called `professionalCloudArchitect`. Our table will keep track of how employees did while sitting the Google Professional Cloud Architect exam. Once you have populated the text field as follows, click **SUBMIT** to create the table:

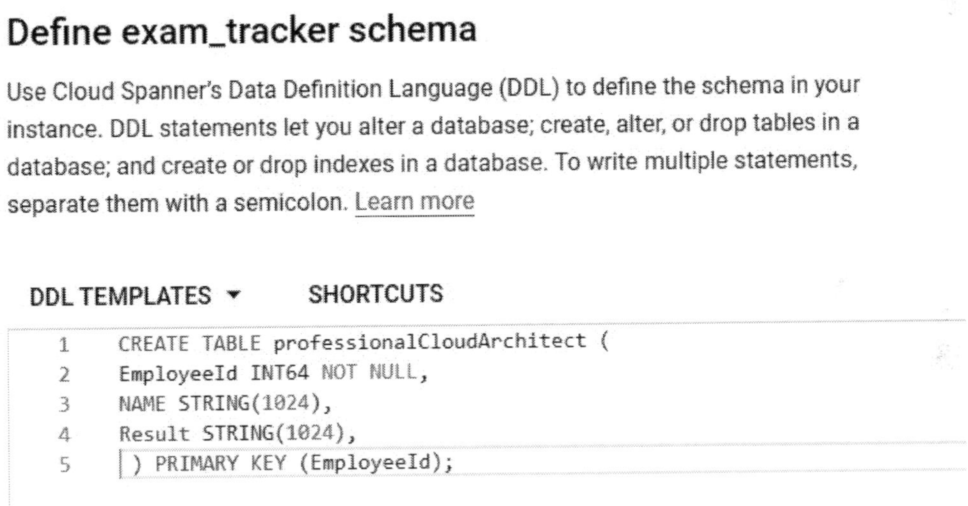

Define exam_tracker schema

Use Cloud Spanner's Data Definition Language (DDL) to define the schema in your instance. DDL statements let you alter a database; create, alter, or drop tables in a database; and create or drop indexes in a database. To write multiple statements, separate them with a semicolon. Learn more

DDL TEMPLATES ▾   SHORTCUTS

```
1    CREATE TABLE professionalCloudArchitect (
2    EmployeeId INT64 NOT NULL,
3    NAME STRING(1024),
4    Result STRING(1024),
5    ) PRIMARY KEY (EmployeeId);
```

Figure 12.4 – Creating a table

5. Now, we can populate it with values by clicking on our new table, browsing to **Data**, and then clicking **Insert**:

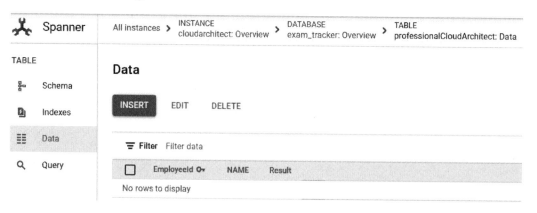

Figure 12.5 – Populating the table

6. The Query Editor will appear and allow us to fill in our table data. Do this by adding the following under the **VALUES** section and clicking **RUN**:

```
INSERT INTO
    professionalCloudArchitect (EmployeeId,
        NAME,
        Result)
VALUES
    (1, 'Brian Gerrard' , 'Pass'),
    (2, 'Konrad Clapa' , 'Pass'),
    (3, 'Joe Bloggs' , 'Pass'),
    (4, 'Paul McDonal' , 'Fail'),
    (5, 'Alison Munro' , 'Fail');
```

Figure 12.6 – Primary key

7. Our table view will now look like this:

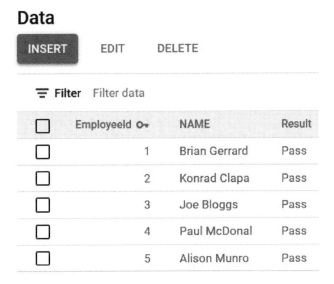

Figure 12.7 – Data

8. Now, let's click on the **Query** tab again and perform a query on our information to see who has passed the exam. Select **RUN** to execute the query:

Figure 12.8 – Query

9. Let's view our results, as follows:

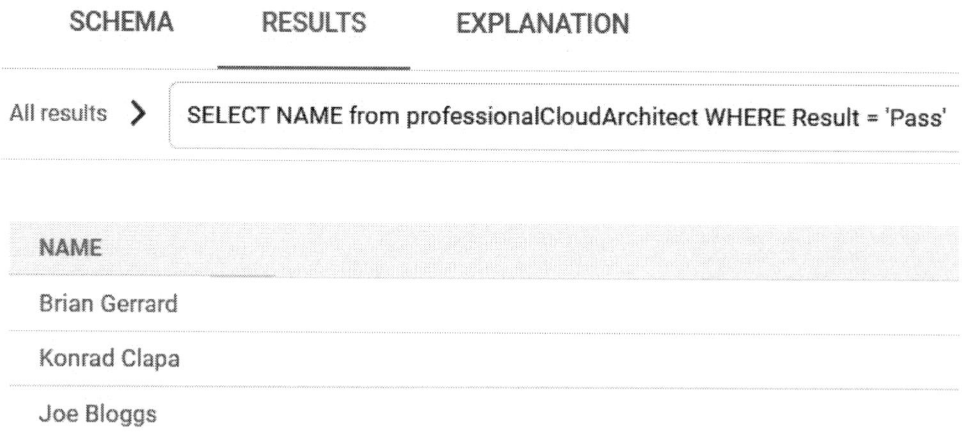

SCHEMA   RESULTS   EXPLANATION

All results **>** | SELECT NAME from professionalCloudArchitect WHERE Result = 'Pass'

NAME
Brian Gerrard
Konrad Clapa
Joe Bloggs

Figure 12.9 – Results

By doing this, we get a list of team members who have passed the exam.

IAM

Access to Google Cloud Spanner is secured with **IAM**. The following is a list of predefined roles, along with a short description for each:

- **Spanner Admin**: This person has complete rights to all Cloud Spanner resources in a project.

- **Spanner Database Admin**: This person has the right to list all Cloud Spanner instances and *create/list/drop* databases in the instances it was created in. They can grant and revoke access to a database in the project, and they can also read and write to all Cloud Spanner databases in the project.

- **Spanner Database Reader**: This person has the right to *read* from the Cloud Spanner database, execute queries on the database, and view the schema for the database.

- **Spanner Database User**: This person has the right to *read* and *write* to a Cloud Spanner database, execute SQL queries on the database, and view and update the schema for the database.

- **Spanner Viewer**: This person has the right to view all Cloud Spanner instances and view all Cloud Spanner databases.

- **Restore Admin**: This person has the right to restore databases from backups.
- **Backup Admin**: This person has the right to *create*, *view*, *update*, and *delete* backups.

Quotas and limits

Cloud Spanner comes with predefined quotas. These default quotas can be changed via the **Navigation** menu and via **IAM & Admin | Quotas**. From this menu, we can review the current quotas and request an increase for these limits. We recommend that you are aware of the limits for each service as this can have an impact on your scalability. For Cloud Spanner, we should be aware of the following limits:

- There is a limit of 2 to 64 characters on the instance ID's length.
- There is a limit of 100 databases per instance.
- There is a limit of 2 to 30 characters on the database ID's length.
- There is a limit of 2 TB storage per node.
- There is a limit of a 10 MB schema size.
- There is a limit of a 10 MB schema change size.
- There is a limit of 5,000 tables per database.
- There is a limit of 1 to 128 characters for the table name's length.
- There is a limit of 1,024 columns per table.
- There is a limit of 1 to 128 characters for the column name's length.
- There is a limit of 10 MB of data per column.
- There is a limit of 16 columns in a table key.
- There is a limit of 10,000 indexes per database.
- There is a limit of 32 indexes per table.
- There is a limit of 16 columns in an index key.
- There is a limit of 1,000 function calls.
- There is a limit of 25 nodes per project, per instance configuration.

Pricing

Cloud Spanner charges for the amount of compute capacity and the amount of storage and network bandwidth that's used. We will be charged for the following:

- For the maximum number of nodes multiplied by the hourly rate. As Spanner has moved to processing units, this might be a fraction of a full node (1,000 processing units are smaller than 1 node).

- The average amount of data in our databases over 1 month. These prices will fluctuate, depending on the location of our instances.

- Egress network traffic for some types of traffic. However, there is no charge for replication or ingress traffic.

- The amount of storage that backups use is also charged over 1 month, multiplied by the monthly rate.

> **Exam Tip**
>
> An important point to remember about Cloud Spanner is that it offers ACID transactions. If an atomic transaction involves two or more pieces of information, then all of the pieces are committed; otherwise, none are.

Bigtable

There is a clue in the name, but Bigtable is GCP's big data NoSQL database service. Bigtable is low latency and can scale to billions of rows and thousands of columns. It's also the database that powers many of Google's core services, such as *Search, Analytics, Maps,* and *Gmail*. This makes Bigtable a great choice for analytics and real-time workloads as it's designed to handle massive workloads at low latency and high throughput.

> **Exam Tip**
>
> Bigtable can support petabytes of data and is suitable for real-time access and analytics workloads. It's a great choice for **Internet of Things (IoT)** applications that require frequent data ingestion or high-speed transactions.

Given Bigtable's massive scalability, we will cover the storage model and architecture. When we discuss Bigtable, we will make references to **HBase**. HBase is effectively an open source implementation of the Bigtable architecture and follows the same design philosophies. Bigtable stores its data in tables, which are stored in a key/value map. Each table is comprised of rows, which will describe a single entity.

Tables are also comprised of columns, which contain individual values for each row. Rows are indexed by a row key, and columns that are related to one another are grouped into a column family. Bigtable only offers basic operations such as *create, read, update,* and *delete.* This means it has some good use cases while also not being great for others. Bigtable should not be used for transaction support – as we mentioned previously, CloudSQL or Spanner would be better suited for OLTP.

The following diagram shows the architecture of Bigtable:

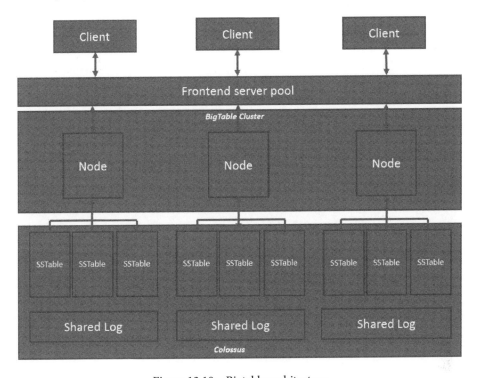

Figure 12.10 – Bigtable architecture

Here, we can see that the client's requests go through a frontend server before they are sent to a Bigtable node. These nodes make up a Bigtable cluster belonging to a Bigtable instance, which acts as a container for the cluster.

Each node in the cluster handles a subset of the requests. We can increase the number of simultaneous requests a cluster can handle by adding more nodes. The preceding diagram only shows a single cluster, but replication can be enabled by adding a second cluster. With a second cluster, we can send different types of traffic to specific clusters and, of course, availability is increased.

To help balance out the workload of queries, Bigtable is sharded into blocks on contiguous rows. These are referred to as tablets and are stored on Google's filesystem – **Colossus** – in **Sorted Strings Table (SSTable)** format. SSTable stores immutable row fragments in a sorted order based on row keys. Each table will be associated with a specific Bigtable node, and writes are stored in the Colossus shared log as soon as they have been acknowledged. We should also note that data is never stored on Bigtable nodes. However, these nodes have pointers to a set of tablets that are stored in Colossus, meaning that if a Bigtable node fails, then no data loss is suffered.

Now that we understand the high-level architecture, let's look at the configuration of Bigtable.

Bigtable configuration

In this section, we will look at the key components that make up Bigtable. We will discuss the following:

- Instances
- Clusters
- Nodes
- Schema
- Replication

Instances

Cloud Bigtable is made up of instances that will contain up to four clusters that our applications can connect to. Each cluster contains nodes. We should imagine an instance as a container for our clusters and nodes. We can modify the number of nodes in our cluster and the number of clusters in our instance. When we create our instance, as expected, we can select the region and zone that we wish to deploy to and we can also select the type of storage, either *SSD* or *HDD*. The location and the storage type are both permanent choices.

Clusters

A Bigtable cluster represents the service in a specific location. Each cluster belongs to a single Bigtable instance and, as we've already mentioned, each instance can have up to four clusters. When our application sends a request to an instance, it is handled by one of the clusters in the instance. Each cluster is located in a single zone, and an instance's clusters must be in unique zones. If our configuration means that we have more than one cluster, then Bigtable will automatically start to replicate our data by storing copies of the data in each of the cluster's zones and synchronizing updates between the copies. To isolate different types of traffic from each other, we can select which cluster we want our application to connect to.

Nodes

Each cluster in a production instance has a minimum of three nodes. Nodes are, as you may expect, compute resources that Bigtable will use to manage our data. Bigtable will try to distribute read and writes evenly across all nodes and also store an equal amount of data on each node. If a Bigtable cluster becomes overloaded, we can add more nodes to improve its performance. Equally, we can scale down and remove nodes.

Schema

It's worth noting that designing a Bigtable schema is very different from designing a schema for a relational database. There are no secondary indices as each table only has one index. Rows are sorted lexicographically by row key (the only index), from the lowest to the highest byte string. If you have two rows in a table, one row may be updated successfully while the other row may fail. Therefore, we should avoid designing schemas that require atomicity across rows. Poor schema designs can be responsible for overall poor Bigtable performance.

> **Exam Tip**
>
> Schemas can also be designed for **time series data**. If we want to measure something along with the time it occurred, then we are building a time series. Data in Bigtable is stored as unstructured columns in rows, with each row having a row key. This makes Bigtable an ideal fit for time series data. When we have to think about schema design patterns for time series, we should use tall and narrow tables, meaning that one event is stored per row. This makes it easier to run queries against our data.

Replication

The availability of data is a very big concern. Bigtable replication copies our data across multiple regions or zones within the same region, thus increasing the availability and durability of our data. Of course, to use replication, we must create an instance with more than one cluster or add clusters to an existing instance. Once this has been set up, Bigtable will begin to replicate straight away and store separate copies of our data in each zone where our instance has a cluster. Since this replication is done in almost real time, it makes for a good backup of our data. Bigtable will perform an automated failover when a cluster becomes unresponsive.

Application profiles

If we require an instance to use replication, then we need to use **application profiles**. By storing settings in these application profiles, we can manage incoming requests from our application and determine how Bigtable handles them. Every Bigtable instance will have a default application profile, but we can also create custom profiles. Our code should be updated to specify which app profile we want our applications to use when we connect to an instance. If we do not specify anything, then Bigtable will use the default profile.

The configuration of our application profiles will affect how an application communicates with an instance that uses replication. There are **routing policies** within an application profile. **Single-cluster routing** will route all the requests to a single cluster in your instance, while **multi-cluster routing** will automatically route traffic to the nearest cluster in an instance. If we create an instance with one cluster, then the default application profile will use single-cluster routing. If we create an instance with two or more clusters, then the default application profile will use multi-cluster routing.

To create an application profile, we must have a Bigtable instance. We can create a custom application profile from the GCP console by browsing to the hamburger menu and going to **Bigtable**, and then clicking on the instance where we wish to create the app profile. Finally, browse to the **Application profiles** option in the left-hand pane and click **CREATE APPLICATION PROFILE**.

In the following screenshot, we are creating an application profile for an instance called **cloudarchitect**:

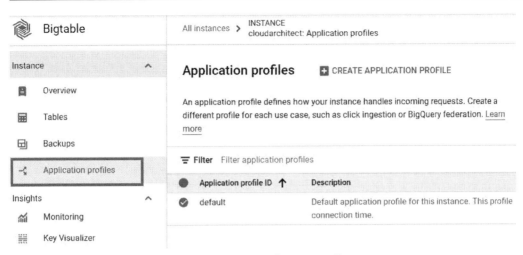

Figure 12.11 – Application profiles

Then, we need to give the profile an **ID** and enter a description if we feel that's necessary. Afterward, we must select the routing policy we require:

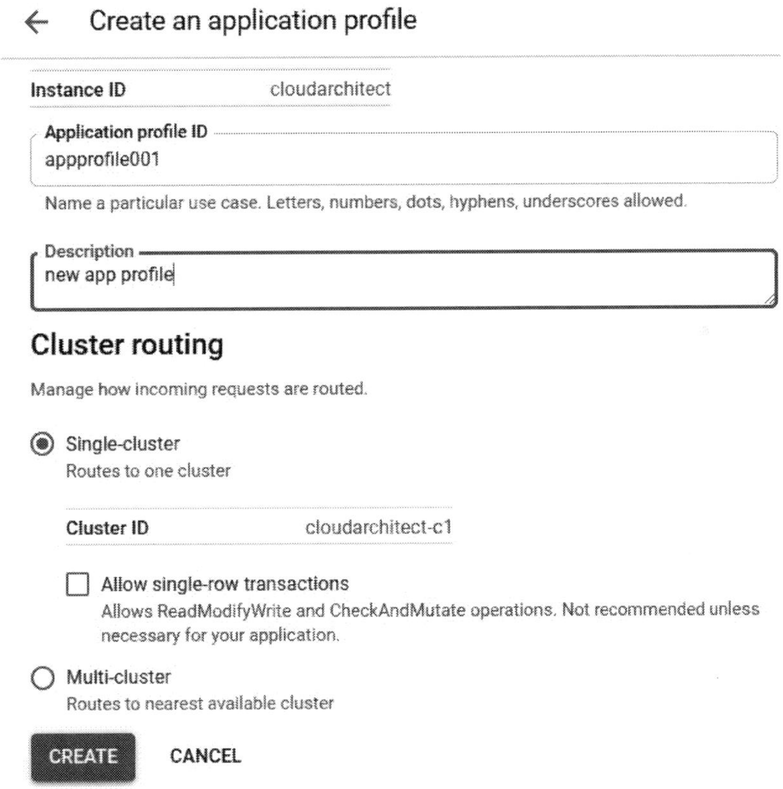

←   Create an application profile

Instance ID   cloudarchitect

Application profile ID
appprofile001

Name a particular use case. Letters, numbers, dots, hyphens, underscores allowed.

Description
new app profile

Cluster routing

Manage how incoming requests are routed.

◉ Single-cluster
     Routes to one cluster

Cluster ID   cloudarchitect-c1

☐ Allow single-row transactions
     Allows ReadModifyWrite and CheckAndMutate operations. Not recommended unless necessary for your application.

○ Multi-cluster
     Routes to nearest available cluster

CREATE   CANCEL

Figure 12.12 – Application profile settings

Note that we can check the box for single-row transactions. Bigtable does not support transactions that atomically update more than one row; however, it can use single-row transactions to complete *read-modify-write* and *conditional writes* operations. Note that this option is only available when using a single-cluster routing policy to prevent conflicts.

Data consistency

One important aspect to understand is that Bigtable is eventually consistent by default, meaning that when we write a change to one of our clusters, we will be able to read that change from other clusters, but only after replication has taken place. To overcome this constraint, we can enable **Read-Your-Writes** consistency when we have replication enabled. This will ensure that an application won't read data that's older than the most recent writes. To achieve Read-Your-Writes consistency for a group of applications, we should use the single-cluster routing policy in our app profiles to route requests to the same cluster. The downside to this, however, means that if a cluster becomes unavailable, then we need to perform the failover manually.

Planning capacity

One important aspect to consider when planning our Bigtable clusters is the trade-off between throughput and latency. For latency-sensitive applications, Google advises that we plan for at least 2x capacity for our application's maximum Bigtable QPS. This is to ensure that Bigtable clusters run at less than 50% CPU usage, therefore offering low latency to frontend services.

> **Exam Tip**
> Capacity planning allows us to provide a buffer for traffic spikes or key-access hotspots, which may cause imbalanced traffic among nodes in the cluster.

Creating a Bigtable instance and table

Let's take a look at creating a Bigtable instance from our GCP console:

1. Browse to **DATABASES | Bigtable**, as shown in the following screenshot:

DATABASES
Bigtable
Datastore
Database Migration
Firestore
Memorystore
Spanner

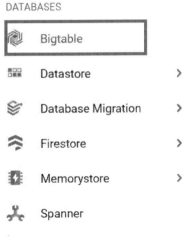

Figure 12.13 – Bigtable

2. Click on **CREATE INSTANCE**:

Bigtable
All instances
Instances
CREATE INSTANCE

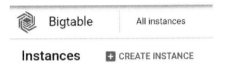

Figure 12.14 – Creating an instance

3. Provide a name and instance ID for our instance and select an instance type. Also, select the type of storage we require:

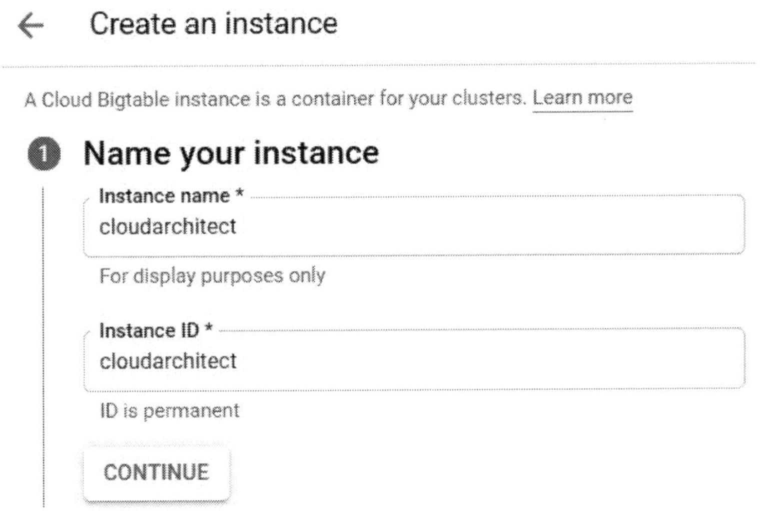

Create an instance
A Cloud Bigtable instance is a container for your clusters. Learn more
1 Name your instance
Instance name *
cloudarchitect
For display purposes only
Instance ID *
cloudarchitect
ID is permanent
CONTINUE

Figure 12.15 – Instance configuration

4. Provide the cluster details; that is, the location and the number of nodes needed. We can also set up replication if needed. Note that we can also select our storage type – either SSD or HDD. This will default to SSD if we do not change it. Click **Done** to accept the cluster changes and click **Create** to complete the instance configuration:

Select a cluster ID

ID is permanent

Cluster ID *

cloudarchitect-c2

Select a location

Choice is permanent. Determines where cluster data is stored. To reduce latency and increase throughput, store your data near the services that need it. Learn more

Region *

europe-west2 (London)   ▼

Zone *

Any   ▼

Allocate nodes

Node count can be updated at any time to meet your cluster's need for data throughput, storage, and rows read per second. For better instance performance, keep your cluster's CPU utilization under the recommended threshold for your app profile routing policy. Contact us if you need to increase your node quota. Learn more

Nodes *

3

Figure 12.16 – Adding a cluster

Once we have our instance and clusters, we can create a table. We touched on this earlier, but Bigtable has a command-line tool called cbt, and creating a table is simplistic when we use it. Once again, we will make assumptions that you are familiar with this tool. Open Cloud Shell so that we can configure the cbt tool. We will look at cbt and Cloud Shell in more detail in *Chapter 16, Google Cloud Management Options*:

1. Before we create a table, run the following syntax to mitigate the need to specify them in future command lines:

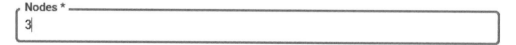

```
echo project = <project ID> ~/.cbtrc
echo instance = <instance ID> >> ~/.cbtrc
```

Here, we have the following:

- `<project ID>` is the ID of the project our Bigtable instance is associated with.

- `<instance ID>` is the ID of our instance.

2. Once this has been configured, we can create a table using some very simple syntax:

```
cbt createtable table001
```

Here, we have created a table called `table001`.

IAM

Access to Google Cloud Bigtable is secured with IAM. The following is a list of predefined roles, along with a short description of each:

- **Bigtable Admin**: This person has rights to all Bigtable features and is where you can create new instances. This role should be used by project administrators.

- **Bigtable User**: This person has read-only access to the data stored within tables. This role should be used by application developers or service accounts.

- **Bigtable Reader**: This person has read-only access to the data stored within tables. This role should be used by data scientists.

- **Bigtable Viewer**: This role should be used to grant the minimal set of permissions for Cloud Bigtable.

Quotas and limits

Google Cloud Bigtable comes with predefined quotas. These default quotas can be changed via the **Navigation** menu and via **IAM & Admin | Quotas**. From this menu, we can review the current quotas and request an increase for these limits. We recommend that you are aware of the limits for each service as this can have an impact on your scalability. For Cloud Bigtable, we should be aware of the following limits:

- There is a limit of 2.5 TB of SSD storage per node.

- There is a limit of 8 TB of HDD storage per node.

- There is a limit of 1,000 tables in each instance.

For Cloud Bigtable, we should also be aware of the following quotas:

- By default, you can provision up to 30 SSD or HDD nodes per zone in each project.

- Numerous operational quotas should be reviewed.

Pricing

Bigtable charges based on several factors:

- Instance types are charged per hour, per node.

- Storage is charged per month and costs vary, depending on the use of SSD or HDD.

- Internet egress rates are charged depending on monthly usage. Ingress traffic is free.

For more specific details, please see the Bigtable pricing URL in the *Further reading* section.

Summary

In this chapter, we covered Cloud Spanner and Bigtable.

In terms of **Cloud Spanner**, we now understand that this is a scalable and globally distributed database. It is strongly consistent and was built to combine the benefits of relational databases with the scalability of a non-relational database. Cloud Spanner can scale across regions for workloads that might have high availability requirements.

We covered **Bigtable** at a high level to make sure you are aware of what is expected in the exam. It is a fully managed NoSQL database service that can scale massively and offers low latency, is ideal for IoT as it can handle high-speed transactions in real time, integrates well with machine learning and analytics, and can support over a petabyte of data.

We have now come to the end of a large chapter with a lot of information to take in. We have looked at the key database services offered by GCP. We advise that you look over the exam tips in this chapter and make sure that you are aware of the main features of each service. Some of the key design decisions that we have spoken about are relational versus non-relational, structured data versus non-structured data, scalability, and SQL versus NoSQL.

In the next chapter, we will look at big data.

Further reading

Read the following articles to find out more about what was covered in this chapter:

- **Cloud Spanner**: https://cloud.google.com/spanner/docs/

- **Cloud Spanner Pricing**: https://cloud.google.com/spanner/pricing

- **Bigtable**: https://cloud.google.com/Bigtable/docs/

- **Bigtable Pricing**: https://cloud.google.com/Bigtable/pricing

13
Analyzing Big Data Options

If you have been looking into cloud computing, then the chances are you have come across the term **big data**. This is used to describe the large volumes of data that modern-day businesses are processing. We are not so worried about the mass of data, but more about how we can use this data. Almost everything carries a digital footprint these days, and there are challenges in ingesting this data and extracting meaningful information. Google offers services that work together to allow us to gather data, process it, and analyze it. The faster we can analyze data, the faster business decisions can be made. Big data is becoming very important to many organizations.

In this chapter, we will cover the following topics:

- End-to-end big data solution
- Pub/Sub
- Dataflow
- BigQuery
- Dataproc
- Cloud IoT
- Cloud Data Fusion
- Datastream

In this chapter, we want to introduce the main Google big data services and concepts to a level expected by the exam. Of course, deeper dives are available.

End-to-end big data solution

Before we begin looking at the services, let's look at a very simple diagram. This represents the end-to-end big data solution. GCP provides us with all of the tools to architect an elastic and scalable service where we can import huge amounts of data, process events, and then execute business rules.

> **Exam Tip**
>
> It is important to understand this flow and which services map to each stage. As we go through this chapter, we will map each big data service to a stage in our end-to-end solution.

We can ingest data from multiple sources, execute code to process this data, and then analyze the data to ensure that we maximize our business capabilities:

Figure 13.1 – End-to-end data flow

Of course, this is a very simplistic view of it and there are complexities when architecting our solutions, but we should expect, at least for the exam, to understand this at a high level. Let's look at the services that map to each stage of the process in more detail.

Cloud Pub/Sub

Pub/Sub is a messaging and event ingestion service that acts as the glue between loosely coupled systems. It allows us to send and receive messages between independent applications while **decoupling** the publishers of events and subscribers to those events. This means that the publishers do not need to know anything about their subscribers. Pub/Sub is fully managed, so it offers scale at ease, making it perfect for a modern stream analytics pipeline.

There are some core concepts that you should understand:

- A **publisher** is an application that will create and send messages to a topic.

- A **topic** is a resource that messages are sent to by publishers.

- A **subscription** represents the stream of messages from a single topic to be delivered to the subscribing application. Subscribers will either receive the message through pull or push, meaning Pub/Sub pushes the messages to the endpoint using a webhook, or the message is pulled by the application using HTTPS requests to the Google API.

- A **message** is data that a publisher will send to a topic. Simply put, it is data in transit through the system.

A publisher can be any application that can make HTTPS requests to `googleapis.com`. This can be existing GCP services, **Internet Of Things (IoT)** devices, or end user applications.

As we mentioned earlier, subscribers receive the messages either through a pull or push delivery method. Similar to publishers, pull subscribers can be any application that can make HTTPS requests to `googleapis.com`. In this case, the subscriber application will initiate requests to Pub/Sub to retrieve messages. On the other hand, push subscribers must be webhook endpoints that can accept `POST` requests over HTTPS.

In this case, Cloud Pub/Sub initiates requests to the subscriber application to deliver messages. Consideration should be given as to the best method for our requirements. As an example, if you are expecting a large volume of messages (for example, more than one message per second), then it is advisable to use the pull delivery method. Alternatively, if you have multiple topics that must be processed by the same webhook, then it is advisable to use the push delivery method:

Figure 13.2 – Push delivery method

To summarize this, let's look at how this works in practice in the preceding diagram. When all of the deliveries are complete, the message will be removed from the queue.

As Cloud Pub/Sub integrates well with other GCP products, it opens up a lot of use cases.

Let's have a look at the most common use cases:

- **Distributed event notifications**: Let's take a service that needs to send a notification whenever there is a new registration. Pub/Sub makes it possible for a downstream service to subscribe and receive notifications of this new registration.

- **Balancing workloads**: Tasks can be distributed among multiple Compute Engine instances.

- **Logging**: Pub/Sub can write logs to multiple systems. For example, if we wish to work with real-time information, we could write to a monitoring system, and if we wish to analyze the data at a later time, we could write to a database.

Creating a topic and a subscription

Pub/Sub can ingest data from several data sources. The following diagram shows the key services that can pass data to Pub/Sub. This is the first step in our solution:

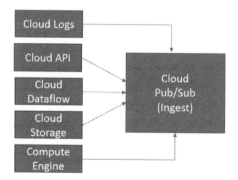

Figure 13.3 – Passing data to Pub/Sub

Now, let's look at creating a Pub/Sub topic and subscription. Then, we will publish a message and pull it via Cloud Shell. Please refer to *Chapter 16, Google Cloud Management Options*, for more information on Cloud Shell. At this point, we are assuming you can open this:

1. From the **Navigation** menu, browse to **BIG DATA | Pub/Sub**, as shown in the following screenshot:

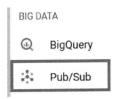

Figure 13.4 – Selecting Pub/Sub

2. Click on **CREATE TOPIC**:

Figure 13.5 – Creating a topic

3. Provide a **Topic ID**. In this example, we will name it `newTopic`. Click **CREATE TOPIC**, as shown in the following screenshot:

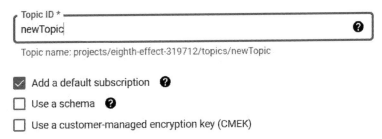

Figure 13.6 – Entering a Topic ID

4. Select **Create subscription**, as shown in the following screenshot:

Figure 13.7 – Create subscription

5.   Provide a **Subscription ID**. In this example, we will call it `newSub`. We will leave the rest of the settings as their default settings, but we should note what each of these is:

• **Message retention duration**: Pub/Sub will try to deliver the message within a maximum of 7 days. After that, the message will be deleted is no longer accessible.

• **Subscription expiration**: If there are no active connections or pull/push successes, then the subscription expires.

• **Acknowledgment Deadline**: The subscriber should acknowledge the message within a specific timeframe; otherwise, Pub/Sub will attempt to deliver this message.

Notice that we keep **Delivery Type** set to **Pull**, as shown in the following screenshot:

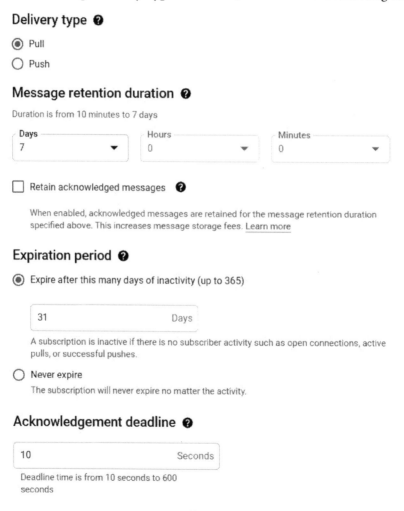

Figure 13.8 – Subscription settings

6. Browse back to **Topics** and click on the topics we recently created. Scroll to the bottom, select the **MESSAGES** tab, and select **PUBLISH MESSAGE**:

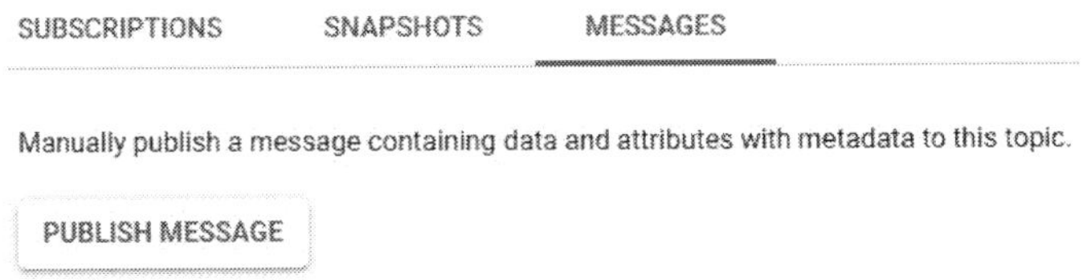

Figure 13.9 – Browsing to messages

7. Enter the message's content and select **PUBLISH**, as shown in the following screenshot:

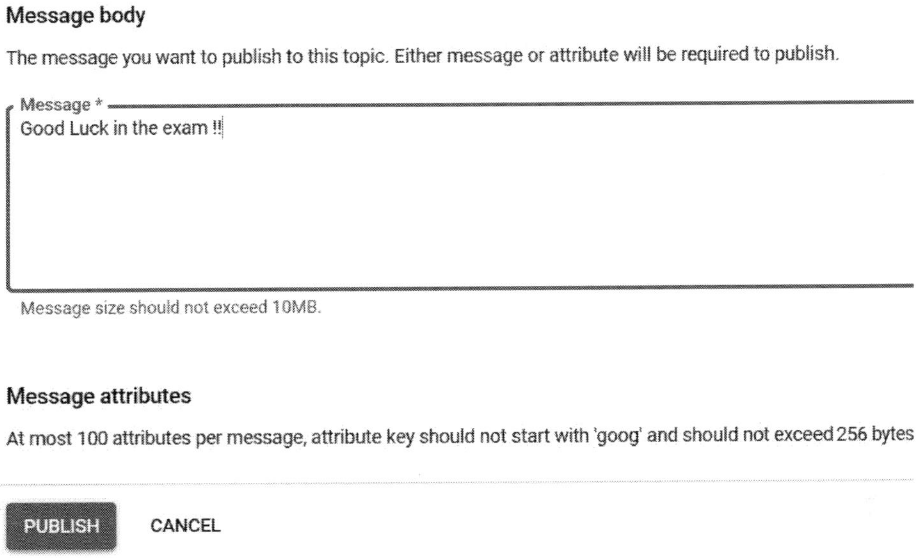

Figure 13.10 – Publishing a message

8. From Cloud Shell, we can now pull down the message:

```
gcparchitectbook@cloudshell:~ (eighth-effect-319712)$ gcloud pubsub subscriptions pull --auto-ack newSub
```

DATA	MESSAGE_ID	ORDERING_KEY	ATTRIBUTES	DELIVERY_ATTEMPT
Good Luck in the exam !!	2629643884009593			

Figure 13.11 – Cloud Shell output

This concludes how to publish and retrieve messages to and from Pub/Sub.

Pub/Sub Lite

While Pub/Sub should be our default solution for most application integration use cases, GCP does offer Pub/Sub Lite for applications when a lower cost justifies some operational overhead. It offers fewer features, lower availability, and there is a requirement to manually reserve and manage resource capacity. However, using Pub/Sub Lite for a system with a single subscription could be up to 85% cheaper.

Some of the other main differences between the products are as follows:

- Pub/Sub routes messages globally, whereas Lite routes messages zonally.

- Pub/Sub topics and subscriptions are global resources, whereas with Lite, they are zonal resources.

- Pub/Sub scales automatically, whereas Lite requires us to manually provision capacity.

IAM

Access to Pub/Sub is secured with IAM. Let's have a look at the list of predefined roles, along with a short description of each:

- **Pubsub Publisher**: This has permission to publish a topic.

- **Pubsub Subscriber**: This has permission to consume a subscription or attach a subscription to a topic.

- **Pubsub Viewer**: This has the right to list topics and subscriptions.

- **Pubsub Editor**: This has the right to create, delete, and update topics, as well as create, delete, and update subscriptions.

- **Pubsub Admin**: This has the right to retrieve and set IAM policies for topics and subscriptions.

Quotas and limits

Pub/Sub comes with some limits. We recommend that you are aware of the limits for each service as this can have an impact on your scalability. For Pub/Sub, we should be aware of the following limits:

- There is a limit of 10,000 topics and 10,000 subscriptions per project.

- There is a limit of 10,000 attached subscriptions per topic.

- There is a limit of 1,000 messages and a 10 MB total size per publishing request.

- There is a limit of 10 MB per message.

Pricing

Pub/Sub is billed per message ingestion and delivery. There is also a storage charge for retained acknowledged messages.

In this section, we looked at Pub/Sub and Pub/Sub Lite. In the next section, we'll look at Cloud Dataflow.

Cloud Dataflow

Cloud Dataflow is a service based on Apache Beam, which is an open source software for creating data processing pipelines. A pipeline is essentially a piece of code that determines how we wish to process our data. Once these pipelines have been constructed and input into the service, they become a Dataflow job. This is where we can process the data that's been ingested by Pub/Sub. It will perform steps to change our data from one format to another and can transform both real-time streams or historical batch data. Dataflow is completely serverless and fully managed. It will spin up the necessary resources to execute our Dataflow job and then delete these resources when the job is complete. As an example, a pipeline job might be made up of several steps. If a specific step needs to be executed on 15 machines in parallel, then Dataflow will automatically scale to these 15 machines and remove them when the job is complete. These resources are based on Compute Engine and are referred to as workers, and Cloud Storage is used as a temporary staging area and I/O. These resources are based on our location settings.

> **Exam Tip**
> Dataflow will transform and enrich data in stream and batch modes. Its serverless architecture can be used to shard and process very large batch datasets or a high volume of live streams in parallel.

Cloud Dataflow is the next stage of our end-to-end solution and will process the data that's passed by **Cloud Pub/Sub**. Let's look at how this impacts our service designs from *Figure 13.3*:

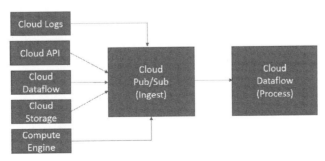

Figure 13.12 – Service design

Now, let's create a streaming pipeline using one of Google's open source Dataflow templates.

Here, we have a Pub/Sub subscription and we wish to write the data to a data warehouse service for analysis. In this example, we will use BigQuery to analyze our data. We will discuss this service in the next section. We need Dataflow to convert JSON-formatted messages from Pub/Sub into BigQuery elements. For this example, we will use a Google public GCP project, which has **Pub/Sub Topics** set up. We will also assume that we have a BigQuery table ready for the data to be written to:

1. From the **Navigation** menu, browse to **BIG DATA | Dataflow**:

Figure 13.13 – Browsing to Dataflow

2. Click on **CREATE JOB FROM TEMPLATE**:

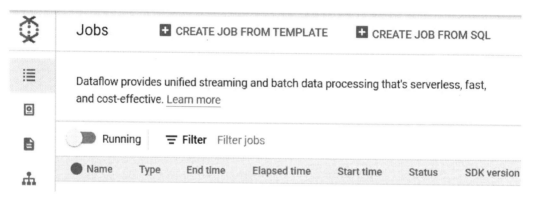

Figure 13.14 – CREATE JOB FROM TEMPLATE

3. Now, we can populate the required parameters for our Dataflow job:

- Select a location to deploy our Dataflow workers to and store our metadata in. We will leave this as the default setting.

- Insert the Pub/Sub input topic. This is a public project that's made available by Google as part of the template.

- Insert the BigQuery output table where our data will be written.

- Insert a Cloud Storage bucket to store temporary files:

Figure 13.15 – Create job from template

Once you have selected the dataflow template, we need to populate additional required parameters. We need to enter a valid Pub/Sub topic. In the following example, we are using a public GCP-managed topic. We also need to enter a BigQuery table to output the data to and then a location for temporary files to be written to. In our example, we are using a Cloud Storage bucket called `cloudarchitectbookupdate`:

Input Pub/Sub topic *

projects/pubsub-public-data/topics/taxirides-realtime

The Pub/Sub topic to read the input from. Ex: projects/your-project-id/topics/your-topic-name

BigQuery output table *

eighth-effect-319712:taxirides.realtime

The location of the BigQuery table to write the output to. If you reuse an existing table, it will be overwritten. The table's schema must match the input JSON objects. Ex: your-project:your-dataset.your-table

Temporary location *

gs://cloudarchitectbookupdate/temp

Path and filename prefix for writing temporary files. Ex: gs://your-bucket/temp

Encryption

◉ Google-managed encryption key
  No configuration required

○ Customer-managed encryption key (CMEK)
  Manage via Google Cloud Key Management Service

⌄ SHOW OPTIONAL PARAMETERS

`RUN JOB`

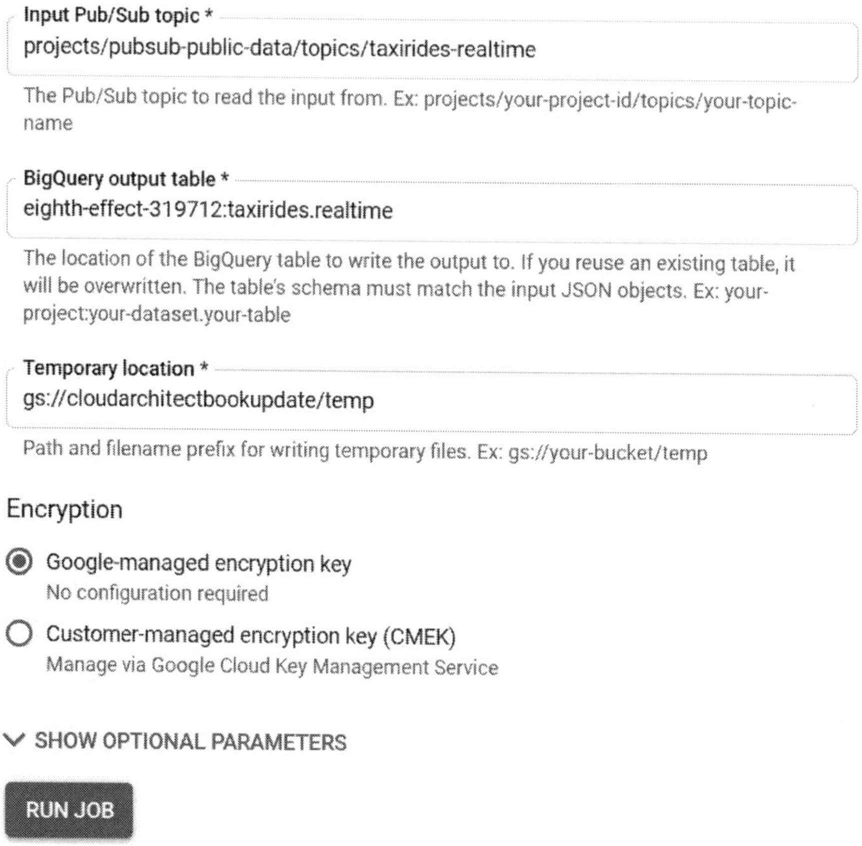

Figure 13.16 – Additional options

4. Once we have run the job, we will see the flowchart as output to see its status. This chart shows the stages of our pipeline. It reads JSON-formatted messages from a Cloud Pub/Sub topic, transforms them using a JavaScript user-defined function, and then writes them to our BigQuery table. This is a quick way to move Cloud Pub/Sub data to BigQuery:

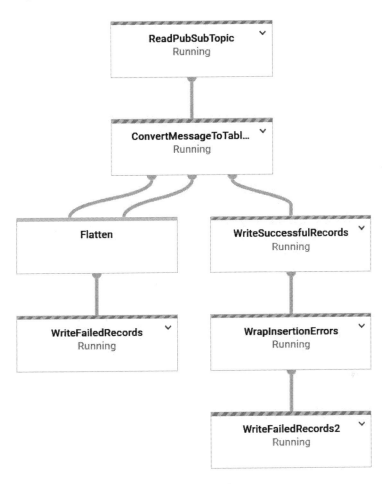

Figure 13.17 – Graph view

5. If we go to our BigQuery table and run a SQL query, we will see that we are pulling in data from the Pub/Sub topic (note that your table will be named differently):

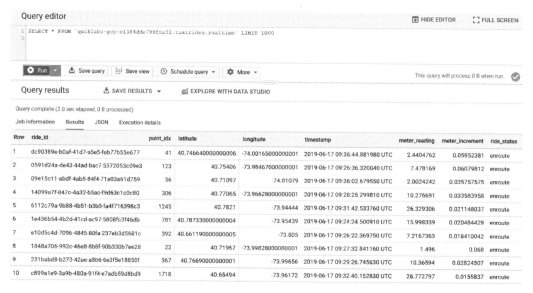

Figure 13.18 – Query results

Of course, this query would be refined rather than us selecting all.

One additional important thing to note is that although the preceding example has built a pipeline job from a template, this is only one of the options available. This option allows us to quickly start with no coding. However, GCP offers us the option to build pipelines using the following languages:

- Java and Maven
- Python
- SQL

IAM

Access to Cloud Dataflow is secured with IAM. Let's have a look at the list of predefined roles, along with a short description of each:

- **Dataflow Admin**: This has the right to create and manage Dataflow jobs.
- **Dataflow Developer**: This has the right to execute and manipulate Dataflow jobs.

- **Dataflow Viewer**: This has read-only rights to all Dataflow-related resources.
- **Dataflow Worker**: This has rights for a GCE service account to execute work units for a Dataflow pipeline.

Quotas and limits

Google Cloud Dataflow comes with predefined quotas. These default quotas can be changed via the **Navigation** menu and **IAM & Admin | Quotas**. From this menu, we can review the current quotas and request an increase to these limits. We recommend that you are aware of the limits for each service as this can have an impact on your scalability. For Cloud Dataflow, we should be aware of the following limits:

- Dataflow uses Compute Engine to execute pipeline code, and then we are subject to Compute Engine quotas.
- There is a limit of 1,000 workers per pipeline.
- There is a limit of 10 MB for a job creation request.
- There is a limit of 20,000 side input shards.

Pricing

Dataflow is billed in per-second increments on a per-job basis. Prices vary by region, depending on the location.

BigQuery

BigQuery is a fully managed, serverless analytics service. It can scale to petabytes of data and is ideal for data warehouse workloads. It is the analysis stage of our solution, and once Dataflow processes our data, BigQuery will provide value to our business by querying large volumes of data in a very short period. Queries are executed in the SQL language, so it will be easy to use for many. We should emphasize that BigQuery is enterprise-scale and can perform large SQL queries extremely fast – all without the need for us to provision any underlying infrastructure.

> **Exam Tip**
> BigQuery is ideal for data warehouse workloads as it has the capacity for PB of storage.

BigQuery features

In this section, we will take a look at datasets and tables. These are two important concepts of BigQuery, and we need to understand them to be successful in the exam.

Datasets

Datasets are used to organize and control access to tables and views. We require at least one dataset before we can load data into BigQuery. Dataset names are unique to each project, and we are required to specify a location. Locations can be either regional or multi-regional, and we cannot change our location once the dataset has been created. Some consideration should be taken when selecting a location, depending on the export or ingestion requirements. For example, if we plan to query data from an external data source such as Cloud Storage, the data we are querying must be in the same location as our BigQuery dataset.

We can create a new dataset by browsing to the hamburger menu | **BIG DATA** | **BigQuery**, and then **SQL Workplace**. Finally, click the three dots beside our project and select **Create Dataset**:

Figure 13.19 – Selecting a dataset location

An additional consideration when creating a dataset is whether or not to apply a default table expiration. BigQuery charges for both data storage and per query. We should think about setting an expiration date if our tables will be for temporary use. The following example shows the same screenshot as the preceding one after **Data location** has been selected:

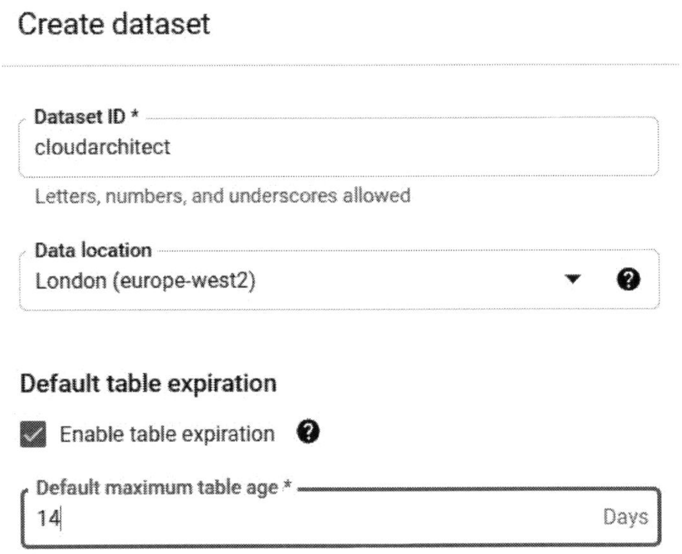

Figure 13.20 – Default table expiration

We are setting an expiration value of 14 days for every table in our dataset.

Tables

Once we have created a dataset, we can create a table and load data into it. Tables will contain individual records that are organized into rows. Each table is defined by a schema that will describe the column names and data types; for example, a string or integer. The schema is decided when we create our table. We can also set an expiration date for our tables when we create them. If we set an expiration value when we create our dataset, then this value will be overwritten by the expiration value that's set when the table is created. If no value is set on either, then the table will never expire.

Partitioned tables make it easier to manage and query data. These are tables that are split into smaller partitions, meaning it will improve the query's performance and reduce costs. This is because the number of bytes that are read by a query is also reduced.

BigQuery offers three types of table partitioning:

- **Ingestion time**: BigQuery will automatically load data into daily, data-based partitions.

- **Time-Unit Column**: These allow us to partition a table on the **DATE, TIMESTAMP**, or **DATETIME** column.

- **Integer Range**: These allow us to partition a table based on the ranges of values in an **integer** column.

> **Exam Tip**
>
> It is possible to set expiration data on partitioned tables. Use this if you have, for example, a requirement to delete sensitive data after a while.

Federated queries

To send a query statement to an external database and receive the result as a temporary table, we can use Federated queries. These will use the BigQuery Connection API and establish a connection with an external database. This allows us to use the EXTERNAL_ QUERY function in our standard SQL query to send a statement to the external database, using that database's SQL dialect. The results will be transformed into BigQuery standard SQL data types.

Connected Sheets

Just as a reminder, Google Sheets is an online spreadsheet application by Google. Connected Sheets lets us analyze data from a Google Sheet without needing to know SQL. We can access, analyze, and share billions of rows of BigQuery data from our Google Sheet spreadsheet. This can be useful if we want to collaborate with our partners or analysts within a recognizable spreadsheet interface or provide a single source of truth without further spreadsheet exports. Connected Sheets will execute the BigQuery queries on our behalf, via a request or a schedule, and save the results in our spreadsheet for analysis.

Storage and compute separation

BigQuery separates storage and compute. By decoupling these components, we can select the storage and processing solutions that are best for our organization as each of them can scale independently, therefore offering a real elastic data warehouse solution.

Materialized views

To increase performance and efficiency, BigQuery offers materialized views, which are precomputed views that will routinely cache the results of our queries. BigQuery uses these precomputed results and, whenever possible, reads only the delta changes from the base table to compute up-to-date results. Using these views can significantly enhance the performance of workloads that have common characteristics.

BigQuery BI Engine

BigQuery BI Engine is a **Business Intelligence** (**BI**) service built into BigQuery that allows us to analyze data that has been stored in BigQuery. It offers sub-second query response time with high concurrency. Additionally, we can build dashboards and reports that are backed by BigQuery, without impacting performance or security. It can integrate into Google tools such as Data Studio (which we will look at later in this chapter) and Connected Sheets, or third-party BI tools such as Microsoft's Power BI or Tableau.

BigQuery ML Engine

BigQuery ML is a **Machine Learning** (**ML**) service that allows us to create and execute ML models in BigQuery using SQL queries. Machine learning will be discussed in more detail in *Chapter 14, Putting Machine Learning to Work*.

BigQuery GIS

BigQuery GIS allows us to augment our analytics workflows with location intelligence. By using geography data types and standard SQL geography functions, we can analyze and visualize geospatial data in BigQuery. This can be a real benefit for organizations where decisions are based on location data.

BigQuery Omni

At the time of writing, this feature is in preview. However, it is worth us highlighting the service for your information. BigQuery Omni is a multi-cloud analytics solution that allows us to analyze data across Azure, AWS, and GCP all within the BigQuery UI. BigQuery Omni is powered by Anthos, which means we do not have to manage any underlying infrastructure. We will discuss Anthos in *Chapter 8, Managing Cloud-Native Workloads with Anthos*.

Using BigQuery

Let's look at the power of BigQuery. Google offers several example datasets for public use so that you can get a feel for BigQuery. In this example, we will use a dataset called **Chicago Taxi Trips** and execute a query to see which drop-off areas give the highest tip:

1. Browse to **BIG DATA | BigQuery** in the GCP console, as shown in the following screenshot:

Figure 13.21 – Selecting BigQuery

2. Expand **ADD DATA** and select **Explore public datasets**, as shown in the following screenshot:

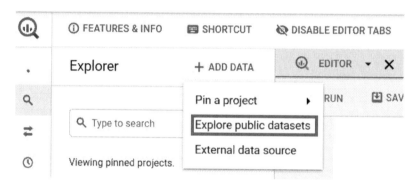

Figure 13.22 – Explore public datasets

3. In the marketplace, search for `taxi` and select the **Chicago Taxi Trips** dataset:

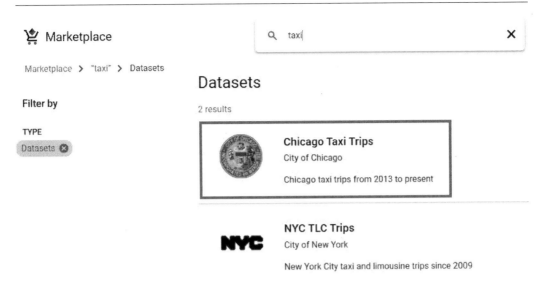

Figure 13.23 – Searching the marketplace

4. View the dataset:

Figure 13.24 – Public dataset

5. You will now see the public datasets that are available for our use. Browse to the Chicago Taxi Dataset:

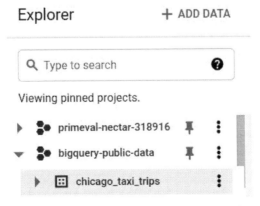

Figure 13.25 – Dataset available in the console

6. Now, we can compose a new query on this dataset. This query will provide some valuable information. We will retrieve both the average and the highest tip given to drivers, grouped by drop-off communities. We can see that this query uses standard SQL language and that ANSI 2011 is supported:

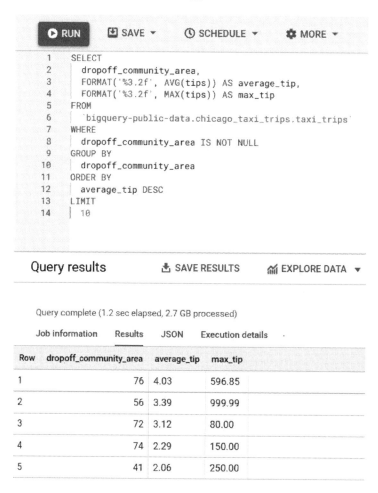

Figure 13.26 – Dataset query

Notice from the results that we have processed the query in only 1.2 seconds. This may not be a large amount of data that's been queried, but it shows that we can quickly load a dataset and execute our query. There were no prerequisite steps to deploying the infrastructure.

One thing regarding BigQuery that we should mention is that it has a command-line tool called bq. We will look at bq in more detail in *Chapter 16, Google Cloud Management Options*.

Importing and exporting data

The preceding example was based on a public dataset. BigQuery allows us to upload data from the console or Cloud Shell. Let's look at using the console to upload a CSV file we have locally. In this example, we will use an example dataset named **london_bikes**. We will also use a CSV called `london_bikes.csv`:

1. From our BigQuery dataset, we can click on the plus (+) icon to create a new table, as shown in the following screenshot:

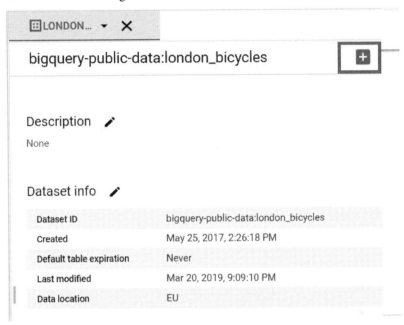

Figure 13.27 – Adding a table

2. We are then given several methods to create our table. Select **Upload** and browse to the location of our CSV file:

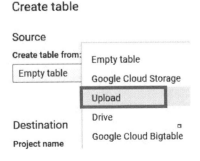

Figure 13.28 – Upload

3. Then, we can populate the dataset we want to add the table to and build our schema. In this example, we are adding entries to our schema with different types. Here, we can see that **start_station_name** and num are both **STRING**:

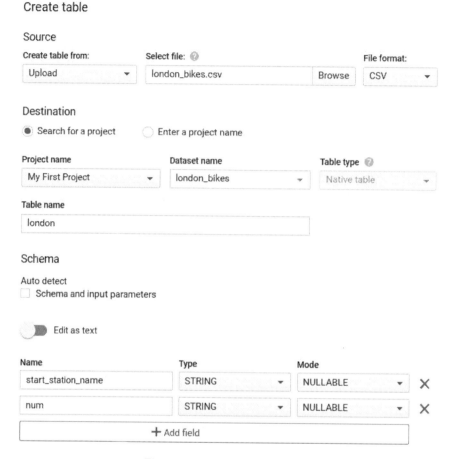

Figure 13.29 – Importing a table

Sometimes, we will also need to export our tables to an external source as well. This is also a very simple process.

Let's export our table to a Cloud Storage bucket:

1. From our table view, we can click **EXPORT**:

Figure 13.30 – EXPORT

2.   Then, we can populate our bucket name and export it:

Export table to Google Cloud Storage

Select GCS location: ⊘

| ☑ cloudarchitectupdate001/london_bikes.csv | Browse |

Export format: **Compression:**

| CSV ▼ | None ▼ |

Figure 13.31 – Export table to Google Cloud Storage

GCP also offers something called **BigQuery Data Transfer Service**, which will automate the process of moving data into BigQuery on a scheduled basis. After the initial data transfer configuration, the service will automatically load data into BigQuery. Note that it cannot be used for transferring data out of BigQuery.

Storage

Although we are discussing BigQuery as big data, let's remind ourselves that it is also a storage service. There is no need to export older data to another storage platform. With BigQuery, we can enjoy the same inexpensive long-term storage as we would expect from services such as Cloud Storage. So long as we are not editing tables for 90 consecutive days, then our cost will drop by 50%, which would match the cost of the Cloud Storage Nearline class.

We now have some valuable information from our data. By putting our full services together, at a high level, our solution would now look like this:

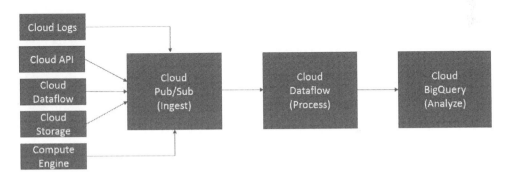

Figure 13.32 – Service diagram

Take a moment to review the preceding diagram and understand the services that are used at each stage. This is important for the exam.

Storage Read API

BigQuery also offers a Storage Read API, which provides fast access to BigQuery-managed table data. This is the third option for accessing table data in BigQuery, alongside the `tabledata.list` or `jobs.getQueryResults` REST API, or bulk data export using BigQuery `extract` jobs, which will export table data to Cloud Storage. When using the Storage Read API, structured data is sent over the wire in a binary serialization format, allowing for additional parallelism, thus improving on the two original options.

IAM

Access to BigQuery is secured with IAM. Let's have a look at the list of predefined roles, along with a short description of each:

- **BigQuery User**: This has the rights to run jobs within the project. It can also create new datasets. Most individuals in an organization should be a user.

- **BigQuery Job User**: This has the rights to run jobs within the project.

- **BigQuery Read Sessions User**: This has the rights to create and read sessions within the project via the BigQuery storage API.

- **BigQuery Data Viewer**: This has the right to read the dataset metadata and list tables in the dataset. It can also read data and metadata from the dataset tables.

- **BigQuery Metadata Viewer**: This has the rights to list all datasets and read metadata for all datasets in the project. It can also list all the tables and views and read the metadata for all the tables and views in the project.

- **BigQuery Data Editor**: This has the right to read the dataset metadata and list tables in the dataset. It can create, update, get, and delete the dataset tables.

- **BigQuery Data Owner**: This has the rights to read, update, and delete the dataset. It can also create, update, get, and delete the dataset tables.

- **BigQuery Admin**: This has the right to manage all the resources within the project.

Quotas and limits

BigQuery comes with predefined quotas. These default quotas can be changed via the **Navigation** menu and **IAM & Admin | Quotas**. From this menu, we can review the current quotas and request an increase to these limits. We recommend that you are aware of the limits for each service, as this can have an impact on your scalability. For BigQuery, we should be aware of the following limits:

- There is a limit of 100 concurrent queries.

- There is a query execution time limit of 6 hours.

- 1,500 maximum number of table operations are allowed per day.

- There is a maximum of 100,000 streamed rows of data per second, per project. This is 500,000 in the US and EU multi-regions.

- A maximum of 300 concurrent API requests per user is allowed.

Pricing

Storage costs for BigQuery are based on the amount of data we store. We can be charged for both active and long-term storage. Of course, long-term storage will be a lower monthly change. Additionally, we are charged for running queries. We are offered two pricing models for queries:

- **On-demand**: This charges based on the amount of data that's processed by each query.

- **Flat-rate**: This allows us to purchase dedicated resources for processing, so we are not charged for individual queries.

Pricing is also determined by the location of our BigQuery dataset. Now, let's look at Dataproc.

Dataproc

Dataproc is GCP's big-data-managed service for running Hadoop and Spark clusters. Hadoop and Spark are open source frameworks that handle data processing for big data applications in a distributed manner. Essentially, they provide massive storage for data, while also providing enormous processing power to handle concurrent processing tasks.

If we refer to the *End-to-end big data solution* section of this chapter, Dataproc is also part of the processing stage. It can be compared to Dataflow; however, Dataproc requires us to provision servers, whereas Dataflow is serverless.

Exam Tip

Dataproc should be chosen over Dataflow if we have an existing Hadoop or Spark Cluster. Also, the skill sets of existing resources are needed. If we need to create new pipeline jobs or process streaming data, then we should select Dataflow.

As an alternative to hosting these services on-premises, Google offers Dataproc, which has many advantages – mainly cost-saving, as you are only charged for what you use, with no large initial outlay for the required processing power and storage. Traditional on-premises Hadoop clusters are generally expensive to run because you are paying for processing power that is not being utilized regularly, and we cannot remove the cluster because our data would also be removed. In comparison, Dataproc moves away from persistent clusters to ephemeral clusters. Dataproc integrates well with Cloud Storage. Therefore, if we have a requirement to run a job, we can spin up our cluster very quickly, process our data, and store it on Cloud Storage in the same region. Then, we can simply delete our cluster. Dataproc clusters are not made to run 24/7 as they are job-specific, and this is where we can gain cost savings. This approach allows us to use different cluster configurations for individual jobs, scale clusters to suit individual jobs or groups of jobs, and reduce any maintenance of the clusters as we are simply spinning up a freshly configured cluster each time we need to run a job.

Exam Tip

The whole point of an ephemeral cluster is to use it only for the job's lifetime.

Architecture

The following diagram shows the high-level architecture of Dataproc:

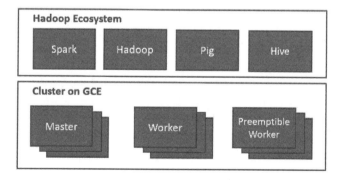

Figure 13.33 – Dataproc

The underlying Dataproc infrastructure is built on Compute Engine, which means we can build on several machine types, depending on our budget, and take advantage of predefined and custom machine types.

> **Exam Tip**
> Cost savings are also increased by using preemptible instances.

When Dataproc clusters are created, we have the option to set a maximum combination of 96 CPU cores and 624 GB RAM. We can also select between SSD and HDD storage. Please refer to *Chapter 4, Working with Google Compute Engine,* for more details on machine types.

In a Dataproc cluster, there are different classes of machines:

- **Master nodes**: This machine will assign and synchronize tasks on worker nodes and process the results.

- **Worker nodes**: These machines will process data. These can be expensive due to high their CPU and memory specifications.

- **Preemptible worker nodes**: These are secondary worker nodes and are optional. They do the same job but lower the per-hour compute costs for non-critical data processing.

When we create a new cluster, we can select different cluster modes:

- **Standard**: This includes one master node and *N* worker nodes. In the event of a Compute Engine failure, in-flight jobs will fail and the filesystem will be inaccessible until the master nodes reboot.

- **High availability**: This includes three master nodes and *N* worker nodes. This is designed to allow uninterrupted operations, despite a Compute Engine failure or reboots.

- **Single node**: This combines both master and worker nodes. This is not suitable for large data processing and should be used for PoC or small-scale non-critical data processing.

By default, when we create a cluster, standard Apache Hadoop ecosystem components will be automatically installed on the cluster:

- Apache Spark

- Apache Hadoop

- Apache Pig

- Apache Hive

- Python

- Java

- **Hadoop Distributed File System (HDFS)**

> **Important Note**
>
> The process of migrating from on-premises to Google Cloud Storage is explained further at `https://cloud.google.com/solutions/migration/hadoop/hadoop-gcp-migration-data`.

We can also specify initialization actions in executables or scripts that Dataproc will run on all the nodes in our cluster immediately after the cluster has been set up. These are often used to set up job dependencies to ensure jobs don't require any dependencies to be installed.

IAM

Access to Dataproc is secured with IAM. Let's have a look at the list of predefined roles, along with a short description of each:

- **Dataproc Editor**: This has full control over Dataproc.

- **Dataproc Viewer**: This has rights to get and list Dataproc machine types, regions, zones, and projects.

- **Dataproc Worker**: This is for service accounts only and provides the minimum permissions necessary to operate with Dataproc.

- **Dataproc Admin**: This role has the same permissions as Editor but can Get and Set Dataproc IAM permissions.

Quotas and limits

As Dataproc clusters utilize other GCP products, Compute Engine's limits and quotas apply to Dataproc. When we create a Dataproc cluster, the compute resources will affect our regional quota limit.

We recommend that you review the *Further reading* section for more information on Compute quotas.

Cloud IoT Core

The **Internet of Things**, or **IoT**, is a collective term for physical objects that are connected to the internet. You are no doubt using many IoT devices today, such as smartwatches, Google Home, or wirelessly controlled light bulbs.

Cloud IoT Core is a fully managed service that allows us to securely connect, manage, and ingest data from devices spread around the globe. It is also completely serverless, meaning no upfront software installation. Cloud IoT Core integrates with other GCP services to offer a complete solution for collecting, processing, and analyzing data in real time. Let's look at the following diagram. It shows us where Cloud IoT Core sits in the overall end-to-end solution we have discussed in this chapter and the protocols that IoT devices can use to communicate with it – MQTT and HTTP:

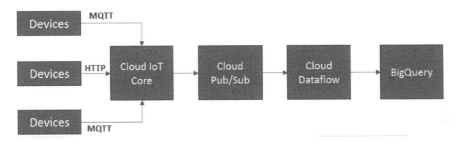

Figure 13.34 – Service diagram

> **Important Note**
>
> **MQTT** is a Pub/Sub protocol and is often used with embedded devices. MQTT is considered data-focused and better suited to IoT.
>
> **HTTP** is a connection-less protocol, and devices will maintain a connection to Cloud IoT Core. HTTP is considered document-focused.

Both protocols communicate with Cloud IoT Core across a **protocol bridge**, which provides the following:

- MQTT and HTTP protocol endpoints
- Automatic load balancing
- Global data access with Pub/Sub

The other key component is the **device manager**. This is used to do the following:

- Register individual devices
- Configure individual devices
- Update and control devices
- Provide role-level access control
- Provide a console and APIs for device deployment and monitoring

IAM

Access to Cloud IoT Core is secured with IAM. Let's have a look at the list of predefined roles, along with a short description of each:

- **Cloudiot Viewer**: This has read-only access to all Cloud IoT resources.
- **Cloudiot Device Controller**: This has access to update the configuration of devices. It does not have the right to create or delete devices.
- **Cloudiot Provisioner**: This has the right to create and delete devices from registries but not to modify the registries.
- **Cloudiot Editor**: This has read-write access to all Cloud IoT resources.
- **Cloudiot Admin**: This has full control over all Cloud IoT resources and permissions.

Quotas and limits

There are many limits for Cloud IoT core, ranging from project limits to device limits, and they are split into three categories:

- **Project, device, and telemetry limits**: These limits refer to the number of devices per project, device metadata, telemetry event payloads, and MQTT connections per device.
- **Rate**: These limits refer to device-to-cloud and cloud-to-device throughput limits, MQTT incoming messages per second and connection, and device manager API limits.
- **Time**: These limits refer to MQTT connection time and timeout limits.

We recommend that you refer to the *Further reading* section for more information.

Pricing

Cloud IoT Core is charged according to the data volume that's used per calendar month. Google recommends using the pricing calculator to estimate the price according to the volume of data that's exchanged.

Data Fusion

Cloud Data Fusion is a fully managed and cloud-native data integration service for quickly building and managing data pipelines. Data Fusion uses Dataproc as the execution environment for these pipelines. The GUI caters to a variety of users, which means that business users, developers, and data scientists can easily build integration solutions that will cleanse, prepare, and transform data. Data fusion also offers a library of preconfigured plugins to extend its capabilities. It is also important to note that it is powered by an open source project called **Cask Data Application Platform (CDAP)**.

Core concepts

Some core Data Fusion concepts are worth highlighting to understand the product and how to use it.

Instances

To begin with, we must create a Cloud Data Fusion instance. Instances run as the Compute Engine service account and Data Fusion executes pipelines using a Dataproc cluster. Instances are a unique deployment of Data Fusion and are created from the GCP Console. At the time of creating, we can decide what type of instance we want to deploy, and the choice will be determined by requirements and cost. There are three options:

- **Developer** instances provide a full-featured edition with zonal availability and limitations on execution environments.

- **Basic** instances provide comprehensive integration capabilities but have limitations on simultaneous pipeline runs and are recommended for non-critical environments.

- **Enterprise** instances also offer comprehensive integration capabilities but there are no limitations on simultaneous pipeline runs and are recommended for critical environments.

Each instance contains a unique and independent Data Fusion deployment that will contain a set of services that handle pipeline life cycle management, orchestration, coordination, and metadata management. Note that before we can create an instance, we will be prompted to enable the API and create credentials:

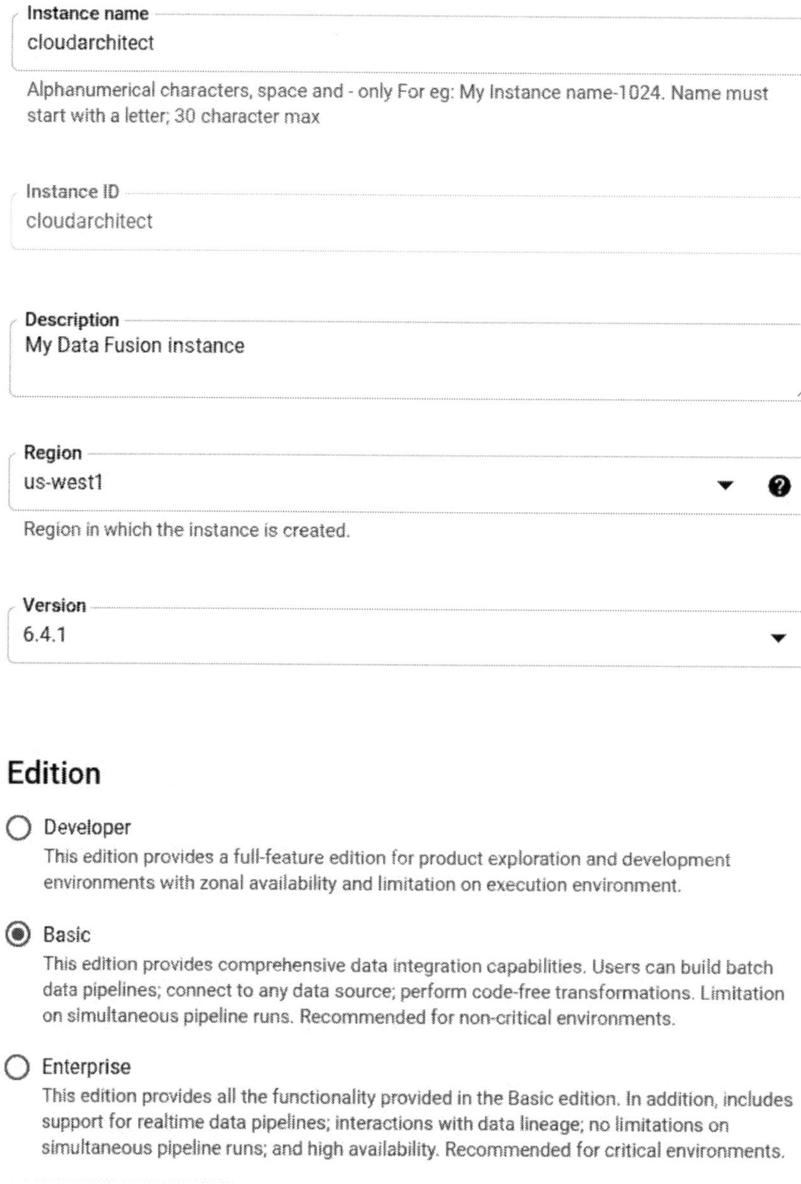

Instance name

cloudarchitect

Alphanumerical characters, space and - only For eg: My Instance name-1024. Name must start with a letter; 30 character max

Instance ID

cloudarchitect

Description

My Data Fusion instance

Region

us-west1

Region in which the instance is created.

Version

6.4.1

Edition

○ Developer
  This edition provides a full-feature edition for product exploration and development environments with zonal availability and limitation on execution environment.

◉ Basic
  This edition provides comprehensive data integration capabilities. Users can build batch data pipelines; connect to any data source; perform code-free transformations. Limitation on simultaneous pipeline runs. Recommended for non-critical environments.

○ Enterprise
  This edition provides all the functionality provided in the Basic edition. In addition, includes support for realtime data pipelines; interactions with data lineage; no limitations on simultaneous pipeline runs; and high availability. Recommended for critical environments.

Figure 13.35 – Selecting an instance edition

Once the instance has been deployed, we can click on the Instance URL, which will open a separate Data Fusion UI, allowing us to view our instance. Let's look at deploying a sample pipeline:

1. From the Data Fusion UI, click **HUB**. This will open a list of plugins that we can utilize to extend the capabilities of Data Fusion:

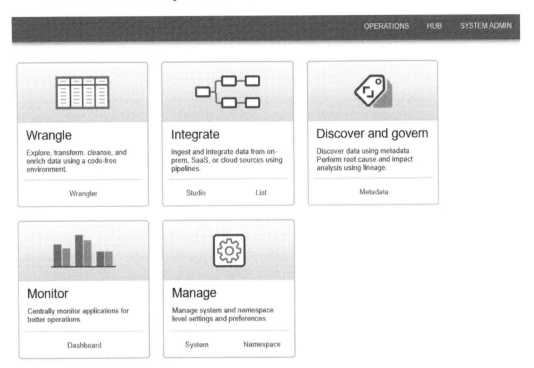

Figure 13.36 – Viewing the instance

2.   Select the **Cloud Data Fusion Quickstart** plugin:

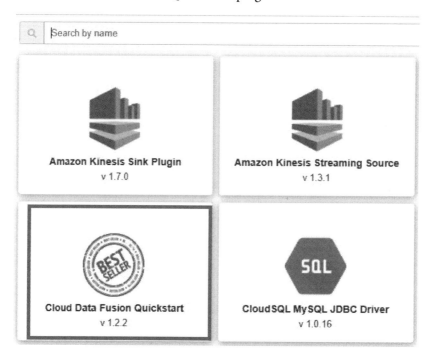

Figure 13.37 – Quickstart plugin

3.   Click **Create**, update the pipeline name if required, and click **Finish**:

Figure 13.38 – Creating a pipeline

4. Click **Customize Pipeline** when prompted. This will take us to our pipeline studio. This is a graphical interface for developing our pipeline. It allows us to drag and drop various plugins onto our canvas. If we click **Deploy** from the top right, it will submit the pipeline to Data Fusion. In this example pipeline, we are reading a JSON file containing New York Times bestseller data from Cloud Storage. It will then run transformations on the file to parse and clean the data. Finally, it will load the top-rated books that have been added in the last week that cost less than $25 into BigQuery:

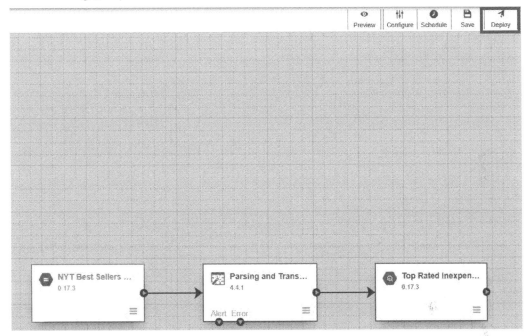

Figure 13.39 – Deploying the pipeline

5. We can then **Run** our pipeline and see the results at the end of the process:

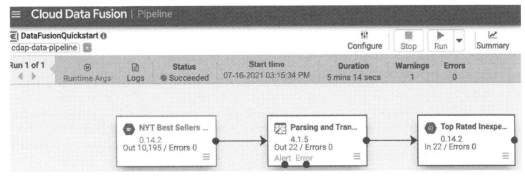

Figure 13.40 – Pipeline results

With that, we have seen how easy it is to get started with Data Fusion.

Execution environments

Cloud Data Fusion will create ephemeral execution environments to run pipelines when we want to manually run our pipelines or if we want our pipelines to run through a schedule or a pipeline state trigger. We have already mentioned that Cloud Data Fusion supports Dataproc as an execution environment. We can choose to run pipelines as MapReduce, Spark, or Spark Streaming programs. Cloud Data Fusion will provision an ephemeral Dataproc cluster in our customer project at the start of a pipeline run. Then, it will execute the pipeline using MapReduce or Spark in the cluster before deleting the cluster once the pipeline's execution is complete.

If we are using technologies such as Terraform to manage existing Dataproc clusters, we can configure Cloud Data Fusion to use these and not provision new clusters.

It is recommended that we use autoscaling policies to increase the cluster's size, not decrease it. Decreasing its size with autoscaling will also remove nodes that hold intermediate data and may cause failure.

Pipelines

Pipelines offer us a way to visually design data and control flows to extract, transform, aggregate, and load data from various data sources – whether that is on-premises or cloud-based. Pipelines allow us to create data processing workflows that can help us solve data ingestion, integration, and migration problems. We can use Cloud Data Fusion to build real-time and batch pipelines.

Pipelines allow us to express our data processing workflows using the logical flow of data and Cloud Data Fusion will handle all the functionality to physically run in an execution environment. The Cloud Data Fusion planner transforms the logical flow into parallel computations by using Apache Spark and Apache Hadoop MapReduce on Dataproc.

Use cases

Data Fusion should be considered for the following use cases:

- Secure Data Lakes on GCP. Data Fusion helps us build scalable, distributed data lakes on GCP.

- Agile data warehouses with BigQuery. Data Fusion can break down data silos and enable the development of data warehouse solutions in BigQuery.

- Unified Analytics. Data Fusion can establish an analytics environment across a variety of on-premises data marts.

IAM

Access to Cloud Data Fusion is secured with IAM. Let's have a look at the list of predefined roles, along with a short description of each:

- **Datafusion Viewer**: This has full access to the Data Fusion UI, along with permissions to view, create, manage and run pipelines.

- **Datafusion Admin**: This has all viewer permissions, plus permissions to create, update, and delete all Data Fusion instances

- **Datafusion Runner**: This is granted to the Dataproc service account so that Dataproc is authorized to communicate the pipeline runner information.

Quotas and limits

There are a few limits worth noting:

- There is a limit of 600 requests per minute from a single user in a single region.

- Data Fusion quotas apply to all pipelines that are executed.

- Data Fusion also stores logs, so Cloud Operations logging quotas apply.

We recommend that you refer to the *Further reading* section for more information.

Pricing

Usage for Data Fusion is measured as the length of time, in minutes, between the time a Cloud Data Fusion instance is created to the time it is deleted. Cloud Data Fusion is billed by the minute, although pricing is defined by the hour. Usage will be measured in hours – for example, 30 minutes is 0.5 hours – to apply hourly pricing to minute-by-minute use.

Now, let's look at the Datastream API.

Datastream API

Datastream is a serverless **change data capture** (CDC) and replication service. It helps us bring in change streams from Oracle or MySQL into Google's data services to support analytics, DB replication, and event-driven architectures. It allows us to synchronize our data across heterogeneous databases and applications with minimal latency and downtime.

Please note that at the time of writing, this product is in the pre-GA phase. However, we felt that it is worth highlighting the service as something to be aware of.

Additional considerations

There are other services offered by Google that we wish to highlight:

- **Dataprep**: This is a web application that allows us to define preparation rules for our data by interfacing with a sample of the data. Like many of the other services we have discussed, Dataprep is serverless, meaning no upfront deployments are required. By default, Dataprep jobs are executed on a Dataflow pipeline. Refer to `https://cloud.google.com/dataprep/` for more information.

- **Datalab**: This is built on Jupyter (formerly IPython), which is an open source web application. Datalab is an interactive data analysis and machine learning environment. We can use this product to visualize and explore data using Python and SQL interactively. This would be treated as part of the data usage stage of our end-to-end solution and would use data that's passed from BigQuery. Datalab is free of charge but runs on Compute Engine instances, so charges will be applicable. For more information, refer to `https://cloud.google.com/datalab/`.

- **Data Studio**: This is a **Business Intelligence** (**BI**) solution that turns your data into informative and easy-to-read dashboards and reports. It is a fully managed visual analytics service. Refer to `https://datastudio.google.com/overview/` for more information.

- **Composer**: Another workflow orchestration service is Cloud Composer. Built on the Apache Airflow open source project, it allows us to create workflows that span across both public cloud and on-premises data centers. Workflows are a series of tasks that are used to ingest, transform, analyze, and utilize data. In Airflow, these workflows are created using what is known as **Directed Acyclic Graphs** (**DAGs**). DAGs represent a group of tasks that we want to schedule and run. Cloud Composer operates using Python, so it is free from cloud vendor lock-in and easy to use. DAGs are created using Python scripts that define tasks and their dependencies in code.

  Similar to Data Fusion, there is a requirement for an environment to execute these workflows. By using Cloud Composer, we can benefit from everything that Airflow offers without the need for any installation or management overhead, so Composer will provision the GCP resources required to run our workflows. This group of components is referred to as a Cloud Composer environment and is based on GKE. You can define the number of nodes in the GKE cluster when creating a Composer environment. For more information, refer to `https://cloud.google.com/composer/docs/concepts/overview`.

- **Looker**: Looker is an enterprise platform that helps us explore and share company data to make more informed business decisions. Using a modeling language called LookML, we can query data to create reports, dashboards, and other patterns of data.

- **Data Catalog**: Without the right tools, dealing with the growing number of data assets within many of today's organizations will be a real challenge. Stakeholders wish to search for insightful data, understand the data, and make the data as useful as possible. Data Catalog is a scalable metadata management service that can catalog the metadata on data assets from BigQuery, Pub/Sub, the Dataproc metastore, and Cloud Storage. For more information, refer to `https://cloud.google.com/data-catalog/docs/concepts`.

While the preceding services are not primary exam topics, we should still be aware of what each service offers.

Summary

In this chapter, we covered the main aspects of big data relating to the exam. We covered each service and showed that these can be used at different stages of our end-to-end solution. We took the time to see how we can configure Pub/Sub, Dataflow, and BigQuery from the GCP console and discussed Dataproc and Cloud IoT Core.

> **Exam Tip**
> The key takeaway from this chapter is to understand which services map to the ingest, process, and analysis stages of data.

Then, we looked at the processing stage of our solution. Cloud Dataflow will deploy Google Compute Engine instances to deploy and execute our Apache Beam pipeline, which will process data from Pub/Sub and pass it onto further stages for analysis or storage. We have shown how we can easily create a pipeline in the GCP console, which pulls information from Pub/Sub for analysis in BigQuery.

After, we covered BigQuery and understood that it is a data warehouse. It is designed to make data analysts more productive, crunching petabytes of data in small amounts of time. It is completely serverless, so we do not have to worry about provisioning any infrastructure before we can use it, which saves a lot of upfront cost and time. We looked at how easy and quick it is to set up a dataset and start to query it.

We also covered Dataproc. We covered the architecture of the service and established that Dataproc is an alternative to hosting Hadoop clusters on-premises. We should now understand that Dataproc can be used to process data that has been injected from Cloud Pub/Sub.

We also covered Cloud IoT Core, which is used to connect IoT devices. We showed you how we can ingest the real-time data that's generated by these devices. Additionally, we discussed data pipelines using Data Fusion and serverless CDC and replication services in Datastream. We also introduced Dataprep, Datalab, Datastudio, Composer, DataCatalog, and Looker.

In the next chapter, we will take a look at machine learning.

Further reading

Read the following articles for more information on the topics that were covered in this chapter:

- **For Cloud Pub/Sub**, refer to the following:

    - **Pub/Sub**: https://cloud.google.com/pubsub/docs/

    - **Pricing**: https://cloud.google.com/pubsub/pricing

    - **Quotas**: https://cloud.google.com/pubsub/quotas

    - **Complex event processing**: https://cloud.google.com/solutions/architecture/complex-event-processing

    - **Use cases**: https://cloud.google.com/pubsub/docs/overview

- **For Cloud Dataflow**, refer to the following:

    - **Dataflow**: https://cloud.google.com/dataflow/docs/

    - **Pricing**: https://cloud.google.com/dataflow/pricing

    - **Quotas**: https://cloud.google.com/dataflow/quotas

- **For BigQuery**, refer to the following:

    - **BigQuery**: https://cloud.google.com/bigquery/docs/

    - **Pricing**: https://cloud.google.com/bigquery/pricing

    - **Quotas**: https://cloud.google.com/bigquery/quotas

- **For Dataproc**, refer to the following:

  - **Dataproc**: `https://cloud.google.com/dataproc/docs/`

  - **Quotas**: `https://cloud.google.com/compute/quotas`

  - **Pricing**: `https://cloud.google.com/dataproc/pricing`

- **For Cloud IoT Core**, refer to the following:

  - **Cloud IoT Core**: `https://cloud.google.com/iot/docs/`

  - **Quotas**: `https://cloud.google.com/iot/quotas`

  - **Pricing**: `https://cloud.google.com/iot/pricing`

- **For Data Fusion**, refer to the following:

  - **Data Fusion**: `https://cloud.google.com/data-fusion/docs/resources`

  - **Quotas**: `https://cloud.google.com/data-fusion/quotas`

  - **Pricing**: `https://cloud.google.com/data-fusion/pricing`

- **For Datastream**, refer to `https://cloud.google.com/datastream`.

14
Putting Machine Learning to Work

As we have already mentioned, **machine learning (ML)** is one of the differentiators of the **Google Cloud Platform (GCP)**. You should pay special attention to this chapter, as you will be learning that you don't actually need to be a data scientist to leverage ML in your applications. Google has options for both beginners and highly experienced consumers. ML can be quite an intimidating topic for many people but, hopefully, we will be able to explain the basic underlying concepts by means of easy examples. Having that understanding, we will then be able to look at the ML services that we can use in GCP. Hopefully, you are as excited about this chapter as we were when writing it.

In this chapter, we will cover the following topics:

- An introduction to AI and ML
- The seven steps of ML
- Learning models
- GCP ML options
- TensorFlow
- Vertex AI

- Pretrained ML models
- Dialogflow
- AutoML

Exam Tip

Interestingly, the topic of ML has been significantly reduced in the exam. There is a new exam that was introduced in 2020, Professional Machine Learning Engineer, that requires a deep knowledge of Google ML services. We still feel the topic is very important and would like you to understand the basics.

As a cloud architect, you should be able to differentiate between different GCP ML services and identify the proper one for your use case. It may be the case that two services satisfy requirements, but *which of them will entail less effort when it comes to their use?* Remember what types of ML models there are and understand the differences. And don't be scared – no one will ask you to develop your own model!

An introduction to AI and ML

Artificial Intelligence (AI) is described as the ability of a digital computer to perform tasks that intelligent human beings can perform. ML is a subset of AI. It is used by machines to make decisions based on data without getting specific programmed instructions. It can be used, for example, to indicate whether an email that's been received is spam, to recognize objects, or to make smart predictions. The ML concept is illustrated in the following diagram:

Figure 14.1 – ML flow

As we can see, ML models rely on mathematical models that have been created from an analysis of samples called **training data**. The process of developing the model is called **model training**. The purpose of the model is to answer our question with the highest possible degree of accuracy. The better the accuracy, the better the model. You may be confused as to how this model is created. We will look at this in the following section.

The seven steps of ML

Google indicates that there are seven steps of ML:

1. Gathering the data
2. Preparing the data
3. Choosing a model
4. Training
5. Evaluation
6. Hyperparameter tuning
7. Prediction

Let's go through each of the steps with an example. Let's say we are training the model to check whether a piece of fruit is an apple or a lemon. We need to choose the features that we will use to train our model. There are lots of possible alternatives, including shape, color, taste, and skin smoothness:

Figure 14.2 – Objects for the ML experiment

For this particular training, we will use color and sugar content. The second measurement is probably not the simplest one to obtain, but for this test, let's assume that we have the proper equipment to do so.

Gathering and preparing the data

Let's start gathering data by buying multiple apples and lemons. We will start with the creation of tables with two features – **color** and **sugar content**.

> **Important Note**
> Color is described in terms of wavelength interval in **nanometers** (**nm**).

This is an example involving a couple of fruits, but we need far more samples in order to obtain accurate predictions:

Color [nm]	Sugar content [g]	Fruit
590	10	Apple
570	2	Lemon
610	15	Apple
500	3	Lemon

At this stage, we should try to visualize the data to make sure we haven't collected too many fruits of one kind; otherwise, the model will be biased toward that fruit.

Now, we need to split the data into **training** and **evaluation data**. The data that's used for training should not be used for evaluation if our model is correct as we will always get good results. A good rule of thumb is that we should use 80% of the data for training and the remaining 20% as evaluation data. Once we have this division, additional steps may be required to prepare the data, such as normalization and deduplication. In our case, these are not required.

Choosing a model

Now, we need to establish which model we want to use. There are thousands of models that have been developed that we can choose from. They can be suitable for images, text, or numerical-based data. The model should be chosen according to the use case. Since we have only two features in our case, the model can be a simple linear model.

Training

Now, we'll get to the heart of ML: the actual training. Let's look at the model we have chosen for training. Here, we have $X = W x Y + b$, where W is **weight** and b is **bias, while X and Y are the features**. During training, we will manipulate the W and b values and use the training data to verify whether we are getting correct predictions. Each of these manipulations is referred to as a training step:

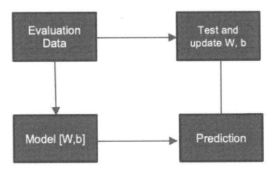

Figure 14.3 – ML training

While at the outset we may obtain poor results, gradually, we will get accurate predictions for the W and b values. If we are not getting the results we anticipated, we may need to choose a more complex model:

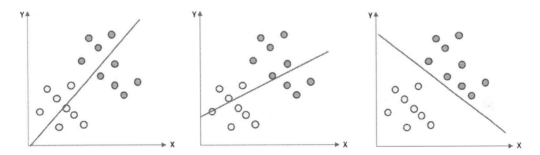

Figure 14.4 – Adjusting weight and bias

In the preceding plots, we can see how the line changes when we manipulate W and b. In the beginning, we may get results that do not appear to be fit for purpose, but eventually, we achieve values with satisfying results.

Evaluation

Once the training is complete, it is time to evaluate the model. This is where our validation data will be used. You will test this data against your trained model and see how correct it is:

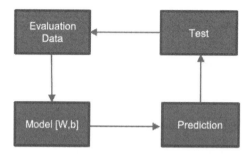

Figure 14.5 – ML evaluation

This is supposed to simulate how the model would work with real-world data.

Hyperparameter tuning

When we were training our models, we made some assumptions regarding parameters. Those parameters are so-called hyperparameters. By tuning them, we can get higher accuracy rates. For example, we can use **learning rate parameters**, which indicate the extent of the changes made to W and b. If these parameters are too small, it can take a long time for our model to converge. If these parameters are too big, our model may never converge, thereby missing the ideal state. The other parameter we might want to tune is how many times we run through the training process. By changing it, we could potentially obtain higher accuracy.

Keep in mind that this process is rather experimental and requires some experience to get it set right. Have a look at the *Further reading* section for more information on hyperparameter tuning.

Prediction

Finally, it is time to use our model to evaluate whether a given fruit is an apple or a lemon based on sugar content and color. There are a couple of ways in which we can do this. As you will see in the *Vertex AI* section of this chapter, we can host our model on GCP and access it via an API whenever we need to make a prediction.

Of course, this is a very simple example, but it should be good enough for you to grasp the idea of how ML works.

Learning models

Now that we have a basic understanding of ML and how to train a model, let's have a look at three types of ML learning. These are as follows:

- Supervised learning
- Unsupervised learning
- Semi-supervised ML

The preceding three types of ML are defined as follows:

- **Supervised learning**: Supervised learning is the most common model. It is used when the training data and validation data are labeled. What the model does is learn how to set a label for input data. It does this based on what it has learned from some labeled training data. We can further classify supervised learning into the following categories:

  - **Classification**: This occurs when the output data is a category, such as *apple*, *pear*, or *orange*.

  - **Regression**: This occurs when the output data is a value, such as *cost* or *temperature*.

- **Unsupervised learning**: Unsupervised learning is used when the training data is not labeled. The model attempts to learn the structure of the data and export information or features that might be useful for classification. Since the data isn't labeled, the accuracy cannot be measured. As an example, the model can be used on data that consists of attributes such as weight and height for people of different genders. The height and weight information can be extracted from the data to perform classification into groups. If you draw a plot from the data, you may observe that the data can be used to create patterns and groups.

  Again, as the labels are not known, we cannot explicitly say which group represents which gender, but we can presume that one of the groups can be represented by males and the other by females. We can further classify unsupervised learning into the following categories:

  - **Clustering**: This occurs when you want to group the data, for example, grouping consumers according to their preference for coffee or tea.

  - **Association**: This occurs when you want to link two different actions or behaviors, for example, a customer buying product *A* also buying product *B*.

- **Semi-supervised ML**: Semi-supervised training occurs when part of the training data is labeled and part of it isn't. You can use a mix of both of the preceding methods. Unsupervised learning can be used to structure the data. Supervised learning can be used to label unlabeled data.

GCP ML options

With GCP, you have multiple options when it comes to leveraging ML. Which one you choose largely depends on your use case and how knowledgeable you are on the topic. The following options are available:

- **TensorFlow (for a data scientist)**: This is an option for those who want to work with ML from scratch. It is a software library that's developed and open-sourced by Google. There are more libraries on the market, but this one is the most popular and is used by other cloud providers for their managed ML services.

- **Vertex AI (for a data scientist)**: This is an option for those who want to train their own models but who use Google for training and predictions. It is a managed TensorFlow/Kubeflow service that offloads all infrastructure and software bits from users.

- **Pretrained ML models (for a developer)**: This is an option for those who want to leverage ML without having any knowledge of it. It allows Google-developed models to be used to perform predictions.

- **AutoML (for a developer)**: This is an option for those who want to leverage ML without having any knowledge of it and where the pretrained models are not fit for purpose. It allows models to be trained by supporting labeled data.

TensorFlow

TensorFlow is the most popular open source ML library in the world for developing and training ML models. As a library, it is now part of the GCP offering and can be used on different platforms. For the development phase, you can use your laptop. For the run phase, you can still use your laptop, a public cloud, or even a mobile device.

As you know, Google has the biggest datasets in the world. For this reason, it developed TensorFlow to be highly scalable. Google uses it for services such as Gmail, Google Search, and Photos. You can have a look at how TensorFlow works using TensorFlow Playground, which is available at the following link: `https://playground.tensorflow.org`:

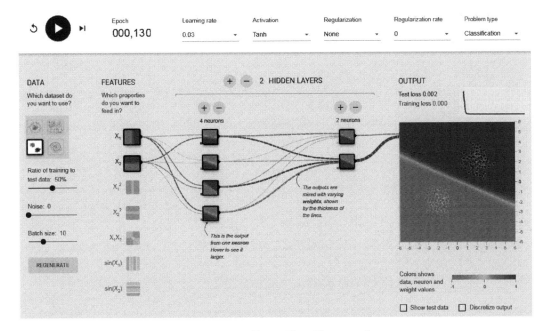

Figure 14.6 – TensorFlow Playground

As you can see, it allows you to choose the type of dataset you want to analyze, and you can experiment with all of the parameters we discussed in the *Seven steps of ML* section. Visualization of the process allows you to understand how changes in parameters affect the final output.

> **Exam Tip**
>
> For the exam, you don't really need to have an in-depth knowledge of TensorFlow. Just be aware of what it is and what it is used for. However, it may be an idea to test TensorFlow Playground.
>
> Even if it is not tested as part of the exam, you may want to have a look at an example of TensorFlow usage. The following video demonstrates how to classify clothing images: `https://www.youtube.com/watch?v=FiNglI1wRNk`.

Cloud Vertex AI

Vertex AI is a Google Cloud AI platform service that allows you to build, deploy and scale ML models with a pretrained or custom tool without worrying about the underlying infrastructure. It is an evolution of the AI Platform service and introduced integration with AutoML.

> **Exam Tip**
>
> Vertex AI was announced at the Google I/O conference in 2021. Lots of Vertex AI features are still in preview at the time of writing this book. We don't anticipate that you will get a question on this in the PCA exam. We still feel this topic is very exciting. If you want to learn more about Vertex AI, check the documentation: `https://cloud.google.com/vertex-ai/docs/start`.

You can accelerate the learning process, since a range of CPU, GPU, and **Tensor Processing Unit** (**TPU**) nodes are supported. It works with multiple frameworks, but the most popular is TensorFlow. As TensorFlow is open source, it allows for portability. Models can be trained locally on limited data and then sent to GCP to train at scale. Vertex AI integrates with other GCP services, such as Cloud Storage for data storage and Cloud Dataflow for data processing.

Using Vertex AI

The following diagram should give you an idea of where Vertex AI fits into the process of developing, deploying, and monitoring your ML model:

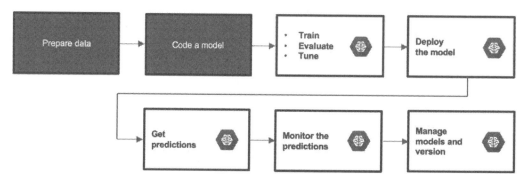

Figure 14.7 – Vertex AI workflow

Now, think about the seven steps we discussed previously. You can see that Vertex AI will allow you to progress from training your model to deploying it in production. From there, the model can be consumed. You will also be able to version your models to see how well each version works.

Cloud TPUs

In this section, we will explain what TPUs are. They are Google's custom-developed **Application-Specific Integrated Circuits (ASICs)**, which are used to speed up ML workloads.

They enhance the performance of linear algebra computation, which is used heavily in ML applications. TPUs facilitate a reduction in model training time from weeks to hours. In the following figure, we can see a rack of servers using TPUs, which was presented at the Google Next conference:

Figure 14.8 – Cloud TPU v3 pod

As indicated by Google, the following factors make your model suitable for being trained with TPUs:

- Models using matrix computations
- Models without custom TensorFlow operations inside the main training loop
- Models that take a long time to train, for example, weeks
- Models with very large batch sizes

In other cases, you may consider using CPUs or GPUs.

Pretrained ML models

Google's pretrained models can be used to perform predictions without us needing any knowledge of how ML works. All of the models are accessible using APIs and can be directly consumed from your application. The data for prediction is delivered using a JSON file or is stored on Cloud Storage. There are currently a number of models available, as follows:

- The Cloud Speech-to-Text API
- The Cloud Text-to-Speech API
- The Cloud Translation API
- The Cloud Natural Language API
- The Cloud Vision API
- The Cloud Video Intelligence API

Let's have a quick look at each of them.

The Cloud Speech-to-Text API

The Cloud Speech-to-Text API empowers developers with the ability to turn speech into text. This API accepts received audio and returns a text transcription. This API can be used synchronously, asynchronously, or in a streaming model. Many languages and dialects are supported. For a full list, check the *Further reading* section.

The Cloud Text-to-Speech API

The Cloud Text-to-Speech API empowers developers with the ability to transform text into a form of **Speech Synthesis Markup Language (SSML)** input into audio data of natural human speech. Many languages are supported, with multiple voices available per language. There are two types of voice to choose from, **Standard** and **WaveNet**, the latter constituting an advanced module that narrows the gap to human speech.

The Cloud Translation API

The Cloud Translation API enables the translation of hundreds of languages. If the language is unknown, the service can auto-detect it. Cloud Translation comes with libraries for the most popular languages, so you can use it directly in your code without using the REST API.

The Cloud Natural Language API

The Cloud Natural Language API allows you to leverage the deep learning models that Google uses for its search engine to analyze text. It is also leveraged by Google Assistant.

It is able to perform the following operations:

- Extract information regarding entities, including places, people, and events
- Categorize the entities
- Perform sentiment analysis
- Perform syntax analysis

> **Exam Tip**
>
> Expect to see questions on the Natural Language API in the exam. Remember that it is an easy way to analyze natural human language. It is quicker to use this than to develop your own model. Keep the preceding capabilities in mind so that you can adapt them to the use case you are given in the exam.

In view of the preceding capabilities, this API can be used for the following use cases.

It can be leveraged to analyze documents, news, social media, or blog posts. In combination with the Speech-to-Text API, it can analyze customer satisfaction from a call center call. Be aware that a limited number of languages are supported. If your language is not supported, you can use the Translation API to convert the text into a supported language.

Let's put this into practice! The API can be accessed both through the REST API and the `gcloud ml language` command, and the text can be provided as a parameter or uploaded from Cloud Storage. For better visualization, we will use a GUI tool provided by Google (`https://cloud.google.com/natural-language`) to analyze some sample text:

```
Packt has released a new book to help IT geeks learn GCP. The
readers really love it!
```

Looking at **Entities,** we can see that five entities have been found. Each entity comes with a **Salience** attribute (ranging from 0–1), which stipulates how important that entity is in the sentence. The higher the value, the more salient it is. For some entities, you also get a Wikipedia link so that you can obtain further information:

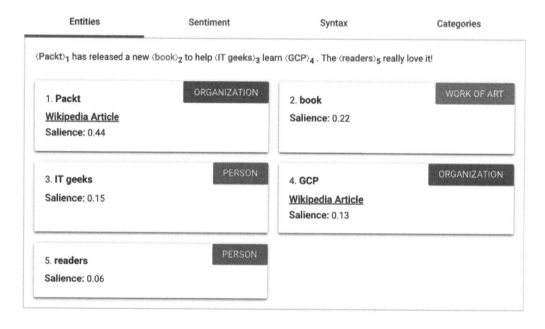

Figure 14.9 – Natural Language API – Entities

For sentiment analysis, we see two **Sentiment** attributes:

- **Score**: Ranging from -1 (very negative) to 1 (very positive)
- **Magnitude**: Ranging from 0 to infinity, showing the strength of the statement:

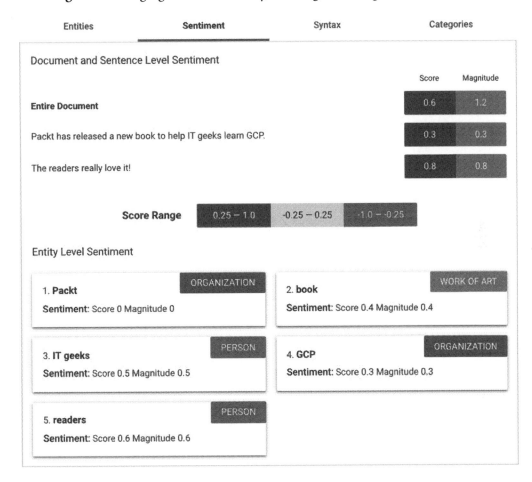

Figure 14.10 – Natural Language API – Sentiment

Now, we change the preceding sentence to the following:

```
Packt has released a new book to help IT geeks learn GCP. The
readers think it is ok.
```

We can see that both **Score** and **Magnitude** have dropped to 0 for the second sentence:

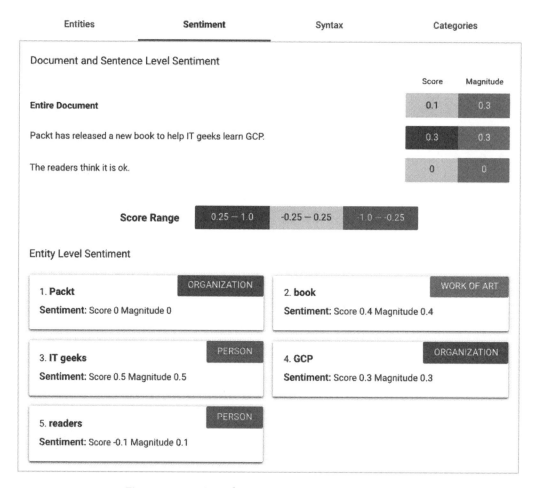

Figure 14.11 – Natural Language API – Sentiment change

The **Syntax** tab shows detailed syntax information:

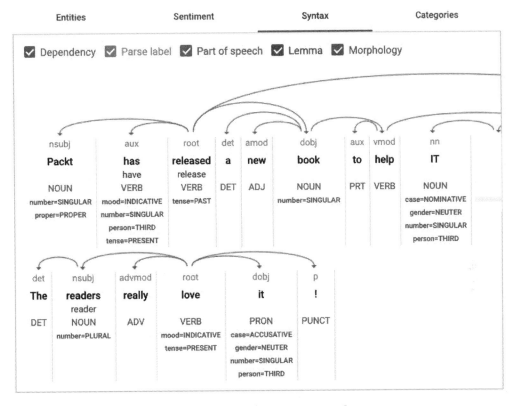

Figure 14.12 – Natural Language API – Syntax

Finally, the text was categorized as **Computer & Electronics** with a **Confidence** value of 0.67:

Figure 14.13 – Natural Language API – Categories

As you can see, this is a very powerful API that can help you perform a deep analysis of text.

Remember that this is still under development and that new features will be added over time.

The Cloud Vision API

The **Cloud Vision API** provides vision detection features, including the following:

- Image labeling

- Face and landmark detection

- **Optical Character Recognition (OCR)**

- Tagging explicit content

You can test this API using `https://cloud.google.com/vision/`. You simply upload the image and see what analysis is possible.

If we look at the **Faces** tab, we can see that a face and a hat were detected correctly. The service was also able to detect the feeling of joy, which I can confirm, as it is me in the photograph having a lot of fun:

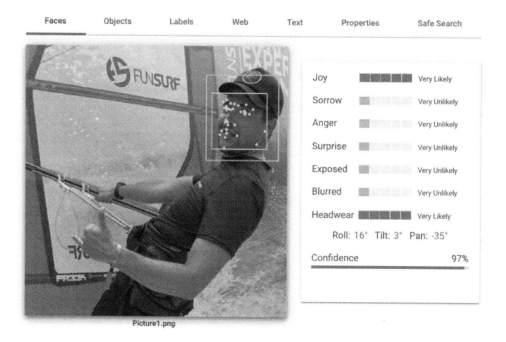

Figure 14.14 – Vision AI – Faces

In the **Objects** tab, we can see that most of the objects have been identified correctly, although I don't remember wearing a skirt that day:

Figure 14.15 – Vision AI – Objects

The **Labels** tab reveals the analysis of how the image is to be labeled. Again, most of the labels make sense, with the exception of the tennis racket:

Figure 14.16 – Vision AI – Labels

When we look at the OCR capabilities, there is some good analysis, especially when we look at **+Block 3**, where the API has detected an **S** from the logo with an odd font:

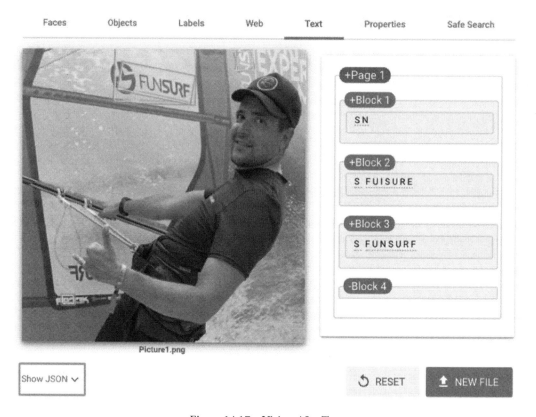

Figure 14.17 – Vision AI – Text

Finally, if we expand the **Show JSON** link under the image, we can also see how the REST API's call and response would appear:

Figure 14.18 – Vision AI – JSON response

As we can see in the preceding screenshot, we get the response in JSON format. This allows us to easily parse it and use the results of the query in the code of the application.

The Cloud Video Intelligence API

Google Cloud Video Intelligence allows you to analyze video that's been uploaded to Cloud Storage.

Currently, the following features are available:

- **Labels**: These detect and label entities, such as animals, plants, and people.
- **Shots**: These detect scene changes within the video and label them.
- **Explicit content**: These are explicit content annotations for pornography.

This can have a number of use cases. Video metadata can be created with labels that describe its content to allow improved searching in media libraries. In addition, videos with inappropriate content can be identified and removed from general access.

Dialogflow

This is actually a tool outside of GCP and has its origins in a product called **Api.ai**. It was developed to perform human-to-computer interaction using natural language processing.

It allows you to create so-called **agents** and **intents** that have definite possible conversation scenarios. Dialogflow is able to train itself on possible variations of phrases that the user uses to demonstrate particular intent. The more phrases that are provided, the better it can learn to trigger the intent:

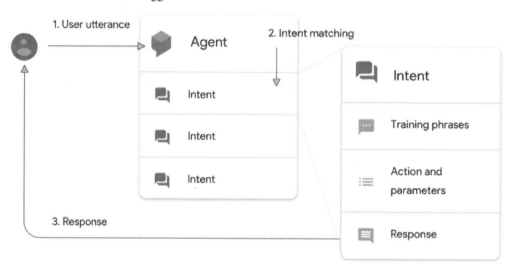

Figure 14.19 – Dialogflow (Source: https://cloud.google.com/dialogflow/docs/intents-overview. License: https://creativecommons.org/licenses/by/4.0/)

When a user calls an intent, the agent can answer with a simple response, or more advanced actions can take place. For example, an intent can be analyzed in relation to defined parameters.

The parameters can get extracted and passed to so-called **fulfillment**, which is basically Firebase functions. The developer can produce Node.js code to integrate with third-party systems outside Dataflow. This can be used to retrieve information or be asked to perform specific actions. As an example, a call can be made to a weather service to get a forecast for a particular location, or a smart home system can be called to turn off the light in the living room. Dialogflow can integrate with your application or website using the REST API, or you can use one of the one-click integrations for applications such as the following:

- Google Assistant
- Slack
- Facebook Messenger
- Twitter
- Skype
- Amazon Alexa
- Microsoft Cortana

Dialogflow comes with three flavors of agents. Which one you choose depends on how advanced your design is:

- **Dialogflow ES**: A standard agent suitable for small-to-medium and simple-to-moderate solutions.
- **Dialogflow CX**: An advanced agent suitable for large and complex solutions.
- **Dialogflow Trial**: This provides features of Dialogflow ES with limited quotas. It is suitable for experimenting.

You can find a detailed comparison of those three agent editions by accessing this link: `https://cloud.google.com/dialogflow/docs/editions`.

AutoML

AutoML comes into play when pretrained models are not fit for purpose. As an example, the Vision API can recognize a sofa, but *what if we want to recognize a particular sofa that our company produces?* The Vision API cannot do that for us.

In such a case, we need to use AutoML or train our own model. As you have probably already guessed, the former is a much easier method. AutoML takes datasets from you, trains and deploys the model, and then serves it through the REST API. This sounds a little bit like magic, right? Take a look at the following diagram:

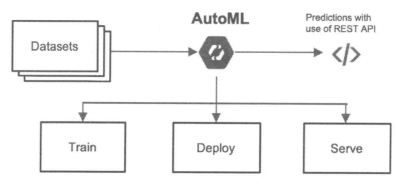

Figure 14.20 – AutoML

Note that there are five services available that allow you to train your custom model:

- **AutoML Vision**: This classifies your images according to your own defined labels.

- **AutoML Translation**: This performs translation queries, returning results specific to your domain.

- **AutoML Natural Language**: This classifies English-language content into a custom set of categories.

- **AutoML Tables**: This turns structured data into predictive insights.

- **AutoML Video Intelligence**: This allows you to classify segments of video.

Let's have a look at an example. See how you would actually use AutoML, using the example of the Vision API, to recognize a table that your company produces. In short, what you would do is the following:

1. Take multiple photos of your table.
2. Upload it to Cloud Storage.
3. Create a CSV file with a label for your photos.
4. Provide the CSV file to AutoML to train the model.

Once the model has been trained, you can access the model through the REST API, as you would with any other pretrained model. Quite amazing, right? Check the *AI adventures* video in the *Further reading* section if you want to see AutoML Vision in action.

Summary

In this chapter, we learned about the ML services offered by GCP. We started with the theory of ML to introduce basic concepts and nomenclature to better understand the actual services. We learned that, depending on your role and use case, you need to make the correct choice as to which service will be the most effective for you to use. One goal can sometimes be achieved using two or more different services. We also learned that you don't need to be a data scientist to leverage ML. Those of you who have very limited knowledge can use pretrained models. If those models are not good enough for your use case, you can try AutoML, which allows new models to be created without us having to develop the model ourselves. We just need to deliver proper datasets to GCP.

Finally, for those of you who have the knowledge and are capable of developing your own models, Vertex AI is the service you can use to develop and host your models.

In the next chapter, we will have a closer look at how to secure our environment in GCP.

Further reading

Read the following articles for more information regarding what was covered in this chapter:

- **ML building blocks**: https://cloud.google.com/products/ai/
- **Dialogflow**: https://cloud.google.com/dialogflow/docs/
- **ML Engine**: https://cloud.google.com/ml-engine/docs/
- **Cloud AutoML**: https://cloud.google.com/automl/docs/
- **TensorFlow**: https://www.tensorflow.org/
- **AI adventures video**: https://www.youtube.com/watch?v=nKW8Ndu7Mjw
- **Speech-to-Text**: https://cloud.google.com/speech-to-text/docs/basics
- **Vertex AI**: https://cloud.google.com/vertex-ai/docs

Section 3: Secure, Manage and Monitor a Google Cloud Solution

In this section we will focus on securing your environment, how to use the various tools to manage GCP, and also how we monitor service operations.

This part of the book comprises the following chapters:

15
Security and Compliance

Security in GCP was built in from the start and certainly not an afterthought! In each service that GCP provides, you will see that security is paramount. In the public cloud era, it's true that a single breach of security can not only cause direct financial implications but can also have a detrimental effect on future business for a company. For this reason, GCP takes the view that the best way is in-depth defense rather than a single piece of technology, and it offers a lot more security than what a customer can usually afford by replicating on-premises. In this chapter, we will look at the key topics that we need to understand to be successful in the exam and try to give an overview of security and the importance GCP places on it.

In this chapter, we will cover the following topics:

- Introduction to security
- Cloud Identity
- Resource Manager
- IAM
- Organization Policies
- Service accounts

- Fire rules and load balancers

- Cloud Security Scanner

- Monitoring and logging

- Encryption

- Penetration testing in GCP

- Industry regulations

- CI/CD security overview

- Additional security services

Introduction to security

Let's start this chapter with a brief introduction to GCP's approach to security. As we mentioned previously, security is not an afterthought and is built into its services. But before we even think about securing our services, we need to acknowledge the fact that GCP has a holistic view of security. This can be seen by restricting physical data center access and using custom hardware and hardened versions of operating systems in the software stack.

> **Important Note**
>
> Google uses custom hardware with security in mind and uses a hardened version of Linux for the software stack, which is monitored for binary modifications and enforces trusted server boots.

Storage is a key service for any cloud provider, and GCP offers encryption at rest by default on all storage services. This can support customer encryption keys or manage keys on behalf of the customer. On physical storage disks, retired disks will have sectors zeroed and if data cannot be deleted, disks are destroyed in a multi-stage crusher. However, note that if a customer deletes data, it can take 180 days to be physically deleted.

Additionally, one of the main security concerns is attacks from outside organizations. To protect us from internet attacks, Google offers the ability to register against the frontend, which will check incoming network connections for correct certificates, and offers protection against **Distributed Denial-of-Service (DDoS)** attacks. In addition, using GCP load balancers will offer extra protection, while cloud VPNs and direct connections offer more encryption options.

Google invests heavily in securing its infrastructure, which is designed in progressive security layers. As a quick reference, let's briefly look at these main infrastructure security layers:

- **Securing Low-Level Infrastructure**: Google incorporates multiple layers of physical protection. As they design and build their data centers, access is limited to a very small group of Google employees. Biometric identification, metal detection, vehicle barriers, and laser-based intrusion detection systems are just some of the technologies used to provide a physical layer of protection.

  In addition to this, Google also designs server boards and networking equipment, allowing Google to vet the vendors they work with and perform audits and validation on security properties provided by the components. Custom hardware security chips allow Google to securely identify and authenticate Google devices at a hardware level.

  Finally, Google uses cryptographic signatures over low-level components such as the kernel, BIOS, and base operating system to ensure server machines are booting the correct software stack.

- **Securing Service Deployment**: A service is an application binary that a developer has written and wants to run on Google's infrastructure. Each service that runs on the Google infrastructure will have an associated service account identity and is used by the clients to ensure communication with the intended server. Google uses cryptographic authentication and authorization for inter-service communication at the application layer.

- **Securing Data Storage**: Google's various storage services can be configured to use keys from a central key management system to encrypt data before it is written to physical storage. This allows Google's infrastructure to isolate itself from potential threats such as malicious disk firmware. Hardware encryption support in the hard drives and SSDs that are used can also track each drive through its life cycle.

- **Securing Internet Communications**: Google's infrastructure consists of large sets of physical machines, connected over LANs and WANs, so there is a need to defend against DoS attacks. This is helped by only exposing a subset of machines directly to external internet traffic. There are also services such as Cloud Armor, which assist in preventing DoS attacks.

  Additionally, things such as multi-factor authentication assist in securing internet communication.

- **Operational Security**: Google also needs to operate the infrastructure securely. Google has code libraries and frameworks that will eliminate XSS vulnerabilities in web apps, as well as tools to automatically detect security bugs. They also offer a Vulnerability Reward Program that pays anyone who can discover bugs and is heavily invested in intrusion detection.

> **Exam Tip**
>
> We will talk about security in more depth than what is expected for you to be successful in the exam; however, it is vital to understand this information for the role of a cloud architect. For the exam, there are several areas that we recommend that you focus on: understanding Cloud IAM roles, understanding what Cloud Identity is, understanding what **Key Management System** (KMS) does, understanding the difference between **Customer-Supplied Encryption Keys** (CSEKs) and **Customer-Managed Encryption Keys** (CMEKs), being aware of encryption at rest and in transit, and being aware of PCI compliance.

Shared responsibility model

Before we look deeper into security options, it is important to point out that like the other main public cloud vendors, GCP has what is known as a shared responsibility agreement. As we touched on previously, Google invests a lot in the security of its infrastructure. However, we, as consumers of the platform, also have responsibilities.

Google is not responsible for what resides in the operating system. It's important to understand the principle of shared responsibility for the exam. Google won't be responsible for everything in your architecture, so we must be prepared to take our share of the responsibility. For the exam, we should understand that the different GCP services that are offered mean that Google and the customer will have different levels of responsibility. As an example, let's look at Cloud Storage. Google will manage the encryption of storage and the hardware providing the service and will allow audit logging. However, it will not be responsible for the content that resides on Cloud Storage or the network security that's used to access it. Likewise, access to and authentication of the content will be the owner's responsibility. Compare this to, let's say, BigQuery, which is a PaaS offering. In this case, Google would take responsibility for network security and authentication.

The following diagram shows what the customer is expected to manage in each service model. From left to right, we can see the difference between fully self-managed on-premises data centers and SaaS offerings:

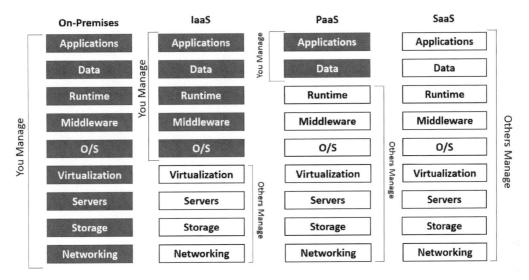

Figure 15.1 – Shared responsibility model

Now that we have introduced security at a high level, let's move on to understanding Cloud Identity in GCP.

Cloud Identity

Cloud Identity is a key GCP service that's offered by Google as an **Identity-as-a-Service (IDaaS)** solution. This is an optional service and a more basic approach can be taken to apply individual permissions to services or projects. However, for enterprise organizations, using an identity service makes far more sense. It enables businesses to manage who has access to their resources and services within a GCP organization, all from a single pane of glass. Cloud Identity can be used as a standalone product for domain-based user accounts and groups. We should note early on in this chapter that Google also offers a similar management pane for Google workspace users. The console works in the same way, and user and domain management have a lot of similarities. You may wish to investigate this further in detail, but for this book and, more importantly, the exam, we will focus solely on GCP Cloud Identity.

Like many on-premises directories that can reduce the overhead of user administration, GCP allows us to centrally manage our users in the cloud through Cloud Identity. It offers a central, single pane of glass to administer users, groups, and settings and is referred to as the Google Admin console. To utilize Cloud Identity, your domain name should be enabled to receive emails, hence allowing your existing web and email addresses to be used as normal. Your GCP organization will have a single Cloud Identity, and the organization is the root node in the resource hierarchy. It is deemed the supernode of your projects.

It should be noted that there are two editions of Cloud Identity. One is free and one is a premium subscription. The premium subscription offers additional features, such as device management and security and application management. A full comparison can be found here: `https://support.google.com/cloudidentity/answer/7431902?hl=en`. Finally, you must understand that Cloud Identity is not controlled through the GCP console, but in fact through the Google Admin console. Once you're logged into the admin console, you will be able to add users, create groups, and assign members and disable users.

The following is a screenshot of what the **Google Admin** console page looks like:

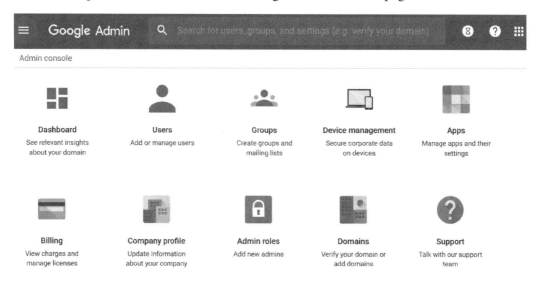

Figure 15.2 – Google Admin console

Adding users manually is classed as overhead in terms of effort and is not scalable if you have a large environment to manage. The whole point of Cloud Identity is to simplify the management of users and groups as it's unlikely that an organization can afford one person to add, remove, and manage things. This is where **Google Cloud Directory Sync (GCDS)** comes in. Many organizations will have an LDAP database such as Microsoft **Active Directory (AD)**. GCDS can synchronize an organization's AD or LDAP database onto Cloud Identity, and it is highly scalable. Synchronization is only one-way – that is, from on-premises to GCP –so your on-site database is never compromised. GCDS allows the administrator to perform delta syncs and scheduled synchronizations and perform tasks manually. If we require permissions to be revoked from a user, or indeed disabled, then the results are immediate.

When we start to use Cloud Identity for authentication, Google stores and manages all authentications and passwords by default, but there is an option to disable this. Two-step verification can be added to this by using multi-factor tools. There is also an alternative to using **Single Sign-On (SSO)**, which is a SAML 2.0-based authentication that also includes **multi-factor authentication (MFA)**. Finally, password complexity can be set within Cloud Identity's password management feature to align with existing policies your business may have:

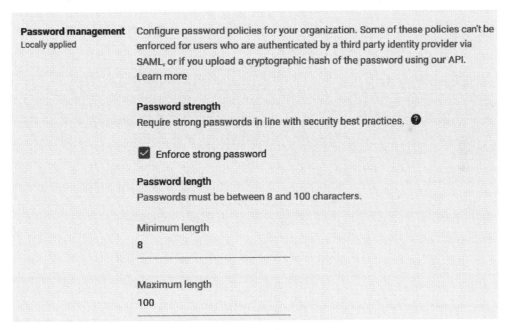

Figure 15.3 – Password management

In the preceding screenshot, we can see an example of the **Password management** screen. In the next section, we will look at GCP Resource Manager.

Resource Manager

GCP Resource Manager allows you to create and manage a hierarchical grouping of objects such as organizations, folders, and projects together. Let's look at an example where we have an organization, brgerrard.co.uk, and several folders underneath that to add to the structure. Folders are optional but can be used to group projects. Access to these folders will work on a hierarchical model, meaning that if you have full access to the Departments folder, then this will be inherited down to, for example, the Google Cloud Architect Project folder, as shown in the following screenshot:

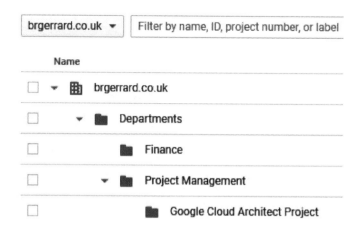

Figure 15.4 – Resource Manager

A good example to think of would be the separation of development, testing, and production environments in GCP. Separate projects for each environment allow you to grant access to only those who need access to the resources. The following screenshot shows how the hierarchy of GCP is set up:

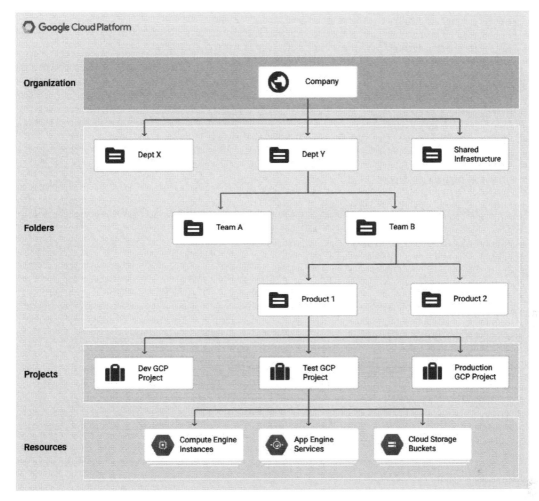

Figure 15.5 – GCP hierarchy (Source: https://cloud.google.com/resource-manager/docs/cloud-platform-resource-hierarchy, License: https://creativecommons.org/licenses/by/4.0/legalcode)

It's important to understand that setting permissions at a higher level results in permission inheritance. For example, granting a user permission to the **Dept Y** folder means that the user will also have the same permissions applied to all subfolders and projects. Therefore, it is important to design your organization and permissions in such a way that they only grant access to the resources that are required to fulfill the requested role.

In the next section, we will look at Identity and Access Management.

Identity and Access Management (IAM)

GCP offers us the ability to create GCP resources and manage who can access them. It also allows us to grant only the specific access that's necessary, to prevent any unwanted access. It allows us to meet any requirements for the separation of duties. This is known as the security principle of least privilege, and we will look at this in detail shortly. First, we will have a look at some key concepts of IAM. In Cloud IAM, we can grant access to members. Members can belong to any one of the following types:

- **Google accounts**: These represent someone who interacts with GCP, such as a developer.

- **Service accounts**: These belong to your application and not an end user. We will look at service accounts in more detail later in this chapter, in the *Service accounts* section.

- **Google groups**: These are named collections of Google accounts and service accounts and are a good way to grant an access policy to a collection of users. A Google group can be used with IAM to grant access to roles. One important exception is that a group can only be assigned the owner role of a project if they are part of the same organization.

- **Google Workspace Domain**: This domain represents a group of all of the Google accounts that have been created in an organization's Google Workspace (Formerly G Suite).

- **Cloud Identity Domain**: Similar to Google Workspace, this domain represents all of the Google accounts in an organization.

The following are some of the concepts that are related to access management:

- **Resources**: Resources are projects, Compute Engine instances, or Cloud Storage buckets.

- **Permissions**: A permission dictates what operations are allowed on a resource and are seen in the form of `<service>.<resource>.<verb>`; for example, `compute.instance.list`. Permissions cannot be assigned directly to a user.

- **Roles**: Roles are a collection of permissions. To provide a user with access to a resource, we grant them a role rather than assigning permissions directly to the user. There are three kinds of roles – that is, **basic**, **predefined**, and **custom** – and we will discuss them later in this chapter. Please note that Basic roles were originally known as *Primitive roles*.

- **IAM Policy**: An IAM policy is a collection of statements that will define who has what type of access. You attach a policy to a resource and use it to enforce access control whenever it is accessed.

> **Important Note**
>
> In IAM, you will grant access to *principles*. These can be one of the following types: Google group, Google account, service account, Cloud Identity, Google Workspace Domain, all authenticated users, or all users.

Now that we have some background knowledge of IAM, let's continue with some examples. We previously mentioned the principle of least privilege, and we now know that we should only grant access to exactly what is necessary.

We'll look at the `Google Cloud Architect Project` folder permissions in the following example. We may have a user who should be able to create projects in all folders, but we may also have another user who should only create projects in a specific folder. In the following screenshot, we are granting the user called `konrad@brgerrard.co.uk` the **Project Creator** role:

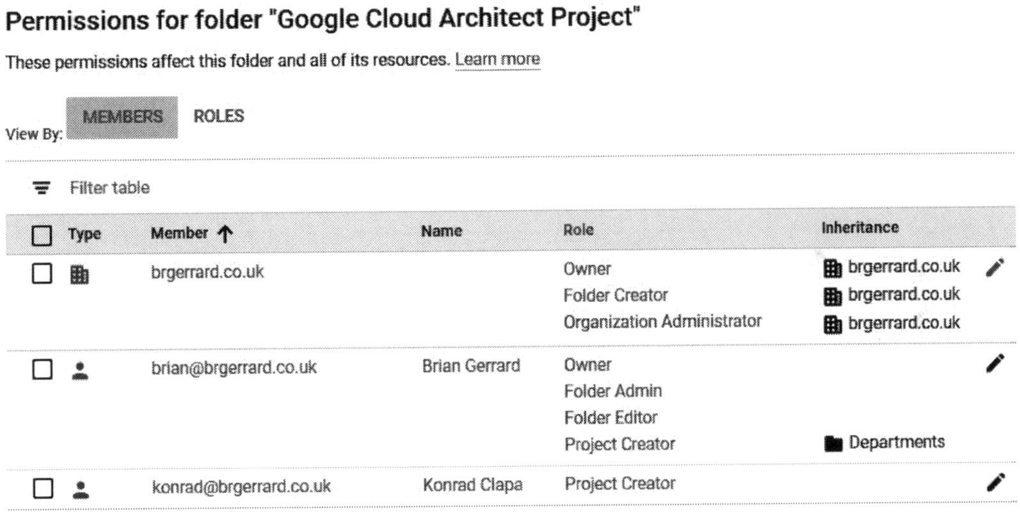

Permissions for folder "Google Cloud Architect Project"

These permissions affect this folder and all of its resources. Learn more

View By: MEMBERS   ROLES

≡ Filter table

	Type	Member ↑	Name	Role	Inheritance
☐	🏢	brgerrard.co.uk		Owner Folder Creator Organization Administrator	🏢 brgerrard.co.uk ✐ 🏢 brgerrard.co.uk 🏢 brgerrard.co.uk
☐	👤	brian@brgerrard.co.uk	Brian Gerrard	Owner Folder Admin Folder Editor Project Creator	✐ 📁 Departments
☐	👤	konrad@brgerrard.co.uk	Konrad Clapa	Project Creator	✐

Figure 15.6 – Applying permissions

Basic roles existed before Cloud IAM. These were legacy **owner**, **editor**, and **viewer** roles. Since these roles are limited, applying any of these roles means granting a wide spectrum of permissions. This does not exactly follow our least-permission principle! However, we should understand that there may be some cases where we wish to use primitive roles. For example, we may work in a small cross-functional team where the granularity of IAM is not required. Similarly, if we are working in a testing or development environment, then we may not wish full granular permissions to be applied.

If we want to be more granular, we should use **predefined** roles and base our roles on job functions. These roles are created and maintained by Google, so permissions are automatically updated as necessary whenever Google Cloud adds new features or services. As an example, here are the predefined roles for **App Engine**:

Figure 15.7 – Predefined roles

If we want to create roles with specific permissions and not the Google-provided collection, then we can utilize **custom** roles. These may provide more granularity according to our requirements, but it should be noted that they are user-managed and therefore come with overhead. They can, however, prevent unwanted access to other resources. Before we create a custom role, we should always check that an existing predefined role – or a combination of predefined roles – doesn't already meet our needs.

Granting access to roles on an individual basis can be tedious, and ideally, we should use groups to control access. As an example, let's create a new group from our Cloud Identity admin console called `Project Creator`. Looking back at *Figure 15.2* from the **Identity and Access Management (IAM)** section, we can do this by browsing to the **Groups** field and clicking **Add new group**:

1.   Give the group a name, as shown in the following screenshot:

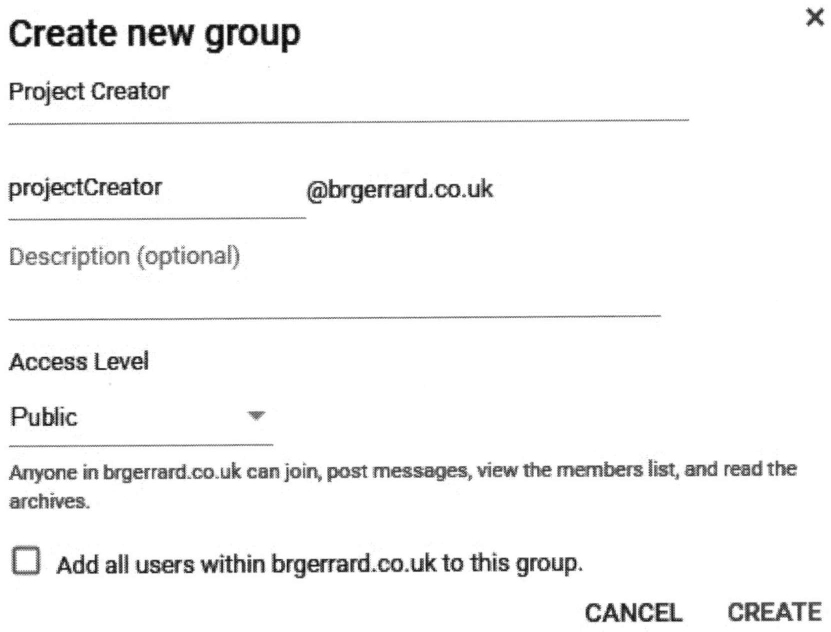

Create new group   ✕

Project Creator

projectCreator   @brgerrard.co.uk

Description (optional)

Access Level

Public   ▼

Anyone in brgerrard.co.uk can join, post messages, view the members list, and read the archives.

☐ Add all users within brgerrard.co.uk to this group.

CANCEL   CREATE

Figure 15.8 – Create new group

2.   Apply this to a resource in our GCP console. In this example, we are assigning the group to a folder:

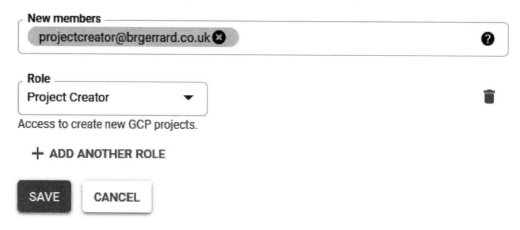

Add members, roles to "Google Cloud Architect Project" folder

Enter one or more members below. Then select a role for these members to grant them access to your resources. Multiple roles allowed. Learn more

New members

projectcreator@brgerrard.co.uk ⊗   ❓

Role

Project Creator   ▼   🗑

Access to create new GCP projects.

+ ADD ANOTHER ROLE

SAVE   CANCEL

Figure 15.9 – Adding group members

Now, we can centrally control permission to our resources rather than drill down into folder structures in our GCP console. This also offers a separation of duties to increase security. Now that we have created our project, we want to allow a user to only create a VM instance.

Let's say that, as a project owner, we want to allow an engineer to create a VM instance, but we want a separate engineer to have read-only access to this compute resource. Again, we can create two new groups in Cloud Identity for this purpose; let's call them vmviewer and vmadmin. We can assign these groups the relevant roles. Using predefined roles means that they are managed by Google, and any additional permissions that are added to a role would mean that your member automatically gets them.

Our vmviewer group is now assigned the **Compute Viewer** role at a project level, as shown in the following screenshot. Note that we also can add a condition. IAM conditions are one or more rules that are used to evaluate as true before the role associated with it is permitted. As an example, you may only want the IAM role to apply during certain hours of the day:

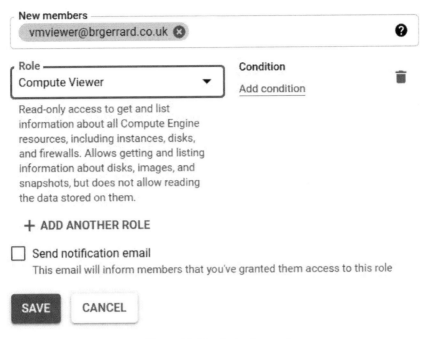

Figure 15.10 – Assigning a role

Our `vmadmin` group has now been assigned the **Compute Instance Admin** role at the project level:

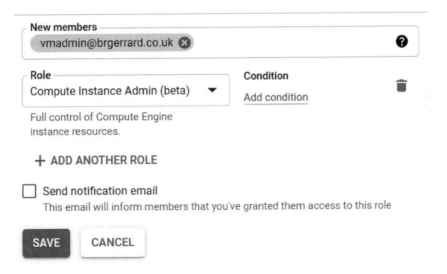

Figure 15.11 – Assigning a role

We can also use the gcloud CLI to add permissions. This command line allows us to manage interactions with GCP APIs. As an example, if I want to assign the `editor` role to `brian@brgerrard.co.uk` within the `redwing` project, then I can run the following command:

```
gcloud projects add-iam-policy-binding redwing -
member='user:brian@brgerrard.co.uk' -role='roles/editor'
```

The output of this command will confirm that `brian@brgerrard.co.uk` has been granted the role of editor.

This `gcloud projects` command line can also be used for many more functions. Please note that we will take a deeper dive into the `gcloud` command line in *Chapter 16, Google Cloud Management Options*.

> **Important Note**
>
> Please refer to the official documentation if you are keen on using this in more depth: `https://cloud.google.com/sdk/gcloud/reference/projects/`.

Finally, regarding IAM, we have spoken about who has permission to perform actions on resources. We should also be mindful of what organizational policies focus on. These policies allow us to set restrictions on resources. An organizational policy would allow us to disable certain options that are available to a user. These restrictions are done using constraints and can be applied to a GCP service or a list of GCP services. For example, let's say that we didn't want a default network to be available. We could set a constraint to skip default network creation, thus preventing any new VM instances on this network.

Previously, we mentioned the importance of service accounts. We will look at these in more depth now.

Service accounts

Service accounts are used to call the API of a service, hence removing users from any direct involvement. They belong to an application or VM instance. By default, every GCP project we create will have a default service account created when we enable our projects to use Compute Engine:

1. We can create a new service account by navigating to **IAM & Admin | IAM | Service accounts** on our GCP console. We can also create a new service account using the gcloud CLI. As an example, let's say we need to have a VM that has access to Cloud Storage. The following screenshot shows us creating a new service account named `AccessCloudStorage`:

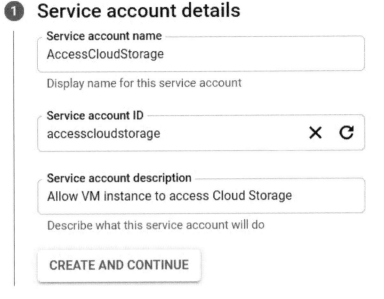

Figure 15.12 – Adding a service account

2. Once we decide that we will be using service accounts for our resources, we can then decide whether we want to grant specific roles to the service account. The following screenshot shows that we have optional choices when assigning a role:

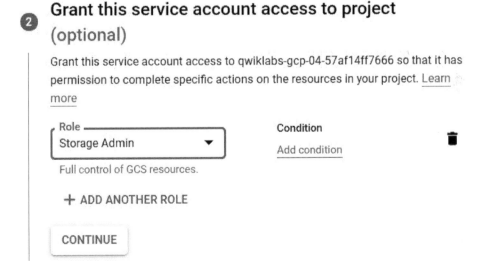

Figure 15.13 – Grant this service account access to project

3. Optionally, we can grant access to users or groups that need to perform actions as this service account:

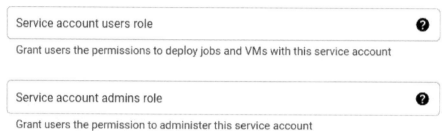

Figure 15.14 – Assigning a role

If we revisit the process of creating our VM instance, we can assign this service account under the **Identity and API access** option:

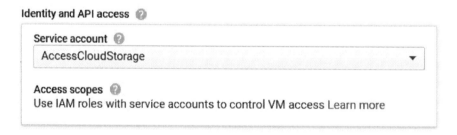

Figure 15.15 – Identity and API access

This will allow the service account to assume the service account identity for authenticating API requests. As we mentioned previously, we can see that we have the option to assign accounts we have created to a service account.

If you select the default service account, you will notice that there is the option to select an access scope. An **access scope** determines the level of access the API call is allowed to a service. It is good practice to select each API access individually per service to improve security. The following is the full list of APIs that are currently available:

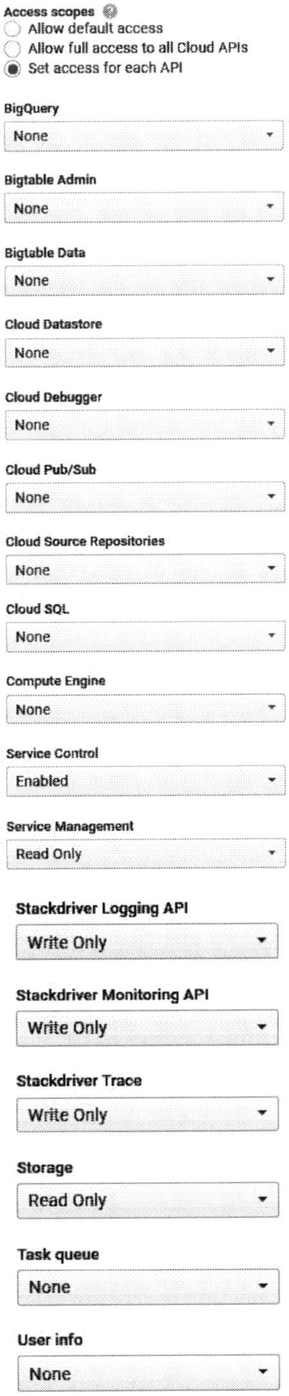

Access scopes ⚙
- ○ Allow default access
- ○ Allow full access to all Cloud APIs
- ● Set access for each API

BigQuery

None ▾

Bigtable Admin

None ▾

Bigtable Data

None ▾

Cloud Datastore

None ▾

Cloud Debugger

None ▾

Cloud Pub/Sub

None ▾

Cloud Source Repositories

None ▾

Cloud SQL

None ▾

Compute Engine

None ▾

Service Control

Enabled ▾

Service Management

Read Only ▾

Stackdriver Logging API

Write Only ▾

Stackdriver Monitoring API

Write Only ▾

Stackdriver Trace

Write Only ▾

Storage

Read Only ▾

Task queue

None ▾

User info

None ▾

Figure 15.16 – List of APIs

Service accounts are managed using service account keys. There are two types of service account keys:

- **Google Cloud-managed**: Google Cloud-managed keys are used by services such as Compute Engine and App Engine and cannot be downloaded.

- **User-managed**: User-managed keys are created and can be downloaded and managed by users of GCP. You are fully responsible for user-managed keys.

We will speak about key management in the *Encryption* section of this chapter.

Before we finish talking about service accounts, one final thing to note is that service accounts should still follow the same principles we learned about for IAM. Service accounts should only get the minimum set of permissions required for that service.

> **Exam Tip**
>
> For the exam, this topic is key so that you understand identities, roles, and resources. We have briefly touched on IAM in previous chapters, but now, we want to look at it in a bit more detail. Some principles to note before you read any further, which will be explained in more detail in this chapter, are as follows: IAM roles are groups of permissions that can be assigned to users, groups, or service accounts; there are different types of roles; we should follow the principle of least privilege; and use groups to control access rather than granting access to individual users, if possible.

In this section, we covered service accounts. We explained that they are a special type of account that removes a user from direct involvement and that they are an important part of Google IAM. In the next section, we will look at access control lists, which are an alternative to IAM.

Cloud Storage access management

On top of using IAM permissions to restrict access to Cloud Storage, it can also be secured using **Access Control Lists (ACLs)**. ACLs should be used when you want to set permissions on objects rather than the whole bucket, for example, to gain access to an individual object in a specific bucket. This is because Cloud IAM would apply permissions to all of the objects in a bucket. It's vital to understand this because, from a manageability perspective, it is not ideal to manage these individually, and if there is a commonality of permissions across all objects in the bucket, then you should use IAM to control access.

An ACL is made up of the permission that defines what can be performed, as well as the scope that defines who can perform the action. When a request is made to a bucket, the ACL will grant the user permissions, if applicable; otherwise, the request will result in a **403 Forbidden** error. An object inside a bucket can only be granted **Owner** or **Reader** permission, as shown in the following screenshot:

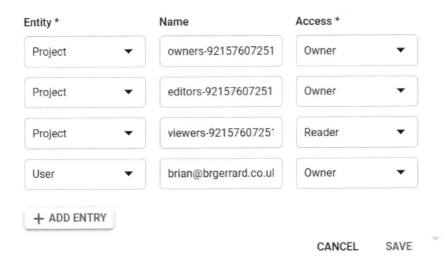

Figure 15.17 – GCP bucket file permissions

> **Important Note**
> On top of the ACLs, GCP also offers legacy roles of Storage Legacy bucket **Owner**, Storage Legacy bucket **Reader**, and Storage Legacy bucket **Writer**.

As with IAM, we should follow the principle of least privilege. If you need to use an ACL, then do not apply the owner role if it is not needed. You should be careful to ensure that buckets are not unnecessarily made public (by assigning the allUser role). Assigning wrong permissions to a bucket is a very typical security gap in the real world and you should think carefully before applying ACLs.

One final piece of information you should be aware of before the exam is the use of signed URLs. This option allows you to grant access to a visitor so that they can upload or download from storage without the need for a Google account. Access can be time-limited, and access can be granted for reads or writes to anyone who has the URL. We can create a signed URL with `gsutil` by running the following command:

```
gsutil signurl -d 10m Desktop/private-key.json gs://example-
bucket/cat.jpeg
```

In this example, we are using `private-key.json` as our service account private key to expose the `cat.jpeg` bucket object from `example-bucket`.

> **Exam Tip**
>
> Remember that we should never grant a user or service more permissions than what's required. Always use the principle of least privilege.

Next, we will look at Organization Policy Service.

Organization Policy Service

Organization Policy Service gives us programmatic control over our organization's cloud resources. This allows for centralized control to configure how our organization's resources are configured. Additionally, it helps our development teams stay within compliance boundaries and helps project owners move quickly without worrying about or breaking compliance.

It is important to highlight that Organization Policies are different from IAM, which we have discussed previously. While IAM focuses on allowing administrators to authorize *who* can act on specific resources based on permissions, Organization Policies focuses on allowing administrators to set restrictions on specific resources to determine how they can be configured. An organization policy is a set of restrictions and as an administrator, we define the policy to enforce restrictions on organizations, folders, or projects.

To define such policies, we would choose a particular type of restriction called a **constraint**. Constraints are applied against a Google Cloud service or a list of services. Essentially, this is a blueprint defining what behaviors are controlled. A constraint has a type, either list or Boolean. As you can guess, a list constraint will evaluate a list of allowed or denied values that have been set by the administrator. For example, this could be an allowed list of IP addresses that can connect to a virtual machine. A Boolean constraint would either enforce or not.

When a policy is set on a resource, all the descendants of that resource will inherit the policy by default. A user with the **Organization Policy Administrator** role can modify this inheritance if exceptions are required.

Violations are when a service acts in a state that is against the organization's policy restrictions. This may occur if a new policy sets a restriction on an action or state that a service is already in.

To create an Organization Policy, navigate to **IAM & Admin | Organization Policies**. This will list the available policies:

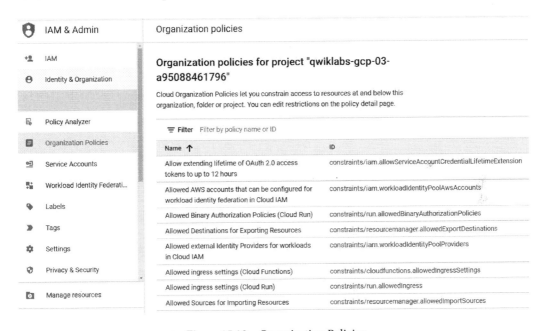

Figure 15.18 – Organization Policies

As an example, the following policy has been selected. Each policy describes the constraint and how it is currently applied. We can see that, by default, it would be inherited. We can edit the policy, if we are permitted to, and change the effective policy:

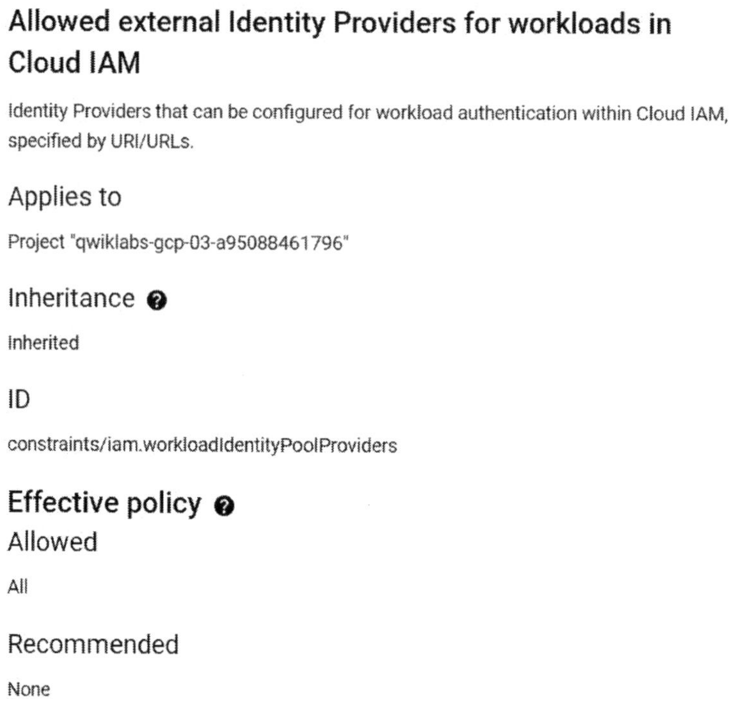

Allowed external Identity Providers for workloads in Cloud IAM

Identity Providers that can be configured for workload authentication within Cloud IAM, specified by URI/URLs.

Applies to

Project "qwiklabs-gcp-03-a95088461796"

Inheritance ❷

Inherited

ID

constraints/iam.workloadIdentityPoolProviders

Effective policy ❷

Allowed

All

Recommended

None

Figure 15.19 – Policy description

To reiterate, Organization Policies are important to understand for exam success. Please ensure that you understand how they differ from IAM.

Next, let's review firewall rules and load balancers.

Firewall rules and load balancers

We already covered networking in *Chapter 10, Networking Options in GCP*, but we would like to recap what is important from a security standpoint.

If Compute Engine instances don't need to communicate with each other, then we should host them on different **Virtual Private Cloud** (**VPC**) networks. Additionally, if we have an application made up of servers on different network tiers, then each server should be on a different subnet. Let's take a traditional web app and database application as an example. We want to segment each tier on a different subnet.

Firewall rules are the obvious choice for securing a network. As you now know, a VPC lets you isolate your network to allow for segmentation between computing resources. Firewall rules let you control the flow of inbound and outbound traffic by allowing or denying the traffic based on direction, source or destination, protocol, and priority. The following screenshot shows the creation of a new firewall rule:

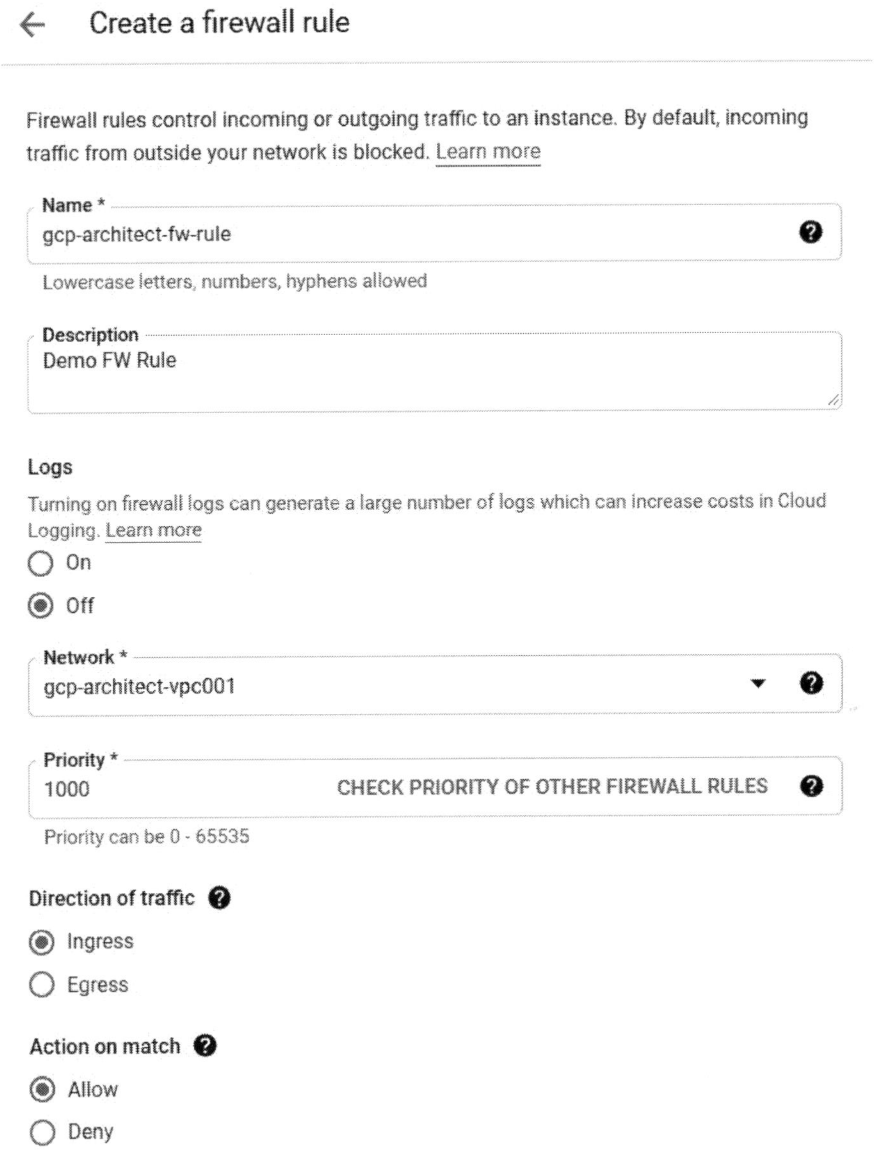

← Create a firewall rule

Firewall rules control incoming or outgoing traffic to an instance. By default, incoming traffic from outside your network is blocked. Learn more

Name *
gcp-architect-fw-rule   ❷

Lowercase letters, numbers, hyphens allowed

Description
Demo FW Rule

Logs

Turning on firewall logs can generate a large number of logs which can increase costs in Cloud Logging. Learn more

○ On

◉ Off

Network *
gcp-architect-vpc001   ▼   ❷

Priority *
1000   CHECK PRIORITY OF OTHER FIREWALL RULES   ❷

Priority can be 0 - 65535

Direction of traffic ❷

◉ Ingress

○ Egress

Action on match ❷

◉ Allow

○ Deny

Figure 15.20 – New firewall rule

It's important to note that firewall rules in GCP are stateful, meaning that if a rule is initiated by an **Allow** rule in one direction, the traffic will automatically be allowed to return. Likewise, you should also understand that all VPCs have two default rules. The first one permits all outgoing connections to any IP address, while the second blocks all incoming traffic. These are assigned the lowest priority, which means they can easily be overwritten by your custom rules. Additional rules that are applied to a new VPC allow ingress connections for all protocols and ports between instances. Others allow ICMP traffic (`ping`/`trace route`), SSH, and RDP from any source to any destination in the VPC.

As with IAM, for firewall rules, we should also use the principle of least privilege. By this, we mean that we should only allow communications that are needed by our applications and tie down anything that's not required. It is seen as good practice to create a rule with a low priority that will block all traffic and then layer the relevant rules on top with a higher priority.

Load balancers in GCP also offer additional security. Load balancers support SSL and HTTPS proxies for encryption in transit. There is a requirement for at least one signed SSL certificate to be installed on the target HTTPS proxy for the load balancer, and you have a choice of using self-managed SSL certificates or Google-managed SSL certificates. It seems obvious but if you need to use HTTPS traffic, then you should select the HTTPS load balancer, but for non-HTTPS traffic, you should use the SSL load balancer.

In the next section, we will introduce Cloud Web Security Scanner.

Cloud Web Security Scanner

It's important to take application security as seriously as we take infrastructure security. Applications are one of the main targets of attacks, and GCP aids in this through the Web Security Scanner service. Of course, we know security is an extremely important topic and Cloud Web Security Scanner supports us in detecting vulnerabilities in our services easily.

When you create a scan, you can set this to scan URLs that your Compute Engine instance, App Engine instance, or GKE instance hosts and likewise exclude URLs. It will detect common vulnerabilities such as flash injection, mixed content, cleartext passwords, and XSS. We can also set a schedule for scans or perform them manually.

> **Important Note**
>
> It should be noted that Cloud Scanner can generate a real load against your application, so performance should be taken into consideration as some scans can take hours to complete. Likewise, caution should be exercised when using this service as it can post comments into the comments section of a web page or generate multiple emails, if prompted, for signup on a page. Therefore, it is good practice to scan your applications in a test environment and have a backup of your application's state before a scan is initiated.

The following screenshot shows us creating a new scan. To begin, we must navigate to **App Engine | Security Scan**. We must then click **Enable API**. We are now ready to create a new scan:

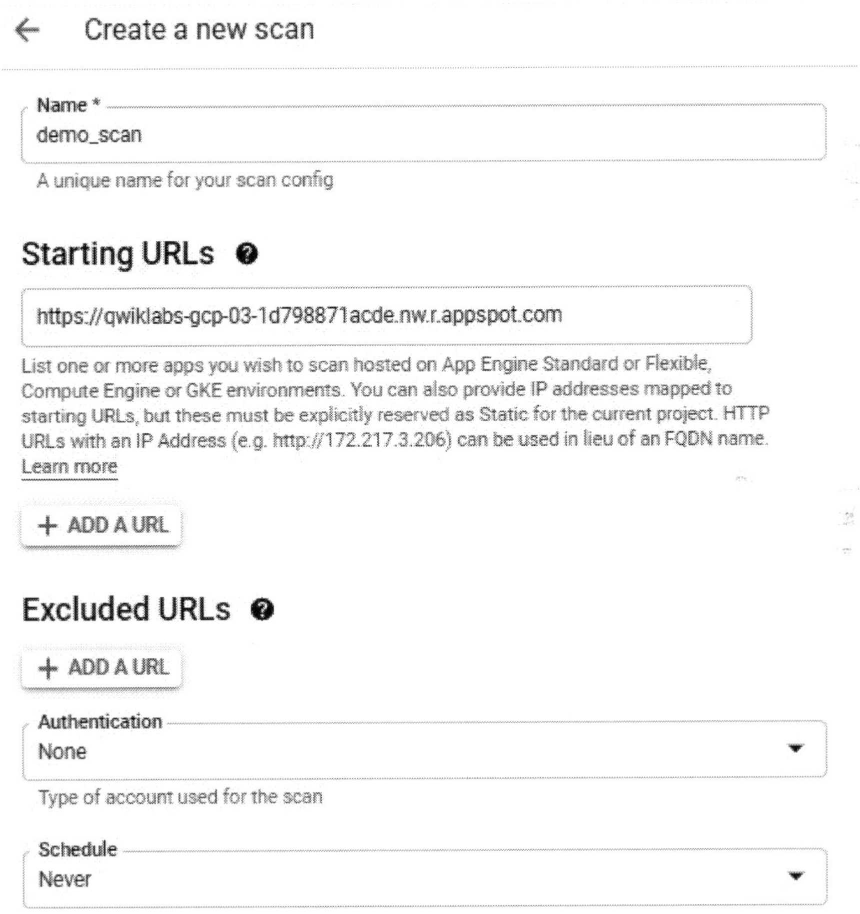

← **Create a new scan**

Name *
demo_scan

A unique name for your scan config

Starting URLs ❷

https://qwiklabs-gcp-03-1d798871acde.nw.r.appspot.com

List one or more apps you wish to scan hosted on App Engine Standard or Flexible, Compute Engine or GKE environments. You can also provide IP addresses mapped to starting URLs, but these must be explicitly reserved as Static for the current project. HTTP URLs with an IP Address (e.g. http://172.217.3.206) can be used in lieu of an FQDN name. Learn more

+ ADD A URL

Excluded URLs ❷

+ ADD A URL

Authentication
None ▼

Type of account used for the scan

Schedule
Never ▼

Figure 15.21 – New security scan

When we have run the scan, we will receive our results, which will flag any vulnerabilities, as shown in the following screenshot. We can also view the scan's date and the duration of the scan:

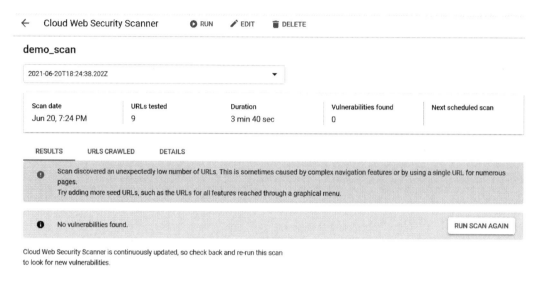

Figure 15.22 – Security scan results

In this section, we looked at Cloud Web Security Scanner and showed you how to set up a new scan. In the next section, we will touch on monitoring and logging.

Monitoring and logging

We will look at monitoring in a lot more detail in *Chapter 17, Monitoring Your Infrastructure*, but it is wise to mention this again in terms of security. Cloud Operations is Google's service for monitoring and managing services, containers, applications, and infrastructure. Cloud Operations offers error reporting, debugging, alerts, tracing, and logging.

Logging assists in securing GCP and minimizing the downtime of your applications. Monitoring allows you to monitor application metrics that can flag an anomaly. Moreover, Cloud Operations Debugger inspects the state of your production data and compares your source code without any performance overhead. Logging allows real-time metrics logging and retains a set period, depending on the log type. If you have security requirements to keep logs for a longer period, then they can be exported to Cloud Storage, which offers inexpensive storage for extended periods.

Encryption

Encryption is a basic form of security for sensitive data. In its simplest form, encryption is the process of turning plaintext data into a scrambled string of characters. We cannot read those strings and, more importantly, a system cannot read them if it doesn't hold the relevant key to decrypt it back to plaintext format.

Encryption is a key element of GCP security. By default, GCP offers encryption at rest, which means that data stored on GCP's storage services is encrypted without any further action from users. This means that there is no additional configuration needed and even if this data did somehow get into the wrong hands, then the data would be unreadable as they wouldn't have the proper encryption key to make sense of the data.

The ability to encrypt sensitive data over GCP assures customers that confidential data will stay just there. At the core of this protection is GCP KMS, which Google uses to manage cryptographic keys for your cloud services. Cloud KMS allows you to generate, use, rotate, and destroy cryptographic keys, which can either be Google-generated or imported from your KMS system. Cloud KMS is integrated with Cloud IAM, so you can manage permissions on individual keys. When we create a new disk, for example, the default option is to use a Google-managed key.

Now, let's take a look at data encryption keys and key encryption keys.

Data encryption keys versus key encryption keys

The key that's used to encrypt a piece of data is known as a **data encryption key (DEK)**. These keys are then wrapped by a **key encryption key (KEK)**. KEKs are stored and managed within Google Cloud's KMS, allowing Google to track and control access from a central point. It isn't possible to export your KEK from KMS, and all of the encryption and decryption of keys must be within KMS. In addition to this, KMS-held keys are backed up for disaster recovery purposes. KEKs are also rotated over a certain period, meaning that a new key is created. This allows GCP to comply with certain regulations, such as **Payment Card Industry Data Security Standard (PCI DSS)**, and is considered a security best practice. GCP will rotate the keys every 90 days by default.

CMEKs versus CSEKs

GCP offers additional methods for managing encryption keys that might fit better with customer security policies.

GCP offers the ability for the customer to manage KEKs, allowing us to control the generation of keys, the rotation of keys, and the expiration of keys. Keys will still be stored in KMS, but we will have control of their life cycle. This is known as CMEK. To organize keys effectively, Google Cloud KMS uses the concept of key rings to group keys together and push inherited permissions to keys.

We can create our key by performing several steps. Let's get started:

1. By browsing to **Security | Key Management** from our GCP console, we can create a new key ring within Cloud KMS. Key rings group keys together. The first thing we must do is enable the IP and then select a key ring location. We can select a region, or we can select **global**. Our decisions will impact the performance of the applications using the key and also the options we have when creating the key. In the following example, we are selecting **global**. A global location is a special multi-region location whereby data centers are spread throughout the world, and it would not be possible to control the exact data centers that are selected. We should only use **global** if our applications are distributed globally, we have infrequent read or writes, and our keys have no geographic residency requirements:

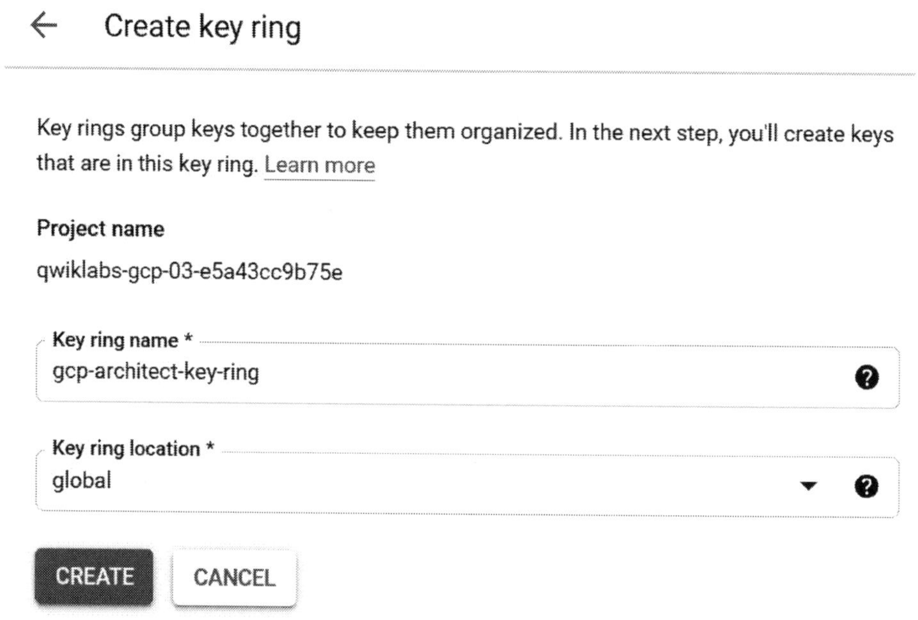

←   Create key ring

Key rings group keys together to keep them organized. In the next step, you'll create keys that are in this key ring. Learn more

Project name

qwiklabs-gcp-03-e5a43cc9b75e

Key ring name *

gcp-architect-key-ring   ❓

Key ring location *

global   ▼ ❓

CREATE   CANCEL

Figure 15.23 – Create key ring

Once we have created the key ring, we will be prompted to create a key. We can create several keys under the key ring, and those keys will be responsible for encrypting and decrypting data. When creating a new key, you can see that we have options for setting the key's purpose; for example, whether the key is only for encryption, decryption, or both.

> **Tip**
> When deciding on which location to choose, network performance should be considered.

2. The first selection we have to make is what type of key we want. We are given options as follows. As we selected a global key ring, we are not able to select externally managed keys. We can see from the descriptions that a generated key is a standard customer-managed encryption key:

What type of key do you want to create?

⦿ Generated key
   A standard customer managed encryption key. The key material will be generated for you.
   Learn more

◯ Imported key
   For importing your key material into GCP. Learn more

◯ Externally managed key
   The key material will be stored in an external key manager. Learn more

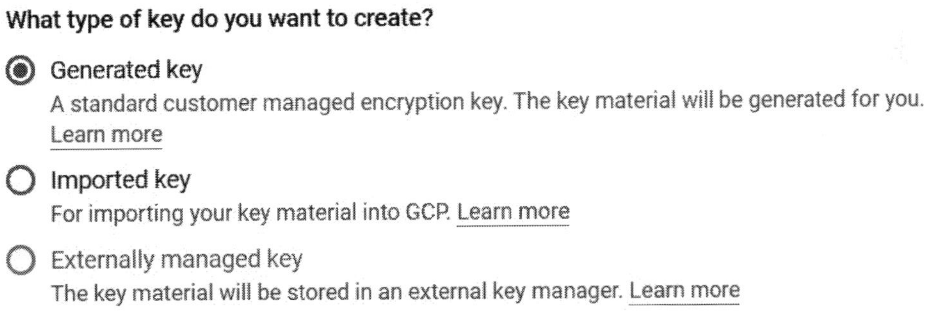

Figure 15.24 – Selecting the type of key

3.   Furthermore, we can select rotation periods and when the validity of the key begins. Once the key has been created, we can manage the rotation period, disable and reenable the key, or delete the key completely through the GCP console. The following screenshot shows us creating a new key:

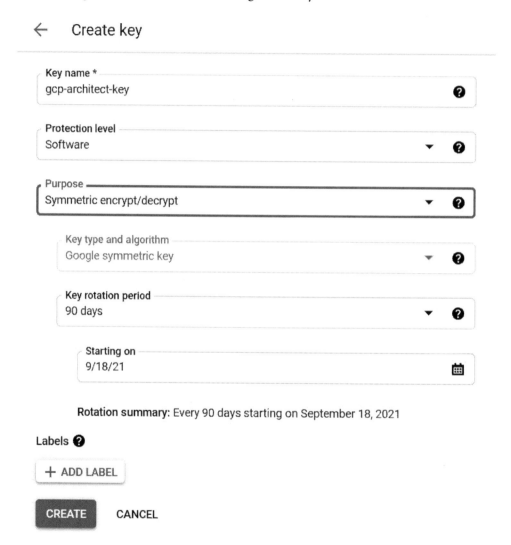

Figure 15.25 – Create key

An important aspect of the KMS key structure is the key version. Each key can have many versions, which are numbered sequentially, starting with 1. We may have files encrypted with the same key but with different key versions. Cloud KMS will automatically identify which version was used for encryption and will use this to decrypt the file if the version is still *enabled*. We will not be able to decrypt the file if the version has been moved to a state of *disabled*, *destroyed*, or *scheduled for destruction*.

4. Now that we have created our key, let's use it. If, for example, we want to create a new disk in GCP, we have several options under the encryption settings. To use our newly created key, we should select **Customer-managed key** and select our key from the drop-down menu when prompted, as shown in the following screenshot:

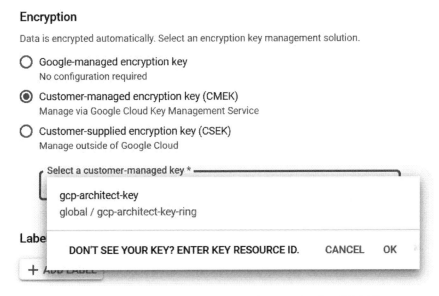

Figure 15.26 – Using Customer-managed encryption key (CMEK)

A second option is available is CSEK, where the key is not stored in KMS, and Google doesn't manage the key. CSEK allows us to provide our own AES-256 key. If we supply this key, Cloud Storage doesn't permanently store it on Google's servers or in any way manage our key. Once we have provided the key for a Cloud Storage operation, then the key is purged from Google's memory. This means that the key would have to be provided each time storage resources were created or used. The customer would have sole responsibility, which means that if the key was lost, then you would be unable to decrypt your data. Here, we would select the **Customer-supplied encryption key (CSEK)** option and input the relevant key.

Now, let's start looking at some industry regulations.

Industry regulations

It's also important to understand that security is more than just firewall rules or encryption. Google needs to adhere to global regulations and third-party certifications. Examples of the regulations that GCP adheres to can be found on their web page at `https://cloud.google.com/security/compliance/#/`. It is recommended that you review this page to familiarize yourself with the various standards that should be met. Some of these will be well-known; for example, regulations from the financial industry such as PCI DSS or the ISO 27017 address, which is responsible for interactions between cloud vendors and customers.

In this section, we will look at PCI compliance.

PCI compliance

Many organizations handle financial transactions, and Google has to go to great lengths to secure information residing on their servers. An example of PCI can tie what we learned previously into a real-life example. If there is a need to set up a specific payment processing environment, then Google can assist in helping customers achieve this. At the core of this architecture would be what we have learned in this chapter. To secure the environment, we should use Resource Manager to create separate projects to segregate our gaming and PCI projects. We can utilize Cloud IAM and apply permissions to those separate projects. Remember the rule of least privilege! We can also secure the environment with firewall rules to restrict the inbound traffic. We want the public to be able to use our payment page, so we need HTTPS traffic to be secured by an HTTP(S) load balancer, and any additional payment processing applications may need bi-directional access to third parties. Take a look at the article at`https://cloud.google.com/solutions/pci-dss-compliance-in-gcp` for more in-depth knowledge of how GCP would handle PCI DSS requirements.

In the next section, we'll review data loss prevention.

Data loss prevention (DLP)

Removing **Personal Identifiable Information** (**PII**) is also a concern within the industry. Cloud DLP provides us with a powerful data and de-identification platform. DLP uses information types, also known as infoTypes, to define what is scanned for. These infoTypes are types of data that are sensitive such as name, email address, credit card number, or identification number. An example of how Cloud DLP can assist us is that we can automatically redact such sensitive data, which may be stored in GCP storage repositories.

We should also note that compliance with the **European Union General Data Protection Regulation** (**GDPR**) is one of Google's top priorities from a security standpoint and that these build-in infoType detectors offer GDPR compliance.

Penetration testing in GCP

It's worth noting that, if you have a requirement to perform penetration testing on your GCP infrastructure, you don't need permission from Google, but you must abide by the Acceptable Use Policy to ensure that tests only target your projects. Interestingly, Google offers an incentive program, should bugs or vulnerabilities be found, and rewards range from $100 to $31,337!

CI/CD security overview

As DevOps becomes increasingly popular, it is important to consider security when we build our pipelines, images, and delivery models. There are some best practices offered by Google Cloud when building your CI/CD pipeline. However, they, like many best practices, are subjective and may not apply to your architecture. Nonetheless, it is important to think about things such as the following:

- **Branching model**: It's important to consider how changes to your code will affect your production environment, so feature branches may be required to test the changes before any merge requests are made in the production code base.

- **Container image vulnerabilities**: When creating an image to be used in your pipeline, it is also important to scan for vulnerabilities when the image is uploaded to an Artifact or Container Registry. Cloud Build can be used in this instance to scan an image once it has been built and then block upload it to an Artifact Registry. This is known as on-demand scanning.

- **Filesystem security**: Even in containers, it is still important to prevent potential attackers from installing their tools. We should avoid running as root inside our container and launch the container in read-only mode.

- The size of our containers should also be considered, not only from a performant standpoint but also from a security standpoint. A small container means a smaller attack surface area. Many larger containers show vulnerabilities relating to programs that are installed but have nothing to do with the application.

Now, let's look at Identity-Aware Proxy.

Identity-Aware Proxy (IAP)

Google offers additional access control to your Cloud Engine instances or applications running on GCP via Cloud IAP. This allows the user's identity to be verified over HTTPS and grants access only if permitted. This service is especially useful for remote workers as it negates the need for a company VPN to authenticate user requests using on-premises networks. Instead, access is via an internet-accessible URL. When remote users need to access an application, a request is forwarded to Cloud IAP, and access will be granted (if permitted). Additionally, without the overhead of a traditional VPN, manageability is simplified for the administrator.

Enabling Cloud IAP is a simple process, but some prerequisites must be met. You will need to configure firewall rules to block access to the VMs that are hosting your application and only allow access through IAP. Next, you need to navigate to **Security | Identity-Aware Proxy** in the GCP console, where you will find a list of your application or Compute Engine resources. Simply click on the blue radio button to enable IAP.

> **Important Note**
> You may be asked for OAuth consent first.

Finally, you can populate the IAP access list with the relevant membership from the information panel that will become available. The following screenshot shows IAP enabled for an HTTPS resource:

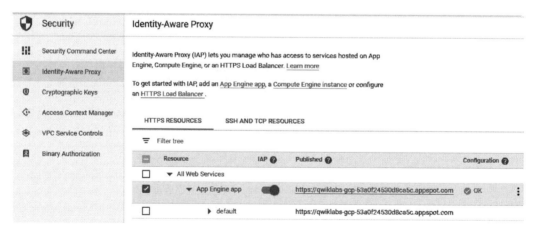

Figure 15.27 – Identity-Aware Proxy

Now that we have provided an overview of IAP, let's look at some important features.

TCP forwarding

IAP has a port forwarding feature that allows us to **Secure Shell (SSH)** or **Remote Desktop for Windows (RDP)** onto our backends from the public internet, which prevents these services from being exposed openly to the internet. We are required to pass authorization and authentication checks before they get to their intended resources, thus reducing the risk of connecting to these services from the internet.

IAP's forwarding feature allows us to connect to random TCP ports on our Compute Engine instances. IAP will then create a listening port on the localhost that forwards all traffic to our instance. IAP will then wrap all traffic from the client in HTTPS and allow access to the interface and port if we successfully pass authentication. This authentication process is based on configured IAM permissions.

There are some limitations that we should be aware of. Port forwarding is not intended for bulk transfer of data, so IAP reserves the right to apply rate limits to prevent misuse of the service. Additionally, after 1 hour of inactivity, IAP will automatically disconnect our session, so applications using this should have logic to handle re-establishing a tunnel after being disconnected.

Access Context Manger

Access Context Manager offers Google Cloud Organization Administrators the ability to define fine-grained, attribute-based access control for projects and resources in GCP. Access Context Manager grants access based on the context of the request, such as the user's identity, the device type, or the IP address. It adds another layer of protection on top of the traditional perimeter security model, whereby anything inside a network is considered trusted. Access Context Manager takes into consideration the mobile workforce and **Bring Your Own Device (BYOD)**, which adds additional attack vectors that are not considered by a perimeter security model.

Chronicle

One of the most recent introductions to Google's security suite is **Chronicle**. Although it is doubtful that we will be quizzed on this in the exam, we felt it was worthwhile to say a few words on this.

Chronicle is a threat detection solution that helps enterprises identify threats at speed and scale. It can search the massive amounts of security and network telemetry data that enterprises generate and provide instant analysis and context on an activity.

Summary

There are much bigger, deeper dives into security, but for the exam, you must understand that security is key to all of Google's services and was not an afterthought. So far, we have covered several services that are offered to make sure that your GCP infrastructure is secure. We introduced Cloud Identity, covered the IAM model, and looked at encryption.

In the next section, we will look at additional security services.

Additional security services

GCP offers several advanced services to help you secure your infrastructure and resources. In this section, we will take a short look at other key services.

Security Command Center (SCC)

SCC gives enterprises an overarching view of their cloud data across several GCP services. The real benefit of SCC comes from it assisting in gathering data and identifying threats, and it can act on these before any business impact occurs. It also provides a dashboard that reflects the overall health of our resources. It can also integrate with other GCP tools such as Cloud Security Scanner and third parties, such as Palo Alto Networks. GCP refers to possible security threats in SCC as *findings*. To access these *findings*, you must have the relevant IAM role, which includes the permissions for the Security Center Findings Viewer, and then browse to the **Findings** tab of the SCC. Of course, like all GCP services, there is API integration, which allows us to list any findings. SCC also lets us use *security* marks, which allow us to annotate assets or findings and search or filter using these marks.

To use SCC, you must view it from your GCP organization. Additionally, you must be an organization administrator and have the Security Center Admin role for the current organization. This allows you to select all of the current and future projects to be included (if you wish). Alternatively, we can include or exclude individual projects, should any security risk be found.

Security Command Center events can be exported to Chronicle, which is purpose-built for security threat detection and investigation. It is built on Google infrastructure, which lets us take advantage of Google's scale to reduce investigation time.

Forseti

Forseti is an open source security tool that assists in securing your GCP environment. It is useful if you wish to monitor resources to ensure that access control is the same as you intended it to be. It can also be used to create an alert when anything changes, via email or a post on a Slack channel. Additionally, it lets you take snapshots of resources so that you always know what your cloud looks like. It can also enforce rules on sensitive GCP resources by comparing a policy with the current state and correcting any violations using GCP APIs.

Cloud Armor

Cloud Armor uses Google's global infrastructure to provide defense at scale against DDoS attacks. It is used to blacklist or whitelist access to your HTTPS load balancer. This can be used to prevent malicious users or traffic from contacting your resources, or – worse – taking control of your VPC based on rule sets. The following screenshot shows a policy that has been set to deny a specific IP and give a 404 error:

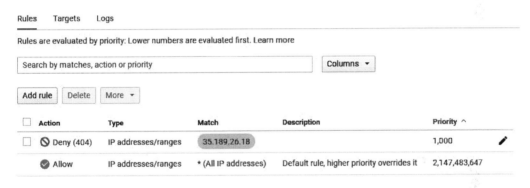

Figure 15.28 – Cloud Armor

By clicking on the **Targets** tab, we can see that the policy is targeting a backend load balancer, as shown in the following screenshot:

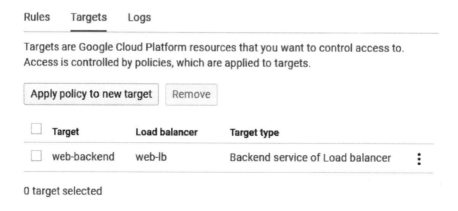

Figure 15.29 – Cloud Armor – Targets

Cloud Armor logs allow us to see any access attempts and tell us which source requested access. We should be aware that these logs are provided through Stackdriver, which was described in the *Monitoring and logging* section of this chapter. This will be covered in more detail in *Chapter 17, Monitoring Your Infrastructure*.

The following screenshot shows some example output from the Cloud Armor logs:

Figure 15.30 – Cloud Armor logs

Secret Manager

Secret Manager is a convenient and secure system that's used to store certificates, passwords, or API keys. Storing this sensitive data in a central location allows for a single source of truth to manage, access, and audit secrets across Google Cloud. Secret Manager also allows access policies to be set for each secret. Additionally, audit logs can be configured for each secret access. This service is an alternative for third-party secret management systems such as Hashicorp Vault.

In this section, we looked at some of the other security services offered by GCP. Not all of them will be questioned in the exam, but it is good to have a high-level understanding of what each service offers.

Summary

There are much bigger, deeper dives into security, but for the exam, we must understand that security is key to all Google's services and was not an afterthought. In this chapter, we looked at many services that GCP offers to make sure our solution is secure. Among other things, we introduced Cloud Identity, covered the IAM model, and looked at encryption. In the next chapter, we will look at Google Cloud Management Options.

> **Exam Tip**
> Remember that we should never grant a user or service more permissions than what is required. Always use the principle of least privilege.

Further reading

Read the following articles for more information on what was covered in this chapter:

- **Cloud Identity**: https://cloud.google.com/identity/docs/
- **IAM**: https://cloud.google.com/iam/docs/
- **Encryption**: https://cloud.google.com/storage/docs/encryption/
- **Cloud IAP**: https://cloud.google.com/iap/docs/
- **Security Command Center**: https://cloud.google.com/security-command-center/docs/

- **Cloud Armor**: `https://cloud.google.com/armor/docs/`

- **Google Cloud Security Foundations Guide**: `https://services.google.com/fh/files/misc/google-cloud-security-foundations-guide.pdf`

- **Best Practices Guides**: `https://cloud.google.com/security/best-practices#section-1`

16
Google Cloud Management Options

This chapter describes how to utilize the various management options available so that you can administer your **Google Cloud Platform (GCP)** services with ease. In the previous chapters, we touched on the command-line tools that are available so that we can manage Google services. In this chapter, we will look at these tools in more detail, which include `gcloud`, `cbt`, `bq`, and `gsutil`.

Exam Tip

You must know about the most efficient command-line tool for managing a particular service. Review and understand each command-line tool in this chapter and ensure that you can quickly map them to a GCP service. For example, if we are asked to create a new storage bucket using a command-line tool, we should know instantly that we need to use `gsutil`.

We also recommend that you take a deeper look at the `gsutil` command lines and understand them so that you can set life cycle policies.

As we cover each management option in this chapter, you can expect to understand how to access it and gain hands-on knowledge from examples. You can also expect to see code-based commands that can be used in the real world but are important to understand for exam success. We will begin by looking at using **application programming interfaces** (**APIs**) and will then look at the remaining tools.

In this chapter, we will introduce the various management options that you can use. Specifically, we will cover the following topics:

- Using APIs to manage resources

- Using Google Cloud Shell

- The GCP **Software Development Kit (SDK)**

- Exploring Cloud Deployment Manager

- Pricing Calculator

- Additional things to consider

Using APIs to manage resources

API usage is extremely common now. APIs are access points to an application that offer developers flexibility in the way they communicate with them, dramatically increasing their efficiency.

> **Important Note**
> GCP offers full documentation on the APIs for their services. We recommend that you check out `https://cloud.google.com/apis/` and click on the specific service you wish to read more about.

APIs use different authentication services, depending on where the API calls come from and the resource(s) they are requesting:

- **API keys**: These are encrypted strings that can be used when API calls don't need to access user data. These are great for getting developers up and running quickly. Keys are created from the GCP console under **APIs & Services | Credentials**. These keys are then used in the API request.

- **OAuth client IDs**: These are based on the scope, meaning that different privileges will be granted to different IDs. This method is used if a developer needs to request user data.

- **Service Accounts**: These belong to an application of a **Virtual Machine (VM)** instance. Please refer to *Chapter 15*, *Security and Compliance*, for more in-depth information on service accounts.

Let's look at an example of using an API. As we mentioned previously, we can browse to **API & Services** from the GCP console and then select **ENABLE APIS AND SERVICES**. If we search for Compute Engine, as shown in the following screenshot, we can select **TRY THIS API**:

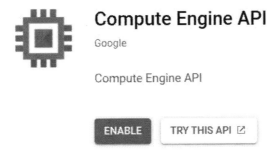

Figure 16.1 – Enabling the API

This will take us to the **Compute Engine API** documentation page. This is a nice feature that GCP offers to assist us in using our API calls for all of its services. If can scroll through the documentation, we will see a list of all the API calls that are related to GCE. Let's look for a method that we can use to create a new instance; that is, under the v1.instances.insert listing:

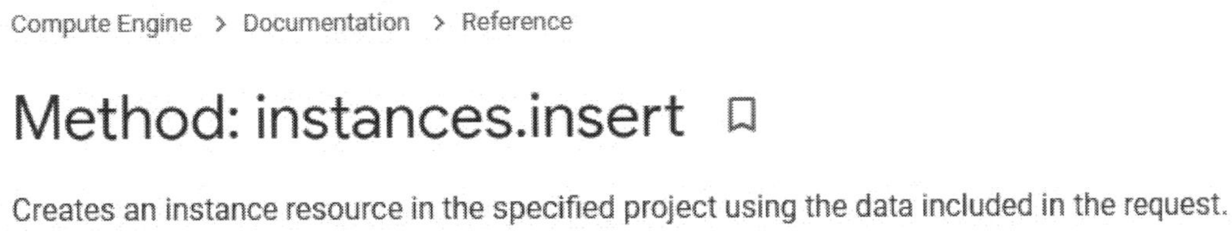

Compute Engine > Documentation > Reference

Method: instances.insert 🔖

Creates an instance resource in the specified project using the data included in the request.

Figure 16.2 – API example

If we click on this method, it will bring us to a page that allows us to request a VM instance via the API. The first thing that we should notice is the menu on the right-hand side, where we can select OAuth 2.0 as our authentication method. This allows us to authorize the API call using the same user we used to log into the GCP console. There is some mandatory information to populate, and this is specified in red:

- **project**: This is the ID of your GCP project.

- **zone**: This is the zone where you would like the VM to reside.

The following screenshot shows an example of these fields populated:

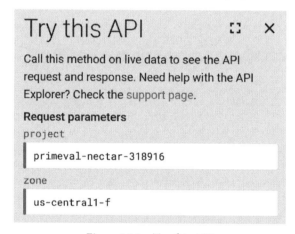

Figure 16.3 – Try this API

We also need to populate the request body with information about our request. Let's look at what is required in the following example. We are required to provide information regarding the machine's type, the machine's name, and the disk and image type:

```
{
    "machineType": "zones/us-central1-f/machineTypes/n1-
standard-1",
    "name": "test001",
    "disks": [
      {
        "initializeParams": {
          "sourceImage": "projects/debian-cloud/global/images/
family/debian-9"
        },
        "boot": true,
```

```
      "interface": "SCSI"
    }
  ],
  "networkInterfaces": [
    {
      "network": "global/networks/default"
    }
  ]
}
```

After its initial validation, we can execute our request by clicking **Authorize and execute**. Response code **200 OK** means that our request was successfully executed:

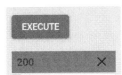

Figure 16.4 – API return code

By taking a closer look, we can see information about the user, URI, and zone:

```
{
  "id": "5737119379050389182",
  "name": "operation-1625514064727-5c6657c67cea7-42560a30-
2bf3bace",
  "zone": "https://www.googleapis.com/compute/v1/projects/
primeval-nectar-318916/zones/us-central1-f",
  "operationType": "insert",
  "targetLink": "https://www.googleapis.com/compute/v1/
projects/primeval-nectar-318916/zones/us-central1-f/instances/
test001",
  "targetId": "6541634553944923838",
  "status": "PENDING",
  "user": "gcparchitectbook@gmail.com",
  "progress": 0,
  "insertTime": "2021-07-05T12:41:06.131-07:00",
```

```
    "selfLink": "https://www.googleapis.com/compute/v1/projects/
primeval-nectar-318916/zones/us-central1-f/operations/
operation-1625514064727-5c6657c67cea7-42560a30-2bf3bace",
    "kind": "compute#operation"
}
```

Now, let's look at another example by creating a new disk. We can simply search for the `v1.instances.insert` method. Again, we have the project and zone to populate. The request body is also required:

```
{
    "name": "newdisk001",
    "sizeGb": 10
}
```

After clicking **Authorize and execute**, we can, once again, see the response:

```
{
    "id": "4514886327875854282",
    "name": "operation-1625514277056-5c665890fb0fa-1bd73387-
5f597370",
    "zone": "https://www.googleapis.com/compute/v1/projects/
primeval-nectar-318916/zones/us-central1-f",
    "operationType": "insert",
    "targetLink": "https://www.googleapis.com/compute/v1/
projects/primeval-nectar-318916/zones/us-central1-f/disks/
newdisk001",
    "targetId": "3511243588531838922",
    "status": "RUNNING",
    "user": "gcparchitectbook@gmail.com",
    "progress": 0,
    "insertTime": "2021-07-05T12:44:37.706-07:00",
    "startTime": "2021-07-05T12:44:37.713-07:00",
    "selfLink": "https://www.googleapis.com/compute/v1/projects/
primeval-nectar-318916/zones/us-central1-f/operations/
operation-1625514277056-5c665890fb0fa-1bd73387-5f597370",
    "kind": "compute#operation"
}
```

We recommend that you explore the GCP API's **Explorer** page to review what APIs are available in the core GCP services. In the upcoming sections, we will be looking at more command-line tools that are available to us.

Using Google Cloud Shell

The main management tool in the GCP suite is Google Cloud Shell. This is a free `g1-small` **Google Compute Engine (GCE)** instance that provides command-line access so that you can manage your GCP infrastructure through a Linux shell. The interesting thing here is that it can be accessed directly from your GCP console simply by clicking on the shell access button at the top-right-hand side:

Figure 16.5 – Initiating Google Cloud Shell

Once activated, the console screen will split in two and Google Cloud Shell will become visible inside the browser:

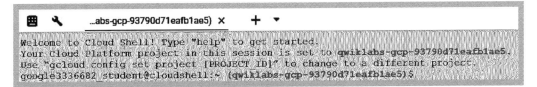

Figure 16.6 – Google Cloud Shell

No additional steps are required for authorization, so we can manage projects and resources securely without the need to install any other management toolset. Moreover, the SDK command lines that we will look at in this chapter are packaged as standard. Additionally, Google Cloud Shell has preinstalled admin tools such as the MySQL client, Docker, and `kubectl`. Finally, your developers can also access different languages, including Go, Python, Node.js, and Ruby. For a full and up-to-date list of features that have been installed, we recommend that you visit `https://cloud.google.com/shell/docs/features#tools`.

Google Cloud Shell comes with 5 GB of persistent disk storage, which is mounted to your `$HOME` directory. This means that you can store scripts or user configurations safely between sessions and install any required packages. Note that anything that's saved outside the `$HOME` directory will be lost when the session terminates; that is, after it has been idle for an hour.

We can upload and download from our local machine using the console shell's settings, as shown in the following screenshot:

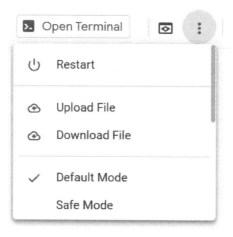

Figure 16.7 – The Upload File and Download File options

Google Cloud Shell's code editor can also be used to browse the folder path from persistent storage. We can easily access this by clicking the pencil icon in the Cloud Shell menu bar:

Figure 16.8 – Cloud Shell menu

From here, we can update our scripts or files directly in Cloud Shell. The Cloud Shell virtual instance also comes with standard Linux-based editors such as nano and vim. Note that, at the time of writing, the code editor is in the beta stage:

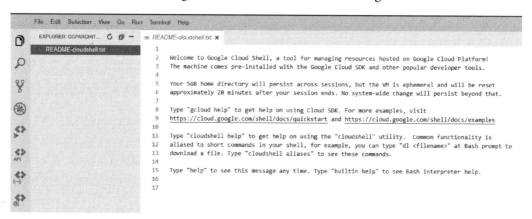

Figure 16.9 – Cloud Shell editor

Now that we have covered Google Cloud Shell, let's move on and look at the GCP SDK.

The GCP SDK

This section will describe how to use the Google Cloud SDK. The SDK is a set of tools that allows you to manage your GCP resources and applications and includes the `gcloud`, `gsutil`, and `bq` command-line tools. There are, as expected, some prerequisites to installing this kit. The SDK can run on Linux, macOS, and Windows OSes and requires you to have Python 2.7.x installed. Some tools that come bundled may have additional requirements. Please refer to `https://cloud.google.com/sdk/install` for specific system and operating system requirements.

gcloud

`gcloud` is the primary command-line tool for GCP and allows you to perform common tasks in your GCP environment. There are many use cases for `gcloud`; for example, creating and managing GCE instances, Cloud SQL instances, Kubernetes Engine clusters, Dataproc clusters, DNS zones, and Cloud Deployment Manager deployments.

When you are using `gcloud` for the first time, it is advisable to check out the usage guidelines. Adding `-h` to a command will offer the following guidelines:

```
google3167498_student@cloudshell:/home (qwiklabs-gcp-cf3e4b1a188f0368)$ gcloud -h
Usage: gcloud [optional flags] <group | command>
  group may be           access-context-manager | alpha | app | asset | auth |
                         beta | bigtable | builds | components | composer |
                         compute | config | container | dataflow | dataproc |
                         datastore | debug | deployment-manager | dns |
                         domains | endpoints | filestore | firebase |
                         functions | iam | iot | kms | logging | ml |
                         ml-engine | organizations | projects | pubsub | redis |
                         resource-manager | services | source | spanner | sql |
                         topic
  command may be         docker | feedback | help | info | init | version

For detailed information on this command and its flags, run:
  gcloud --help
```

Figure 16.10 – gcloud help

For detailed information about this command and its flags, we can run the following command:

```
gcloud --help
```

This will list far more details – try it out and take a look at the output you receive! Press the *spacebar* to continue looking through the detailed output or press Q to exit.

> **Important Note**
>
> gcloud has a command reference for features and resources hosted on GCP, which we recommend that you review. This can be found at https:// cloud.google.com/sdk/gcloud/reference/.

Let's have a look at how we can use gcloud to create a new VM instance.

We will also show you how we can use gcloud to connect to our VM via SSH, create a new disk, and attach it to our VM instance. Follow these steps:

1. To create a VM, we should use the following syntax:

    ```
    gcloud compute instances create <instance name> --zone
    <zone name>
    ```

    Here, <instance name> is the name of your VM instance, and <zone> is the zone where your instance will be deployed.

2. The following example will create a new VM instance named myinstance in zone us-central1-f:

    ```
    gcloud compute instances create myinstance --zone
    us-central1-f
    ```

3. Once we have created our instance, gcloud also allows us to connect to the instance and manage it. This is a thin wrapper around the SSH command that will deal with the authentication and instance name to IP address resolution. The connection will, by default, initiate the SSH session using the user credentials that are running the command:

    ```
    gcloud compute ssh <instance name> --zone <zone name>
    ```

    Here, <instance name> is the name of your GCE VM instance, and <zone> is the zone where your instance will be deployed.

4. The following example will connect to a new VM instance named myinstance in zone us-central1-f using the following SSH command:

    ```
    gcloud compute ssh myinstance --zone us-central1-f
    ```

5. `gcloud` also allows us to perform day 2 operations. As an example, let's add a disk to the VM instance we've already created. First, we need to create the disk using the following syntax:

    ```
    gcloud compute disks create <disk name> --zone <zone
    name>
    ```

    Here, `<disk name>` is the name of the disk we are creating, and `<zone name>` is the zone where the disk will be created.

6. The following example will create a new disk named `newdisk001` in zone `us-central1-f`:

    ```
    gcloud compute disks create newdisk001 --zone
    us-central1-f
    ```

    We should note that, in the preceding example, I didn't use the optional size flag. We should note that the default disk size for a standard HDD is 500 GB. Also, you can see that we have created the disk in the same zone as the instance.

7. Finally, we need to attach the disk to our instance. This can be accomplished using the following syntax:

    ```
    gcloud compute instances attach-disk <instance name>
    attach-disk <disk name> --zone <zone>
    ```

    Here, `<instance name>` is the name of your GCE VM instance, `<disk name>` is the name of the disk you want to attach to your VM instance, and `<zone name>` is the zone your instance resides in.

8. The following example will attach a disk called `newdisk001` to a VM instance called `myinstance` in the `us-central1-f` zone:

    ```
    gcloud compute instances attach-disk myinstance --disk
    newdisk001 --zone us-central1-f
    ```

Finally, it is wise to mention the alpha and beta commands, which you may find in `gcloud`. Alpha commands are typically not production-ready and may still be in the development phase. They may change without any notice, and some are only fully accessible via invitation. Beta commands are typically almost fully developed and being tested in production. However, these may also be changed without notice.

gsutil

In this section, we will describe the usage of `gsutil`. The main purpose of this is to ensure that you understand the primary use case for `gsutil` and show examples of real-life scenarios. `gsutil` is a Python application that can be used to manage Cloud Storage resources and can be triggered from Cloud Shell. By using `gsutil`, we can do the following:

- Create and delete buckets.

- Manage access to these buckets and their objects.

- Copy and move storage data.

- List the contents of a bucket.

- Transfer data in and out of our Cloud Shell instance (note that this is not limited to Cloud Shell).

> **Important Note**
>
> You need to understand that the `gsutil` syntax works in `gsutil <action> gs://<bucket name>/<resource name>` format.
>
> An example of `<action>` could be mb, which is used to create a bucket. Here, `gs://` is the prefix to indicate a resource in Cloud Storage. `<bucket name>/<object name>` could be `cloudarchitect/notes.txt`, for example. For a full range of `gsutil` commands, please refer to `https://cloud.google.com/storage/docs/gsutil`.

Creating a bucket is a good place to start with `gsutil`. Buckets are basic containers where you can store your data. We covered storage in detail in *Chapter 11, Exploring Storage and Database Options in GCP – Part 1.*

Let's look at some examples of common tasks that we can use `gsutil` for. Let's create a bucket, upload some content to it, list some files, and then remove the bucket:

1. The following syntax can be used to create a bucket:

   ```
   gsutil mb -l <zone name> gs://<bucket name>
   ```

   Here, `<zone name>` is the zone where you will be creating your storage bucket, and `<bucket name>` is a globally unique bucket name. In the following example, we will create a bucket called `cloudarchitect001` in the `us-east1` zone:

   ```
   gsutil mb -l us-east1 gs://cloudarchitect001
   ```

2. Now that we have created a new bucket, let's add a file to it. In this example, I will create a new file on my local persistent Google Cloud Shell storage. Let's assume that we have a file called examnotes.txt in our Cloud Shell environment. This can be uploaded as described in the *Using Google Cloud Shell* section. To copy this to our bucket, we can use the following syntax:

```
gsutil cp <file to copy> gs://<bucket name>
```

Here, <file to copy> is the file you wish to copy to your bucket, and <bucket name> is a globally unique bucket name where you want the file to reside. In the following example, we will copy a file called examnotes.txt to a bucket called cloudarchitect001:

```
gsutil cp examnotes.txt gs://cloudarchitect001
```

3. The output from the previous command will confirm the success of this copy. We should also note that options can be specified when using cp to extend the command. For example, the -n option will prevent overwriting the content of existing files. The -r option will copy an entire directory tree and, importantly, -m will allow us to perform a parallel multi-threaded/multi-processing copy. We can list the contents of our bucket to ensure that the file is there using the following syntax:

```
gsutil ls gs://<bucket name>
```

Here, <bucket name> is the name of the bucket you wish to list resources in. Let's list the resources of our cloudarchitect001 bucket:

```
gsutil ls gs://cloudarchitect001
```

4. If we wish to remove files from our bucket, we can use the following syntax:

```
gsutil rm gs://<bucket name>/<object name>
```

Here, <bucket name> is the name of the bucket where our resource resides, and <object name> is the object we wish to remove. Let's remove examnotes.txt from our cloudarchitect001 bucket:

```
gsutil rm gs://cloudarchitect001/examnotes.txt
```

5. Finally, if we wish to remove the bucket completely (remember, resources come at a cost!), we can use the following syntax:

```
gsutil rb gs://<bucket name>
```

Here, `<bucket name>` is the name of the bucket we wish to delete. Let's delete our `cloudarchitect001` bucket:

```
gsutil rb gs://cloudarchitect001
```

Note that we could also run this command with the `-r` flag, which would remove the bucket and all its contents.

bq

Now, let's look at the command-line tools for BigQuery. BigQuery was described in more detail in *Chapter 13, Analyzing Big Data Options*, so in this section, we won't do a deep dive into the service. However, in general, the main way to interact with BigQuery is to load, export, query, view, and manage data. One of the ways we can do this is from Cloud Shell using the bq command-line tool.

> **Important Note**
>
> BigQuery can be complex to use from the bq command line, and it is recommended to review the bq command-line tool reference page for full details: `https://cloud.google.com/bigquery/docs/bq-command-line-tool`.

Let's look at some common use cases. In the following examples, we will create a new dataset, create a table, and then query it:

1. The following syntax is used to create a new dataset in its simplest form:

    ```
    bq --location=<location> mk --dataset <dataset name>
    ```

    Here, `<location>` is the dataset location, and `<dataset name>` is the name of your new dataset. The location can be multi-regional, such as the US or EU, or it can be a regional location, such as `us-west2` or `europe-north1`.

2. Let's create a new dataset called `newdataset` as a multi-regional location of the US:

    ```
    bq --location=US mk --dataset newdataset
    ```

    > **Important Note**
    >
    > Some optional flags can be set. It is good practice to configure the default table's expiration for the default tables of your datasets, the expiration time for your tables, and the partition expiration for your partitioned tables.

3. Now, let's create a new empty table in its simplest form. To do so, we can use the following syntax:

```
bq mk -t <dataset name>.<table name> <schema>
```

Here, `<dataset name>` is the name of the dataset you wish to create a new table in, `<table name>` is the name of the table to be created, and `<schema>` is the inline schema definition in `[FIELD:DATA_TYPE]` format. A path to a JSON file on your local machine can also be used. The `<schema>` parameter may be a bit confusing but, to clarify, this is like a column in an Excel file.

4. Let's create a new table called `newtable` inside our dataset called `newdataset`. We will create two new columns named `examname` and `result` that we will want to populate with character (Unicode) data; that is, `STRING` data:

```
bq mk -t  newdataset.newdataset \
examname:STRING,result:STRING
```

5. Finally, let's look at how we can use bq to run queries. To do so, we need to use the following syntax:

```
bq query '<SQL query>'
```

Here, `<SQL query>` is the SQL query that you wish BigQuery to execute on the data. `<SQL query>` will contain information on the data to query from a specific dataset and table. If we want to connect to a project that isn't set as our default, we can also specify this in our SQL request. If we were to query the full path of the table, it would look as follows:

```
<projects>.<dataset>.<table>
```

To clarify this, let's look at an example. GCP provides some sample datasets and tables that we can make use of. Let's execute a bq query on a table called `Shakespeare` from a dataset called `samples`. The dataset and the table reside under a `public` project that Google allows us to connect to called `bigquery-public-data`.

In this example, we want to see how many times the word `beloved` appears in Shakespeare's works. We will search by the columns in the table, which are `word` and `corpus`. Also, note that we are specifying `#standardSql` as the query type:

```
bq query "#standardSql SELECT word, corpus, COUNT(word) FROM
\'bigquery-public-data.samples.shakespeare\'

WHERE word LIKE '%beloved%' GROUP BY word, corpus"
```

> **Important Note**
>
> Please note that `'` in `\'bigquery-public-data.samples.shakespeare\'` is a backquote, not an apostrophe.

This will return the following results:

```
| word    |        corpus        | f0_ |
+---------+----------------------+-----+
| beloved | cymbeline            |  1  |
| beloved | romeoandjuliet       |  1  |
| beloved | winterstale          |  1  |
| beloved | tamingoftheshrew     |  1  |
| beloved | hamlet               |  1  |
| beloved | twogentlemenofverona |  1  |
| beloved | tempest              |  1  |
| beloved | timonofathens        |  1  |
| beloved | kinglear             |  1  |
| beloved | sonnets              |  1  |
| beloved | coriolanus           |  1  |
| beloved | 1kinghenryiv         |  1  |
| beloved | juliuscaesar         |  1  |
| beloved | 3kinghenryvi         |  1  |
| beloved | antonyandcleopatra   |  1  |
| beloved | comedyoferrors       |  1  |
| beloved | periclesprinceoftyre |  1  |
| beloved | titusandronicus      |  1  |
| beloved | rapeoflucrece        |  1  |
| beloved | measureformeasure    |  1  |
| beloved | midsummersnightsdream |  1  |
| beloved | merchantofvenice     |  1  |
| beloved | asyoulikeit          |  1  |
| beloved | othello              |  1  |
| beloved | troilusandcressida   |  1  |
| beloved | 2kinghenryvi         |  1  |
| beloved | twelfthnight         |  1  |
| beloved | kinghenryviii        |  1  |
+---------+----------------------+-----+
```

Figure 16.11 – bq output

For exam success, we should understand the power of the `bq` command line, but mostly ensure that we understand which command-line tool to use to query BigQuery tables.

cbt

In this section, we will discover the command-line tool for Cloud Bigtable – `cbt`. Written in Go, the CLI allows us to perform basic interactions with Bigtable. Unlike the previous command-line tools we've looked at, we must install this component using Cloud Shell and the `gcloud` command.

Again, we took a deeper look at this service in *Chapter 12, Exploring Storage and Database Options in GCP – Part 2*, but before we look at the command-line tool, we should remind ourselves that Bigtable is a high-performance NoSQL database service that uses instances, clusters, and nodes. Bigtable is a container for your clusters and nodes. Tables belong to these Bigtable instances:

```
gcloud components install cbt
```

Note that if you receive feedback that the Cloud SDK component manager is disabled, then you can also run the following command:

```
sudo apt-get install google-cloud-sdk-cbt
```

You may have noticed that the different tools we have looked at have slightly different syntax and that cbt is no different. The usage of cbt is as follows:

```
cbt <command>
```

Let's look at an example of creating a new instance in Bigtable called myfirstinstance. There are additional flags we must add. Let's look at the syntax:

```
cbt createinstance <instance id> <display name> <cluster id>
<zone> <number of nodes> <storage type>
```

Here, <instance id> is an identifier you wish to give your Bigtable instance, <display name> is the display name of your Bigtable instance, <cluster id> is an identifier for the cluster of nodes, <zone> is the zone that your instances will be deployed in, <number of nodes> is the number of VM instances in the cluster, and <storage type> is the storage type we wish to use for our VM instances. This can be set to either SSD or HDD.

Let's look at the syntax that we'd have if we wanted to create a new instance with an ID of instance001, a display name of myfirstinstance, a cluster ID of cluster001, and three nodes deployed in the europe-west2-a zone using SSD storage:

```
cbt createinstance instance001 myfirstinstance cluster001
europe-west2-a 3 SSD
```

If we look inside our console, we can verify that this has been created correctly:

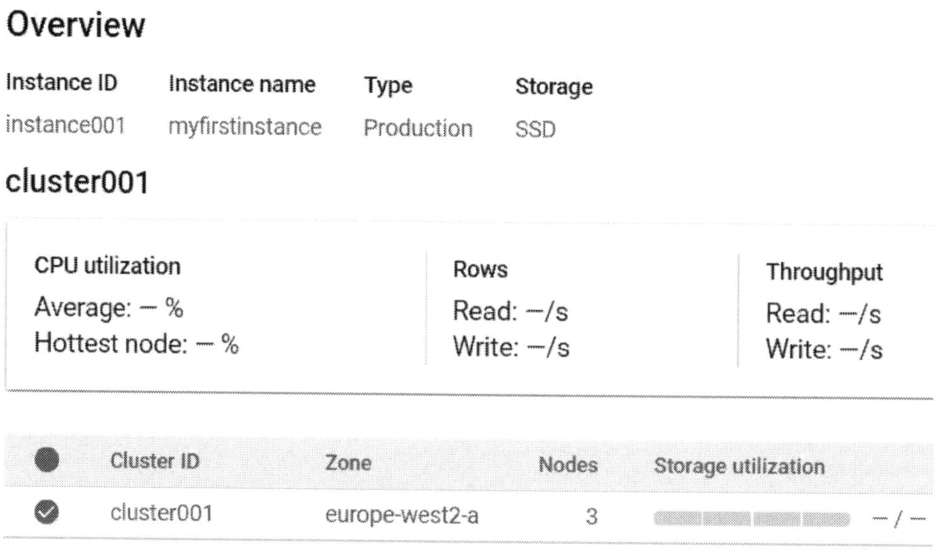

Overview

Instance ID	Instance name	Type	Storage
instance001	myfirstinstance	Production	SSD

cluster001

CPU utilization	Rows	Throughput
Average: — % Hottest node: — %	Read: —/s Write: —/s	Read: —/s Write: —/s

●	Cluster ID	Zone	Nodes	Storage utilization
✓	cluster001	europe-west2-a	3	— / —

Figure 16.12 – Overview

> **Important Note**
>
> You can also use `gcloud` commands to create Bigtable instances. `gcloud` lets us create production or development environments, where developments have limited performance and no SLA. If you need to create a development Bigtable instance, then use `gcloud`.

Exploring Cloud Deployment Manager

In this section, we will look at one of the most useful management tools – Google Cloud Deployment Manager. It's important to understand the concepts of Cloud Deployment Manager for exam success.

Deployment Manager allows us to automate the process of creating and configuring a variety of GCP resources. We can write all the resources our application needs in a declarative format using YAML files, which ensure repeatable deployments with consistent results. YAML is a data sequencing language that humans can easily read. Overall, Deployment Manager can be referred to as **Infrastructure as Code (IaC)**. You may have some experience with tools such as Ansible or Terraform and will recognize that you can nest elements through indentation, rather than any braces or brackets, which are used in some other languages.

> **Exam Tip**
>
> Deployment Manager is a very large topic, and deep-dive courses are available so that you can gain further knowledge. For the exam, we will explain the fundamental knowledge that's needed to be successful.

Some components are fundamental to Deployment Manager. Configuration files contain all the resources we want to deploy, as well as their properties.

A configuration file starts with the resource string and is followed by a list of entries, each of which has the following fields:

- **Name:** The name of the resource we are deploying; for example, `vm001`.

- **Type:** This specifies the base type of this resource. There are many available resource types, and they relate to the type of resource we wish to deploy. For example, the resource type for a new VM instance would be `compute.v1.instance`. Note that `v1` stands for production-ready.

- **Properties:** This specifies the properties that are required to create the resource. For example, if we wish to deploy a new VM instance from the GUI, we need to populate mandatory fields such as OS type, disk type, and image and network interfaces. These would be populated in the `properties` section of a configuration file.

> **Important Note**
>
> A full list of resource types can be found here: `https://cloud.google.com/deployment-manager/docs/configuration/supported-resource-types`.

Let's look at how we can construct our first example configuration file. In the *Using Google Cloud Shell* section of this chapter, we referred to the Cloud Shell editor. Let's open this up and create a new file. To do this, simply right-click on your user ID and select **New File**:

Figure 16.13 – Cloud Shell – New File

Give the file a name – for example, `vm001.yaml` – and click **OK** to create it. We are now ready to edit. In this example, the code will do the following:

- Create a VM in the `europe-west4-a` zone.
- Size it as the `g1-small` machine type.
- Use `centos-6` as our image.
- Create a persistent boot disk.
- Add the VM to the default network.
- Add access configurations as external NATs.

The completed configuration file will look as follows:

```
resources:
- name: vm001
  type: compute.v1.instance
  properties:
```

```
      zone: europe-west4-a
      machineType: https://www.googleapis.com/compute/v1/
projects/primeval-nectar-318916/zones/europe-west4-a/
machineTypes/g1-small
      disks:
      - deviceName: boot
        type: PERSISTENT
        boot: true
        autoDelete: true
        initializeParams:
          sourceImage: https://www.googleapis.com/compute/v1/
projects/centos-cloud/global/images/centos-stream-8-v20210721
      networkInterfaces:
      - network: https://www.googleapis.com/compute/v1/projects/
primeval-nectar-318916/global/networks/default
      accessConfigs:
      - name: External NAT
        type: ONE_TO_ONE_NAT
```

Now, let's save it and use this configuration file to deploy a VM. Again, we will use the Cloud Shell tool to execute this using the Deployment Manager command-line syntax:

```
gcloud deployment-manager deployments create <deployment name>
--config <config file>
```

Here, <deployment name> is the name of your overall deployment name. Remember that the VM instance name is specified in our configuration file and that <config file> is the name of the configuration file we created previously. Let's look at an example of creating a new deployment called deployment01 using our vm001.yaml configuration file:

```
gcloud deployment-manager deployments create deployment01
--config vm001.yaml
```

If we browse to **Deployment Manager** in our GCP console, we can confirm that this was deployed:

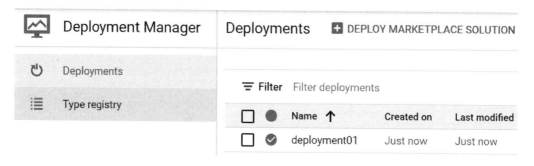

Figure 16.14 – Deployment Manager

We can also browse to Compute Engine in our GCP console and confirm that the VM instance exists:

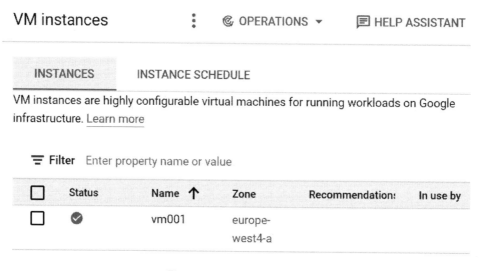

Figure 16.15 – VM instance

So, although we have taken time to create a configuration file, we have only deployed a single VM instance. Deployment Manager allows us to deploy full environments. To do this, we should use templates. A template allows us to abstract part of a configuration file into individual building blocks that can be reused across deployments.

A template is a separate file from your configuration file. It is also written in a different language – either Jinja or Python – and is imported and used as a type in a configuration file.

Templates allow us to pass variables from our configuration files, which means they can stay pretty static, and we can just pass in the edited variables from our configuration file. We need to modify our configuration file to reflect the fact that we want to call a template file. This can be done by adding a path from the template to the top of our configuration file. We can also edit the configuration file to reflect the variables we want to pass.

Let's look at an example. We want to keep a static template for creating `debian-9` VMs, but we want to pass variables such as the hostname, zone, and machine type. Let's create a new configuration YAML file as follows. Let's call it `createdbytemplate.yaml`. Note that we have added the `vm-template.jinja` file as a type and that our variables are set as properties:

```yaml
imports:

- path: vm-template.jinja


resources:

- name: newinstance

  type: vm-template.jinja

  properties:

    name: createdbytemplate

    zone: europe-west4-a
    type: g1-small
```

Now, we need to configure our template file, which will contain the values of our variables to be passed through. Note that our hostname, machine type, and zone are set inside our brackets in the following format:

```
{{ properties["variable name"] }}
```

Here, `variable name` is the string that's passed from the configuration file. The following code is our Jinja template file:

```
resources:
- name: {{ properties["name"] }}
  type: compute.v1.instance
  properties:
    zone: {{ properties["zone"] }}
    machineType: zones/{{ properties["zone"] }}/machineTypes/{{ properties["type"] }}
    disks:
    - deviceName: boot
      type: PERSISTENT
      boot: true
      autoDelete: true
      initializeParams:
        sourceImage: projects/debian-cloud/global/images/family/debian-9
    networkInterfaces:
    - network: global/networks/default
```

We can save this and call it `vm-template.jinja`. Now, we can use our `gcloud` commands to call our `createdbytemplate.yaml` file:

```
gcloud deployment-manager deployments create templatedeployment
--config createdbytemplate.yaml
```

Now, we can check our console to verify that we have a new VM called `createdbytemplate`:

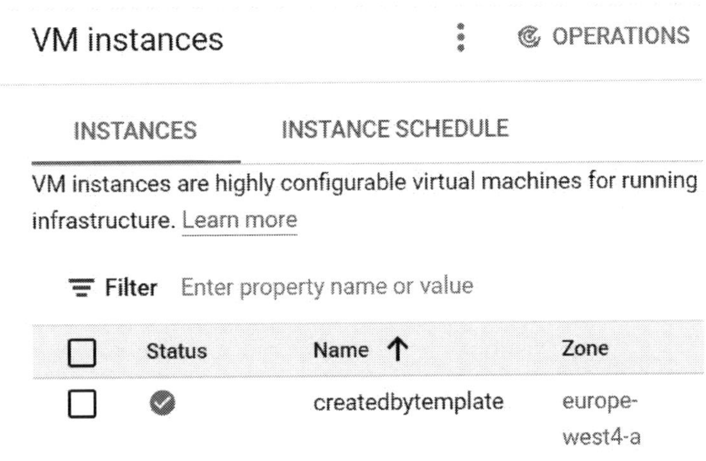

VM instances   ⋮   ⓒ OPERATIONS

INSTANCES   INSTANCE SCHEDULE

VM instances are highly configurable virtual machines for running infrastructure. Learn more

≡ Filter   Enter property name or value

	Status	Name ↑	Zone
☐	✓	createdbytemplate	europe-west4-a

Figure 16.16 – New VM instance

We can also specify the variable properties in our gcloud command. In the following example, we have a new template called vm-template1.jinja, which is expecting variables for a hostname and a zone:

```
resources:
- name: {{ properties["name"] }}
  type: compute.v1.instance
  properties:
    zone: {{ properties["zone"] }}
    machineType: zones/{{ properties ["zone"] }}/machineTypes/
g1-small
    disks:
    - deviceName: boot
      type: PERSISTENT
      boot: true
      autoDelete: true
      initializeParams:
        sourceImage: projects/centos-cloud/global/images/
centos-stream-8-v20210721
    networkInterfaces:
    - network: global/networks/default
    accessConfigs:
    - name: External NAT
      type: ONE_TO_ONE_NAT
```

Once again, let's use our `gcloud` commands to create this. However, we need to specify the name as vm002 and the zone as `europe-west4-a`:

```
gcloud deployment-manager deployments create
deployment002 --template vm-template1.jinja --properties
name:vm002,zone:europe-west4-a
```

Let's check our GCP console and confirm that we now have a VM instance called vm002 in the `europe-west4-a` zone:

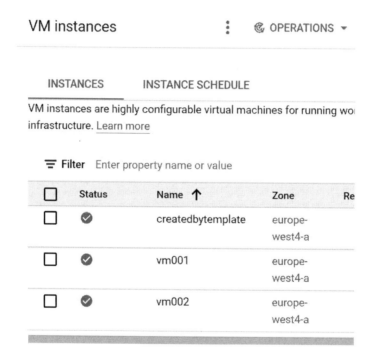

Figure 16.17 – Instances

So far, we have only looked at single VM deployments, but we can also deploy multiple VMs via Deployment Manager.

Let's look at an example where we want to deploy a three-tier application made up of a web application and a DB server in different zones. We can expand on our previous templates to add the information that's required. Note that we are now specifying three separate resources. Let's create a new template file called vm-template2.jinja:

```
resources:
- name: {{ properties["webname"] }}
  type: compute.v1.instance
```

```
  properties:
    zone: {{ properties["webzone"] }}
    machineType: zones/{{ properties ["webzone"] }}/
machineTypes/{{ properties["type"] }}
    disks:
    - deviceName: boot
      type: PERSISTENT
      boot: true
      autoDelete: true
      initializeParams:
        sourceImage: projects/centos-cloud/global/images/
centos-stream-8-v20210701
    networkInterfaces:
    - network: global/networks/default
    accessConfigs:
    - name: External NAT
      type: ONE_TO_ONE_NAT


- name: {{ properties["appname"] }}
  type: compute.v1.instance
  properties:
    zone: {{ properties["appzone"] }}
    machineType: zones/{{ properties ["appzone"] }}/
machineTypes/{{ properties["type"] }}
    disks:
    - deviceName: boot
      type: PERSISTENT
      boot: true
      autoDelete: true
      initializeParams:
        sourceImage: projects/centos-cloud/global/images/
centos-stream-8-v20210701
    networkInterfaces:
    - network: global/networks/default
    accessConfigs:
    - name: External NAT
```

```
        type: ONE_TO_ONE_NAT

- name: {{ properties["dbname"] }}
  type: compute.v1.instance
  properties:
    zone: {{ properties["dbzone"] }}
    machineType: zones/{{ properties ["dbzone"] }}/
machineTypes/{{ properties["type"] }}
    disks:
    - deviceName: boot
      type: PERSISTENT
      boot: true
      autoDelete: true
      initializeParams:
        sourceImage: projects/centos-cloud/global/images/
centos-stream-8-v20210701
    networkInterfaces:
    - network: global/networks/default
    accessConfigs:
    - name: External NAT
      type: ONE_TO_ONE_NAT
```

Now, we need to update our configuration file. Let's create a new file and call it `multi.yaml`. Let's add the following text:

```
imports:
  - path: vm-template2.jinja

resources:
- name: newinstance
  type: vm-template2.jinja
  properties:
    webname: web001
    webzone: europe-west2-a
    appname: app001
    appzone: europe-west4-b
```

```
    dbname: db001
    dbzone: europe-west6-c
    type: g1-small
```

Now, we can run the following command to trigger a deployment called
`multideployment`:

```
gcloud deployment-manager deployments create multideployment
--config multi.yaml
```

Now, let's check our results from Cloud Shell:

```
The fingerprint of the deployment is NdvSfAvJTKQnTfuTYocnBQ==
Waiting for create [operation-1556477906253-5879bc0b3f6a3-e71eb3bb-b27e918e]...done.
Create operation operation-1556477906253-5879bc0b3f6a3-e71eb3bb-b27e918e completed successfully.
NAME     TYPE                   STATE       ERRORS  INTENT
app001   compute.v1.instance    COMPLETED   []
db001    compute.v1.instance    COMPLETED   []
web001   compute.v1.instance    COMPLETED   []
```

Figure 16.18 – Multideployment

We can confirm our deployment via the GCP console. Let's check out the **Deployment
Manager** menu, where we can see that our deployments have been successful:

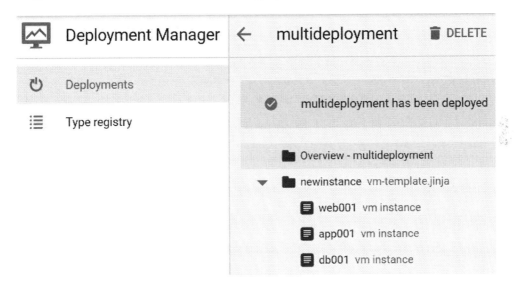

Figure 16.19 – Result

We can also see that each VM instance has been deployed to the correct zone:

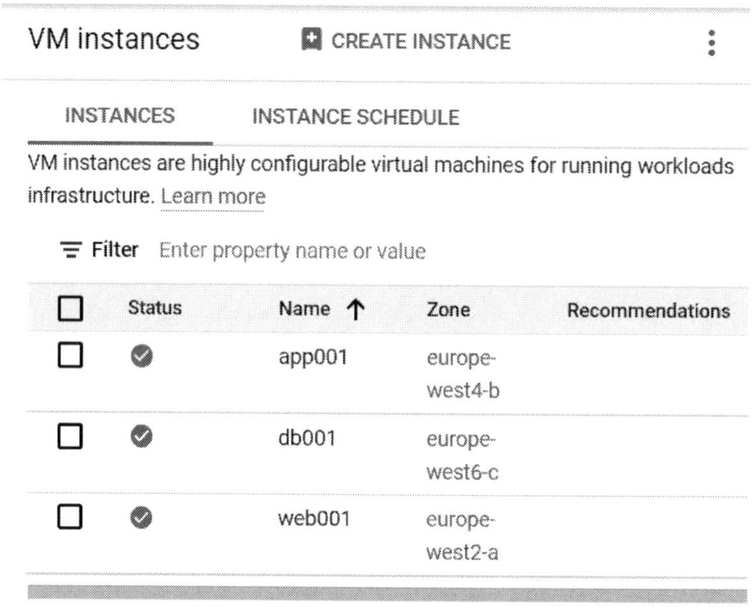

	Status	Name ↑	Zone	Recommendations
☐	✔	app001	europe-west4-b	
☐	✔	db001	europe-west6-c	
☐	✔	web001	europe-west2-a	

Figure 16.20 – Instances

This is how we can configure a template for VM instance types only. We can also extend our template to other types of services, such as networking. As a final example, let's look at how to create a template and configuration file to create a networking and firewall ruleset. In this example, we need to have three separate templates: one for our network, one for our subnetwork, and one for our firewall rule.

Let's look at our network first. This is pretty simple. Note that we are now using a type of `compute.v1.network` and that we have single properties. We set this to `false` to avoid automatically creating a corresponding subnetwork. The name is a variable that's passed from our configuration file. Let's save this file as `network.jinja`:

```
resources:
- name: {{ env["name"] }}
  type: compute.v1.network
  properties:
    autoCreateSubnetworks: false
```

Next, we can create a subnetwork template. Again, we have the name as a variable, which will be passed from our configuration file. We will also be passing information about the IP range and the network to attach it to, which we will create using the `network.jinja` template, as well as the region to create the subnet in. Let's save this as `subnet.jinja`:

```
resources:
- name: {{ env["name"] }}
  type: compute.v1.subnetwork
  properties:
    ipCidrRange: {{ properties["iprange"] }}
    network: {{ properties["network"] }}
    region: {{ properties["region"] }}
```

Finally, let's create a template so that we can create a firewall rule. Once again, we will pass the name from our configuration file, but this time, we will append the name with a hardcoded value. We will also set the network to attach this to and pass in the protocol for our firewall rule. Let's save this template as `firewall.jinja`:

```
resources:
- name: {{ env["name"] }}-firewall-rule
  type: compute.v1.firewall
  properties:
    network: {{ properties["network"] }}
    sourceRanges: ["0.0.0.0/0"]
    allowed:
    - IPProtocol: {{ properties["Protocol"] }}
      ports: ["80"]
```

Now, we need our configuration file. We will import all three of our templates rather than a single file, as we did in the previous examples. There is no real complexity to this – we just add an extra line for each template to import. One of the key things to note here is to make sure we connect the subnet and firewall rule to the correct network. We can pass the variable as follows:

```
$(ref.custom-net.selfLink)
```

Here, `custom-net` is the name of the network we are creating. This name is passed as a variable. Let's save this configuration file as `config.yaml`:

```
imports:
- path: network.jinja
- path: subnet.jinja
- path: firewall.jinja


resources:
- name: custom-net
  type: network.jinja


- name: custom-subnet
  type: subnet.jinja
  properties:
    iprange: 10.10.0.0/16
    network: $(ref.custom-net.selfLink)
    region: us-central1


- name: custom
  type: firewall.jinja
  properties:
    network: $(ref.custom-net.selfLink)
    Protocol: TCP
```

Finally, let's upload these files to our Cloud Shell environment and trigger the `gcloud` commands that we have become familiar with:

```
gcloud deployment-manager deployments create networking
--config config.yaml
```

Let's see what the output of this command looks like in Cloud Shell:

```
The fingerprint of the deployment is 2A6YxCYsxQ_e04Se7N6Rpw==
Waiting for create [operation-1556741126674-587d909dcd9bd-c1d90539-9a25356a]...done.
Create operation operation-1556741126674-587d909dcd9bd-c1d90539-9a25356a completed successfully.
NAME                 TYPE                    STATE       ERRORS  INTENT
custom-firewall-rule compute.v1.firewall     COMPLETED   []
custom-net           compute.v1.network      COMPLETED   []
custom-subnet        compute.v1.subnetwork   COMPLETED   []
```

Figure 16.21 – Google Cloud Shell output

There is one final file that we should also discuss. A schema file is used as a guide to show users how to interact with and use your template. For example, let's look at a configuration file that will require a zone to be passed as a variable to the template. We can provide our users with information on how it is used, and which variables need to be set:

```
info:
    title: VM Instance Template
    author: Cloud Architect
    description: Creates a new instance
    version: 0.1

imports:
    - path: vm-template.jinja

required:
    - zone

properties:
    zone:
        type: string
        description: zone where VM will reside
```

> **Important Note**
>
> Some great Deployment Manager examples are provided by Google, which we can download and use in our free-tier environment. We recommend that you download and look at a further, more complex, Cloud Deployment Manager template at `https://github.com/GoogleCloudPlatform/deploymentmanager-samples`.

In the next section, we will look at an alternative to Cloud Deployment Manager: Terraform.

Terraform

Terraform is an open source tool that lets us provision Google Cloud resources in a declarative manner. We should note that it is not exclusive to Google Cloud. Terraform can deploy resources in AWS, Azure, and VMware, to name a few vendors. Like Cloud Deployment Manager, Terraform also uses an IaC approach and keeps a note of the desired state that we want our environment to look like. No modifications should be made to the backend and Terraform should be the source of truth. This is similar to Deployment Manager, which creates manifest files that store information about our deployed resources. Terraform, however, uses its structured language called **HashiCorp Configuration Language** (HCL), which is an alternative to the YAML file approach we looked at in the previous section. This can bring a bit of a steeper learning curve for those looking at IaC for the first time. Terraform integrates with GCP using a provider that is responsible for understanding API interactions with the underlying infrastructure. The Google provider for Terraform is used to configure our GCP infrastructure and is jointly maintained by the Terraform team at Google and the Terraform team at HashiCorp, though they do accept community contributions!

With Google Cloud Shell, Terraform is automatically authenticated and we can begin experimenting with it straight from Terraform's Google Provider documentation pages. Many of the examples have **Open in Google Cloud Shell** buttons, allowing us to launch an interactive Cloud Shell session with the example loaded and Terraform ready to use.

Now, let's look at an example of deploying a Cloud Storage bucket. We will not go into details about the Terraform HCL code as it is outside the scope of this book, but it is good to get a high-level idea of what it looks like. Terraform has some main commands to deploy a resource. First, we must run `terraform init`, which will look for the specific providers we need and download them. One of the benefits of Terraform is its drift detection, whereby running the next Terraform commands `terraform plan`, will present the difference between the configuration we want to apply against what is deployed. When we run the plan, it does not deploy anything. To execute the plan, we must run the `terraform apply` command.

For our example, we will look at creating a Google Storage bucket. Let's clone some code from GitHub for the Terraform modules by executing the `git clone` command from the repository at `https://github.com/terraform-google-modules/terraform-google-cloud-storage`.

Next, we must change directories to `/terraform-google-cloud-storage/examples/simple_bucket` and run `terraform init`, which will look for the specific providers we need and download them:

```
Initializing the backend...

Initializing provider plugins...
- Finding hashicorp/google versions matching ">= 3.43.0, < 4.0.0"...
- Installing hashicorp/google v3.74.0...
- Installed hashicorp/google v3.74.0 (self-signed, key ID 34365D9472D7468F)

Partner and community providers are signed by their developers.
If you'd like to know more about provider signing, you can read about it here:
https://www.terraform.io/docs/cli/plugins/signing.html

Terraform has created a lock file .terraform.lock.hcl to record the provider
selections it made above. Include this file in your version control repository
so that Terraform can guarantee to make the same selections by default when
you run "terraform init" in the future.

Terraform has been successfully initialized!
```

Figure 16.22 – terraform init output

When we run the `terraform plan` command, we will be prompted for a bucket name and the ID of our project. It will not deploy anything. In this example, we can see that we are creating a new multi-region bucket called `cloudarchitectupdate001` in the EU location:

```
Terraform will perform the following actions:

  # google_storage_bucket.bucket will be created
  + resource "google_storage_bucket" "bucket" {
      + bucket_policy_only          = (known after apply)
      + force_destroy               = false
      + id                          = (known after apply)
      + location                    = "EU"
      + name                        = "cloudarchitectupdate001"
      + project                     = "primeval-nectar-318916"
      + self_link                   = (known after apply)
      + storage_class               = "STANDARD"
      + uniform_bucket_level_access = true
      + url                         = (known after apply)

      + versioning {
          + enabled = true
        }
    }

Plan: 1 to add, 0 to change, 0 to destroy.
```

Figure 16.23 – terraform plan output

To execute the plan, we must run the `terraform apply` command. The output will look similar to the following:

```
google_storage_bucket.bucket: Creating...
google_storage_bucket.bucket: Creation complete after 1s [id=cloudarchitectupdate001]

Apply complete! Resources: 1 added, 0 changed, 0 destroyed.
```

Figure 16.24 – terraform apply output

Finally, we can browse to **Cloud Storage** in our console and confirm that our new bucket has been created in the correct location:

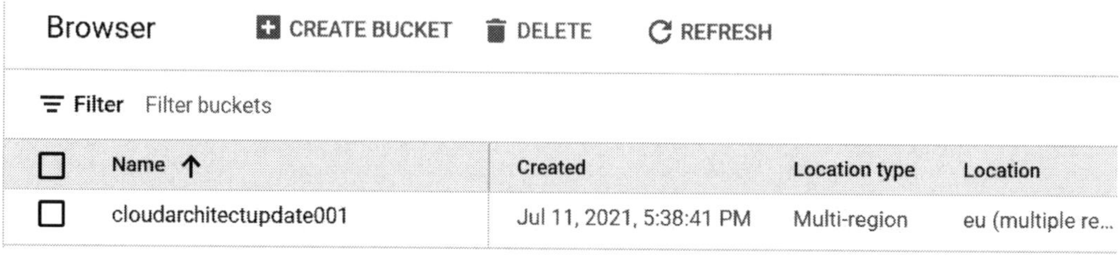

Figure 16.25 – Google Cloud Storage bucket

Of course, this is a very simple example, but you can deploy a much more complex set of resources with multiple VMs, GKE clusters, load balancers, and so on. If you feel intimidated by the complexity of syntax of Terraform templates, do not worry! Google comes with a set of already existing templates that you can use and learn from.

Cloud Foundation Toolkit

Cloud Foundation Toolkit (CFT) (`https://cloud.google.com/foundation-toolkit`) offers ready-made templates for both Deployment Manager and Terraform. The code from the previous Terraform example, which was used to create the Cloud Storage bucket, came directly from these off-the-shelf templates. They are designed so that we can quickly build repeatable enterprise-ready foundations inside our Cloud platform. These templates are time-saving tools that we can build on to customize in a way that can add value to our business. They also free us to focus on the applications rather than tedious infrastructure tasks.

In the next section, we will look at Pricing Calculator.

Pricing Calculator

Google offers help when it comes to calculating the cost of running your apps in GCP. Instead of checking the prices in the documentation of each service, you can use the GCP Pricing Calculator. This calculator is available online via `https://cloud.google.com/products/calculator`. It allows you to choose the services and configuration you want to use for your application. You can also add your estimated storage and network requirements. The total price will be calculated for you:

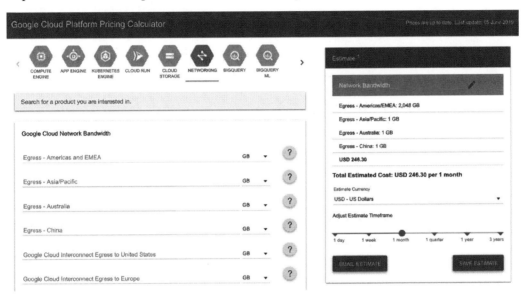

Figure 16.26 – Pricing Calculator

Here, you can see an example of the cost for five nodes on the GKE cluster with 500 GB disk space. To add your estimated egress networking traffic, simply choose the **NETWORKING** icon and define where your traffic will go:

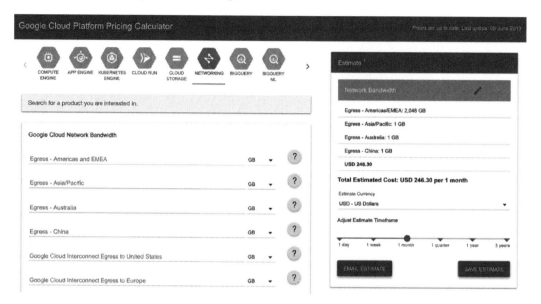

Figure 16.27 – Pricing Calculator – Networking

Let's look at another example, this time for **Cloud Storage**. In this example, we are showing you how much it will cost to use 1 TB of Cloud Storage in Singapore. We have estimated that we will have 500,000 class A and 500,000 class B operations per month. Please note that when you are adding operations into the calculator, it expects the figure in millions. In our example, we have put 0.5 million:

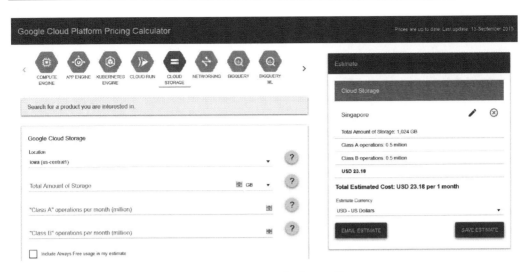

Figure 16.28 – Pricing Calculator – Storage

We encourage you to navigate to this website and familiarize yourself with different examples.

Additional things to consider

There are additional management tools that we need to consider. For the exam, it is also important to be aware of the following:

- **Cloud Source Repositories**: These are fully featured GitHub repositories that are hosted on GCP and support the collaborative development of an application. You can use the `gcloud` commands to create code, commit code, and manage new repositories. More information can be found at `https://cloud.google.com/source-repositories/docs/`.

- **Cloud Build**: This is a GCP CI/CD service that will execute your builds on the GCP infrastructure. It can import source code from Google Cloud Storage, Cloud Source Repositories, GitHub, or Bitbucket. More information can be found in *Chapter 6, Managing Kubernetes Clusters with Google Kubernetes Engine*, and here: `https://cloud.google.com/cloud-build/docs/`.

- **Cloud Scheduler**: This is a fully managed cron job scheduler service. It can be used to trigger jobs on App Engine, send Pub/Sub messages, or even hit HTTP(S) endpoints.

- **Container Registry**: This provides us with private Docker repository storage on our GCP platform. We can use the `gcloud` commands to push images to our registry, and then we can pull these images using an HTTP endpoint from any GCE instance or even our hardware. More information can be found in *Chapter 6, Managing Kubernetes Clusters with Google Kubernetes Engine.*

- **Cloud Endpoints**: This acts as an API management system that allows us to manage our APIs on any Google Cloud backend. Once you have deployed your API in Cloud Endpoints, you can create a developer portal that users can interact with and access and view documentation.

Summary

In this chapter, we looked over the main management tools that can be used to manage GCP services. It's important to reiterate that you should understand which services can be managed by which command-line tool and the basic command-line structure. Let's review what we would use each tool for:

- `gcloud` can be used to manage many GCP services, but it is most commonly used to manage Compute Engine VM instances, Cloud SQL instances, Kubernetes Engine clusters, and Cloud Deployment Manager deployments.

- Use `cbt` to manage Bigtable.

- Use `bq` to manage BigQuery.

- Use `gsutil` to manage Cloud Storage. We need to understand the different syntax for creating buckets, copying data, and removing buckets.

- Deployment Manager can be used to automate a variety of GCP services within templates and configuration files.

- Pricing Calculator.

Remember that Google offers a free tier where you can use these command-line tools and familiarize yourself with creating and managing different services.

In the next chapter, we will look at how to monitor our GCP services.

Further reading

Read the following articles for more information about what was covered in this chapter:

- **APIs Explorer**: `https://developers.google.com/apis-explorer/#p/`
- **gsutil**: `https://cloud.google.com/storage/docs/gsutil`
- **cbt**: `https://cloud.google.com/bigtable/docs/quickstart-cbt`
- **gcloud**: `https://cloud.google.com/sdk/gcloud/`
- **bq**: `https://cloud.google.com/bigquery/docs/bq-command-line-tool`
- **Cloud Deployment Manager**: `https://cloud.google.com/deployment-manager/docs/`

17
Monitoring Your Infrastructure

In this chapter, we will look at GCP monitoring. We will discuss what Google Cloud's operations suite (formerly known as **Stackdriver**) is and why you need it. We will explain all of the services that it offers. We will also go through some basic configurations that will give you a good understanding of how you can leverage it in order to monitor your Google Cloud services, such as **Google Compute Engine** (GCE) or **Google Kubernetes Engine** (GKE).

The following topics will be covered in this chapter:

- Introduction to Google Cloud's operations suite
- Configuring Google Cloud's operations suite
- Cloud Monitoring
- Cloud Logging
- **Application Performance Management (APM)**

> **Exam Tips**
>
> Monitoring is a massive topic and can feel somewhat overwhelming. Once you understand the three main functionalities of Google Cloud's operations suite, which are monitoring, logging, and APM, we want you to focus on what you will be tested on in the exam. Make sure that you know which GCP services you can monitor with Google Cloud's operations suite. Pay special attention to **GCE**, both in terms of performance and availability monitoring. Understand audit logs well, and make sure that you know how to track who made the changes to your project and the associated resources. Log in to the GCP console and browse the activity and audit logs. Anticipate that you may be asked about where to find particular types of logs! Finally, Qwiklabs will allow you to understand the service better, and we strongly recommend that you have a look at the available labs.

Technical requirements

In order to gain hands-on experience with Google Cloud's operations suite, we recommend that you use Qwiklabs. The Google Cloud operations suite quest can be found here: `https://www.qwiklabs.com/quests/35?locale=en`.

> **Important Note**
>
> You need to purchase credits in order to enroll for the quest.

Introduction to Google Cloud's operations suite

We have already learned about a number of services, and now it is time to take a closer look at the monitoring options. Google comes with a GCP-integrated tool called Google Cloud's operations suite (formerly known as Stackdriver). Stackdriver was founded in 2012 as a **Software-as-a-Service (SaaS)** platform that would allow consistent monitoring across different cloud layers. In 2014, it was acquired by Google and made publicly available in 2016 as a GCP service.

Currently, Google Cloud's operations suite can monitor both GCP and AWS. However, integration with the former is much more robust. Google Cloud's operations suite is a set of tools that provides the following services:

- Monitoring
- Logging

- Debugging
- Tracing
- Error Reporting
- Profiling

Monitoring and Logging are agentless, but in order to obtain more informative metrics and logs, an agent should be installed. There are actually two types of agents that can be installed on your instances: a Monitoring agent, based on the `collectd` software, and a Logging agent, based on the `fluentd` software.

In the following diagram, you can see a schema, which highlights a GCE VM instance and the agents that are installed on top of it. The VM instance, by default, talks to Logging and Monitoring. The agents report to their respective services:

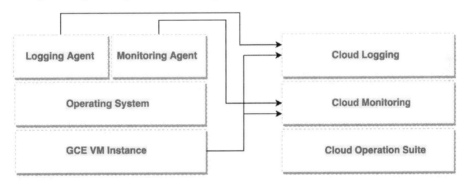

Figure 17.1 – Google Cloud's operations suite

GCP is a developer-oriented platform, and it provides a lot of monitoring-related services that can be directly integrated with your application. Google Cloud's operations suite allows you to monitor both the infrastructure and the applications. It is very important to understand that developers need to consider monitoring and logging from the very outset when designing applications. For each of the programming languages that are supported, there are libraries that facilitate log integration with Google Cloud's operations suite. Make sure that you check out the languages that are supported so that you can take full advantage of them!

In this chapter, we will have a look at how Google Cloud's operations suite is used to monitor GCP. Remember to read this chapter carefully and perform the recommended Qwiklabs, as this is a key exam topic.

Now that we have a basic understanding of what Google Cloud's operations suite is, let's have a look at the cost of each service.

Cost

With Google Cloud's operations suite, you only pay for what you use. The cost can be controlled using Cloud Billing reports and alerts.

The following Google Cloud operations suite services can be used for free:

- Cloud Debugger
- Error Reporting
- Cloud Profiler

The following services may incur costs once monthly limits have been exceeded:

- Cloud Logging
- Cloud Monitoring
- Cloud Trace

We don't include the actual prices on purpose, given that they may change.

> **Important Note**
>
> Check the following link to learn about the most recent and detailed pricing list: `https://cloud.google.com/monitoring#pricing`.

Configuring Google Cloud's operations suite

> **Exam Tip**
>
> For Stackdriver, there was a need to manually create a monitoring workspace. After Google Cloud's operations suite was introduced, there was no more need to do it. When you navigate to Cloud Monitoring from the Google Console, you will see the project has been enabled for monitoring automatically after it was created and has become a so-called **scoping project**.

Google Cloud's operations suite is enabled on a project-by-project basis. Best practice says that if you are going to use just one project, you should enable it for that project. If you have more than one project, you should have a separate project just for monitoring. This is called a scoping project. From that project, you will be able to indicate which other projects you would like to monitor. Those will become **monitored projects**. Remember, you are not charged for additional projects, so this will not entail any additional costs.

Now, let's have a look at how to start working with Google Cloud's operations suite:

1. From the hamburger menu, go to **Monitoring**. Next, choose **Overview**:

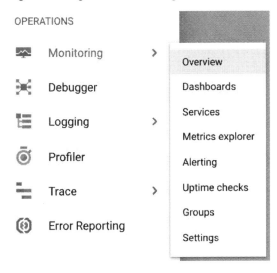

Figure 17.2 – Access Cloud Monitoring

2. This brings you to the Cloud Monitoring main screen. As you can see, you have a well-formatted board that sums up the most important information related to your GCP resource monitoring, such as resource **Dashboards**, incident **Uptime checks**, and so on:

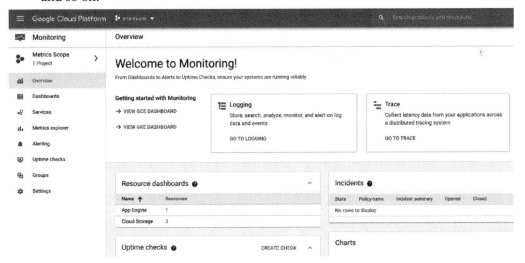

Figure 17.3 – Cloud Monitoring Overview screen

3. In the scenario of multiple projects, enable monitoring for each project by clicking on **Metrics Scope** in the left pane and then on the **Add Cloud projects to metrics scope** link (`https://console.cloud.google.com/monitoring/settings/add-projects?project=pca-exam-314409`):

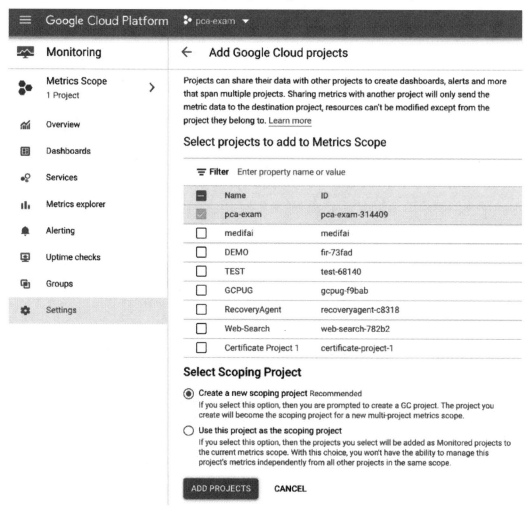

Figure 17.4 – Add Google Cloud projects

Now we can see the metrics scope settings with our projects. You can either add the project to be monitored by the current scoping project or create a new scoping project. When you are ready with selecting the projects, click on the **ADD PROJECTS** button:

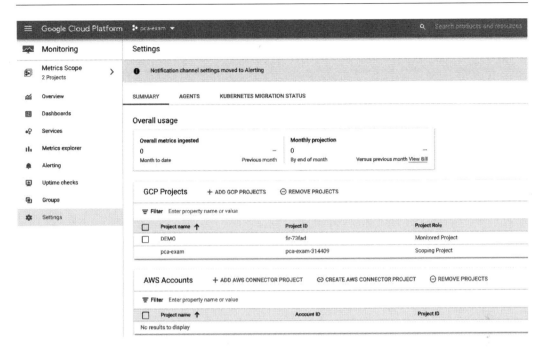

Figure 17.5 – Metrics Scope – Settings

4. You can choose whether you want to monitor AWS resources. That will require the creation of an IAM role in AWS, with listed permissions. If you only work with GCP, then you can launch monitoring by clicking on **Skip AWS Setup**.

Exam Tip

Google Cloud operations suite is also capable of monitoring logging data for your AWS accounts. You must associate your AWS resources with a Google Cloud project. This project serves as a connector to AWS.

Now that we have configured Google Cloud's operations suite, let's look at the monitoring service.

Cloud Monitoring

With the Monitoring service, you can discover and monitor all GCP resources and services. The Monitoring console allows you to view all of your resources, create alerting policies, and view uptime checks, groups, and custom dashboards. It also allows you to navigate to the debug, trace, logging, and error reporting consoles.

Let's have a look at what can be configured from here. We will look into the following topics:

- Groups
- Dashboards
- Alerting policies
- Change screen
- Uptime checks
- Monitoring agents

Groups

Resources such as VM instances, applications, and databases can be grouped into logical groups. This allows us to manage them together and display them in dashboards. Constraints are used to define the criteria to filter the resources. They can be based on names, regions, applications, and so on. The groups can be nested in one another, and the nesting can be six levels deep:

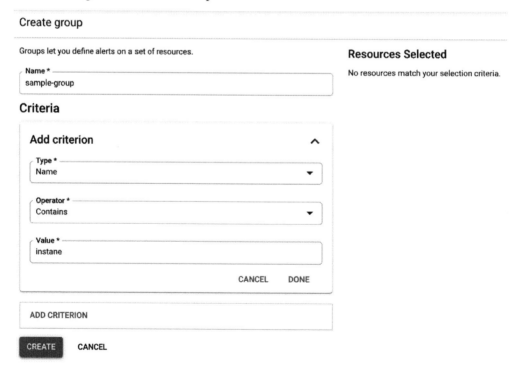

Figure 17.6 – Create group

The preceding screenshot shows the screen for creating a new group. We can use multiple criteria to filter the resources that we want to be added to the group.

Dashboards

Dashboards allow us to give visibility to different metrics in a single pane of glass. We can create multiple dashboards that contain charts based on **predefined** or **user-defined metrics**. This allows us to create customized boards with the most important metrics. The charts visualize the metrics, allowing a good understanding of how your environment performs.

Note that, for VM instances, we can also see agent-based metrics on top of standard metrics. The agent-based metrics will be listed when you go to **Dashboards** and click on the **+CREATE DASHBOARD** button. Next, choose one of the charts from the library and click on the **Metric** dropdown:

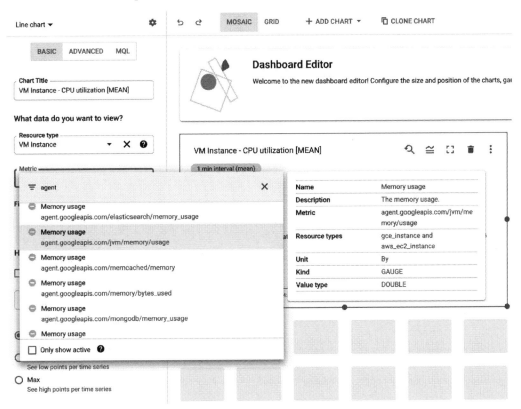

Figure 17.7 – Dashboards

Alerting policies

Alerting policies can be configured in order to create notifications when event and metric thresholds are reached. The policies can have one or more conditions to trigger the alert and will create an incident that is visible in the Cloud Monitoring console.

The following actions can be selected to address the open incident:

- **Acknowledge**
- **Silence Associated condition**
- **View Policy**
- **Edit Alerting Policy**

The menu for these actions opens once you click on the three-dots icon in the right-hand corner:

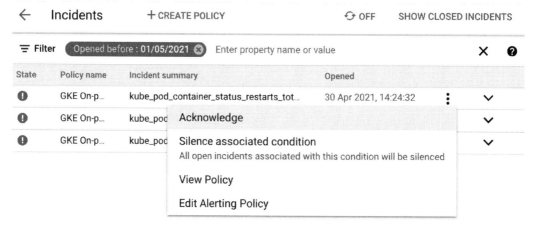

Figure 17.8 – Alerting policies

The incident can be acknowledged as a known issue or resolved. In terms of notifications, email, SMS, and many other forms can be configured. The channel to be used can be chosen from the drop-down menu, as shown in the following screenshot:

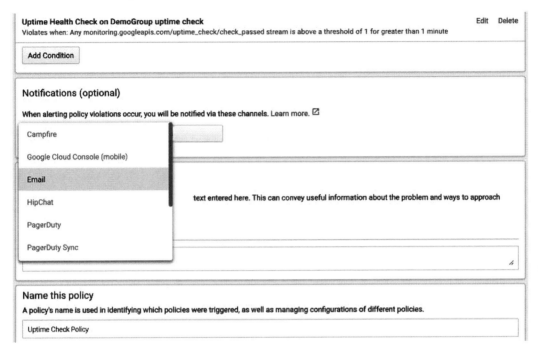

Figure 17.9 – Notifications

To further guide the operations to a possible solution, documentation links can also be attached to the alert.

Uptime checks

Uptime checks are used for checking the availability of your services from different locations around the globe. They can be combined with alerting policies and are displayed in the dashboards. Checks can be done using HTTP, HTTPS, or TCP, and are possible for URLs, App Engine, **Elastic Load Balancing** (**ELB**), Kubernetes' load balancer service, and Amazon EC2 and GCE instances. The probing interval can be set to 1, 5, 10, or 15 minutes:

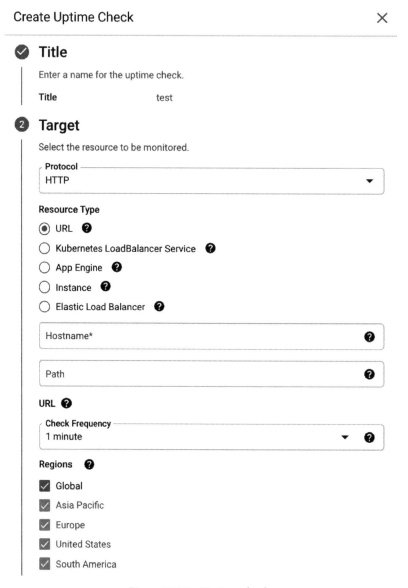

Figure 17.10 – Uptime check

You also need to choose from which regions the checks will be performed. You need to have at least three regions checked:

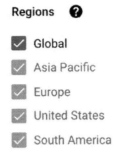

Figure 17.11 – Regions

In the further section, you can add the host header, change the port, add custom headers, and encrypt them. You can also add authentication if applicable:

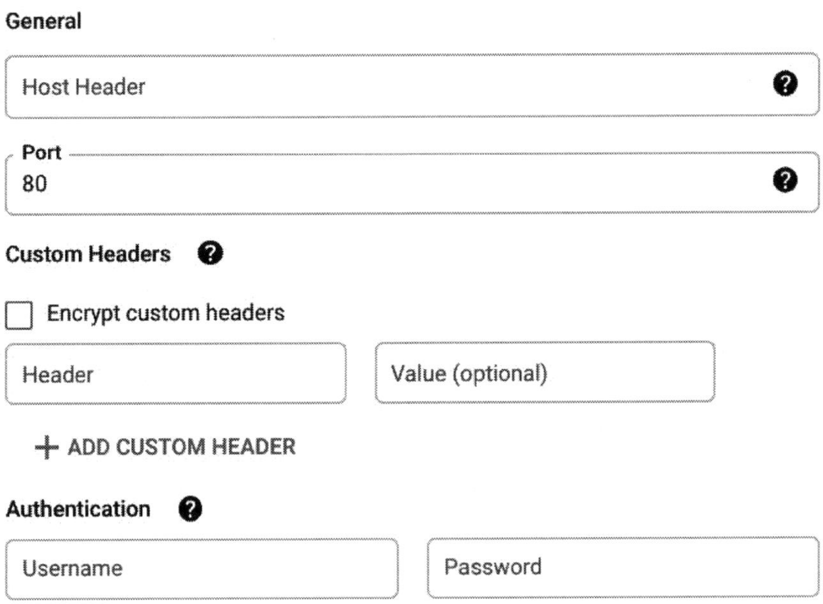

General

Host Header   ❓

Port
80   ❓

Custom Headers ❓

☐ Encrypt custom headers

Header   Value (optional)

╋ ADD CUSTOM HEADER

Authentication ❓

Username   Password

Figure 17.12 – Advanced settings

In the **Response Validation** section, you can set **Response Timeout** and set up the content matching for the response:

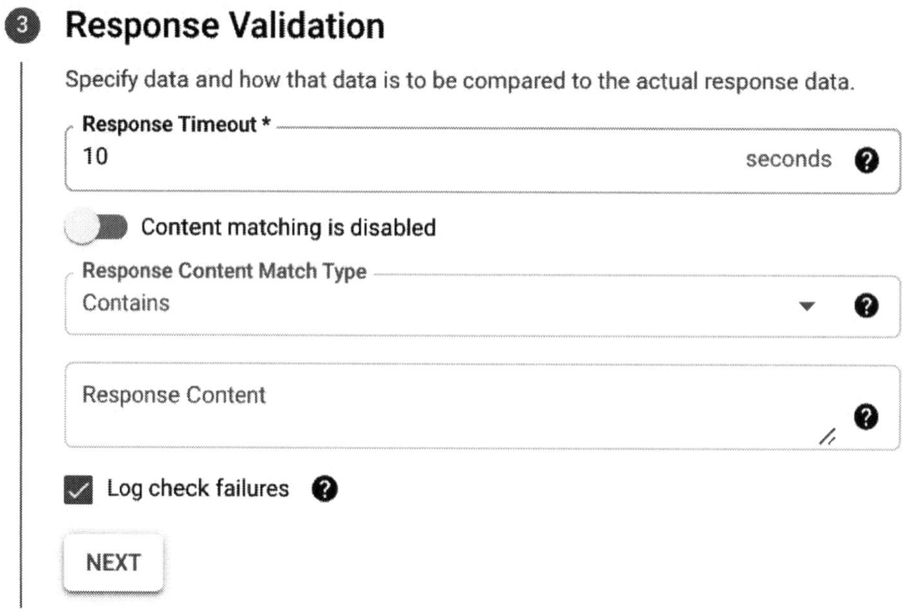

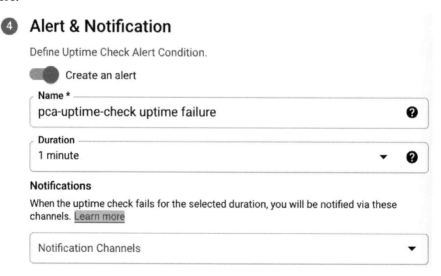

Figure 17.13 – Response Validation

Finally, you can set up alerts and notifications. You can choose which notification channel should be used to send the notification. If no channel exists yet, you can create a new one from here:

Figure 17.14 – Alert & Notification

> **Exam Tip**
>
> Remember that, for the uptime check to work, the firewall rules need to be created. To check the IPs of the uptime servers, go to the uptime check console and download the list of rules. For details on how to do it, check the documentation: `https://cloud.google.com/monitoring/uptime-checks/`.

Monitoring agents

To get more out of Cloud Monitoring, a Monitoring agent can be installed on the instance to collect additional metrics. By default, the Monitoring agent collects disk, CPU, network, and process metrics; however, additional metrics can also be collected.

The Monitoring agent is a `collectd`-based agent that can be installed both on GCP and AWS instances. The agent can be also configured to monitor many applications, including the Apache web server, Tomcat, Kafka, Memcached, and Redis.

The installation of the agent on Linux is very straightforward and requires the following two commands to be executed:

```
curl -sSO https://dl.google.com/cloudagents/add-monitoring-agent-repo.sh
sudo bash add-monitoring-agent-repo.sh --also-install
```

To install the agent on a Windows machine, run the following command in PowerShell:

```
(New-Object Net.WebClient).DownloadFile("https://repo.stackdriver.com/windows/StackdriverMonitoring-GCM-46.exe",
"${env:UserProfile}\StackdriverMonitoring-GCM-46.exe") &
"${env:UserProfile}\StackdriverMonitoring-GCM-46.exe"
```

More instructions can be found at `https://cloud.google.com/monitoring/agent/install-agent#agent-install-windows`.

> **Exam Tip**
>
> To monitor the instance memory, you need to use the Monitoring agent!

Cloud Logging

Cloud Logging is the second most important service. It allows you to store and analyze logs, as well as events coming from GCP and AWS. Based on the logs, alerts can be created. It also provides a robust API, allowing logs to be both managed and injected. This means that any third-party application can leverage Google Cloud's operations suite for logging purposes. The gathered logs are visible in the Legacy Logs Viewer, where they can be filtered and exported for further analysis or archival purposes, or integrated with third-party solutions. There are a number of types of logs, and some of them are not enabled by default. Log-based metrics use log entries and can be leveraged to create dashboard charts and custom alerts. Now, let's take a closer look at how to use logging. We will be looking at the following topics:

- Logs Viewer
- Basic log filtering
- Advanced filtering
- Exporting logs
- Logging agent
- Log-based metrics
- Cloud Audit Logs
- Activity
- Retention

Legacy Logs Viewer

> **Exam Tip**
>
> The **Legacy Logs Viewer** is a tool that was used in Stackdriver. You can still access it from Google Cloud's operations suite. The new iteration of this tool has a completely new user experience called the **Logs Explorer**. We will have a look at it in the following section. Keep this section for reference in case you get such a question on the exam.

The Legacy Logs Viewer is a console that allows you to view, filter, and export logs. Keep in mind that logs are associated with a single GCP project:

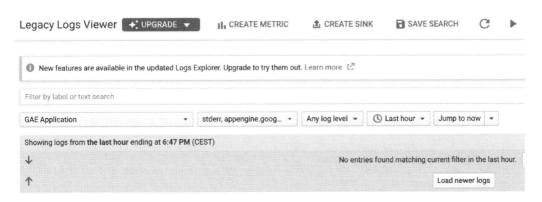

Figure 17.15 – Legacy Logs Viewer

To be able to view logs from other projects, you need to switch the view. An API can be used to get logs from multiple projects. The logs can be filtered, using either basic or advanced filtering, to pinpoint the exact event.

Logs Explorer

The Logs Explorer is a new tool from the Google Cloud operations suite that allows you to inspect your GCP logs. It pops up as the default pane when you open the Cloud Logging service in the GCP console:

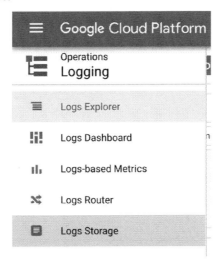

Figure 17.16 – Accessing Cloud Logging

With the Logs Explorer, you can choose to view the logs in two different scopes:

- Scope by project – allows you to search and view logs from a single project

- Scope by storage – allows you to view logs from a bucket that was used as a sink

The second option is very convenient as it allows you to get the same experience from browsing the sink logs as you would get for the logs that still reside in the project:

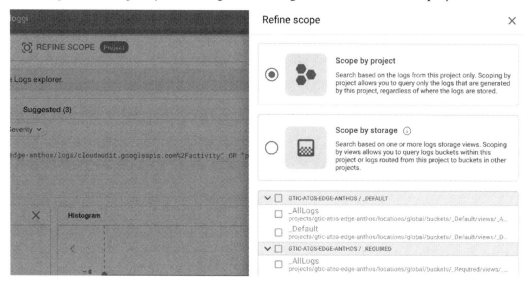

Figure 17.17 – Refine scope

To find the logs you are interested in, you can define a query by simply choosing a filter and then a value from the list of the objects that the filter selected:

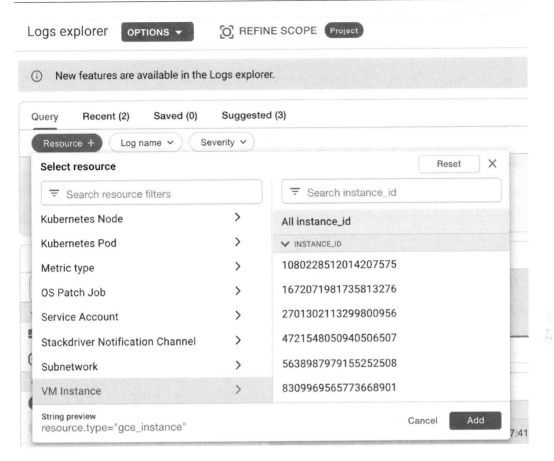

Figure 17.18 – Resource filters

The second filter allows you to choose the type of logs to be displayed, as shown in the following screenshot:

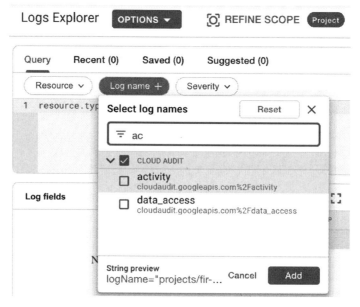

Figure 17.19 – Log name

The third filter allows the level of severity to be chosen:

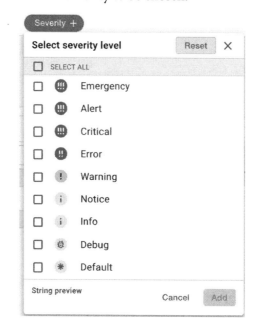

Figure 17.20 – Severity

From the top-right link, you can go to the menu where you can choose the time range:

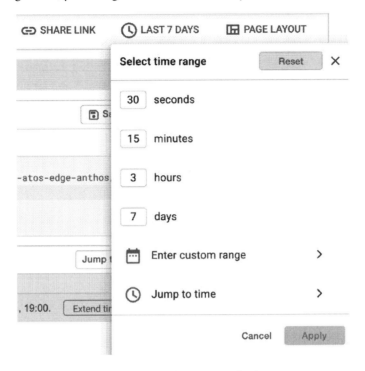

Figure 17.21 – Time range selection

You can also choose from predefined time spans or a custom one. Finally, when we run the query, we get the logs that show when the machine was started:

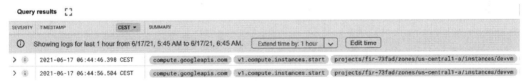

Figure 17.22 – Filtered logs

The severity in this case is at the INFO level.

The preceding example shows logs with a resource type of the GCE instance and a severity of INFO and higher.

Exporting logs

Log entries that are received by logging can be exported (copied) to Cloud Storage buckets, BigQuery data sets, and Cloud Pub/Sub topics. You export logs by configuring log sinks, which then continue to export log entries as they arrive in logging. A sink includes a destination and a filter that selects the log entries to be exported. Remember that only the logs that were created after the sink configuration will be exported:

1. To set up an export, go to **Logs Router** in the Cloud Logging window and click on **CREATE SINK**:

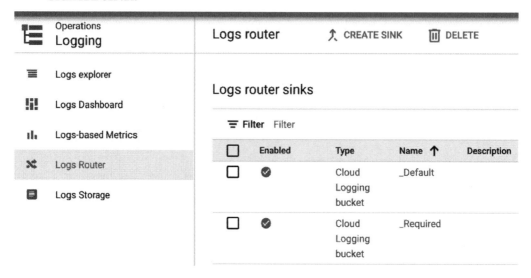

Figure 17.23 – Logs Router

2. In **Sink details**, fill in the name of the sink and description:

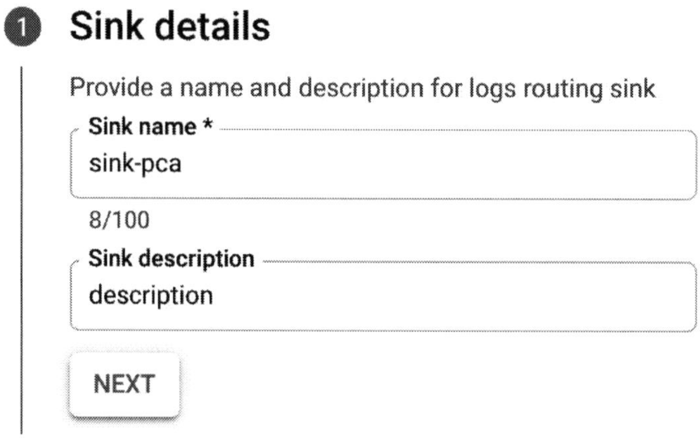

① Sink details

Provide a name and description for logs routing sink

Sink name *

sink-pca

8/100

Sink description

description

NEXT

Figure 17.24 – Sink details

3. In the **Sink destination** section, you can choose the service that you want to sink to. These include the following:

- **Cloud Logging bucket**
- **BigQuery data set**
- **Cloud Storage bucket**
- **Cloud Pub/Sub topic**
- **Splunk**
- **Other project**:

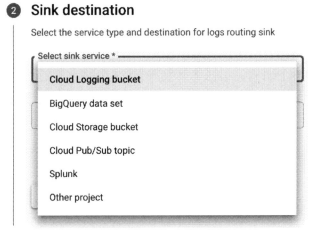

Figure 17.25 – Sink destination

4. In choosing the logs to include in the sink section, you can add a filter to define which logs you want to sink. If you leave this blank, all logs will be included. We can use the simple filter we already created. This will give us logs for GCE VM instances:

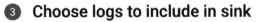

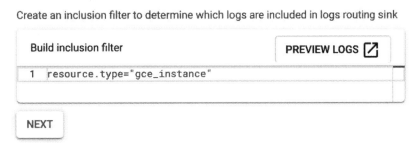

Figure 17.26 – Choose logs to include in sink

5. If you want to check the filters functions correctly, click on **PREVIEW LOGS**. This will bring you to the Logs Explorer:

Figure 17.27 – Logs preview

6. As we can see, all GCE logs are now visible, as the filter did not specify any additional parameters, such as log types.

7. Finally, you may wish to exclude some logs from the sink. In this section, you choose the exclusion filter name. By setting the exclusion rate, you can decide what percentage of the log should be filtered out. A rate of 100% means that all logs that match the filter will be excluded:

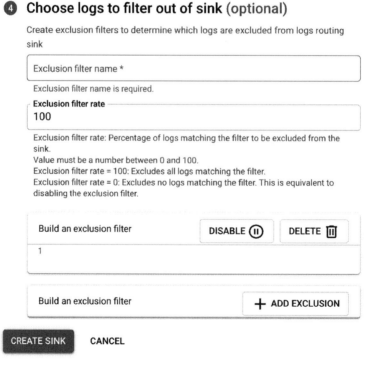

Figure 17.28 – Choose logs to filter out of sink

8. You might now wonder why I would want to export the logs. There are a couple of use cases for exporting the logs:

- BigQuery can be used for analytics and queries using SQL.

- A Pub/Sub export allows integration with third-party solutions.

- A Cloud Storage export is the most cost-effective option for archiving the logs.

You might use a dedicated **Security Information and Event Management (SIEM)** tool such as Splunk for further logs analysis.

Logging agent

The Logging agent is an application that is based on `fluentd`, and both Linux and Windows machines are supported. It allows the streaming of logs from common third-party applications and system software to Cloud Logging. The agent is included in the images for App Engine and GKE. For Compute Engine and Amazon EC2, it needs to be installed. Installation of the agent on Linux is very simple, and requires the following two commands to be executed:

```
curl -sSO https://dl.google.com/cloudagents/add-logging-agent-
repo.sh
sudo bash add-logging-agent-repo.sh --also-install
```

By default, the agent streams logs for predefined applications. `google-fluentd.conf` can be modified to indicate additional logs that should be streamed.

Ops Agent

You might wonder why you need to install two agents to get both the monitoring and logging functionality. Google is trying to solve this by introducing a single agent called the **Ops Agent**.

At the time of writing, the Ops Agent is a pre-GA offering and is not yet fully supported by Google. The Ops Agent is a combination of the Logging and Monitoring agents. It provides higher throughput and improved resource efficiency. As this still has a limited number of features supported, consult the documentation first before migrating to the Ops Agent: `https://cloud.google.com/stackdriver/docs/solutions/agents/ops-agent`.

Log-based metrics

Logs can be used to create log-based metrics. Cloud Logging can accumulate logs that are defined by the filter every time a match appears. This data is then exposed to Monitoring and can be used further to create dashboards and alert policies.

As an example, logs containing a particular 404 error message can be counted during a period of 1 minute and exposed as a metric.

The log-based metric can either be system metrics or user-defined:

- **System metrics**: These are predefined by Cloud Logging.

- **User-defined metrics**: These metrics are created by a user on a project-by-project basis, based on the filtering criteria.

In the following screenshot, we can see an example of system and user-defined metrics:

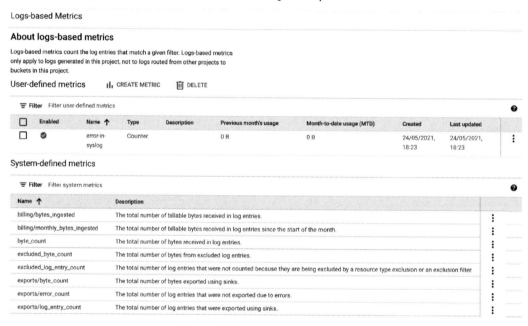

Figure 17.29 – Log-based metrics

Cloud Audit Logs

To understand better *who did what?*, *where?*, and *when?*, Cloud Audit Logs can be used. The logs are stored per project, folder, or organization, and are of the following types:

- Admin Activity
- System Event
- Data Access
- Policy Denied

The first two are enabled by default and cannot be deactivated. The third one is disabled by default, as it can generate a massive amount of information. Audit logs are generated for most of the GCP services. To get the full list of services, refer to the following documentation: `https://cloud.google.com/logging/docs/audit/`.

The logs can be accessed from the Legacy Logs Viewer, just like any other log, but specific permissions are required to view them. The following are short descriptions of each type of audit log that we mentioned previously:

- **Admin Activity audit logs**: This contains information about actions on modifying resources' metadata or configuration. These may include, for example, the creation of a VM instance or changes to the permissions. To view the logs, Logging/Logs Viewer or Project/Viewer roles are required. To see only those logs under basic filtering, choose the `activity` log type.

- **System Event audit logs**: This contains information on system events for Compute Engine. This may be, for example, the live migration of a VM instance. To view the logs, Logging/Logs Viewer or Project/Viewer roles are required. To see only those logs under basic filtering, choose the `system_events` log type.

- **Data Access audit logs**: This contains information on the creation, modification, or reading of user-provided data. To view the logs, Logging/Private Logs Viewer or Project/Owner roles are required. To see only those logs under basic filtering, choose the `data_access` log type.

- **Policy Denied audit logs**: This records logs when access is denied to a user or service account due to a security policy violation. These logs are generated by default and your Cloud project is charged for the logs storage. To view these logs, Logging/Logs Viewer or Project/Viewer roles are required.

In the following screenshot, you can see an example of filtering for the Admin Activity audit logs:

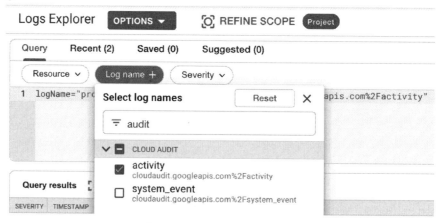

Figure 17.30 – Logs Explorer

While there is no charge for Admin Activity and System Event logs, Data Access logs can incur additional charges when enabled. BigQuery has its own Data Access logs, which are handled separately and cannot be disabled.

Activity

The audit logs can be also viewed from the **ACTIVITY** tab in the main GCP console screen, which is outside the Google Cloud operations suite console. From the main GCP console screen, click on **ACTIVITY** in the top-left corner, which will bring you to the log list, as shown in the following screenshot:

HOME PREVIEW	DASHBOARD	ACTIVITY	RECOMMENDATIONS	

Today

2:32 PM	Set IAM policy on project	service-agent-manager@system.gserviceaccount.com assigned role dialogflow.serviceAgent to serviceAccoun...	⌄
2:32 PM	google.cloud.dialogflow.v3alpha1.Agents.CreateAgent	konradclapa@gmail.com has executed google.cloud.dialogflow.v3alpha1.Agents.CreateAgent on us-central1	⌄
2:32 PM	google.cloud.dialogflow.cx.v3.SecuritySettingsService.CreateLocationSe...	konradclapa@gmail.com has executed google.cloud.dialogflow.cx.v3.SecuritySettingsService.CreateLocationS...	⌄
2:23 PM	Completed: google.api.serviceusage.v1.ServiceUsage.EnableService	google.api.serviceusage.v1.ServiceUsage.EnableService was executed on dialogflow.googleapis.com	⌄
2:23 PM	google.api.serviceusage.v1.ServiceUsage.EnableService	konradclapa@gmail.com has executed google.api.serviceusage.v1.ServiceUsage.EnableService on dialogflow.g...	⌄
2:01 PM	google.monitoring.dashboard.v1.DashboardsService.CreateDashboard	konradclapa@gmail.com has executed google.monitoring.dashboard.v1.DashboardsService.CreateDashboard ...	⌄
12:41 PM	google.longrunning.Operations.GetOperation	konradclapa@gmail.com has executed google.longrunning.Operations.GetOperation	⌄
12:41 PM	Completed: google.api.serviceusage.v1.ServiceUsage.BatchEnableServi...	konradclapa@gmail.com has executed google.api.serviceusage.v1.ServiceUsage.BatchEnableServices on servi...	⌄
12:41 PM	google.longrunning.Operations.GetOperation	konradclapa@gmail.com has executed google.longrunning.Operations.GetOperation	⌄
12:41 PM	Set IAM policy on project	service-agent-manager@system.gserviceaccount.com assigned role cloudscheduler.serviceAgent to serviceAc...	⌄
12:41 PM	Set IAM policy on project	service-agent-manager@system.gserviceaccount.com failed to set the IAM policy.	⌄
12:41 PM	Set IAM policy on project	service-agent-manager@system.gserviceaccount.com assigned role editor to serviceAccount:1094548570820...	⌄
12:41 PM	google.longrunning.Operations.GetOperation	konradclapa@gmail.com has executed google.longrunning.Operations.GetOperation	⌄
12:41 PM	google.api.serviceusage.v1.ServiceUsage.BatchEnableServices	konradclapa@gmail.com has executed google.api.serviceusage.v1.ServiceUsage.BatchEnableServices on servi...	⌄
12:30 PM	Completed: Update App Engine module	konradclapa@gmail.com updated default	⌄
12:30 PM	Update App Engine module	konradclapa@gmail.com updated default	⌄
12:21 PM	Completed: Update App Engine module	konradclapa@gmail.com updated default	⌄
12:21 PM	Update App Engine module	konradclapa@gmail.com updated default	⌄

Figure 17.31 – ACTIVITY

The logs are abbreviated and can be filtered by categories, resources, and time periods. By selecting the entries, you can see further details. To narrow down the list of logs, you can use predefined filters, which you will find in the top-right corner. Select the filter and press **OK** to apply, as shown in the following screenshot:

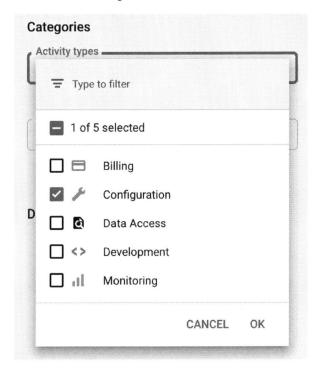

Figure 17.32 – Activity categories

Retention

Retention defines how long the logs are stored in Cloud Logging. After the stipulated period, the logs are removed. Depending on the log types, the retention time differs. Refer to the following list of log types and their retention periods:

- **Admin Activity**: 400 days
- **Data Access**: 30 days
- **System Event**: 400 days
- **Policy Denied**: 30 days

Note that the logs can be exported and archived for longer periods. We have explained how to export logs in the *Exporting logs* section of this chapter.

Google Cloud's operations suite for GKE

Google Cloud's operations suite for GKE is an evolution of GKE Legacy Logging and Monitoring that was deprecated and decommissioned on March 31, 2021.

Cloud Operations for GKE provides observability capabilities for GKE clusters both at the cluster and workload level. It shows you all the most important GKE cluster resources and allows you to drill down to the logs generated by the workload containers.

For all new GKE clusters, the feature is enabled by default. You have, however, a choice to decide what level of monitoring and logging you want to have. Note you can either limit it to the logging and monitoring of the system (a Kubernetes cluster) only or also include the workload (application). All options are visible in the GKE cluster provisioning wizard after clicking on the dropdown in the **Select logging and monitoring type** form. Those options available are as follows:

- **System and workload logging and monitoring**
- **System logging and monitoring only (beta)**
- **System and workload logging only (Monitoring disabled)**
- **System monitoring only (Logging disabled):**

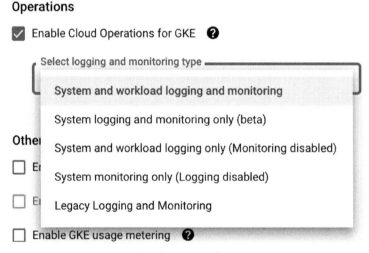

Figure 17.33 – GKE logging and monitoring types

Even though **Legacy and Logging and Monitoring** is still visible on the screen, it should not be used anymore.

GKE dashboard

> **Tip**
> Note that at the time of writing this book, Google Cloud's operations suite for GKE is available only for GKE clusters running on Google Cloud. This means that it does not include GKE clusters running on-premises or bare-metal servers.

The GKE dashboard is a single pane of glass for the most important metrics for the GKE clusters, including the following:

- Timeline with opened alerts for the GKE clusters

- Metrics such as CPU, memory, and disk utilization for the namespaces, nodes, workloads, services, pods, and containers

- Logs for pods and containers:

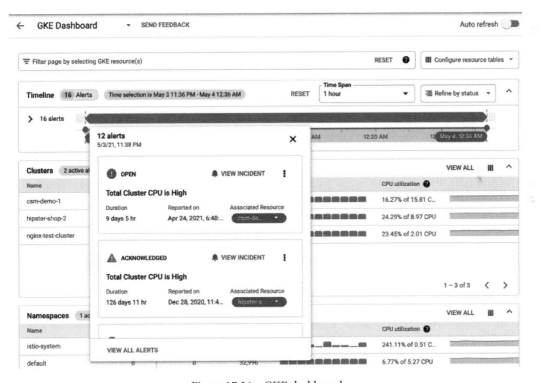

Figure 17.34 – GKE dashboard

The GKE dashboard consolidates all the essential information about your GKE cluster and workloads in a single window. It is very handy to navigate through the Kubernetes resources and pinpoint the issue affecting your application.

APM

APM is a set of tools that developers use to give them some insight into how fast and how reliably they can run an application. It consists of three services:

- Trace
- Debugger
- Profiler

These tools are integrated into the code of the application. The application does not need to be hosted on GCP but can run in any cloud or even on-premises, as long as connectivity is available. APM originates from Google's **Site Reliability Engineering** (**SRE**) team toolset. So, it is high time that we got into the shoes of SRE!

Trace

Cloud Trace allows you to track latencies in your microservices application. It shows you the overall time of the application responses but can also show detailed delays for each of the microservices. This allows you to pinpoint the root cause of the latency.

The traces are displayed in the GCP console, and analysis reports can be generated. By default, it is installed on **Google App Engine** (**GAE**) standard, but it can be used with GCE, GKE, GAE flexible, and non-GCP machines. The tracing mechanism needs to be incorporated using the Cloud Trace SDK or API.

Debugger

This allows you to debug errors in the code of your application, without stopping the application. Developers can request a real-time snapshot of a running application, capturing the call stack and local variables. Debug log points can be injected into the code to display additional information. These can even be done in production, without affecting the end users.

By default, it is installed on GAE standard, but it can be used with GCE, GKE, GAE flexible, and non-GCP machines. It does not require a Logging agent.

Profiler

Cloud Profiler shows you how many resources your code consumes. With the changes in the code in your application, there may be an unexpected rise in the demand for resources. Profiler allows you to pinpoint those issues, even in production. It uses a piece of code called the **profiler agent** that is attached to the main code of your application, and it periodically sends information on resource usage. It currently supports Java, Go, and Node.js, and can be used with GCE, GKE, GAE flexible, and non-GCP machines. The following screenshot presents an example of Cloud Profiler with the CPU profile:

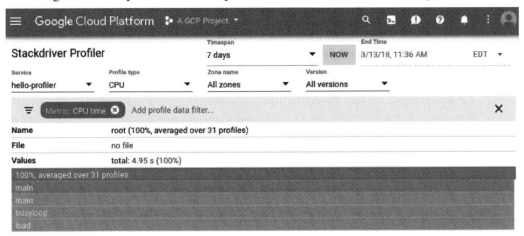

Figure 17.35 – Profiler (Source: https://cloud.google.com/profiler/docs/quickstart. License: https://creativecommons.org/licenses/by/4.0/legalcode)

Error Reporting

Error Reporting allows you to collect and aggregate errors that are produced by your applications in a single place. The collected errors can be grouped and displayed in a centralized interface. This way, you can see how many crashes have occurred over a specific time period.

The service works in a very similar way to Cloud Logging, but it allows you to filter only the most important errors and pinpoint the root cause of the crash. Error Reporting works with Cloud Functions, App Engine, GCE, GKE, and AWS EC2. It is, by default, enabled for the App Engine standard environment. Multiple languages, such as Go, Java, .NET, Node. js, PHP, Python, and Ruby are supported. There are two ways to leverage error reporting:

- You can use the Cloud Logging API and send properly formatted error messages.
- You can call the dedicated Error Reporting API.

Information in Error Reporting is retained for 30 days.

Summary

In this chapter, we learned about Google Cloud's operations suite and how to monitor GCP services, resources, and applications. There are three main functionalities that we looked into: **Monitoring**, **Logging**, and **APM**.

To enhance monitoring and logging capabilities, install agents on the instances. Monitoring allows predefined metrics to be monitored. Logging allows you to create log-based metrics. Alert policies can be created on conditions, and they can send notifications to endpoints of your choosing. Tracing facilitates an understanding of the latency of your application components, including microservices and load balancers. Debugging allows you to look at a snapshot of the code that is causing an error, without stopping the application. Profiler shows how many resources are used by different components of the application. Finally, Error Reporting aggregates the error logs of the application and displays them on timescale charts.

In the exam, some questions may refer you to several case studies with which you should be familiar before you take the exam. These case studies explain fictitious business and solution concepts. In the next chapter, we will cover how to find these case studies, and we will look at an example case study and analyze it, in order to design an appropriate solution.

Further reading

If you want to learn more about Google Cloud's operations suite, use the official Google documentation:

- **Google Cloud's operations suite docs**: `https://cloud.google.com/stackdriver/docs/`

- **Monitoring agent**: `https://cloud.google.com/monitoring/agent/`

- **Logging agent**: `https://cloud.google.com/logging/docs/agent/`

- **Debugger**: `https://cloud.google.com/debugger/docs/setup/python`

- **Profiler**: `https://cloud.google.com/profiler/docs/about-profiler`

- **Error Reporting**: `https://cloud.google.com/error-reporting/docs/setup/compute-engine`

Section 4: Exam Focus

This section will focus on an example case study and mock questions. This will help you to understand the exam in a more practical manner.

This part of the book comprises the following chapters:

- *Chapter 18, Case Studies*
- *Chapter 19, Test Your Knowledge*

18
Case Studies

As we mentioned way back in *Chapter 1, GCP Cloud Architect Professional*, the Google Professional Architect exam involves referring to a certain set of case studies. Around 30% of the exam questions will relate to one or more of these case studies. Although you have access to these case studies before you sit the exam, you will not know which case studies will appear in the exam. However, you will have access to them in the exam, so there is no need to memorize each one! Think of it as Google being nice to us and giving us extra preparation material. During the exam, when you are asked a question about a case study, you will have a split screen and will be able to view the case study and question simultaneously.

We will cover the following topics in the chapter:

- Understanding how to approach the exam case studies
- What are we looking for in the case studies?
- Additional case studies

Understanding how to approach the exam case studies

The questions will clearly state the case study that you need to refer to. At the time of writing, there are four case studies available from the exam guide web page. Although some of the names may be familiar from the previous version of the exam, these have changed significantly since the original exam's release:

- **Mountkirk Games**: `https://services.google.com/fh/files/blogs/master_case_study_mountkirk_games.pdf`

- **Helicopter Racing League**: `https://services.google.com/fh/files/blogs/master_case_study_helicopter_racing_league.pdf`

- **EHR Healthcare**: `https://services.google.com/fh/files/blogs/master_case_study_ehr_healthcare.pdf`

- **TerramEarth**: `https://services.google.com/fh/files/blogs/master_case_study_terramearth.pdf`

It is important to read over these case studies before the exam. You should make this a part of your study plan. Each case study refers to a business that needs to integrate with **Google Cloud Platform (GCP)**. You will find a business overview and a solution concept, and it is your job to map these concepts and requirements to GCP services.

The main objective, when looking through these case studies, is to try to allocate keywords that you can map to GCP services. However, there is also a lot of information that is there simply to fill out the case study. It is important to separate what information is not needed and what is important. For example, if there is a requirement to build a reliable and reproducible environment, it might be wise to start thinking along the lines of Cloud Deployment Manager, which offers you a repeatable deployment process. Likewise, if the technical requirements suggest the company wants to be able to scale up or down based on demand, then we might be inclined to think of autoscalers, load balancers, and managed instance groups. Understanding the use case of each service is key to the case studies. The good thing is that we get to review the case studies upfront!

In this chapter, we will look at one of the aforementioned case studies in detail to try and show exactly what they are looking for from you in the exam, as well as how you should look to process the information you receive and try to map it to relevant GCP services.

> **Important Note**
>
> While you are reading the case study, it is recommended that you also refer to the GCP solutions page: `https://cloud.google.com/solutions`.
>
> Additionally, it is recommended that you refer to the GCP architecture center for the reference architecture: `https://cloud.google.com/architecture/`.

What are we looking for in the case studies?

Let's look closely at one of the case studies presented by Google Cloud. We have selected Mountkirk Games. On the initial first pass of reading this case study, we can see that it's broken down into six distinct sections, so let's look at each in more detail:

- Company overview
- Solution concept
- Existing technical environment
- Business requirements
- Technical requirements
- Executive statement

The excerpts in each section reference the text of the case studies. As a reminder, the full documents can be viewed at the URLs mentioned at the beginning of this chapter.

Company overview

Let's look at the company overview:

> *"Mountkirk Games makes online, session-based, multiplayer games for mobile platforms. They have recently started expanding to other platforms after successfully migrating their on-premises environments to Google Cloud.*
>
> *Their most recent endeavor is to create a retro-style first-person shooter (FPS) game that allows hundreds of simultaneous players to join a geo-specific digital arena from multiple platforms and locations. A real-time digital banner will display a global leaderboard of all the top players across every active arena."*

Source: `https://services.google.com/fh/files/blogs/master_case_study_mountkirk_games.pdf`.

License: `https://creativecommons.org/licenses/by/4.0/legalcode`.

So, what information can be taken from here that will help us form a solution architecture? Well, we can see this overview is driving us to think about mobile platforms, so we should start to think about a starting point for architecture for mobile games, as well as what should be the frontend architecture and what should be the backend architecture. We can see that we need to be able to cope with multiplayer requirements, which may require complicated interrelated tables. We also need to store sessions, so we need to look into the kind of configuration we need for this, as well as some other key elements such as multiple platforms and locations. We also require a leaderboard, which we can do by breaking down components. Finally, we should be thinking about the user experience. The speed of the queries going to our backend has a direct impact on the end users, as well as the success of our game overall.

The first paragraph informs us that the core business is online games for mobile platforms. Immediately, we should be aware that mobile games platforms generate a large amount of real-time data and have a large number of devices connecting to them, all of which will come from different types of connections (Wi-Fi, 3G-5G, and so on). This is a pretty unique industry.

The second paragraph starts to hint at some potential GCP services. For example, it mentions that there will be a real-time digital banner with a leaderboard of top players. We can try to translate this into GCP services that fit this architecture:

- We will need a streaming service. What service do we know can handle streaming processing patterns? If you are thinking about **Pub/Sub**, then that would be correct.

- How can we transform these events into a leaderboard? We may need a **Dataflow** pipeline to cleanse the data and ensure the message is well formed before transforming it into structured data.

- That transformation could then be added to a **BigQuery** table format that matches someone's username to the number of *kills* to list the top players.

- **Data Studio** could also be used to create an interactive leaderboard that consumes and presents data from BigQuery.

This is just something to get us thinking about architecture. There may be arguments that we don't require Dataflow and that BigQuery could directly query data from a cloud storage bucket, but would this be a scalable design? Would this require us to revisit this if events from mobile devices were to introduce added fields?

Solution concept

Now, let's look at the solution concept:

> *"Mountkirk Games is building a new multiplayer game that they expect to be very popular. They plan to deploy the game's backend on Google Kubernetes Engine so they can scale rapidly and use Google's global load balancer to route players to the closest regional game arenas. To keep the global leaderboard in sync, they plan to use a multi-region Spanner cluster."*

Source: `https://services.google.com/fh/files/blogs/master_case_study_mountkirk_games.pdf`.

License: `https://creativecommons.org/licenses/by/4.0/legalcode`.

The solution concept only offers us a few lines of information, yet it still provides us with key information. They are telling us that there are some services they require the design to use, but why do they wish to use these? Additionally, we should be thinking about which services should be designed as the frontend and backend components of a typical gaming infrastructure.

Let's take the frontend as an example. They wish to use Google Kubernetes Engine (GKE) but there are various other options they could use. They could use App Engine or Cloud Run, which would also offer full integration with cloud load balancing. However, both of these are fully managed, while GKE offers developers more control and there is also a history of games being deployed on a massive scale on GKE using the *dedicated gaming server* approach:

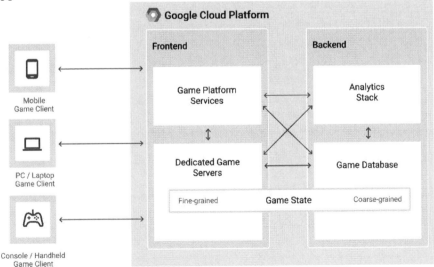

Figure 18.1 – Gaming architecture (courtesy of https://cloud.google.com/architecture/mobile-gaming-analysis-telemetry, License: https://creativecommons.org/licenses/by/4.0/legalcode)

Existing technical environment

Now, let's review the existing environment and requirements:

"The existing environment was recently migrated to Google Cloud, and five games came across using lift-and-shift virtual machine migrations, with a few minor exceptions.

Each new game exists in an isolated Google Cloud project nested below a folder that maintains most of the permissions and network policies. Legacy games with low traffic have been consolidated into a single project. There are also separate environments for development and testing."

Source: `https://services.google.com/fh/files/blogs/master_case_study_mountkirk_games.pdf.`

License: `https://creativecommons.org/licenses/by/4.0/legalcode.`

Business requirements

Now, let's look at the business requirements:

"Support multiple gaming platforms.

Support multiple regions.

Support rapid iteration of game features. Minimize latency.

Optimize for dynamic scaling.

Use managed services and pooled resources.

Minimize costs."

Source: `https://services.google.com/fh/files/blogs/master_case_study_mountkirk_games.pdf.`

License: `https://creativecommons.org/licenses/by/4.0/legalcode.`

Technical requirements

We now have several technical requirements:

"Dynamically scale based on game activity.

Publish scoring data on a near-real-time global leaderboard.

Store game activity logs in structured files for future analysis.

Use GPU processing to render graphics server-side for multi-platform support.

Support eventual migration of legacy games to this new platform."

Source: `https://services.google.com/fh/files/blogs/master_case_study_mountkirk_games.pdf`.

License: `https://creativecommons.org/licenses/by/4.0/legalcode`.

What kind of services spring to mind when you read these requirements? There are some keywords or phrases on almost every line: dynamically scale, logs, migration, and latency, to name a few. We should map these to GCP services. For example, if we can see requirements to scale on game activity, we may start to think of services that can meet this demand. For example, Pub/Sub is capable of ingesting events from mobile devices and scale as required.

Executive summary

The final section of our case study is the executive summary:

"Our last game was the first time we used Google Cloud, and it was a tremendous success. We were able to analyze player behavior and game telemetry in ways that we never could before. This success allowed us to bet on a full migration to the cloud and to start building all-new games using cloud-native design principles. Our new game is our most ambitious to date and will open up doors for us to support more gaming platforms beyond mobile. Latency is our top priority, although cost management is the next most important challenge. As with our first cloud-based game, we have grown to expect the cloud to enable advanced analytics capabilities so we can rapidly iterate on our deployments of bug fixes and new functionality."

Source: `https://services.google.com/fh/files/blogs/master_case_study_mountkirk_games.pdf`.

License: `https://creativecommons.org/licenses/by/4.0/legalcode`.

There is a clear message that latency and cost management are the primary concern for the executives. They are also focused on releasing new iterations as quickly as possible and this should draw our minds to DevOps principles. Analytics is also mentioned as something important, but could this help us with the cost savings? Investing in a proper design related to our analytics output format can lead to significant cost savings. Can **BigQuery** help us here?

Forming a solution

After the first pass, we have managed to extract several keywords and map them to specific GCP services. The next step is to try and form a solution out of this. How do these services link to each other to make a usable design that will relate to the requirements set out by the company? The exam will not ask you to make an end-to-end solution – it will ask you which services are more appropriate to meet the needs of the specific question. However, having an idea of how to do this will also stand you in good stead as a GCP cloud architect.

The analytics platform

One of the key takeaways from the case study is that we will be dealing with mobile data streaming at a high rate, but we will also be dealing with some batch data. Let's take a quick look at the Google Solutions web page for guidance. If we look at the mobile guide at `https://cloud.google.com/architecture/mobile-gaming-analysis-telemetry`, we will see that there is a reference architecture for building a mobile gaming analytics platform. Let's focus on how we can handle real-time events from mobile devices. If we look at the following diagram, we can see that it mirrors our requirements:

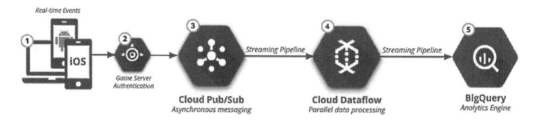

Figure 18.2 – Real-time processing of events (courtesy of https://cloud.google.com/architecture/mobile-gaming-analysis-telemetry, License: https://creativecommons.org/licenses/by/4.0/legalcode)

We can see that using Cloud Pub/Sub helps us process data on the fly with its event-driven design. This is an ideal service for ingesting real-time event streams and can be consumed by multiple destinations. Pub/Sub also acts as a queue to fetch new messages and push them to the next service in the pipeline. This is performed instantly as the messages arrive.

We also have to accommodate batch data. Again, this reference architecture shows us exactly how to accomplish this. Mobile devices can upload their data to Cloud Storage, which is a cost-effective way to store object data:

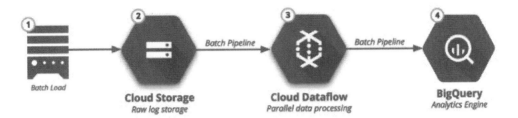

Figure 18.3 – Batch processing events and logs (courtesy of https://cloud.google.com/solutions/mobile/ mobile-gaming-analysis-telemetry, License: https://creativecommons.org/licenses/by/4.0/legalcode)

The next step in this process is Cloud Dataflow, which is acting as our data processing service. We can create separate pipeline jobs to process both real-time and batch data to ensure the data is well formed and matches the BigQuery schema. Dataflow has a time windowing trigger that allows it to process events based on the actual time they occur, as opposed to when they were sent or received.

Finally, BigQuery helps us with our analytics requirements and reporting large data. BigQuery is a managed service and it can provide rapid scaling, both of which are demanded by the executive summary.

The following diagram shows an example of a Dataflow pipeline processing data and mapping our *userId to the number of kills* and presenting it in a BigQuery table format. We can now visually see how this can help meet our requirement of a real-time leaderboard:

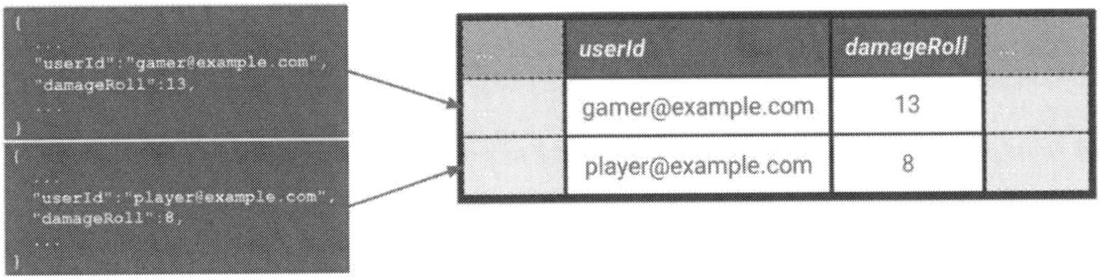

...	userId	damageRoll	...
	gamer@example.com	13	
	player@example.com	8	

Figure 18.4 – Batch processing events and logs (courtesy of https://cloud.google.com/solutions/mobile/ mobile-gaming-analysis-telemetry, License: https://creativecommons.org/licenses/by/4.0/legalcode)

The frontend platform

Our frontend requirements are pretty clear. We need to use GKE to scale rapidly and also use a global load balancer to route players to a regional game arena.

We touched on this earlier in this chapter, but why are we specifically required to use GKE when we have other options that may meet requirements, such as using managed services? Well, in short, Google recommends using Kubernetes to deploy production-scale fleets of **dedicated game servers**. These dedicated servers provide the game logic and help minimize the latency perceived by the user. The client game apps will generally communicate directly with these game servers.

Using GKE, we can design a scalable architecture for running session-based multiplayer servers. This architecture allows us to meet another key technical requirement by dynamically scaling on game activity. A scaling manager process will automatically start and stop VM instances that are used as GKE nodes, as demand requires. All of the machine's configurations can be handled by managed instance groups.

The backend platform

Our backend services will only interface with frontend and backend services; that is, clients will not interact directly with these services. We are also required to use Cloud Spanner to keep our leaderboard in sync. Cloud Spanner will provide global consistency that keeps player history or inventory for players all over the world. However, Cloud Spanner alone is not suitable for maintaining a frequently updated leaderboard. For this, we should look to introduce something such as Redis and periodically save high scores to long-term storage as necessary. By using Cloud **Memorystore**, we can achieve this requirement:

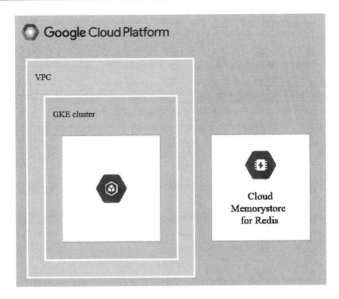

Figure 18.5 – Leaderboard infrastructure (courtesy of https://cloud.google.com/architecture/using-memorystore-for-redis-as-a-leaderboard, License: https://creativecommons.org/licenses/by/4.0/legalcode)

The preceding diagram shows the infrastructure of a leaderboard. A leaderboard can consist of a GKE cluster inside a VPC network and a separate Memorystore instance.

Other considerations

In the technical requirements, it was noted that the eventual migration of legacy games should be supported in our design. We have been told legacy games have been consolidated into a single project, which is helpful as we should have these environments segregated, and we can destroy this after the migration has taken place. Google offers a migration guide for this, which can be found at `https://cloud.google.com/architecture/dedicated-game-server-migration-guide`.

Summary of Mountkirk

Now that we have formed a solution, we can be confident that we understand the business needs and how to use the appropriate services. You should be mindful not to expect a simple link between what we see in the case study and what the question is. It will not always be as simple as, for example, which storage service best fits the requirements. Some questions may reference the case study but could add additional requirements that do not appear in the case study; for example, what IAM policy could Mountkirk use to isolate development and production? Nothing in the case study specifically mentions IAM, but we should still expect to see questions like these.

Additional case studies

We would also like to look at the other three case studies available at the time of writing. We hope you now have a clear idea of how to break these case studies down and understand that the key is to locate keywords that help us map to GCP services. We will not go into so much depth for the other cases, but we hope you will begin to form solutions without guidance as you read through the case studies.

EHR Healthcare

We will now look at the EHR Healthcare case study. Again, we will review what can be gleaned from the online documentation. At the end of the case study, we will provide an analysis. We would like you to write down the services that jump out to you as you are reading and compare your findings to our analysis:

Company overview:

> "EHR Healthcare is a leading provider of electronic health record software to the medical industry. EHR Healthcare provides their software as a service to multi-national medical offices, hospitals, and insurance providers."

Solution concept:

> "Due to rapid changes in the healthcare and insurance industry, EHR Healthcare's business has been growing exponentially year over year. They need to be able to scale their environment, adapt their disaster recovery plan, and roll out new continuous deployment capabilities to update their software at a fast pace. Google Cloud has been chosen to replace their current colocation facilities."

Existing technical environment:

> "EHR's software is currently hosted in multiple colocation facilities. The lease on one of the data centers is about to expire.
>
> Customer-facing applications are web-based, and many have recently been containerized to run on a group of Kubernetes clusters. Data is stored in a mixture of relational and NoSQL databases (MySQL, MS SQL Server, Redis, and MongoDB).
>
> EHR is hosting several legacy file- and API-based integrations with insurance providers on-premises. These systems are scheduled to be replaced over the next several years. There is no plan to upgrade or move these systems at the current time.

Users are managed via Microsoft Active Directory. Monitoring is currently being done via various open source tools. Alerts are sent via email and are often ignored."

Business requirements:

"On-board new insurance providers as quickly as possible.

Provide a minimum of 99.9% availability for all customer-facing systems.

Provide centralized visibility and proactive action on system performance and usage.

Increase ability to provide insights into healthcare trends.

Reduce latency to all customers.

Maintain regulatory compliance.

Decrease infrastructure administration costs.

Make predictions and generate reports on industry trends based on provider data."

Technical requirements:

"Maintain legacy interfaces to insurance providers with connectivity to both on-premises systems and cloud providers.

Provide a consistent way to manage customer-facing applications that are container-based.

Provide a secure and high-performance connection between on-premises systems and Google Cloud.

Provide consistent logging, log retention, monitoring, and alerting capabilities.

Maintain and manage multiple container-based environments.

Dynamically scale and provision new environments.

Create interfaces to ingest and process data from new providers."

Executive statement:

> *"Our on-premises strategy has worked for years but has required a major investment of time and money in training our team on distinctly different systems, managing similar but separate environments, and responding to outages. Many of these outages have been a result of misconfigured systems, inadequate capacity to manage spikes in traffic, and inconsistent monitoring practices. We want to use Google Cloud to leverage a scalable, resilient platform that can span multiple environments seamlessly and provide a consistent and stable user experience that positions us for future growth."*

Source: `https://services.google.com/fh/files/blogs/master_case_ study_ehr_healthcare.pdf`.

License: `https://creativecommons.org/licenses/by/4.0/legalcode`.

Analysis

Again, there's a lot of information to take in here. But let's focus on getting the keywords and try to form a picture about which services would be used.

Let's try to summarize what this is telling us. We know that they are providing health record software to the medical industry and we know it is providing SaaS solutions to medical offices and more. Let's take a closer look at the case study. A few things should stick out:

- They are moving from an on-premises infrastructure to a cloud-based one and have containerized their web-based applications. They also want to decrease infrastructure administration costs while dynamically scaling when needed. Scaling is also something mentioned in our executive summary as causing issues and the customer-facing applications must be container-based. We should think about **GKE** here. GKE offers a simple way to use their existing containerized applications to deploy and scale their customer-facing web apps. Using GKE means that the infrastructure underneath GKE is not only hosted but managed as well, providing the cost savings from the hosting they require. In addition to this, we can deploy our web app as a load-balanced set of replicas that can scale to the customer's needs.

- Looking at the business requirements, one of the things that quickly jumps out is that they must centralize visibility on their system performance and usage. We can also see that there is a similar requirement in the technical requirements where they need consistent monitoring and alerting capabilities. These should scream out **Google Cloud operations**. Cloud Logging and Cloud Monitoring allow us to search, analyze, monitor, and alert on data and events. They also require log retention. For cost-saving, we could utilize **Cloud Storage**.

- They also require a high-performance connection between their on-premises systems and GCP, so we should be thinking about **Google Cloud Hybrid Connectivity** options here, specifically around dedicated interconnect, which is synonymous with *high performance*.

- The solution concept mentions adapting their **Disaster Recovery (DR)** plan. It also mentions that data is stored on a mixture of relational and NoSQL databases. When we think of DR with databases, we should be thinking about multi-region, highly available instances. **Cloud SQL** instances offer high availability through synchronous replication to persistent disks in different zones.

- The solution concept also mentions continuous deployment capabilities. At this point, we should be thinking about all things CI/CD and **Cloud Build** and **Artifact Registry**. These two products will also help with the requirement to maintain and manage multiple container-based environments.

- The solution also needs to maintain regulatory compliance. HIPPA, for example, is a US set of standards for protecting health information that can identify individuals. To comply with this, we can use **Cloud Identity** for customer organizations. As they are currently using an Active Directory database for user management, we can easily integrate with Cloud Identity to use groups to access project resources and require authentication to modify or use them.

- They are also looking to ingest and process data from new providers. Can we think about what GCP services may help us? Yes – **Pub/Sub** for ingesting? **BigQuery** for processing?

What other services jump out at you when you look at this case study? Perhaps you have noticed a requirement for predicting industry trends and you are beginning to think about BigQuery ML. Try to think about how these all work together. This particular case study seems to be heavily focused on scaling and alerting, so think about how GKE and Google Cloud operations can help here.

TerramEarth

We will now look at the TerramEarth case study. Again, we will review what can be gleaned from the online documentation. At the end of the case study, we will provide an analysis. We would like you to write down the services that jump out to you as you are reading and compare your findings to our analysis:

Company overview:

> *"TerramEarth manufactures heavy equipment for the mining and agricultural industries. They currently have over 500 dealers and service centers in 100 countries. Their mission is to build products that make their customers more productive."*

Solution concept:

> *"There are 2 million TerramEarth vehicles in operation currently, and we see 20% yearly growth. Vehicles collect telemetry data from many sensors during operation. A small subset of critical data is transmitted from the vehicles in real time to facilitate fleet management. The rest of the sensor data is collected, compressed, and uploaded daily when the vehicles return to home base. Each vehicle usually generates 200 to 500 megabytes of data per day."*

Existing technical environment:

> *"TerramEarth's vehicle data aggregation and analysis infrastructure resides in Google Cloud and serves clients from all around the world. A growing amount of sensor data is captured from their two main manufacturing plants and sent to private data centers that contain their legacy inventory and logistics management systems. The private data centers have multiple network interconnects configured to Google Cloud. The web frontend for dealers and customers is running in Google Cloud and allows access to stock management and analytics."*

Business requirements:

> *"Predict and detect vehicle malfunction and rapidly ship parts to dealerships for just-in-time repair where possible.*
>
> *Decrease cloud operational costs and adapt to seasonality.*
>
> *Increase speed and reliability of development workflow.*

Allow remote developers to be productive without compromising code or data security.

Create a flexible and scalable platform for developers to create custom API services for dealers and partners."

Technical requirements:

"Create a new abstraction layer for HTTP API access to their legacy systems to enable a gradual move into the cloud without disrupting operations.

Modernize all CI/CD pipelines to allow developers to deploy container-based workloads in highly scalable environments.

Allow developers to run experiments without compromising security and governance requirements.

Create a self-service portal for internal and partner developers to create new projects, request resources for data analytics jobs, and centrally manage access to the API endpoints.

Use cloud-native solutions for keys and secrets management and optimize for identity-based access.

Improve and standardize tools necessary for application and network monitoring and troubleshooting."

Executive statement:

"Our competitive advantage has always been our focus on the customer, with our ability to provide excellent customer service and minimize vehicle downtimes. After moving multiple systems into Google Cloud, we are seeking new ways to provide best-in-class online fleet management services to our customers and improve the operations of our dealerships. Our 5-year strategic plan is to create a partner ecosystem of new products by enabling access to our data, increasing autonomous operation capabilities of our vehicles, and creating a path to move the remaining legacy systems to the cloud."

Source: https://services.google.com/fh/files/blogs/master_case_study_terramearth.pdf.

License: https://creativecommons.org/licenses/by/4.0/legalcode.

Analysis

The first thing we should be conscious of is that we are looking at a company where telemetry data is particularly important. We need to automatically collect geolocation and other sensor data from a large fleet of vehicles, which means we want to derive meaning from that data to make it productive for the business. We can process telemetric data by using a pipeline. We also need to look at what products we can use for each processing state. Let's get started:

- **Data input**: We should think of **Pub/Sub**, **BigQuery**, **Cloud Storage** import or streaming transfers, and **Cloud Logging**. Pub/Sub is an excellent choice for this scenario as it delivers real-time and reliable messaging in one global service.

- **Processing**: We should think of **Dataflow** and **Pub/Sub** here. This stage is where we transform the data into a format that is appropriate for storage. Incoming data can be processed in two modes – streaming or batch. In terms of mapping to our solution concept, this can be in real time for our critical data; the rest of the sensor data can be uploaded daily. Dataflow can process both streamed data and batch data.

- **Storage**: We should think of **Cloud Storage**, **BigQuery**, or **Bigtable**. Here, we will store long-term data.

- **Visualization and analysis**: We should think of **BigQuery** and **Cloud SQL**.

What other key points stick out and what services would be a good match? APIs are mentioned a few times in the scenario – for developers to create custom API services and a self-service portal for internal and partner developers. Our minds could be thinking about **Cloud Endpoints** or **Apigee** and which service is a more natural fit for these requirements. In this scenario, Apigee could be a more appropriate solution. Although the Cloud Endpoints portal allows us to create a developer portal that can produce a web page that can interact with our APIs, this service will only work on GCP. The requirements state that we should also support partner developers. The Apigee documentation tells us that "*The developer portal is the face of your API program, providing everything that internal, partner, and third-party developers need.*"

Security is, of course, a key concern of our company. They also specify in the requirements that they wish to "*Use cloud-native solutions for keys and secrets management and optimize for identity-based access.*" We know that Cloud **Key Management Service (KMS)** can support a range of compliance mandates that require specific key management procedures. This is done in a scalable and cloud-native way. For identity-based access, we should be thinking of **Cloud Identity**.

Finally, predictions are referenced in the requirements. We should consider ML services to meet these requirements.

Helicopter Racing League

We will now look at the Helicopter Racing League case study. Again, we will review what can be found in the online documentation. At the end of the case study, we will provide an analysis. We would like you to write down the services that jump out to you as you are reading and compare your findings to our analysis.

Company overview:

> *"Helicopter Racing League (HRL) is a global sports league for competitive helicopter racing. Each year HRL holds the world championship and several regional league competitions where teams compete to earn a spot in the world championship. HRL offers a paid service to stream the races all over the world with live telemetry and predictions throughout each race."*

Solution concept:

> *"HRL wants to migrate their existing service to a new platform to expand their use of managed AI and ML services to facilitate race predictions. Additionally, as new fans engage with the sport, particularly in emerging regions, they want to move the serving of their content, both real-time and recorded, closer to their users."*

Existing technical environment:

> *"HRL is a public cloud-first company; the core of their mission-critical applications runs on their current public cloud provider. Video recording and editing are performed at the race tracks, and the content is encoded and transcoded, where needed, in the cloud.*
>
> *Enterprise-grade connectivity and local compute are provided by truck-mounted mobile data centers. Their race prediction services are hosted exclusively on their existing public cloud provider. Their existing technical environment is as follows:*
>
> *Existing content is stored in an object storage service on their existing public cloud provider.*
>
> *Video encoding and transcoding are performed on VMs created for each job.*
>
> *Race predictions are performed using TensorFlow running on VMs in the current public cloud provider."*

Business requirements:

> "HRL's owners want to expand their predictive capabilities and reduce latency for their viewers in emerging markets. Their requirements are as follows:
>
> Support the ability to expose the predictive models to partners.
>
> Increase predictive capabilities during and before races:
>
> Race results.
>
> Mechanical failures.
>
> Crowd sentiment.
>
> Increase telemetry and create additional insights.
>
> Measure fan engagement with new predictions.
>
> Enhance global availability and quality of the broadcasts.
>
> Increase the number of concurrent viewers.
>
> Minimize operational complexity.
>
> Ensure compliance with regulations.
>
> Create a merchandising revenue stream."

Technical requirements:

> "Maintain or increase prediction throughput and accuracy.
>
> Reduce viewer latency.
>
> Increase transcoding performance.
>
> Create real-time analytics of viewer consumption patterns and engagement.
>
> Create a data mart to process large volumes of race data."

Executive statement:

> *"Our CEO, S. Hawke, wants to bring high-adrenaline racing to fans all around the world. We listen to our fans, and they want enhanced video streams that include predictions of events within the race (for example, overtaking). Our current platform allows us to predict race outcomes but lacks the facility to support real-time predictions during races and the capacity to process season-long results."*

Source: `https://services.google.com/fh/files/blogs/master_case_study_helicopter_racing_league.pdf.`

License: `https://creativecommons.org/licenses/by/4.0/legalcode.`

Analysis

The first thing you should notice in the requirements is that this is a case study where **Machine Learning (ML)** is really important. Their drive is to provide in-game predictions for their race cars. An ML model can be deployed to production to service these predictions – offering either **offline or online predictions**. Of course, here, it is clear we require online predictions.

Again, to meet these requirements, we must think about how we ingest the data and how it is transformed and enriched. As soon as we see ML as a requirement, we should think of **TensorFlow**, which will implement and train the ML model. We also need something such as **Pub/Sub** to ingest the events and **Dataflow** to process the data. **Cloud Machine Learning Engine** can be used for feedback predation analysis. We can also think about the **Vertex AI platform**, which is a serverless platform that can train, tune, and serve TensorFlow models at scale. This can assist us with our online predictions.

Latency is also a concern here and the company wants to reduce this for their viewers as much as possible. For real-time predictions, it becomes really important as the viewer will expect this immediately. To optimize our models for serving, we should think about using smaller models by reducing the number of input features and ensuring all the irrelevant parts of the model are removed. Additionally, we should think about storing the events in a low-latency database such as **Bigtable**.

What else can you find that sticks out to you? We would be interested to hear about your designs!

Summary

At this point, you have an overview of what to expect regarding the exam's case studies. In this chapter, we broke down the Mountkirk case study section by section and identified the keywords that we can map to services. For the remaining case studies, we hope you have been able to go through each one in its entirety and also extract the keywords.

We can't provide answers in this chapter but we want to show that keywords can be mapped to services, which will give you an advantage for the exam. It also forces us to make sure we understand a service and what its main use case is. As we can see, data is a very important topic in these use cases. Make sure that you understand the options for processing the data and ensuring it is in a format that can be used for analytics. This is your final reminder to use `https://cloud.google.com/architecture` as this can be extremely good for tying your use cases to services.

> **Exam Tip**
>
> Remember, there is no need to provide an end-to-end solution design to be successful in this exam, but understanding the use cases of each GCP service is a key objective.

Further reading

To learn more about what was covered in this chapter, take a look at the following resources:

- **Solutions**: `https://cloud.google.com/solutions/`
- **Architecture**: `https://cloud.google.com/architecture/`
- **More solutions**: `http://gcp.solutions/`

Test Your Knowledge

It is high time to test your knowledge on what you have learned. Here are four mock exams to help you. Good luck!

Mock test one

1. Company X needs to keep their data available for auditing purposes for 5 years. They don't plan to access this storage more than once a year. Which storage option should they choose?

   A. Google Cloud Bigtable

   B. Google Cloud Multi-Regional Storage

   C. Google Cloud Archive Storage

   D. Google Cloud Nearline Storage

   E. Google Cloud BigQuery

2. Company X wants to choose a proper storage system for IoT sensor data. There are 2,000 sensors that send temperature data every second. Company X would like to perform further analysis of the accumulated data. Please select the most appropriate choice:

   A. Google Cloud Bigtable

   B. Google Cloud Datastore

C. Google Cloud Spanner

D. Google Cloud SQL

3.   You have deployed a virtual machine instance to GCP in project X. Specific configuration and software have been installed on this instance. In order to share this image with other teams that only have access to project Z, what would you advise?

A. Create a snapshot. Use the snapshot to create a custom image. Share the image with the other projects.

B. Create a snapshot and store it on Google storage.

C. Use a third-party tool to perform a file-level backup of the instance. Copy the image to Google storage. Import the image to project Z.

D. Use Google Transfer Services.

4.   Company X is looking to analyze data. They are using a hybrid cloud mixture of on-premises and GCP infrastructure and need to analyze both stream and batch data. Select the appropriate GCP service that will allow them to achieve this requirement:

A. Google Cloud Dataproc

B. Google Cloud BigQuery

C. Google Cloud Compute Engine and Apache Airflow

D. Google Cloud Dataflow

5.   Company X is using Hadoop to analyze data. They are using a hybrid cloud mixture of on-premises and GCP infrastructure. They want to move the data analysis to GCP, but they want to migrate it with minimal effort. Which service should they use?

A. Google Cloud Dataproc

B. Google Cloud Dataflow

C. Google Cloud Composer

D. Google Compute Engine

6. Customer X is storing data on Google Datastore. They are using a hybrid cloud mixture of on-premises and GCP infrastructure. Applications on both platforms are needed to access Datastore. Which solution should be used to enable access?

    A. Use Google-managed keys for GCP instances. Use user-managed keys for on-premises instances.

    B. Use Google-managed keys for all instances.

    C. Use Google-managed keys for GCP instances. Use Firebase authentication for on-premises instances.

    D. Use Google-managed keys for GCP instances. Use a third-party tool for on-premises instances.

7. Company X is using GCP with a number of configured projects. They have special requirements vis-à-vis billing visibility and management. Based on the following statement, select the appropriate answer: A CTO should be able to control the budget for different projects, while a project manager should be able to see billing information for their project only.

    A. Set the billing administrator role to the CTO for all the projects that they manage. Set the billing viewer role to the project manager for their project.

    B. Set the billing administrator role to the program manager for a random project. Set the billing viewer role to the project manager for their project.

    C. Set the billing administrator role to the program and project managers.

    D. Set the owner role to the program and project managers.

8. You are monitoring a service with uptime checks. The services are reported as unavailable from different GCP regions. You know that the service is up and running. How can you solve the monitoring issues?

    A. Download the source IPs from the uptime check console and create an ingress firewall rule for the service.

    B. Download the source IPs from the uptime check console and create an egress firewall rule for the service.

    C. Use a third-party tool, outside GCP, to create the uptime checks.

    D. Install Cloud operations monitoring agents on all instances that are hosting the service.

9. Company X is looking to create a development and production environment in GCP. What would be the best practice to separate those environments?

    A. Create two separate projects for each environment. Give the development team access to the development project only. Give the operation team access to production only.

    B. Create two separate projects for each environment. Give the development team and the production team access to both projects.

    C. Create one project and two VPCs. Give the development team and the production team access to that project.

    D. Create two separate Google accounts for each team.

10. Company X wants to perform an analysis of data coming from sensors. The data can arrive out of order. You need to make sure that the data is in the correct order. Which services should be used to minimize the effort?

    A. IoT Core, Pub/Sub, and Dataflow

    B. IoT Core, Pub/Sub, and Dataproc

    C. IoT Core, Pub/Sub, and **Google Kubernetes Engine (GKE)**

    D. IoT Core, Pub/Subs, and GCE

11. Company X has deployed an application using App Engine. They want to release a new version of that application to production. They want to test that application on only one set of users. What is the most appropriate solution?

    A. Deploy a new version of the application. Use traffic splitting to redirect part of the requests to the new version.

    B. Deploy the application to a separate project and direct the user to use a new URL to connect to it.

    C. Migrate the application to GKE and use blue-green deployment.

    D. Migrate the application to GKE and use rolling updates.

12. Company X is using the App Engine flexible environment. They have deployed a new version of the application. The application crashed. The code is stored in GitHub. How would the fastest recovery be performed?

    A. Delete the new application and deploy a new application from GitHub.

    B. Roll back the application to a previous release.

C. Split the traffic between the old and new releases, 10% to 90%.

D. Open a ticket with GCP support to roll back the application to the previous release.

13. Company X is using Google Cloud's operations suite to monitor their GCP environment. They want to store the logs and be able to analyze them. What would be the best solution for them?

A. Create a sink to Pub/Sub.

B. Create a sink to Spanner.

C. Create a sink to BigQuery.

D. Create a sink to Bigtable.

14. Company X is using a GKE cluster. You wish to increase the number of nodes in the cluster. What would be the most appropriate command to run?

A. Run the `gcloud container clusters increase` command to change the number of nodes.

B. Run the `gcloud container clusters resize` command to change the number of nodes.

C. Run the `kubectl container cluster scale` command to change the number of nodes.

D. Run the `gcloud container cluster resize` command to change the number of nodes.

15. Company X wants to migrate their MySQL database to the cloud. They would like to use managed services. Select the most appropriate choice.

A. Use a Compute Engine instance and deploy MySQL.

B. Use a App Engine instance and deploy MySQL.

C. Use Cloud SQL.

D. Use Cloud Spanner.

16. Company X is creating an application that will analyze the comments on their Facebook profiles. They want to use the easiest way to analyze whether there are any negative comments. Which service should they use?

A. TensorFlow

B. Google AutoML

C. Google ML Engine

D. The Natural Language API

17. Company X wants to leverage ML in order to estimate the cost of the materials, based on past data. What type of model should they use?

A. Regression

B. Classification

C. Multi-class classification model

18. Company X wants to set alerts for project budgets. What is the best way to achieve this?

A. Create budget alerts with the desired percentage.

B. Create a ticket with Google Support to set hard quotas.

C. Create a cron job to check the billing and send an email if a threshold is exceeded.

D. Set a limit on credit cards that are attached to the account.

19. Company X wants to store data in Cloud Storage. The data will be accessed once every quarter. After a year, the data will be archived. What is the most cost-effective solution?

A. Store the data in a multi-regional bucket. Set the auto-archiving policy to 365 days.

B. Store the data in a regional bucket. Set the auto-archiving policy to 365 days.

C. Store the data in a Nearline bucket. Set the object life cycle policy to move the data to the Archive bucket after 365 days.

D. Store the data in the Nearline bucket. Create a cron job to move the data to the Archive bucket after 365 days.

20. Company X wants to set up a static website. What is the fastest and most cost-effective solution?

A. Use Cloud Launcher to deploy Apache Server.

B. Use App Engine with a predefined web server.

C. Use Cloud Compute Engine and a startup script to install Apache Server.

D. Use Cloud Storage to host content.

Mock test two

1. Company X wants a standardized re-deployable Hadoop cluster, with options that a managed service doesn't offer. Which solution would be best suited?

   A. A Cloud API

   B. Deployment Manager

   C. Dataflow

   D. TensorFlow

2. Company X is looking to connect their backend platform to a managed NoSQL database service. There is an expectation that the databases could grow into PB scale. As an architect, they ask you which is the best GCP service to fit these requirements without needing to refactor any applications. What is the best fit?

   A. MySQL

   B. Bigtable

   C. Firebase

   D. Redis

3. Select the different types of service accounts (choose three):

   A. User-managed

   B. Automated

   C. Google-managed

   D. G Suite

   E. Google APIs

4. Company X has two projects, separated by different VPCs that need to be able to communicate with one another. Which network service allows this?

   A. VPC peering

   B. Cloud Load Balancing

   C. Dedicated Interconnect

   D. VPN

5.   Company X is looking to use containers in the cloud. They want to continue to be developer-focused and have a code-first strategy. What is the best solution?

A. App Engine standard

B. Containers on Compute Engine

C. Cloud Run

D. App Engine flexible

6.   Your IT manager is looking at cloud vendor data storage services. His DBA has informed him that the principal requirements are strong consistency and high availability, with the potential to grow to PB scale. What is the best storage solution?

A. Cloud SQL

B. Cloud Storage

C. Cloud Datastore

D. Cloud Spanner

7.   Company X needs to be PCI-compliant. Which combination of GCP services would help to meet these requirements?

A. Cloud Monitoring, Cloud Trace, and Cloud Spanner

B. Cloud Monitoring, Cloud Logging, and BigQuery

C. Cloud Error Reporting, Cloud Debugger, and Datastore

D. Cloud Tagging, Cloud Trace, and BigQuery

8.   A storage engineer for Company X needs to migrate data from his AWS S3 bucket to his GCP storage bucket. What is the best solution for this?

A. Storage Transfer Service

B. Transfer Appliance

C. Online transfer

D. BigQuery data transfer

9. A company web page is serving users all over the globe. They want to make sure that users will always get content in the most efficient manner, regardless of where they are located. Which load-balancing solution would best fit these requirements?

A. Network Load Balancing

B. Internal Load Balancing

C. HTTP(S) Load Balancing

D. TCP Proxy Load Balancing

10. Company X is looking to the cloud to achieve autoscaling. They wish to deploy over multiple zones in a standardized manner, while also benefiting from load balancing. What GCP service best suits this scenario?

A. Deployment Manager

B. Managed instance groups

C. Google Compute Engine manager

D. Instance fleet

11. You are creating new firewall rules and wish to identify specific targets according to their use, for example, a web server. Which filter should you use?

A. Zones

B. Network tags

C. Instance groups

D. Targets

12. You have deployed an instance into the same VPC as already-existing instances. When you try to use SSH to connect to the external IP address, the connection is refused. Why might this be?

A. The firewall rule to allow SSH is restricted to internal traffic only.

B. There is no external IP allocated to the instance.

C. You do not have the correct custom **Identity and Access Management (IAM)** role to initiate SSH.

D. You should use the Google API for external SSH.

13. At the moment, your IT department is seeing lots of bugs reported whenever a new software update is released for the company's internal timesheet application. These bugs were not spotted during QA. You have been asked to design a new strategy that will keep the bugs to a minimum and regain confidence in the IT department. Which option best suits this scenario?

    A. Advise that you should only deploy updates once per year.

    B. Deploy only part of the update to production.

    C. Perform the tests more times during QA.

    D. Use canary deployment methods.

14. Your company is looking to connect its onsite networks to a GCP VPC in order to dynamically exchange routes between each site. Which service would you advise?

    A. Cloud Router

    B. Cloud Interconnect

    C. External peering

    D. Cloud DNS

15. You plan to connect VPC networks using VPC peering. What network mode is best suited?

    A. Auto mode networks

    B. VPC VPN networks

    C. Custom mode

    D. Sub-networking mode

16. You have been tasked with researching different methods to extend your on-premises network to your GCP VPC network. You are reminded by your manager that your network bandwidth is 1 Gbps. What would be the best option?

    A. Dedicated Interconnect

    B. Partner Interconnect

    C. VPC Interconnect

    D. VPN Interconnect

17. Company X wants to extend their data center to the cloud. You have been hired as an external consultant to advise on the best hybrid connectivity option. They advise you that they need access to private compute resources on GCP but are not worried about encryption at the application level. What option best corresponds to their needs?

   A. Cloud VPN

   B. Partner Interconnect

   C. Direct Peering

   D. Carrier Peering

18. You want to serve all of your content with low latency, worldwide. Which GCP service should you use?

   A. Cloud CDN

   B. Cloud VPN

   C. Google CloudFront

   D. Cloud Endpoints

19. You wish to load balance your systems based on incoming ports. What load balancing concept should you use?

   A. Network Load Balancing

   B. TCP Load Balancing

   C. HTTP(S) Load Balancing

   D. SSL Proxy Load balancing

20. You are looking to allow access to publish messages to a Cloud Pub/Sub topic. Your security team reminds you that you should be as granular as possible. Which type of IAM role should you use?

   A. Primitive role

   B. Predefined role

   C. Custom role

   D. Policy-based role

   E. Topic role

Mock test three

1. You build a container image using the Cloud Build service. You want to access information such as the Google Cloud project where their image is built. What is the recommended way to do it?

    A. Use substitutions in your build config file to substitute specific variables at build time.

    B. Run a `gcloud` command in your build.

    C. Run an API call to get the information.

    D. It is not possible to access this information.

2. You are running a web application on a Linux distribution. You want to completely remove the overhead of patching the operating system. Which option best suits your requirements?

    A. Containerize the application and use managed base images.

    B. Make the VMs read-only.

    C. Use an Alpine (stripped-down) image for your VMs.

    D. Use Google's OS patching service.

3. You are tasked with containerizing a classic LAMP application. What would be the best practice you should follow (choose two options)?

    A. Package a single app per container.

    B. Package all apps into a single container.

    C. Remove unnecessary tools.

    D. Use public images.

4. You moved your application to GKE and want to see how the application reacts to faults caused by a single microservice not being available. What is the easiest way to do this?

    A. Write a script that will randomly kill microservices.

    B. Enable Istio on the GKE cluster and use fault injection.

    C. Deploy the application from a YAML file that was edited to remove the code related to the microservice you want to test.

    D. Move the microservice to a GCE VM and power off the VM during the tests.

5. You are adding a new feature to your application and decided to use Cloud Functions. Your application is on a GCE VM running within a VPC. The Cloud Function needs direct network access to that VM. How can this be achieved?

    A. Use private services access.

    B. User Serverless VPC Access.

    C. Use Private Google Access.

    D. Use Private Service Connect for Google APIs.

6. You want to scale your **Managed Instance Group (MIG)** based on a custom metric you created. Which option suits your requirements?

    A. Create a Cloud schedule and Cloud function to query the metric and then scale the MIG.

    B. Create a Cloud operations suite alert to trigger the scale out event.

    C. Set up your MIG to export the custom metric from all VMs in the group.

    D. Custom metrics are not supported by MIGs.

7. You want to measure how well your web application hosted on a GKE cluster is performing. Which option best suits your needs?

    A. Periodically perform a survey of customer satisfaction among the users.

    B. Create Cloud Monitoring health checks.

    C. Use a third-party SaaS solution to perform periodic checks of HTTP 400 responses.

    D. Define and set SLIs and SLOs using Cloud Monitoring.

8. You want to make sure only authenticated and authorized users can access your application running on a GKE cluster. What is the Google-recommended design?

    A. Create a frontend container with proprietary authentication and an authorization mechanism.

    B. Use Identity-Aware Proxy and GKE Ingress.

    C. Move your application to Cloud Run and set up authorization.

    D. Integrate your application with Active Directory using LDAP.

9. You want to securely connect to your GCE VMs using RDP and SSH from the public internet. What is the best practice?

   A. Use IAP TCP forwarding.

   B. Set a public IP address on all the VMs.

   C. Use VPN tunnel to the VM.

   D. Install a third-party remote desktop tool on the VMs.

10. Your company is located in one of the European countries where the GCP region is available. You will be serving customers from that country. You want to make sure you don't allow the deployment of resources outside of that GCP region. How can this be achieved?

    A. Use organization policies.

    B. Disable other regions from the Google Console in the Admin menu.

    C. Disable other regions using the `gcloud regions disallow` command.

    D. Disable other regions in the billing account settings.

11. As per the CIS Benchmarks, you want to disallow some VMs to use external IP addresses. How can this be achieved?

    A. Use organization policies.

    B. Set metadata on the GCP project.

    C. Configure VPC as private.

    D. Configure the subnet as private.

12. You want your cloud-native application to be able to access GCP services in a secure way. What is the Google-recommended way to do it?

    A. Store the Google service account tokens in Kubernetes Secrets.

    B. Store the Google service account tokens in the container image.

    C. Store the Google service account tokens in a private container registry.

    D. Use Workload Identity.

13. You are planning to deploy a landing zone for your new customer. The customer wants to make sure that there is a clear separation of duties between the Network and Compute teams. Which architecture will you use?

A. Shared VPC in a single-host project and multiple service projects

B. Single VPC per project

C. Single VPC and multiple-project with VPC peering to that single project

D. Single VPC and multiple-project with VPN tunnels to that single project

14. You want to run your application in containers and be able to move it across your hybrid and multi-cloud landscape. By default, the application will run in GCP. You want to make sure that the application will scale automatically. Which service should you choose?

A. Google Compute Engine

B. Google App Engine

C. Google Cloud Run

D. Google Cloud Functions

15. You are running your cloud-native workloads in a hybrid environment with GKE and an on-premises Kubernetes cluster. You want to make sure the Kubernetes clusters are configured in a unified way. How can this be achieved?

A. Apply Kubernetes `ConfigMaps` on each of the clusters.

B. Attach your on-premises clusters to Anthos and use Config Management.

C. Install Istio on all your clusters and use CRDs.

D. Install Config Connector on all your clusters and use CRDs.

16. You are designing a cloud-native application that will store data that needs to be queried by other applications running in Google Cloud. You decided to use Cloud Run. What is the best storage option?

A. Store the data on a GCS bucket.

B. Move the app to GKE instead and use PVC.

C. Connect from Cloud Run to the Cloud SQL service.

D. Cloud Run does not allow you to store persistent data.

17. You want to load-balance user traffic between Cloud Run services running in two GCP regions. What is the Google-recommended practice?

    A. Use serverless **Network Endpoint Groups (NEGs)** and the External HTTP(S) load balancer.

    B. Use Anthos Service Mesh.

    C. Use Anthos ingress.

    D. Use a multi-cluster service.

18. You are developing an in-house application and want the application to send the logs to Cloud Logging. Which option best suits your needs?

    A. Install a custom Fluentd agent on your instances.

    B. Configure the Cloud Logging agent to include your application logs.

    C. Create a cron job and script that will call the Cloud Logging API to send the logs periodically.

    D. It is not possible to collect custom logs with the Cloud Logging agent.

19. You want to distribute user traffic between services that run on different Anthos GKE clusters. Which option best suits your needs?

    A. Use a multi-cluster service.

    B. Use Anthos Multi Cluster Ingress.

    C. Use a third-party ingress running on a separate GKE cluster.

    D. Use a Network Load Balancer.

20. You have deployed a new revision of your application to Cloud Run. You see that the change made in the new revision contains a bug in the interface. You want to revert to the previous revision as quickly as possible. Select the correct way to do this:

    A. SSH to the container and change the code.

    B. Use the `MANAGE TRAFFIC` function to set that previous revision's traffic percentage to `100`.

    C. Revert the changes in the code, build a new container image, and deploy a new revision.

    D. Delete the service and redeploy it with the container image used for previous revision.

Mock test four

1. OS Login can be enabled and disabled by setting metadata values at which level (select all that count)?

    A. VM

    B. Project

    C. Organization

    D. Folder

2. As a security analyst, you are looking for the ability to define fine-grained attribute-based access control for projects and resources. Which service offers this ability?

    A. Access Context Manager

    B. Cloud Armor

    C. Organization Policy Service

    D. Data Loss Prevention

3. A storage admin has provided you with information regarding a new Cloud Storage bucket that you requested. You use Cloud Shell to set a retention period of 1 month, but receive an error similar to the following: **400 cannot be set for a bucket that has a retention policy**. What is the most likely issue?

    A. Buckets only support a retention period in seconds.

    B. You do not have full permissions on the bucket.

    C. The bucket has versioning enabled.

    D. The bucket is using a customer-managed encryption key.

4. You have created and modified a persistent boot disk and are required to save the state for creating new instances. What does GCP offer to assist you?

    A. Instance templates

    B. Local SSDs

    C. Public images

    D. Custom images

5. You wish to create a BigQuery table. What source options are available (select all that are applicable)?

   A. Upload

   B. Empty table

   C. Google Cloud Storage

   D. Cloud Spanner

   E. Bigtable

   F. Pub/Sub event

6. You want to use off-the-shelf templates to deploy GCP resources. A colleague recommended the **Cloud Foundation Toolkit** (**CFT**). What does this provide (select all that are applicable)?

   A. Templates for Deployment Manager

   B. Access to Cloud Shell with ct and bq installed

   C. Templates for Terraform

   D. Templates for Cloud Formation

7. You currently run your enterprise applications on VMware on-premises. You want them to run in Google Cloud as soon as possible. What service can assist you?

   A. Cloud Migration Services

   B. Creating an Interconnect network and performing vMotion

   C. Migrate for Compute Engine

   D. Cloud operations suite

8. You have been given the responsibility to design a highly available solution that will securely connect your on-premises network to your VPC network. What service should you look to utilize?

   A. Cloud VPC

   B. Cloud Routing

   C. HA Tunneling

   D. HA VPN

9. You currently have access to Compute Engine instances that are dedicated to hosting only your project's VMs, but you have been asked whether there is any way to reduce the cost. During your investigation, you notice that not all the VMs are using all their resources. What can you look into in more detail to assist in reducing the cost?

    A. Shared responsibility model

    B. Overcommitting CPU on sole-tenant VMs

    C. Migrate to an HPC-ready VM instance

    D. Overcommitting memory on a sole-tenant VM

10. You are required to move disk data across to a different project. What is the correct procedure?

    A. Create a backup of the disk in project A, create a new disk in project B based on the backed-up disk, and attach a new disk to the instance in project B.

    B. Back up the VM in project A, sync the VM to project B, and power on the backup in project B.

    C. Create a snapshot of the disk in project A, edit the snapshot configuration to point towards project b, and edit the instance in project B to consume the snapshot.

    D. Create a snapshot of the disk in project A, create a new disk in project B based on the snapshot, and attach a new disk to the instance in project B.

11. Your company is looking for a solution to transform lightweight data as it arrives and store it as structured data. What services could best fit this scenario?

    A. Cloud Storage, Cloud Run, and BigQuery

    B. Pub/Sub, Dataflow, and Bigtable

    C. Cloud Storage, BigQuery, and Cloud Run

    D. Dataflow, Pub/Sub, and Bigtable

12. You are creating a new project for some developers. You wish to restrict them from deploying resources to a particular location. What IAM feature should you use?

    A. Workload Identity

    B. Labels

    C. Resource retention policies

    D. Organizational policies

13. You are setting up a new dataset in BigQuery and want to optimize storage. One of your colleagues states it would be nice to remove unneeded tables and partitions. What should you set?

   A. Table expiration

   B. Table deletion policies

   C. Query optimization policy

   D. Dataset expiration

14. You have been asked to investigate a hybrid connectivity solution that matches the following requirements:

   · Low latency

   · Highly available

   · Large-data transfers

   Which service best fits your needs?

   A. Interconnect

   B. Peering

   C. VPC

   D. VPN

15. You are required to migrate TBs of data from your on-premises machines to an existing cloud storage bucket. You want to perform this in a single transfer. What is the most suited service?

   A. Cloud Storage Transfer Service

   B. Transfer Appliance

   C. BigQuery Data Transfer Service

   D. Cloud Storage Transfer appliance

16. You have been tasked with setting up replication in Cloud SQL. You have been told the main requirement is to improve read performance by making replicas available closer to your application's region. Which type of replication should you choose?

   A. HA read replicas

   B. Cross-region read replicas

   C. External read replicas

   D. Multi-region read replicas

17. You have a latency-sensitive application using Bigtable and want to prevent imbalanced traffic among the nodes in the cluster. What is the recommendation from Google to achieve this?

    A. Ensure your cluster has Bigtable QPS enabled.

    B. Ensure your cluster runs at less than 50% memory usage.

    C. Ensure your cluster runs at less than 50% CPU load.

    D. Ensure your cluster has Bigtable GPS disabled.

18. You are developing a software service in GCP backends and want to expose the API to be consumed only by other developers that you trust. Which service best fits your needs?

    A. Apigee

    B. Cloud APIs service

    C. Cloud Endpoints

    D. GKE

19. You are looking for a Google service where you can import source code from Cloud Storage and then produce a container image. Which service fits your needs?

    A. Cloud Run

    B. Cloud Pipelines

    C. Cloud CI/CD

    D. Cloud Build

20. Which hybrid connectivity service uses BGP for your VPC networks?

    A. Cloud Router

    B. Cloud Interconnect

    C. Cloud Network Connectivity Center

    D. Cloud

Answers to mock test one

1. **C**: Archive storage is the most cost-effective option. For more information, refer to `https://cloud.google.com/storage/`.

2. **A**: Bigtable is a petabyte-scale, fully managed NoSQL database service for large analytical and operational workloads. It is ideal for ad technology, financial technology, and IoT. For more information, refer to `https://cloud.google.com/bigtable/`.

3. **A**: Custom images can be created from snapshots and shared across projects. For more information, refer to `https://cloud.google.com/compute/docs/images/create-delete-deprecate-private-images`.

4. **D**: *"Cloud Dataflow is a fully managed service for transforming and enriching data in stream* (`https://cloud.google.com/solutions/big-data/stream-analytics/`) *(real-time) and batch (historical) modes with equal reliability and expressiveness – no more complex workarounds or compromises needed. And with its serverless approach to resource provisioning and management, you have access to virtually limitless capacity to solve your biggest data processing challenges, while paying only for what you use."* For more information, refer to `https://cloud.google.com/dataflow/`:

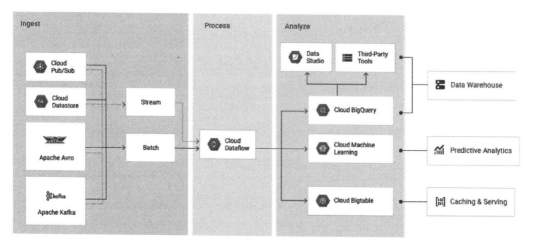

Figure 19.1 – Dataflow diagram (Source: https://cloud.google.com/dataflow/.
License: https://creativecommons.org/licenses/by/4.0/legalcode)

5. **A:** Cloud Dataproc is a fast, easy-to-use, fully managed cloud service for running Apache Spark and Apache Hadoop clusters in a simpler, more cost-efficient way. For more information, refer to `https://cloud.google.com/dataproc/`:

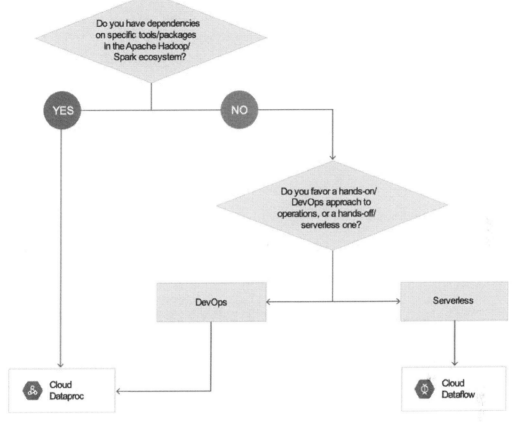

Figure 19.2 – Dataproc diagram (Source: https://cloud.google.com/dataproc/.
License: https://creativecommons.org/licenses/by/4.0/legalcode)

6. **A**: Refer to the following diagram to understand the best practices:

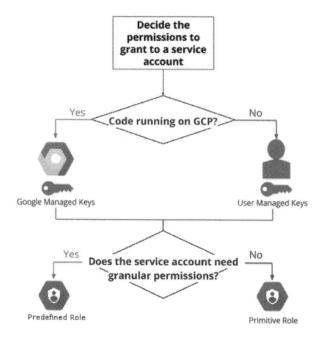

Figure 19.3 – Service accounts (Source: https://cloud.google.com/iam/docs/understanding-service-accounts. License: https://creativecommons.org/licenses/by/4.0/legalcode)

7. **A**: IAM best practice is to set the minimum-required privileges. For more information, refer to `https://cloud.google.com/blog/products/gcp/iam-best-practice-guides-available-now`.

8. **A**: You need to open firewall rules to allow uptime checks. For more information, refer to `https://cloud.google.com/monitoring/uptime-checks/using-uptime-checks#get-ips`:

Figure 19.4 – Uptime checks (Source: https://cloud.google.com/monitoring/uptime-checks/#monitoring_uptime_check_list_ips-console. License: https://creativecommons.org/licenses/by/4.0/legalcode)

"Your use of uptime checks is affected by any firewalls protecting your service:

If the resource you are checking isn't publicly available, you must configure the resource's firewall to permit incoming traffic from the uptime check servers. Refer to Getting uptime-check IP addresses at `https://cloud.google.com/monitoring/uptime-checks/using-uptime-checks#get-ips` *to download a list of the IP addresses.*

If the resource you are checking doesn't have an external IP address, uptime checks are unable to reach it."

9. **A:** Based on best practice with the fewest possible privileges. For more information, refer to `https://cloud.google.com/docs/enterprise/best-practices-for-enterprise-organizations`.

10. **A:** Dataflow will accommodate the processing of late data. Dataflow is a managed Apache Beam service.

    However, data isn't always guaranteed to arrive in a pipeline chronologically or at predictable intervals. Beam tracks a watermark, which is the system's notion of when all data in a certain window can be expected to have arrived in the pipeline. Once the watermark progresses past the end of a window, any further element that arrives with a timestamp in that window is considered late data. For more information, refer to `https://beam.apache.org/documentation/programming-guide/`.

11. **A:** Use traffic splitting to redirect a subset of traffic to the correct version of the application. For more information, refer to `https://cloud.google.com/appengine/docs/standard/python/splitting-traffic`.

12. **B:** The fastest way is to roll back the application.

    "We don't want to mess around with our code; we need to fix this right now. Users are upset! Go back to the list of versions and check the box next to the version that was deployed first. Now, click the MAKE DEFAULT button located above the list. Traffic immediately switches over to the stable version. Crisis averted!

    That was easy.

    You can now delete the buggy version by checking the box next to the version and then clicking the DELETE button located above the list."

    For more information, refer to `https://cloud.google.com/community/tutorials/how-to-roll-your-app-engine-managed-vms-app-back-to-a-previous-version-part-1`.

13. **C**: BigQuery datasets provide big data analysis capabilities. For more information, refer to `https://cloud.google.com/logging/docs/export/configure_export_v2` and `https://cloud.google.com/logging/`.

14. **B**: The `gcloud container clusters resize` parameter is used for resizing the GKE cluster. For more information, refer to `https://cloud.google.com/sdk/gcloud/reference/container/clusters/resize`.

15. **C**: *"Cloud SQL is a fully managed database service that makes it easy to set up, maintain, manage, and administer your relational PostgreSQL and MySQL databases in the cloud."* For more information, refer to `https://cloud.google.com/sql/`.

16. **D**: Sentiment analysis inspects the given text and identifies the prevailing emotional opinion within the text, especially with a view to determining a writer's attitude as positive, negative, or neutral. For more information, refer to `https://cloud.google.com/natural-language/docs/analyzing-sentiment`.

17. **A**: For more information, refer to `https://developers.google.com/machine-learning/crash-course/descending-into-ml/linear-regression`.

18. **A**: *"You can apply budget alerts to either a billing account or a project, and you can set the budget alert at a specific amount or match it to the previous month's spend. The alerts will be sent to billing administrators and billing account users when spending exceeds a percentage of your budget."* For more information, refer to `https://cloud.google.com/billing/docs/how-to/budgets`.

19. **C**: For more information, refer to `https://cloud.google.com/storage/docs/lifecycle`.

20. **D**: For more information, refer to `https://cloud.google.com/storage/docs/static-website`.

Answers to mock test two

1. **B**: Deployment Manager. Requirements are a non-managed service and one that is standardized. Deployment Manager allows for repeatable deployments. For more information, refer to `https://cloud.google.com/deployment-manager/` `https://cloud.google.com/deployment-manager/`.

2.   **B**: Bigtable and Redis are the only NoSQL options. The keyword here is "refactor."

3.   **A, C, E**: For more information, refer to `https://cloud.google.com/iam/docs/service-accounts`.

4.   **A**: VPC peering allows connectivity across two VPC networks, regardless of whether or not they belong to the same project. For more information, refer to `https://cloud.google.com/vpc/docs/using-vpc-peering`.

5.   **D**: App Engine's flexible environment is developer-focused and has a code-first strategy. For more information, refer to `https://cloud.google.com/appengine/docs/flexible/`.

6.   **D**: Cloud Spanner can scale into PT of data and fits the requirements for high availability and strong consistency. For more information, refer to `https://cloud.google.com/spanner/`.

7.   **B**: Cloud Monitoring, Cloud Logging, and BigQuery. For more information, refer to `https://cloud.google.com/blog/products/gcp/oro-how-gcp-smoothed-our-path-to-pci-dss-compliance`.

8.   **A**: Storage Transfer Service. For more information, refer to `https://cloud.google.com/storage-transfer/docs/overview`.

9.   **C**: HTTP(S) Load Balancing. For more information, refer to `https://cloud.google.com/load-balancing/docs/choosing-load-balancer`

10. **B**: Managed instance groups; specifically, regional managed instance groups let you improve availability by spreading instances across multiple zones with a region. For more information, refer to `https://cloud.google.com/compute/docs/instance-groups/distributing-instances-with-regional-instance-groups`.

11. **B**: Tags that are put onto GCE instances can also be used to determine the firewall rule on both inbound and outbound rules. If a web server is applied to a VM and added to the firewall rule, then it will be impacted. For more information, refer to `https://cloud.google.com/vpc/docs/firewalls`.

12. **A**: The default VPC rules have `default-allow-internal` specified, which permits incoming connections to a VM instance from others in the same network. For more information, refer to `https://cloud.google.com/vpc/docs/firewalls#default_firewall_rules`.

13. **D**: Use canary deployment methods. For more information, refer to `https://cloud.google.com/blog/products/gcp/how-release-canaries-can-save-your-bacon-cre-life-lessons?hl=de`.

14. **A**: A Cloud Router uses BGP to learn new subnets in your VPC and announces them on your on-premises network. For more information, refer to `https://cloud.google.com/router/docs/concepts/overview`.

15. **C**: Custom mode networks. For more information, refer to `https://cloud.google.com/vpc/docs/vpc`.

16. **B**: Partner Interconnect. Dedicated Interconnect requires 10 GB, and the other options do not exist. For more information, refer to `https://cloud.google.com/interconnect/docs/how-to/choose-type`.

17. **A**: Cloud VPN satisfies requirements. If application-level encryption is needed, then Partner Interconnect or Direct Interconnect should be considered. If there is a requirement to connect to G Suite, then Carrier Peering should be considered. For more information, refer to `https://cloud.google.com/hybrid-connectivity/`.

18. **A**: Cloud Content Delivery Network caches in numerous locations around the world, thereby yielding reduced latency. For more information, refer to `https://cloud.google.com/cdn/docs/overview`.

19. **A**: Network Load Balancing can balance loads on your system based on the incoming address, port, and protocol type. For more information, refer to `https://cloud.google.com/load-balancing/docs/network/`.

20. **B**: Predefined role. For more information, refer to `https://cloud.google.com/iam/docs/overview`.

Answers to mock test three

1. **A**: *"Substitutions are helpful for variables whose value isn't known until build time, or to reuse an existing build request with different variable values. Cloud Build provides built-in substitutions or you can define your own substitutions. Use substitutions in your build's steps and images to resolve their values at build time."* For more information, refer to `https://cloud.google.com/build/docs/configuring-builds/substitute-variable-values`.

2. **A**: Managed base images follow security best practices – in addition to being maintained with regular patching and testing, they can be rebuilt from scratch reproducibly. By comparing them to the original source, we can verify that no flaws were introduced. For more information, refer to `https://cloud.google.com/blog/products/containers-kubernetes/exploring-container-security-let-google-do-the-patching-with-new-managed-base-images`.

3. **A** and **C**: *"When you start working with containers, it's a common mistake to treat them as virtual machines that can run many different things simultaneously. A container can work this way but doing so reduces most of the advantages of the container model. Because a container is designed to have the same life cycle as the app it hosts, each of your containers should contain only one app." "To protect your apps from attackers, try to reduce the attack surface of your app by removing any unnecessary tools. For example, remove utilities like netcat, which you can use to create a reverse shell inside your system. If netcat is not in the container, the attacker has to find another way."*

    For more information, refer to `https://cloud.google.com/architecture/best-practices-for-building-containers`.

4. **B**: Istio allows you to inject faults to test the resiliency of your application.

    For more information, refer to `https://istio.io/latest/docs/tasks/traffic-management/fault-injection/`.

5. **B**: *"Serverless VPC Access enables you to connect from a serverless environment on Google Cloud (Cloud Run, Cloud Functions, or the App Engine standard environment) directly to your VPC network. This connection makes it possible for your serverless environment to access Compute Engine VM instances, Memorystore instances, and any other resources with an internal IP address."*

    For more information, refer to `https://cloud.google.com/vpc/docs/private-access-options` and `https://cloud.google.com/vpc/docs/configure-serverless-vpc-access`.

6. **C**: *"You can create custom metrics using Cloud Monitoring and write your own monitoring data to the Monitoring service. This gives you side-by-side access to standard Google Cloud data and your custom monitoring data, with a familiar data structure and consistent query syntax. If you have a custom metric, you can choose to scale based on the data from these metrics."*

    For more information, refer to `https://cloud.google.com/compute/docs/autoscaler/scaling-stackdriver-monitoring-metrics`.

7. **D**: *"Service monitoring has a set of core concepts, which are introduced here:*

    - **Service-Level Indicator (SLI)**: *a measurement of performance*

    - **Service-Level Objective (SLO)**: *a statement of desired performance"*

    For more information, refer to `https://cloud.google.com/stackdriver/docs/solutions/slo-monitoring` and `https://sre.google/sre-book/service-level-objectives/`.

8. **B**: When an application or resource is protected by IAP, it can only be accessed through the proxy by members (`https://cloud.google.com/iam/docs/overview#concepts_related_identity`), also known as users, who have the correct **Identity and Access Management (IAM)** role (`https://cloud.google.com/iam/docs/understanding-roles`). When you grant a user access to an application or resource by IAP, they're subject to the fine-grained access controls implemented by the product in use without requiring a VPN. When a user tries to access an IAP-secured resource, IAP performs authentication and authorization checks.

    For more information, refer to `https://cloud.google.com/iap/docs/concepts-overview`.

    IAP is integrated through Ingress for GKE. This integration enables you to control resource-level access for employees instead of using a VPN.

    For more information, refer to `https://cloud.google.com/iap/docs/cloud-iap-context-aware-access-howto`.

9. **A**: If you are connecting from anywhere over the public internet, it's best to enable Identity-Aware Proxy TCP forwarding for your project.

    For more information, refer to `https://cloud.google.com/compute/docs/instances/connecting-to-windows`.

10. **A**: Policies to restrict public IP addresses but allow some exceptions.

11. **A**: By default, all VM instances are allowed to use external IP addresses.

    The allowed/denied list of VM instances must be identified by the VM instance name, in the form: `projects/PROJECT_ID/zones/ZONE/instances/INSTANCE`.

    For more information, refer to `https://cloud.google.com/resource-manager/docs/organization-policy/org-policy-constraints`.

12. **D**: Workload Identity is the recommended way to access Google Cloud services from applications running within GKE, due to its improved security properties and manageability. For information about alternative ways to access Google Cloud APIs from GKE, refer to `https://cloud.google.com/kubernetes-engine/docs/how-to/workload-identity`.

13. **A:** *"Shared VPC lets organization administrators delegate administrative responsibilities, such as creating and managing instances, to Service Project Admins while maintaining centralized control over network resources such as subnets, routes, and firewalls."* For more information, refer to `https://cloud.google.com/vpc/docs/shared-vpc`.

14. **C:** Knative provides an open API and runtime environment that enables you to run your serverless workloads anywhere you choose – fully managed on Google Cloud, on Anthos on **Google Kubernetes Engine** (**GKE**), or on your own Kubernetes cluster. Knative makes it easy to start with Cloud Run and later move to Cloud Run for Anthos, or start in your own Kubernetes cluster and migrate to Cloud Run in the future. By using Knative as the underlying platform, you can move your workloads freely across platforms, while significantly reducing the switching costs. For more information, refer to `https://cloud.google.com/knative`.

15. **B:** *"With Anthos Config Management, you can create a common configuration across all your infrastructure, including custom policies, and apply it both on-premises and across clouds. Anthos Config Management evaluates changes and rolls them out to all Kubernetes clusters so that your desired state is always reflected."*

    For more information, refer to `https://cloud.google.com/anthos/config-management`.

16. **C:** Cloud SQL is a fully managed database service that helps you set up, maintain, manage, and administer your relational databases in the cloud. For more information, refer to `https://cloud.google.com/sql/docs/mysql/connect-run`.

17. **A:** "A **Network Endpoint Group** (**NEG**) *specifies a group of backend endpoints for a load balancer. A serverless NEG is a backend that points to a Cloud Run* (`https://cloud.google.com/run/docs`), *App Engine* (`https://cloud.google.com/appengine/docs`), *or Cloud Functions* (`https://cloud.google.com/functions/docs`) *service."*

    "If a backend service contains several NEGs, the load balancer balances traffic by forwarding requests to the serverless NEG in the closest available region. However, backend services can only contain one serverless NEG per region. To make your Cloud Run service available from multiple regions, you will need to set up cross-region routing. You should be able to use a single URL scheme that works anywhere in the world yet serves user requests from the region closest to the user. If the closest region is unavailable or is short on capacity, the request will be routed to a different region."

    For more information, refer to `https://cloud.google.com/load-balancing/docs/https/setting-up-https-serverless#multi_region_lb`.

18. **B**: Besides the list of default logs (`https://cloud.google.com/logging/docs/agent/default-logs`) that the Logging agent streams by default, you can customize the Logging agent to send additional logs to Logging or to adjust agent settings by adding input configurations.

    For more information, refer to `https://cloud.google.com/logging/docs/agent/logging/configuration#configure`.

19. **B**: "**Multi Cluster Ingress (MCI)** *is a cloud-hosted multi-cluster Ingress controller for Anthos GKE clusters. It's a Google-hosted service that supports deploying shared load balancing resources across clusters and across regions.*" *For more information, refer to* `https://cloud.google.com/kubernetes-engine/docs/concepts/multi-cluster-ingress`.

20. **B**: Cloud Run allows you to specify which revisions should receive traffic and to specify traffic percentages that are received by a revision. This feature allows you to roll back to a previous revision, gradually roll out a revision, and split traffic between multiple revisions.

    For more information, refer to `https://cloud.google.com/run/docs/rollouts-rollbacks-traffic-migration`.

Answers to mock test four

1. **A** and **B**: Metadata values can be added at the VM and project level. For more information, refer to `https://cloud.google.com/compute/docs/instances/managing-instance-access`.

2. **A**: Access Context Manager offers fine-grained, attribute-based access control for projects or resources. For more information, refer to `https://cloud.google.com/access-context-manager/docs/overview`.

3. **C**: Retention policies cannot be enabled if versioning is set, as they are mutually exclusive features. For more information, refer to `https://cloud.google.com/storage/docs/bucket-lock`.

4. **D**: Custom images meet our requirements to save the state of our boot disk and create new instances based on this. For more information, refer to `https://cloud.google.com/compute/docs/images/create-delete-deprecate-private-images`.

5. **A**, **B**, **C**, and **E** are all applicable selections when creating a BigQuery table:

Figure 19.5 – BigQuery options

6. **A and C**: For more information, refer to `https://cloud.google.com/foundation-toolkit`. The **Cloud Foundation Toolkit** (**CFT**) offers templates for both Deployment Manager and Terraform.

7. **C**: For more information, refer to `https://cloud.google.com/migrate/compute-engine/docs/4.2/getting-started`. Migrate for Compute Engine can help to migrate from on-premises VMware private clouds into GCP.

8. **D**: For more information, refer to `https://cloud.google.com/network-connectivity/docs/vpn/concepts/overview#ha-vpn`.

9. **B**: For more information, refer to `https://cloud.google.com/compute/docs/nodes/overcommitting-cpus-sole-tenant-vms`. Overcommitting CPU on sole-tenant machines allows us to share CPU resources across our VMs and therefore reduce cost.

10. **D**: This is the correct procedure for moving disk data across projects. For more information, refer to `https://cloud.google.com/compute/docs/disks/create-snapshots`.

11. **A**: "Lightweight" is the keyword here. Lightweight data transformation is a use case for Cloud Run. Cloud Run transforms lightweight data as it arrives and stores it as unstructured data. In this example, a file can be uploaded to Cloud Storage, and an event is triggered and delivered to a Cloud Run service. Data is then structured and stored in a BigQuery table. As answer A is the only option that mentions Cloud Run, this is the correct answer. For more information, refer to `https://cloud.google.com/run`.

12. **D**: Organizational policies can help us restrict where GCP resources are deployed. For more information, refer to `https://cloud.google.com/resource-manager/docs/organization-policy/defining-locations`.

13. **A**: For more information, refer to `https://cloud.google.com/bigquery/docs/best-practices-storage`. Setting a table expiration time on our Big Query table will delete data when the time is exceeded. This option is useful if you need access to only the most recent data. It is also useful if you are experimenting with data and do not need to preserve it.

14. **A**: Interconnect fulfills the requirements for low-latency, highly available, large-data transfers. For more information, refer to `https://cloud.google.com/network-connectivity/docs/interconnect#docs`.

15. **A**: The Cloud Storage Transfer Service is ideal for one-off transfers of TBs' worth of data. For more information, refer to `https://cloud.google.com/storage-transfer/docs/on-prem-overview`.

16. **B**: Cross-region read replicas are a great fit for this use case. For more information, refer to `https://cloud.google.com/sql/docs/mysql/replication`.

17. **B**: For more information, refer to `https://cloud.google.com/bigtable/docs/performance`. This capacity also provides a buffer for traffic spikes or key-access hotspots, which can cause imbalanced traffic among nodes in the cluster.

18. **C**: For more information, refer to `https://cloud.google.com/endpoints`. Cloud Endpoints lets us develop APIs on any GCP backend and then share our APIs with other developers.

19. **D**: For more information, refer to `https://cloud.google.com/build/docs/overview`. Cloud Build can import from various sources and deliver artifacts as part of a serverless CI/CD pipeline.

20. **A**: Cloud routes use BGP. For more information, refer to `https://cloud.google.com/network-connectivity/docs/router/concepts/overview`.

Index

T

Packt.com

Subscribe to our online digital library for full access to over 7,000 books and videos, as well as industry leading tools to help you plan your personal development and advance your career. For more information, please visit our website.

Why subscribe?

- Spend less time learning and more time coding with practical eBooks and Videos from over 4,000 industry professionals

- Improve your learning with Skill Plans built especially for you

- Get a free eBook or video every month

- Fully searchable for easy access to vital information

- Copy and paste, print, and bookmark content

Did you know that Packt offers eBook versions of every book published, with PDF and ePub files available? You can upgrade to the eBook version at packt.com and as a print book customer, you are entitled to a discount on the eBook copy. Get in touch with us at customercare@packtpub.com for more details.

At www.packt.com, you can also read a collection of free technical articles, sign up for a range of free newsletters, and receive exclusive discounts and offers on Packt books and eBooks.

Other Books You May Enjoy

If you enjoyed this book, you may be interested in these other books by Packt:

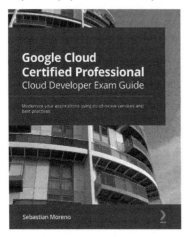

Google Cloud Certified Professional Cloud Developer Exam Guide

Sebastian Moreno

ISBN: 978-1-80056-099-4

- Get to grips with the fundamentals of Google Cloud Platform development
- Discover security best practices for applications in the cloud
- Find ways to create and modernize legacy applications
- Understand how to manage data and databases in Google Cloud
- Explore best practices for site reliability engineering, monitoring, logging, and debugging
- Become well-versed with the practical implementation of GCP with the help of a case study

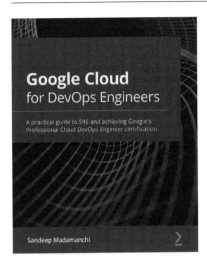

Google Cloud for DevOps Engineers

Sandeep Madamanchi

ISBN: 978-1-83921-801-9

- Categorize user journeys and explore different ways to measure SLIs
- Explore the four golden signals for monitoring a user-facing system
- Understand psychological safety along with other SRE cultural practices
- Create containers with build triggers and manual invocations
- Delve into Kubernetes workloads and potential deployment strategies
- Secure GKE clusters via private clusters, Binary Authorization, and shielded GKE nodes
- Get to grips with monitoring, Metrics Explorer, uptime checks, and alerting
- Discover how logs are ingested via the Cloud Logging API

Packt is searching for authors like you

If you're interested in becoming an author for Packt, please visit `authors.packtpub.com` and apply today. We have worked with thousands of developers and tech professionals, just like you, to help them share their insight with the global tech community. You can make a general application, apply for a specific hot topic that we are recruiting an author for, or submit your own idea.

Share Your Thoughts

Now you've finished *Professional Cloud Architect Google Cloud Certification Guide*, we'd love to hear your thoughts! Scan the QR code below to go straight to the Amazon review page for this book and share your feedback or leave a review on the site that you purchased it from.

https://packt.link/r/1801812292

Your review is important to us and the tech community and will help us make sure we're delivering excellent quality content.